Imperialism & Orientalism

Imperialism & Orientalism

A Documentary Sourcebook

Edited and introduced by

Barbara Harlow
& Mia Carter

BLACKWELL
Publishers

First published 1999

2 4 6 8 10 9 7 5 3 1

Blackwell Publishers Inc.
350 Main Street
Malden, Massachusetts 02148
USA

Blackwell Publishers Ltd
108 Cowley Road
Oxford OX4 1JF
UK

Library of Congress Cataloging-in-Publication Data
Imperialism and Orientalism: a reader / edited and introduced by
   Barbara Harlow and Mia Carter.
      p. cm.
   Includes bibliographical references and index.
   ISBN 1-55786-710-0 (alk. paper). – ISBN 1-55786-711-9 (pbk.:
alk. paper)
    1. Asia–History–18th century. 2. Asia–History–19th century.
3. Middle East–History–19th century. 4. Africa–History–19th
century. 5. Imperialism. I. Harlow, Barbara, 1948– .
II. Carter, Mia.
DS33.7.I45   1999
950′.3–dc21   98-28671
                                       CIP

British Library Cataloguing in Publication Data

A CIP catalogue record for this book is available from the
British Library

Typeset in 9 on 10.5 pt Ehrhardt
by Best-set Typesetter Ltd., Hong Kong
Printed in Great Britain by T J International, Padstow, Cornwall

This book is printed on acid-free paper

Contents

Illustrations

Acknowledgments

Our four years of rummaging in the "archives of empire" have been both arduous and ardent, onerous and obsessive. Every dusty tome, each brittle page, all the pictures – engraved and moving alike, were grounds for more research and more rejoicing, more jobbing and jubilation. We want now to thank those friends, colleagues, readers, and students, who have in their various ways assisted in the travails and shared in the enthusiasms of this project. Rachel Jennings, Dannielle Andrews, and Nabeel Zuberi provided research assistance in 1995–6 (Rachel and Nabeel with the support of University of Texas Special Research Grants and Dannielle with the aid of a Graduate Opportunity Program Research Grant). The following year Purnima Bose and Sumitra Rajkumar continued in their stead with equal expertise and energy. The students in the graduate seminar on "Orientalism and Imperialism" taught by Barbara in UT's English Department and the Program in Comparative Literature in fall 1995 were stalwarts in the stacks and their research must be recommended: Victoria Burton, Chris Busiel, Susan Harris, Mary Harvan, Ellie Higgins, Shirin Khanmohamadi, Rebecca Lorins, Luz Elena Ramirez, Sandy Soto, Tamsin Todd, and Stan Walker. Mia would like to thank her students in the "Twentieth-Century British Novel" class and her graduate and undergraduate "Post-Colonial Voices" classes – especially the undergraduates who put up with being flooded with xeroxes and happily discovered the wonders of the third floor at the PCL. Mia's special thanks to Esther Chung Bagot for the regularly and generously shared bursts of energy (especially helpful towards the end!); Ranjana Natarajan for her fierce sense of realism and her fighting spirit; to Jennifer Wenzel for being inspirational; and to Sumitra and Nabeel for many years of love. In spring 1996, we presented a synopsis of our project to the English Graduate Student Colloquium; the turnout and the feedback were more than encouraging. Similarly, our presentation to UT's South Asian Seminar Series in fall 1996 generated debate, bibliography and lasting collaborations; special thanks to Sagaree Sengupta, Gail Minault, and Janice Leoshko.

We want to thank those who invited us to share our work with them and all those who listened and responded. Barbara presented excerpts from the archive in talks at Bowling Green State University, University of California at San Diego, Swarthmore College, Indiana University, University of Minnesota, and at the 1996 meeting of MELUS in Honolulu. The contributions from members of the audiences following those discussions were invaluable to chasing down still more references. Mia thanks James Kelman for listening to the "kitchen table" presentation and offering enthusiasm, encouragement, and support.

But there were other less organized supports as well – ongoing, sporadic, and incisive. Nels Johnson and Sarah Graham Brown over the four years had new ideas, antiquarian erudition, and made the odd visit to Tipu's Tiger and Ali Pali in store in London. Chris Maziar put up with a lot of hand-waving and unfinished sentences from Barbara and shared cartoons, transparencies, and most of all lasting friendship. Ann Harlow and Ruthie Gilmore followed many of the sorties by email. Liam and Ari heroically endured and continued to offer the grouchy one hugs, even at her snarliest. And Brian Doherty did it all: supplied juice, coffee, and wondrous morsels; proof-read, provided the portable thesaurus services, and warm support; and best of all, remained Mia's friend.

The "archives of empire" couldn't have been assembled in this way though without the stunning collections of UT's General Libraries – the PCL (Perry-Castaneda Library), the HRC (Harry Ransom Humanities Research Center), as well as the libraries in Fine Arts, Architecture, and the Life Sciences, not to mention the truly amazing electronic resources (including Britannica Online, UTCAT, and Biography Find) that the library staff has made available to the university community. The members of that staff, from the circulation desk to the storage facility, have been exemplary in their anticipation of and response to the idiosyncratic demands of teachers and students alike. We salute them. So too, we want to acknowledge Jim Garrison, Chair of the Department of English, who provided us some fine space for doing this project. Memorable Sunday mornings in Parlin 202 saw some good work, some good exchanges, and reflections of empires past and present.

Finally, it was Simon Prosser's idea in the first place that sent us off to the "archives of empire." We want to thank him for getting it all going. And thank you now to our current Blackwell editors, Susan Rabinowitz and Katie Byrne in the US, and Simon Eckley in the UK who shared our enthusiasm for the project. Our desk editor, Helen Rappaport, was the best! She has been brilliant and thorough and her insights have brought a whole new outlook to the reader. We look forward to future work with her.

And, last but hardly least, we want to admit to the pains and perils of this extended collaboration and applaud the privilege and pleasure of working together. We couldn't have done it without each other.

In concluding, we want to remember our friend and colleague, Lora Romero.

Mia Carter and Barbara Harlow
April 1998

The authors and publishers gratefully acknowledge the following for permission to reproduce copyright material:

Oxford University Press, Oxford for *The Evolution of India and Pakistan, 1858–1947: Select Documents*, ed. C. H. Philips, H. L. Singh, and B. N. Pandey (1962); and *History of the Congo Reform Movement* by E. D. Morel, William Roger Louis, and Jean Stengers (1968).

Oxford University Press, New Delhi for *The Politics of the British Annexation of India*, ed. Michael Fisher (1993) and *Sir William Jones: A Reader*, ed. Satya Pachori (1993).

Frank Cass and Company, 900 Eastern Avenue, Ilford, Essex, England for *The Dual Mandate in British Tropical Africa* by Lord Frederick Lugard (1965). Copyright Frank Cass & Co. Ltd.

Grove/Atlantic, Inc., New York for *The Black Diaries: An Account of Roger Casement's Life and Times with a Collection of His Diaries and Public Writings*, eds Peter Singleton-Gates and Maurice Girodias (1959).

David Higham Associates for *Queen Victoria in Her Letters and Journals* by Christopher Hibbert (London: Murray, 1984).

Introduction

General Description

Imperialism and Orientalism: A Documentary Sourcebook assembles a selection of cultural and historical documents that provided the ideological and political grounds for the European, and especially British, colonial project throughout the nineteenth century. Since the publication of Edward Said's *Orientalism* in 1979, the controversial issues of orientalism and the practices of orientalists have figured critically in determining the contemporary definitions of the fields of literary and cultural studies, and in the connected disciplines of history, anthropology, geography, and political science, as well as in area studies related to Africa, South Asia, and the Middle East. *Imperialism and Orientalism* compiles texts that underwrote the orientalist endeavor, and locates for students, critics, and teachers of the subject some of the documentary parameters of an archive for use as both a pedagogical resource and a compass for possible future research. These documents, however, are but a mere preliminary sampling from the vast archives of empire, and this reader is designed as an introduction to those resources.

The sourcebook is divided into five parts: 1 From Company to Crown; 2 The Opening of the Suez Canal; 3 The Great Game; 4 The Scramble for Africa; and 6 Victoria. Each part, according to the specificities of the issues posed by the particular historical circumstances and geographical conditions, includes such documents as official policy statements, political speeches and government papers, journalistic accounts and editorial opinions, as well as personal narratives, private memoirs and literary extracts. Some maps, drawings and cartoons further illustrate the complex of plans and accomplishments that determined the imperial adventure and its accompanying orientalist discourse. The very diversity of materials provides important evidence of the myriad ways in which imperialism was prosecuted as well as of the multiple means through which it was packaged and publicized.

Organization

The sourcebook is organized into five parts, which provide both geographical coordinates and historical markers for the makings of an imperium across the nineteenth century. The collection focuses primarily on the British Empire, but imperialism was a larger European enterprise and thus reference is also made to the competition between France and Britain – from the building of the Suez Canal, to the incident at Fashoda – to secure their respective global status and predetermine the international status quo.

The parts themselves represent crucial moments and extended trajectories, the times and places of decisive encounters and the contiguities of momentous events. We do, however, proceed chronologically: "From Company to Crown" deals with a century of English engagements in India; "The Opening of the Suez Canal" is organized around the construction and celebration of that feat's accomplishment and the new routes of empire that it opened. Important among those routes was that to India, and so we continue with "The Great Game," and the struggle in Central Asia for the Indian subcontinent. But the Suez Canal, in connecting Europe with India, also divided the African continent from the Asian and the new route to India both shortcut the journey round the Cape of Good Hope and altered the terms of European claims – or the "scramble" – to Africa. What was happening in the oriental reaches of empire was nonetheless just as disorienting at home, and so we conclude with "Victoria," in which the paeans to empire were tempered with domestic controversies over just what should be the definitions of England and Englishness – definitions that had territorial, cultural, political, social, and economic ramifications.

The outline we have used here is hardly exhaustive, although we have endeavored to cover as much territory as possible and dig as deeply as probable towards a working anthology such as this one. If not exhaustive, however, the sections and subsections are meant to be in some preliminary way exemplary, perhaps indicating directions toward future projects that could well identify other such incidents or itineraries and excavate still more of the foundations, remnants, and detritus of the imperial edifice and its social, political, and literary constructs.

Each of the parts is subdivided into chapters, to allow for more detailed examination of specific issues that contributed to the imperial agenda and its history. Each chapter begins with an introduction that identifies and contextualizes some of the larger debates and discourses that grounded the historical events illustrated by the documents – which are numbered cumulatively throughout the book – and is accompanied by a list of additional reading, featuring works contemporary to the historical narrative and references to later inquiries and critiques, as well as literary renderings. In addition, where appropriate, brief filmographies suggest supplementary materials. Empire played – and indeed continues to play – an important role in shaping the global and popular imagination at the end of the twentieth century.

Resources

The making of empire, coinciding as it did with what Benedict Anderson, in *Imagined Communities: Reflections on the Origin and Spread of Nationalism* (London, 1983) has called the age of "print capitalism," was assiduously documented, meticulously recorded, and just as imaginatively illustrated. We have attempted in our selections to suggest just how sedimented and kaleidoscopic that textual enterprise was, and have drawn on resources ranging from legislative annals such as *Hansard's Parliamentary Debates* or East India Company materials, to personal narratives and contemporary commentary. But if the proponents of empire were fluent in the proselytizing and celebrating of their mission, its opponents were no less voluble in their castigations and critiques, and the debates raged importantly in the journals and reviews of the time. Even as today, citizenries turn to the popular and academic presses and news media to

inform themselves and chastise their politicians, nineteenth-century readers turned to the writings of opinion-makers and policy-hacks in the current periodicals. These publications themselves constitute both a history and a historical record.

Contemporary Applications

And empire, while it may appear to have been "dismantled" in the post-World War Two era of decolonization, continues to provide the antecedents and lessons for the present age of "globalization" and neo-liberalism. Over the four years that we have worked on this project the continuities between the "civilizing mission" and contemporary debates over "humanitarian interventionism," from imperialism to the "new world order," found repeated instantiation in current events and newspaper headlines. The Boer War, for example, was recalled as South Africa held its first free elections in 1994. Hong Kong, one of Britain's few remaining colonial territories, was returned with much pomp to China in summer 1997, calling up a surge of nostalgia for the glory days of Empire. That same summer, India celebrated the fiftieth anniversary of its independence – or, for other observers, lamented its 50 years of partition. The Congo Reform Association which had protested abuses under Leopold II's dominion was replaced by French troops, UN delegations, and human rights organizations, first in response to the genocide in Rwanda in 1994, and again following Laurent Kabila's overthrow of Zaire's dictator Mobutu. And controversy over the Nike Company's treatment of its "native" Vietnamese workers reminded us of the frequently unfortunate relationship between free markets and indentured service and the fallibility of treaties and international and regional trading blocs. A new "great game" rages again in the renewed contest in and over the Central Asian republics following the demise of the Soviet Union. The remains of empire, in other words, are there in the archives, but the imperial specter has not been buried, nor does it rest quietly in the present with these lessons from the past.

Part I

From Company to Crown 1757–1857

Chapter One

The British East India Company

Introduction

From its inception at the beginning of the seventeenth century, the British East India Company combined military and commercial methods of institutional organization and administration; what began as a corporate enterprise soon evolved into a massively armed colonial empire. The Company's history is characterized by intrigue, national and personal ambition, double-dealing, and even kidnapping and hostage-taking as means of insuring successful treaty negotiations. Great Britain's knowledge of Indian trade was itself acquired by an act of piracy on the high seas when Sir Francis Drake captured five Portuguese vessels containing treasures of the East and detailed documents on trade routes and procedures. The Company also financed itself for a number of years by illegally importing opium to China; Chinese resistance to Britain's drug trade led to the Opium Wars (1839–42, 1856–60) and its seizure of Hong Kong. The East India Company was also used by British families as a disciplinary institution for incorrigible sons. "Naughty" Robert Clive, a delinquent and leader of a local protection racket at home, was sent

to India to improve himself; he eventually earned a knighthood for his military and administrative services on the Company's behalf.

Early on in the Company's history, aggressive protection of its monopoly status was one of the corporation's chief aims; free trade was discouraged and eventually outlawed. Private competitors were eliminated, like Captain Kidd, who was executed for piracy (1701), or incorporated, like Thomas "Diamond" Pitt, an interloper who had individually obtained trading rights from Indian rulers. Upon his return to England, Pitt was tried, fined, and then hired as a senior administrator by the Company; the former rogue eventually became the Governor of Fort Saint George. Critics of the Company were not always critics of colonialism *per se*; often those voicing displeasure were protesting monopolistic policies and practices and the Company's unchecked and extensive military powers which, some argued, usurped the powers of the King and Crown. Others objected to the enhancement of the Nabobs' – the Company's newly made millionaires – individual fortunes; they believed the Company's profits should enrich the kingdom and the state. Those who were critical of the Company's policies of annexation, land settlement, and seizure, argued that native communities and traditions were being debased and destroyed.

The East India Act of 1773 initiated the restructuring of the Company by providing a system of checks and balances with its placement of a supervisory Council. The act also limited the colonial administration's ability to wage war and negotiate treaties and allowed Company employees to be tried at home in His Majesty's Court for offenses made in India, a change that would dramatically affect the future of Governor-General Warren Hastings. Despite progressive legal and administrative reforms, disparaging assessments of the native rulers continued and were expansively represented and broadly disseminated; charges of native misgovernment and mismanagement became the rationale for the continued seizure of Indian territories. The reformers' assessments of native rulers' tyrannical despotism and their wide-ranging descriptions of the under-developed Indian character or nature, supported the representation of the British administration of India as a mission of charity, civilization, and uplift.

Expansionism and increased involvement in the colony's domestic politics engaged the Company in the manufacture of political theory and governmental policy; India was used as a laboratory for imperialistic rule, international economics, and colonial administration. Company improvements included the expansion of the Indian rail, telegraph, and postal systems, all of which served both administrative and military aims. For example, the rail system was used to provide famine relief and to ease and improve the transportation of military staff and supplies; the telegraph system was used to observe famine conditions and to improve military and surveillance operations. Many reformers believed the British were destined to rule India; they would develop ideal systems of government with the aim of leading the Indians away from despotism and towards democracy. The Government of India Act of 1833 transferred the Company to the Crown and exemplified the new administrative focus on the direct government of India.

This section on the British East India Company also contains chapters on Eastern (Tipu Sultan) and Western (Warren Hastings) "Despots," Orientalism, and the British Campaigns to reform the Indian practices of thuggee and sati/suttee.

MC

Additional Reading

Chadhuri, K. N. *The Trading World of Asia and the English East India Company, 1600–1760.* Cambridge, 1978.

Clapham, J. H. *Economic History of Modern Britain*, 3 vols. Cambridge, 1939.
Clive Museum. *Treasures from India: The Clive Collection at Powis Castle.* New York, 1987.
Dodwell, H. H. *Dupleix and Clive: The Beginning of Empire.* London, 1968 (Orig. Pub. 1920).
Gardner, Brian. *The East India Company: A History.* London, 1971.
Keay, John. *The Honourable Company: A History of the English East India Company.* London, 1991.
Lucas, Samuel. *Dacoitee in Excelsis; or, The Spoiliation of Oude by the East India Company.* London, 1857.
Moir, Martin, *A General Guide to the India Office Records.* London, 1988.
Philips, C. H. *The East India Company, 1784–1834.* Manchester, 1961.
Sutherland, Lucy Stuart. *The East India Company in 18th Century Politics.* Oxford, 1952.

1 Timeline of Significant Events

1600	Establishment of the British East India Company
1746–54	Anglo-French contest in the Carnatic
1754	French recall Dupleix
1757	Battle of Plassey
1769	Foundation of the Royal Academy
1772	Warren Hastings Governor of Bengal
1774	Clive commits suicide
1775	Beginning of American War of Independence
1776	Adam Smith's *The Wealth of Nations* published
1767–99	Anglo-Mysore Wars
1782	British acquisition of Mysore districts
1785	Warren Hastings resigns
1786–94	Impeachment proceedings against Warren Hastings
1786	Cornwallis replaces Hastings
1789	Fall of the Bastille
1792	Treaty of Seringapatam
1793	Company's Charter Act
	Execution of Louis XVI
1798	Battle of Seringapatam
	Battle of the Nile
1801	Oudh territories ceded
1804	Napoleon made Emperor
1812	Napoleon's Russian Expedition
1813	Emendation of East India Company Charter allowing missionary work in India
1815	Napoleon defeated at Waterloo
1829	Suttee (sati) officially outlawed by Lord William Cavendish Bentinck
1830	Thuggee outlawed

1832	First Reform Act
1833	Abolition of slavery throughout the British Empire
1837	Accession of Queen Victoria
1843	Sindh annexed
1849	Punjab annexed
1851	Great Exhibition at the Crystal Palace
1853	Nagpur annexed
1854–6	Crimean War
1856	Oudh annexed
1857	Sepoy Rebellion/Indian Mutiny
1858	Queen Victoria proclaimed Empress of India

2   The Governors and Governors-General of India

Governors of the Presidency of Fort William

1758	Robert Clive
1760	John Holwell
1760	Henry Vansittart
1764	John Spencer
1765	Lord Clive
1767	Henry Verelst
1769	John Cartier
1772	Warren Hastings

Governors-General of Bengal (with authority over Madras and Bombay)

1773	Warren Hastings
1785	Sir John Macpherson
1786	Lord Cornwallis
1793	Sir John Shore
1798	Lord Mornington (Lord Richard Wellesley)
1805	Lord Cornwallis
1805	Sir George Barlow
1807	Lord Minto
1813	Lord Moira (Lord Hastings)
1823	John Adam
1823	Lord Amherst
1828	Lord William Cavendish Bentinck

Governors-General of India and Governors of Bengal

1833	Lord William Cavendish Bentinck
1835	Sir Charles Metcalfe

Governors-General of India and Governors of Bengal

1836	Lord Auckland
1842	Lord Ellenborough
1844	Sir Henry Hardinge (Lord Hardinge)
1848	Lord Dalhousie

Governors-General of India

1854	Lord Dalhousie
1856	Lord Canning

3   List of the Nawabs of Bengal

1740–56	Alivardi Khan
1756–7	Seraja-daula
1757–60	Mir Jafar Khan
1760–3	Mir Kasim Khan
1763–5	Mir Jafar Khan (restored)
1765–6	Najm-ud-daula
1766–70	Saif-ud-daula

4   "Agreement between the Nabob Nudjum-Ul-Dowlah and the Company" (August 12, 1765)

The King having been graciously pleased to grant to the English Company the Dewanny of Bengal, Behar, and Orissa, with the revenues thereof, as a free gift for ever, on certain conditions, whereof one is that there shall be a sufficient allowance out of the said revenues for supporting the expenses of the Nizamut: be it known to all whom it may concern, that I do agree to accept of the annual sum of Sicca rupees 53,86,131-9, as an adequate allowance for the support of the Nizamut, which is to be regularly paid as follows, viz.: the sum of rupees 17,78,854-1, for all my household expenses, servants, etc., and the remaining sum of rupees 36,07,277-8, for the maintenance of such horse, sepoys, peons, bercundauzes, etc., as may be thought necessary for my suwarry and the support of my dignity only, should such an expense hereafter be found necessary to be kept up, but on no account ever to exceed that amount: and having a perfect reliance on ul-Miaeen Dowla, I desire he may have the disbursing of the above sum of rupees 36,07,277-8, for the purposes before-mentioned. This Agreement (by the blessing of God) I hope will be inviolably observed, as long as the English Company's factories continue in Bengal.

Fort William, 30th September 1765

(A true copy)

(Signed) ALEXANDER CAMPBELL, SSC

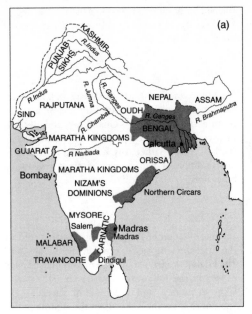

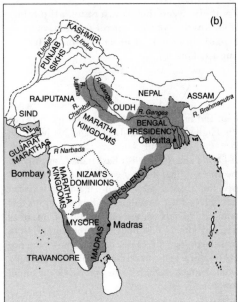

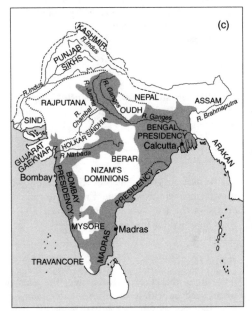

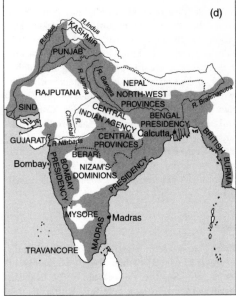

Map 1a–d India under British control (shaded area): (a) under Cornwallis, 1792; (b) under Wellesley, 1799; (c) under Lord Hastings, 1823; (d) under Dalhousie, 1856.

Treaty between the Nawab Shujau-d daula, of Oudh, the Nawab Najmu-d daula, of Bengal, and the East India Company, 16 August, 1765

Article 1

A PERPETUAL and universal peace, sincere friendship, and firm union shall be established between His Highness Shujah-ul-Dowla and his heirs, on the one part, and His Excellency Nudjum-ul-Dowla and the English East India Company on the other; so that the said contracting powers shall give the greatest attention to maintain between themselves, their dominions and their subjects this reciprocal friendship, without permitting, on either side, any kind of hostilities to be committed, from henceforth, for any cause, or under any pretence whatsoever, and everything shall be carefully avoided which might hereafter prejudice the union now happily established.

Article 2

In case the dominions of His Highness Shujah-ul-Dowla shall at any time hereafter be attacked, His Excellency Nudjum-ul-Dowla and the English Company shall assist him with a part or the whole of their forces, according to the exigency of his affairs, and so far as may be consistent with their own security, and if the dominions of his Excellency Nudjum-ul-Dowla or the English Company, shall be attacked, His Highness shall, in like manner, assist them with a part or the whole of his forces. In the case of the English Company's forces being employed in His Highness's service, the extraordinary expense of the same is to be defrayed by him.

Article 3

His Highness solemnly engages never to entertain or receive Cossim Ally Khan, the late Soubahdar of Bengal, etc., Sombre, the assassin of the English, nor any of the European deserters, within his dominions, nor to give the least countenance, support, or protection to them. He likewise solemnly engages to deliver up to the English whatever European may in future desert from them into his country.

Article 4

The King Shah Aalum shall remain in full possession of Cora, and such part of the Province of Illiabad as he now possesses, which are ceded to His Majesty, as a royal demesne, for the support of his dignity and expenses.

Article 5

His Highness Shujah-ul-Dowla engages, in a most solemn manner, to continue Bulwant Sing in the zemindarries of Benares, Ghazepore, and all those districts he possessed at the time he came over to the late Nabob Jaffier Ally Khan and the English, on condition of his paying the same revenue as heretofore.

Article 6

In consideration of the great expense incurred by the English Company in carrying on the late war, His Highness agrees to pay them (50) fifty lakhs of rupees in the following manner; viz. (12) twelve lakhs in money, and a deposit of jewels to the amount of (8) eight lakhs, upon the signing of this Treaty, (5) five lakhs one month after, and the remaining (25) twenty-five lakhs by monthly payments, so as that the whole may be discharged in (13) thirteen months from the date hereof.

Article 8

His Highness shall allow the English Company to carry on a trade, duty free, throughout the whole of his dominions.

Article 9

All the relations and subjects of His Highness, who in any manner assisted the English during the course of the late war, shall be forgiven, and no ways molested for the same.

Article 10

As soon as this Treaty is executed, the English forces shall be withdrawn from the dominions of His Highness, except such as may be necessary for the garrison of Chumar, or for the defence and protection of the King in the city of Illiabad, if His Majesty should require a force for that purpose.

Source: Arthur Berriedale Keith (ed.). *Speeches and Documents on India Policy, 1750–1921* vol. 1. London: Oxford University Press, 1992, pp. 27–30.

5 East India Company Act (1773)

[. . .] VII AND, for the better management of the said United Company's affairs in India, be it further enacted by the authority aforesaid, that, for the government of the Presidency of Fort William in Bengal, there shall be appointed a Governor-General, and four counsellors; and that the whole civil and military government of the said Presidency, and also the ordering, management and government of all the territorial acquisitions and revenues in the kingdoms of Bengal, Behar, and Orissa, shall, during such time as the territorial acquisitions and revenues shall remain in the possession of the said United Company, be, and are hereby vested in the said Governor-General and Council of the said Presidency of Fort William in Bengal, in like manner, to all intents and purposes whatsoever, as the same now are, or at any time heretofore might have been exercised by the President and Council, or Select Committee, in the said kingdoms.

VIII And be it enacted by the authority aforesaid, that in all cases whatsoever wherein any difference of opinion shall arise upon any question proposed in any consultation, the said Governor-General and Council shall be bound and concluded by the opinion and decision of the major part of those present: And if it shall happen that, by the death or removal, or by the absence, of any of the members of the said Council, such Governor-General and Council shall happen to be equally divided; then, and in every such case, the said Governor-General, or, in his absence, the eldest counsellor present, shall have a casting voice, and his opinion shall be decisive and conclusive.

IX And be it further enacted by the authority aforesaid, that the said Governor-General and Council, or the major part of them, shall have, and they are hereby authorized to have, power of superintending and controlling the government and management of the Presidencies of Madras, Bombay, and Bencoolen respectively, so far and insomuch as that it shall be lawful for any President and Council of Madras, Bombay, or Bencoolen, for the time being, to make any orders for commencing hostilities, or declaring or making war, against any Indian princes or powers, or for negotiating or concluding any treaty of peace, or other treaty, with any such Indian princes or powers, without the consent and approbation of the said Governor-General and Council first had and obtained, except in such cases of imminent necessity as would render it dangerous to postpone such hostilities or treaties until the orders from the Governor-General and Council might arrive; and except in such cases where the said Presidents and Councils respectively shall have received special orders from the said United Company; and any President and Council of Madras, Bombay, or Bencoolen, who shall offend in any of the cases aforesaid, shall be liable to be suspended from his or their office by the order of the said Governor-General and Council; and every President and Council of Madras, Bombay, and Bencoolen, for the time being, shall, and they are hereby respectively directed and required, to pay due obedience to such orders as they shall receive, touching the premises from the said Governor-General and Council for the time being, and constantly and diligently to transmit to the said Governor-General and Council advice and intelligence of all transactions and matters whatsoever that shall come to their knowledge, relating to the government, revenues, or interest, of the said United Company; and the said Governor-General and Council for the time being shall, and they are hereby directed and required to pay due obedience to all such orders as they shall receive from the Court of Directors of the said United Company, and to correspond, from time to time, and constantly and diligently transmit to the said Court an exact particular of all advices or intelligence, and of all transactions and matters whatsoever, that shall come to their knowledge, relating to the government, commerce, revenues, or interest, of the said United Company; and the Court of Directors of the said Company, or their successors, shall, and they are hereby directed and required, from time to time, before the expiration of fourteen days after the receiving any such letters or advices, to give in and deliver unto the High Treasurer, or Commissioners of His Majesty's Treasury for the time being, a true and exact copy of such parts of the said letters or advices as shall any way relate to the management of the revenues of the said Company; and in like manner to give in and deliver to one of His Majesty's Principal Secretaries of State for the time being a true and exact copy of all such parts of the said letters or advices as shall any way relate to the civil or military affairs and government of the said Company; all which copies shall be fairly written, and shall be signed by two or more of the Directors of the said Company.

X And it is hereby further enacted, that Warren Hastings, Esquire, shall be the first Governor-General; and that Lieutenant-General John Clavering, the Honourable George Monson, Richard Barwell, Esquire, and Philip Francis,

Esquire, shall be the four first counsellors; and they, and each of them, shall hold and continue in his and their respective offices for and during the term of five years from the time of their arrival at Fort William in Bengal, and taking upon them the government of the said Presidency, and shall not be removable, in the meantime, except by His Majesty, his heirs and successors, upon representation made by the Court of Directors of the said United Company for the time being: and in case of the avoidance of the office of such Governor-General by death, resignation, or removal, his place shall, during the remainder of the term aforesaid, as often as the case shall happen, be supplied by the person of the Council who stands next in rank to such Governor-General; and, in case of the death, removal, resignation, or promotion, of any of the said Council, the Directors of the said United Company are hereby empowered, for and during the remainder of the said term of five years, to nominate and appoint, by and with the consent of His Majesty, his heirs and successors, to be signified under his or their sign manual, a person to succeed to the office so become vacant in the said Council; and until such appointment shall be made, all the powers and authorities vested in the Governor-General and Council shall rest and continue in, and be exercised and executed by, the Governor-General and Council remaining and surviving; and from and after the expiration of the said term of five years, the power of nominating and removing the succeeding Governor-General and Council shall be vested in the Directors of the said United Company.

XIII   And whereas His late Majesty King George the Second did, by his letters patent, bearing date at Westminster the eighth day of January, in the twenty-sixth year of his reign, grant unto the said United Company of Merchants of England trading to the East Indies his royal charter, thereby, amongst other things, constituting and establishing courts of civil, criminal, and ecclesiastical jurisdiction, at the said United Company's respective settlements at Madras-patnam, Bombay on the island of Bombay, and Fort William in Bengal; which said charter does not sufficiently provide for the due administration of justice in such manner as the state and condition of the Company's Presidency of Fort William in Bengal, so long as the said Company shall continue in the possession of the territorial acquisitions before mentioned, do and must require; be it therefore enacted by the authority aforesaid, that it shall and may be lawful for His Majesty, by charter, or letters patent under the great seal of Great Britain, to erect and establish a supreme court of judicature at Fort William afore-

said, to consist of a chief justice and three other judges, being barristers in England or Ireland, of not less than five years standing, to be named from time to time by His Majesty, his heirs and successors; which said Supreme Court of Judicature shall have, and the same Court is hereby declared to have, full power and authority to exercise and perform all civil, criminal, admiralty, and ecclesiastical jurisdiction, and to appoint such clerks, and other ministerial officers of the said Court, with such reasonable salaries, as shall be approved of by the said Governor-General and Council; and to form and establish such rules of practice, and such rules for the process of the said Court, and to do all such other things as shall be found necessary for the administration of justice, and the due execution of all or any of the powers which, by the said charter, shall or may be granted and committed to the said Court; and also shall be, at all times, a court of record, and shall be a court of oyer and terminer, and gaol delivery, in and for the said town of Calcutta, and factory of Fort William, in Bengal aforesaid, and the limits thereof, and the factories subordinate thereto.

XIV   Provided nevertheless, and be it further enacted by the authority aforesaid, that the said new charter which His Majesty is herein-before empowered to grant, and the jurisdiction, powers, and authorities, to be thereby established shall and may extend to all British subjects who shall reside in the kingdoms or provinces of Bengal, Behar, and Orissa, or any of them, under the protection of the said United Company; and the same charter shall be competent and effectual; and the Supreme Court of Judicature therein, and thereby to be established, shall have full power and authority to hear and determine all complaints against any of His Majesty's subjects for any crimes, misdemeanours, or oppressions, committed, or to be committed; and also to entertain, hear, and determine, any suits or actions whatsoever, against any of His Majesty's subjects in Bengal, Behar, and Orissa, and any suit, action or complaint against any person who shall, at the time when such debt, or cause of action, or complaint, shall have arisen, have been employed by, or shall then have been, directly or indirectly, in the service of the said United Company or of any of His Majesty's subjects.

XXIII   And be it further enacted by the authority aforesaid, that no Governor-General, or any of the Council of the said United Company's Presidency of Fort William in Bengal, or any Chief Justice, or any of the Judges of the Supreme Court of Judicature at Fort William aforesaid, shall directly, or indirectly, by themselves, or by any other person or persons for his or their use, or on his or their behalf accept, receive, or take, of or from any person or persons, in any manner, or on any account whatsoever, any present, gift, donation, gratuity, or reward pecuniary or otherwise, or any promise or engagement for any present, gift, donation, gratuity, or reward; and that no Governor-General, or any of the said Council, or any Chief Justice or Judge of the said Court, shall carry on, be concerned in, or have any dealing or transactions, by way of traffick or commerce of any kind whatsoever, either for his or their use or benefit, profit or advantage, or for the benefit or advantage of any other person or persons whatsoever (the trade and commerce of the said United Company only excepted); any usage or custom to the contrary thereof in anywise notwithstanding.

XXIV   And be it further enacted by the authority aforesaid, that from and after the first day of August, one thousand seven hundred and seventy-four, no person holding or exercising any civil or military office under the Crown, or the said United Company in the East Indies, shall accept, receive, or take, direct or indirectly, by himself, or any other person or persons on his behalf, or for his use or benefit, of and from any of the Indian princes or powers, or their ministers or agents (or any of the natives of Asia), any present, gift, donation, gratuity, or reward, pecuniary or otherwise, upon any account or on any pretence whatsoever; or any promise or engagement for any present, gift, donation, gratuity or reward; and if any person, holding or exercising any such civil or military office, shall be guilty of any such offence, and shall be thereof legally convicted in such Supreme Court at Calcutta, or in the Mayor's Court in any other of the said United Company's settlements where such offence shall have been committed; every such person so convicted, shall forfeit double the value of such present, gift, donation, gratuity, or reward, so taken and received; one moiety of which forfeiture shall be to the said United Company, and the other moiety to him or them who shall inform or prosecute for the same; and also shall and may be sent to England, by the order of the Governor and Council of the Presidency or settlement where the offender shall be convicted, unless such person so convicted shall give sufficient security to remove him or themselves within twelve months after such conviction.

XXXVI   And be it further enacted by the authority aforesaid, that it shall and may be lawful for the Governor-General and Council of the said United Company's settlement at Fort William in Bengal, from time to time, to make and issue such rules, ordinances, and regulations, for the good or-der and civil government of the said United Company's settlement at Fort William aforesaid, and other factories and places subordinate, or to be subordinate thereto, as shall be deemed just and reasonable (such rules, ordinances, and regulations, not being repugnant to the laws of the realm), and to set, impose, inflict, and levy, reasonable fines and forfeitures for the breach or non-observance of such rules, ordinances, and regulations; but nevertheless the same, or any of them, shall not be valid, or of any force or effect, until the same shall be duly registered and published in the said Supreme Court of Judicature, which shall be, by the said new charter, established, with the consent and approbation of the said Court, which registry shall not be made until the expiration of twenty days after the same shall be openly published, and a copy thereof affixed in some conspicuous part of the court-house or place where the said Supreme Court shall be held; and from and immediately after such registry as aforesaid, the same shall be good and valid in law; but, nevertheless, it shall be lawful for any person or persons in India to appeal therefrom to his Majesty, his heirs or successors, in Council, who are hereby empowered, if they think fit, to set aside and repeal any such rules, ordinances, and regulations respectively, so as such appeal, or notice thereof, be lodged in the said new Court of Judicature, within the space of sixty days after the time of the registering and publishing the same; and it shall be lawful for any person or persons in England to appeal therefrom in like manner, within sixty days after the publishing the same in England; and it is hereby directed and required that a copy of such rules, ordinances, and regulations, from time to time, as the same shall be so received, shall be affixed in some conspicuous and public place in the India House, there to remain and be resorted to as occasion shall require; yet nevertheless, such appeal shall not obstruct, impede, or hinder the immediate execution of any rule, ordinance, or regulation, so made and registered as aforesaid, until the same shall appear to have been set aside or repealed, upon the hearing and determination of such appeal.

XXXVII   Provided always, and be it enacted by the authority aforesaid, that the said Governor-General and Council shall, and they are hereby required, from time to time, to transmit copies of all such rules, ordinances, and regulations, as they shall make and issue, to one of His Majesty's principal Secretaries of State for the time being, and that it shall and may be lawful to and for His Majesty, his heirs and successors, from time to time, as they shall think necessary, to signify to the said

United Company, under his or their sign manual, his or their disapprobation and disallowance of all such rules, ordinances, and regulations; and that from and immediately after the time that such disapprobation shall be duly registered and published in the said Supreme Court of Judicature at Fort William in Bengal, all such rules, ordinances, and regulations, shall be null and void; but in case His Majesty, his heirs and successors, shall not, within the space of two years from the making of such rules, ordinances, and regulations, signify his or their disapprobation or disallowance thereof, as aforesaid, that then, and in that case, all such rules, ordinances, and regulations, shall be valid and effectual, and have full force.

XXXVIII   And be it further enacted by the authority aforesaid, that the Governor-General and Council for the time being of the said United Company's settlement at Fort William aforesaid, and the Chief Justice and other Judges of the said Supreme Court of Judicature, shall and may, and they are hereby respectively declared to be, and to have full power and authority to act as justices of the peace for the said settlement, and for the several settlements and factories subordinate thereto; and to do and transact all matters and things which to the office of a justice or justices of the peace do belong and appertain; and for that purpose the said Governor-General and Council are hereby authorized and empowered to hold quarter-sessions within the said settlement of Fort William aforesaid, four times in every year, and the same shall be at all times a court of record.

XXXIX   And be it further enacted by the authority aforesaid, that if any Governor-General, President, or Governor, or Council of any of the said Company's principal or other settlements in India, or the Chief Justice, or any of the Judges of the said Supreme Court of Judicature, to be by the said new charter established, or of any other court in any of the said United Company's settlements, or any other person or persons who now are, or heretofore have been employed by or in the service of the said United Company, in any civil or military station, office, or capacity, or who have or claim, or heretofore have had or claimed, any power or authority, or jurisdiction, by or from the said United Company, or any of His Majesty's subjects residing in India, shall commit any offence against this act, or shall have been, or shall be guilty of, any crime, misdemeanour, or offence, committed against any of His Majesty's subjects, or any of the inhabitants of India within their respective jurisdictions, all such crimes, offences and misdemeanours, may be respectively inquired of, heard, tried, and deter-

mined in His Majesty's Court of King's Bench, and all such persons so offending, and not having been before tried for the same offence in India, shall, on conviction, in any such case as is not otherwise specially provided for by this Act, be liable to such fine or corporal punishment as the said Court shall think fit; and moreover shall be liable, at the discretion of the said Court, to be adjudged to be incapable of serving the said United Company in any office, civil or military; and all and every such crimes, offences, and misdemeanours, as aforesaid, may be alleged to be committed, and may be laid, inquired of, and tried in the county of Middlesex.

XL   And whereas the provisions made by former laws for the hearing and determining in England offences committed in India have been found ineffectual, by reason of the difficulty of proving in this kingdom matters done there; be it further enacted by the authority aforesaid, that in all cases of indictments or informations, laid or exhibited in the said Court of King's Bench, for misdemeanours or offences committed in India, it shall and may be lawful for His Majesty's said Court, upon motion to be made on behalf of the prosecutor, or of the defendant or defendants, to award a writ or writs of mandamus, requiring the Chief Justice and Judges of the said Supreme Court of Judicature for the time being, or the Judges of the Mayor's Court at Madras, Bombay, or Bencoolen, as the case may require, who are hereby respectively authorized and required accordingly to hold a court, with all convenient speed, for the examination of witnesses, and receiving other proofs concerning the matters charged in such indictments or informations respectively; and, in the meantime, to cause such public notice to be given of the holding of the said Court, and to issue such summons or other process, as may be requisite for the attendance of witnesses, and of the agents or counsel, of all or any of the parties respectively, and to adjourn, from time to time as occasion may require; and such examination as aforesaid shall be then and there openly and publicly taken viva voce in the said Court, upon the respective oaths of witnesses, and the oaths of skilful interpreters, administered according to the forms of their several religions; and shall, by some sworn officer of such Court, be reduced into one or more writing or writings on parchment in case any duplicate or duplicates should be required by or on behalf of any of the parties interested, and shall be sent to His Majesty, in his Court of King's Bench, closed up, and under the seals of two or more of the judges of the said Court, and one or more of the said judges shall deliver the same to the agent or agents of the party or parties requiring the same; which said agent or agents (or in case of his or their death, the person into whose hands the same shall come) shall deliver the same to one of the clerks in court of His Majesty's Court of King's Bench, in the public office, and make oath that he received the same from the hands of one or more of the judges of such court in India (or if such agent be dead, in what manner the same came into his hands): and that the same has not been opened, or altered, since he so received it (which said oath such clerk in court is hereby authorized and required to administer): and such depositions, being duly taken and returned, according to the true intent and meaning of this Act, shall be allowed and read, and shall be deemed as good and competent evidence as if such witness had been present, and sworn and examined viva voce at any trial for such crimes or misdemeanours, as aforesaid, in His Majesty's said Court of King's Bench, any law or usage to the contrary notwithstanding; and all parties concerned shall be entitled to take copies of such depositions at their own costs and charges.

XLI   And be it further enacted by the authority aforesaid, that in case the said Chief Justice, or Judges of the said Supreme Court of Judicature, or any of them, for the time being, shall commit any offence against this Act, or be guilty of any corrupt practice, or other crime, offence, or misdemeanour, in the execution of their respective offices, it shall and may be lawful for His Majesty's said Court of King's Bench in England, upon an information or indictment laid or exhibited in the said Court for such crime, offence, or misdemeanour, upon motion to be made in the said Court, to award such writ or writs of mandamus, as aforesaid, requiring the Governor-General, and Council of the said United Company's settlement at Fort William aforesaid, who are hereby respectively authorized and required accordingly to assemble themselves in a reasonable time, and to cause all such proceedings to be had and made as are herein-before respectively directed and prescribed concerning the examination of witnesses; and such examination, so taken, shall be returned and proceeded upon in the same manner, in all respects as if the several directions herein-before prescribed and enacted in that behalf were again repeated.

Source: Arthur Berriedale Keith (ed.). *Speeches and Documents on India Policy, 1750–1921*, vol. 1. London: Oxford University Press, 1992, pp. 45–59.

6   James Mill: The Constitution of the East India Company (1817)

When the competitors for Indian commerce were united into one corporate body, and the privilege of exclusive trade was founded on legislative authority, the business of the East India Company became regular and uniform. Their capital, composed of the shares of the subscribers, was a fixed and definite sum: Of the modes of dealing, adapted to the nature of the business, little information remained to be acquired: Their proceedings were reduced to an established routine, or a series of operations periodically recurring: A general description, therefore, of the plan upon which the Company conducted themselves, and a statement of its principal results, appear to comprehend every thing which falls within the design of a history of that commercial body, during a period of several years.

When a number of individuals unite themselves in any common interest, reason suggests, that they themselves should manage as much as it is convenient for them to manage; and that they should make choice of persons to execute for them such parts of the business as cannot be conveniently transacted by themselves.

It was upon this principle, that the adventurers in the trade to India originally framed the constitution of their Company. They met in assemblies, which were called Courts of Proprietors, and transacted certain parts of the common business: And they chose a certain number of persons, belonging to their own body, and who were called Committees, to manage for them other parts of the business, which they could not so well perform themselves. The whole of the managing business, therefore, or the whole of the government, was in the hands of,

First The Proprietors, assembled in general court;

Secondly The Committees, called afterwards the Directors, assembled in their special courts.

At the time of the award of the Earl of Godolphin, power was distributed between these assemblies according to the following plan:

To have a vote in the Court of Proprietors, that is, any share in its power, it was necessary to be the owner of 500*l* of the Company's stock: and no additional share, contrary to a more early regulation, gave any advantage, or more to any single proprietor than a single vote.

The Directors were twenty-four in number: No person was competent to be chosen as a Director who possessed less than 2,000*l* of the Company's stock: And of these Directors, one was Chairman, and another Deputy-Chairman, presiding in the Courts.

The Directors were chosen annually by the Proprietors in their General Court; and no Director could serve for more than a year, except by re-election.

Four Courts of Proprietors, or General Courts, were held regularly in each year, in the month of December, March, June, and September, respectively; the Directors might summon Courts at other times, as often as they saw cause, and were bound to summon Courts within ten days, upon a requisition signed by any nine of the Proprietors, qualified to vote.

The Courts of Directors, of whom thirteen were requisite to constitute a Court, were held by appointment of the Directors themselves, as often, and at such times and places, as they might deem expedient for the dispatch of affairs.

According to this constitution, the supreme power was vested in the Court of Proprietors. In the first place, they held the legislative power entire: All laws and regulations, all determinations of dividend, all grants of money, were made by the Court of Proprietors. To act under their ordinances, and manage the business of routine, was the department reserved for the Court of Directors. In the second place, the supreme power was secured to the Court of Proprietors, by the important power of displacing, annually, the persons whom they chose to act in their behalf.

In this constitution, if the Court of Proprietors be regarded as representing the general body of the people, the Court of Directors as representing an aristocratical senate, and the Chairman as representing the sovereign, we have an image of the British constitution; a system, in which the forms of the different species of government, the monarchical, aristocratical, and democratical, are mixed and combined.

In the constitution, however, of the East India Company, the power allotted to the democratical part was so great, that a small portion may seem to have been reserved to the other two. Not only were the sovereignty, and the aristocracy, both elective, but they were elected from year to year; that is, were in a state of complete dependence upon the democratical part. This was not all: no decrees, but those of the democracy, were binding, at least in the last resort; the aristocracy, therefore, and monarchy, were subordinate, and subject. Under

the common impression of democratic ambition, irregularity, and violence, it might be concluded, that the democratic assembly would grasp at the whole of the power; would constrain and disturb the proceedings of the Chairmen, and Directors; would deliberate with violence and animosity; and exhibit all the confusion, precipitation, and imprudence, which are so commonly ascribed to the exercise of popular power.

The actual result is extremely different from what the common modes of reasoning incite common minds to infer. Notwithstanding the power which, by the theory of the constitution, was thus reserved to the popular part of the system, all power has centered in the Court of Directors; and the government of the Company has been an oligarchy, in fact. So far from meddling too much, the Court of Proprietors have not attended to the common affairs even sufficiently for the business of inspection: And the known principles of human nature abundantly secured that unfortunate result. To watch, to scrutinize, to inquire, is labour, and labour is pain. To confide, to take for granted that all is well, is easy, is exempt from labour, and, to the great mass of mankind, comparatively delightful. On all ordinary occasions, on all occasions which present not a powerful motive to action, the great mass of mankind are sure to be led by the soft and agreeable feeling. And if they who act have only sufficient prudence to avoid those occurrences which are calculated to rouse the people on account of whom they act, the people will allow them abundant scope to manage the common concerns in a way conformable to their own liking and advantage. It is thus that all constitutions, however democratically formed, have a tendency to become oligarchical in practice. By the numerous body, who constitute the democracy, the objects of ambition are beheld at so great a distance, and the competition for them is shared with so great a number, that in general they make but a feeble impression upon their minds: The small number, on the other hand, entrusted with the management, feel so immediately the advantages, and their affections are so powerfully engaged by the presence, of their object, that they easily concentrate their views, and point their energies with perfect constancy in the selfish direction. The apathy and inattention of the people, on the one hand, and the interested activity of the rulers on the other, are two powers, the action of which may always be counted upon; nor has the art of government as yet exemplified, however the science may or may not have discovered, any certain means by which the unhappy effects of that action may be prevented.[1]

For conducting the affairs of the Company, the Directors divided themselves into parties, called Committees; and the business into as many separate shares.

The first was the Committee of Correspondence, of which the business was more confidential, as well as extensive, than that of any of the rest. Its duties were, to study the advices from India, and to prepare answers for the inspection of the Court of Directors: To report upon the number of ships expedient for the trade of the season, and the stations proper for each: To report upon the number of servants, civil and military, in the different stations abroad; on the demand for alterations, and the applications made for leave of absence, or leave to return: All complaints of grievances, and all pecuniary demands on the Company, were decided upon in the first instance by this Committee, which nominated to all places, in the treasury, and in the secretary's, examiner's, and auditor's offices. It performed, in fact, the prime and governing business of the Company: The rest was secondary and subordinate.

The next Committee was that of Law-suits; of which the business was to deliberate and direct in all cases of litigation; and to examine the bills of law charges. It is not a little remarkable that there should be work of this description sufficient to engross the time of a committee.

The third was the Committee of Treasury. Its business was, to provide, agreeably to the orders of the Court, for the payment of dividends and interest on bonds; to negociate the Company's loans; to purchase gold and silver for exportation: to affix the Company's seal to bonds and other deeds; to examine monthly, or oftener, the balance of cash; and to decide, in the first instance, on applications respecting the loss of bonds, on pecuniary questions in general, and the delivery of unregistered diamonds and bullion.

The Committee of Warehouses was the fourth. The business of importation was the principal part of its charge. It framed the orders for the species of goods of which the investment or importation was intended to consist: It had the superintendance of the servants employed in the inspection of the purchases; determined upon the modes of shipping and conveyance; superintended the landing and warehousing of the goods; arranged the order of sales; and deliberated generally upon the means of promoting and improving the trade.

The fifth was the Committee of Accounts: of whose duties the principal were, to examine bills of exchange, and money certificates; to compare advices with bills; to examine the estimates, and accounts of cash and stock; and to superintend the office of the accountant, and the office of transfer, in which are effected the transfers of the Company's stock and annuities, and in which the foreign letters of attorney for that purpose are examined.

A committee, called the Committee of Buying, was the sixth. Its business was, to superintend the purchase and preparation of the standard articles of export, of which lead and woolens constituted the chief; to contract with the dyers and other tradesmen; to audit their accounts, and keep charge of the goods till deposited in the ships for exportation.

The Committee of the House was the seventh, and its business was mostly of an inferior and ministerial nature. The alterations and repairs of the buildings, regulations for the attendance of the several officers and clerks, the appointment of the inferior servants of the House, and the control of the secretary's accounts for domestic disbursements, were included in its province.

The eighth Committee, that of Shipping, had the charge of purchasing stores, and all other articles of export, except the grand articles appropriated to the Committee of Buying; the business of hiring ships, and of ascertaining the qualifications of their commanders and officers; of distributing the outward cargoes; of fixing seamen's wages; of issuing orders for building, repairing, and fitting out the ships, packets, &c. of which the Company were proprietors; and of regulating and determining the tonage allowed for private trade, to the commanders and officers of the Company's ships.

The ninth was the Committee of Private Trade; and its occupation was to adjust the accounts of freight, and other charges, payable on the goods exported for private account, in the chartered ships of the Company; to regulate the indulgences to private trade homeward; and, by examining the commanders of ships, and other inquiries, to ascertain how far the regulations of the Company had been violated or obeyed.

---

1 Not in the East India Company alone; in the Bank of England also, the constitution of which is similar, oligarchy has always prevailed. Nor will the circumstances be found to differ in any joint stock association in the history of British Commerce. So little does experience countenance the dangerous maxim, of the people's being always eager to grasp at too much power, that the great difficulty, in regard to good government, is, to get them really to exercise that degree of power, their own exercise of which good government absolutely requires.

The tenth Committee was of a characteristic description. It was the Committee for preventing the growth of Private Trade. Its business was to take cognizance of all instances in which the licence, granted by the Company for private trade, was exceeded; to decide upon the controversies to which the encroachments of the private traders gave birth; and to make application of the penalties which were provided for transgression. So closely, however, did the provinces of this and the preceding Committee border upon one another; and so little, in truth, were their boundaries defined, that the business of the one was not unfrequently transferred to the other.

[. . .] The powers exercised by the Governor or President and Council, were, in the first place, those of masters in regard to servants over all the persons who were in the employment of the Company; and as the Company were the sole master, without fellow or competitor, and those under them had adopted their service as the business of their lives, the power of the master, in reality, and in the majority of cases, extended to almost every thing valuable to man. With regard to such of their countrymen, as were not in their service, the Company were armed with powers to seize them, to keep them in confinement, and send them to England, an extent of authority which amounted to confiscation of goods, to imprisonment, and what to a European constitution is the natural effect of any long confinement under an Indian climate, actual death. At an early period of the Company's history, it had been deemed necessary to intrust them with the powers of martial law, for the government of the troops which they maintained in defence of their factories and presidencies; and by a charter of Charles II, granted them in 1661, the Presidents and Councils in their factories were empowered to exercise civil and criminal jurisdiction according to the laws of England. Under this sanction they had exercised judicial powers, during all the changes which their affairs had undergone; but at last it appeared desirable that so important an article of their authority should rest on a better foundation. In the year 1726 a charter was granted, by which the Company were permitted to establish a Mayor's Court at each of their three presidencies, Bombay, Madras, and Calcutta; consisting of a mayor and nine aldermen, empowered to decide in civil cases of all descriptions. From this jurisdiction, the President and Council were erected into a Court of Appeal. They were also vested with the power of holding Courts of Quarter Sessions for the exercise of penal judicature, in all cases, excepting those of high treason. And a Court of Requests,

or Court of Conscience, was instituted, for the decision, by summary procedure, of pecuniary questions of inconsiderable amount.

This reform in the judicature of India was not attended with all the beneficial effects which were probably expected from it. Negligence was left to corrupt the business of detail. The charter is said to have been procured by the influence of an individual, for the extension of his own authority; and when his ends were gained, his solicitude expired. The persons appointed to fill the judicial offices were the servants of the Company, bred to commerce, and nursed in its details: while a manuscript book of instructions comprised the whole of the assistance which the wisdom of the King and the Company provided to guide uninstructed men in the administration of justice.

Nor was the obscurity of the English law, and the inexperience of the judges, the only source of the many evils which the new arrangements continued, or produced. Jealousy arose between the Councils, and the Mayor's Courts. The Councils complained that the Courts encroached upon their authority; and the Courts complained that they were oppressed by the Councils. The most violent dissensions often prevailed; and many of the members of the Mayor's Courts quitted the service, and went home with their animosities and complaints.

Besides the above-mentioned tribunals established by the Company for the administration of the British laws to the British people in India, they erected, in the capacity of Zemindar of the district around Calcutta, the usual Zemindary Courts, for the administration of the Indian laws to the Indian people. The Phousdary Court, for the trial of crimes; and the Cutcherry for civil causes; beside the Collector's Court for matters of revenue. The judges, in these tribunals, were servants of the Company, appointed by the Governor and Council, and holding their offices during pleasure; the rule of judgment was the supposed usage of the country, and the discretion of the court; and the mode of procedure was summary. Punishments extended to fine; imprisonment; labour upon the roads in chains for a limited time, or for life; and flagellation, either to a limited degree, or death. The ideas of honour, prevalent among the natives, induced the Mogul government to forbid the European mode of capital punishment, by hanging in the case of a Mussulman. In compensation, however, it had no objection to his being whipped to death; and the flagellants in India are said to be so dexterous, as to kill a man with a few strokes of the chawbuck.

The executive and judicial functions were combined in the Councils, at the Indian presidencies; the powers even of justices of the peace being granted to the Members of Council, and to them alone. If complaints were not wanting of the oppression by these authorities upon their fellow-servants; it is abundantly evident that the Company were judge in their own cause in all cases in which the dispute existed between them and any other party.

The President was Commander-in-Chief of the Military Force maintained within his presidency. It consisted, partly of the recruits sent out in the ships of the Company; partly of deserters from the other European nations settled in India, French, Dutch, and Portuguese; and partly, at least at Bombay and Surat, of Topasses, or persons whom we may denominate Indo-Portuguese, either the mixed produce of Portuguese and Indian parents, or converts to the Portuguese, from the Indian, faith. These were troops disciplined and uniformed; besides whom, the natives were already, to a small extent, employed by the Company in military service, and called Sepoys, from the Indian term Sipahi, equivalent to soldier. They were made to use the musket, but remained chiefly armed in the fashion of the country, with sword and target; they wore the Indian dress, the turban, *cabay* or vest, and long drawers; and were provided with native officers according to the custom of the country; but ultimately all under English command. It had not as yet been attempted to train them to the European discipline, in which it was possible to render them so expert and steady; but considerable service was derived from them; and under the conduct of European leaders they were found capable of facing danger with great constancy and firmness. What at this time was the average number at each presidency, is not particularly stated. It is mentioned, that at the time when the presidency was established at Calcutta in 1707, an effort was made to augment the garrison to 300 men.

The President was the organ of correspondence, by letter, or otherwise, with the country powers. It rested with him to communicate to the Council the account of what he thus transacted, at any time, and in any form, which he deemed expedient; and from this no slight accession to his power was derived.

The several denominations of the Company's servants in India were writers, factors, junior merchants, and senior merchants: the business of the writers, as the term, in some degree, imports, was that of clerking, with the inferior details of commerce; and when dominion succeeded, of government. In the capacity of writers they remained during five years. The first promotion was to the rank of factor; the next to that of junior merchant; in each of which the period of service was three years. After this extent of service, they became senior merchants. And out of the class of senior merchants were taken by seniority the members of the Council, and, when no particular appointment interfered, even the presidents themselves.

Shortly after the first great era, in the history of the British commerce with India, the nation was delivered from the destructive burthen of the long war with France which preceded the treaty of Utrecht: And though the accession of a new family to the throne, and the resentments which one party of statesmen had to gratify against another, kept the minds of men for a time in a feverish anxiety, not the most favourable to the persevering studies and pursuits on which the triumphs of industry depend, the commerce and wealth of the nation made rapid advances.

Source: James Mill. *The History of British India.* Chicago: University of Chicago Press, 1975; (orig. London: 1817 pub.), pp. 331–9, 346–51.

Note

James Mill (1773–1836), was a prominent philosopher, historian, and economist–the son of a Scottish Presbyterian minister and abolitionist. He was also a theorist and practitioner of Utilitarianism, a combined scientific and humanistic approach to politics, economics, and social concerns. Together with Jeremy Bentham he established *The Edinburgh Review*, and in 1826 Mill was a co-founder of the University of London. James Mill's intellectual and philosophical commitments would later have a great influence on the writing and thinking of his son, John Stuart Mill.

7   Government of India Act, 1833

[. . .] III   Provided always, and be it enacted, that from and after the said twenty-second day of April one thousand eight hundred and thirty-four the exclusive right of trading with the Dominions of the Emperor of China, and of trading in tea, continued to the said Company by the said Act of the fifty-third year of King George the Third, shall cease.

IV   And be it enacted, that the said Company shall, with all convenient speed after the said twenty-second day of April one thousand eight hundred and thirty-four, close their commercial business, and make sale of all their merchandize and effects at home and abroad, distinguished in their account books as commercial assets, and all their warehouses, lands, tenements, hereditaments, and property whatsoever which may not be retained for the purposes of the Government of the said territories, and get in all debts due to them on account of the commercial branch of their affairs, and reduce their commercial establishments as the same shall become unnecessary, and discontinue and abstain from all commercial business which shall not be incident to the closing of their actual concerns, and to the conversion into money of the property hereinbefore directed to be sold, or which shall not be carried on for the purposes of the said Government.

XXXIX   And be it enacted, that the superintendence, direction, and control of the whole civil and military Government of all the said territories and revenues in India shall be and is hereby invested in a Governor-General and Counsellors, to be styled "The Governor General of India in Council."

XL   And be it enacted, that there shall be four ordinary members of the said Council, three of whom shall from time to time be appointed by the said Court of Directors from amongst such persons as shall be or shall have been servants of the said Company; and each of the said three ordinary members of Council shall at the time of his appointment have been in the service of the said Company for at least ten years; and if he shall be in the military service of the said Company, he shall not during his continuance in office as a member of Council hold any military command, or be employed in actual military duties; and that the fourth ordinary member of Council shall from time to time be appointed from amongst persons who shall not be servants of the said Company by the said Court of Directors, subject to the approbation of His Majesty, to be signified in writing by his royal Sign Manual, countersigned by the President of the said Board; provided that such last-mentioned Member of Council shall not be entitled to sit or vote in the said Council except at meetings thereof for making laws and regulations; and it shall be lawful for the said Court of Directors to appoint the Commander-in-Chief of the Company's forces in India, and if there shall be no such Commander-in-Chief, or the offices of such Commander-in-Chief and of Governor-General of India shall be vested in the same person, then the Commander-in-Chief of the forces on the Bengal establishment, to be an extraordinary member of the said Council, and such extraordinary member of Council shall have rank and precedence at the Council Board, next after the Governor-General.

XLI   And be it enacted, that the person who shall be Governor-General of the Presidency of Fort William in Bengal on the twenty-second day of April one thousand eight hundred and thirty four shall be the first Governor-General of India under this act, and such persons as shall be members of Council of the same Presidency on that day shall be respectively members of the Council constituted by this Act.

XLII   And be it enacted, that all vacancies happening in the office of Governor-General of India shall from time to time be filled up by the said Court of Directors, subject to the approbation of His Majesty, to be signified in writing by his royal Sign Manual, countersigned by the President of the said Board.

XLIII   And be it enacted, that the said Governor-General in Council shall have power to make laws and regulations for repealing, amending, or altering any laws or regulations whatever now in force or hereafter to be in force in the said territories or any part thereof, and to make laws and regulations for all persons, whether British or native, foreigners or others, and for all courts of justice, whether established by His Majesty's charters or otherwise, and the jurisdictions thereof, and for all places and things whatsoever within and throughout the whole and every part of the said territories, and for all servants of the said Company within the dominions of princes and states in alliance with the said Company; save and except that the said Governor-General in Council shall not have the power of making any laws or regulations which shall in any way repeal, vary, suspend, or affect any of the provisions of this act, or any of the provisions of the acts for punishing mutiny and desertion of officers and soldiers, whether in the service of His Majesty or the said Company, or any provisions of any act hereafter to be passed in anywise affecting the said Company or the said territories or the inhabitants thereof, or any laws or regulations which shall in any way affect any prerogative of the Crown, or the authority of Parliament, or the constitution or rights of the said Company, or any part of the unwritten laws or constitution of the United Kingdom of Great Britain and Ireland, whereon may depend in any degree the allegiance of any person to the Crown of the United Kingdom, or the sovereignty or dominion of the said Crown over any part of the said territories.

LI Provided always, and be it enacted, that nothing herein contained shall extend to affect in any way the right of Parliament to make laws for the said territories and for all the inhabitants thereof; and it is expressly declared that a full, complete, and constantly existing right and power is intended to be reserved to Parliament to control, supersede, or prevent all proceedings and acts whatsoever of the said Governor-General in Council, and to repeal and alter at any time any law or regulation whatsoever made by the said Governor-General in Council, and in all respects to legislate for the said territories and all the inhabitants thereof in as full and ample a manner as if this Act had not been passed; and the better to enable Parliament to exercise at all times such right and power, all laws and regulations made by the said Governor-General in Council shall be transmitted to England, and laid before both Houses of Parliament, in the same manner as is now by law provided concerning the rules and regulations made by the several governments in India.

LII And be it enacted, that all enactments, provisions, matters, and things relating to the Governor-General of Fort William in Bengal in Council and the Governor-General of Fort William in Bengal alone, respectively, in any other act or acts contained, so far as the same are now in force, and not repealed by or repugnant to the provisions of this act, shall continue and be in force and be applicable to the Governor-General of India in Council, and to the Governor-General of India alone, respectively.

LIII And whereas it is expedient that, subject to such special arrangements as local circumstances may require, a general system of judicial establishments and police, to which all persons whatsoever, as well Europeans as natives, may be subject, should be established in the said territories at an early period, and that such laws as may be applicable in common to all classes of the inhabitants of the said territories, due regard being had to the rights, feelings, and peculiar usages of the people, should be enacted, and that all laws and customs having the force of law within the same territories should be ascertained and consolidated, and as occasion may require amended; be it therefore enacted, that the said Governor-General of India in Council shall, as soon as conveniently may be after the passing of this act, issue a commission, and from time to time commissions, to such persons as the said Court of Directors, with the approbation of the said Board of Commissioners, shall recommend for that purpose, and to such other persons, if necessary, as the said Governor-General in Council

shall think fit, all such persons, not exceeding in the whole at any one time five in number, and to be styled "the Indian Law Commissioners," with all such powers as shall be necessary for the purposes hereinafter mentioned; and the said Commissioners shall fully inquire into the jurisdiction, powers, and rules of the existing Courts of Justice and police establishments in the said territories, and all existing forms of judicial procedure, and into the nature and operation of all law, whether civil or criminal, written or customary, prevailing and in force in any part of the said territories, and whereto any inhabitants of the said territories, whether Europeans or others, are now subject: and the said Commissioners shall from time to time make reports, in which they shall fully set forth the result of their said inquiries, and shall from time to time suggest such alterations as may in their opinion be beneficially made in the said Courts of Justice and police establishments, forms of judicial procedure and laws, due regard being had to the distinction of castes, difference of religion, and the manners and opinions prevailing among different races and in different parts of the said territories.

LXXXI And be it enacted, that it shall be lawful for any natural-born subjects of His Majesty to proceed by sea to any port or place having a Custom-house establishment within the said territories, and to reside thereat, or to proceed to and reside in or pass through any part of such of the said territories as were under the Government of the said Company on the first day of January one thousand eight hundred, and in any part of the countries ceded by the Nabob of the Carnatic, of the Province of Cuttack, and of the settlements of Singapore and Malacca, without any licence whatever; provided that all subjects of His Majesty not natives of the said territories shall, on their arrival in any part of the said territories from any port of place not within the said territories, make known in writing their names, places of destination, and objects of pursuit in India, to the chief officer of the Customs or other officer authorized for that purpose at such port or place as aforesaid.

LXXXV And whereas the removal of restrictions on the intercourse of Europeans with the said territories will render it necessary to provide against any mischief or dangers that may arise therefrom, be it therefore enacted, that the said Governor-General in Council shall and he is hereby required, by law or regulations, to provide with all convenient speed for the protection of the natives of the said territories from insult and outrage in their persons, religions, or opinions.

LXXXVII And be it enacted, that no native of the said territories, nor any natural-born subject of His Majesty resident therein, shall, by reason only of his religion, place of birth, descent, colour, or any of them, be disabled from holding any place, or employment under the said Company.

CIII And whereas it is expedient to provide for the due qualifications of persons to be employed in the Civil Service of the said Company in the said territories, be it therefore enacted, that the said Governor-General of India in Council shall as soon as may be after the first day of January in every year, make and transmit to the said Court of Directors a prospective estimate of the number of persons, who in the opinion of the said Governor-General in Council, will be necessary, in addition to those already in India or likely to return from Europe, to supply the expected vacancies in the civil establishments of the respective governments in India in such one of the subsequent years as shall be fixed in the rules and regulations hereinafter mentioned; and it shall be lawful for the said Board of Commissioners to reduce such estimate, so that the reasons for such reduction be given to the said Court of Directors; and in the month of June in every year, if the said estimate shall have been then received by the said Board, and if not, then within one month after such estimate shall have been received, the said Board of Commissioners shall certify to the said Court of Directors what number of persons shall be nominated as candidates for admission, and what number of students shall be admitted to the College of the said Company at Haileybury in the then current year, but so that at least four such candidates, no one of whom shall be under the age of seventeen or above the age of twenty years, be nominated, and no more than one student admitted for every such expected vacancy in the said civil establishments, according to such estimate or reduced estimate as aforesaid; and it shall be lawful for the said Court of Directors to nominate such a number of candidates for admission to the said College as shall be mentioned in the Certificate of the said Board; and if the said Court of Directors shall not within one month after the receipt of such Certificate nominate the whole number mentioned therein, it shall be lawful for the said Board of Commissioners to nominate so many as shall be necessary to supply the deficiency.

CV And be it enacted, that the said Candidates for admission to the said College shall be subjected to an examination in such branches of knowledge and by such examiners as the said Board shall direct, and shall be classed in a list to be prepared by the examiners, and the Candidates whose names shall stand highest in such list shall be admitted by the said Court as students in the said College until the number to be admitted for that year, according to the Certificate of the said Board, be supplied.

Source: Arthur Berriedale Keith, (ed.): *Speeches and Documents on India Policy, 1750–1921*, vol. 1. London: Oxford University Press 1922, pp. 266–74.

8 Thomas Babington Macaulay: "A Speech Delivered in the House of Commons on the 10th of July, 1833"

On Wednesday, the 10th of July, 1833, Mr Charles Grant, President of the Board of Control, moved that the bill for effecting an arrangement with the India Company, and for the better government of His Majesty's Indian territories, should be read a second time. The motion was carried without a division, but not without a long debate, in the course of which the following Speech was made:

The Company had united in itself two characters, the character of trader and the character of sovereign. Between the trader and the sovereign there was a long and complicated account, almost every item of which furnished matter for litigation. While the monopoly continued, indeed, litigation was averted. The effect of the monopoly was to satisfy the claims both of commerce and of territory at the expense of a third party, the English people; to secure at once funds for the dividend of the stockholder, and funds for the government of the Indian empire, by means of a heavy tax on the tea consumed in this country. But, when the third party would no longer bear this charge, all the great financial questions which had, at the cost of that third party, been kept in abeyance, were opened in an instant. The connection between the Company in its mercantile capacity, and the same Company in its political capacity, was dissolved. Even if the Company were permitted, as has been suggested, to govern India and at the same time to trade with China, no advances would be made from the profits of its Chinese trade for the support of its Indian government. It was in consideration of the exclusive privilege that the Company had hitherto been required to make those advances; it was by the exclusive privilege that the Company had been enabled to make them. When that privilege was taken away, it would be unreasonable in the Legislature to impose such an obligation, and impossible for the Company to fulfil it. The whole system of loans from commerce to territory, and repayments from territory to commerce, must cease. Each party must rest altogether on its own resources. It was, therefore, absolutely necessary to ascertain what resources each party possessed, to bring the long and intricate account between them to a close, and to assign to each a fair portion of assets and liabilities. There was vast property. How much of that property was applicable to purposes of state? How much was applicable to a dividend? There were debts to the amount of many millions. Which of these were the debts of the government that ruled at Calcutta? Which of the great mercantile house that bought tea at Canton? Were the creditors to look to the land revenues of India for their money? Or were they entitled to put executions into the warehouses behind Bishopsgate Street?

[. . .] We come, then, to the great question. Is it desirable to retain the Company as an organ of government for India? I think that it is desirable. The question is, I acknowledge, beset with difficulties. We have to solve one of the hardest problems in politics. We are trying to make brick without straw, to bring a clean thing out of an unclean, to give a good government to a people to whom we cannot give a free government. In this country, in any neighboring country, it is easy to frame securities against oppression. In Europe you have the materials of good government everywhere ready to your hands. The people are everywhere perfectly competent to hold some share, not in every country an equal share, but some share, of political power. If the question were, What is the best mode of securing good government in Europe? the merest smatterer in politics would answer, representative institutions. In India you cannot have representative institutions. Of all the innumerable speculators who have offered their suggestions on Indian politics, not a single one, as far as I know, however democratical his opinions may be, has ever maintained the possibility of giving, at the present time, such institutions to India. One gentleman, extremely well acquainted with the affairs of our Eastern Empire, a most valuable servant of the Company, and the author of a History of India, which, though certainly not free from faults, is, I think, on the whole, the greatest historical work which has appeared in our language since that of Gibbon – I mean Mr Mill – was examined on this point. That gentleman is well known to be a very bold and uncompromising politician. He has writ-

ten strongly, far too strongly, I think, in favour of pure democracy. He has gone so far as to maintain that no nation which has not a representative legislature, chosen by universal suffrage, enjoys security against oppression. But when he was asked before the Committee of last year whether he thought representative government practicable in India, his answer was, "Utterly out of the question." This, then, is the state in which we are. We have to frame a good government for a country into which, by universal acknowledgment, we cannot introduce those institutions which all our habits, which all the reasonings of European philosophers, which all the history of our own part of the world would lead us to consider as the one great security for good government. We have to ingraft on despotism those blessings which are the natural fruits of liberty. In these circumstances, sir, it behooves us to be cautious, even to the verge of timidity. The light of political science and of history are withdrawn: we are walking in darkness: we do not distinctly see whither we are going. It is the wisdom of a man so situated to feel his way, and not to plant his foot till he is well assured that the ground before him is firm.

Some things, however, in the midst of this obscurity, I can see with clearness. I can see, for example, that it is desirable that the authority exercised in this country over the Indian government should be divided between two bodies, between a minister or a board appointed by the Crown, and some other body independent of the Crown. If India is to be a dependency of England, to be at war with our enemies, to be at peace with our allies, to be protected by the English navy from maritime aggression, to have a portion of the English army mixed with its sepoys, it plainly follows that the King, to whom the constitution gives the direction of foreign affairs, and the command of the military and naval forces, ought to have a share in the direction of the Indian government. Yet, on the other hand, that a revenue of twenty millions a year, an army of two hundred thousand men, a civil service abounding with lucrative situations, should be left to the disposal of the Crown, without any check whatever, is what no Minister, I conceive, would venture to propose. This House is indeed the check provided by the constitution on the abuse of the royal prerogative. But that this House is, or is likely ever to be, an efficient check on abuses practised in India, I altogether deny. We have, as I believe we all feel, quite business enough. If we were to undertake the task of looking into Indian affairs as we look into British affairs, if we were to have Indian budgets and Indian estimates, if

we were to go into the Indian currency question
and the Indian Bank Charter, if to our disputes
about Belgium and Holland, Don Pedro and Don
Miguel, were to be added disputes about the debts
of the Guicowar and the disorders of Mysore, the
ex-King of the Afghans and the Maharajah Runjeet
Singh; if we were to have one night occupied by the
embezzlements of the Benares mint, and another
by the panic in the Calcutta money-market; if the
questions of Suttee or no Suttee, Pilgrim tax or no
Pilgrim tax, Ryotwary or Zemindary, half Batta or
whole Batta, were to be debated at the same length
at which we have debated Church reform and the
assessed taxes, twenty-four hours a day and three
hundred and sixty-five days a year would be too
short a time for the discharge of our duties. The
House, it is plain, has not the necessary time to
settle these matters; nor has it the necessary knowledge; nor has it the motives to acquire that
knowledge. The late change in its constitution has
made it, I believe, a much more faithful representative of the English people. But it is as far as ever
from being a representative of the Indian people. A
broken head in Cold Bath Fields produces a greater
sensation among us than three pitched battles in
India. A few weeks ago we had to decide on a claim
brought by an individual against the revenues of
India. If it had been an English question, the walls
would scarcely have held the Members who would
have flocked to the division. It was an Indian question; and we could scarcely, by dint of supplication,
make a House. Even when my right honorable
friend, the President of the Board of Control, gave
his able and interesting explanation of the plan
which he intended to propose for the government
of a hundred millions of human beings, the attendance was not so large as I have often seen it on the
turnpike bill or a railroad bill.

[. . .] That empire is itself the strangest of all
political anomalies. That a handful of adventurers
from an island in the Atlantic should have subju-
gated a vast country divided from the place of their
birth by half the globe; a country which, at no very
distant period, was merely the subject of fable to
the nations of Europe; a country never before violated by the most renowned of Western conquerors; a country which Trajan never entered; a
country lying beyond the point where the phalanx
of Alexander refused to proceed; that we should
govern a territory ten thousand miles from us; a
territory larger and more populous than France,
Spain, Italy, and Germany put together; a territory,
the present clear revenue of which exceeds the
present clear revenue of any state in the world,

France excepted; a territory inhabited by men differing from us in race, color, language, manners,
morals, religion; these are prodigies to which the
world has seen nothing similar. Reason is confounded. We interrogate the past in vain. General
rules are useless where the whole is one vast exception. The Company is an anomaly; but it is part of
a system where everything is anomaly. It is the
strangest of all governments; but it is designed for
the strangest of all Empires.

[. . .] In what state, then, did we find India? And
what have we made India? We found society
throughout that vast country in a state to which
history scarcely furnishes a parallel. The nearest
parallel would, perhaps, be the state of Europe during the fifth century. The Mogul empire in the
time of the successors of Aurungzebe, like the
Roman empire in the time of the successors of
Theodosius, was sinking under the vices of a bad
internal administration, and under the assaults of
barbarous invaders. At Delhi, as at Ravenna, there
was a mock sovereign, immured in a gorgeous
state-prison. He was suffered to indulge in every
sensual pleasure. He was adored with servile
prostrations. He assumed and bestowed the most
magnificent titles. But, in fact, he was a mere pup-
pet in the hands of some ambitious subject. While
the Honorii and Augustuli of the East, surrounded
by their fawning eunuchs, revelled and dozed without knowing or caring what might pass beyond the
walls of their palace gardens, the provinces had
ceased to respect a government which could neither
punish nor protect them. Society was a chaos. Its
restless and shifting elements formed themselves
every moment into some new combination, which
the next moment dissolved. In the course of a
single generation a hundred dynasties grew up,
flourished, decayed, were extinguished, were forgotten. Every adventurer who could muster a troop
of horse might aspire to a throne. Every palace was
every year the scene of conspiracies, treasons, revolutions, parricides. Meanwhile a rapid succession
of Alarics and Attilas passed over the defenceless
empire. A Persian invader penetrated to Delhi, and
carried back in triumph the most precious treasures
of the House of Tamerlane. The Afghan soon followed, by the same track, to glean whatever the
Persian had spared. The Jauts established themselves on the Jumna. The Seiks devasted Lahore.
Every part of India, from Tanjore to the Himalayas, was laid under contribution by the Mahrattas.
The people were ground down to the dust by the
oppressor without and the oppressor within; by the
robber from whom the Nabob was unable to pro-

tect them, by the Nabob who took whatever the robber had left to them. All the evils of despotism, and all the evils of anarchy, pressed at once on that miserable race. They knew nothing of government but its exactions. Desolation was in their imperial cities, and famine all along the banks of their broad and redundant rivers. It seemed that a few more years would suffice to efface all traces of the opulence and civilization of an earlier age.

Source: Lady Trevelyan (ed.). *Macaulay: Miscellaneous Works*, vol. 5. New York: Harper and Bros, 1880 pp. 132–3, 141–5, 148–9.

Note

Thomas Babington Macaulay (1800–59), like John Stuart Mill, was the son of a Presbyterian minister; he was also a Whig parliamentarian and social and political reformer. Macaulay served as the secretary for the Board of Control for the East India Company. In 1834, he was appointed to the Supreme Council of India, where he argued on behalf of the legal equality of Europeans and Indians. During his tenure, Macaulay also established a national system of education in India, advocated the freedom of the Indian press, and drafted the Indian Penal Code. He later served as Secretary of War (1839–41). Upon his return to England, Macaulay combined his parliamentary duties with scholarly activities, writing essays, political commentary, and histories. One of his best known historical works includes his multi-volume, *The History of England from the Accession of James II* (1849–59).

Chapter Two

Oriental Despotisms and Political Economies

Introduction

From the granting of its charter by Queen Elizabeth I in 1600 to the transfer of its rule to the British crown in 1858, the British East India Company had traded with and presided over an ever expanding territory across the British subcontinent. Its very practices – at once commercial, political, judicial, cultural, and legislative – provided important, if controversial, examples to the elaboration of inquiries into political economy and philosophies of history during those two and a half centuries. The proponents of mercantilism (or government regulation of trade) argued, for example, with the expounders of laissez-faire and free (unregulated) trade (see Smith, 1776). Challengers to Eastern cultures condemned their tendency toward "oriental despotism," and ascribed their susceptibility to conquest to an inherent failure to advance beyond the "Asiatic mode of production" (see Marx, 1853). The debates over the different forms of proper government and governability between East and West, between Europe and the "Orient," provided grounds for the continuing contest over power and suzerainty and the very question of just

how – and less and less whether – Britain should rule India.

The term "despotism" is derived from the Greek, *despotes*, meaning both head of the family and master of slaves, but the formula "oriental despotism" went on in the European Enlightenment to acquire the further specifications of the idea of the unchecked power of an agrarian emperor, to be found largely in Asia, ruling through an administrative elite, and supported by the labor of slaves. The concept of "oriental despotism" figured importantly in the considerations of the proper practice of British rule in India – whether in the inquiry into Warren Hastings' activities as the first Governor-General of India, or in the legends that emerged around the militant resistance of Tipu Sultan to continued British encroachments on local sovereignties.

Warren Hastings like Robert Clive, was central to the early history of the East India Company; both men are considered Founding Fathers of the British Raj. Hastings' career with the Company spanned the eras of unfettered monopoly trade, aggressive imperial expansionism, and corporate and institutional reform; he is generally described as an effective administrator who was caught up in the shifting tides of policy revision and political change. Hastings' career with the Company was assuredly influenced by the spectacular military campaigns of the Clive era. Clive's uninhibited ability to judge situations, make bold and frequently risky decisions involving treaty negotiations, declarations of war, and seizures of native rulers' territories, influenced the domestic interpretations of the armed conflicts of the Hastings era. Hastings was far more scholarly, cautious, and conservative than "Naughty Clive"; however, his reputation in Great Britain was affected by his association with the financial corruption of the Nabobs – the Indian-derived nickname for the Company's newly created millionaires. Hastings' career was also dramatically affected by the Parliamentary Whigs' anti-expansionist and free trade/ open market sympathies. The Whig-supported East India Act of 1773 (see Chapter 1) changed the nature of the Governor-General's administrative power; unlike his governorship of Fort William, Hastings was now subject to the supervision of the Company-appointed Council.

Hastings' questionable behavior during his Governor-Generalship included his extension of the opium trade with China – he used opium profits to finance military campaigns; his requisitioning of treasures from the Begum of Oude; his autonomous decision- and policy-making; his alleged warmongering; and his ambiguous involvement in the trial and eventual execution of Raja Nand Kumar (or Maharaja Nandakumar), who had accused Hastings of bribing him for more than one-third of a million rupees. Nand Kumar claimed to have a letter from Hastings that would support his charges against the Governor-General. The case was put before the newly instituted Supreme Court; the justice serving was a schoolmate and close friend of Hastings. In the course of the proceedings, another Indian suddenly accused Nand Kumar of forgery; the Hastings-accuser was tried, found guilty, and executed. Warren Hastings did nothing to prevent or prohibit Nand Kumar's capital punishment.

Hastings defended his administrative decisions and declared his commitment to and enjoyment of his professional position ("I have catched the desire of applause in public life"). This line of self-defense continued in his *Memoirs Relative to the State of India*. There, Hastings explained that he had inherited an institution which was growing and changing before his eyes; his decisions were always made, he argued, with the best interests of the British empire in mind. This argument did not persuade Whig Parliamentarian Edmund Burke, who initiated impeachment proceedings against

Hastings in 1786. Burke charged Hastings with a series of crimes: abuse of powers, "bribery, oppression, and tyranny"; "avarice, rapacity, pride, cruelty, ferocity, malignity of temper, haughtiness, insolence" and "blackness" of heart. Burke's high-flown moralistic rhetoric almost suggests that Hastings had become infected by a racial-viral disease, something very closely related to "Oriental despotism." For Burke, one of Hastings' great sins was his alleged abandonment of Western values and ethics. Rather than upholding British constitutional and humanistic values, Hastings had succumbed to "geographical morality."

Tipu Sultan (Tippu Sultan, Tippoo Sultan) was variously acknowledged as at once a ruler loved and respected by his own people and an infamous tyrant and treacherous opponent to Company projects for India. As Lord Cornwallis described him, "Strange, is it not, that [Tipu] should have alienated the high and mighty who are backed by sword and wealth, only to find a place in the hearts of the vast multitude which counts for nothing." Cornwallis, Governor-General in India from 1786 to 1793, had himself been involved in wars with Tipu Sultan. Born in 1750, Tipu succeeded his father Haidar Ali to rule over Mysore state. Like his father, he assisted in building up the area's military might and in revitalizing the revenue administration, fostering trade and agriculture, and introducing social reforms, such as the opposition to bonded labor. The independence of father and son, however, was not appreciated by representatives of the Company, and a series of wars – sometimes referred to as the Anglo-Mysore Wars – from 1767 to 1799 eventually brought about the subjugation of the Mysore state. The third Anglo-Mysore War, from 1790 to 1791, had been concluded with the Treaty of Seringapatam in 1792, in which not only half of Tipu's dominions were ceded to his foes, but two of his sons were taken as hostages "for a due performance of the treaty." Subsequently, Tipu Sultan, already impressed by what he knew of the example of the French Revolution, entered into "intercourse" with the French, much to the alarm of the British. Tipu even exchanged letters with Napoleon Bonaparte who in 1798 had brought his campaign to Egypt, with the eventual plan of overtaking the British and reaching India itself. As the 1798–9 correspondence between Tipu and the Company makes clear, issues of territory, political allegiances, and military preparations were paramount to their conflicted relationship. The fourth and final Anglo-Mysore War was concluded on May 4, 1799, with the capture of Seringapatam and Tipu's death in battle. But, as pointed out by the Duke of Wellington, the fear remained that "Tipu's memory will live long after the world has ceased to remember you and me."

MC and BH

Additional Reading

Ahmad, Aijaz. "Marx on India," in *In Theory*. London and New York, 1992.

Ali, B. Shaikh. *Tipu Sultan: A Study in Diplomacy and Confrontation*. Mysore, 1982.

Anderson, Perry. *Lineages of the Absolutist State*. London, 1974.

Burke, Edmund. *The Complete Works of the Right Honorable Edmund Burke*. Boston, 1866.

East India Company. *The War with Tippoo Sultan* (1800). Lahore, 1977.

Embree, Ainslie T. *Imagining India: Essays on Indian History*. Delhi, 1989.

Fernandes, Praxy. *The Tigers of Mysore: A Biography of Hyder Ali and Tipu Sultan*. New Delhi, 1991.

Feiling, Keith. *Warren Hastings*. London, 1954.

Marshall, Peter James. *The Impeachment of Warren Hastings*. London, 1965.

Marx, Karl. "On Imperialism in India," two letters to the *New York Daily Tribune*, June 25 and August 8 1853.

Moon, Penderel. *Warren Hastings and British India*. New York, 1947.

O'Leary, Brendan. *The Asiatic Mode of Production: Oriental Despotism, Historical Materialism and Indian History*. Oxford, 1989.

Scott, David. "Colonial Governmentality," in *Social Text*, 43: 191–220 (1995).

Smith, Adam. *An Inquiry into the Nature and Causes of the Wealth of Nations*. London, 1776, part 3, chapter VII.

Stokes, Eric. *The English Utilitarians and India*. Oxford, 1959.

Suleri, Sara. "Reading the Trial of Warren Hastings" and "Edmund Burke and the Indian Sublime," in *The Rhetoric of English India*. Chicago, 1992.

Sultan, Tippoo. *Authentic Memoirs of Tippoo Sultan* (1799). Delhi, 1979.

Thapar, Romila. "Ideology and the Interpretation of Early Indian History," in *Interpreting Early India*. Delhi, 1993.

Wittfogel, Karl. *Oriental Despotism*. New Haven, 1957.

Film

Zoltan Korda. *The Drum* (1938).

9   Robert Orme: "Of the Government and People of Indostan" (1782)

Nature of the Government of Indostan in general

Whoever considers the vast extent of the empire of Indostan, will easily conceive, that the influence of the emperor, however despotic, can but faintly reach those parts of his dominion which lay at the greatest distance from his capital.

This extent has occasioned the division of the whole kingdom into distinct provinces, over each of which the Mogul appoints a Viceroy.

These Viceroys are, in their provinces, called Nabobs; and their territories are again subdivided into particular districts, many of which are under the government of Rajahs. These are the descendants of such Gentoo Princes, who, before the conquest of the kingdom, ruled over the same districts.

The Gentoos, having vastly the superiority in numbers throughout the kingdom, have obliged the Moors to submit to this regulation in their government.

The Nabobs ought annually to remit to the throne the revenues of their provinces, which are either ascertained at a fixed sum, or are to be the total produce of the country, authenticated by regular accounts, after deductions made for the expenses of the government.

If the officers of the throne are satisfied, which is oftener effected by intrigue, than by the justice of his administration, the Nabob continues in favour; if not, another is appointed to succeed him.

A new appointed Nabob set out from Delhi, riding with his back turned to the head of his elephant; his attendants asked him the reason of that uncustomary posture; he said that he was looking out for his successor.

On the temper of the Nabob or his favourites, depends the happiness or misery of the province. On the temper of the King or his ministers, depends the security of the Nabob and his favourites.

The Rajahs who govern in particular districts, are, notwithstanding their hereditary right, subject to the caprice and power of the Nabob, as the army is with him.

Even this appointment of Viceroys was found too weak a representation of the royal power in the extreme parts of the kingdom; to which orders from the court are three months in arriving.

This insurmountable inconvenience occasioned the subjecting several provinces, with their distinct Nabobs, to the authority of one, who is deemed the highest representative of the Mogul.

Princes of this rank are called Subahs. Nizamalmuluck was Subah of the Decan (or southern) provinces. He had under his government all the countries lying to the south of Aurengabad, bordered on the west by the Morattoes and the Malabar coast, to the eastward extending to the sea. The Nabobs of Condanore, Cudapah, Carnatica, Yalore, etc. the Kings of Tritchinopoly, Mysore, Tanjore, are subject to this Subahship. Here is a subject ruling a larger empire than any in Europe, excepting that of the Muscovite.

The consequence of so large a dominion at such a distance from the capital has been, that an active, wily prince could overwhelm the empire itself, which Nizamalmuluck actually did, by bringing Thamas Kouli Khan into the kingdom.

Allaverdy Khan the Prince of Bengal is a Subah. He too lies at a vast distance from Delhi. He is a great warrior, and has never paid the court any tribute. The Morattoes were sent as freebooters into his country, to divert him from attempting the throne itself. He has, notwithstanding, been able to add to his dominion the whole province of Patna, which before was dependant only on the King. His relations are at this time the Nabobs of that province.

Thus the contumacy of Viceregents resisting their sovereign, or battling amongst themselves, is continually productive of such scenes of bloodshed, and of such deplorable devastations, as no other nation in the universe is subject to.

If the subjects of a despotic power are everywhere miserable, the miseries of the people of Indostan are multiplied by the incapacity of the power to control the vast extent of its dominion.

Particular Government of the Provinces

Every province is governed by a subordination of officers, who hold from no other power than that of the Nabob.

Nabob (derived from *Naib*, a word signifying deputy) is a title which, at Delhi, none but those who are styled thus in a commission given by the King, dare to assume. In distant provinces Nabobs have governed, who have been registered as dead at Delhi. A Nabob, although appointed by a Subah, ought to have his commission confirmed by the King, or one with an authentic commission appears to supplant him. He then depends upon his own force, or the support of his Subah, and a war between the competitors ensues.

A Nabob is so far despotic in his government, as he can rely upon the protection of his sovereign or his superior. Secure of this, he has nothing to apprehend, but poison or assassination from the treachery or resentment of his subjects.

Nabobs more particularly attach themselves to the command of the army, and leave the civil administration to the Duan.

Duan is properly the judge of the province in civil matters. This office is commonly devolved on a Gentoo, in provinces which by their vicinity or importance to the throne, are more immediately subject to its attention. This officer holds his commission from the King. But by the nature of the government of Indostan, where all look only to one head, he is never more than an assistant: he may be a spy; he cannot be a rival to the power of the Nabob.

He therefore comprehends in his person the offices of Prime Minister, Lord Chancellor, and Secretary of State, without presuming to advise, judge, or issue orders, but according to the will of his master, or to the influence which he has over it. Under the Duan is an officer called the Buggshi, or Buxey, who is the paymaster of the troops, and the disburser of all the public expences of the government. This must be a post of great advantage. The Buxey has under him an Amuldar, who is the overseer and manager of all the occasions of expense.

Revenues, imposts, and taxes, are levied throughout the country, by the appearance, if not by the force of the soldiers. The other officers of the province are therefore more immediately military.

Phousdar signifies the commander of a detached body of the army, and in the military government, is a title next to that of the Nabob. As the governors of particular parts of the province have always some troops under their command, such governors are called Phousdars; although very often the Nabob himself holds no more than this rank at the court of Delhi, from whence all addresses to the rulers of inferior provinces, make use only of this term.

Pollygar, from the word Pollum, which signifies a town situated in a wood, is the governor of such a town and the country about it; and is likewise become the title of all who rule any considerable town, commanding a large district of land. This term is only used on the coast of Coromandel. In other provinces of the empire, all such governors pass under the general title of Zemindars.

A Havildar is the officer placed by the government to superintend a small village.

The Havildar plunders the village, and is himself fleeced by the Zemindar; the Zemindar by the Phousdar; the Phousdar by the Nabob, or his Duan. The Duan is the Nabob's head slave; and the Nabob compounds on the best terms he can make, with his Subah, or the throne. Wherever this gradation is interrupted, bloodshed ensues.

Kellidar is the governor or commander of a fort.

Munsubbar is now a title of honour held from the throne, and exalted according to the number of horsemen which he is permitted in his commission to command. There are Munsubbars of ten thousand, and others of two hundred and fifty. This title originally signified a commissioned officer, who by favour from the throne had obtained a particular district of lands, to be allotted for his maintenance instead of a salary.

Zemindar, derived from Zemin, the word signifying lands, is the proprietor of a tract of land given in inheritance by the King or the Nabob, and who stipulates the revenue which he is to pay for the peaceable possession of it. Such Zemindars are not now to be frequently met with; but the title everywhere: it is transferred to all the little superintendants or officers under the Phousdar.

Cazee is the Mahomedan judge ecclesiastical, who supports and is supported by the *Alcoran*. He is extremely venerated.

In treating upon the administration of justice in Indostan, farther lights will be thrown upon this subject of the government of the provinces.

Source: Robert Orme (1728–1801). *Historical Fragments of the Mogul Empire.* New Delhi: Associated Publishing House, pp. 255–9 (orig. pub. 1782).

Note

Robert Orme (1728–1801) was initially employed as an East India Company writer in 1742; he later became a member of the Madras Council (1754–8). Orme was also a friend of Robert Clive and his fortunes rose and fell alongside the illustrious warrior-merchant and notorious Nabob; he would eventually have charges of extortion leveled against him. Years later, Orme was employed as the historiographer for the East India Company (1769).

10   Warren Hastings: *Memoirs Relative to the State of India* (1786)

I shall add some reflections upon the general subject of the political interests of the Company, or of the British nation in India, which I deem connected with the scope and design of this review, or are connected with the actual state of our affairs; and if in these also I shall appear to speak too much of myself, let it be remembered, that the whole of this composition is in effect a portion of the history of my own life, in those events of it which were blended with the public. Besides, I am not sure that the Company possessed a political character, or can be said to have conducted their intercourse with other nations on any system of established policy, before the period in which I was appointed to the principal administration of their affairs.

I know how readily many will both allow the position, and reprobate the system, and admit me for its author, for the sake of reprobating me also for it. I am not its author, the seed of this wonderful production was sown by the hand of calamity. It was nourished by fortune, and cultivated, and shaped (if I may venture to change the figure) by necessity. Its first existence was commercial; it obtained, in its growth, the sudden accession of military strength and territorial dominion, to which its political adjunct was inevitable. It is useless to inquire whether the Company, or the nation, has derived any substantial benefit from the change, since it is impossible to retrace the perilous and wonderful paths by which they have attained their present elevation, and to re-descend to the humble and undreaded character of trading adventurers. Perhaps the term of the national existence in India may have become susceptible of a shorter duration by it; but it is that state which it must henceforth maintain, and it must therefore adopt those principles which are necessary to its preservation in that state. To explain those principles, and to shew the necessity of their construction to the duration of the British dominion in India, is foreign from the present design, as it is perhaps too late to attempt it with any chance of its application to any purpose of utility. Yet so much as I have said, was necessary to obviate the common objection, to which every measure and every maxim are liable, which are built on a different ground from that which exists only in the idea of those who look upon the East India Company still as a body of merchants, and consider commerce as their only object.

I have been represented to the public as a man of ambition, and as too apt to be misled by projects of conquest. Though the only two facts on which this imputation has originated, have been refuted on the clearest conviction, and this in the principal instance is universally acknowledged; the imputation still remains; and I much fear that it has served, with others equally opposite to truth, for the ground of a recent and great national measure, most unfortunate in its construction, if such were the causes of it.

I can affirm that the charge, so far as it respects myself, and I fear that I stand too conspicuous a mark before my fellow-servants to be missed, or not to have been the aim of its intended direction, is wholly and absolutely false, as it is inconsistent with any motive to which it could be ascribed of pride, avarice or thirst of power; for what profit or advantage could I have acquired, or hoped to acquire, for instance, in a Marattah war; or what reputation in any war, the operations of which must necessarily depend on another, and him either taken in his turn from the roster, or with a choice divided at the most between two or three officers standing at the head of the list of the army? The first acts of the government of Bengal, when I presided over it, were well known at the time to have been of my formation, or formed on principles which I was allowed to dictate. These consisted of a variety of regulations, which included every department of the service, and composed a system as complete as a mind incompetent like my own, though possessed of very superior aids, could form, of military, political, productive, economical, and judicial connection. I found the Treasury empty, the revenue declining, the expenses unchecked, and the whole nation yet languishing under the recent effects of a mortal famine. Neither was this a season for war, nor, occupied as I was in it, would candor impute to me even a possible disposition to war. The land required years of quiet to restore its population and culture; and all my acts were acts of peace. I was busied in raising a great and weighty fabric of which all the parts were yet loose and destitute of the superior weight which was to give them their mutual support; and (if I may so express myself) their collateral strength. A tempest, or an earthquake could not be more fatal to a builder whose walls were uncovered, and his unfinished columns trembling in the breeze, than the ravages or terrors of war would have been to me and to all my hopes.

I laid my plans before the Court of Directors, and called upon them to give me the powers which were requisite for their accomplishment and duration. These were silently denied me, and those which I before possessed, feeble as they were, were taken from me. Had I been allowed the means which I required, I will inform my readers of the use to which I intended to apply them. I should have sought no accession of territory. I should have rejected the offer of any which would have enlarged our line of defence, without a more than proportionate augmentation of defensive strength and revenue. I should have encouraged, but not solicited, new alliances; and should have rendered that of our government an object of solicitation, by the example of those which already existed. To these I should have observed, as my religion, every principle of good faith; and where they were deficient in the conditions of mutual and equal dependance, I should have endeavoured to render them complete; and this rule I did actually apply to practice in the treaty which I formed with the Nabob Shujah o' Dowlah in the year 1773.

With respect to the provinces of the Company's dominion under my government, I should have studied to augment both their value and strength by an augmentation of their inhabitants and cultivation. This is not a mere phantasy of speculation. The means were most easy, if the power and trust were allowed to use them. Every region of Indostan, even at that time groaned under different degrees of oppression, desolation, and insecurity. The famine which had wasted the provinces of Bengal had raged with equal severity in other parts, and in some with greater, and the remembrance of it yet dwelt on the minds of the inhabitants with every impression of horror and apprehension. I would have afforded an asylum in Bengal, with lands and stock, to all the emigrants of other countries; I would have employed emissaries for their first encouragement; and I would have provided a perpetual and proclaimed incentive to them in the security of the community from foreign molestation, and of the individual members from mutual wrong; to which purpose, the regulations already established were sufficient, with power only competent to enforce them. And for the same purpose and with a professed view to it, I early recommended, even so early as the year 1773, the erection of public granaries on the plan since happily commenced.

Those who have been in the long habits of familiar communication with me, whether by letter or by discourse, will know that the sentiments which I have been describing are of as old a date as that of my late office in the first appointment and state of it; and to every candid reader I appeal for his conviction of their effect, if I had been permitted to follow their direction: for what man is there so immovably attached to his native soil, as to prefer it, under the scourge of oppression, the miseries of want, and the desolation of war, embittering or destroying every natural affection, and ultimately invading the source of life itself, to a state of peace, of external tranquillity, and internal protection; of assured plenty, and all the blessings of domestic increase?

Those who have seen, as I did, in a time of profound peace, the wretched inhabitants of the Carnatic, of every age, sex, and condition, tumultuously thronging round the walls of Fort St George, and lying for many successive days and nights on the burning soil, without covering or food, on a casual rumour, falsely excited, of an approaching enemy, will feelingly attest the truth of the contrast which I have exhibited in one part of it, and will readily draw the conclusion which I have drawn from it, even without attending to the rest. That such a state as I have described would have been attained without imperfection or alloy. I do not pretend to suppose; but I confidently maintain, that under an equal vigorous, and fixed administration, determined on the execution of such a plan to its accomplishment, it would have been attainable, even with common talents prosecuting it, to a degree as nearly approaching to perfection as human life is capable of receiving. The submissive character of the people; the fewness of their wants; the facility with which the soil and climate, unaided by exertions of labour, can supply them; the abundant resources of subsistence and trafficable wealth which may be drawn from the natural productions, and from the manufactures, both of established usage and of new introduction, to which no men upon earth can bend their minds with a readier accommodation; and above all, the defences with which nature has armed the land, in its mountainous and hilly borders, its bay, its innumerable intersections of rivers, and inoffensive or unpowerful neighbours; are advantages which no united state upon earth possesses in an equal degree; and which leave little to the duty of the magistrate; in effect, nothing but attention, protection, and forbearance.

But though I profess the doctrine of peace, I by no means pretend to have followed it with so implicit a devotion as to make sacrifices to it. I have never yielded a substantial right which I could assert, or submitted to a wrong which I could repel, with a moral assurance of success proportioned to the magnitude of either; and I can allude to instances in which I should have deemed it criminal not to have hazarded both the public safety and my own, in a crisis of uncommon and adequate emergency, or in an occasion of dangerous example.

I have ever deemed it even more unsafe than dishonourable to sue for peace; and more consistent with the love of peace to be the aggressor, in certain cases, than to see preparations of intended hostility, and wait for their maturity, and for their open effect to repel it. The faith of treaties I have ever held inviolate. Of this I have given the most ample and public testimonies in my conduct to the Nabob Shujah o' Dowlah, to the Nabob Assof o' Dowlah, the Nabob Walla Jah, to the Rana of Gohid, to the Nabob Nizam Ally Cawn, Raja Futty Sing, and Mahdajee Sindia; and I have had the satisfaction of seeing the policy, as well as the moral rectitude, of this practice justified by the exemplary sufferings of all who have deviated from it, in acts of perfidy to myself, or to the government over

which I presided during the time that I have had charge of it.

If in this display of my own character, I shall appear to have transgressed the bounds of modesty, I shall not decline the charge, nor fear to aggravate it by adding, that I have never yet planned or authorised any military operation, or series of operations, which has not been attended with complete success, in the attainment of its professed objects; and that I have never, in any period of my life, engaged in a negotiation which I did not see terminate as I wished and expected; and let this conclusion be offered as an undeniable proof of the propriety and efficacy of the principles on which I have regulated my conduct in both.

It would not be either an unpleasing or an unprofitable employment to turn from the survey of our neighbours, and from the contemplation of their views, interests, powers, resources and to look back on our own; mixing with the reflections obvious to our habits of thinking, those which would occur to the people with whom we have been engaged in past hostility, or who may expect to be eventually concerned with us, whether as friends or foes, in future operations. Very different would be the observations made by a spectator in such a point of view, from those which pass in the mind of a mere individual, through the clouded medium of his own wants and feelings, and with the terrors and discontents of his fellow-citizens aggravating his own; and such, perhaps, as the following would be his reflections, as the different objects of his contemplation passed in succession before him.

No state can carry on extensive military operations for any length of time, without imposing some burdens upon its subjects, or subjecting them to consequent inconveniencies; and those that suffer will complain, and condemn measures which create partial exigency, without considering their object and tendency. To the complaints of individuals, the adherents of party will superadd their accusations, exaggerate the temporary evil that exists, and darken, by despondency, the bright expectations of a future period. Such particularly has been the case in Bengal; and murmurs, suspicions, and despair, have been transmitted from India to England.

In proportion as our distresses have been, or have appeared to be, pressing, the power, resources, and advantages of our enemies have been supposed to accumulate; and an idea is adopted without reflection, that the cause which diminishes our resources, operates on one side only, without producing a similar effect on the strength of our enemies; as if it were in their power to marshall armies, and undertake military expeditions, without any augmentation of expense or distress to individuals. With as limited a judgement men are apt to draw conclusions from the errors and deficiencies of government, and the mismanagement of military operations, not reflecting that our adversaries have also their difficulties to surmount, which arise out of the imperfection of human policy and the depravations of self-interest; and that the fortune of contending states, as of simple individuals, as often turns on the different effects of their mutual blunders and misconduct, as on the superiority of skill and exertion.

But widely different is the estimate formed by those whom necessity has led us to oppose or attack of our strength and resources. They behold with astonishment the exertions that have been made from the banks of the Ganges; and reasoning as we have done from their own distresses, lament the necessity that has engaged them in wars with a power capable of making such exertions, and whose reresources, instead of being diminished, must appear to them to augment. Instead of being able to extend their incursions to the capital of our dominions, which at a period little remote from the establishment of the Company's authority they did with success; they find themselves attacked in the center of their own territories, and all their exertions required for the defence of them. They find, notwithstanding the temporary success they have derived from accident or mismanagement, that we have fresh armies ready to take the field, and that whilst our spirit is unabated, our strength is sufficient to give efficacy to its resolutions.

The conclusion I would draw from these premises is, that the vigorous exertions which we have made for the defence and security of our own possessions, have impressed an idea of our strength and resources among the powers of India, which will, more than any other motive, contribute to establish the present peace on firm foundation; to show that if our resources have suffered a diminution, those of the states with which we have been engaged in war, have felt, in probably a greater degree, the same inconvenience; finally, to evince the propriety of those exertions, notwithstanding the expense with which they have been made, by the event itself, which had evidently proved to all the powers of Hindostan and Deccan, assisted by our great European enemy the French, have not been able to destroy the solid fabric of the English power in the East, nor even to deprive it of any portion of the territories over which its control extends.

Source: Warren Hastings. *Memoirs Relative to the State of India.* New Delhi: Oxford and IBH Pub. Co., 1973, pp. 55–63 (orig. pub. 1786).

11   Edmund Burke: "On the Impeachment of Warren Hastings, 15–19 February 1788"

My Lords,

The gentlemen who have it in command to support the impeachment against Mr Hastings, late Governor-General of Bengal, have directed me to open a general view of the grounds upon which the Commons have proceeded in their charge against him; to open a general view of the extent, the magnitude, the nature, the tendency, and effect of the crimes with which they have charged him; and they have also directed me to give such an explanation, as, with their aid, I may be enabled to give, of such circumstances, preceding or concomitant with the crimes with which they charge him, as may tend to explain whatever may be found obscure in the charges as they stand. And they have further commanded me, and enabled me, I hope and trust, to give to your lordships such an explanation of anything in the laws, customs, opinions and manners, of the people concerned, and who are the objects of the crimes with which they charge him, as may tend to remove all doubt and ambiguity from the minds of your lordships upon these subjects. The several articles as they appear before you, will be opened by the other gentlemen with more distinctness, and without doubt with infinitely more particularity, when they come to apply the evidence that they adduce to each charge. This is the plan, my lords, that we mean to pursue on the great charge which is now before your lordships.

My lords, I confess that in this business I come before your lordships with a considerable degree of animation, because I think it is a most auspicious circumstance in a prosecution like this, in which the honour of this kingdom and that of many nations is involved, that from the commencement of our preliminary process to the hour of this solemn trial, not the smallest difference of opinion has arisen between the two houses. My lords, there were persons who, looking rather upon what was to be found in the journals of parliament than what was to be expected from the public justice of parliament, had formed hopes consolatory to them and unfavourable to us. There were persons who entertained hopes that the corruptions of India should have escaped amongst the dissensions of parliament: but they are disappointed. They will be disappointed in all the rest of their expectations which they had formed upon everything except the merits of the cause. The Commons will not have the melancholy and unsocial glory of having acted a right part in an imperfect work. What the greatest inquest of the nation has begun, its highest tribunal will accomplish. Justice will be done to India. It is true your lordships will have your full share in this great and glorious work; but we shall always consider that any honour that is divided with your lordships will be more than doubled to ourselves.

[. . .] My lords, the powers which Mr Hastings is charged with having abused are the powers delegated to him by the East India Company. The East India Company itself acts under two sorts of powers, derived from two sources. The first source of its power is under a charter which the Crown was authorized by act of parliament to grant. The next is from several grants and charters indeed, as well as that great fundamental charter which it derived from the Emperor of the Moguls, the person with whose dominions they are chiefly conversant; particularly the great charter by which they acquired the high stewardship of the kingdoms of Bengal, Behar, and Orissa, in 1765. Under those two charters they act. As to the first, it is from that charter that they derive the capacity by which they can be considered as a public body at all, or capable of any public function; it is from thence they acquire the capacity to take any other charter, to acquire any other offices, or to hold any other possessions. This being the root and origin of their power, it makes them responsible to the party from whom that power is derived. As they have emanated from the supreme power of this kingdom, they themselves are responsible – their body as a corporate body, themselves as individuals – and the whole body and train of their servants are responsible, to the high justice of this kingdom. In delegating great power to the India Company, this kingdom has not released its sovereignty. On the contrary, its responsibility is increased by the greatness and sacredness of the power given. For this power they are and must be responsible; and I hope this day your lordships will show that this nation never did give a power without imposing a proportionable degree of responsibility.

As to the other power, which they derived from the Mogul empire by various charters from that crown, and particularly by the charter of 1765, by which they obtained the office of lord high steward, as I said, or diwan, of the kingdoms of Bengal, Behar, and Orissa, by that charter they bound themselves, and bound exclusively all their servants, to perform all the duties belonging to that new office. And by the ties belonging to that new relation they were bound to observe the laws, rights, usages and customs, of the natives, and to pursue their benefit in all things; which was the nature, institution, and purpose, of the office which they received. If the power of the sovereign from whom they derived these powers should be by any misfortune in human affairs annihilated or suspended, the duty of the people below, which they acquired under his charter, is not suspended, is not annihilated, but remains in all its force; and, for the responsibility, they are thrown back upon that country from whence their original power, and along with it their responsibility, both emanated in one and the same act. For when the Company acquired that office in India, an English corporation became an integral part of the Mogul empire. When Great Britain assented to that grant virtually, and afterwards took advantage of it, Great Britain made a virtual act of union with that country, by which they bound themselves as securities for their subjects, to preserve the people in all rights, laws and liberties, which their natural original sovereign was bound to enforce, if he had been in a condition to enforce it. So that the two duties flowing from two different sources are now united in one, and come to have justice called for them at the bar of this House, before the supreme royal justice of this kingdom, from whence originally their powers were derived.

It may be a little necessary, when we are stating the powers they have derived from their charter, and which we state Mr Hastings to have abused, to state, in as short and as comprehensive words as I can (for the matter is large indeed) what the constitution of the Company is, and particularly what its constitution is in reference to its Indian service; where the great theatre of the abuse was situated, and where those abuses were committed.

Your lordships will recollect that the East India Company – and therefore I shall spare you a long history of that, hoping and trusting that your lordships will think it is not to inform you, but to revive circumstances in your memory, that I enter into this detail – the East India Company had its origin about the latter end of the reign of Elizabeth, a period when all sorts of companies, inventions, and monopolies, were in fashion. And at that time the Company was sent out with large, extensive powers for increasing the commerce and the honour of this country: for to increase its commerce without increasing its honour and reputation would have been thought at that time, and will be thought now, a bad bargain for the country. But their powers were under that charter confined merely to commercial affairs. By degrees, as the theatre of the operation was distant, as its intercourse was with many great, some barbarous, and all of them armed nations, where not only the sovereign but the subjects were also armed in all places, it was found necessary to enlarge their powers. The first power they obtained was a power of naval discipline in their ships – a power which has been since dropped. The next was a power of law martial. The next was a power of civil, and to a degree of criminal, jurisdiction within their own factory, within their own settlements, over their own people and their own servants. The next was – and there was a stretch indeed – the power of peace and war; those great, high prerogatives of sovereignty which never were known before to be parted with to any subjects. But those high sovereign powers were given to the East India Company. So that when it had acquired them all, which it did about the end of the reign of Charles the Second, the East India Company did not seem to be merely a company formed for the extension of the British commerce, but in reality a delegation of the whole power and sovereignty of this kingdom sent into the East. In that light the Company began undoubtedly to be considered, and ought to be considered, as a subordinate sovereign power; that is, sovereign with regard to the objects which it touched, subordinate with regard to the power from whence this great trust was derived.

When the East India Company once appeared in that light, things happened to it totally different from what has happened in all other ordinary affairs, and from what has happened in all the remote mysteries of politicians, or been dreamed of in the world. For, in all other countries, a political body that acts as a commonwealth is first settled, and trade follows as a necessary consequence of the protection obtained by political power. But here the affair was reversed: the constitution of the Company began in commerce and ended in empire; and where powers of peace and war are given, it wants but time and circumstance to make this supersede every other, and the affairs of commerce fall into their proper rank and situation. And accordingly it did happen that, the possession and power of assertion of these great authorities coin-

ciding with the improved state of Europe, with the improved state of arts and the improved state of laws, and (what is much more material) the improved state of military discipline; that coinciding with the general fall of Asia, with the relaxation and dissolution of its government, with the fall of its warlike spirit, and the total disuse almost of all parts of military discipline; those coinciding, the India Company became what it is, a great empire carrying on subordinately under the public authority a great commerce; it became that thing which was supposed by the Roman law so unsuitable – the same power was a trader, the same power was a lord.

In this situation, the India Company, however, still preserved traces of its original mercantile character, and the whole exterior order of its service is still carried on upon a mercantile plan and mercantile principles: in fact, it is a state in the disguise of a merchant, a great public office in the disguise of a counting-house. Accordingly the whole order and series, as I observed, is commercial: while the principal, inward, real part of the Company is entirely political. Accordingly the Company's service – of which the order and discipline is necessary to be explained to your lordships, that you may see in what manner the abuses have affected it – is commercial.

In the first place, all the persons who go abroad in the Company's service enter as clerks in the counting-house, and are called by a name to correspond to it – writers. In that condition they are obliged to serve five years. The next step is that of a factor, in which they are obliged to serve three years. The next step they take is that of a junior merchant, in which they are obliged to serve three years more. Then they become a senior merchant, which is the highest stage of advance in the Company's service, as a rank by which they had pretensions, before the year 1774, to the Council, to the succession of the Presidency, and to whatever other honours the Company has to bestow. Therefore the Company followed this idea in the particulars of their service; having originally established factories in certain places, which factories by degrees grew to the name of Presidencies and Councils, in proportion as the power and influence of the Company increased, and as the political began to dominate over the mercantile. And so it continued till the year 1773, when the legislature broke in, for proper reasons urging them to it, upon that order of the service, and appointed to the superior part persons who were not entitled to it – however some might have been, – by the course and order of service, such as Mr Hastings was. But, whatever title they had from thence, their legal title was derived from an express act of parliament, nominating them to that Presidency. In all other respects, the whole course of the service denominated by act of parliament does remain upon that footing – that is, a commercial footing.

Your lordships see here a regular system, a regular order, a regular course of gradation, which requires eleven years before persons can arrive at the highest trusts and situations in the Company's service. You will therefore be utterly astonished when you know that, after so long a service and so long a probation was required, things very different have happened, and that in a much shorter time persons have been seen returning to this kingdom with great and affluent fortunes. It will be necessary for you to consider, and it will be a great part of your inquiry, when we come before you to substantiate evidence against Mr Hastings, to know how that order came to be broken down completely, so that scarce a trace of it for any good purpose remains. For, though I will not deny that any order in a state may be superseded by the Presidency, when any great parts and talents upon superior exigencies are called forth, yet I must say the order of that service was formed upon wise principles. It gave the persons who were put in that course of probation an opportunity, if circumstances enabled them, of acquiring experience; it gave those who watched them a constant inspection upon them in all their progress; it gave them the necessity of acquiring a character in proportion to their standing, that all they had gained by years should not be lost by misconduct. It was a great, substantial regulation fit to be observed; but scarcely a trace of it remains to be discovered. For Mr Hastings first broke through that service by making offices which had no reference to gradation, but which were superior in profit to those which the highest gradation might have acquired. He established whole systems of offices, and especially the systems of offices established in 1781, which being new none of the rules of gradation applied to them, and he filled them in such a manner as suited best his own views and purposes; so that in effect the whole of that order, whatever merit was in it, was by him broken down and subverted. The consequence was that persons in the most immature stages of life have been put to conduct affairs which required the greatest maturity of judgement and the greatest possible temper and moderation; and effects consequent have followed upon it. So far with respect to that order of the Company's service.

My lords, I must remark, before I go farther, that there is something peculiar in the service of the East India Company, and different from that of any other nation that has ever transferred its power from one country to another. The East India Company in India is not the British nation. When the Tartars entered into China and into Hindustan – when all the Goths and Vandals entered into Europe – when the Normans came into England – they came as a nation. The Company in India does not exist as a nation. Nobody can go there that does not go in its service. Therefore the English nation in India is nothing but a seminary for the succession of officers. They are a nation of place-men. They are a republic, a commonwealth, without a people. They are a state made up wholly of magistrates. The consequence of which is, that there is no people to control, to watch, to balance against the power of office. The power of office, so far as the English nation is concerned, is the sole power in the country. There is no corrective upon it whatever. The consequence of which is, that, being a kingdom of magistrates, the *esprit de corps* is strong in it – the spirit of the body by which they consider themselves as having a common interest, and a common interest, separated both from the country that sent them out and from the country in which they are, and where there is no control by persons who understand their language, who understand their manners, or can apply their conduct to the laws of the country. Such control does not exist in India. Therefore confederacy is easy, and has been general among them; and therefore your lordships are not to expect that that should happen in such a body which never happened in the world in any body or corporation, namely, that they should ever be a proper check and control upon themselves: it is not in the nature of things. There is a monopoly with an *esprit de corps* at home, called the India Company, and there is an *esprit de corps* abroad; and both those systems are united into one body, animated with the same spirit, that is, with the corporate spirit, which never was a spirit which corrected itself in any time or circumstance in the world, and which is such a thing as has not happened to the Moors, to the Portuguese, to the Romans – to go to any old or new examples. It has not happened in any one time or circumstance in the world, except in this. And out of that has issued a series of abuses, at the head of which Mr Hastings has put himself, against the authority of the East India Company at home and every authority in this country.

My lords, the next circumstance is – and which is curious too – that the emoluments of office do not in any degree correspond with the trust. For, under the name of junior merchant, and senior merchant, and writer, and those other little names of a counting-house, you have great magistrates; you have the administrators of revenues truly royal; you have judges civil, and in a great degree criminal, who pass judgements upon the greatest properties of the country. You have all these under these names; and the emoluments that belong to them are so weak, so inadequate to the dignity of the character, that it is impossible – I may say of that service that it is absolutely impossible – for the subordinate parts of it to exist, to hope to exist, as Englishmen who look at their home as their ultimate resource – to exist in a state of incorruption. In that service the rule that prevails in many other countries is reversed. In other countries, often the greatest situations are attended with but little emoluments; because glory, fame, reputation, the love, the tears of joy, the honest applause of their country, pay those great and weighty labours which in great situations are sometimes required from the commonwealth; but all other countries pay in money what cannot be paid in fame and reputation. But it is the reverse with the India Company. All the subordinate parts of the gradation are officers, who, notwithstanding the weight and importance of the offices and dignities entrusted to them, are miserably provided for; and the heads, the chiefs, have great emoluments, securing them against every mode of temptation. And this is the thing Mr Hastings has abused. He was at the head of the service. He has corrupted his hands and sullied his government with bribes. He has used oppression and tyranny in the place of legal government; and, instead of endeavouring to find honest, honourable, and adequate rewards for the persons who served the public, he has left them to prey upon it without the smallest degree of control. He has neither supplied nor taken care to supply, with that unbounded licence which he used over the public revenues, an honest scale of emoluments, suited to the vastness of the power given to the Company's service. He has not employed the public revenue for that purpose; but has left them at large to prey upon the country, and find themselves emoluments as they could. These are the defects of that service. There is no honest emolument, in much the greater part of it, correspondent to the nature and answerable to the expectations of the people who serve. There is an unbounded licence in almost all other respects; and, as one of the honestest and ablest servants of the Company said to me, it resembled the service of the Mahrattas – little pay, but unbounded licence to plunder. This is the pay of the Company's service; a service opened to all dishonest emolument, shut up to all things that are honest and fair. I do not say that the salaries would not sound well here; but when you consider the nature of the trusts, the dignity of the situation whatever the name of it is, the powers that are granted, and the hopes that every man has of establishing himself at home, it is a source of infinite grievance, of infinite abuse; and we charge Mr Hastings, instead of stopping up, instead of endeavouring to regulate, instead of endeavouring to correct, so grievous and enormous an error, with having increased every part of it.

My lords, the next circumstance which distinguishes the East India Company is the youth of the persons who are employed in the system of that service. They have almost universally been sent out at that period of life, to begin their progress and career in active life and in the use of power, which in all other places has been employed in the course of a rigid education. They have been sent there in fact – to put it in a few words – with a perilous independence, with too inordinate expectations, and with boundless power. They are schoolboys without tutors; they are minors without guardians. The world is let loose upon them with all its temptations; and they are let loose upon the world, with all the powers that despotism can give. This is the situation of the Company's servants. [. . .] My lords, you have now heard the principles upon which Mr Hastings governs the part of Asia subjected to the British empire. You have heard his opinion of "the mean and depraved state" of those who are subject to it. You have heard his lecture upon arbitrary power, which he states to be the constitution of Asia. You hear the application that he makes of it; and you hear the practices which he employs to justify it, and who the persons were the authority of whose examples he professes to follow. Do your lordships really think that the nation would bear, that any human creature would bear, to hear an English governor defend himself upon such principles? For, if he can defend himself upon such principles, no man has any security for anything but by being totally independent of the British Government. Here he has declared his opinion that he is a despotic prince, that he is to use arbitrary power; and of course all his acts are covered with that shield. "I know," says he, "the constitution of Asia only from its practices." Will your lordships ever bear the corrupt practices of mankind made the principles of government? It will be your pride and glory to teach men that they are to confirm their practices to principles, and not to draw their principles from the corrupt practices of any man whatever. Was there ever heard, or could it be conceived, that a man would dare to mention the practices of all the villains, all the mad usurpers, all the thieves and robbers, in Asia, that he should gather them all up, and form the whole mass of abuses into one code and call it the duty of a British governor? I believe that till this time so audacious a thing was never attempted by mankind.

He to have arbitrary power! My lords, the East India Company have not arbitrary power to give him; the King has no arbitrary power to give him; your lordships have not; nor the Commons; nor the whole legislature. We have no arbitrary power to give, because arbitrary power is the thing which neither any man can hold nor any man can give away. No man can govern himself by his own will, much less can he be governed by the will of others. We are all born in subjection, all born equally, high and low, governors and governed, in subjection to one great, immutable, pre-existent law, prior to all our devices and prior to all our contrivances, paramount to our very being itself, by which we are knit and connected in the eternal frame of the universe, out of which we cannot stir.

This great law does not arise from our conventions or compacts; on the contrary, it gives to our conventions and compacts all the force and sanction they can have; it does not arise from our vain institutions. Every good gift is of God, all power is of God; and He who has given the power, and from whom it alone originates, will never suffer the exercise of it to be practised upon any less solid foundation than the power itself. Therefore, will it be imagined, if this be true, that He will suffer this great gift of government, the greatest, the best, that was ever given by God to mankind, to be the plaything and the sport of the feeble will of a man, who, by a blasphemous, absurd, and petulant usurpation, would place his own feeble, contemptible, ridiculous will in the place of the Divine wisdom and justice? No, my lords. It is not to be had by conquest; for by conquest, which is a more immediate designation of the hand of God, the conqueror only succeeds to all the painful duties and subordination to the power of God which belonged to the sovereign that held the country before. He cannot have it by succession; for no man can succeed to fraud, rapine, and violence, neither by compact, covenant, or submission, nor by any other means, can arbitrary power be conveyed to any man. Those who give and those who receive arbitrary power are alike criminal, and there is no man but is bound to resist it to the best of his power, wherever it shall show its

face to the world. Nothing but absolute impotence can justify men in not resisting it to the best of their power.

Law and arbitrary power are at eternal enmity. Name me a magistrate, and I will name property; name me power, and I will name protection. It is a contradiction in terms, it is blasphemy in religion, it is wickedness in politics, to say that any man can have arbitrary power. Judges are guided and governed by the eternal laws of justice, to which we are all subject. We may bite our chains if we will, but we shall be made to know ourselves, and be taught that man is born to be governed by law; and he that will substitute will in the place of it is an enemy to God. . . .

Therefore I charge Mr Hastings – and we shall charge him afterwards, when we come to bring the evidence more directly and fully home – with having destroyed, for private purposes, the whole system of government by the six provincial councils which he had no right to destroy.

I charge him with having delegated away from himself that power which the act of parliament had directed him to preserve inalienably in himself.

I charge him with having formed a committee to be mere instruments and tools, at the enormous expense of £62,000 per annum.

I charge him with having appointed a person their diwan, to whom these Englishmen were to be subservient tools, whose name was – to his own knowledge, by the general voice of the Company, by the recorded official transactions, by everything that can make a man known – abhorred and detested, stamped with infamy; and I charge him with the whole power which he had thus separated from the Council General and from the provincial councils.

I charge him with taking bribes of Gunga Govind Sing.

I charge him with not having done that bribe-service which fidelity, even in iniquity, requires at the hands of the worst of men.

I charge him with having robbed those people of whom he took the bribes.

I charge him with having fraudulently alienated the fortunes of widows.

I charge him with having, without right, title, or purchase, taken the lands of orphans and given them to wicked persons under him.

I charge him with having removed the natural guardians of a minor Raja, and given his zemindary to that wicked person, Deby Sing.

I charge him – his wickedness being known to himself and all the world – with having committed to Deby Sing the management of three great provinces; and with having thereby wasted the country, destroyed the landed interest, cruelly harassed the peasants, burnt their houses, seized their crops, tortured and degraded their persons, and destroyed the honour of the whole female race of that country.

In the name of the Commons of England, I charge all this villany upon Warren Hastings in this last moment of my application to you.

My lords, what is it that we want here to a great act of national justice? Do we want a cause, my lords? You have the cause of oppressed princes, of undone women of the first rank, of desolated provinces and of wasted kingdoms.

Do you want a criminal, my lords? When was there so much iniquity ever laid to the charge of any one? No, my lords, you must not look to punish any delinquent in India more. Warren Hastings has not left substance enough in India to nourish such another delinquent.

My lords, is it a prosecutor that you want? You have before you the Commons of Great Britain as prosecutors; and I believe, my lords, that the sun, in his beneficent progress round the world, does not behold a more glorious sight than that of men, separated from a remote people by the material bounds and barriers of nature, united by the bond of a social and moral community; – all the Commons of England resenting as their own the indignities and cruelties that are offered to all the people of India.

Do we want a tribunal? My lords, no example of antiquity, nothing in the modern world, nothing in the range of human imagination, can supply us with a tribunal like this. My lords, here we see virtually, in the mind's eye, that sacred majesty of the Crown, under whose authority you sit and whose power you exercise. We see in that invisible authority, what we all feel in reality and life, the beneficent powers and protecting justice of his Majesty. We have here the heir apparent to the Crown, such as the fond wishes of the people of England wish an heir apparent of the Crown to be. We have here all the branches of the royal family, in a situation between majesty and subjection, between the Crown and the subject, offering a pledge in that situation for the support of the rights of the Crown and the liberties of the people, both which extremities they touch. My lords, we have a great hereditary peerage here; those who have their own honour, the honour of their ancestors and of their posterity, to guard; and who will justify, as they have always justified, that provision in the constitution by which justice is made an hereditary office. My lords, we have here a new nobility, who have

risen and exalted themselves by various merits, by great military services, which have extended the fame of this country from the rising to the setting sun. We have those who, by various civil merits and various civil talents, have been exalted to a situation which they well deserve, and in which they will justify the favour of their sovereign and the good opinion of their fellow-subjects, and make them rejoice to see those virtuous characters, that were the other day upon a level with them, now exalted above them in rank, but feeling with them in sympathy what they felt in common before. We have persons exalted from the practice of the law, from the place in which they administered high though subordinate justice, to a seat here, to enlighten with their knowledge and to strengthen with their votes those principles which have distinguished the courts in which they have presided.

My lords, you have before you the lights of our religion – you have the bishops of England. My lords, you have that true image of the primitive church in its ancient form, in its ancient ordinances, purified from the superstitions and the vices which a long succession of ages will bring upon the best institutions. You have the representatives of that religion which says that "God is love," that the very vital spirit of its institution is charity; a religion which so much hates oppression, that, when the God whom we adore appeared in human form, he did not appear in a form of greatness and majesty, but in sympathy with the lowest of the people; and thereby made it a firm and ruling principle that their welfare was the object of all government, since the person who was the master of nature chose to appear himself in a subordinate situation. These are the considerations which influence them, which animate them and will animate them against all oppression; knowing that he who is called first among them, and first among us all, both of the flock that is fed and of those who feed it, made himself "the servant of all."

My lords, these are the securities that we have in all the constituent parts of the body of this house. We know them, we reckon, we rest, upon them; and commit safely the interests of India and of humanity into their hands. Therefore it is with confidence that, ordered by the Commons,

I impeach Warren Hastings, Esquire, of high crimes and misdemeanours.

I impeach him in the name of the Commons of Great Britain in Parliament assembled, whose parliamentary trust he has betrayed.

I impeach him in the name of all the Commons of Great Britain, whose national character he has dishonoured.

I impeach him in the name of the people of India, whose laws, rights, and liberties, he has subverted, whose properties he has destroyed, whose country he has laid waste and desolate.

I impeach him in the name and by virtue of those eternal laws of justice which he has violated.

I impeach him in the name of human nature itself, which he has cruelly outraged, injured, and oppressed, in both sexes, in every age, rank, situation, and condition of life.

Source: Arthur Berriedale Keith (ed.). *Speeches and Documents on Indian Policy, 1750–1921.* Delhi: Anmol Publishers, 1985, pp. 114–15, 120–32, 147–55.

Note

Edmund Burke (1765–82) was a prominent Whig parliamentarian. He began his career with a secretarial appointment to the Marquess of Rockingham in 1765, the same year that the Marquess entered the House of Commons as Prime Minister. Burke's persuasive arguments were central in convincing Prime Minister William Pitt (the younger) and the House of Commons to initiate impeachment proceedings against William Hastings in 1787. In addition to his fiery rhetorical prosecution of the former Governor-General of India, Burke was known for his conciliatory attitudes towards the American colonies during the taxation revolt of 1765–6 and for his advocacy of party politics. Burke also drafted the failed East India Bill of 1783, which proposed an independent board of governance for the India colony.

Edmund Burke was also a prominent scholar; his best known works include his highly influential *A Philosophical Enquiry into the Origin of Our Ideas of the Sublime and the Beautiful* (1757), and his critique of republicanism and revolution, *Reflections on the Revolution in France* (1790).

12 Warren Hastings: "The Address in his Defence" (June 2, 1791)

My Lords, in the course of this trial, my accusers, to excite a popular odium against me, have called me the abettor or usurper of arbitrary power. I certainly did not use the words arbitrary power in the sense which has been imputed to me. The language, it is true, was not my own, for I was indebted for that part of my Defence to the assistance of a friend; but this I can aver, that nothing more was meant by arbitrary power than discretionary power. I considered myself and Council as invested with that discretionary power which commanders-

in-chief have over their armies, which the Legislature has lately conferred, in a greater extent, on Lord Cornwallis, singly, and which all Governments have in their legislative capacity over the property of their subjects. I never considered that my will or caprice was to be the guide to my conduct; but that I was responsible for the use of the authority with which I was invested to those who had conferred it on me.

My Lords, let me be tried by this rule: – did I act prudently and consistently with the interest of my superiors and of the people whom I governed? Whatever may be your Lordships' opinion upon this question, I can with a safe conscience declare to all the world that my intentions were perfectly upright, and biassed by no selfish considerations whatever. [. . .]

I must entreat your Lordships to remember that, at the time I formed an intention to levy a fine upon Cheyt Sing, and when I consented to the resumption of the Begum's treasure, our government was in the utmost distress for money. I need not, in this place, enter into a minute detail of the several armies we then had in the field, or of the various demands upon me for immediate supplies of treasure; it is sufficient to say, that the distress was as great as it was possible to be without an actual state of bankruptcy and insolvency. It was very natural, under such circumstances, for me to avail myself of every just means of supply which fortune might throw in my way. It might and, I may say, it actually did incline me to act with greater promptitude and decision than I should otherwise have done.

My Lords, it will depend upon your Lordships to give me what degree of credit you please. Whether I intended, for a moment, to apply any one of the sums received by me to my own use, is a point which can be known only to God and my own conscience. I can solemnly and with a pure conscience affirm that I never did harbour such a thought for an instant. And permit me to add, my Lords, that I was too intent upon the means to be employed for preserving India to Great Britain, from the hour in which I was informed that France meant to strain every nerve to dispute that empire with us, to bestow a thought upon myself or my own private fortune. [. . .]

My Lords, I will not detain your Lordships by adverting for any length to the story, told by the Manager who opened the general charge, relative to the horrid cruelties practised on the natives of Dhee Jumla by Deby Sing. It will be sufficient to say that the Manager never ventured to introduce this story in the form of a charge, though pressed and urged to do so in the strongest possible terms, both in and out of Parliament.

Mr Paterson, on whose authority he relied for the truth of his assertions, and with whom he said he wished to go down to posterity, has had the generosity to write to my attorney in Calcutta, for my information, that he felt the sincerest concern to find his reports turned to my disadvantage, as I had acted as might be expected from a man of humanity, throughout all the transactions in which Deby Sing was concerned. Had the cruelties which the Manager stated really been inflicted, it was not possible, as he very well knew at the time, to impute them even by any kind of forced construction to me. My Lords, it is a fact that I was the first person to give Mr Paterson an ill opinion of Deby Sing, whose conduct upon former occasions had left an unfavourable and, perhaps, an unjust impression upon my mind. In employing Deby Sing, I certainly yielded up my opinion to that of Mr Anderson and Mr Shore, who had better opportunities of knowing him than I could have. In the course of the inquiry into his conduct, he received neither favour nor countenance from me, nor from any member of the Board. That inquiry was carried on principally when I was at Lucknow, and was not completed during my government, though it was commenced and continued with every possible solemnity, and with the sincerest desire, on my part and on the part of my colleagues, to do strict and impartial justice. The result I have read in England; and it certainly appears, that, though the man was not entirely innocent, the extent of his guilt bore no sort of proportion to the magnitude of the charges against him. In particular, it proved that the most horrible of those horrible acts, so artfully detailed and with such effect in this place, never were committed at all. Here I leave the subject, convinced that every one of your Lordships must feel for the unparalleled injustice that was done to me by the introduction and propagation of that atrocious calumny.

My Lords, I will not now detain your Lordships by offering many remarks upon the gross injustice that I also sustained, in having been compelled to appear at your Lordships' bar to justify acts which have received the repeated approbation of the King's Ministers and, virtually, of the late House of Commons. My Lords, it is perfectly true that the Articles to which I allude are not insisted upon, or, in other words, that they are abandoned. But I feel the injury most sensibly, and the expense of defending myself against them has been intolerable. [. . .]

When Great Britain was involved in a complicated war, and her governments in India had, besides European enemies, a confederacy of all the principal powers of India armed against them, I gave the then Minister of this kingdom constant information of all the measures which I had taken, in conjunction with my colleagues in the government, to repel the dangers which pressed us, the motive and objects of those measures, the consequences expected from them, and the measures which I had further in contemplation. And it has since afforded me more than common pleasure to reflect, that every successive letter verified the expectations and the promises of the preceding.

If I had given evidence in my defence, I should have called upon the noble Lord to have produced all my letters in his possession – those, and my letters to the court of Directors. But my letters to Lord North, in a most striking manner, would have shown how careful I was to expose all my actions to their knowledge; and, consequently, how little apprehension I could have felt that there was anything in them that could be deemed reprehensible. In all instances which might have been deemed of a doubtful nature, these communications were virtual references for their sanction or for their future prohibition. If I received neither, their silence was a confirmation, and had more than the effect of an order; since, with their tacit approbation of them, I had imposed upon myself the prior obligation of my own conception of their propriety. Were I therefore for a moment to suppose that the acts with which I am charged and which I so communicated – for I communicated all – to the court of Directors, were intrinsically wrong, yet from such proofs it is evident that I thought them right; and therefore the worst that could be said of them, as they could affect me, is, that they were errors of judgment. [. . .]

Two great sources of revenue, opium and salt, were of my creation. The first, which I am accused for not having made more productive, amounts at this time yearly to the net income of 120,000*l*. The last – and all my colleagues in the Council refused to share with me in the responsibility attendant upon a new system – to the yearly net income of above 800,000*l*.

To sum up all – I maintained the provinces of my immediate administration in a state of peace, plenty and security, when every other member of the British empire was involved in external wars or civil tumult.

In a dreadful season of famine, which visited all the neighbouring states of India during three successive years, I repressed it in its first approach to the countries of the British dominion, and by timely and continued regulations prevented its return. [. . .]

And, lastly, I raised the collective annual income of the Company's possessions under my administration from three to five millions sterling – not of temporary and forced exaction, but of an easy, continued, and still existing production – the surest evidence of a good government, improving agriculture and increased population.

To the Commons of England, in whose name I am arraigned for desolating the provinces of their dominion in India, I dare to reply, that they are – and their representatives annually persist in telling them so – the most flourishing of all the states in India. It was I who made them so. The valour of others acquired – I enlarged and gave shape and consistency to – the dominion which you hold there. I preserved it. I sent forth its armies with an effectual but an economical hand, through unknown and hostile regions, to the support of your other possessions – to the retrieval of one from degradation and dishonour, and of the other from utter loss and subjection.

I maintained the wars which were of your formation, or of that of others – not of mine [. . .] I gave you all; and you have rewarded me with confiscation, disgrace, and a life of impeachment.

Source: Geoffrey Carnall and Colin Nicholson (eds). The Impeachment of Warren Hastings: Papers from a Bicentenary Commemoration. Edinburgh: Edinburgh University Press, pp. 23–8.

13   G. A. Henty: Descriptions of Tippoo (1890s)

While some of our wars in India are open to the charge that they were undertaken on slight provocation, and were forced on by us in order that we might have an excuse for annexation, our struggle with Tippoo Saib was, on the other hand, marked by a long endurance of wrong, and a toleration of abominable cruelties perpetrated upon Englishmen and our native allies. Hyder Ali was a conqueror of the true Eastern type; he was ambitious in the extreme, he dreamed of becoming the Lord of the whole of Southern India, he was an able leader, and, though ruthless where it was his policy to strike terror, he was not cruel from choice. His son, Tippoo, on the contrary, revelled in acts of the most abominable cruelty. It would seem that he

massacred for the very pleasure of massacring, and hundreds of British captives were killed by famine, poison, or torture, simply to gratify his lust for murder. Patience was shown towards this monster until patience became a fault, and our inaction was naturally ascribed by him to fear. Had firmness been shown by Lord Cornwallis, when Seringapatam was practically in his power, the second war would have been avoided and thousands of lives spared. The blunder was a costly one to us, for the work had to be done all over again, and the fault of Lord Cornwallis retrieved by the energy and firmness of the Marquis of Wellesley. (Preface)

Tippoo, on the other hand, is a human tiger; he delights in torturing his victims, and slays his prisoners from pure love of bloodshed. He is proud of the title of "Tiger"; his footstool is a tiger's head, and the uniforms of his infantry are a sort of imitation of a tiger's stripes. He has military talent, and showed great judgment in command of his division–indeed most of the successes gained during the last war were his work. Since then he had laboured incessantly to improve his army; numbers of regiments have been raised, composed of the captives off from here and from the west coast. They are drilled in European fashion by the English captives he still holds in his hands. (chapter V: "War Declared")

Source: G. A. Henty. The Tiger of Mysore: A Story of the War with Tippoo Saib. London and Glasgow: Blackie and Son Limited, (189?), Preface and p. 83.

Note

George Alfred Henty (1832–1902) was an English writer of boy's adventure stories at the end of the nineteenth century. In addition to his tales in such popular magazines as *Boy's Own*, his more than 40 novels covered the reaches of the empire, from India to Australia, including Egypt and southern Africa, and involved boys in the battles at Mysore, in the Mutiny, in the Afghan War, the Boer War, Napoleon's campaign, and with Gordon at Khartoum (see related sections).

14   Maj. Alexander Dirom: "Treaties of Peace, and Review of the Consequences of the War" (1792)

PRELIMINARY articles of a treaty of peace concluded between the allied armies and Tippoo Sultan.

ARTICLE I

One half of the dominions of which Tippoo Sultan was in possession before the war, to be ceded to the allies from the countries adjacent, according to their situation.

ARTICLE II

Three crores and thirty lacs of rupees, to be paid by Tippoo Sultan, either in gold mohurs, pagodas, or bullion.

1st One crore and sixty-five lacs, to be paid immediately.

2nd One crore and sixty-five lacs, to be paid in three payments, not exceeding four months each.

ARTICLE III

All prisoners of the four powers, from the time of Hyder Ally, to be unequivocally restored.

ARTICLE IV

Two of Tippoo Sultan's three eldest sons to be given as hostages for a due performance of the treaty.

ARTICLE V

When they shall arrive in camp, with the articles of this treaty, under the seal of the Sultan, a counterpart shall be sent from the three powers. Hostilities shall cease, and terms of a treaty of alliance and perpetual friendship shall be agreed upon.

These were the terms, which, after different conferences with the vakeels, were dictated by Earl Cornwallis to Tippoo Sultan, and to which he found it necessary to submit. They were sent to him on the 22nd, and returned by him, signed and sealed, the night of the 23rd of February.

The allies, Hurry Punt on the part of the Mahrattas, and the Nizam's son, Secunder Jaw, and his minister Azeem-ul-Omrah, on the part of the Nizam, are said to have conducted themselves with the greatest moderation and propriety in the negotiation, and on every occasion on which they had been consulted during the war. And such was the ascendancy gained by a plain and upright conduct in all public transactions, by condescension in all points of form and religious prejudice, and by firmness in all the material operations in the field, that they professed the most perfect confidence in Lord Cornwallis, and declared their willingness to proceed with the siege, or readiness to agree to any

terms of peace his Lordship should think fit to conclude with the Sultan.

Tippoo is said to have been prevailed upon with infinite difficulty to subscribe to the terms of peace; and now that all was settled, the uneasiness in the seraglio became extreme in parting with the boys, who were to be sent out as hostages. The Sultan was again entreated to request they might be allowed to remain another day, in order to make suitable preparations for their departure, and Lord Cornwallis, who had dispensed with their coming at the time the treaty was sent, had again the goodness to grant his request.

The vakeels had been instructed to acquaint Tippoo that his Lordship would wait upon the Princes as soon as they came to their tents; and besides the guards and attendants, about 200, allowed to be sent with them, that his Lordship would appoint a careful officer, with a battalion of Sepoys, for their protection. The Sultan sent in answer, "that he was fully sensible of his Lordship's goodness; that he could not agree to his being at the trouble to go first to wait on his sons; and having the most perfect reliance on his honour, it was his own particular desire and request, that he would be pleased to allow them to be brought at once to his tent, and delivered into his own hands."

On the 26th about noon, the Princes left the fort, which appeared to be manned as they went out, and everywhere crowded with people, who, from curiosity or affection, had come to see them depart. The Sultan himself, was on the rampart above the gateway. They were saluted by the fort on leaving it, and with twenty-one guns from the park as they approached our camp, where the part of the line they passed, was turned out to receive them. The vakeels conducted them to the tents which had been sent from the fort for their accommodation, and pitched near the mosque redoubt, where they were met by Sir John Kennaway, the Mahratta and Nizam's vakeels, and from thence accompanied by them to head quarters.

The Princes were each mounted on an elephant richly caparisoned, and seated in a silver howder, and were attended by their father's vakeels, and the persons already mentioned, also on elephants. The procession was led by several camel harcarras, and seven standard-bearers, carrying small green flags suspended from rockets, followed by one hundred pikemen, with spears inlaid with silver. Their guard of two hundred Sepoys, and a party of horse, brought up the rear. In this order they approached headquarters, where the battalion of Bengal Sepoys, commanded by Captain Welch, appointed for their guard, formed a street to receive them.

Lord Cornwallis, attended by his staff, and some of the principal officers of the army, met the Princes at the door of his large tent as they dismounted from the elephants; and, after embracing them, led them in, one in each hand, to the tent; the eldest, Abdul Kalick, was about ten, the youngest, Mooza-ud-Deen, about eight years of age. When they were seated on each side of Lord Cornwallis, Gullam Ally, the head vakeel, addressed his Lordship as follows. "These children were this morning the sons of the Sultan my master; their situation is now changed, and they must look up to your Lordship as their father."

Lord Cornwallis, who had received the boys as if they had been his own sons, anxiously assured the vakeel and the young Princes themselves, that every attention possible would be shewn to them, and the greatest care taken of their persons. Their little faces brightened up; the scene became highly interesting; and not only their attendants, but all the spectators were delighted to see that any fears they might have harboured were removed, and that they would soon be reconciled to their change of situation, and to their new friends.

The Princes were dressed in long white muslin gowns, and red turbans. They had several rows of large pearls round their necks, from which was suspended an ornament consisting of a ruby and an emerald of considerable size, surrounded by large brilliants; and in their turbans, each had a sprig of rich pearls. Bred up from their infancy with infinite care, and instructed in their manners to imitate the reserve and politeness of age, it astonished all present to see the correctness and propriety of their conduct. The eldest boy, rather dark in his colour, with thick lips, a small flattish nose, and a long thoughtful countenance, was less admired than the youngest, who is remarkably fair, with regular features, a small round face, large full eyes, and a more animated appearance. Placed too, on the right hand of Lord Cornwallis, he was said to be the favourite son, and the Sultan's intended heir. His mother (a sister of Burham-ud-Deen's, who was killed at Sattimungulum), a beautiful delicate, woman, had died of fright and apprehension, a few days after the attack of the lines. This melancholy event made the situation of the youngest boy doubly interesting, and, with the other circumstances, occasioned his attracting by much the most notice. After some conversation, his Lordship presented a handsome gold watch to each of the Princes, with which they seemed much pleased. Beetle-nut and otter of roses, according to the eastern custom, being then distributed, he led them back to their elephants, embraced them again, and they returned, escorted by their suite and the battalion, to their tents.

Next day, the 27th; Lord Cornwallis, attended as yesterday, went to pay the Princes a visit at their tents, pitched near the mosque redoubt, within the green canaut or wall, used by the Sultan in the field, of which we had so often traced the marks during the war.

The canaut of canvas, scollopped at top, was painted of a beautiful sea-green colour, with rich ornamented borders, and formed an elegant inclosure for the tents. It was thrown open to the front, and within it the pikemen, Sepoys, etc. of the Princes' guard formed a street to a tent, whence they came out and met Lord Cornwallis. After embracing them, he led them, one in each hand, into the tent, where chairs were placed for his Lordship, themselves, and his suite. Sir John Kennaway, the Mahratta and the Nizam's vakeels, also attended the conference.

The eldest boy, now seated on his Lordship's right hand, appeared less serious than yesterday; and when he spoke, was not only graceful in his manner, but had a most affable, animated appearance. The youngest, however, appeared to be the favourite with the vakeels; and, at the desire of Gullam Ally, repeated, or rather recited some verses in Arabic, which he had learned by heart from the Koran, and afterwards some verses in Persian, which he did with great ease and confidence, and shewed he had made great progress in his education.

Each of the Princes presented his Lordship with a fine Persian sword, and in return he gave the eldest a fuzee, and the youngest a pair of pistols, of very fine and curious workmanship. Some jewels, shawls, and rich presents were then offered to his Lordship as matter of form; after which, beetle-nut and otter of roses being distributed, the Princes conducted his Lordship without the tent, when he embraced them and took his leave.

The tent in which the Princes received Lord Cornwallis, was lined with fine chintz, and the floor covered with white cloth. The attendants sprinkled rose water during the audience; and there was a degree of state, order, and magnificence in every thing, much superior to what had been seen amongst our allies. The guard of Sepoys drawn up without, was clothed in uniform, and not only regularly and well armed, but, compared to the rabble of infantry in the service of the other native powers, appeared well disciplined and in high order.

From what passed this day, and the lead taken by the eldest son, it seemed uncertain which of them might be intended for Tippoo's heir. Perhaps, and most probably neither; for Hyder Saib, about twenty years of age, has always been said to be

Tippoo's eldest son; had been educated accordingly, and had accompanied his father constantly during the war, till lately, when he was sent on a separate command, and distinguished himself very eminently in the relief of Gurramconda. The vakeels, however, asserted that he was not a legitimate son, nor in favour with Tippoo, from being of an unpromising disposition; but there is reason to suspect that they were directed to make this sacrifice of truth to policy, in order to prevent the demand of Hyder Saib as one of the hostages, which, to a prince at his time of life, must have been extremely disagreeable; though the others, from their early age, would feel less in that situation, and would not suffer essentially by removal from their father's care.

Hyder Saib is, from all accounts, a most promising youth, and should he be destined to succeed to the kingdom of Mysore, it may be hoped that the misfortunes which the inordinate ambition of his father has brought upon their family, will lead him to recur to the prudence of his grandfather; and that his reign, as well as the remainder of Tippoo's life, will be employed rather to preserve and improve what remains, than to attempt to recover the half which they have lost of the extensive dominions so lately acquired by the wisdom and valour of old Hyder.

Source: Major Dirom. *A Narrative of the Campaign in India which terminated the War with Tippoo Sultan in 1792.* New Delhi: Asian Educational Services, 1985, pp. 225–32, (orig. pub. 1792).

Note

Alexander Dirom (d. 1830) began his military career in the West Indies and in 1786 was sent to Madras as Deputy Adjutant-General of British forces in India. He served under Cornwallis at the siege of Bangalore and the battle at Seringapatam. He published his account of the campaign against Tipu Sultan on his return to England in 1792.

15   Selected Letters Between Tipu Sultan and Company Governors-General (1799)

To Tipu Sultan, Written on the 16th January, 1799

Your Highness has already been furnished by Lord Clive with a translation of the declaration of War, issued by the *Sublime Porte* against the French, in consequence of their having violated the sacred obligation of Treaty with the *Grand Signior*, and of their having invaded Egypt, in contempt of every principle of good faith, and of the law of Nations. You have also received from me a translation of the Manifesto, published by the *Porte* on the same occasion, exposing in just colours, the overbearing and arrogant spirit, as well as the treachery and falsehood which the French have disclosed in their conduct towards all mankind and especially towards the *Sublime Porte*.

The *Porte*, justly outraged by an aggression so atrocious and unprecedented as the invasion of Egypt, has now united in a common cause with the British Nation, for the purpose of curbing the intemperance of the French, and the *Grand Signior* having learnt the unfortunate alliance, which Your Highness has contracted with his enemies the French, against his friends and Allies the British Nation, His Highness resolved, from motives of friendship towards you, as well as towards the British Nation, to warn you, in an amicable letter, of the dangers of this fatal connection and to exhort you to manifest your zeal for the Mussalman faith, by renouncing all intercourse with the common enemy of every religion, and the aggressor of the Head of the Muhammadans.

Accordingly this letter (the testimony of friendship, and the fruit of wisdom, piety, and faithful zeal) was delivered by the ministers of the *Porte*, under the *Grand Signior*'s orders, to Mr Spencer Smith, the British Minister, resident at Constantinople, by whom it was transmitted to Honourable Mr Duncan, the Governor of Bombay, who has forwarded it to Lord Clive; the day before yesterday, this letter reached Madras, and a translation accompanied it, by which I learnt the valuable lessons of prudence and truth which it contains. I now forward it to Your Highness; you will read and consider it with the respectful attention, which it demands; there you will find the same friendly admonitions respecting the dangerous views of the French Nation which I have already submitted to your consideration.

When your discerning mind shall have duly examined this respected letter, you will no doubt draw the following conclusions from it:

Firstly: That all the maxims of public law, honour and religion, are despised and profaned by the French Nation, who consider all the thrones of the world, and every system of civil order and religious faith, as the sport and prey of their boundless ambition, insatiable rapine, and indiscriminate sacrilege.

Secondly: That the French have insulted and assaulted the acknowledged Head of the

Muhammadan Faith, and that they have wantonly raised an unprovoked and cruel war in the heart of that country, which is revered by every Mussalman, as the repository of the most sacred monuments of the Muhammadan Faith.

Thirdly: That a firm, honourable, and intimate alliance and friendship now subsists between the *Grand Signior* and the British Nation, for the express purpose of opposing a barrier to the excesses of the French.

Fourthly: That the *Grand Signior* is fully apprised of the intercourse and connection, unhappily established between Your Highness and the French, for purposes hostile to the British Nation, that he offers to Your Highness the salutary fruit of that experience which he has already acquired of the ruinous effects of French intrigue, treachery and deceit; and that he admonishes you, not to flatter yourself with the vain hope of friendly aid from those, who (even if they had escaped from the valour and skill of the British Forces) could never have reached you, until they had profaned the Tomb of your Prophet, and overthrown the foundation of your religion.

May the admonition of the Head of your own faith, dispose your mind to the pacific propositions, which I have repeatedly but in vain, submitted to your wisdom! and may you at length receive the Ambassador, who will be empowered to conclude the definite arrangement of all differences between you and the Allies, and to secure the tranquillity of India against the disturbers of the world!

(Signed) Mornington (Marquess Wellesley)

Letter from Sultan Salim, to the Indian Sovereign, Tipu Sultan, Dated Constantinople, the 20th September, 1798 Delivered to Mr Spencer Smith, His Britannic Majesty's Minister Plenipotentiary etc.

We take this opportunity to acquaint Your Majesty, when the French Republic was engaged in a war with most of the powers of Europe within this latter period, our *Sublime Porte* not only took no part against them, but, regardful of the ancient amity existing with that Nation adopted a system of the strictest neutrality and showed them even such acts of countenance as have given rise to complaints on the part of other Courts.

Thus friendly disposed towards them and reposing a confidence in those sentiments of friendship which they appeared to profess for us, we gave no ear to many propositions and advantageous offers, which had been made to us to side with the bellig-

erent powers, but pursuant to our maxims of moderation and justice, we abstained from breaking with them without direct motive and firmly observed the line of neutrality; all which is well-known to the world.

In this posture of things, when, the French having witnessed the greatest marks of attention from our *Sublime Porte*, a perfect reciprocity was naturally expected on their side, when no cause existed to interrupt the continuance of the peace between the two nations, they all of a sudden have exhibited the unprovoked and treacherous proceedings, of which the following is a sketch:

They began to prepare a Fleet in one of their harbours, called Toulon, with most extraordinary mystery, and when completely fitted out and ready for Sea, embarked a large body of troops, and they put also on board several people, versed in the Arabic Language, and who had been in Egypt before; they gave the command of that armament to one of their Generals, named Buonaparte, who first went to the Island of Malta, of which he took possession and thence proceeded direct for Alexandria, where being arrived on the 17th *Muharram*, all of a sudden landed his troops, and entered the town by open force, publishing soon after manifestoes in Arabic among the different tribes, stating in substance that the object of their enterprise was not to declare war against the *Ottoman Porte*, but to attack the *Beys* of Egypt, for insults and injuries they had committed against the French merchants in the time past; that peace with the Ottoman Empire was permanent, that those of the Arabs, who should join, would meet with the best treatment: but such, as showed opposition would suffer death: with this further insinuation, made in different quarters, but more particularly to certain Courts at amity with us, that the expedition against the *Beys* was with the privity and consent of our *Sublime Porte*; which is a horrible falsity. After this they also took possession of Rosetta, not hesitating to engage in a pitched battle with the Ottoman troops, who had been detached from Cairo to assist the invaded.

It is standing law amongst all Nations, not to encroach upon other's territories, whilst they are supposed to be at peace. When any such events take place as lead to a rupture, the motives, so tending, are previously made known between the parties, nor are any open aggressions attempted against their respective dominions, until a formal declaration of war takes place.

Whilst, therefore, no interruption of the peace, nor the smallest symptom of misunderstanding appeared between our *Sublime Porte* and the French

Republic, a conduct, so audacious, so unprovoked, and so deceitfully sudden on their part, is an undeniable trait of the most extreme insult and treachery.

The province of Egypt is considered as a region of general veneration, from the immediate proximity of the noble city of Mecca, the Qiblah of the Mussalmans, (the point of the compass to which all Turks turn their face in performing their prayers) and the sacred town of Medina, where the Tomb of our blessed Prophet is fixed; the inhabitants of both these sacred cities deriving from thence their subsistence.

Independent of this, it has been actually discovered from several letters, which have been intercepted, that the further project of the French is to divide Arabia into various Republics; to attack the whole Mahomedan sect, in its religion and country: and by a gradual progression, to extirpate all Mussalmans from the face of the earth.

It is for these cogent motives and considerations that we have determined to repel this enemy and to adopt every vigorous measure against these persecutors of the faith; we placing all confidence in the Omnipotent God, the source of all succour, and in the intercession of him, who is the glory of Prophets.

Now it being certain, that in addition to the general ties of religion, the bonds of amity and good understanding have ever been firm and permanent with Your Majesty, so justly tamed for your zeal and attachment to our faith; and that more than once such public acts of friendly attention have been practised between us, as to have cemented the connection subsisting between the two countries.

We, therefore, sincerely hope from Your Majesty's dignified disposition that you will not refuse entering into concert with us, and giving, our *Sublime Porte* every possible assistance, by such an exertion of zeal, as your firmness and natural attachment to such a cause cannot fail to excite.

We understand, that in consequence of certain secret intrigues, carried on by the French in India, (after their accustomed system) in order to destroy the settlements and to sow dissensions in the provinces of the English there, a strict connection is expected to take effect between them and Your Majesty for whose service they are to send over a corps of troops by the way of Egypt.

We are persuaded, that the tendency of the French plans cannot in the present days escape Your Majesty's penetration and notice, and that no manner of regard will be given to their deceitful insinuations on your side; and whereas the Court of Great Britain is actually at war with them and our

Sublime Porte engaged on the other hand in repelling their aggressions, consequently the French are enemies to both; and such a reciprocity of interest must exist between those Courts, as ought to make both parties eager to afford every mutual succour which a common cause requires.

It is well-known that the French bent upon the overthrow of all sects and religions, have invented a new doctrine under the name of Liberty; they themselves professing no other belief but that of *dahris*; (Epicureans, or Pythagoreans) that they have not even spared the territories of the Pope of Rome, a country, since time immemorial held in great reverence by all the European Nations; that they have wrested and shared, with others the whole Venitian State, notwithstanding that fellow Republic and not only abstained from taking part against them, but had rendered them service during the course of the war, thus effacing the name of the Republic of Venice from the annals of history.

There is no doubt that their present attempt against the Ottomans, as well as their ulterior designs, (dictated by their avaricious view towards Oriental riches) tend to make a general conquest of that country (which may God never suffer to take effect!) and to expel every Mussalman from it, under pretence of annoying the English. Their end is to be once admitted in India and then to develop what really lies in their hearts, just as they have done in every place, where they have been able to acquire a footing.

In a word, they are a Nation, whose deceitful intrigues and perfidious pursuits know no bounds. They are intent on nothing, but on depriving people of their lives and properties, and on persecuting religion, wherever their arms can reach.

Upon all this, therefore, coming to Your Majesty's knowledge, it is sincerely hoped, that you will not refuse every needful exertion towards assisting your Brethren Mussalmans, according to the obligations of religion and towards defending Hindustan itself, against the effect of French machinations.

Should it be true, as we hear, that an intimate connection has taken place between your Court and that Nation, we hope, that by weighing present circumstances as well as every future inconvenience, which would result from such a measure, Your Majesty will beware against it, and in the event of your having harboured any idea of joining with them, or of moving against Great Britain, you will lay such resolution aside.

We make it our especial request, that Your Majesty will please to refrain from entering into any measures against the English or lending any compliant ear to the French.

Should there exist any subject of complaint with the English, please do communicate it, certain as you may be, of the employment of every good office on our side to compromise the same; we wish to see the connection above alluded to, exchanged in favour of Great Britain.

We confidently expect that upon consideration of all that is stated in this communication and of the necessity of assisting your Brethren Mussalmans in this general cause of religion, as well as of cooperating towards the above precious Province being delivered from the hands of the enemy, Your Majesty will employ every means, which your natural zeal will point out, to assist the common cause, as to corroborate, by that means, the ancient good understanding so happily existing between our Empires.

> Certified translation and copy, (Signed)
> Spencer Smith

A true copy, (Signed) J. A. Grant, Sub-Secretary.

From Tipu Sultan To The Governor-General Received on the 13th February, 1799

I have been much gratified by the agreeable receipt of your Lordship's two friendly letters, the first brought by a Camel-man, the last by a *Harkara*, and understood their contents. The letter of the Prince, in station like Jamshed; with angels as his guards, with troops numerous as the stars; the sun illumining the world of the heaven of empire and dominion; the luminary giving splendour to the universe of the firmament of glory and power; the Sultan of the sea and the land; the King of Rome (i.e. the Grand Signior) be his Empire and his power perpetual; addressed to me, which reached you through the British Envoy and which you transmitted has arrived. Being frequently disposed to make excursions and hunt, I am accordingly proceeding upon a hunting excursion; you will be pleased to despatch Major Doveton (about whose coming your friendly pen has repeatedly written) slightly attended (or unattended).

Always continue to gratify me by friendly letters, notifying your welfare.

Declaration of the Right Honourable the Governor-General-in-Council

For all the Forces and Affairs of the British Nation in the East Indies, on behalf of the Honourable the East India Company, and the Allies of the said Company, Their Highnesses the Nizam and the Peshwa.

A solemn Treaty of peace and friendship was concluded at Seringapatam between the Honourable Company and the *Nawwab* Asaf Jah and the Peshwa on the one part, and *Nawwab* Tipu Sultan, on the other part, and from that day all commotion and hostility ceased. Since that day, the three Allied States have invariably manifested a sacred regard for the obligations, contracted under that Treaty with the *Nawwab* Tipu Sultan; of this uniform disposition, abundant proofs have been afforded by each of the Allies: whatever differences have arisen, with regard to the limits of the territory of Mysore, have been amicably adjusted, without difficulty, and with the most exact attention to the principles of equity, and to the stipulations of Treaty; such has been the solicitude of the Allies for the preservation of tranquillity, that they have viewed with forbearance, for some years past, various embassies and military preparations on the part of Tipu Sultan, of a tendency so evidently hostile to the interests of the Allies, as would have justified them, not only in the most serious remonstrances, but even in an appeal to arms. On the part of the British Government, every endeavour has been employed to conciliate the confidence of the Sultan, and to mitigate his vindictive spirit, by the most unequivocal acknowledgement and confirmation of his just rights and by the removal of every cause of jealousy which might tend to interrupt the continuance of peace. These pacific sentiments have been most particularly manifested in the Governor-General's recent decision on Tipu Sultan's claim to the District of Wynaad, and in the negotiation, opened by his Lordship, with regard to the districts of Amerah and Souleah. In every instance the conduct of the British Government in India towards Tipu Sultan has been the natural result of those principles of moderation, justice and good faith, which the legislature of Great Britain, and the Honourable the East India Company have firmly established as the unalterable rule of their intercourse with the Native Princes and States of India.

The exemplary good faith and the pacific disposition of the Allies, since the conclusion of the Treaty of Seringapatam, have never been disputed even by Tipu Sultan. Far from having attempted to allege even the pretext of a complaint against their conduct, he has constantly acknowledged their justice, sincerity and good faith, and has professed, in the most cordial terms, his desire to maintain and strengthen the foundations of harmony and concord with them.

In the midst of these amicable professions, on the part of Tipu Sultan, and at the moment when the British Government had issued orders for the confirmation of his claim to Wynaad, it was with astonishment and indignation that the Allies discovered the engagements, which he had contracted with the French Nation, in direct violation of the Treaty of Seringapatam, as well as of his own most solemn and recent protestations of friendships towards the Allies.

Under the mask of these specious professions, and of a pretended veneration for the obligations of Treaty, Tipu Sultan despatched Ambassadors to the Isle of France, who, in a period of profound peace in India, proposed and concluded, in his name, an offensive alliance with the French, for the avowed purpose of commencing a War of aggression against the Company, and consequently against the Peshwa and the Nizam, the Allies of the Company.

The Ambassadors in the name of Tipu Sultan demanded military succours from the French and actually levied a military force in the Isle of France, with the declared view of prosecuting the intended war.

When the Ambassadors returned in a French ship of war from the Isle of France, Tipu Sultan suffered the military force, which they had levied, for the avowed purpose of making war upon the Allies to land in his country and finally he admitted it into his army; by these personal acts ratifying and confirming the proceedings of his Ambassadors. This military force, however, was not sufficiently powerful to enable him immediately to attempt his declared purpose of attacking the Company's possessions; but in the meanwhile he advanced his hostile preparations, conformably to his engagements with the French, and he was ready to move his army into the Company's territories, whenever he might obtain from France the effectual succours, which he had assiduously solicited from that nation.

But the providence of God, and the victorious arms of the British Nation frustrated his vain hopes, and checked the presumptuous career of the French in Egypt at the moment when he anxiously expected their arrival on the coast of Malabar.

The British Government, the Nizam, and the Peshwa had not omitted the necessary precaution of assembling their forces for the joint protection of their respective dominions. The strict principles of self-defence would have justified the Allies, at that period of time, in making an immediate attack upon

the territories of Tipu Sultan; but even the happy intelligence of the glorious success of the British fleet at the mouths of the Nile, did not abate the anxious desire of the Allies to maintain the relations of amity and peace with Tipu Sultan; they attempted by a moderate representation, to recall him to a sense of his obligations, and of the genuine principles of prudence and policy; and they employed every effort to open the channels of negotiation and to facilitate the means of amicable accommodation. With these salutary views, the Governor-General on the 8th November 1798, in the name of the Allies proposed to despatch an Ambassador to Tipu Sultan for the purpose of renewing the bonds of friendship and of concluding such an arrangement as might afford effectual security against any future interruption of the public tranquillity and His Lordship repeated the same proposal on the 10th of December 1798.

Tipu Sultan declined, by various evasions and subterfuges, this friendly and moderate advance on the part of the Allies, and he manifested an evident disposition to reject the means of pacific accommodation, by suddenly breaking up, in the month of December, the conferences, which had commenced with respect to the districts of Amerah and Souleah, and by interrupting the intercourse between his subjects and those of the Company on their respective frontiers. On the 9th of January 1799, the Governor-General, being arrived at Fort St George (notwithstanding these discouraging circumstances in the conduct of Tipu Sultan) renewed with increased earnestness the expression of His Lordship's anxious desire to despatch an Ambassador to the Sultan.

The Governor-General expressly solicited the Sultan to reply within one day to this letter; and as it involved no proposition either injurious to the rights, dignity, or honour of the Sultan, or in any degree novel or complicated, either in form or substance, it could not require a longer consideration, the Governor-General waited with the utmost solicitude for an answer to the reasonable and distinct proposition contained in his letter of the 9th January, 1799.

Tipu Sultan, however, who must have received the said letter before the 17th of January, remained silent, although the Governor-General had plainly apprised the Prince, that dangerous consequences would result from delay. In the meanwhile the season for military operations had already advanced to so late a period, as to render a speedy decision indispensible to the security of the Allies.

Under these circumstances on the 3rd of February (twelve days having elapsed from the period, when an answer might have been received from Seringapatam to the Governor-General's letter of the 9th of January). His Lordship declared to the Allies, that the necessary measures must now be adopted without delay for securing such advantages, as should place the common safety of the Allies beyond the reach of the insincerity of Tipu Sultan and the violence of the French. *With this view the Governor-General, on the 3rd of February, issued orders to the British Armies to march and signified to the Commander of His Majesty's squadron that the obstinate silence of the Sultan must be considered as a rejection of the proposed negotiation.*

At length, on the 13th of February a letter from Tipu Sultan reached the Governor-General in which the Sultan signifies to His Lordship "that being frequently disposed to hunt, he was accordingly proceeding upon a hunting excursion," adding "that the Governor-General would be pleased to despatch Major Doveton to him, unattended".

The Allies will not dwell on the peculiar phrases of this letter; but it must be evident in all the States of India that the answer of the Sultan has been deferred to this late period of the Season with no other view than to preclude the Allies by insidious delays from the benefit of those advantages, which their combined military operations would enable them to secure; on those advantages alone (under the recent experience of Tipu Sultan's violation of the Treaty of Seringapatam, and under the peculiar circumstances of that Prince's alliance with the French) can the Allies now venture to rely for the faithful execution of any Treaty of Peace concluded with Tipu Sultan.

The Allies cannot suffer Tipu Sultan to profit by his own studied and systematic delay, nor to impede such a disposition of their military and naval force as shall appear best calculated to give effect to their just views.

Bound by the sacred obligations of public faith professing the most amicable disposition and undisturbed in the possession of those Dominions secured to him by Treaty, Tipu Sultan wantonly violated the relations of amity and peace and compelled the Allies to arm in defence of their rights, their happiness and their honour.

For a period of three months he obstinately rejected every pacific overture, in the hourly expectation of receiving that succour, which he had eagerly solicited for the prosecution of his favourite purposes of ambition and revenge; disappointed in his hopes of immediate vengeance, and conquest, he now resorts to subterfuge and procrastination; and by a tardy, reluctant, and insidious acquiescence in a proposition, which he had so long and repeatedly declined, he endeavours to frustrate the precautions of the Allies, and to protract every effectual operation, until some change of circumstance and of season shall revive his expectations of disturbing the tranquillity of India, by favouring the irruption of a French Army.

The Allies are equally prepared to repel his violence and to counteract his artifices and delays. The Allies are, therefore, resolved to place their army in such a position as shall afford adequate protection against any artifice or insincerity and shall preclude the return of that danger which has so lately menaced their possessions. The Allies, however, retaining an anxious desire to effect an adjustment with Tipu Sultan, Lieutenant General Harris, Commander-in-Chief of His Majesty's and the Honourable Company's Forces on the Coast of Coromandel and Malabar, is authorized to receive any Embassy which Tipu Sultan may despatch to the Headquarters of the British Army and to concert a treaty on such conditions, as appear to the Allies to be indispensibly necessary for the establishment of a secure and permanent peace.

By order of the Right Honourable the Governor-General.

Fort St George: February 22, 1799

Source: Secret Correspondance of Tipu Sultan. Compiled by Kabir Kausar. New Delhi: Light and Life Publishers, 1980, pp. 253–65.

Chapter Three

Orientalism: The East as a Career

Introduction

Edward Said has argued that "orientalism" was a "Western style for dominating, restructuring, and having authority over the Orient" (1978: 3), but "orientalism," as Said and others have demonstrated, has had its own disciplinary history in the course of the last two centuries in the Euro-American academy. Sir William Jones (1746–94), for example, is often credited with founding father status of comparative literature. A scholar – and perhaps an exemplar of Henry Clerval, the orientalist in Mary Shelley's *Frankenstein* – of Eastern languages and cultures, Jones was the first president of the Asiatic Society of Bengal, established in 1784. His translations of literary and legal works from Arabic, Persian, and Sanskrit, were decisive in determining one approach – that of the "orientalist" – to the question of how the British might rule India. By contrast, Lord Thomas Babington Macaulay argued the imperative of a more "anglicist" emphasis: natives should learn the English language and British ways rather than British civil servants and Company officials specializing in orientalist studies. The role of the "scholar" in the imperial project from the beginning was not without its challenges. As William Jones described it in a letter from India to Viscount Althorp in 1783: "Of myself I will only say that, disliking as I did,

the politicks and parties of Britain, I am very glad to be out of their way, and to amuse myself a few years in this wonderful country. The substantial good, that I can do, will not, I fear, be very great, as the character of a reformer is too invidious for one to assume; but should I live to return, I may indeed be useful in supplying the legislature with just and accurate intelligence for the reformation of this imperfect judicature" (Calcutta, October 14, 1783).

The debate – circular, disciplinary, commercial, as well as political – continued throughout the century and functions currently, a century later, even in considerations of "post-colonial" and other "area" studies. Jones's Asiatic Society, however, would go on at that time to propagate not only its methodologies and ideologies, but other societies as well. Max Müller, the German anthropologist whose career developed in England in the latter half of the nineteenth century, spoke eloquently to the point in his address to the 1874 meeting of the second session of the International Congress of Orientalists:

No one likes to be asked, what business he has to exist, and yet, whatever we do, whether singly or in concert with others, the first question which the world never fails to address to us, is . . . Why are you here? . . . What is the good of an International Congress of Orientalists?

BH

Additional Reading

Cannon, Garland Hampton. *The Life and Mind of Oriental Jones: Sir William Jones, The Father of Modern Linguistics*. Cambridge, 1990.

Disraeli, Benjamin. *Sybil, or the Two Nations*. London, 1845.

Hegel, G. W. F. "India," in *The Philosophy of History*. 1822.

Jones, Sir William. *The Letters of Sir William Jones*, ed. Garland Cannon. (2 vols). Oxford, 1970.

Lowe, Lisa, *Critical Terrains: French and British Orientalisms*. Ithaca and London, 1991.

Mukherjee, Soumyendra Nath. *Sir William Jones: A Study in Eighteenth-Century British Attitudes to India*. Bashir Bagh, Hyderabad, 1987.

Müller, Max. *India, What Can It Teach Us?* London, 1833.

Trevelyan, Charles. *"On the Education of the People of India"* (pamphlet). London, 1838.

Said, Edward. *Orientalism*. New York, 1978.

Suleri, Sara. *The Rhetoric of English India*. Chicago, 1992.

Schwab, Raymond. *The Oriental Renaissance*, trans. Gene Patterson-Black and Victor Reinking. New York, 1984.

Viswanathan, Gauri. *Masks of Conquest: Literary Study and British Rule in India*. New York, 1989.

Thapar, Romila. *Interpreting Early India*. Delhi, 1993.

16   Col. Henry Yule and A. C. Burnell: Definitions of "Baboo," "Nabob," and "Pundit" (1886)

BABOO, s. Beng. and H. *Bābū* [Skt. *vapra*, a father]. Properly a term of respect attached to a name, like *Master* or *Mr*, and formerly in some parts of Hindustan applied to certain persons of distinction. Its application as a term of respect is now almost or altogether confined to Lower Bengal (though C. P. Brown states that it is also used in S. India for "Sir, My lord, your Honour"). In Bengal and elsewhere, among Anglo-Indians, it is often used with a slight savour of disparagement, as characterizing a superficially cultivated, but too often effeminate, Bengali. And from the extensive employment of the class, to which the term was applied as a title, in the capacity of clerks in English offices, the word has come often to signify "a native clerk who writes English."

1781   "I said . . . From my youth to this day I am a servant to the English. I have never gone to any Rajahs or Bauboos nor will I go to them." – Depn. of *Dooud Sing*, Commandant. In *Narr. of Insurn. at Banaras* in 1781. Calc. 1782. Reprinted at Roorkee, 1853. App., p. 165.

1782   "*Cantoo* Baboo" appears as a subscriber to a famine fund at Madras for 200 Sicca Rupees. – *India Gazette*, Oct. 12.

1791   "Here Edmund was making a monstrous ado, About some bloody Letter and Conta Bah-Booh." *Letters of Simkin the Second*, 147.

1803   ". . . Calling on Mr. Neave I found there Baboo Dheep Narrain, brother to Oodit Narrain, Rajah at Benares." – *Lord Valentia's Travels*, i. 112.

1824   ". . . the immense convent-like mansion of some of the more wealthy Baboos . . ." – *Heber*, i. 31, ed. 1844.

1834   "The Babbo and other Tales, descriptive of Society in India." – Smith & Elder, London. (By Augustus Prinsep.)

1850   "If instruction were sought for from them (the Mohammedan historians) we should no longer hear bombastic Baboos, enjoying under our Government the highest degree of personal liberty . . . rave about patriotism, and the degradation of their present position." – *Sir H. M. Elliot*, Orig. Preface to *Mahom. Historians of India*, in Dowson's ed., I. xxii.

c.1866.

"But I'd sooner be robbed by a tall man who showed me a yard of steel,
Than be fleeced by a sneaking Baboo, with a peon and badge at his heel."

Sir A. C. Lyall, *The Old Pindaree*.

1873   "The pliable, plastic, receptive Baboo of Bengal eagerly avails himself of this system (of English education) partly from a servile wish to please the *Sahib logue*, and partly from a desire to obtain a Government appointment." – *Fraser's Mag.*, August, 209.

1880   "English officers who have become de-Europeanised from long residence among undomesticated natives. . . . Such officials are what Lord Lytton calls White Baboos." – *Aberigh-Mackay, Twenty-one Days*, p. 104.

N.B. – In Java and the further East *bābū* means a nurse or female servant (Javanese word).

NABÓB, s. Port. *Nabâbo*, and Fr. *Nabab*, from Hind. *Nawāb*, which is the Ar. pl. of sing. *Nāyab* (see NAIB), a deputy, and was applied in a singular sense to a delegate of the supreme chief, viz. to a Viceroy or supreme chief, viz. to a Viceroy or chief Governor under the Great Mogul *e.g.* the *Nawāb* of Surat, the *Nawāb* of Oudh, the *Nawāb* of Arcot, the *Nawāb Nazim* of Bengal. From this use it became a title of rank without necessarily having any office attached. It is now a title occasionally conferred, like a peerage, on Mohammedan gentlemen of distinction and good service, as *Rāī* and *Rājā* are upon Hindus.

Nabob is used in two ways: (a) simply as a corruption and representative of *Nawāb*. We get it direct from the Port. *nabâbo*, see quotation from Bluteau below. (b) It began to be applied in the 18th century, when the transactions of Clive made the epithet familiar in England, to Anglo-Indians who returned with fortunes from the East; and Foote's play of "The Nabob" (*Nábob*) (1768) aided in giving general currency to the word in this sense.

(a)

1604 ". . . delante del Nauabo quo es justicia mayor." – *Guerrero, Relacion,* 70.

1615 "There was as Nababo in Surat a certain Persian Mahommedan (*Mouro Parsio*) called Mocarre Bethião, who had come to Goa in the time of the Viceroy Ruy Lourenço de Tavora, and who being treated with much familiarity and kindness by the Portuguese . . . came to confess that it could not but be that truth was with their Law. . . ." – *Bocurro,* p. 354.

1616 "Catechumeni ergo parentes viros aliquot inducunt honestos et assessores Nauabi, id est, judicis supremi, cui consiliarii erant, uti et Progregi, ut libellum famosum adversus Pinnerum spargerent." – *Jarric, Thesaurus,* iii. 378.

1652 "The Nabab was sitting, according to the custom of the Country, barefoot, like one of our Taylors, with a great number of Papers sticking between his Toes, and others between the Fingers of his left hand, which Papers he drew sometimes from between his Toes, sometimes from between his Fingers, and order'd what answers should be given to every one." – *Tavernier,* E. T. ii. 99; [ed. *Ball,* i. 291].

1653 ". . . il prend la qualité de Nabab qui vault autant à dire que monseigneur." – *De la Boullaye-le-Gouz* (ed. 1657), 142.

1666 "The ill-dealing of the Nabab proceeded from a scurvy trick that was play'd me by three Canary-birds at the Great Mogul's Court. The story whereof was thus in short . . ." – *Tavernier,* E.T. ii. 57; [ed. *Ball,* i. 134].

1673 "Gaining by these steps a nearer intimacy with the Nabob, he cut the new Business out every day." – *Fryer,* 183.

1675 "But when we were purposing next day to depart, there came letters out of the Moorish Camp from the Nabab, the field-marshal of the Great Mogul. . . ." – *Heiden Vervaarlijke Schíp-Breuk,* 52.

1682 ". . . Ray Nundelall ye Nábabs *Duan,* who gave me a most courteous reception, rising up and taking of me by ye hands, and ye like at my departure, which I am informed is a greater favour than he has ever shown to any *Franke.* . . ." – *Hedges, Diary,* Oct. 27; [Hak. Soc. i. 42]. Hedges writes *Nabob, Nabab, Navab, Navob.*

1716 "Nabâbo. Termo do Mogol. He o Titolo do Ministro que he Cabeca." – *Bluteau,* s.v.

1727 "A few years ago, the Nabob or Vice-Roy of *Chormondel,* who resides at *Chickakal,* and who superintends that Country for the Mogul, for some Disgust he had received from the Inhabitants of Diu Islands, would have made a Present of them to the Colony of Fort St. George." – *A. Hamilton,* i. 374; [ed. 1744].

1742 "We have had a great man called the Nabob (who is the next person in dignity to the Great Mogul) to visit the Governor. . . . His lady, with all her women attendance, came the night before him. All the guns fired round the fort upon her arrival, as well as upon his; *he* and *she* are Moors, whose women are never seen by any man upon earth except their husbands." – Letter from Madras in *Mrs. Delany's Life,* ii. 169.

1743 "Every governor of a fort, and every commander of a district had assumed the title of Nabob . . . one day after having received the homage of several of these little lords, Nizam ul muluck said that he had that day seen no less than eighteen Nabobs in the Carnatic." – *Orme,* Reprint, Bk. i.

1752 "Agreed . . . that a present should be made the Nobab that might prove satisfactory." – In *Long,* 33.

1773
"And though my years have passed in this hard duty,
No Benefit acquired – no Nabob's booty."
Epilogue at Fort Marlborough, by II.
Marsden, in *Mem.* 9.

1787
"Of armaments by flood and field;
Of Nabobs you have made to yield."
Ritson, in *Life and Letters,* i. 124.

1807 "Some say that he is a Tailor who brought out a long bill against some of Lord Wellesley's staff, and was in consequence provided for; others say he was an adventurer, and sold knicknacks to the Nabob of Oude." – *Sir T. Munro,* in *Life,* i. 371.

1809 "I was surprised that I had heard nothing from the Nawaub of the Carnatic." – *Ld. Valentia,* i. 381.

*c.*1858
Le vieux Nabab et la Begum d'Arkato."
Leconte de Lisle, ed. 1872, p. 156.

(b)

1764   "Mogul Pitt and Nabob Bute." – *Horace Walpole, Letters*, ed. 1857, iv. 222 (*Stanf. Dict.*).]

1773   "I regretted the decay of respect for men of family, and that a Nabob would not carry an election from them.

"JOHNSON: Why, sir, the Nabob will carry it by means of his wealth, in a country where money is highly valued, as it must he where nothing can be had without money; but if it comes to personal preference, the man of family will always carry it." – *Boswell, Journal of a Tour to the Hebrides*, under Aug. 25.

1777   "In such a revolution . . . it was impossible but that a number of individuals should have acquired large property. They did acquire it; and with it they seem to have obtained the detestation of their countrymen, and the appellation of nabobs as a term of reproach. – *Price's Tracts*, i. 13.

1780   "The Intrigues of a Nabob, or Bengal the Fittest Soil for the Growth of Lust, Injustice, and Dishonesty. Dedicated to the Hon. the Court of Directors of the East India Company. By Henry Fred. Thompson. Printed for the Author." (A base book).

1783   "The office given to a young man going to India is of trifling consequence. But he that goes out an insignificant boy, in a few years returns a great Nabob. Mr. Hastings says he has two hundred and fifty of that kind of raw material, who expect to be speedily manufactured into the merchantlike quality I mention." *Burke, Speech on Fox's E. I. Bill*, in *Works and Corr.*, ed. 1852, iii. 506.

1787   "The speakers for him (Hastings) were Burgess, who has completely done for himself in one day; Nichols, a lawyer; Mr Vansittart, a nabob; Alderman Le Mosurier, a smuggler from Jersey; . . . and Dempster, who is one of the good-natured candid men who connect themselves with every bad man they can find." – *Ld. Minto*, in *Life*, &c., i. 126.

1848   "'Isn't he very rich?' said Rebecca.

"'They say all Indian Nabobs are enormously rich.'" – *Vanity Fair*, ed. 1867, i. 17.

1872   "Ce train de vie facile . . . suffit à me faire décerner . . . le surnom de Nabob par les bourgeois et les visiteurs de la petite ville." – *Rev. des Deux Mondes*, xcviii. 938.

1874   "At that time (*c.*1830) the Royal Society was very differently composed from what it is now. Any wealthy or well-known person, any MP . . . or East Indian Nabob, who wished to have FRS added to his name, was sure to obtain admittance." – *Geikie, Life of Murchison*, i. 197.

1878   ". . . A Tunis? – interrompit le duc. . . . Alors pourquoi ce nom de Nabab? – Bah! les Parisiens n'y regardent pas de si près. Pour eux tout riche étranger est un Nabab, n'importe d'où il vienne." – *Le Nabab, par Alph. Daudet*, ch. i.

It is purism quite erroneously applied when we find Nabob in this sense miswritten *Nawab*; thus:

1878   "These were days when India, little known still in the land that rules it, was less known than it had been in the previous generation, which had seen Warren Hastings impeached, and burghs bought and sold by Anglo-Indian Nawabs." – *Smith's Life of Dr John Wilson*, 30.

But there is no question of purism in the following delicious passage:

1878   "If . . . the spirited proprietor of the Daily Telegraph had been informed that our aid of their friends the Turks would have taken the form of a tax upon paper, and a concession of the Levis to act as Commanders of Regiments of Bashi-Bozouks, with a request to the Generalissimo to place them in as forward a position as Nabob was given in the host of King David, the harp in Peterborough Court would not have twanged long to the tune of a crusade in behalf of the Sultan of Turkey." – *Truth*, April 11, p. 470. In this passage in which the wit is equalled only by the scriptural knowledge, observe that *Nabob* = Naboth, and *Naboth* = Uriah.

PUNDIT, s. Skt. *paṇḍita*, "a learned man." Properly a man learned in Sanskrit lore. The Pundit of the Supreme Court was a Hindu Law-Officer, whose duty it was to advise the English Judges when needful on questions of Hindu Law. The office became extinct on the constitution of the "High Court," superseding the Supreme Court and Sudder Court, under the Queen's Letters Patent of May 14, 1862.

In the Mahratta and Telegu countries, the word *Paṇḍit* is usually pronounced *Pant* (in English colloquial *Punt*); but in this form it has, as with many other Indian words in like case, lost its original significance, and become a mere personal title, familiar in Mahratta history, *e.g.* the Nānā Dhundo*pant* of evil fame.

Within the last 30 or 35 years the term has acquired in India a peculiar application to the natives trained in the use of instruments, who have been employed beyond the British Indian frontier in surveying regions inaccessible to Europeans. This application originated in the fact that two of the earliest men to be so employed, the explorations by one of whom acquired great celebrity, were masters of village schools in our Himālayan provinces. And the title *Pundit* is popularly employed there much as *Dominie* used to be in Scotland. The *Pundit* who brought so much fame on the title was the late Nain Singh, CSI. (See Markham, *Memoir of Indian Surveys*, 2nd ed. 148 *seqq.*)

1574 "I hereby give notice that . . . I hold it good, and it is my pleasure, and therefore I enjoin on all the pandits (*panditos*) and Gentoo physicians (*phisicos gentios*) that they ride not through this City (of Goa) or the suburbs thereof on horseback, nor in andors and palanquins, on pain of paying; on the first offence 10 *cruzados*, and on the second 20, *pera o sapal*, with the forfeiture of such horses, andors, or palanquins, and on the third they shall become the galley-slaves of the King my Lord. . . ." – *Procl.* of the Governor *Antonio Moriz Barreto*, in *Archiv. Port. Orient.* Fascic. 5, p. 899.

1604 ". . . llamando tãbien on su compania los Põditos, le presentaron al Nauabo." – *Guerrero, Relaçion*, 70.

1616 ". . . Brachmanao una cum Panditis comparentes, simile quid iam inde ab orbis exordio in Indostane visum negant." – *Jarric, Thesaurus*, iii. 81–82.

1663 "A Pendet Brachman or *Heathen* Doctor whom I had put to serve my Agah . . . would needs make his Panegyrick . . . and at last concluded seriously with this: *When you put your Foot into the Stirrup, My Lord, and when you march on Horseback in the front of the Cavalry, the Earth trembleth under your Feet, the eight Elephants that hold it up upon their Heads not being able to support it.*" – *Bernier*, E.T., 85; [ed. *Constable*, 264].

1688 "Je feignis donc d'être malade, et d'avoir la fièvre on fit venir aussitôt un Pandite ou médicin Gentil." – *Dellon, Rel. de l'Inq. de Goa*, 214.

1785 "I can no longer bear to be at the mercy of our pundits, who deal out Hindu law as they please; and make it at reasonable rates, when they cannot find it ready made." – Letter of *Sir W. Jones*, in Mem. by *Ld. Teignmouth*, 1807, ii. 67.

1791 "Il était au moment de s'embarquer pour l'Angleterre, plein de perplexité et d'ennui, lorsque les brames de Bénarés lui apprirent que le brame supérieur de la fameuse pagode de Jagrenat . . . était seul capable de resoudre toutes les questions de la Société royale de Londres. C'était en effet le plus fameux pandect, ou docteur, dont on eût jamais oui parler." – *B. de St. Pierre, La Chaumière Indienne*. The preceding exquisite passagé shows that the blunder which drew forth Macaulay's flaming wrath, in the quotation lower down, was not a new one.

1798 ". . . the most learned of the Pundits or Bramin lawyers, were called up from different parts of Bengal." – *Raynal, Hist*, i. 42.

1856 "Besides . . . being a Pundit of learning, he (Sir David Brewster) is a bundle of talents of various kinds." – *Life and Letters of Sydney Dobell*, ii. 14.

1860 "Mr. Vizetelly next makes me say that the principle of limitation is found 'amongst the Pandects of the Benares. . . .' The Benares he probably supposes to be some Oriental nation. What he supposes their Pandects to be, I shall not presume to guess. . . . If Mr. Vizetelly had consulted the Unitarian Report, he would have seen that I spoke of the Pundits of Benares, and he might without any very long and costly research have learned where Benares is and what a Pundit is." – *Macaulay*, Preface to his *Speeches*.

1877 "Colonel Y–. Since Nain Singh's absence from this country precludes my having the pleasure of handing to him in person, this, the Victoria or Patron's Medal, which has been awarded to him, . . . I beg to place it in your charge for transmission to the Pundit." – *Address* by *Sir R. Alcock*, Prest. R. Geog. Soc., May 28.

"Colonel Y – in reply, said: . . . Though I do not know Nain Singh personally, I know his work. . . . He is not a topographical automaton, or merely one of a great multitude of native employés with an average qualification. His observations have added a larger amount of important knowledge to the map of Asia than those of any other living man, and his journals form an exceedingly interesting book of travels. It will afford me great pleasure to take steps for the transmission of the Medal through an official channel to the Pundit." – *Reply to the President*, same date.

Source: Col. Henry Yule and A. C. Burnell. *Hobson-Jobson: A Glossary of Colloquial Anglo-Indian Words and Phrases*. New Delhi: Munshiram Manoharlal, 1994, pp. 610–12 (orig. pub. 1886).

Note

Captain Henry Yule (1820–89) received a commission in the Bengal Engineers in 1838 and served during the Sikh wars of 1845–6 and 1848–9. He later held several political appointments in India. Although he officially retired in 1862, he served as a member of the Council of India from 1875 until his death. He devoted his later life to his interest in geography, as a member of the Hakluyt Society, publishing an annotated version of the journey of Marco Polo in 1871. He was knighted in 1889.

Arthur Coke Burnell (1840–82) was the son of an East India Company official. He joined the Indian Civil Service in 1860 and served as a district judge. He later became interested in Sanskrit writing and spent several years cataloguing the Sanskript manuscripts in the library of the Maharajah of Tanjore.

Since its publication in 1886, *Hobson-Jobson* has become a standard reference – and a nomer – for the diction and vocabulary of the English lexical reconstructions of nearly two centuries of British history in India.

17   William Jones: "A Discourse on the Institution of a Society for Inquiring into the History, Civil and Natural, the Antiquities, Arts, Sciences, and Literature of Asia" (1784)

Gentlemen

When I was at sea last August, on my voyage to this country, which I had long and ardently desired to visit, I found one evening, on inspecting the observations of the day, that *India* lay before us, and *Persia* on our left, whilst a breeze from *Arabia* blew nearly on our stern. A situation so pleasing in itself, and to me so new, could not fail to awaken a train of reflections in a mind, which had early been accustomed to contemplate with delight the eventful histories and agreeable fictions of this eastern world. It gave me inexpressible pleasure to find myself in the midst of so noble an amphitheatre, almost encircled by the vast regions of *Asia*, which has ever been esteemed the nurse of sciences, the inventress of delightful and useful arts, the scene of glorious actions, fertile in the productions of human genius, abounding in natural wonders, and infinitely diversified in the forms of religion and government, in the laws, customs, and languages, as well as in the features and complexions, of men. I could not help remarking, how important and extensive a field was yet unexplored, and how many solid advantages unimproved; and when I considered, with pain, that, in this fluctuating, imperfect, and limited condition of life, such inquiries and improvements could only be made by the united efforts of many, who are not easily brought, without some pressing inducement or strong impulse, to converge in a common point, I consoled myself with a hope, founded on opinions which it might have the appearance of flattery to mention, that, if in any country or community, such a union could be effected, it was among my countrymen in *Bengal*, with some of whom I already had, and with most was desirous

of having, the pleasure of being intimately acquainted.

You have realized that hope, gentlemen, and even anticipated a declaration of my wishes, by your alacrity in laying the foundation of a society for inquiring into the history and antiquities, the natural productions, arts, sciences, and literature of *Asia*. I may confidently foretell, that an institution so likely to afford entertainment, and convey knowledge, to mankind, will advance to maturity by slow, yet certain, degrees; as the Royal Society, which at first was only a meeting of a few literary friends at *Oxford*, rose gradually to that splendid zenith, at which a *Halley* was their secretary, and a *Newton* their president.

Although it is my humble opinion, that, in order to ensure our success and permanence, we must keep a middle course between a languid remissness, and an over zealous activity, and that the tree, which you have auspiciously planted, will produce fairer blossoms, and more exquisite fruit, if it be not at first exposed to too great a glare of sunshine, yet I take the liberty of submitting to your consideration a few general ideas on the plan of our society; assuring you, that, whether you reject or approve them, your correction will give me both pleasure and instruction, as your flattering attentions have already conferred on me the highest honour.

It is your design, I conceive, to take an ample space for your learned investigations, bounding them only by the geographical limits of *Asia*; so that, considering *Hindustan* as a centre, and turning your eyes in idea to the North, you have on your right, many important kingdoms in the Eastern peninsula, the ancient and wonderful empire of *China* with all her *Tartarian* dependencies, and that of *Japan*, which the cluster of precious islands, in which many singular curiosities have too long been concealed: before you lies that prodigious chain of mountains, which formerly perhaps were a barrier against the violence of the sea, and beyond them the very interesting country of *Tibet*, and the vast regions of *Tartary*, from which, as from the *Trojan* house of the poets, have issued so many consummate warriors, whose domain has extended at least from the banks of the *Ilissus* to the mouths of the *Ganges*: on your left are the beautiful and celebrated provinces of *Iran* or *Persia*, the unmeasured, and perhaps unmeasurable deserts of *Arabia*, and the once flourishing kingdom of *Yemen*, with the pleasant isles that the *Arabs* have subdued or colonized; and farther westward, the *Asiatick* dominions of the *Turkish* sultans, whose moon seems approaching rapidly to its wane. – By this great circumference, the field of your useful researches will be inclosed; but, since *Egypt* had unquestionably an old connexion with this country, if not with *China*, since the language and literature of the *Abyssinians* bear a manifest affinity to those of *Asia*, since the *Arabian* arms prevailed along the *African* coast of the *Mediterranean*, and even erected a powerful dynasty on the continent *of Europe*, you may not be displeased occasionally to follow the streams of *Asiatick* learning a little beyond its natural boundary; and, if it be necessary or convenient, that a short name or epithet be given to our society, in order to distinguish it in the world, that of *Asiatick* appears both classical and proper, whether we consider the place or the object of the institution, and preferable to *Oriental*, which is in truth a word merely relative, and, though commonly used in *Europe*, conveys no very distinct idea.

If now it be asked, what are the intended objects of our inquiries within these spacious limits, we answer, MAN and NATURE; whatever is performed by the one, or produced by the other. Human knowledge has been elegantly analysed according to the three great faculties of the mind, *memory*, *reason*, and *imagination*, which we constantly find employed in arranging and retaining, comparing and distinguishing, combining and diversifying, the ideas, which we receive through our senses, or acquire by reflection; hence the three main branches of learning are *history*, *science*, and *art*: the first comprehends either an account of natural productions, or the genuine records of empires and states; the second embraces the whole circle of pure and mixed mathematicks, together with ethicks and law, as far as they depend on the reasoning faculty; and the third includes all the beauties of imagery and the charms of invention, displayed in modulated language, or represented by colour, figure, or sound.

Agreeably to this analysis, you will investigate whatever is rare in the stupendous fabrick of nature, will correct the geography of *Asia* by new observations and discoveries; will trace the annals, and even traditions, of those nations, who from time to time have people or desolated it; and will bring to light their various forms of government, with their institutions civil and religious; you will examine their improvements and methods in arithmetick and geometry, in trigonometry, mensuration, mechanicks, opticks, astronomy, and general physicks; their systems of morality, grammar, rhetorick, and dialectick; their skill in chirurgery and medicine, and their advancement, whatever it may be, in anatomy and chymistry. To this you will

add researches into their agriculture, manufactures, trade; and, whilst your inquire with pleasure into their musick, architecture, painting, and poetry, will not neglect those inferior arts, by which the comforts and even elegances of social life are supplied or improved. You may observe, that I have omitted their languages, the diversity and difficulty of which are a sad obstacle to the progress of useful knowledge; but I have ever considered languages as the mere instruments of real learning, and think them improperly confounded with learning itself: the attainment of them is, however, indispensably necessary; and if to the *Persian, Armenian, Turkish*, and *Arabick*, could be added not only the *Sanscrit*, the treasures of which we may now hope to see unlocked, but even the *Chinese, Tartarian, Japanese*, and the various insular dialects, an immense mine would then be open, in which we might labour with equal delight and advantage.

Having submitted to you these imperfect thoughts on the *limits* and *objects* of our future society, I request your permission to add a few hints on the *conduct* of it in its present immature state.

Lucian begins one of his satirical pieces against historians, with declaring that the only true proposition in his work was, that it should contain nothing true; and perhaps it may be advisable at first, in order to prevent any difference of sentiment on particular points not immediately before us, to establish but one rule, namely, to have no rules at all. This only I mean, that, in the infancy of any society, there ought to be no confinement, no trouble, no expense, no unnecessary formality. Let us, if you please, for the present, have weekly evening meetings in this hall, for the purpose of hearing original papers read on such subjects, as fall within the circle of our inquiries. Let all curious and learned men be invited to send their tracts to our secretary, for which they ought immediately to receive our thanks; and if, towards the end of each year, we should be supplied with a sufficiency of valuable materials to fill a volume, let us present our *Asiatick* miscellany to the literary world, who have derived so much pleasure and information from the agreeable work of *Kœmpfer*, than which we can scarce propose a better model, that they will accept with eagerness any fresh entertainment of the same kind. You will not perhaps be disposed to admit mere translations of considerable length, except of such unpublished essays or treatises as may be transmitted to us by native authors; but, whether you will enrol as members any number of learned natives, you will hereafter decide, with many other questions as they happen to arise; and you will think, I presume, that all questions should be decided on a ballot, by a majority of two thirds, and that nine members should be requisite to constitute a board for such decisions. These points, however, and all others I submit entirely, gentlemen, to your determination, having neither wish nor pretension to claim any more than my single right of suffrage. One thing only, as essential to your dignity, I recommend with earnestness, on no account to admit a new member, who has not expressed a voluntary desire to become so; and in that case, you will not require, I suppose, any other qualification than a love of knowledge, and a zeal for the promotion of it.

Your institution, I am persuaded, will ripen of itself, and your meetings will be amply supplied with interesting and amusing papers, as soon as the object of your inquiries shall be generally known. There are, it may not be delicate to name them, but there are many, from whose important studies I cannot but conceive high expectations; and, as far as mere labour will avail, I sincerely promise, that, if in my allotted sphere of jurisprudence, or in any intellectual excursion, that I may have leisure to make, I should be so fortunate as to collect, by accident, either fruits or flowers, which may seem valuable or pleasing, I shall offer my humble *Nezr* to your society with as much respectful zeal as to the greatest potentate on earth.

Source: Satya S. Pachori (ed.). *Sir William Jones: A Reader.* Delhi: Oxford University Press, 1993, pp. 170–2.

Note

William Jones (1746–94) was knighted in 1783 and a year later sailed for Calcutta. He had studied languages previously at Oxford and been admitted to the Bar. A year after his arrival in India, he founded the Asiatic Society of Bengal. His commitment to comparative law and linguistics has had both political and literary consequences – in terms of questions of governance (see Part III) and the development of the study of comparative literature in the Euro-American academy.

18   Thomas Babington Macaulay: Minute on Indian Education (February 2, 1835)

As it seems to be the opinion of some of the gentlemen who compose the Committee of Public Instruction, that the course which they have hitherto pursued was strictly prescribed by the British Parliament in 1813, and as, if that opinion be correct, a legislative Act will be necessary to warrant a change, I have thought it right to refrain from taking any part in the preparation of the adverse statements which are now before us, and to reserve what I had to say on the subject till it should come before me as a member of the Council of India.

It does not appear to me that the Act of Parliament can, by any art of construction, be made to bear the meaning which has been assigned to it. It contains nothing about the particular languages or sciences which are to be studied. A sum is set apart "for the revival and promotion of literature and the encouragement of the learned natives of India, and for the introduction and promotion of a knowledge of the sciences among the inhabitants of the British territories." It is argued, or rather taken for granted, that by literature the Parliament can have only meant Arabic and Sanscrit literature, that they never would have given the honourable appellation of a "learned native" to a native who was familiar with the poetry of Milton, the metaphysics of Locke, and the physics of Newton; but that they meant to designate by that name only such persons as might have studied in the sacred books of the Hindoos all the usages of cusa-grass, and all the mysteries of absorption into the Deity. This does not appear to be a very satisfactory interpretation. To take a parallel case; suppose that the Pacha of Egypt, a country once superior in knowledge to the nations of Europe, but now sunk far below them, were to appropriate a sum for the purpose of "reviving and promoting literature, and encouraging learned natives of Egypt," would anybody infer that he meant the youth of his pachalic to give years to the study of hieroglyphics, to search into all the doctrines disguised under the fable of Osiris, and to ascertain with all possible accuracy the ritual with which cats and onions were anciently adored? Would he be justly charged with inconsistency, if, instead of employing his young subjects in deciphering obelisks, he were to order them to be instructed in the English and French languages, and in all the sciences to which those languages are the chief keys?

The words on which the supporters of the old system rely do not bear them out, and other words follow which seem to be quite decisive on the other side. This lac of rupees is set apart, not only for "reviving literature in India," the phrase on which their whole interpretation is founded, but also for "the introduction and promotion of a knowledge of the sciences among the inhabitants of the British territories," – words which are alone sufficient to authorize all the changes for which I contend.

If the Council agree in my construction, no legislative Act will be necessary. If they differ from me, I will prepare a short Act rescinding that clause of the Charter of 1813, from which the difficulty arises.

The argument which I have been considering affects only the form of proceeding. But the admirers of the Oriental system of education have used another argument, which, if we admit it to be valid, is decisive against all change. They conceive that the public faith is pledged to the present system, and that to alter the appropriation of any of the funds which have hitherto been spent in encouraging the study of Arabic and Sanscrit would be downright spoliation. It is not easy to understand by what process of reasoning they can have arrived at this conclusion. The grants which are made from the public purse for the encouragement of literature differed in no respect from the grants which are made from the same purse for other objects of real or supposed utility. We found a sanatarium on a spot which we suppose to be healthy. Do we thereby pledge ourselves to keep a sanatarium there, if the result should not answer our expectation? We commence the erection of a pier. Is it a violation of the public faith to stop the works, if we afterwards see reason to believe that the building will be useless? The rights of property are undoubtedly sacred. But nothing endangers those rights so much as the practice, now unhappily too common, of attributing them to things to which they do not belong. Those who would impart to abuses the sanctity of property are in truth imparting to the institution of property the unpopularity and fragility of abuses. If the Government has given to any person a formal assurance; nay, if the Government has excited in any person's mind a reasonable expectation that he shall receive a certain income as a teacher or a learner of Sanscrit or Arabic, I would respect that person's pecuniary interests – I would rather err on the side of liberality to individuals than suffer the public faith to be called in question. But to talk of a Government pledging itself to teach certain languages and certain sciences, though those languages may become useless, though those sciences may be exploded, seems to me quite unmeaning. There is not a single word in any public instructions from which it can be inferred that the Indian Government ever intended to give any pledge on this subject, or ever considered the destination of these funds as unalterably fixed. But, had it been otherwise, I should have denied the competence of our predecessors to bind us by any pledge on such a subject. Suppose that a Government had in the last century enacted

in the most solemn manner that all its subjects should, to the end of time, be inoculated for the small-pox: would that Government be bound to persist in the practice after Jenner's discovery? These promises, of which nobody claims the performance, and from which nobody can grant a release; these vested rights, which vest in nobody; this property without proprietors; this robbery, which makes nobody poorer, may be comprehended by persons of higher faculties than mine – I consider this plea merely as a set form of words, regularly used both in England and India, in defence of every abuse for which no other plea can be set up.

I hold this lac of rupees to be quite at the disposal of the Governor-General in Council, for the purpose of promoting learning in India, in any way which may be thought most advisable. I hold his Lordship to be quite as free to direct that it shall no longer be employed in encouraging Arabic and Sanscrit, as he is to direct that the reward for killing tigers in Mysore shall be diminished, or that no more public money shall be expended on the chanting at the cathedral.

We now come to the gist of the matter. We have a fund to be employed as Government shall direct for the intellectual improvement of the people of this country. The simple question is, what is the most useful way of employing it?

All parties seem to be agreed on one point, that the dialects commonly spoken among the natives of this part of India contain neither Literary nor scientific information, and are, moreover so poor and rude that, until they are enriched from some other quarter, it will not be easy to translate any valuable work into them. It seems to be admitted on all sides that the intellectual improvement of those classes of the people who have the means of pursuing higher studies can at present be effected only by means of some language not vernacular amongst them.

What, then, shall that language be? One half of the Committee maintain that it should be the English. The other half strongly recommend the Arabic and Sanscrit. The whole question seems to me to be, which language is the best worth knowing?

I have no knowledge of either Sanscrit or Arabic. – But I have done what I could to form a correct estimate of their value. I have read translations of the most celebrated Arabic and Sanscrit works. I have conversed both here and at home with men distinguished by their proficiency in the Eastern tongues. I am quite ready to take the Oriental learning at the valuation of the Orientalists themselves. I have never found one among them who could deny that a single shelf of a good European library was worth the whole native literature of India and Arabia. The intrinsic superiority of the Western literature is, indeed, fully admitted by those members of the Committee who support the Oriental plan of education.

It will hardly be disputed, I suppose, that the department of literature in which the Eastern writers stand highest is poetry. And I certainly never met with any Orientalist who ventured to maintain that the Arabic and Sanscrit poetry could be compared to that of the great European nations. But, when we pass from works of imagination to works in which facts are recorded and general principles investigated, the superiority of the Europeans becomes absolutely immeasurable. It is, I believe, no exaggeration to say, that all the historical information which has been collected from all the books written in the Sanscrit language is less valuable than what may be found in the most paltry abridgments used at preparatory schools in England. In every branch of physical or moral philosophy the relative position of the two nations is nearly the same.

How, then, stands the case? We have to educate a people who cannot at present be educated by means of their mother-tongue. We must teach them some foreign language. The claims of our own language it is hardly necessary to recapitulate. It stands preeminent even among the languages of the West. It abounds with works of imagination not inferior to the noblest which Greece has bequeathed to us; with models of every species of eloquence; with historical compositions, which, considered merely as narratives, have seldom been surpassed, and which, considered as vehicles of ethical and political instruction, have never been equalled; with just and lively representations of human life and human nature; with the most profound speculations on metaphysics, morals, government, jurisprudence, and trade; with full and correct information respecting every experimental science which tends to preserve the health, to increase the comfort, or to expand the intellect of man. Whoever knows that language, has ready access to all the vast intellectual wealth, which all the wisest nations of the earth have created and hoarded in the course of ninety generations. It may safely be said that the literature now extant in that language is of far greater value than all the literature which three hundred years ago was extant in all the languages of the world together. Nor is this all. In India, English is the language spoken by the ruling class. It is spoken by the higher class of

natives at the seats of Government. It is likely to become the language of commerce throughout the seas of the East. It is the language of two great European communities which are rising, the one in the south of Africa, the other in Australasia; communities which are every year becoming more important, and more closely connected with our Indian empire. Whether we look at the intrinsic value of our literature, or at the particular situation of this country, we shall see the strongest reason to think that, of all foreign tongues, the English tongue is that which would be the most useful to our native subjects.

The question now before us is simply whether, when it is in our power to teach this language, we shall teach languages in which, by universal confession, there are no books on any subject which deserve to be compared to our own; whether, when we can teach European science, we shall teach systems which, by universal confession, whenever they differ from those of Europe, differ for the worse; and whether, when we can patronise sound Philosophy and true History, we shall countenance, at the public expense medical doctrines which would disgrace an English Farrier – Astronomy, which would move laughter in girls at an English boarding school – History, abounding with kings thirty feet high, and reigns thirty thousand years long – and Geography, made up of seas of treacle and seas of butter.

We are not without experience to guide us. History furnishes several analogous cases, and they all teach the same lesson. There are in modern times, to go no further, two memorable instances of a great impulse given to the mind of a whole society – of prejudices overthrown – of knowledge diffused – of taste purified – of arts and sciences planted in countries which had recently been ignorant and barbarous.

The first instance to which I refer is the great revival of letters among the Western nations at the close of the fifteenth and the beginning of the sixteenth century. At that time almost everything that was worth reading was contained in the writings of the ancient Greeks and Romans. Had our ancestors acted as the Committee of Public Instruction has hitherto acted; had they neglected the language of Cicero and Tacitus; had they confined their attention to the old dialects of our own island; had they printed nothing and taught nothing at the universities but Chronicles in Anglo-Saxon and Romances in Norman-French, would England have been what she now is? What the Greek and Latin were to the contemporaries of More and Ascham, our tongue is to the people of India. The literature of

England is now more valuable than that of classical antiquity. I doubt whether the Sanscrit literature be as valuable as that of our Saxon and Norman progenitors. In some departments – in History, for example – I am certain that it is much less so.

Another instance may be said to be still before our eyes. Within the last hundred and twenty years, a nation which had previously been in a state as barbarous as that in which our ancestors were before the Crusades, has gradually emerged from the ignorance in which it was sunk, and has taken its place among civilised communities – I speak of Russia. There is now in that country a large educated class, abounding with persons fit to serve the state in the highest functions, and in nowise inferior to the most accomplished men who adorn the best circles of Paris and London. There is reason to hope that this vast empire, which in the time of our grandfathers was probably behind the Punjab, may, in the time of our grandchildren, be pressing close on France and Britain in the career of improvement. And how was this change effected? Not by flattering national prejudices; not by feeding the mind of the young Muscovite with the old woman's stories which his rude fathers had believed: not by filling his head with lying legends about St Nicholas: not by encouraging him to study the great question, whether the world was or was not created on the 13th of September: not by calling him "a learned native," when he has mastered all these points of knowledge: but by teaching him those foreign languages in which the greatest mass of information had been laid up, and thus putting all that information within his reach. The languages of Western Europe civilized Russia. I cannot doubt that they will do for the Hindoo what they have done for the Tartar.

And what are the arguments against that course which seems to be alike recommended by theory and by experience? It is said that we ought to secure the co-operation of the native public, and that we can do this only by teaching Sanscrit and Arabic.

I can by no means admit that, when a nation of high intellectual attainments undertakes to superintend the education of a nation comparatively ignorant, the learners are absolutely to prescribe the course which is to be taken by the teachers. It is not necessary, however, to say anything on this subject. For it is proved by unanswerable evidence that we are not at present securing the co-operation of the natives. It would be bad enough to consult their intellectual taste at the expense of their intellectual health. But we are consulting neither – we are withholding from them the learning for which they are craving; we are forcing on them the mock-learning which they nauseate.

This is proved by the fact that we are forced to pay our Arabic and Sanscrit students, while those who learn English are willing to pay us. All the declamations in the world about the love and reverence of the natives for their sacred dialects will never, in the mind of any impartial person, outweigh the undisputed fact, that we cannot find, in all our vast empire, a single student who will let us teach him those dialects unless we will pay him.

I have now before me the accounts of the Madrassa for one month – the month of December, 1833. The Arabic students appear to have been seventy-seven in number. All receive stipends from the public. The whole amount paid to them is above 500 rupees a month. On the other side of the account stands the following item: Deduct amount realised from the out-students of English for the months of May, June, and July last, 103 rupees.

I have been told that it is merely from want of local experience that I am surprised at these phenomena, and that it is not the fashion for students in India to study at their own charges. This only confirms me in my opinion. Nothing is more certain than that it never can in any part of the world be necessary to pay men for doing what they think pleasant and profitable. India is no exception to this rule. The people of India do not require to be paid for eating rice when they are hungry, or for wearing woollen cloth in the cold season. To come nearer to the case before us, the children who learn their letters and a little elementary Arithmetic from the village schoolmaster are not paid by him. He is paid for teaching them. Why, then, is it necessary to pay people to learn Sanscrit and Arabic? Evidently because it is universally felt that the Sanscrit and Arabic are languages the knowledge of which does not compensate for the trouble of acquiring them. On all such subjects the state of the market is the decisive test.

Other evidence is not wanting, if other evidence were required. A petition was presented last year to the Committee by several ex-students of the Sanscrit College. The petitioners stated they had studied in the college ten or twelve years; that they had made themselves acquainted with Hindoo literature and science; that they had received certificates of proficiency: and what is the fruit of all this? "Notwithstanding such testimonials," they say, "we have but little prospect of bettering our condition without the kind assistance of your Honourable Committee, the indifference with which we are generally looked upon by our countrymen leaving no hope of encouragement and assistance from them." They therefore beg that they may be recommended to the Governor-General for places under the Government, not places of high dignity or emolument, but such as may just enable them to exist. "We want means," they say, "for a decent living, and for our progressive improvement, which, however, we cannot obtain without the assistance of Government, by whom we have been educated and maintained from childhood." They conclude by representing, very pathetically, that they are sure that it was never the intention of Government, after behaving so liberally to them during their education, to abandon them to destitution and neglect.

I have been used to see petitions to Government for compensation. All these petitions, even the most unreasonable of them, proceeded on the supposition that some loss had been sustained – that some wrong had been inflicted. These are surely the first petitioners who ever demanded compensation for having been educated gratis – for having been supported by the public during twelve years, and then sent forth into the world well-furnished with literature and science. They represent their education as an injury which gives them a claim on the Government for redress, as an injury for which the stipends paid to them during the infliction were a very inadequate compensation. And I doubt not that they are in the right. They have wasted the best years of life in learning what procures for them neither bread nor respect. Surely we might, with advantage, have saved the cost of making these persons useless and miserable; surely, men may be brought up to be burdens to the public and objects of contempt to their neighbours at a somewhat smaller charge to the state. But such is our policy. We do not even stand neuter in the contest between truth and falsehood. We are not content to leave the natives to the influence of their own hereditary prejudices. To the natural difficulties which obstruct the progress of sound science in the East we add fresh difficulties of our own making. Bounties and premiums, such as ought not to be given even for the propagation of truth, we lavish on false taste and false philosophy.

By acting thus we create the very evil which we fear. We are making that opposition which we do not find. What we spend on the Arabic and Sanscrit colleges is not merely a dead loss to the cause of truth: it is the bounty-money paid to raise up champions of error. It goes to form a nest, not merely of helpless place-hunters, but of bigots prompted alike by passion and by interest to raise a cry against every useful scheme of education. If there should be any opposition among the natives

to the change which I recommend, that opposition will be the effect of our own system. It will be headed by persons supported by our stipends and trained in our colleges. The longer we persevere in our present course, the more formidable will that opposition be. It will be every year re-inforced by recruits whom we are paying. From the native society left to itself we have no difficulties to apprehend; all the murmuring will come from that oriental interest which we have, by artificial means, called into being and nursed into strength.

There is yet another fact, which is alone sufficient to prove that the feeling of the native public, when left to itself, is not such as the supporters of the old system represent it to be. The Committee have thought fit to lay out above a lac of rupees in printing Arabic and Sanscrit books. Those books find no purchasers. It is very rarely that a single copy is disposed of. Twenty-three thousand volumes, most of them folios and quartos, fill the libraries, or rather the lumber-rooms, of this body. The Committee contrive to get rid of some portion of their vast stock of Oriental literature by giving books away. But they cannot give so fast as they print. About twenty thousand rupees a year are spent in adding fresh masses of waste paper to a hoard which, I should think, is already sufficiently ample. During the last three years, about sixty thousand rupees have been expended in this manner. The sale of Arabic and Sanscrit books, during those three years, has not yielded quite one thousand rupees. In the mean time the School-book Society is selling seven or eight thousand English volumes every year, and not only pays the expenses of printing, but realizes a profit of 20 per cent on its outlay.

The fact that the Hindoo law is to be learned chiefly from Sanscrit books, and the Mahomedan law from Arabic books, has been much insisted on, but seems not to bear at all on the question. We are commanded by Parliament to ascertain and digest the laws of India. The assistance of a law commission has been given to us for that purpose. As soon as the code is promulgated, the Shasters and the Hedeya will be useless to a Moonsiff or Sudder Ameen. I hope and trust that, before the boys who are now entering at the Madrassa and the Sancrit college have completed their studies, this great work will be finished. It would be manifestly absurd to educate the rising generation with a view to a state of things which we mean to alter before they reach manhood.

But there is yet another argument which seems even more untenable. It is said that the Sanscrit and Arabic are the languages in which the sacred books of a hundred millions of people are written, and that they are, on that account, entitled to peculiar encouragement. Assuredly it is the duty of the British Government in India to be not only tolerant, but neutral on all religious questions. But to encourage the study of a literature admitted to be of small intrinsic value only because that literature inculcates the most serious errors on the most important subjects, is a course hardly reconcilable with reason, with morality, or even with that very neutrality which ought, as we all agree, to be sacredly preserved. It is confessed that a language is barren of useful knowledge. We are told to teach it because it is fruitful of monstrous superstitions. We are to teach false history, false astronomy, false medicine, because we find them in company with a false religion. We abstain, and I trust shall always abstain, from giving any public encouragement to those who are engaged in the work of converting natives to Christianity. And, while we act thus, can we reasonably and decently bribe men out of the revenues of the state to waste their youth in learning how they are to purify themselves after touching an ass, or what text of the Vedas they are to repeat to expiate the crime of killing a goat?

It is taken for granted by the advocates of Oriental learning that no native of this country can possibly attain more than a mere smattering of English. They do not attempt to prove this; but they perpetually insinuate it. They designate the education which their opponents recommend as a mere spelling-book education. They assume it as undeniable, that the question is between a profound knowledge of Hindoo and Arabian literature and science on the one side, and a superficial knowledge of the rudiments of English on the other. This is not merely an assumption, but an assumption contrary to all reason and experience. We know that foreigners of all nations do learn our language sufficiently to have access to all the most abstruse knowledge which it contains, sufficiently to relish even the more delicate graces of our most idiomatic writers. There are in this very town natives who are quite competent to discuss political or scientific questions with fluency and precision in the English language. I have heard the very question on which I am now writing discussed by native gentlemen with a liberality and an intelligence which would do credit to any member of the Committee of Public Instruction. Indeed, it is unusual to find, even in the literary circles of the continent, any foreigner who can express himself in English with so much facility and correctness as we find in many Hindoos. Nobody, I suppose, will contend

that English is so difficult to a Hindoo as Greek to an Englishman. Yet an intelligent English youth, in a much smaller number of years than our unfortunate pupils pass at the Sanscrit college, becomes able to read, to enjoy, and even to imitate, not unhappily, the composition of the best Greek authors. Less than half the time which enables an English youth to read Herodotus and Sophocles ought to enable a Hindoo to read Hume and Milton.

To sum up what I have said: I think it clear that we are not fettered by the Act of Parliament of 1813; that we are not fettered by any pledge expressed or implied; that we are free to employ our funds as we choose; that we ought to employ them in teaching what is best worth knowing; that English is better worth knowing than Sanscrit or Arabic; that the natives are desirous to be taught English, and are not desirous to be taught Sanscrit or Arabic; that neither as the languages of law, nor as the languages of religion, have the Sanscrit and Arabic any peculiar claim to our encouragement; that it is possible to make natives of this country thoroughly good English scholars, and that to this end our efforts ought to be directed.

In one point I fully agree with the gentlemen to whose general views I am opposed. I feel, with them, that it is impossible for us, with our limited means, to attempt to educate the body of the people. We must at present do our best to form a class who may be interpreters between us and the millions whom we govern; a class of persons, Indian in blood and colour, but English in taste, in opinions, in morals, and in intellect. To that class we may leave it to refine the vernacular dialects of the country, to enrich those dialects with terms of science borrowed from the Western nomenclature, and to render them by degrees fit vehicles for conveying knowledge to the great mass of the population.

I would strictly respect all existing interest. I would deal even generously with all individuals who have had fair reason to expect a pecuniary provision. But I would strike at the root of the bad system which has hitherto been fostered by us. I would at once stop the printing of Arabic and Sanscrit books; I would abolish the Madrassa and the Sanscrit college at Calcutta. Benares is the great seat of Brahmanical learning; Delhi, of Arabic learning. If we retain the Sanscrit college at Benares and the Mahomedan college at Delhi, we do enough, and much more than enough in my opinion, for the Eastern languages. If the Benares and Delhi colleges should be retained, I would at least recommend that no stipend shall be given to any students who may hereafter repair thither, but that the people shall be left to make their own choice between the rival systems of education without being bribed by us to learn what they have no desire to know. The funds which would thus be placed at our disposal would enable us to give larger encouragement to the Hindoo college at Calcutta, and to establish in the principal cities throughout the Presidencies of Fort William and Agra schools in which the English language might be well and thoroughly taught.

If the decision of his Lordship in Council should be such as I anticipate, I shall enter on the performance of my duties with the greatest zeal and alacrity. If, on the other hand, it be the opinion of the Government that the present system ought to remain unchanged, I beg that I may be permitted to retire from the chair of the Committee. I feel that I could not be of the smallest use there – I feel, also, that I should be lending my countenance to what I firmly believe to be a mere delusion. I believe that the present system tends, not to accelerate the progress of truth, but to delay the natural death of expiring errors. I conceive that we have at present no right to the respectable name of a Board of Public Instruction. We are a Board for wasting public money, for printing books which are of less value than the paper on which they are printed was while it was blank; for giving artificial encouragement to absurd history, absurd metaphysics, absurd physics, absurd theology; for raising up a breed of scholars who find their scholarship an encumbrance and a blemish, who live on the public while they are receiving their education, and whose education is so utterly useless to them that, when they have received it, they must either starve or live on the public all the rest of their lives. Entertaining these opinions, I am naturally desirous to decline all share in the responsibility of a body which, unless it alters its whole mode of proceeding, I must consider not merely as useless, but as positively noxious.

Source: Thomas Babington Macaulay. *Selected Writings*, ed. John Clive and Thomas Pinney. Chicago: University of Chicago Press, 1972, pp. 237–51 (orig. pub. 1898).

Note

Thomas Babington Macaulay (1800–1859), was a dominant critic – and advocate as well as historian – of imperial ambitions, both scholastic and political. He wrote voluminously on the topic and its multiple ramifications. He served in India from 1834 to 1838, and later as a member of Parliament. His "minute" on Indian education was – and remains – a critical and much cited contribution to the debate on the respective roles of Indian and English traditions in the issues of government and instruction. Should the English, for example (and as a William Jones argued) learn from and about their Indian subjects? or vice versa? And what consequences would such considerations bring to the existing relations between colonizer and colonized? (see Part III).

19   Friedrich Max Müller: "The Aryan Section" (1876)

[. . .] The danger of all scientific work at present, not only among Oriental scholars, but, as far as I can see, everywhere, is the tendency to extreme specialisation. Our age shows in that respect a decided reaction against the spirit of a former age, which those with grey heads among us can still remember, an age represented in Germany by such names as Humboldt, Ritter, Böckh, Johannes Müller, Bopp, Bunsen, and others; men who look to us like giants, carrying a weight of knowledge far too heavy for the shoulders of such mortals as now be; aye, men who *were* giants, but whose chief strength consisted in this, that they were never entirely absorbed or bewildered by special researches, but kept their eye steadily on the highest objects of all human knowledge; who could trace the vast outlines of the kosmos of nature or the kosmos of the mind with an unwavering hand, and to whose maps and guide books we must still recur, whenever we are in danger of losing our way in the mazes of minute research. At the present moment such works as Humboldt's Kosmos, or Bopp's Comparative Grammar, or Bunsen's Christianity and Mankind, would be impossible. No one would dare to write them, for fear of not knowing the exact depth at which the *Protogenes Haeckelii* has lately been discovered or the lengthening of a vowel in the *Samhitapâtha* of the *Rig-veda*. It is quite right that this should be so, at least, for a time; but all rivers, all brooks, all rills, are meant to flow into the ocean, and all special knowledge, to keep it from stagnation, must have an outlet into the general knowledge of the world. Knowledge for its own sake, as it is sometimes called, is the most dangerous idol that a student can worship. We despise the miser who amasses money for the sake of money, but still more contemptible is the intellectual miser who hoards up knowledge instead of spending it, though, with regard to most of our knowledge, we may be well assured and satisfied that, as we brought nothing into the world, so we may carry nothing out.

Against this danger of mistaking the means for the end, of making bricks without making mortar, of working for ourselves instead of working for others, meetings such as our own, bringing together so large a number of the first Oriental scholars of Europe, seem to me a most excellent safe-guard. They draw us out of our shell, away from our common routine, away from that small orbit of thought in which each of us moves day after day, and make us realise more fully, that there are other stars moving all around us in our little universe, that we all belong to one celestial system, or to one terrestrial commonwealth, and that, if we want to see real progress made in that work with which we are more specially entrusted, the reconquest of the Eastern world, we must work with one another, for one another, like members of one body, like soldiers of one army, guided by common principles, striving after common purposes, and sustained by common sympathies. Oriental literature is of such enormous dimensions that our small army of scholars can occupy certain prominent positions only; but those points, like the stations of a trigonometrical survey, ought to be carefully chosen, so as to be able to work in harmony together. I hope that in that respect our Congress may prove of special benefit. We shall hear, each of us, from others, what they wish us to do. "Why don't you finish this?" "Why don't you publish that?" are questions which we have already heard asked by many of our friends. We shall be able to avoid what happens so often, that two men collect materials for exactly the same work, and we may possibly hear of some combined effort to carry out great works, which can only be carried out *viribus unitis*, and of which I may at least mention one, a translation of the *Sacred Books of Mankind*. Important progress has already been made for setting on foot this great undertaking, an undertaking which I think the world has a right to demand from Oriental scholars, but which can only be carried out by joint action. This Congress has helped us to lay the foundation-stone, and I trust that at our next Congress we shall be able to produce some tangible results.

I now come to the second point. A Congress enables us to tell the world what we have been doing. This, it seems to me, is particularly needful with regard to Oriental studies which, with the exception of Hebrew, still stand outside the pale of our schools and Universities, and are cultivated by the very smallest number of students. And yet, I make bold to say, that during the last hundred, and still more during the last fifty years, Oriental studies have contributed more than any other branch of scientific research to change, to purify, to clear, and intensify the intellectual atmosphere of Europe, and to widen our horizon in all that pertains to the Science of Man, in history, philology, theology, and philosophy. We have not only conquered and annexed new worlds to the ancient empire of learning, but we have leavened the old world with ideas that are already fermenting even in the daily bread of our schools and Universities. Most of those here present know that I am not exaggerating; but as the world is sceptical while listening to orations *pro domo*, I shall attempt to make good my assertions.

At first, the study of Oriental literature was a matter of curiosity only, and it is so still to a great extent, particularly in England. Sir William Jones, whose name is the only one among Oriental scholars that has ever obtained a real popularity in England, represents most worthily that phase of Oriental studies. Read only the two volumes of his Life, and they will certainly leave on your mind the distinct impression that Sir William Jones was not only a man of extensive learning and refined taste, but undoubtedly a very great man – one in a million. He was a good classical scholar of the old school, a well-read historian, a thoughtful lawyer, a clear-headed politician, and a true gentleman, in the old sense of the word. He moved in the best, I mean the most cultivated society, the great writers and thinkers of the day listened to him with respect, and say what you like, we still live by his grace, we still draw on that stock of general interest which he excited in the English mind for Eastern subjects.

Yet the interest which Sir William Jones took in Oriental literature was purely aesthetic. He chose what was beautiful in Persian and translated it, as he would translate an ode of Horace. He was charmed with Kâlidâsa's play of Sakuntala – and who is not? – and he left us his classical reproduction of one of the finest of Eastern gems. Being a judge in India, he thought it his duty to acquaint himself with the native law-books in their original language, and he gave us his masterly translation of the Laws of Manu. Sir William Jones was fully aware of the startling similarity between Sanskrit, Latin, and Greek. More than a hundred years ago, in a letter written to Prince Adam Czartoryski, in the year 1770, he says: "Many learned investigators of antiquity are fully persuaded that a very old and almost primeval language was in use among the northern nations, from which not only the Celtic dialect, but even Greek and Latin are derived; in fact we find πατήρ and μήτηρ in Persian, nor is θυγάτηρ so far removed from *dookter*, or even ὄνομα and *nomen* from Persian *nâm*, as to make it ridiculous to suppose that they sprang from the same root." "We must confess," he adds, "that these researches are very obscure and uncertain, and, you will allow, not so agreeable as an ode of Hafez, or an elegy of Amr'alkeis." In a letter, dated 1787, he says: "You will be surprised at the resemblance between Sanskrit and both Greek and Latin."

Colebrooke also, the great successor of Sir William Jones, was fully aware of the relationship between Sanskrit, Greek, Latin, German, and even Slavonic. I possess some curious MS notes of his, of the year 1801 or 1802, containing long lists of words, expressive of the most essential ideas of primitive life, and which he proved to be identical in Sanskrit, Greek, Latin, German, and Slavonic.

Yet neither Colebrooke nor Sir William Jones perceived the full import of these facts. Sir William Jones died young; Colebrooke's energies, marvellous as they were, were partly absorbed by official work, so that it was left to German and French scholars to bring to light the full wealth of the mine which those great English scholars had been the first to open. We know now that in language, and in all that is implied by language, India and Europe are one; but to prove this, against the incredulity of all the greatest scholars of the day, was no easy matter. It could be done effectually in one way only, viz. by giving to Oriental studies a strictly scientific character, by requiring from Oriental students not only the devotion of an *amateur*, but the same thoroughness, minuteness, and critical accuracy which were long considered the exclusive property of Greek and Latin scholars. I could not think of giving here a history of the work done during the last fifty years. It has been admirably described in Benfey's "History of the Science of Language." Even if I attempted to give merely the names of those who have been most distinguished by really original discoveries – the names of Bopp, Pott, Grimm, Burnouf, Rawlinson, Miklosich, Benfey, Kuhn, Zeuss, Whitley Stokes – I am afraid my list would be considered very incomplete.

But let us look at what has been achieved by these men, and many others who followed their banners! The East, formerly a land of dreams, of fables, and fairies, has become to us a land of unmistakeable reality; the curtain between the West and the East has been lifted, and our old forgotten home stands before us again in bright colours and definite outlines. Two worlds, separated for thousands of years, have been reunited as by a magical spell, and we feel rich in a past that may well be the pride of our noble Aryan family. We say no longer vaguely and poetically *Ex Oriente Lux*, but we know that all the most vital elements of our knowledge and civilisation, – our languages, our alphabets, our figures, our weights and measures, our art, our religion, our traditions, our very nursery stories, came to us from the East; and we must confess that but for the rays of Eastern light, whether Aryan, or Semitic, or Hamitic, that called forth the hidden germs of the dark and dreary West, Europe, now the very light of the world, might have remained for ever a barren and forgotten promontory of the primeval Asiatic continent. We live indeed in a new world, the barrier between the West and the East, that seemed insurmountable, has vanished. The East is ours, we are its heirs, and claim by right our share in its inheritance.

[. . .] I have so far dwelt chiefly on the powerful influence which the East, and more particularly India, has exercised on the intellectual life and work of the West. But the progress of Oriental scholarship in Europe, and the discovery of that spiritual relationship which binds India and England together, has likewise produced practical effects of the greatest moment in the East. The Hindus, in their first intercourse with English scholars, placed before them the treasures of their native literature with all the natural pride of a nation that considered itself the oldest, the wisest, the most enlightened nation in the world. For a time, but for a short time only, the claims of their literature to a fabulous antiquity were admitted, and dazzled by the unexpected discovery of a new classical literature, people raved about the beauty of Sanskrit poetry in truly Oriental strains. Then followed a sudden reaction; and the natives themselves, on becoming more and more acquainted with European history and literature, began to feel the childishness of their claims, and to be almost ashamed of their own classics. This was a national misfortune. A people that cannot feel some pride in the past, in its history and literature, loses the mainstay of its national character. When Germany was in the very depth of its political degradation, it turned to its ancient literature, and drew hope for the future from the study of the past. Something of the same kind is now passing in India. A new taste, not without some political ingredients, has sprung up for the ancient literature of the country; a more intelligent appreciation of their real merits has taken the place of the extravagant admiration for the masterworks of their old poets; there is a revival in the study of Sanskrit, a surprising activity in the republication of Sanskrit texts, and there are traces among the Hindus of a growing feeling, not very different from that which Tacitus described, when he said of the Germans; "Who would go to Germany, a country without natural beauty, with a wretched climate, miserable to cultivate or to look at – *unless it be his fatherland?*"

Even the discovery that Sanskrit, English, Greek, and Latin are cognate languages, has not been without its influence on the scholars and thinkers, on the leaders of public opinion, in India. They, more than others, had felt for the time most keenly the intellectual superiority of the West, and they rose again in their own estimation by learning that physically, or, at all events, intellectually, they had been and might be again, the peers of Greeks and Romans and Saxons. These silent influences often escape the eye of the politician and the historian, but at critical moments they may decide the fate of whole nations and empires.

Now it seems to me that, first of all, our Universities, and I think again chiefly of Oxford, might do much more for missions than they do at present. If we had a sufficient staff of professors for Eastern languages, we could prepare young missionaries for their work, and we should be able to send out from time to time such men as Patteson, the Bishop of Melanesia, who was every inch an Oxford man. And in these missionaries we might have not only apostles of religion and civilisation, but at the same time, the most valuable pioneers of scientific research. I know there are some authorities at home who declare that such a combination is impossible, or at least undesirable; that a man cannot serve two masters, and that a missionary must do his own work and nothing else. Nothing, I believe, can be more mistaken. First of all, some of our most efficient missionaries have been those who have done also the most excellent work as scholars, and whenever I have conversed on this subject with missionaries who have seen active service, they all agree that they cannot be converting all day long, and that nothing is more refreshing and invigorating to them than some literary or scientific work. Now what I should like to see is this: I should like to see ten or twenty of our non-resident fellowships, which at present are doing more harm than good, assigned to missionary work, to be given to young men who have taken their degree, and who, whether laymen or clergymen, are willing to work as assistant missionaries on distant stations; with the distinct understanding, that they should devote some of their time to scientific work, whether the

study of languages, or flowers, or stars, and that they should send home every year some account of their labours. These men would be like scientific consuls, to whom students at home might apply for information and help. They would have opportunities of distinguishing themselves by really useful work, far more than in London, and after ten years, they might either return to Europe with a well-established reputation, or if they find that they have a real call for missionary work, devote all their life to it. Though to my own mind there is no nobler work than that of a missionary, yet I believe that some such connection with the Universities and men of science would raise their position, would call out more general interest, and secure to the missionary cause the good-will of those whose will is apt to become law.

Thirdly, I think that Oriental studies have a claim on the colonies and the colonial governments. The English colonies are scattered all over the globe, and many of them in localities where an immense deal of useful scientific work might be done, and would be done with the slightest encouragement from the local authorities, and something like a systematic supervision on the part of the Colonial Office at home. Some years ago I ventured to address the Colonial Secretary of State on this subject, and a letter was sent out in consequence to all the English colonies, inviting information on the languages, monuments, customs, and traditions of the native races. Some most valuable reports have been sent home during the last five or six years, but when it was suggested that these reports should be published in a permanent form, the expense that would have been required for printing every year a volume of Colonial Reports, and which would not have amounted to more than a few hundred pounds for all the colonies of the British Empire, part of it to be recovered by the sale of the book, was considered too large.

Source: Robert K. Douglas (ed.). *Transactions of the Second Session of the International Congress of Orientalists.* Nendeln, Liechtenstein: Kraus Reprint, 1968, pp. 79–83, 188–9, 192–4 (orig. pub. 1876).

Note

Friedrich Max Müller (1823–1900) was a distinguished orientalist and philologist of German background who settled in Oxford in 1848, where he had a long academic career. He was important in representing the importance of the "East" in the elaborations of academic and institutional efforts of the empire. His work takes, for example, the early efforts of Jones as proponent of the "Asiatic" school through Macaulay's arguments on behalf of "Anglicization," through to the more procedural directions of later nineteenth-century scholars. Müller was the author of *Chips from a German Workshop* (1867) and *India, What Can It Teach Us?* (1883).

Chapter Four

Laws and Order: The Cases of Thuggee and Sati

Introduction

Eighteenth- and nineteenth-century orientalist scholarship, represented here by the works of Robert Orme and Thomas Babington Macaulay, depicts India as a lawless and chaotic land, inhabited by various despotic governments and roving bands of thugs and bandits; it is characterized by a myriad of superstitions and contradictory religious beliefs and troubled by a history of bribery and corruption, which served as poor imitations of civil jurisprudence. Orme concludes that no existing Indian codes of law can amend the nation's elaborate disorder. Macaulay, on the other hand, describes the pre-existing laws of India as being implemented by super-succession; the Indian legal system, he argues, has been imported, put into place by the nation's various conquerors. He suggests that a more aggressive, precise, and consistent penal code be implemented to amend the colonial nation's motley inherited legal traditions. Macaulay declares that the British penal code will be the superior juridical import; its enlightened qualities will be immediately recognized when translated into native languages.

"Evidence" of the dramatic need for British forms of law and government in India could be found in the sensational representations of the nation's criminality. In addition to the alleged inconsistency of native laws, its landscape was represented as being peopled by "villains as subtle, rapacious, and cruel, as any who are to be met in the records of human depravity." The former description is taken from Captain, later Major-General W. H. Sleeman's accounts of Indian criminality, which combines police surveillance and the practices of orientalist scholarship. Sleeman's *The Ramaseeana, or Vocabulary of the Thugs Language* (1839) catalogues the density and variety of the thug vocabulary as a means of displaying the intricacy of the thugs' criminal genius and the totality of India's outlaw culture. In Sleeman's history of "that extraordinary fraternity of assassins," *The Thugs or Phansigars of India* (1839), he describes the extensiveness of banditry in the colony and outlines a plan for its suppression: "Every arrest brought to light new combinations and associations of these professed assassins, and discovered new scenes in which their dreadful trade was at work. It was obvious that nothing but a general system, undertaken by a paramount power, strong enough to bear down all opposition by interested native chiefs, could ever eradicate such well-organized villainy." The representations of thuggee served to document the need for an expansive and aggressive police force in the colony; Fanny Parks Parlby's *Wanderings of A Pilgrim* (1850; see bibliography) describes the circulation of an 1829 pamphlet, "The Confessions of a Thug," to the judges of various colonial stations. Popular representations of thuggee were distributed in paintings and etchings and are evident in twentieth-century representations like the films *Gunga Din* and the Beatles' *Help!* The vivid representations and administrative discourses on thuggee, native criminality, advanced policing systems, and legal reform also inflamed the imaginations of politicians and statesmen in Great Britain. The working class and Irish "hooligans" at home were the subjects of equally zealous reform campaigns and would, in the near future, receive similar kinds of public interest and administrative scrutiny (see chapter 18, In the Streets).

Sati (or suttee), the customary Hindu practice of widow immolation, similarly captured the attention and imaginations of British administrators and reformers. In his "Minute" proposing its abolition, William Bentinck – Governor-General of India from 1828 to 1835 – describes at some length the several considerations that led him to propose the legislative act. Despite the risks such an action threatened, the beneficial advantages, he claims, were more substantial. The perils were real, however, and included a certain circumspection with regard to interfering in native religious practices, lest such intrusion be viewed by native observers with a well-grounded suspicion of further incursion, or even, more risky still for British rule, lead to open opposition, even resistance from within the ranks of the sepoys in the British army in India. Women would again be the issue in the latter half of the century, when the subjects of polygamy and child marriage figured in the legislative debates (see chapter 11, The Game and Its Rules). But for Bentinck at the time, the abolition of sati was nonetheless not so much an innovation as a considered response to the authority of precedent and the imperatives of humanity and "civilization"; it would be carried out not only for the "benefit of the Hindus" themselves, in the establishment of a "purer morality," but would additionally serve to "wash out a foul stain upon British rule."

Although sati had much earlier been prescribed in the annals of Hindu law (translated by H. T. Colebrooke) under the rubric of the "duties of a faithful widow," duties that included "dying with or after her husband," there were in India at the time local advocates of its proscription. In petitions and addresses, in particular from the reformer Raja Ram Mohan Roy and his supporters, the argument was that the law itself had been egregiously misapplied in a "system of female destruction": "While in fact fulfilling the suggestion of their jealousy, they [Hindu princes] pretended to justify this hideous practice by quoting some passages from authorities of evidently inferior weight, sanctioning the wilful ascent of a widow on the flaming pile of her husband, as if they were offering such female sacrifices in obedience to the dictates of the Shastrus and not from the influence of jealousy."

But if the observance of sati was officially abolished in India in 1829, European observations of the practice persisted throughout the century, from the notice of thuggee expert W. H. Sleeman (*Rambles and Recollections*, 1844), to Jules Verne, whose Phileas Fogg saves a Bombay widow from such destruction, a woman who will then accompany the traveler and his companion Passepartout through the rest of their journey in *Around the World in Eighty Days* (1873). Hegel too had made the practice a part of his "philosophy of history," and Charles Dickens, whose own journal *Household Words* had published several articles on the custom, reenacted it after another fashion in the immolation of Miss Havisham in *Great Expectations* (1861). Sati's reproduction also became the basis for a mid-century advertising of Egyptian cigarettes: "With only a Suttee's passion/To do their duty and burn." More recently, Gerald Crich, the zealous and pragmatic modernist anti-hero of D. H. Lawrence's twentieth-century *Women in Love* (1917), looked back with nostalgia to the "good old days" of Indian widow sacrifice as he contemplated the financial burden of supporting the Crich Coal Mine's dependent widows. Since the nineteenth century, according to Lata Mani, the "abolition of sati (widow immolation) by the British in 1829 has become a founding moment in the history of women in modern India" (p. 89).

MC and BH

Additional Reading

Bose, Shilo Chunder. *The Hindus As They Are: A Description of the Manners, Customs, and Inner Life of Hindoo Society in Bengal*. London, 1881.

Dickens, Charles. "Heathen and Christian Burial," *Household Words*, 1:2 (1850).

——. "Suttee in China," *All the Year Round*, 127:6 (1861).

Hall, Stuart, et al. *Policing the Crisis: Mugging, The State, and Law and Order*. London, 1978.

Hamburger, Joseph. *Macaulay and the Whig Tradition*. Chicago, 1976.

Hutton, James. *Thugs and Dacoits of India*. Delhi, 1981 repr.; (orig. pub. London, 1857).

Lively, Jack and John Collwyn Rees. *Utilitarian Logic and Politics: James Mill's Essay on Government, Macaulay's Critique, and the Ensuing Debate*. Oxford, 1978.

Mani, Lata. "Contentious Traditions: The Debate on Sati in Colonial India," in *Recasting Women: Essays in Indian Colonial History*, ed. Kumkum Sangari and Sudesh Vaid. New Brunswick, NJ, 1990.

Morely, William Hook. *The Administration of Justice in British India: Its Past History and Present State*. London, 1858.

Parlby, Fanny Parks. "A Kutcherry or Kachahri," chapter xiii in *The Wanderings of a Pilgrim in Search of the Picturesque*. Karachi, 1975 repr.; (orig. pub. London, 1850).

Spivak, Gayatri Chakravorty. "Can the Subaltern Speak?," in *Marxism and the Interpretation of Culture*, ed. Cary Nelson and Lawrence Grossberg. Urbana and Chicago, 1988.

Stratton Hawley, John, ed. *Sati, the Blessing and the Curse: The Burning of Wives in India*. Oxford, 1994.

Srivastava, Ramesh Chandra. *Development of the Judicial System in India Under the East India Company, 1833–1858*. Lucknow, 1971.

Thompson, Edward. *Suttee: A Historical and Philosophical Enquiry into the Hindu Rite of Widow Burning*. Boston, 1928.

Wightman, Archibald John. *No Friend for Travelers*. London, 1975.

(See also ch. 18, related bibliography)

Films

George Stevens. *Gunga Din* (1930).

Rowland V. Lee and Graham Cutts. *The Sign of Four* (1932).

Richard Lester. *Help!* (1965).

Stephen Spielberg. *Indiana Jones and the Temple of Doom* (1984).

Shekhar Kapur. *The Bandit Queen* (1995).

20   Robert Orme: "Of the Laws and Justice of Indostan" (1782)

Of the Laws of Indostan

A government depending upon no other principle than the will of one, cannot be supposed to admit any absolute laws into its constitution; for these would often interfere with that will.

There are no digests or codes of laws existing in Indostan: the Tartars who conquered this country could scarcely read or write; and when they found it impossible to convert them to Mahomedanism, left the Gentoos at liberty to follow their own religion.

To both these people (the lords and slaves of this empire) custom and religion have given all the regulations which are at this time observed in Indostan. The sanction of such impressions continue the policies of this empire, such as they are, with a constancy not exceeded in legislatures founded upon the best of principles.

A detail of these customs and policies is not to be expected. A whole life spent in such enquiries, would at the end remain ignorant of the hundredth part of them: every province has fifty sects of Gentoos; and every sect adheres to different observances. My intent is only to give a general idea of the sources of civil and criminal cases, and of the methods of process by which they are adjudged.

Of Civil Cases

It is a maxim, that civil institutions will always be found infinitely more circumscribed, and much less complicated, in despotic States, than in those of liberty. If these in Indostan are found less frequent than in freer governments, they certainly are more than could be expected in one so absolute: and this I shall endeavour to account for.

No property in lands admits of disputes concerning them. The slavery to which the rights of parent and husband subjects the female (who neither amongst the Moors or Gentoos is suffered to appear before any of the other sex, except her nearest relations) abolishes at once all suits of dowries, divorce, jointures, and settlements: but if these two of the fundamental causes of dispute are removed, the other two remain; commerce and inheritances are permitted, and naturally produce contentions.

Inheritances and Commerce Permitted; and from hence Civil Cases Arise in Indostan

Although the notion of absolute power admits of nothing which can be sanctified from its grasp, whence the king, as in other despotic States, may, if he pleases, become heir to any man in his kingdom; yet custom has not established this right to him in Indostan; and these perhaps are the reasons why neither the Moors or Gentoos have been subjected to it.

1   All the political institutions of the Gentoos are so blended with the idea of religion, that this is generally effected where these are concerned. The softness of manners which these people receive from the climate, has fixed all their attention to the solaces of a domestic life. There are not more tender parents, or better masters, in the world: such a people will make wills in favour of their offspring: and the prince finds himself restrained by policy from establishing a right so utterly shocking to the nature and disposition of the subject. He is likewise restrained by religion: the name of God invoked in the testament of a Gentoo, gives it as sacred an authority as with those who have better notions of a deity; and the Brachman is too much interested, as father of a family, to sanctify a practice which

would affect his own property. Thus the Gentoo princes were never seen to assert this right, excepting when avarice had got so far the ascendant, as not only to confound all their notions of policy, but even to make them look on religion as the prejudice of education.

2   The Moors, in the first outrages of conquest, doubtless possessed themselves of all kinds of property: but when the Gentoos would not be converted, and were left to the observance of their own rites, the right of testaments was continued, and still subsists amongst them. The Gentoos, by their subtilty and application, find many means of gaining wealth under the Moors; and this wealth they devolve by will to their male children. The obstacles which these may meet with in taking possession, will be explained hereafter.

3   The idea of being fellow-conquerors; the complacency arising from perpetual victories; the immense wealth which these conquests afforded; might have been the causes which prevented the first Mahomedan princes of Indostan, from establishing amongst those of their own religion, this utmost effort of absolute power. They were contented with knowing that they had at all times the power to seize, without declaring that they intended to inherit every man's property.

4   When the kingdom came to be divided into distinct provinces; when many of these provinces rendered their Nabobs almost independent of the throne; it would have been the height of impolicy to have attempted such an institution; it would have been impossible to have effected it.

5   Had the throne attempted such violence upon such subjects as were more immediately within its reach, the next province, or, if not that, one beyond it, would have afforded an asylum, where a part of the persecuted wealth, bestowed with address, could not fail to procure safety and protection to the remainder; especially if the heirs, as they doubtlessly would, took sanctuary with princes, who either were dissatisfied with, or disregarded, the authority of the court: hence confusions and revolts may be strengthened, if not produced.

6   If a Nabob thought his power sufficiently established to perpetrate, and should attempt the violence of such acquisitions, the subject would remove to the government of the neighbouring prince, whom he would probably find in a state of war with him from whose outrages he had fled.

If the right of inheritance in the sovereign were as chimerical a notion as it appears inconsistent with the existence of a powerful nation, I should not have insisted upon these conjectures; but this right is certainly established in the dominions of the Turk: and the emperor of Japan is not only the absolute lord of the property of his subjects, but is likewise so, in the utmost signification of the term, over their persons, which he massacres and tortures at his pleasure, at some times exterminating a whole city for the offence of a single man.

The different methods of inheritance amongst the Gentoos, are settled by their religion, according to the different casts by which they are distinguished. In general, the females are recommended to the care of the brothers; and these are commonly ordered to divide equally: sometimes first cousins, especially if born under the same roof, share equally with the brothers: sometimes the first wife of the deceased is entrusted with the management of the whole estate during life – a custom attended with no consequences prejudicial to the children, as she cannot enter into a second marriage. It is always recommended by the parent, that the house, if in a way of trade, be not divided; and as surely it happens, that divisions ensue amongst the heirs.

If the rights of inheritance are seen to be a source from whence a multiplicity of litigations may arise in Indostan, the free exercise of commerce will be found to produce still more frequent occasions of dispute.

The varied and extensive commerce which exists in Indostan, both by sea and land, is more than can be imagined by those who are unacquainted with the multiplicity and value of the productions of this wealthy empire: the high roads are full of caravans; the navigable rivers of boats; the sea-coasts of barques; and ships with the richest cargoes make voyages from one part of the kingdom to another.

Spirit of the Moors and the Gentoos, in Litigious Contentions

It may not be thought unnecessary to view the dispositions of the people of Indostan in litigious contentions.

The Moors hold the office of a scribe in contempt: commerce therefore cannot be held by them in honour. The Moors who engage in it have nothing but the name of the merchant; the business is transacted by some subtile Gentoo, who, when he wants his master to confirm a bargain, is sure to find him in the women's apartment, or falling asleep over his Kaloon. Nothing is so indolent as a Moor out of the track of ambition: he will readily compromise a cause, if he entertains the least doubt of gaining it; and if there is a necessity of prosecuting it, he sends a Gentoo to the Durbar, as his representative solicitor.

That pusillanimity and sensibility of spirit, which renders the Gentoos incapable of supporting the contentions of danger, disposes them as much to prosecute litigious contests. No people are of more inveterate and steady resentments in civil disputes. The only instance in which they seem to have a contempt for money, is their profusion of it in procuring the redress and revenge of injuries at the bar of justice. Although they can, with great resignation, see themselves plundered to the utmost by their superiors, they become mad with impatience when they think themselves defrauded of any part of their property by their equals. Nothing can be more adapted to the feminine spirit of a Gentoo, than the animosities of a law-suit.

Of the Administration of Justice in Civil Cases

The superiority of their numbers in every province of Indostan, may have first given rise to the custom of devolving the office of Duan upon a Gentoo: and the sense of their superior industry and abilities may have confirmed this custom; which nevertheless is not so absolute as to exclude the Moors entirely: if any favourite of the Nabob have application and capacity equal to the task, his being a Moor will certainly give him that preference, which a kind of necessity alone seems to have established amongst the Gentoos.

The Duan is, by his office, the chief judge of the province: from whose tribunal no appeal is made, as by suffering him to preside in the seat of judgment, it is known that the Nabob will confirm his decrees.

A Nabob, who through humanity is led to inquire into the condition of his subjects, may sometimes be seen to preside at the Durbar in person; during which time the Duan has no authority but what the countenance of his master gives him.

No man is refused access to the Durbar, or seat of judgment; which is exposed to a large area, capable of containing the multitude: here justice, or the appearance of it, is administered upon all but festival days, by the Duan, if the Nabob is absent; or by a deputy, in the absence of the Duan.

The plaintiff discovers himself by crying aloud, Justice! Justice! until attention is given to his importunate clamours. He is then ordered to be silent, and to advance before his judge; to whom, after having prostrated himself, and made his offering of a piece of money, he tells his story in the plainest manner, with great humility of voice and gesture,

and without any of those oratorical embellishments which compose an art in freer nations.

The wealth, the consequence, the interest, or the address of the party, become now the only considerations. He visits his judge in private, and gives the jar of oil: his adversary bestows the hog, which breaks it. The friends who can influence, intercede; and, excepting where the case is so manifestly proved as to brand the failure of redress with glaring infamy (a restraint which human nature is born to reverence) the value of the bribe ascertains the justice of the cause.

This is so avowed a practice, that if a stranger should enquire, how much it would cost him to recover a just debt from a creditor who evaded payment, he would everywhere receive the same answer – the government will keep one-fourth, and give you the rest.

Still the forms of justice subsist: witnesses are heard; but brow-beaten and removed: proofs of writing produced; but deemed forgeries and rejected, until the way is cleared for a decision, which becomes totally or partially favourable, in proportion to the methods which have been used to render it such; but still with some attention to the consequences of a judgment, which would be of too flagrant iniquity not to produce universal detestation and resentment.

The quickness of decisions which prevails in Indostan, as well as in all other despotic governments, ought no longer to be admired. As soon as the judge is ready, everything that is necessary is ready: there are no tedious briefs of cases, no various interpretations of an infinity of laws, no methodized forms, and no harangues to keep the parties longer in suspense.

Providence has, at particular seasons, blessed the miseries of these people with the presence of a righteous judge. The vast reverence and reputation which such have acquired, are but too melancholy a proof of the infrequency of such a character. The history of their judgments and decisions is transmitted down to posterity, and is quoted with a visible complacency on every occasion. Stories of this nature supply the place of proverbs in the conversations of all the people of Indostan, and are applied by them with great propriety.

Of Arbitrations

The abuses of public justice naturally produced the preference of private arbitrations: these would soon have removed all causes from the tribunal of the sovereign; all arbitrations are therefore prohibited, excepting under the inspections and restrictions of the Durbar, which confirms such umpire as are desired, or elects such as are dreaded, conformable to the complacency or displeasure which have been inspired by the address of the parties.

Many of the causes which arise from the intricacies in commercial accounts, are referred to arbitration, as the attention necessary to scrutinize them would employ too much time at the Durbar. These are sometimes decided with sufficient candour, as the umpire capable of such a task are not always the immediate instruments of the government.

An Objection Answered

It may be objected, that the strict attention given to the forms of justice in Indostan, appears inconsistent with the nature of a government acknowledged to be despotic.

These forms would, without doubt, be despised, were not the inhabitants of the province less subjected to the will of their Nabob, than the vicegerent himself is dependent upon the will of his sovereign.

A government depending upon the will of one, exists no longer if another absolute will exists in any part of it; that part immediately becomes a separate kingdom. This is openly the case in the revolts of Indostan whilst they last; and sometimes is secretly so in the dominions of such vicegerents, who, relying on their power, distance, or address, think that they have little to fear from the throne; but at the same time do not openly give defiance to it.

The Nabob is commissioned to represent his prince as a steward, who is bound to take all measures for the preservation and increase of his master's estate. It would be absurd to imagine that the emperor should delegate to any subject the power of plundering and murdering at pleasure: this monstrous privilege is acknowledged in none but himself, and others must use oblique means to attain it. The last resource from injustice lays at the throne, which has been often seen to recall a Nabob, when the cries of a province have been loud enough to penetrate its recesses.

It is well known that the emperor is commonly the most ignorant man in his dominions, of the transactions of his government. The lordly minister who thus excludes all affairs from his master's inspection, subjects them as much to his own. The cabals, the caprice, the revolutions of a court, are every hour to be dreaded by every vicegerent, if not of overgrown authority; and he is never without enemies and rivals ready to exaggerate all pretexts for supplanting him.

From the impression of these restraints, such as they are, the forms of justice are revered in all the governments of Indostan, as much as the reality of it is abused.

Monstrous Abuse of the Forms of Justice

From the impression of such restraints, we likewise see no act of violence committed but under the mask of justice.

As soon as a man becomes conspicuous for his possessions, and begins to despise keeping measures with the Durbar, by neglecting to supply the voluntary contributions which are expected from him; instead of giving him poison, which would not answer the end proposed, as his treasures are buried, he is beset with spies, commonly of his own domestics, who report even to the minutest of his actions: offers from discontented parties are made to him; a commerce with the enemies of the province is proposed; if he avoids these snares, a profitable post in the government is tendered to him; which if he accepts, his ruin is at hand, as the slightest of the villanies practised in every branch of it, becomes foundation sufficient to render him a public criminal: should he have escaped this too, it remains that some more glaring and desperate measure of iniquitous justice hurry him to destruction. Let the following example suggest and supply the many which might be produced.

A very wealthy house of Gentoo bankers were admonished at Muxadavad of the Nabob's necessities for money: and better versed in the arts of amassing, than in the methods necessary to preserve their riches, they presented a sum much more agreeable to their own avarice, than to the expectations of their persecutors. None of the usual snares were likely to succeed with people of their excessive caution. One of the dead bodies, which are continually floating upon the river Ganges, happened to be thrown ashore under the wall of their dwelling-house; which was immediately surrounded by the officers of the civil magistrate, and nothing heard but execrations against these devoted criminals, who were proclaimed the murderers of a son of Mahomed. The chief of the house was hurried away to a dungeon prepared for his reception; where, after having thrice endured the scourge, he compromised the price of his liberty, and the remission of his pretended crime, for the sum of fifty thousand rupees. This man I personally knew.

Warned by such examples, the more intelligent man of condition sees at once the necessity of ingratiating himself into the favour of his prince by making acceptable offerings, proportioned to his fortune. It would not be credited, that the family of Tuttichchund, shortly after his death, gave in one present to the Nabob of Bengal, the sum of three hundred thousand pounds sterling! were it not known that this man, by having managed the mint and treasury of the province for forty years successively, was become the richest private subject in the empire.

General Idea of the Oppression of the Government

Imitation has conveyed the unhappy system of oppression which prevails in the government of Indostan throughout all ranks of the people, from the highest even to the lowest subject of the empire. Every head of a village calls his habitation the Durbar, and plunders of their meal and roots the wretches of his precinct: from him the Zemindar extorts the small pittance of silver, which his penurious tyranny has scraped together: the Phousdar seizes upon the greatest share of the Zemindar's collections, and then secures the favour of his Nabob by voluntary contributions, which leave him not possessed of the half of his rapines and exactions: the Nabob fixes his rapacious eye on every portion of wealth which appears in his province, and never fails to carry off part of it: by large deductions from these acquisitions, he purchases security from his superiors, or maintains it against them at the expense of a war.

Subject to such oppressions, property in Indostan is seldom seen to descend to the third generation.

Of Criminal Cases, and of the Justice Administered in Them

It now remains to speak of the justice administered in criminal cases.

These meet with severer and more various punishments amongst the Gentoos, who are guided by their own caprice in appointing them, than amongst the Moors, who are directed by their *Alcoran* – a law which, amongst its absurdities, has not admitted that of cruelty in the punishment of crimes.

The punishment of all offences is executed immediately after conviction; and the proofs of this conviction are generally attended to with more justice than prevails in any other cases: perhaps, because the guilty have seldom anything but their lives to lose.

Murders and robberies upon the highway incur death; other felonies, labour during life, and the scourge, a mulct, or imprisonment.

The offices in the civil magistrate are comprised in an institution, which is too peculiar to Indostan to be expressed by any word in our language.

In every city, and in every considerable town, is appointed a guard, directed by proper officers, whose duty it is to coerce and punish all such crimes and misdemeanors as affect the policy of that district, and are at the same time of too infamous or of too insignificant a nature to be admitted before the more solemn tribunal of the Durbar. These ministers of justice are called the Catwall; and a building bearing the same name is allotted for their constant resort.

At this place are perpetually heard the clamours of the populace: some demanding redress for the injury of a blow, or a bad name; others for a fraud in the commerce of farthings: one wants assistance to take, another has taken a thief: some offering themselves for bondsmen; others called upon for witnesses. The cries of wretches under the scourge, and the groans of expiring criminals, complete a scene of perfect misery and confusion.

After these employments of the day, parties are sent from the Catwall, to patrol and watch through the town by night.

The intelligence which the Catwall constantly receives, of every transaction which passes within the limits of its jurisdiction, renders it very capable of assisting the superior powers of the government in their system of oppressions.

Gentoos who have commerce with public women; Moors who are addicted to drinking spirituous liquors; all persons who hazard money in gaming; – such are subject to be narrowly watched by the Catwall; and, when detected, find that nothing but money can exempt them from public disgrace.

In such governments where the superiors are lost to all sense of humanity, the most execrable of villanies are perpetrated by this institution, designed to prevent them.

The Catwall enters into treaty with a band of robbers, who receive from hence the intelligence necessary to direct their exploits, and in return pay to it a stipulated portion of their acquisitions: besides the concessions necessary to secure impunity when detected, one part of the band is appointed to break into houses, another assaults the traveller upon the road, a third the merchant upon the river: I have seen these regulated villains commit murders in the face of day, with such desperate audacity as nothing but the confidence of protection could inspire.

In jurisdictions of narrow limits and little importance, it is customary to blend the Durbar and Catwall in one tribunal. In these all causes wherein money and property are in contention, those wherein the terror of his presence is necessary to support the intended extortions, – such are brought before the governor of the district, who leaves to inferior ministers the execution of what are properly the duties of the Catwall.

Some Reflections

Having brought to a conclusion this essay on the government and people of Indostan, I cannot refrain from making the reflections which so obviously arise from the subject.

Christianity vindicates all its glories, all its honour, and all its reverence, when we behold the most horrid impieties avowed amongst the nations on whom its influence does not shine, as actions necessary in the common conduct of life: I mean poisonings, treachery, and assassinations, in the sons of ambition; rapines, cruelty, and extortions, in the ministers of justice.

I leave divines to vindicate, by more sanctified reflections, the cause of their religion and their God.

The sons of Liberty may here behold the mighty ills to which the slaves of a despotic power must be subject: the spirit darkened and depressed by ignorance and fear; the body tortured and tormented by punishments inflicted without justice and without measure: such a contrast to the blessings of liberty, heightens at once the sense of our happiness, and our zeal for the preservation of it.

Source: Robert Orme. *Historical Fragments of the Mogul Empire.* New Delhi: Associated Publishing House, 1974, pp. 280–91; (orig. pub. 1782).

21   Thomas Babington Macaulay: "Introductory Report upon the Indian Penal Code" (1837)

TO THE RIGHT HONORABLE GEORGE LORD AUCKLAND, C.G.C.B., GOVERNOR-GENERAL OF INDIA IN COUNCIL.

MY LORD, – The Penal Code which, according to the orders of government of the 15th of June, 1835, we had the honor to lay before your Lordship in Council on the 2d of May last has now been printed under our superintendence, and has, as well as the Notes, been carefully revised and corrected by us while in the press.

The time which has been employed in framing this body of law will not be thought long by any person who is acquainted with the nature of the labour which such works require, and with the history of other works of the same kind. We should, however, have been able to lay it before your Lordship in Council many months earlier but for a succession of unfortunate circumstances against which it was impossible to provide. During a great part of the year 1836, the Commission was rendered almost entirely inefficient by the ill-health of a majority of the members; and we were altogether deprived of the valuable services of our colleague, Mr Cameron, at the very time when those services were most needed.

It is hardly necessary for us to entreat your Lordship in Council to examine with candor the work which we now submit to you. To the ignorant and inexperienced, the task in which we have been engaged may appear easy and simple. But the members of the Indian government are doubtless well aware that it is among the most difficult tasks in which the human mind can be employed; that persons placed in circumstances far more favourable than ours have attempted it with very doubtful success; that the best codes extant, if malignantly criticised, will be found to furnish matter for censure in every page; that the most copious and precise of human languages furnish but a very imperfect machinery to the legislator; that, in a work so extensive and complicated as that on which we have been employed, there will inevitably be, in spite of the most anxious care, some omissions and some inconsistencies; and that we have done as much as could reasonably be expected from us if we have furnished the government with that which may, by suggestions from experienced and judicious persons, be improved into a good code.

Your Lordship in Council will be prepared to find in this performance those defects which must necessarily be found in the first portion of a code. Such is the relation which exists between the different parts of the law that no part can be brought to perfection while the other parts remain rude. The penal code cannot be clear and explicit while the substantive civil law and the law of procedure are dark and confused. While the rights of individuals and the powers of public functionaries are uncertain, it cannot always be certain whether those rights have been attacked or those powers exceeded.

Your Lordship in Council will perceive that the system of penal law which we propose is not a digest of any existing system, and that no existing system has furnished us even with a groundwork. We trust that your Lordship in Council will not hence infer that we have neglected to inquire, as we are commanded to do by Parliament, into the present state of that part of the law, or that in other parts of our labors we are likely to recommend unsparing innovation, and the entire sweeping-away of ancient usages. We are perfectly aware of the value of that sanction which long prescription and national feeling give to institutions. We are perfectly aware that law-givers ought not to disregard even the unreasonable prejudices of those for whom they legislate. So sensible are we of the importance of these considerations that, though there are not the same objections to innovation in penal legislation as to innovation affecting vested rights of property, yet, if we had found India in possession of a system of criminal law which the people regarded with partiality, we should have been inclined rather to ascertain it, to digest it, and moderately to correct it than to propose a system fundamentally different.

But it appears to us that none of the systems of penal law established in British India has any claim to our attention, except what it may derive from its own intrinsic excellence. All those systems are foreign. All were introduced by conquerors differing in race, manners, language, and religion from the great mass of the people. The criminal law of the Hindoos was long ago superseded, through the greater part of the territories now subject to the Company, by that of the Mahometans, and is certainly the last system of criminal law which an enlightened and humane government would be disposed to revive. The Mahometan criminal law has in its turn been superseded, to a great extent, by the British Regulations. Indeed, in the territories subject to the Presidency of Bombay, the criminal law of the Mahometans, as well as that of the Hindoos, has been altogether discarded, except in one particular class of cases; and even in such cases it is not imperative on the judge to pay any attention to it. The British Regulations, having been made by three different legislatures, contain, as might be expected, very different provisions. Thus, in Bengal, serious forgeries are punishable with imprisonment for a term double of the term fixed for perjury; in the Bombay Presidency, on the contrary, perjury is punishable with imprisonment for a term double of the term fixed for the most aggravated forgeries; in the Madras Presidency, the two offences are exactly on the same footing. In the Bombay Presidency, the escape of a convict is pun-

ished with imprisonment for a term double of the term assigned to that offence in the two other presidencies; while a coiner is punished with little more than half the imprisonment assigned to his offence in the other two presidencies. In Bengal, the purchasing of regimental necessaries from soldiers is not punishable except at Calcutta, and is there punishable with a fine of only fifty rupees. In the Madras Presidency, it is punishable with a fine of forty rupees. In the Bombay Presidency, it is punishable with imprisonment for four years. In Bengal, the vending of stamps without a license is punishable with a moderate fine; and the purchasing of stamps from a person not licensed to sell them is not punished at all. In the Madras Presidency, the vendor is punished with a short imprisonment; but there also the purchaser is not punished at all. In the Bombay Presidency, both the vendor and the purchaser are liable to imprisonment for five years, and to flogging.

Thus widely do the systems of penal law now established in British India differ from each other; nor can we recommend any one of the three systems as furnishing even the rudiments of a good code. The penal law of Bengal and of the Madras Presidency is, in fact, Mahometan law, which has gradually been distorted to such an extent as to deprive it of all title to the religious veneration of Mahometans, yet which retains enough of its original peculiarities to perplex and encumber the administration of justice. In substance it now differs at least as widely from the Mahometan penal law as the penal law of England differs from the penal law of France. Yet technical terms and nice distinctions borrowed from the Mahometan law are still retained. Nothing is more usual than for the courts to ask the law officers what punishment the Mahometan law prescribes in a hypothetical case, and then to inflict that punishment on a person who is not within that hypothetical case, and who by the Mahometan law would be liable either to a different punishment or to no punishment. We by no means presume to condemn the policy which led the British government to retain, and gradually to modify, the system of criminal jurisprudence which it found established in these provinces. But it is evident that a body of law thus formed must, considered merely as a body of law, be defective and inconvenient.

The penal law of the Bombay Presidency is all contained in the Regulations; and is almost all to be found in one extensive Regulation.[1] The government of that presidency appears to have been fully sensible of the great advantage which must arise

1 Bombay Regulation XIV of 1827.

from placing the whole law in a written form before those who are to administer and those who are to obey it; and, whatever may be the imperfections of the execution, high praise is due to the design. The course which we recommend to the government, and which some persons may perhaps consider as too daring, has already been tried at Bombay, and has not produced any of those effects which timid minds are disposed to anticipate even from the most reasonable and useful innovations. Throughout a large territory, inhabited, to a great extent, by a newly conquered population, all the ancient systems of penal law were at once superseded by a code, and this without the smallest sign of discontent among the people.

It would have given us great pleasure to have found that code such as we could with propriety have taken as the groundwork of a code for all India. But we regret to say that the penal law of the Bombay Presidency has over the penal law of the other presidencies no superiority, except that of being digested. In framing it, the principles according to which crimes ought to be classified and punishments apportioned have been less regarded than in the legislation of Bengal and Madras. The secret destroying of any property, though it may not be worth a single rupee, is punishable with imprisonment for five years. Unlawful confinement, though it may last only for a quarter of an hour, is punishable with imprisonment for five years. Every conspiracy to injure or impoverish any person is punishable with imprisonment for ten years; so that a man who engages in a design as atrocious as the Gunpowder Plot, and one who is party to a scheme for putting off an unsound horse on a purchaser, are classed together, and are liable to exactly the same punishment. Under this law, if two men concert a petty theft, and afterwards repent of their purpose and abandon it, each of them is liable to twenty times the punishment of the actual theft. All assaults which cause a severe shock to the mental feelings of the sufferer are classed with the atrocious crime of rape, and are liable to the punishment of rape; that is, if the courts shall think fit, to imprisonment for fourteen years. The breaking of the window of a house, the dashing to pieces a china cup within a house, the riding over a field of grain in hunting, are classed with the crime of arson, and are punishable, incredible as it may appear, with death. The following is the law on the subject, "Any person who shall wilfully and wrongfully set fire to or otherwise damage or destroy any part of a dwelling-house or building appertaining thereto, or property contained in a dwelling-house, or building or enclosure appertaining thereto, or crops standing or reaped in the field, shall be liable to any of the punishments specified in section iii of this Regulation." The section to which reference is made contains a list of the punishments authorized by the Bombay code, and at the head of that list stands "Death."

But these errors, the effects probably of inadvertence, are not, in our opinion, the most serious faults of the penal code of Bombay. That code contains enactments which it is impossible to excuse on the ground of inadvertence – enactments the language of which shows that when they were framed their whole effect was fully understood, and which appear to us to be directly opposed to the first principles of penal law. One of the first principles of penal law is this, that person who merely conceals a crime after it has been committed ought not to be punished as if he had himself committed it. By the Bombay code, the concealment after the fact of murder is punishable as murder; the concealment after the fact of gang-robbery is punishable as gang-robbery; and this, though the concealment after the fact of the most cruel mutilations, and of the most atrocious robberies committed by not more than four persons, is not punished at all.

If there be any distinction which more than any other it behooves the legislator to bear constantly in mind, it is the distinction between harm voluntarily caused and harm involuntarily caused. Negligence, indeed, often causes mischief, and often deserves punishment. But to punish a man whose negligence has produced some evil which he never contemplated as if he had produced the same evil knowingly and with deliberate malice is a course which, as far as we are aware, no jurist has ever recommended in theory, and which we are confident that no society would tolerate in practice. It is, however, provided by the Bombay code that the "unintentional commission of any act punishable by that code shall be punished according to the court's judgement of the culpable disregard of injury to others evinced by the person committing the said act; but the punishment for such unintentional commission shall not exceed that prescribed for the offence committed."

We have said enough to show that it is owing not at all to the law, but solely to the discretion and humanity of the judges, that great cruelty and injustice is not daily perpetrated in the Criminal Courts of the Bombay Presidency.

Many important classes of offences are altogether unnoticed by the Bombay code; and this omission appears to us to be very ill supplied by one sweeping clause, which arms the courts with almost unlimited power to punish as they think fit offences against morality, or against the peace and good order of society, if those offences are penal by the religious law of the offender. This clause does not apply to people who profess a religion with which a system of penal jurisprudence is not inseparably connected. And from this state of the law some singular consequences follow. For example, a Mahometan is punishable for adultery: a Christian is at liberty to commit adultery with impunity.

Such is the state of the penal law in the Mofussil. In the meantime the population which lives within the local jurisdiction of the courts established by the Royal Charters is subject to the English Criminal Law, that is to say, to a very artificial and complicated system – to a foreign system – to a system which was framed without the smallest reference to India – to a system which, even in the country for which it was framed, is generally considered as requiring extensive reform – to a system, finally, which has just been pronounced by a Commission composed of able and learned English lawyers to be so defective that it can be reformed only by being entirely taken to pieces and reconstructed.

Under these circumstances we have not thought it desirable to take as the groundwork of the code any of the systems of law now in force in any part of India. We have, indeed, to the best of our ability, compared the code with all those systems, and we have taken suggestions from all; but we have not adopted a single provision merely because it formed a part of any of those systems. We have also compared our work with the most celebrated systems of Western jurisprudence, as far as the very scanty means of information which were accessible to us in this country enabled us to do so. We have derived much valuable assistance from the French code, and from the decisions of the French courts of justice on questions touching the construction of that code. We have derived assistance still more valuable from the code of Louisiana, prepared by the late Mr Livingston. We are the more desirous to acknowledge our obligations to that eminent jurist, because we have found ourselves under the necessity of combating his opinions on some important questions.

The reasons for those provisions which appear to us to require explanation or defence will be found appended to the Code in the form of notes. Should your Lordship in Council wish for fuller information as to the considerations by which we have been guided in framing any part of the law, we shall be ready to afford it.

One peculiarity in the manner in which this code is framed will immediately strike your Lordship in Council – we mean the copious use of illustrations. These illustrations will, we trust, greatly facilitate the understanding of the law, and will at the same time often serve as a defence of the law. In our definitions we have repeatedly found ourselves under the necessity of sacrificing neatness and perspicuity to precision, and of using harsh expressions because we could find no other expressions which would convey our whole meaning, and no more than our whole meaning. Such definitions standing by themselves might repel and perplex the reader, and would perhaps be fully comprehended only by a few students after long application. Yet such definitions are found, and must be found, in every system of law which aims at accuracy. A legislator may, if he thinks fit, avoid such definitions, and by avoiding them he will give a smoother and more attractive appearance to his workmanship; but in that case he flinches from a duty which he ought to perform, and which somebody must perform. If this necessary but most disagreeable work be not performed by the law-giver once for all, it must be constantly performed in a rude and imperfect manner by every judge in the empire, and will probably to performed by no two judges in the same way. We have therefore thought it right not to shrink from the task of framing these unpleasing but indispensable parts of a code. And we hope that when each of these definitions is followed by a collection of cases falling under it, and of cases which, though at first sight they appear to fall under it, do not really fall under it, the definition and the reasons which led to the adoption of it will be readily understood. The illustrations will lead the mind of the student through the same steps by which the minds of those who framed the law proceeded, and may sometimes show him that a phrase which may have struck him as uncouth, or a distinction which he may have thought idle, was deliberately adopted for the purpose of including or excluding a large class of important cases. In the study of geometry it is constantly found that a theorem which, read by itself, conveyed no distinct meaning to the mind, becomes perfectly clear as soon as the reader casts his eye over the statement of the individual case taken for the purpose of demonstration. Our illustrations, we trust, will in a similar manner facilitate the study of the law.

There are two things which a legislator should always have in view while he is framing laws; the one is, that they should be, as far as possible, precise: the other, that they should be easily understood. To unite precision and simplicity in definitions intended to include large classes of things, and to exclude others very similar to many of those which are included, will often be utterly impossible. Under such circumstances it is not easy to say what is the best course. That a law, and especially a penal law, should be drawn in words which convey no meaning to the people who are to obey it, is an evil. On the other hand, a loosely-worded law is no law, and to whatever extent a legislature uses vague expressions, to that extent it abdicates its functions, and resigns the power of making law to the courts of justice.

On the whole, we are inclined to think that the best course is that which we have adopted. We have, in framing our definitions, thought principally of making them precise, and have not shrunk from rugged or intricate phraseology when such phraseology appeared to us to be necessary to precision. If it appeared to us that our language was likely to perplex an ordinary reader, we added as many illustrations as we thought necessary for the purpose of explaining it. The definitions and enacting clauses contain the whole law. The illustrations make nothing law which would not be law without them. They only exhibit the law in full action, and show what its effects will be on the events of common life.

Thus the code will be at once a statute-book and a collection of decided cases. The decided cases in the code will differ from the decided cases in the English law-books in two most important points. In the first place, our illustrations are never intended to supply any omission in the written law, nor do they ever, in our opinion, put a strain on the written law. They are merely instances of the practical application of the written law to the affairs of mankind. Secondly, they are cases decided not by the judges but by the legislature, by those who make the law, and who must know more certainly than any judge can know what the law is which they mean to make.

The power of construing the law in cases in which there is any real reason to doubt what the law is amounts to the power of making the law. On this ground the Roman jurists maintained that the office of interpreting the law in doubtful matters necessarily belonged to the legislature. The contrary opinion was censured by them with great force of reason, though in language perhaps too bitter and sarcastic for the gravity of a code. "Eorum vanam subtilitatem tam risimus quam corrigendam esse censuimus. Si ceim in præsenti leges condere soli imperatori concessum est, et leges interpretari solo dignum imperio esse oportet. Quis legum ænigmata solvere et omnibus aperire idoneus esse videbitur nisi is cui legislatorem esse concessum est? Explosis itaque his ridiculosis ambiguitatibus tam conditor quam interpres legum solus imperator juste existimabitur."

The decisions on particular cases which we have annexed to the provisions of the code resemble the imperial rescripts in this, that they proceed from the same authority from which the provisions themselves proceed. They differ from the imperial rescripts in this most important circumstance, that they are not made *ex post facto*, that they cannot therefore be made to serve any particular turn, that the persons condemned or absolved by them are purely imaginary persons, and that, therefore, whatever may be thought of the wisdom of any judgment which we have passed, there can be no doubt of its impartiality.

The publication of this collection of cases decided by legislative authority will, we hope, greatly limit the power which the courts of justice possess of putting their own sense on the laws. But we are sensible that neither this collection nor any other can be sufficiently extensive to settle every question which may be raised as to the construction of the code. Such questions will certainly arise, and, unless proper precautions be taken, the decisions on such questions will accumulate till they form a body of law of far greater bulk than that which has been adopted by the legislature. Nor is this the worst. While the judicial system of British India continues to be what it now is, these decisions will render the law not only bulky, but uncertain and contradictory. There are at present eight chief courts subject to the legislative power of your Lordship in Council, four established by Royal Charter, and four which derive their authority from the Company. Every one of these tribunals is perfectly independent of the others. Every one of them is at liberty to put its own construction on the law; and it is not to be expected that they will always adopt the same construction. Under so inconvenient a system there will inevitably be, in the course of a few years, a large collection of decisions diametrically opposed to each other, and all of equal authority.

How the powers and mutual relations of these courts may be placed on a better footing, and whether it be possible or desirable to have in India a single tribunal empowered to expound the code in the last resort, are questions which must shortly engage the attention of the Law Commission. But whether the present judicial organization be retained or not, it is most desirable that measures should be taken to prevent the written law from being overlaid by an immense weight of comments and decisions. We conceive that it is proper for us, at the time at which we lay before your Lordship in

Council the first part of the Indian code, to offer such suggestions as have occurred to us on this important subject.

We do not think it desirable that the Indian legislature should, like the Roman emperors, decide doubtful points of law which have actually been mooted in cases pending before the tribunals. In criminal cases, with which we are now more immediately concerned, we think that the accused party ought always to have the advantage of a doubt on a point of law, if that doubt be entertained after mature consideration by the highest judicial authority, as well as of a doubt on a matter of fact. In civil suits which are actually pending, we think it, on the whole, desirable to leave to the courts the office of deciding doubtful questions of law which have actually arisen in the course of litigation. But every case in which the construction put by a judge on any part of the code is set aside by any of those tribunals from which at present there is no appeal in India, and every case in which there is a difference of opinion in a court composed of several judges as to the construction of any part of the code, ought to be forthwith reported to the legislature. Every judge of every rank whose duty it is to administer the law as contained in the code should be enjoined to report to his official superiors every doubt which he may entertain as to any question of construction which may have arisen in his court. Of these doubts, all which are not obviously unreasonable ought to be periodically reported by the highest judicial authorities to the legislature. All the questions thus reported to the government might with advantage be referred for examination to the Law Commission, if that Commission should be a permanent body. In some cases it will be found that the law is already sufficiently clear, and that any misconstruction which may have taken place is to be attributed to weakness, carelessness, wrong-headedness or corruption on the part of an individual, and is not likely to occur again. In such cases it will be unnecessary to make any change in the code. Sometimes it will be found that a case has arisen respecting which the code is silent. In such a case it will be proper to supply the omission. Sometimes it may be found that the code is inconsistent with itself. If so, the inconsistency ought to be removed. Sometimes it will be found that the words of the law are not sufficiently precise. In such a case it will be proper to substitute others. Sometimes it will be found that the language of the law, though it is as precise as the subject admits, is not so clear that a person of ordinary intelligence can see its whole meaning. In these cases it will generally be expedient to add illustrations, such as

may distinctly show in what sense the legislature intends the law to be understood, and may render it impossible that the same question, or any similar question, should ever again occasion difference of opinion. In this manner every successive edition of the code will solve all the important questions as to the construction of the code which have arisen since the appearance of the edition immediately preceding. Important questions, particularly questions about which courts of the highest rank have pronounced opposite decisions, ought to be settled without delay; and no point of law ought to continue to be a doubtful point more than three or four years after it has been mooted in a court of justice. An addition of a very few pages to the code will stand in the place of several volumes of reports, and will be of far more value than such reports, inasmuch as the additions to the code will proceed from the legislature, and will be of unquestionable authority; whereas the reports would only give the opinions of the judges, which other judges might venture to set aside.

It appears to us also highly desirable that, if the code shall be adopted, all those penal laws which the Indian legislature may from time to time find it necessary to pass should be framed in such a manner as to fit into the code. Their language ought to be that of the code. No word ought to be used in any other sense than that in which it is used in the code. The very part of the code in which the new law is to be inserted ought to be indicated. If the new law rescinds or modifies any provision of the code, that provision ought to be indicated. In fact, the new law ought, from the day on which it is passed, to be part of the code, and to affect all the other provisions of the code, and to be affected by them as if it were actually a clause of the original code. In the next edition of the code, the new law ought to appear in its proper place.

For reasons which have been fully stated to your Lordship in Council in another communication, we have not inserted in the code any clause declaring to what places and to what classes of persons it shall apply.

Your Lordship in Council will see that we have not proposed to except from the operation of this code any of the ancient sovereign houses of India residing within the Company's territories. Whether any such exception ought to be made is a question which, without a more accurate knowledge than we possess of existing treaties, of the sense in which those treaties have been understood, of the history of negotiations, of the temper and of the power of particular families, and of the feeling of the body of the people towards those families, we could not venture to decide. We will only beg permission most respectfully to observe that every such exception is an evil; that it is an evil that any man should be above the law; that it is a still greater evil that the public should be taught to regard as a high and enviable distinction the privilege of being above the law; that the longer such privileges are suffered to last, the more difficult it is to take them away; that there can scarcely ever be a fairer opportunity for taking them away then at the time when the government promulgates a new code binding alike on persons of different races and religions; and that we greatly doubt whether any consideration, except that of public faith solemnly pledged, deserves to be weighed against the advantages of equal justice.

The peculiar state of public feeling in this country may render it advisable to frame the law of procedure in such a manner that families of high rank may be dispensed, as far as possible, from the necessity of performing acts which are here regarded; however unreasonably, as humiliating. But though it may be proper to make wide distinctions as respects form, there ought in our opinion to be, as respects substance, no distinctions except those which the government is bound by express engagements to make. That a man of rank should be examined with particular ceremonies or in a particular place may, in the present state of Indian society, be highly expedient. But that a man of any rank should be allowed to commit crimes with impunity must in every state of society be most pernicious.

The provisions of the code will be applicable to offences committed by soldiers, as well as to offences committed by other members of the community. But for those purely military offences which soldiers only can commit, we have made no provision. It appears to us desirable that this part of the law should be taken up separately, and we have been given to understand that your Lordship in Council has determined that it shall be so taken up. But we have, as your Lordship in Council will perceive, made provision for punishing persons who, not being themselves subject to martial law, abet soldiers in the breach of military discipline.

Your Lordship in Council will observe that in many parts of the penal code we have referred to the code of procedure, which as yet is not in existence; and hence it may possibly be supposed to be our opinion that, till the code of procedure is framed, the penal code cannot come into operation. Such, however, is not our meaning. We conceive that almost the whole of the penal code, such as we now lay it before your Lordship, might be made law, at least in the Mofussil, without any considerable change in the existing rules of procedure. Should your Lordship in Council agree with us in this opinion, we shall be prepared to suggest those changes which it would be necessary immediately to make.

In conclusion, we beg respectfully to suggest that, if your Lordship in Council is disposed to adopt the code which we have framed, it is most desirable that the native population should, with as little delay as possible, be furnished with good versions of it in their own languages. Such versions, in our opinion, can be produced only by the combined labours of enlightened Europeans and natives; and it is not probable that men competent to execute all the translations which will be required would be found in any single province of India. We are sensible that the difficulty of procuring good translations will be great; but we believe that the means at the disposal of your Lordship in Council are sufficient to overcome every difficulty; and we are confident that your Lordship in Council will not grudge anything that may be necessary for the purpose of enabling the people who are placed under your care to know what that law is according to which they are required to live.

We have the honour to be, my Lord, Your Lordship's most obedient humble servants,

T. B. Macaulay, J. M. Macleod,
G. W. Anderson, F. Millett.
Indian Law Commission,
October 14, 1837.

Source: Lady Trevelyan (ed.), *Macaulay: Miscellaneous Works.* New York: Harper and Bros, 1880, pp. 161–77.

---

22 Capt. William H. Sleeman: Thug vocabulary (1839)

Adhoreea Any person who has separated himself from a party whom the Thugs have murdered or intend to murder, and thereby escaped them.

Agasee A turban. A Thug never moves out without his turban, except in Bengal perhaps. If a turban is set on fire, it threatens great evil, and the gang must if near home, return and wait seven days; if at a distance, an offering of goor is made, and the individual to whom the turban belonged, alone returns home. If the turban falls off it is an omen almost as bad, and requires the same sacrifices.

Aulae A Thug, in contradistinction to Beeto, any person not a Thug. When Thugs wish to ascertain whether the persons they meet are Thugs or not, they accost them with "Aulae Bhae Ram Ram," in Hindoo. This to anyone but a Thug would seem the common salutation of "Peace to thee, friend," but it would be instantly recognized by a Thug. Any man that should reply in the same manner would be quite safe.

Cheeha A coward, timid Thug, one who shows sympathy or fear.

Baroonee An old and venerable Thug woman, who is much respected by the fraternity.

Bhurtote A strangler.

Bunar Same as Baee. Bad news, untoward discovery of the Thugs' proceedings: also a road unsafe for Thugs.

Buneana To stain with blood a cloth or any other thing.

Bunij Ladhna Literally, to load the goods; technically, to murder the travellers.

Ihirnee The signal for strangling; this is commonly given either by the leader of the gang, or the Beiha, who has chosen the place for the murder.

Guthonie A knot in a turban, or any other piece of cloth in which money or jewels may be concealed.

Raba Any trick of Thugs.

Rooh An affix to the number of persons killed in any affair; a single person killed is an Eeloo, when two persons are killed, the affair is a Bhitree, three Singhor, four Behra, five Puchrooh, six Chehrooh, and so on.

Sotha The person employed to inveigle travellers; always the most eloquent and persuasive man they can find.

To Strangle

Dhurdalna	Dhurohurkurna	Jheer Dalna
Leepurna	Ooharna	
Parna Khna	Tubae dalna	Wahurna

Source: Capt. William Henry Sleeman. *The Thugs or Phansigars of India: History of the Rise and Progress*, vol. 2. Philadelphia: Carey and Hart, 1839, q. v.

Note

Captain William Henry "Thuggee" Sleeman (1788–1856) served as Chief Agent under Lord William Cavendish Bentinck, the Governor-General of India (1833–5) and famous reformer. Sleeman combined his orientalist interests with his professional military duties; he solicited incriminating evidence from captured thugs and collected their vocabulary and phrases for his own scholarship. Sleeman is credited with having "exterminated" the Thugs and bandits of India. Between 1831 and 1837, over 3,000 thugs were captured; more than 400 of them were executed. Close to 500 thugs gave state evidence, and the remainder were transported or imprisoned for life. Sleeman published his memoirs, *Rambles and Recollections of an Indian Official* in 1844. He was promoted to Major and knighted by Queen Victoria for his Indian service.

23 Capt. William H. Sleeman: "The Suppression of Thuggee" (1839)

Our readers will almost deem it impossible that such organised gangs of murderers, amounting to several thousands, could carry on their villainy almost undiscovered so long; for two or three centuries at least. The difficulty, however, nearly vanishes when we reflect on the mode of travelling in India [. . .] and on the peculiar system of the Thugs. In the first place they seldom murder near their own homes; but even this would be a point of little importance when we consider, secondly, that travellers, and generally from a distant part of the country, are their victims: thirdly, that they invariably murder before they rob.

Lastly, they avoid exciting suspicion by being careful to leave behind them no marks even of a crime having been committed. The travellers who became their victims were men seeking for service; or returning home with the savings of years; merchants going on business to a distant town; or others journeying either for business or pleasure. They might be murdered in the morning twilight within half a mile of the serai or village in which they had passed the night; while the Thugs who watched and had marked them for their prey were encamped at a short distance. No one missed them: the people of the serai or village which they had left took it for granted that they had proceeded on their way; and those of the next halting-place in advance were ignorant of their approach. It is not till days, weeks, months, or even years had passed away that their relations, hearing nothing of their arrival at their intended destinations, make inquiries, and it is seldom that they can ascertain even the place about which the travellers were probably murdered. Unless the inquiry be made within a short time, and there may have been something in the appearance or equipage of the travellers to attract attention, the villagers and others who reside along the road would not recollect whether those inquired for had passed or not. But even supposing (as has occasionally occurred) that the relations succeed in tracing the travellers to a certain spot, beyond which all clue is lost; this gives a moral certainty that they have been murdered at no great distance, that is, within a few miles adjacent. But how, within such a space, are they to pitch upon the spot where the bodies are interred? – and more – where are the murderers? probably hundreds of miles away; and even should they by chance be again encamped on the very spot, what means are there of detection? In ordinary thefts, and by local thieves, the tracing and discovery of stolen property affords a very powerful means of bringing the matter home to the perpetrators; but this has but little effect against Thugs. They contrive to obtain full knowledge of the persons, residence, and destination of those they murder, and are careful not to dispose of any recognisable articles where they might by chance be perceived. Such as have any peculiar marks are destroyed.

Considering all these circumstances, it is not astonishing that so little has been done towards suppressing this association of miscreants. The fact is, that until these five or six years, no one had any correct notion of its extent: all that was known up to that period was, that travellers were occasionally enticed and murdered by people called Thugs, who assumed the garb of inoffensive wayfarers. By some extraordinary chance, such as one of the victims having made his escape, or some of the stolen property being unexpectedly recognised, or one of the gang having turned informer in consequence of a quarrel for the division of the spoil, a few of these miscreants were occasionally discovered and punished. Even had the various governments into which India is divided, been aware of the extent of the evil and anxious to destroy it, they would have been unable to do so: insulated efforts would have produced little or no benefit; the jealousies which existed would have prevented their combining for the purpose; and for a century and a half or more, there has not existed any paramount power which could devise a general plan of operations, and compel the rest to submit to it.

Other causes are not wanting which tended to prevent any attempts being made, even in detail, to arrest the proceedings of the different gangs of Thugs. Some of the native chiefs knowingly harboured and protected them as a source of revenue from which they derived considerable sums annually out of the profits of their plunder. The Thugs lived in villages like other people, and generally cultivated small portions of ground to maintain appearances: so that the native chiefs, if questioned, pretended of course to know nothing of their real character; asserting that these people lived, cultivated, and paid their rent like others, and accounting for the absence of most of the male population during several months, by saying that they went for service and returned periodically with the amount of their earnings. In other cases, native chiefs who would have readily punished a gang of thieves when apprehended, were deterred from doing so by superstitious dread. The Thugs always endeavoured to impress the belief that they were acting according to the injunctions of their deity Bhowanee, and that all who opposed them would feel the vengeance of their goddess. The few instances in which Thugs were put to death by native chiefs were generally cases of personal vengeance, because these villains had murdered some relation or dependent of the chief, and were by good fortune apprehended immediately, "in the red-hand." It has unfortunately in several instances occurred that after punishing Thugs, the chief himself, his son, or some relation has died within a short time: whether some of the Thug fraternity took secret means to insure such an occurrence, cannot be ascertained; but they seized all such opportunities to substantiate the belief which they endeavoured to inculcate. In general, a native chief would merely extort a sum of money from the Thugs, or keep them in confinement for a short time, after which they were released; and not unfrequently they were discharged at once. Their own superstition however, as has just been explained, is now beginning to operate against them.

[. . .] Though the British Indian government was free from the superstitions or the corruptions which prevented the native chiefs from punishing Thugs, it was not the less hampered by prejudices of its own, and by real difficulties which lay in the way of the object desired. Regarding the prejudices alluded to, it is necessary to explain a little of the secret springs that actuated the government. The members at the head of the administration have always had a tolerably correct idea of the oppressive nature of the British rule in India, and of the light in which it is held by the natives; but it has always been a primary object to prevent this knowledge from reaching the English public. To effect this, the reports forwarded to the Court of Directors, have always descanted on the admirable system of internal government which has been established in their territories; the blessings which the native subjects enjoy; and their consequent gratitude. The feeling descends through the various ranks of government servants, who generally take their cue accordingly. It may be observed too, that the majority of the officers of government, civil or military, are extremely ignorant of the natives of India, and of their real sentiments; and are therefore easily misled by a few designing favourites, who alone possess their ear, and have their own ends to serve.

To acknowledge, even had they been fully aware of it, the existence of such an evil as Thuggee over the whole of the British provinces, was by no means agreeable to the government, it would have contradicted their repeated assertions and representations. If an evil could be suppressed quietly and without incurring any additional expense, it would have been a source of deep satisfaction; but the proceedings of government have almost warranted a belief that they would prefer the existence of an evil, provided it were not generally known, even to the discovery of a remedy, if this should tend to produce a considerable sensation and excite inquiry. We could at least instance several public officers who have brought considerable annoyance upon themselves by too broadly bringing to notice the existence of evils, or the enormous extent to which crimes of the deepest dye, such as murders, gang robbery, and others, are perpetrated. Appearances are, however, kept up. The zeal and ability of the officer are praised, and his praiseworthy motives duly appreciated; but then come certain remarks indicating an "apprehension of his being misinformed"; doubts that "the evil is not so bad as he has represented"; with a concluding observation that copies of the correspondence will be sent to the superintendent of police, judge of circuit, or some superior officer, who will be desired to report on the subject. This individual, if he have any tact, or any thing to hope or fear from the favour of government, frames his report according to what he sees is wished or expected from him; states the district to be not in worse order than others (which perhaps is true enough, owing to the vigorous measures of the magistrate in question, by which crime has been abated); and, by a careful adjustment of words and phrases, contrives to do away entirely with the impression which, in accordance with truth, ought to have been received. Occasionally, where the magistrate has persisted in his representations, the affair has actually ended by his removal, while his successor has reaped the full benefit of his exertions, and gained the entire credit of them.

[. . .] But even when an insulated gang was actually brought to justice, it was but a drop in the ocean towards the suppression of Thuggee: nor would, nor will any thing effect this, but a general system, which shall be in operation all over India. Different magistrates might receive information which, if it were combined and compared together, might prove of the greatest value, but which becomes useless when frittered away among separate officers, who have no communication with each other. The whole business too was so little understood, that few could bring themselves to credit the extent of such an organized system of murder. Although sufficient was known, so far back as 1810, to induce the commander-in-chief to issue a general order to the native soldiery who went on leave, urging them to take bills on the different treasuries for the amount of their savings, instead of carrying cash for fear of being robbed on the road, yet year after year passed, and men did not join their corps: but it was always supposed they had deserted, and little suspicion apparently was entertained of their being murdered, which however, was since discovered to have been the case in almost every instance. The scattered residences of the Thugs was another obstacle, and rendered them much more difficult to deal with than ordinary criminals, who inhabit the same locality. The members of a single gang often came from different parts of the country, some of which were hundreds of miles asunder. Numbers of them, perhaps the greater part, were residents of foreign states over which the magistrates had no control; and, although the British government might have requested the co-operation of the different princes, little or no good would have been effected. Even a system of Thug police, such as has now been established, if confined to the British provinces, could have been of no permanent use. The Thugs would have emigrated for the time to the native states, and although the crime might for a while cease in the British territories, as soon as the special Thug police was abolished, those miscreants would all have returned and prosecuted their trade as vigorously as ever.

Occasionally when a gang, residents of a foreign territory, were arrested, and moral proof against them was strong, but legal proof, according to the English system, failing; if the government made them over to their native chief in the hope that he would punish them, this usually ended in their being released by paying a sum of money – sometimes without. On the other hand, when British subjects were apprehended on a Thug expedition in a native state, they sometimes contrived, by flattering English prejudices, to obtain the protection of the functionaries. The established creed of the government is the superior excellence of their own administration, and the blessings enjoyed by their native subjects; and they descant largely on the tyranny and oppression in all native states. This is well known to the native dependents and officials, who play their part accordingly. With many of them the Thugs maintained a good understanding, and when any of those wretches, residents of British territories, were arrested by a native chief, a pitiable story was presented to some English functionary of "poor innocent British subjects on a trading expedition," or something of the sort, having been confined by a tyrannical chief, in order to extort money from them. Of course, a due proportion of compliments and flattery of the English was mixed up with the representation, and this would produce, often without the slightest inquiry, a strong letter from the English functionary to the native chief on the injustice of his proceedings, and generally insured the release of the Thugs.

Measures of the British Government in India for the Suppression of Thuggee

We now proceed to notice the measures taken by the British authorities in India for the suppression of Thuggee. The writer in the Foreign Quarterly Review, upon whose authority as well as that of Captain Sleeman, the following statements are made, seems to have had access to the most authentic original sources of information.

The state of society in India being such as we have just described, it is not surprising that so well organized a system of murder and robbery as that of the Thugs should have remained so long in full vigour.

Things had gone on in this way for years, chequered occasionally by the vigorous attempt of some individual functionary to eradicate the evil, but without any solid benefit. The most notorious of these efforts was an attack made by Messrs Halhed and Stockwell, in the year 1812, on the stronghold of a large body of Thugs, in the province of Sindouse, in the Gualior territory. They had formed a large village there, whence they issued annually on their excursions, and paid a regular tribute to that state for their protection. Many were killed; but the greater part, being driven away, scattered themselves all over India, joining other gangs or forming new ones wherever they went: so that the enterprise, from not being followed up on a system of information derived from some of those who were captured, actually in its results produced more evil than good.

The next event which occurred, and which ultimately laid the foundation of the successful measures that have been since pursued, was the arrest of a gang of a hundred and fifteen, near Jubulpoor, in 1823; it was accomplished by the following means. A noted leader of Thugs, named Kulian, was in the Jubulpoor gaol. Seeing the proof strong against him, he offered to turn informer to save himself; and was promised his life in the event of his doing good service. He accordingly desired his brother, Motee, to accompany the first large gang he should meet, travelling in that direction; to note well the murders and places where the bodies should be buried: and, as the gang approached Jubulpoor, to give information to Mr Molony, agent to the governor-general. The gang which Motee joined was that of Dhunnee Khan: he strictly fulfilled his instructions, and 'caused the apprehension of the whole; this has been already related; and also how Dhunnee Khan contrived to persuade Mr Molony to order their release. In despair at this, Motee followed the gang, and, by dint of frightening some of them with assurances of speedy re-apprehension, persuaded a few to return with him to Mr Molony, and declare what they really were. On this additional evidence, a large police force was sent after the gang, and succeeded in capturing a hundred and three, who were safely lodged in gaol. Mr Molony unfortunately died soon after this: his successor apparently did not know how to proceed in the case, until Mr F. C. Smith took it up in 1830, shortly after his appointment as governor-general's agent at Jubulpoor; seventy-five were convicted; the others having died in gaol, excepting some who were made informers.

Another considerable gang was apprehended in the same territories in 1826 by Captain Wardlow, employed there as a civil officer; a third by Captain Sleeman, in Bhopal, in the beginning of 1830; and a fourth by Major Borthwick, political agent of Mahidpoor.

Of all these gangs, some of the members, frightened at what had already occurred, turned approvers, in order to save themselves; but the evidence of these men, in particular of a Brahmin approver, named Ferringhea, was perfectly astounding, and laid open a scene of barefaced villainy which could scarcely be credited: nevertheless, every statement hitherto made by them, and by others, have been corroborated.

The disclosures made by these different approvers, and the information given, threw open so fine a field for a general plan of operations, that the matter was warmly taken up by Mr Smith, agent to the governor-general, and Captain Sleeman, district officer of Nursingpoor, each zealously co-operating with the other. On the 21st September, 1830, Mr Smith wrote to government, and intimated the necessity of some such plan: but the eyes of the latter had been opened, and before the receipt of Mr Smith's dispatch, a letter from government, dated 8th October, was addressed to him, requesting his opinion on the subject. In reply, he submitted a plan, of which the following is an outline.

1st   That an officer, to be termed superintendent of operations against Thuggee, should be appointed, with power to send out parties to apprehend those against whom he might have information in any part of the country.
2nd The superintendent to commit all whom he deems guilty for trial, before the governor-general's agent in the Saugor and Nerbudda territories.
3rd   Lists to be made out against all upon whom suspicion rests, and sent to the different English functionaries.
4th   The residents at native courts also to give their assistance.

The draught likewise contains several minor provisions regarding the search for dead bodies; rewards to those who deserve such a mark of approbation; penalties for harbouring Thugs; prevention of abuses by approvers; and other clauses not worth enumerating here, although highly useful in practice.

[. . .] Still, the more that was done the more seemed requisite to do. Every arrest brought to light new combinations and associations of these professed assassins, and discovered new scenes in which their dreadful trade was at work. It was obvious that nothing but a general system, undertaken by a paramount power, strong enough to bear down all opposition by interested native chiefs, could ever eradicate such well-organized villainy; and the other members of government at length succeeded in persuaded Lord William Bentinck that it was incumbent upon a government calling itself enlightened to take the lead in so good a work; and that a moderate expense would be well bestowed in suppressing an association which was causing the annual murder of some thousands of his fellow creatures. In prosecution of the extended system of operations, Captain Sleeman was in January, 1835, relieved altogether from ordinary civil duties, and appointed superintendent; and several additional officers were nominated to act under him in various parts of the country.

Jubulpoor, the residence of the agent to the governor-general in the Saugor and Nerbudda territories, was appointed Captain Sleeman's headquarters. All Thugs apprehended within those territories Jeypoor, Hyderabad, Nagpoor, and other contiguous native states, are tried by the agent at Jubulpoor. Those of Oude and Indore by the residents of those courts; and such as have committed crimes in what are called the regulation provinces, are tried by the officers who are there stationed. Operations have lately extended into Bombay, Madras, the eastern parts of Bengal, and the north westernmost parts of the Indian continent; and there is no doubt that, to ensure complete success it will be necessary to nominate additional superintendents as well as subordinate officers for each of these divisions: to which should be added functionaries specially appointed for the trial of those committed.

The success of the combined operations has been beyond hope; and if properly followed up, it will be almost impossible for a Thug to remain at large. The mode of proceeding is, to take the deposition of those who turn approvers, wherever this may happen to be. These men are then required to give, to the best of their recollection, a full account of every expedition on which they have been, mentioning the dates of every one, and the detail of every murder; together with the names of those who had formed the gangs, their residence, caste, etc., etc. All this is registered in the office of the general-superintendent, and lists of those to be apprehended are sent to the different subordinate officers, who are all provided with approvers and guards. These officers also take the depositions in full of all whom they may apprehend, copies of which are sent to the general-superintendent. It is obvious that when depositions, thus taken almost simultaneously from different people hundreds of miles apart, who have had no means of collusion, and none of them expecting to be apprehended, agree in describing the same scenes and the same actors, it is obviously next to impossible to refuse belief. But another test is applied. When a Thug is arrested, he is brought direct to the officers' residence, and placed in a row between unconcerned people. The approvers, who have been detained at the stations, are then sent for singly, and required to point out any individual of the party whom they may know. If they all fix on the same individual, and their statements also agree with those previously made by others, it is impossible that better evidence can be had.

We mention this, because we are aware that a prejudice has gone forth against the mode of conducting both the previous investigations and the sessions part of the business in Thug trials. That a man who has only seen or heard the latter should have some suspicions is not surprising; for the whole evidence of events long past is given so glibly, that it appears to bear strong marks of fabrication. But in fact the sessions part of the business is the least to be relied on: if that were all a man had before him to enable him to form his judgment, few Thugs would have been punished: before the trials come on, the approvers have all been brought together; have had opportunities of seeing the prisoners, and of fabricating what tales they please. But this they dare not do; they know well that what passes in the sessions, though the actual trial, yet serves chiefly to inspect the papers and operations of the subordinate officers, in order to ascertain that all has been correctly conducted; and that in reality, the previous proceedings form the evidence mainly relied upon. The whole association of Thugs is, in fact, different from that of any other known villains in existence. Their system is such, that they are beyond the reach of the ordinary tribunals of the country, and a special system must be put in force against them. That some petty abuses have been committed, we allow. Money has occasionally been extorted from people, under threat of accusing them of being Thugs; and others, though innocent, have suffered a temporary imprisonment. But there is no system, however well organized, that may not be open to imperfections; and what are such evils as the above, which are the sum total of all that has occurred, to ridding the world of some hundreds of professed assassins.

We are fully convinced, after taking everthing into consideration, that there are no trials in which a man may with so safe a conscience pronounce sentence, as those of the Thugs; in proof of which we have only to refer to the table in p. 38 of Captain Sleeman's work. No less than eleven different functionaries, judicial and political, are there mentioned as having held Thug trials; yet the general result is the same in all, as to the proportion found guilty and acquitted. We could mention many individual instances in proof of the correctness of the information obtained and evidence brought forward, but will content ourselves with one very striking case from Hyderabad. About eighty Thugs had been arrested in various parts of that kingdom by different parties of approvers; they were collected into a gang and sent off to Jubulpoor under a guard. As they were passing the residence of the local governor of one of the Hyderabad provinces, he gave in charge to the guard eleven men whom he had apprehended on suspicion. The whole were safely brought to Jubulpoor; but it so happened that the papers and documents relating to their arrest had not been received by the time of their arrival; and the officer commanding the guard made no report as to whence the different men who composed the gang under his charge had been received; they were, therefore, as a matter of course, supposed to be all Thugs who had been arrested by the approvers. Nevertheless the usual form was proceeded in, i. e. the approvers who remained at Jubulpoor were sent for singly to inspect the gang; all were recognized to be Thugs excepting eleven men, of whom the approvers said they knew nothing. On the receipt of the documents a few days afterwards, these eleven proved to be the party given in charge to the guard by the local governor, with whose arrest the approvers had no concern.

Then success which has attended the exertions of the officers employed to suppress this crime, has hitherto equalled the most sanguine expectations. In most parts of central India, Bundlecund, Boglecund, and from Allahabad to the Himalayah, Thuggee now scarcely exists: the great proof of which is, that the servants of English gentlemen, and Sepahees, who go on leave into those parts of the country, have, during the last three years, all returned in safety; whereas previously, not a year passed without many of them being missed. We mention these two classes, for their movements only can we correctly ascertain; but it is a fair inference that other natives have travelled in equal safety. There can be no doubt that if the British government will pursue vigorous measures for a few years, the system will, with proper supervision on the part of the ordinary police, be completely eradicated, never again to rise; but if exertions are slackened, and any fully initiated Thugs left at large, they would infallibly raise new gangs, and Thuggee would again flourish all over India. It is certainly incumbent on a government which assumes to itself the character of enlightened, and which is now paramount in India, to exert itself for the suppression of such an atrocious system. It is impossible to ascertain with accuracy the extent to which it has been carried annually, and, could it be done, the statement would scarcely be credited. Reckoning the number of Thugs in all India to be ten thousand, and that, on the average, each Thug murders three victims a year, this will give an amount of thirty thousand murders annually committed for many years past, of which, till lately, scarcely any thing was known. Frightfully enormous as this may appear, it is probable that both estimates are under the mark, which is warranted by what appears on the trials, where, of course, but a small portion of the crimes actually committed are proved.

In the sessions of 1836, lately held by the Honourable F. I. Shore at Jubulpoor, two hundred and forty-one prisoners were convicted of the murder of four hundred and seventy-four individuals, of whose corpses three hundred and fourteen were disinterred, and inquests held upon them.

The results have been hitherto highly satisfactory. Within these few years more than two thousand Thugs have been arrested by the officers attached to the Jubulpoor and Central India establishment alone. Of these about three hundred have been made approvers; eighteen hundred and three were committed for trial. Of these four hundred and nineteen were sentenced to death; one thousand and eighty to transportation for life;[1] ninety-five to imprisonment for life; leaving two hundred and nine, who were either sentenced to limited imprisonment, allowed to turn approvers, died in gaol, or were otherwise disposed of. Only twenty-one of the whole have been acquitted; and this proves the extraordinary care with which the cases are prepared by the officers to whom this duty has been intrusted, and the strong nature of the evidence adduced. We cannot but wish them every success in exterminating a system which spares neither sex nor age; whose members never abandon their profession as long as they possess the power to engage in an expedition; who watch for their prey like wild beasts or vultures; and talk of the principal scenes of their crimes as a sportsman would of his favourite preserves. We trust also that no miserable fit of economy on the part of government may arise to thwart the measures in progress, but that every co-operation will be given to those praiseworthy exertions.

Source: Capt. William H. "Thuggee" Sleeman. *The Thugs or Phansigars of India: History of the Rise and Progress.* Philadelphia, PA: Carey and Hart, 1839, pp. 52–8, 62–7, 68–75.

---

24   William Cavendish Bentinck: Minute on Sati, November 8, 1829 and Sati Regulation of the Bengal Code (1829)

Whether the question be to continue or discontinue the practice of suttee, the decision is equally sur-

---

1 These sentences are at once carried into execution, and not commuted, as is so common in England.

---

rounded by an awful responsibility. To consent to the consignment, year after year, of hundreds of innocent victims to a cruel and untimely end, when the power exists of preventing it, is a predicament which no conscience can contemplate without horror. But on the other hand, if heretofore received opinions are to be considered of any value, to put to hazard, by a contrary course, the very safety of the British empire in India, and to extinguish at once all hopes of those great improvements affecting the condition, not of hundreds and thousands, but of millions, which can only be expected from the continuance of our supremacy; is an alternative which, even in the light of humanity itself, may be considered as a still greater evil. It is upon this first and highest consideration alone, the good of mankind, that the tolerance of this inhuman and impious rite can, in my opinion, be justified on the part of the government of a civilized nation. While the solution of this question is appalling from the unparalleled magnitude of its possible results, the considerations belonging to it are such as to make even the stoutest mind distrust its decision. On the one side, religion, humanity under the most appalling form, as well as vanity and ambition, in short all the most powerful influences over the human heart, are arrayed to bias and mislead the judgment. On the other side, the sanction of countless ages, the example of all the Mussulman conquerors, the unanimous concurrence in the same policy of our own most able rulers, together with the universal veneration of the people, seem authoritatively to forbid, both to feeling and to reason, any interference on the exercise of their natural prerogative. In venturing to be the first to deviate from this practice, it becomes me to show, that nothing has been yielded to feeling, but that reason, and reason alone, has governed the decision. So far indeed from presuming to condemn the conduct of my predecessors, I am ready to say, that in the same circumstances, I should have acted as they have done. So far from being chargeable with political rashness, as this departure from an established policy might infer, I hope to be able so completely to prove the safety of the measure, as even to render unnecessary any calculation of the degree of risk, which for the attainment of so great a benefit, might wisely and justly be incurred. So far also from being the sole champion of a great and dangerous innovation, I shall be able to prove that the vast preponderance of present authority has long been in favour of abolition. Past experience indeed ought to prevent me, above all men, from coming lightly to so positive a conclusion. When Governor of Madras, I saw, in the mutiny of Vellore, the dreadful consequences of a supposed violation of religious customs upon the minds of the native population and soldiery: I cannot forget that I was then the innocent victim of that unfortunate catastrophe, and I might reasonably dread, when the responsibility would justly attach to me in the event of failure, a recurrence of the same fate. Prudence and self-interest would counsel me to tread in the footsteps of my predecessors. But in a case of such momentous importance to humanity and civilization, that man must be reckless of all his present or future happiness who could listen to the dictates of so wicked and selfish a policy. With the firm undoubting conviction entertained upon this question, I should be guilty of little short of the crime of multiplied murder, if I could hesitate in the performance of this solemn obligation. I have been already stung with this feeling. Every day's delay adds a victim to the dreadful list, which might perhaps have been prevented by a more early submission of the present question. But during the whole of the present year, much public agitation has been excited, and when discontent is abroad, when exaggerations of all kinds are busily circulated, and when the native army have been under a degree of alarm, lest their allowances should suffer with that of their European officers, it would have been unwise to have given a handle to artful and designing enemies to disturb the public peace. The recent measures of government for protecting the interests of the sepoys against the late reduction of companies, will have removed all apprehension of the intentions of government; and the consideration of this circumstance having been the sole cause of hesitation on my part, I will now proceed, praying the blessing of God upon our counsels, to state the grounds upon which my opinion has been formed.

We have now before us two reports of the Nizamat Adalat with statements of suttees in 1827 and 1828, exhibiting a decrease of 54 in the latter year as compared with 1827, and a still greater proportion as compared with former years. If this diminution could be ascribed to any change of opinion upon the question, produced by the progress of education or civilization, the fact would be most satisfactory; and to disturb this sure though slow process of self correction would be most impolite and unwise. But I think it may be safely affirmed, that though in Calcutta truth may be said to have made a considerable advance among the higher orders; yet in respect to the population at large, no change whatever has taken place, and that from these causes at least no hope of the abandonment of the rite can be rationally entertained.

The decrease, if it be real may be the result of less sickly seasons, as the increase in 1824 and 1825 was of the greater prevalence of cholera. But it is probably in a greater measure due to the more open discouragement of the practice given by the greater part of the European functionaries in latter years; the effect of which would be to produce corresponding activity in the police officers, by which either the number would be really diminished, or would be made to appear so in the returns.

It seems to be the very general opinion that our interference has hitherto done more harm than good, by lending a sort of sanction to the ceremony, while it has undoubtedly tended to cripple the efforts of magistrates and others to prevent the practice.

I think it will clearly appear, from a perusal of the documents annexed to this minute, and from the facts which I shall have to adduce, that the passive submission of the people to the influence and power beyond the law, which in fact and practically may be and is often exercised without opposition by every public officer, is so great, that the suppression of the rite would be completely effected by a tacit sanction alone on the part of government. This mode of extinguishing has been recommended by many of those whose advice has been asked, and no doubt this, in several respects might be a preferable course, as being equally effectual, while more silent, not exciting the alarm which might possibly come from a public enactment, and from which, in case of failure, it would be easy to retreat with less inconvenience and without any compromise of character. But this course is clearly not open to government, bound by parliament to rule by law, and not by their good pleasure. Under the present position of the British empire moreover, it may be fairly doubted, if any such underhand proceeding would be really good policy. When we had powerful neighbours and had greater reason to doubt our own security, expediency might recommend an indirect and more cautious proceeding, but now that we are supreme my opinion is decidedly in favour of an open, avowed and general prohibition, resting altogether upon the moral goodness of the act, and our power to enforce it, and so decided is my feeling against any half measure, that were I not convinced of the safety of total abolition, I certainly should have advised the cessation of all interference.

Of all those who have given their advice against the abolition of the rite, and have described the ill effects likely to ensue from it, there is no one to whom I am disposed to pay greater deference than

Mr Horace Wilson. I purposely select his opinion, because, independently of his vast knowledge of oriental literature, it has fallen to his lot, as secretary to the Hindu College, and possessing the general esteem both of the parents and of the youths, to have more confidential intercourse with natives of all classes, than any man in India. While his opportunity of obtaining information has been great beyond all others, his talents and judgement enable him to form a just estimate of its value. I shall state the most forcible of his reasons, and how far I do and do not agree with him.

First Mr Wilson considered it to be a dangerous evasion of the real difficulties, to attempt to prove that suttees are not "essentially a part of the Hindu religion" – I entirely agree in this opinion. The question is, not what the rite is, but what it is supposed to be; and I have no doubt that the conscientious belief of every order of Hindus, with few exceptions, regard it as sacred.

Second Mr Wilson thinks that the attempt to put down the practice will inspire extensive dissatisfaction. I agree also in this opinion. He does not imagine that the promulgated prohibition will lead to any immediate and overt act of insubordination, but that affrays and much agitation of the public mind must ensue. But he conceives, that, if once they suspect that it is the intention of the British government to abandon this hitherto inviolate principle of allowing the most complete toleration in matter of religion, that there will arise, in the mind of all, so deep a distrust of our ulterior designs, that they will no longer be tractable to any arrangement intended for their improvement and that the principles of morality as well as of a more virtuous and exalted rule of action, now actively inculcated by European education and knowledge, will receive a fatal check. I must acknowledge that a similar opinion as to the probable excitation of a deep distrust of our future intentions was mentioned to me in conversation by that enlightened native, Rammohan Roy, a warm advocate for the abolition of suttees, and of all other superstitions and corruptions, engrafted on the Hindu religion, which he considers originally to have been a pure deism. It was his opinion that the practice might be suppressed, quietly and unobservedly, by increasing the difficulties, and by the indirect agency of the police. He apprehended that any public enactment would give rise to general apprehension, that the reasoning would be, "While the English were contending for power, they deemed it politic to allow universal toleration, and to respect our religion; but having obtained the supremacy, their first act is a violation of their professions, and the next

will probably be like the Mahomedan conquerors, to force upon us their own religion."

Admitting, as I am always disposed to do, that much truth is contained in these remarks, but not all assenting to the conclusions which though not described, bear the most unfavourable import, I shall now enquire into the evil and the extent of danger which may practically result from this measure.

It must be first observed, that of the 463 suttees occurring in the whole of the presidency of Fort William, 420 took place in Bengal, Bihar and Orissa, or what are termed the lower provinces, and of these latter, 287 in the Calcutta division alone.

It might be very difficult to make a stranger to India understand, much less believe, that in a population of so many millions of people, as the Calcutta division includes, and the same may be said of all the lower provinces, so great is the want of courage and of vigour of character, and such the habitual submission of centuries, that insurrection or hostile opposition to the will of the ruling power may be affirmed to be an impossible danger. I speak of the population taken separately from the army, and may add for the information of the stranger, and also in support of my assertion that few of the natives of the lower provinces are to be found in our military ranks. I therefore, at once deny the danger in toto, in reference to this part of our territories, where the practice principally obtains. If, however, security were wanting against extensive popular tumult or revolution, I should say that the permanent settlement, which though a failure in many other respects and its most important essentials, has this great advantage at least, of having created a vast body of rich landed proprietors, deeply interested in the continuance of the British dominion, and having complete command over the mass of the people, and, in respect to the apprehension of ulterior views, I cannot believe that it could last but for the moment. The same large proprietary body, connected for the most part with Calcutta, can have no fears of the kind, and through their interpretation of our intentions, and that of their numerous dependants, and agents, the public mind could not long remain in a state of deception.

Were the scene of this sad destruction of human life laid in the upper instead of the lower provinces, in the midst of a bold and manly people, I might speak with less confidence upon the question of safety. In these provinces the suttees amount to 43 only – upon a population of neary twenty millions. It cannot be expected that any general feeling, where combination of any kind is so unusual, could be excited in defence of a rite, in which so few participate, a rite also, notoriously made too often subservient to views of personal interest on the part of the other members of the family.

It is stated by Mr Wilson that interference with infanticide and the capital punisment of Brahmins offer a fallacious analogy with the prohibition now proposed. The distinction is not perceptible to my judgement. The former practice, though confined to particular families, is probably viewed as a religious custom; and as for the latter, the necessity of the enactment proves the general existence of the exception, and it is impossible to conceive a more direct and open violation of the shastras or one more at variance with the general feelings of the Hindu population. To this day, in all Hindu states, the life of Brahmins is, I believe, still held sacred.

But I have taken up too much time in giving my own opinions, when those of the greatest experience, and the highest official authority are upon our records. In the report of the Nizamat Adalat for 1828, four out of five of the judges recommended to the governor-general in council the immediate abolition of the practice, and attest its safety. The fifth judge, though not opposed to the opinions of the rest of the bench, did not feel then prepared to give his entire assent. In the report of this year, the measure has come up with the unanimous recommendation of the court. The two superintendents of police for the upper and lower provinces, Mr Walter Ewer, and Mr Charles Barwell, have in the strongest terms expressed their opinion that the suppression might be effected without the least danger. The former officer has urged the measure upon the attention of government in the most forcible manner. No documents exist to show the opinions of the public functionaries in the interior, but I am informed that nine-tenths are in favour of the abolition.

How again are these opinions supported by practical experience?

Within the limits of the supreme court at Calcutta, not a suttee has taken place since the time of Sir John Anstruther.

In the Delhi territory, Sir Charles Metcalfe never permitted a suttee to be performed.

In Jessore, one of the districts of the Calcutta division, in 1824 there were 30 suttees, in 1825 – 16, in 1826 – 3, in 1827 and 1828 there were none. To no other cause can this be assigned, than to a power beyond the law, exercised by the acting magistrate, against which, however, no public remonstrance was made. Mr Pigou has been since appointed to Cuttack, and has pursued the same

strong interference as in Jessore, but his course, although most humane, was properly arrested, as being illegal, by the commissioners. Though the case of Jessore is perhaps one of the strongest examples of efficacious and unopposed interposition, I really believe that there are few districts in which the same arbitrary power is not exercised to prevent the practice. In the last week, in the report of the acting commissioner, Mr Smith, he states that in Ghazipur in the last year 16, and in the preceding years 7 suttees had been prevented by the persuasions, or rather it should be said by the threats of the police.

Innumerable cases of the same kind might be obtained from the public records.

It is stated in the letter of the collector of Gaya, Mr Trotter, but upon what authority I have omitted to enquire, that the Peishwa (I presume he means the ex-Peishwa Baji Rao) would not allow the rite to be performed, and that in Tanjore it is equally interdicted. These facts, if true, would be positive proofs at least that no unanimity exists among the Hindus upon the point of religious obligations.

Having made enquiries also how far suttees are permitted in the European foreign settlements, I find, from Dr Carey, that at Chinsurah no such sacrifices had ever been permitted by the Dutch government; that within the limits of Chandernagore itself they were also prevented, but allowed to be performed in the British territories. The Danish government of Serampore has not forbidden the rite in conformity to the example of the British government.

It is a very important fact, that though representations have been made by the disappointed party to superior authority, it does not appear that a single instance of direct opposition to the execution of the prohibitory orders of our civil functionaries has ever occurred. How then can it be reasonably feared that to the government itself, from whom all authority is derived, and whose power is now universally considered to be irresistible, anything bearing the semblance of resistance can be manifest. Mr Wilson also is of opinion that no immediate overt act of insubordination would follow the publication of the edict. The regulations of government may be evaded, the police may be corrupted, but even here the price paid as hush money will operate as a penalty indirectly forwarding the objects of government.

I venture then to think it completely proved that, from the native population, nothing of extensive combination or even of partial opposition may be expected from the abolition.

It is, however, a very different and much more important question, how far the feelings of the native army might take alarm, how far the rite may be in general observance by them, and whether as in the case of Vellore, designing persons might not make use of the circumstance either for the purpose of immediate revolt, or of sowing the seeds of permanent disaffection. Reflecting upon the vast disproportion of numbers between our native and European troops, it was obvious that there might be, in any general combination of the former, the greatest danger to the state, and it became necessary therefore to use every precaution to ascertain the impression likely to be made upon the minds of the native soldiery.

Before I detail to council the means I have taken to satisfy my mind upon this very important branch of the enquiry, I shall beg leave to advert to the name of Lord Hastings. It is impossible but that to his most humane, benevolent, and enlightened mind, this practice must have been often the subject of deep and anxious meditation. It was consequently a circumstance of ill omen and severe disappointment not to have found, upon the records, the valuable advice and direction of his long experience and wisdom. It is true that during the greater part of his administration, he was engaged in war, when the introduction of such a measure would have been highly injudicious. To his successor, Lord Amherst, also the same obstacle was opposed. I am however fortunate in possessing a letter from Lord Hastings to a friend in England upon suttees, and from the following extract, dated 21st November 1825, I am induced to believe that, had he remained in India, this practice would long since have been suppressed. "The subject which you wish to discuss is one which must interest one's feeling most deeply; but it is also one of extreme nicety. When I mention that in one of the years during my administration of government in India, above eight hundred widows sacrificed themselves within the provinces comprised in the presidency of Bengal, to which number I very much suspect, that very many not notified to the magistrates should be added, I will hope to have credit for being acutely sensible to such an outrage against humanity. At the same time, I was aware how much danger might attend the endeavouring to suppress, forcibly, a practice so rooted in the religious belief of the natives. No men of low caste are admitted into the ranks of the Bengal army. Therefore the whole of that formidable body must be regarded as blindly partial to a custom which they consider equally referable to family honour and to points of faith. To attempt the extinction of the horrid superstition, without being supported in the procedure by a real concurrence on the part of the army, would be distinctly perilous. I have no scruple to say, that I did believe, I could have carried with me the assent of the army towards such an object. That persuasion, however, arose from circumstances which gave me peculiar influence over the native troops.

Lord Hastings left India in 1823. It is quite certain that the government of that time were much more strongly impressed with the risk of the undertaking, than is now very generally felt. It would have been fortunate could this measure have proceeded under the auspices of that distinguished noble-man, and that the state might have had the benefit of the influence which undoubtedly he possessed, in a peculiar degree, over the native troops. Since that period, however, six years have elapsed. Within the territories all has been peaceful and prosperous, while without, Ava and Bharatpur, to whom alone a strange sort of consequence was ascribed by public opinions, have been made to acknowledge our supremacy. In this interval, experience has enlarged our knowledge, and has given us surer data upon which to distinguish truth from illusion, and to ascertain the real circumstances of our position and power. It is upon these that the concurring opinion of the officers of the civil and military services at large having been founded, is entitled to our utmost confidence.

I have the honour to lay before council the copy of a circular addressed to forty-nine officers, pointed out to me by the secretary to government in the military department, as being from their judgement and experience the best enabled to appreciate the effect of the proposed measure upon the native army, together with their answers. For more easy reference, an abstract of each answer is annexed in a separate paper and classed with those to the same purport.

It appears – first, that of those whose opinions are directly adverse to all interference, whatever, with the practice, the number is only five. Secondly, of those who are favourable to abolition, but averse to absolute and direct prohibition under the authority of the government, the number is twelve. Thirdly, of those who are favourable to abolition, to be effected by the indirect interference of magistrates and other public officers, the number is eight. Fourthly, of those who advocate the total, immediate and public suppression of the practice, the number is twenty-eight.

It will be observed also, of those who are against an open and direct prohibition, few entertain any fear of immediate danger. They refer to a distinct and undefined evil. I can conceive the possibility of the expression of dissatisfaction and anger being immediately manifested upon this supposed attack on their religious usages; but the distant danger seems to me altogether groundless, provided that perfect respect continues to be paid to all their innocent rites and ceremonies, and provided also, that a kind and considerate regard be continued to their worldly interests and comforts.

I trust therefore that the council will agree with me in the satisfactory nature of this statement, and that they will partake in the perfect confidence which it has given me of the expediency and safety of the abolition.

In the answer of one of the military officers, Lieutenant-Colonel Todd, he has recommended that the tax on pilgrims should be simultaneously given up, for the purpose of affording an un-doubted proof of our disinterestedness and of our desire to remove every obnoxious obstacle to the gratification of their religious duties. A very con-siderable revenue is raised from this head; but if it were to be the price of satisfaction and confidence to the Hindus, and of the removal of all distrust of our present and future intentions, the sacrifice might be a measure of good policy. The objections that must be entertained by all to the principle of the tax, which in England has latterly excited very great reprobation, formed an additional motive for the enquiry. I enclose the copy of a circular letter addressed to different individuals at present in charge of the districts where the tax is collected, or who have had opportunities from their local knowl-edge of forming a judgement upon this question. It will be seen that opinions vary, but upon a review of the whole, my conviction is that, in connection with the present measure, it is inexpedient to repeal the tax. It is a subject upon which I shall not neglect to bestow more attention than I have been able to do. An abstract of these opinions is annexed to this minute.

I have now to submit for the consideration of council the draft of a regulation enacting the aboli-tion of suttees. It is accompanied by a paper con-taining the remarks and suggestions of the judges of the Nizamat Adalat. In this paper is repeated the unanimous opinion of the court in favour of the proposed measure. The suggestions of the Nizamat Adalat are, in some measure, at variance with a principal object I had in view of preventing colli-sion between the parties to the suttee and the of-ficers of police. It is only in the previous processes or during the actual performance of the rite, when the feelings of all may be more or less roused to a high degree of excitement, that I apprehend the

possibility of affray, or of acts of violence, through an indiscreet and injudicious exercise of authority. It seemed to me prudent, therefore, that the police in the first instance should warn and advise, but not forcibly prohibit, and if the suttee, in defiance of this notice, were performed, that a report should be made to the magistrate, who would summon the parties and proceed as in any other case of crime. The sadar court appear to think these precautions unnecessary and I hope they may be so, but, in the beginning, we cannot, I think, proceed with too much circumspection. Upon the same principle, in order to guard against a too hasty or severe a sen-tence, emanating from extreme zeal on the part of the local judge, I have proposed that the case should only be cognizable by the commissioner of circuit. These are, however, questions which I should wish to see discussed in council. The other recommendations of the court are well worthy of our adoption.

I have now brought this paper to a close, and I trust I have redeemed my pledge of not allowing, in the consideration of this question, passion or feel-ing to have any part. I trust it will appear that due weight has been given to all difficulties and objec-tions; that facts have been stated with truth and impartiality; that the conclusion to which I have come is completely borne out, both by reason and authority. It may be justly asserted that the govern-ment, in this act, will only be following, not preced-ing the tide of public opinion, long flowing in this direction: and when we have taken into considera-tion the experience and wisdom of that highest public tribunal, the Nizamat Adalat, who in unison with our wisest and ablest public functionaries have been, year after year, almost soliciting the govern-ment to pass this act, the moral and political re-sponsibility of not abolishing this practice far surpasses in my judgment that of the opposite course.

But discarding, as I have done, every inviting appeal from sympathy and humanity, and having given my verdict, I may now be permitted to ex-press the anxious feelings with which I desire the success of this measure.

The first and primary object of my heart is the benefit of the Hindus. I know nothing so important to the improvement of their future conditions, as the establishment of a purer morality, whatever their belief, and a more just conception of the will of God. The first step to this better understanding will be dissociation of religious belief and practice from blood and murder. They will then, when no longer under this brutalizing excitement, view with more calmness, acknowledged truths. They will see that there can be no inconsistency in the ways of providence, that to the command received as divine by all races of men, "No innocent blood shall be spilt," there can be no exception, and when they shall have been convinced of the error of this first and most criminal of their customs, may it not be hoped, that others which stand in the way of their improvement may likewise pass away, and that (with) this emancipation from those chains and shackles upon their minds and actions, they may no longer continue as they have done, the slaves of every foreign conqueror, but that they may assume their just places among the great families of mankind. I disavow in these remarks or in this measure any view whatever to conversion to our own faith. I write and feel as a legislator for the Hindus, and as I believe many enlightened Hindus think and feel.

Descending from these higher considerations, it cannot be a dishonest ambition that the government of which I form a part, should have the credit of an act, which is to wash out a foul stain upon British rule, and to stay the sacrifice of humanity and justice to a doubtful expediency; and finally, as a branch of the general administration of the empire, I may be permitted to feel deeply anxious, that our course shall be in accordance with the noble example set to us by the British government at home and that the adaptation, where practicable, to the circumstances of this vast Indian population, of the same enlightened principles, may promote here as well as there, the general prosperity, and may exalt the character of our nation.

Sati Regulation XVII, A.D. 1829 of the Bengal Code, 4 December 1829

A regulation for declaring the practice of suttee, or of burning or burying alive the widows of Hindus, illegal, and punishable by the criminal courts, passed by the governor-general in council on the 4th December 1829, corresponding with the 20th Aughun 1236 Bengal era; the 23rd Aughun 1237 Fasli; the 21st Aughun 1237 Vilayati; the 8th Aughun 1886 Samavat; and the 6th Jamadi-us-Sani 1245 Hegira.

I The practice of suttee, or of burning or burying alive the widows of Hindus, is revolting to the feelings of human nature; it is nowhere enjoined by the religion of the Hindus as an imperative duty; on the contrary a life of purity and retirement on the part of the widow is more especially and preferably inculcated, and by a vast majority of that people throughout India the practice is not kept up, nor observed; in some extensive districts it does not

exist: in those in which it has been most frequent it is notorious that in many instances acts of atrocity have been perpetrated which have been shocking to the Hindus themselves, and in their eyes unlawful and wicked. The measures hitherto adopted to discourage and prevent such acts have failed of success, and the governor-general in council is deeply impressed that the conviction that the abuses in question cannot be effectually put an end to without abolishing the practice altogether. Actuated by these considerations the governor-general in council, without intending to depart from one of the first and most important principles of the system of British government in India, that all classes of the people be secure in the observance of their religious usages so long as that system can be adhered to without violation of the paramount dictates of justice and humanity, has deemed it right to establish the following rules, which are hereby enacted to be in force from the time of their promulgation throughout the territories immediately subject to the presidence of Fort William.

II The practice of suttee, or of burning or burying alive the widows of Hindus, is hereby declared illegal, and punishable by the criminal courts.

III First. All zamindars, or other proprietors of land, whether malguzari or lakhiraj; ali sadar farmers and under-renters of land of every description; all dependent taluqdars; all naibs and other local agents; all native officers employed in the collection of the revenue and rents of land on the part of government, or the court of wards; and all munduls or other headmen of villages are hereby declared especially accountable for the immediate communication to the officers of the nearest police station of any intended sacrifice of the nature described in the foregoing section; and any zamindar, or other description of persons above noticed, to whom such responsibility is declared to attach, who may be convicted of wilfully neglecting or delaying to furnish the information above required, shall be liable to be fined by the magistrate or joint magistrate in any sum not exceeding two hundred rupees, and in default of payment to be confined for any period of imprisonment not exceeding six months.

Secondly. Immediately on receiving intelligence that the sacrifice declared illegal by this regulation is likely to occur, the police darogha shall either repair in person to the spot, or depute his mohurrir or jamadar, accompanied by one or more burkundazes of Hindu religion, and it shall be the duty of the police-officers to announce to the persons assembled for the performance of ceremony, that it is illegal; and to endeavour to prevail on them to disperse, explaining to them that in the event of their persisting in it they will involve themselves in a crime, and become subject to punishment by the criminal courts. Should the parties assembled proceed in defiance of these remonstrances to carry the ceremony into effect, it shall be the duty of the police-officers to use all lawful means in their power to prevent the sacrifice from taking place, and to apprehend the principle persons aiding and abetting in the performance of it, and in the event of the police-officers being unable to apprehend them, they shall endeavour to ascertain their names and places of abode, and shall immediately communicate the whole of the particulars to the magistrate for his orders.

Thirdly. Should intelligence of a sacrifice have been carried into effect before their arrival at the spot, they will nevertheless institute a full enquiry into the circumstances of the case, in like manner as on all other occasions of unnatural death, and report them for the information and orders of the magistrate or joint magistrate, to whom they may be subordinate.

IV   First. On the receipt of the reports required to be made by the police daroghas, under the provisions of the foregoing section, the magistrate or joint magistrate of the jurisdiction in which the sacrifice may have taken place, shall enquire into the circumstances of the case, and shall adopt the necessary measures for bringing the parties concerned in promoting it to trial before the court of circuit.

Secondly. It is hereby declared, that after the promulgation of this regulation all persons convicted of aiding and abetting in the sacrifice of a Hindu widow, by burning or burying her alive, whether the sacrifice be voluntary on her part or not, shall be deemed guilty of culpable homicide, and shall be liable to punishment by fine or by both fine and imprisonment, at the discretion of the court of circuit, according to the nature and circumstance of the case, and the degree of guilt established against the offender; nor shall it be held to be any plea of justification that he or she was desired by the party sacrificed to assist in putting her to death.

Thirdly. Persons committed to take their trial before the court of circuit for the offence abovementioned shall be admitted to bail or not, at the discretion of the magistrate or joint magistrate, subject to the general rules in force in regard to the admission of bail.

V   It is further deemed necessary to declare, that nothing contained in this regulation shall be construed to preclude the court of Nizamat Adalat

from passing sentence of death on persons convicted of using violence or compulsion, or of having assisted in burning or burying alive a Hindu widow while labouring under a state of intoxication, or stupefaction, or other cause impeding the exercise of her free will, when, from the aggravated nature of the offence, proved against the prisoner, the court may see no circumstances to render him or her proper object of mercy.

Source: V. N. Datta. Sati: A Historical, Social and Philosophical Enquiry into the Hindu Rite of Widow Burning. New Delhi: Manohar, 1988, pp. 335–53 (orig. pub. 1829).

Note

Lord William Cavendish Bentinck (1774–1839) was British Governor-General in Madras from 1828 to 1835. As administrator he introduced numerous innovations and reforms to British rule in India at the time, including financial reform, the representation of Indians in government (see Part III), and the suppression of such practices as thuggee (see this chapter) and sati.

25   Digest of Hindu Law: The Duties of a Faithful Widow (1789)

Section 1: On dying with or after her husband

123

ANAGIRAS: That woman who, on the death of her husband, ascends the *same* burning pile with him, is exalted to heaven, as equal in virtue to ARUNDHATI.

2   She who follows her husband *to another world*, shall dwell in a region of joy for so many years as there are hairs on the human body, or thirty-five millions.

3   As a serpent-catcher forcibly draws a snake from his hole, thus, drawing her lord *from a region of torment*, she enjoys delight together with him.

4   The woman who follows her husband *to the pile*, expiates the sins of three generations, on the paternal and maternal side, of that family to which she was given while a virgin.

5   There, having the best of husbands, *herself* best *of women*, enjoying the best delights, she partakes of bliss with her husband *in a celestial abode*, as long as fourteen INDRAS reign.

6 Even though the man had slain a priest, or returned evil for good, or killed an intimate friend, the woman expiates those crimes: this has been declared by ANGIRAS.

7 No other effectual duty is known for virtuous women, at any time after the death of their lords, except casting themselves into the same fire.

8 As long as a woman, *in her successive transmigrations*, shall decline burning herself, like a faithful wife, on the *same* fire with her deceased lord, so long shall she be not exempted from *springing again to life in* the body of some female animal.

9 When their lords have departed at the *fated* time of *attaining* heaven, no other way but entering the *same* fire is known for women whose virtuous conduct and whose thoughts have been devoted to their husbands, and who fear the dangers of separation.

124

The *Mahabharata*: Those who have slighted their former lord through an evil disposition, or have remained at all times averse from their husbands.

If they follow their lords at the *proper* time, in such a mode are all purified from lust, wrath, fear, and avarice.

125

VYASA: Learn the power of that widow, who, hearing that her husband has deceased, and been burned in another region, speedily casts herself into the fire:

2 Though he have sunk to a region of torment, be restrained in dreadful bonds, have reached the place of anguish, be seized by the imps of YAMA;
3 Be exhausted of strength, and afflicted and tortured for his crimes; still, as a serpent-catcher unerringly drags a serpent from his hole;
4 So does she draw her husband *from hell*, and ascend to heaven by the power of devotion.

There, with the best of husbands, lauded by the choirs of APSARAS,

5 She sports with her husband, as long as fourteen INDRAS reign.

126

The *Brahme-purana*: No other way is known for a virtuous woman, after the death of her husband; the separate cremation of her husband would be lost, *to all religious intents*.

2 If her lord die in another country, let the faithful wife place his sandals on her breasts, and pure, enter the fire.
3 The faithful widow is pronounced no suicide by the *recited* text of the *Rigveda*: when three days of mourning are passed, she obtains legal obsequies.

127

Vrihat Narediya purana: Mothers of infant children, pregnant women, they who have not menstruated, and they who are actually unclean, ascend not the funeral pile, O lovely princess!

128

VRIHASPATI: The mother of an infant child may not relinquish the care of her infant to ascend *the pile*; nor *may* a woman in her courses, nor one who *lately* brought forth a child, *burn herself* with her husband; a pregnant widow must preserve the embryo.

The husband may employ, in every sort of business, his wife who has borne a son, when she has bathed after twenty nights from the child-birth; and her who has borne a daughter, when she has bathed after a month.

MENU: A man of the sacerdotal class becomes pure in ten days; of the warlike, in twelve; of the commercial, in fifteen; of the servile, in a month.

129

GOTAMA: A woman of the sacerdotal class cannot go *with her husband to another world*, ascending a separate pile.

130

The *Bhawishya-purana*: If, indeed, *her* husband die after the third night of her uncleanness, the corpse, O twice-born men, should be kept one night, that she may follow him in death.

131

VYASA: If the faithful wife reside at a place which may be reached in one day, and notice be given *her of her husband's death*, the ceremony of burning her lord should not be performed so long as her arrival may be *expected*.

Section 2: On the duties of widows choosing to survive their husbands

132

VRIHASPATI: A wife is considered as half the body *of her husband*, equally sharing the fruit of pure and impure acts: whether she ascend *the pile* after him, or survive for the benefit of her husband, she is a faithful wife.

133

VISHNU: After the death of her husband, a wife must practise austerities, or ascend *the pile* after him.

134

PRACHETAS: An anchorite, a student in theology, and a widow, must avoid the leaf of the betel, inunctions, and feeding from vessels of zinc.

The *Ayur Veda*: When oil is applied to the crown of the head, and reaches all the limbs, if both arms be sufficiently wetted with water, it is called *abhyanga*.

2 If the oil sparingly reach the limbs, and the arms be not sufficiently wetted, it is *mashti*, a distinct inunction (*abhyanga*) intended for the head (*mastaca*) and the rest of the limbs.

135

Smriti: Only one meal each day should ever be made *by a widow*, not a second repast by any means; and a widowed woman, sleeping on a bed, would cause her husband to fall *from a region of joy*:

2 She must not again use perfumed substances: but daily make offerings for her husband, with *cusa* grass, *tila*, and water.

3 In the month of *Vaisac'ha*, *Cartica*, and *Magha*, let her observe special fasts, perform ablutions, make gifts, travel to places of pilgrimage, and repeatedly utter the name of VISHNU.

136

The *Matsya purana* declares veneration due to faithful women:

Therefore should faithful women be venerated like deities by all men; *for*, through their merits, the three worlds are governed by the king.

137

HARITA: Leaving her husband's favourite abode, keeping her tongue, hands, feet, and *other* organs in subjection, strict in her conduct, *all* day mourning her husband, with harsh duties, devotion, and fasts to the end of her life, a widow victoriously gains her husband's abode and repeatedly acquires the same mansion with her lord as is thus declared:

"That faithful woman who practises harsh duties after the death of her lord, cancels all her sins, and acquires the same mansion with her lord."

138

VRIHASPATI: Strict in austerities and rigid devotion, firm in avoiding sensuality, and ever patient and liberal, a widow attains heaven even though she have no son.

139

MENU: Let her emaciate her body, by living voluntarily on pure flowers, roots, and fruit; but let her not, when her lord is deceased, even pronounce the name of another man.

2 Let her continue till death forgiving all injuries, performing harsh duties, avoiding every sensual pleasure, and cheerfully practising the incomparable rules of virtue, which have been followed by such women as were devoted to only one husband.

140

MENU: Many thousands of *Brahmanas*, having avoided sensuality from their early youth, and having left no issue in their families, have ascended, *nevertheless*, to heaven.

141

MENU: And, like those abstemious men, a virtuous wife ascends to heaven, though she have no child, if, after the decease of her lord, she devote herself to pious austerity.

142

MENU: But a widow who, from a wish to bear children, slights her *deceased* husband *by marrying again*, brings disgrace on herself here below; and shall be excluded from the seat of her lord.

143

MENU: Issue begotten on a woman by any other *than her husband* is here declared to be no progeny of her's, no more than a child begotten on the wife of another man belongs to the begetter; nor is a second husband allowed, in any part *of this code*, to a virtuous woman.

144

YAMA: Let her continue as long as she lives, performing austere duties, avoiding every sensual pleasure, and cheerfully practising those rules of virtue which have been followed by such women as were devoted to *one only husband*.

2   Neither in the *Veda*, nor in the sacred code, is religious seclusion allowed to a woman; her own duties, practised with a husband of equal class, are indeed her religious rites: this is a settled rule.

3   Eighty-eight thousand holy Sages of the sacerdotal class, superior to sensual appetites, and having left no issue in their families, have ascended, *nevertheless*, to heaven.

4   Like them, a *betrothed* damsel, become a widow, and devoting herself to pious austerity, shall attain heaven, though she have no son: this MENU, sprung from the self-existent, has declared.

145

CATYAYANA: Though her husband die guilty of many crimes, if she remain ever firm in virtuous conduct, obsequiously honouring her spiritual parents.

2   And devoting herself to pious austerity after the death of her husband, that faithful widow is exalted to heaven, as equal in virtue to ARUNDHATI.

Source: Book IV, Chapter 3 of *Digest of Hindu Law*. Translated from the Original Sanscrit by H. T. Colebrooke, Esq., vol. 2, 4th edn. Madras: J. Higginbotham, 1874, pp. 153–61.

Note

In addition to his translation of the *Digest of Hindu Law*, the Sanskrit scholar Henry Thomas Colebrooke (1765–1837) wrote numerous studies of the history, literature and religions of ancient India.

Part II

The Opening of the Suez Canal

Chapter Five

The "Master Builder" of the Canal:
Ferdinand De Lesseps

Introduction

Ferdinand de Lesseps' career, like Warren Hastings', was characterized by soaring accomplishments and great notoriety and scandal. The indomitable visionary who was nicknamed "Le Grand Français," was bold enough to implement Napoleon Bonaparte's dream of building a canal across the isthmus of Suez which would serve as a "short cut" to the riches of the East. For some, De Lesseps was a great diplomatic genius; for others, he was a devious schemer, double-dealer, and cheat. De Lesseps' letters and journal entries represent him as a major player, an unswervingly confident man who was fully aware of his charms and absolutely unafraid of using them in pursuit of his goals. De Lesseps saw himself as someone who was destined for greatness which, in his eyes, was the family tradition. In his journal entries, De Lesseps reads Egyptian meteors and ancient texts as evidence that he, and he alone, was destined to build the Canal.

De Lesseps' uncle Barthélemy was a military hero of the grand manner who became Civil Governor of Moscow; he was also a favorite in the court of Louis XVI. His father Mathieu was Napoleon's Commissary-General at the Port of Cadiz in Egypt and, later, at Alexandria. Napoleon made the senior De Lesseps a Count for his patriotism and loyal service; young Ferdinand grew up in the atmosphere of national glory, great comfort, and wealth. De Lesseps' childhood contacts assisted him in his adult endeavors. Mohammed Said Pasha had been a close associate of his father and De Lesseps and Ismail Pasha had been youthful friends. De Lesseps took advantage of this intimacy to convince the Egyptian leaders that they should financially support his canal plan. He impressed Ismail Pasha with fantastic images of Egypt's restored glory; the Suez Canal would be a monument that would rival the Great Pyramids.

De Lesseps campaigned all over Europe, advertising the international and universal benefits of the Suez Canal. Commerce was the primary reason the European nations should invest in the Canal, and commerce would also be the answer to the Western nations' concerns about competition and control in times of peace and war. The nations' self-interest and determination to protect their trade would, he argued, be the ideal deterrent to war. The journalists' and politicians' uncertainties about the Suez Canal and its political consequences appear to be related to the recent wars and the volatility of present alliances. Some of De Lesseps' audience also seemed to be concerned about the smooth-talking Frenchman himself.

When the Canal was completed, the British were one of its primary users and beneficiaries. Despite Prime Minister Palmerston and numerous politicians' formerly vehement objections to the Canal, Great Britain soon demonstrated its appreciation. In 1870, De Lesseps was awarded the Grand Cross of the Star of India by Queen Victoria; he was also ordained a freeman by the City of London and presented a Gold medal at the Crystal Palace by Albert, the Prince of Wales. The glorious celebrations which inaugurated the Canal's opening would soon dissipate and the difficult job of administering its use and determining rights of passage, taxation, and ownership would cloud the horizon for years to come.

De Lesseps' success with the building of the Suez Canal also dramatically affected his future. Unable to rest on his laurels, De Lesseps felt compelled to out-do his own legacy when he took on the project of building the Panama Canal. His questionable financial maneuverings and dramatic, but extremely dangerous and costly engineering decisions doomed the second canal project and thousands of its workers and proved catastrophic for its shareholders and the French government, as well. When the Company was forced to liquidate in 1889, the country was nearly bankrupted; many individual fortunes were ruined. De Lesseps and his son Charles were accused of bribery, found guilty, and later acquitted. De Lesseps' life reflects the productive and destructive nature of his, and the era's, enterprising energies.

MC

Additional Reading

Anonymous. "The Suez Canal," *The Edinburgh Review*, January 1856, pp. 235–67.
Anonymous. "Suez and Euphrates Routes," *Quarterly Review*, July–Oct. 1857, pp. 354–97.
Beatty, Charles. *Ferdinand De Lesseps: A Biographical Study*. London, 1956.
Bolt, Jonathan. *To Culebra: A Play in Two Acts*. Salt Lake City, 1989.
Kinross, Lord John Patrick Balfour. *Between Two Seas. The Creation of the Suez Canal*. London, 1968.
Marlowe, John. *World Ditch: The Making of the Suez Canal*. New York, 1964.

26   Timeline of Significant Events

1830	French invade Algeria
1834	Egyptian–Syrian War
1842	Spanish Civil War
1850	Mohammed-Ali dies; Abbas Pasha succeeds him
1853–6	Crimean War
1854	Viceroy approves De Lesseps' plan for Suez Canal
	Act of Concession granted to De Lesseps
1855	Lord Palmerston, British Prime Minister
1856	Commission approves De Lesseps' plan
1857–8	Indian Rebellion
1858	Lord Derby, British Prime Minister
	Canal debated in the House of Commons; majority opposes Canal

	Universal Company of the Maritime Suez Canal founded
	Lord Palmerston again Prime Minister
1863	Said Pasha dies; Ismail Pasha succeeds him
1865	Cholera plague in Egypt
	Lord Palmerston dies; Lord John Russell succeeds him
	De Lesseps' grandson dies of cholera
1864	Riots on the isthmus of the Suez Canal
1866	Sultan ratifies Act of Concession
1869	Suez Canal completed
	Nov.: The Canal Inauguration
1870	De Lesseps honored by Queen Victoria in London
1871	Debut of Verdi's *Aïda* at the Cairo Opera House

27   Ferdinand de Lesseps: *The Suez Canal: Letters and Documents Descriptive of Its Rise and Progress in 1854–56* (1876)

The Suez Canal

1   To M. S. W. Ruyssenaers, Consul-General for Holland in Egypt

PARIS, July 8, 1852

THREE years ago, after my mission to Rome as Envoy Extraordinary, I asked for and obtained leave from my office as Minister Plenipotentiary.

Since 1849, I have studied incessantly, under all its aspects, a question which was already in my mind when we first became friends in Egypt twenty years ago.

I confess that my scheme is still a mere dream, and I do not shut my eyes to the fact that so long as I alone believe it to be possible, it is virtually impossible.

To make the public take it up it requires a support still wanting to it, and I ask for your assistance with a view to obtaining that support.

The scheme in question is the cutting of a canal through the Isthmus of Suez. This has been thought of from the earliest historical times, and for that very reason is looked upon as impracticable. Geographical dictionaries inform us indeed that the project would have been executed long ago but for insurmountable obstacles.

I enclose a minute, the result of my former and more recent studies, which I have had translated into Arabic by my friend Duchenoud, the best interpreter to the Government. It is strictly

Plate 1   "Ferdinand de Lesseps bestrides his canal" (n. d.); from Lord John Patrick Balfour Kinross *Between Two Seas: The Creation of the Suez Canal*. London: John Murray, 1968.

confidential, and you must judge whether the present Viceroy, Abbas Pacha, is likely to recognise its importance for Egypt and to aid in its execution.

2   To the Same

PARIS, November 15, 1852

WHEN you wrote to me that there was no chance of getting Abbas Pacha to entertain the idea of the Suez Canal, I communicated my project to my friend M. Benoit Fould, the financier, who was about to take part in the formation of a Crédit Mobilier at Constantinople. He was struck with the grandeur of the scheme and with the advantage of including the privilege of making the Suez Canal amongst the concessions to be demanded of Turkey.

The agent sent to Constantinople met with such difficulties as led to the abandonment of the project. One argument brought to bear against it was the impossibility of taking the initiative in a work to be executed in Egypt, where the Viceroy alone has a right to undertake it.

Under these circumstances I shall lay aside my minute on the Canal until a more convenient season, and occupy myself meanwhile with agriculture and in building a model farm on a property recently acquired by my mother-in-law, Madame Delamalle.

3   To the Same

LA CHENAIE, September 15, 1854

I WAS busy amongst bricklayers and carpenters, superintending the addition of a storey to Agnes Sorel's old manor house, when the postman, bringing the Paris mail, appeared in the courtyard. My letters and papers were handed up to me by the workmen, and my surprise was great on reading of the death of Abbas Pacha and the accession to power of the friend of our youth, the intelligent and warm-hearted Mohammed Said. I hurried down from the scaffolding, and at once wrote to congratulate the new Viceroy. I told him that I had retired from politics, and should avail myself of my leisure to pay my respects to him as soon as he would let me know the date of his return from Constantinople after his investiture.

He lost no time in replying, and fixed the beginning of November for our meeting at Alexandria. I wish you to be one of the first to know that I shall be punctual at the place of meeting. How delightful it will be for us to be together again in dear old Egypt! Not a word to any one, before I arrive, on the Canal project.

4   To Madame Delamalle, Paris (Journal)

ALEXANDRIA, November 7, 1854

I LANDED at Alexandria at eight o'clock a.m., from the Messageries packet Le Lycurgue. I was met, on behalf of the Viceroy, by my friend Ruyssenaers, Consul-General for Holland, and Hafouz Pacha, Minister of Marine. I got into a state carriage, which was to take me to one of his Highness's villas, a league from Alexandria, on the Mahmoudieh Canal; and thinking it as well not to pass through Alexandria without calling at the French Consulate, I delivered some despatches to M. Sabatier, of which I had taken charge in Paris, where nothing had been said of my Canal project, as I had mentioned it to no one, not even to my brother, secretary to the Minister of Foreign Affairs. I was very well received by M. Sabatier, who begged me, should I remain a night in Alexandria, to take up my quarters in the French palace, which had been commenced under my own superintendence in 1835, when I was at the head of the French Consulate-General.

I then proceeded on my way to Villa Cérisy, with my escort of Kawas and Sais, and on my arrival I found an entire staff of servants drawn up on the staircase, who saluted me three times by stretching their right hand to the ground and then raising it to their forehead. They were Turks and Arabs, under the control of a Greek valet de chambre and a Marseillaise cook named Ferdinand.

Here is a description of my residence, of which I myself witnessed the construction by M. de Cérisy, the celebrated French naval engineer, founder of the Arsenal of Alexandria, from which he has turned out twelve vessels of the line and twelve frigates in a short space of time. Under Mehemet Ali, M. de Cérisy contributed much to the enfranchisement of Egypt. The chief pavilion rises from the centre of a beautiful garden between two avenues, one leading to the plain of Alexandria, on the side of the Rosetta Gate, the other to the Mahmoudieh Canal. This pavilion was occupied a few days back by the princess who has recently presented Said Pacha with a son, named Toussoum. The reception-rooms and dining-room are on the ground floor; and on the first storey we have the drawing-room, a very cheerful apartment, with luxurious divans all round and four large windows overlooking the two avenues; the bedroom, with a soft canopied couch and fine yellow lampas curtains, fringed and embroidered with gold, and supplemented by double inner curtains of worked net; a first dressing-room, well stocked with perfumes and with rose-wood and marble furniture;

and beyond that again a second dressing-room, not less elegant, provided with a large basin, a silver ewer, and long soft towels, embroidered with gold, hanging from pegs.

I had just inspected my quarters when some friends of the Viceroy came in. I made them talk of the habits of Said Pacha since his accession; of his tastes, his mental tendencies, the persons about him, who was in favour and who in disfavour: all matters which it is well to be informed of beforehand when the guest of a prince. These gentlemen told me that since his return from Constantinople the Viceroy has often spoken of my visit, and has talked to those about him of his old friendship for me. I was informed that he had waited for me to accompany him on a journey he is about to make to Cairo, by way of the Desert of Libya, at the head of an army of 10,000 men. This trip will certainly be interesting, and will take eight or ten days. The start is fixed for next Sunday.

Presently additional servants arrived, including a Kaouadji bachi (chief coffee-maker), accompanied by several assistants; and a Chiboukchi bachi (superintendent of pipes), escorted by four acolytes with their insignia, consisting of a dozen long pipes with large amber bowls set with diamonds. The office of these men is no sinecure, for in well-ordered homes, belonging to great Turkish seigneurs, fresh pipes and little cups of coffee (findjanes) are served to every visitor.

Now came one of the Viceroy's officers to inform me that his Highness would receive me at noon in his palace of Gabbari.

I reflected that, having known the prince when he was in a totally different position, it would be desirable to treat him with the respectful deference always so acceptable to the human heart. I therefore wore my dress coat, with my medals, decorations, and orders.

The Viceroy received my very cordially, and talked about his childhood: of the way in which I had sometimes protected him from his father's severities; of the persecution and misery he had endured in the reign of Abbas Pacha; and, lastly, of his desire to do good and restore prosperity to Egypt. I congratulated him on his intentions, adding that it must be for some good end that Providence had entrusted the most despotic Government in the world to a prince who had received a good education when young, and had subsequently been sorely tried by adversity. I also expressed my conviction that he would be worthy of his mission.

The approaching march through the desert, amongst the Bedouin tribes, was discussed, and it was agreed that I should join the expedition without having to make any preparations myself.

I returned by way of Alexandria, and paid a second visit to M. Sabatier, meeting at his house all the officers of the Consulate-General and some old French friends, who, one and all, welcomed me enthusiastically.

Later I went to the French Post-office, still presided over by M. Gérardin, whom I had myself appointed eighteen years ago, at the time of the inauguration of the packet-boat service by M. Philibert Conte, son of the celebrated Postmaster-General.

Then came a grand dinner at the hospitable mansion of the Pastrés, who had invited the "ban" and "arrière-ban" of my old friends in Egypt to meet me.

On returning to my pavilion at eleven at night I found my entire staff of servants drawn up as before, and the head cook called my attention to a well-spread table decked with flowers. He told me he had orders to serve a similar meal morning and evening, and I replied that I should only require breakfast, and was now going to my room. Two footmen offered to assist me to ascend the brilliantly-illuminated staircase, and I accepted their services with the gravity and indifference proper to the guest of a Sovereign accustomed to similar attentions.

November 8th

I was up at five this morning, and opened the two windows of my room, shaded by the branches of trees the names of which I am unable to give. The air was laden with the scent of their blossoms and of the jasmines lining the avenue leading to the canal, beyond which, though the sun had not yet risen, I could see Lake Mareotis swept by a deliciously soft fresh breeze.

I went to make a morning visit to the Viceroy, and he left his apartments as soon as he heard of my arrival. We seated ourselves on a comfortable sofa in a gallery opening on to the garden. After we had had a pipe and some coffee my host led me to the balcony of the gallery to show me a regiment of his guard, which was to accompany him on his journey. We then went into the garden to try some revolving pistols I had brought him from France.

Our walk ended I told Mohammed Said I must leave him to receive some people at his house, whom I had invited in his name. He thanked me for doing the honours of *my* house so well.

Later I called on the Viceroy's brother, Halim Pacha, whose house is near my own. The young prince speaks French fluently, and said that, from what he had heard of me, he was sure we should soon be good friends, as we were both fond of riding and hunting. He is to be of our party in the desert, and will take his falcons and greyhounds with him. He palaced his servants and weapons at my disposal.

November 9th

I went this morning to see the Viceroy at his father's palace at Raz-el-Tyn, on the further side of the port, and he invited me to assist at the first audience of the new Consul-General for Sardinia, who was about to present his credentials.

After the ceremony we retired to the private apartments, where we had a long and very interesting conversation on the best principles of government; but not a word was said about the Suez Canal, a subject I shall not broach until I am quite sure of my ground and the scheme is sufficiently matured for the prince to adopt it as his own rather than mine.

I must act with the greater prudence that Ruyssenaers remembers having heard Said Pacha remark, before his accession to power, that if ever he became Viceroy of Egypt he should follow the example of his father, Mehemet Ali, who had declined to have anything to do with cutting a canal across the Isthmus because of the difficulties it might lead to with England.

This is not an encouraging precedent; but I am confident of success.

November 11th

This morning I received a fine horse from the Viceroy, for which he sent to Syria, and I was informed that there would be a review of troops this morning on a plain between Alexandria and Lake Mareotis. I mounted and joined my host. Soliman Pacha superintended the manœuvres, which included field exercise. As we were galloping along, a diamond ornament fell from the prince's cartridge-box; but he would not have it picked up, and we rode on.

November 12th

The Viceroy sent me word that his troops are to begin their march to Cairo, under his leadership, to-day, and he has given orders to his aide-de-camp to bring me to his first halting-place to-morrow.

[. . .]   November 14th

I was on foot at five o'clock this morning; the soldiers were beginning to leave their tents; and the vast moon-lit plains, though bare and desolate, were not entirely without beauty.

Hearing the Viceroy's voice I went to wish him good morning. We smoked a pipe together, drank some coffee, and mounted our horses ready to re-ceive the expected troops, who soon came up, fresh and in good condition, having left Alexandria yesterday morning with only three biscuits for each man. The Arabs are very temperate, and seem to thrive on their abstinence. The review over, we all returned to our tents.

I was interrupted by a visit from Halim Pacha, the Viceroy's brother, who has pitched his tent a league from our camp. He tells me that his Bedouin scouts report having sighted herds of gazelles two or three hours' march off, and that he proposes arranging a hunt for the day on which we resume our journey.

At ten o'clock we were summoned to breakfast by the Viceroy, and went to his tent with Halim Pacha.

Directly after our meal, Prince Halim's horses were brought round, and he returned to his camp. We retired at the same time, and, saddling my horse, I galloped about over the level plains and occasional hills near the camp. On one side the desert stretched away as far as the eye could reach, whilst on the other it was bounded by Lake Mareotis, with the sea beyond. Presently a large jackal started up almost from beneath my horse's feet, and I followed it at close quarters for some ten minutes, nearly touching it with the end of my whip, but finally losing sight of it in the brush-wood. It had probably taken up its position at a good starting-point for nocturnal visits to our camp in search of food.

On my return I found the Viceroy outside his tent, and, dismounting, I went with him to an how-itzer, planted 450 metres from a target, on which two companies of light infantry were trying their skill. Several shells had been thrown, but, though often near the mark, none had actually hit it.

And now night closed in upon the camp, and the watch-fires were lit. The Viceroy's military band struck up airs and marches of every nationality, including the "Marseillaise" and the "Hymn of Riégo." The Egyptians, the most lively nation on earth, grouped themselves before their tents and sang their national airs, beating time with their hands. The Viceroy, who had lost his appetite, probably because of the failure of his gunners, retired to his own tent, and sent his dinner to me in mine!

November 15th

I was not dressed at five o'clock this morning. Any one who had happened to see me outside my tent in my red dressing-gown, like the robe of a Scherif of Mecca, washing my arms up to the elbows, would have taken me for a true believer, and in the time of the Inquisition I should have been burnt alive; for you know that washing the arms to the elbow was one of the high misdemeanours punishable with tortures and *autos da fé*.

The camp soon began to show signs of life, and the freshness of the air gave notice of the approaching sunrise. I put on something warmer than my dressing-gown, and returned to my observatory. The horizon was already illuminated by the first rays of the dawn, and the east, on the right, was clear and bright, whilst the west was still dark and cloudy.

Suddenly to the left of my tent I beheld a rainbow of the most brilliant colours, the ends dipping, one into the east, the other into the west. I confess that my heart beat violently, and I was obliged to check myself from jumping to the conclusion that this sign of the covenant alluded to in the Scriptures was a proof of the moment having arrived for the true union of the West and East, and that this day was marked out for the success of my scheme.

The Viceroy's approach roused me from my dream, and we wished each other good morning with a hearty shake of the hand, in thoroughly French style. He told me he thought of adopting my suggestion of yesterday, and riding to some of the neighbouring heights to examine the dispositions of his camp. We mounted, preceded by two lancers and followed by an aide-de-camp. Arrived on a prominent hill, strewn with relics of ancient stone constructions, the Viceroy decided that it would be a good place from which to arrange the start of to-morrow; so he sent an aide-de-camp to order his tent and carriage to be brought to him. The latter is a kind of omnibus, with sleeping accommodation inside, and is drawn by six mules. The mules brought the carriage to the top of the hill at a gallop, and we sat down beneath its shade.

The Viceroy had a circular parapet of stones, picked up on the spot, erected opposite to us by some of his light infantry. An embrasure was then made, through which a cannon was pointed, and a salute fired for the benefit of the rest of the troops arriving from Alexandria. The heads of the columns could be seen beyond the camp.

At half-past ten, the Viceroy having breakfasted before he started, I went to get something to eat with Zulfikar Pacha. I wanted to show my host that his horse, the sturdy qualities of which I had proved on the first day of the journey, was a first-rate jumper; so, as I saluted him, I made my steed clear the stone parapet with one bound, and gallop down the slope to my tent. As you will see, this piece of imprudence probably had something to do with my winning the necessary approbation of the viceroy's suite for my scheme. The Generals, with

whom I breakfasted, complimented me, and I noticed that I had gained greatly in their esteem by my boldness.

I thought the Viceroy was now sufficiently prepared by my previous conversations to recognise the advantage to every Government of having great works of public utility executed by financial companies, and, encouraged by the happy omen of the rainbow, I hoped that the day would not pass over without a decision on the subject of the Suez Canal.

At five p.m. I remounted and returned to the Viceroy's tent, again clearing the parapet. His Highness was in a very good humour, and taking my hand, which he held for a moment in his own, he made me sit down beside him on his divan. We were alone, and through the door of the tent we could see the beautiful setting of that sun the rising of which had affected me so deeply in the morning. I felt strong in my composure and self-control at a moment when I was about to broach a question on which hung my whole future. My studies and reflections on the Canal between the two seas rose clearly before my mind, and the execution seemed to me so practicable that I did not doubt I should be able to make the prince share my conviction. I propounded my scheme without entering into details, laying stress on the chief facts and arguments set forth in my minute, which I could have repeated from end to end. Mohammed Said listened with interest to my explanations. I begged him if he had any doubts to be good enough to communicate them to me. He brought forward several objections with considerable intelligence, to which I replied in a satisfactory manner, for he said at last: *"I am convinced; I accept your plan. We will talk about the means of its execution during the rest of the journey. Consider the matter settled. You may rely upon me."*

Thereupon he sent for his Generals, made them sit down on chairs opposite to us, and repeated the conversation he had just had with me, inviting them to give their opinion on the proposals of *his friend*. These impromptu counsellers, better able to pronounce on an equestrian evolution than on a vast enterprise of which they could not in the least appreciate the significance, opened their great eyes, and, turning towards me, seemed to be thinking that their master's friend, whom they had just seen clear a wall on horseback with so much ease, could not but give good advice. Whilst the Viceroy was speaking to them they raised their hands to their foreheads every now and then in sign of assent.

The dinner-tray now appeared, and with one accord we plunged our spoons into the same bowl, which contained some first-rate soup. This is a faithful account of the most important negotiation I ever made or am ever likely to make.

Towards eight o'clock I took leave of the Viceroy, who told me we should start again to-morrow morning, and I returned to my tent. Zulfikar Pacha guessed my success as soon as he saw me, and rejoiced with me. The Viceroy's playmate in his childhood and the most intimate friend of his mature years, he has done much to contribute to the favourable result just obtained.

I was not inclined for sleep, so I set about working up my notes on the journey, and putting the finishing touches to an *impromptu* minute asked for by the Sultan, which had already been drawn up for two years.

This is the minute, dated Mareia Camp, November 15, 1854, and addressed to his Highness Mohammed Said, Viceroy of Egypt and its dependencies:

The scheme of uniting the Mediterranean and the Red Sea, by means of a navigable canal, suggested itself to all the great men who have ruled over or passed through Egypt, including – Sesostris, Alexander, Cæsar, the Arab conqueror Amrou, Napoleon I, and Mohammed Ali.

A canal effecting a junction between the two seas, via the Nile, existed for a period of unknown duration under the ancient Egyptian dynasties; during a second period of 445 years, from the first successors of Alexander and the Roman conquest to about the fourth century before the Mohammedan era; and, lastly, during a third period of 130 years, after the Arab conquest.

On his arrival in Egypt Napoleon appointed a commission of engineers to ascertain whether it would be possible to restore and improve the old route. The question was answered in the affirmative; and when M. Lepère presented him with the report of the commission, the Emperor observed: "It is a grand work; and though I cannot execute it now, the day may come when the Turkish Government will glory in accomplishing it."

The moment for the fulfilment of Napoleon's prophecy has arrived. The making of the Suez Canal is beyond doubt destined to contribute more than anything else to the stability of the Ottoman Empire, and to give the lie to those who proclaim its decline and approaching ruin by proving that it is possessed of prolific vitality and capable of adding a brilliant page to the history of civilization.

Why, I ask, did the Western nations and their rulers combine as one man to secure the possession of Constantinople to the Sultan? Why did the Power which menaced that possession meet with the armed opposition of Europe? Because the importance of the passage from the Black Sea to the Mediterranean is such, that the European Power commanding it would dominate over every other, and would upset the balance of power, which it is to the interest of each one to maintain.

But suppose a similar though yet more important position be established on some other point of the Ottoman Empire; suppose Egypt to be converted into the highway of commerce by the opening of the Suez Canal; would not a doubly impregnable situation be created in the East? for, afraid of seeing any one of themselves in possession of the new passage at some future date, would not the European Powers look upon the maintenance of its neutrality as a vital necessity?

Fifty years ago M. Lepère said he should require ten thousand men for four years and thirty or forty million francs for the restoration of the old indirect canal. He thought, moreover, that it would be possible to cut across the isthmus from Suez to Pelusium in a direct line.

M. Paulin Talabot, who was associated, as surveying engineer for a maritime canal society, with the equally celebrated Stephenson and Negrelli, advocated the indirect route from Alexandria to Suez, and proposed using the *barrage* already existing for the passage of the Nile. He estimated the total cost at 130 million francs for the canal and twenty million for the port and roadstead of Suez.

Linant Bey, the able director for some thirty years of the canal works of Egypt, who has made the Suez Canal question the study of his life in the country itself, and whose opinion is therefore worthy of serious respect, proposed cutting through the isthmus, at its narrowest part, in an almost direct line, establishing a large internal port in the basin of Lake Timsah, and rendering the harbours of Suez and Pelusium accessible to the largest vessels.

Gallice Bey, general of engineers and founder and director of the fortifications of Alexandria, presented Mohammed Ali with a canal scheme coinciding entirely with that proposed by Linant Bey.

Mougel Bey, director of works at the *barrage* of the Nile and chief engineer *des ponts et chaussées*, also had some conversation with Mohammed Ali on the possibility and desirability of making a maritime canal; and in 1840, at the request of Count Walewski, then on a mission in Egypt, he was commissioned to take some preliminary measures in Europe, which were, however, prevented by political events from leading to any definite results.

A careful survey would decide which would be the best route; and the scheme having once been recognised as possible, nothing remains to be done but to choose the readiest means for carrying it out.

None of the necessary operations, difficult though they may be, are really formidable to modern science. There can be no fear nowadays of their failure. The whole affair is, in fact, reduced to a mere question of pounds, shillings, and pence – a question which will, without doubt, be readily solved by the modern spirit of enterprise and association, that is to say, if the advantages to result from its solution are at all proportionate to the cost.

Now it is quite easy to prove that the cost of the Suez Canal, even on the largest estimate, will not be out of proportion with its value, shortening, as it must do, by more than half the distance between India and the principal countries of Europe and America.

To illustrate this fact I add the following table, drawn up by M. Cordier, Professor of Geology:

NAMES OF THE CHIEF PORTS OF EUROPE AND AMERICA		LEAGUES		Difference
		Via the Suez Canal	Viâ the Atlantic	
Constantinople	*Distance from Bombay*	1,800	6,100	4,300
Malta		2,062	5,800	3,778
Trieste		2,340	5,980	3,620
Marseilles		2,374	5,650	3,276
Cadiz		2,224	5,200	2,976
Lisbon		2,500	2,350	2,830
Bordeaux		2,800	6,650	2,850
Havre		2,824	5,800	2,976
London		3,100	5,950	2,850
Liverpool		3,050	5,900	2,850
Amsterdam		3,100	5,950	2,850
St Petersburg		3,700	6,550	2,850
New York		3,761	6,200	2,439
New Orleans		3,724	6,450	2,726

With such figures before us comment is useless, for they demonstrate that Europe and the United States are alike interested in the opening of the Suez Canal and in the maintenance of its strict and inviolable neutrality.

Mohammed Said is already convinced that no scheme can compare either in grandeur or in practical utility with that in question. What lustre it would reflect upon his reign! What an inexhaustible source of wealth it would be to Egypt! Whilst the names of the sovereigns who built up the pyramids, those monuments of human vanity, are unknown or forgotten, that of the prince who should inaugurate the great maritime canal would go down from age to age, and be blessed by the most remote generations!

The pilgrimage to Mecca henceforth rendered not only possible but easy to all Mussulmans, an immense impulse given to steam navigation and travelling generally, the countries on the Red Sea, Persian Gulf, the east coast of Africa, Spain, Cochin China, Japan, the empire of China, the Philippine Islands, Australia, and the vast archipelago now attracting emigration from the Old World brought 3,000 leagues nearer alike to the Mediterranean, the north of Europe, and to America, such would be the immediate results of the opening of the Suez Canal.

It has been estimated that six million tons of European and American shipping annually pass round the Cape of Good Hope and Cape Horn; and if only one-half went through the Canal, there would be an annual saving to commerce of 150 million francs.

There can be no doubt that the Suez Canal will lead to a considerable increase of tonnage; but counting upon three million tons only, an annual produce of thirty million francs will be obtained by levying a toll of ten francs per ton, which might be reduced in proportion to the increase of traffic.

Before closing this note, I must remind your Highness that preparations are actually being made in America for making new routes between the Atlantic and Pacific, and at the same time call your attention to the inevitable results to commerce generally, and that of Turkey in particular, should the isthmus separating the Red Sea from the Mediterranean remain closed for any length of time after the opening of the proposed American lines.

The chief difference between the Isthmus of Panama and that of Suez would appear to be that the mountainous nature of the former presents insuperable difficulties to the construction of a continuous ship canal, whereas on the latter such a canal would be the best solution of the difficulty. For America a kind of compromise has been made, the route consisting partly of a canal and partly of a railway. Now if, with a view to effecting only a partial success, the nations chiefly interested have come forward at once in a case where the advantages to be obtained are fewer and the expenses far greater than they would be in the Suez Canal scheme, and if the conventions for insuring the neutrality of the American route were accepted without difficulty, are we not forced to conclude that the moment has come for considering the question of the Isthmus of Suez? that the scheme for a canal which is of far more importance to the whole world than the Panama line, is perfectly secure from any real opposition, and that, in our efforts to carry it out, we shall be supported by universal sympathy and by the active and energetic co-operation of enlightened men of every nationality?

(Signed)   FERDINAND DE LESSEPS

[. . .]

9   To Richard Cobden, Esq., M. P., London

CAIRO, *December* 3, 1854
As the friend of peace and of the Anglo-French alliance I am going to tell you some news which will aid in realising the words, *Aperire terram gentibus.*

I arrived in Egypt a short time back, as the invited guest of the Viceroy, with whom, since his boyhood, I have been on terms of friendship, and I have had an opportunity of calling his attention to the advantages which would result to the commerce of the world and the prosperity of Egypt from the opening of a maritime canal between the Mediterranean and the Red Sea. Mohammed Said has understood the importance of this great enterprise, and wishing to see it carried into execution, he has authorised me to form a company of capitalists of all nations. I forward you a translation of the Firman of Concession. The Viceroy has requested me to communicate it to her Britannic Majesty's Agent and Consul-General as well as to the other Consuls-General in Egypt.

Some people maintain that the Viceroy's project will meet with opposition in England. I cannot believe it. Under existing circumstances your statesmen must be too enlightened for me to admit such an hypothesis. What! England monopolises half the general commerce with India and China; she possesses an immense empire in Asia; she can reduce by one-third the charges on her commerce and the distance from her metropolis by one half, and she will not have it done! And why? In order to prevent the countries on the Mediterranean from profiting by their geographical situation to carry on a little more commerce in the Oriental seas than they do at present, she will deprive herself of the advantages, material and political, of this new communication, merely because others are more favourably situated than herself, as if geographical position were everything, as if, having regard to all the circumstances, England had not more to gain by this work than all the other Powers put together. Lastly, England deprecates, it is said, the diminution in the number

of vessels trading with India which will result from the reduction by more than one-third of the length of the voyage. Has not our experience with railways proved, in a manner surpassing the expectations of the most sanguine, that the abbreviation of distances and of the duration of journeys lead to an immense increase in the number of passengers and the amount of traffic?

It is difficult to understand why those who admit this last objection do not advise the English Government to compel vessels for India to take the Cape Horn route, for it would employ more ships and turn out better sailors than that of the Cape of Good Hope.

If, though it seems impossible, the difficulties with which we are threatened have actually arisen, I hope that public spirit, so powerful in England, will soon have done justice to interested opposition and superannuated objections.

Allow me, in case of need, to count upon your legitimate influence. I have already written to our friend M. Arles Dufour, Secretary-General to the Imperial Commission at the Universal Exhibition of Paris, asking him to communicate with you.

[. . .]

12   To M. Arles Dufour, Paris

CAIRO, December 14th
THE Viceroy wrote by the very first mail after his arrival at Cairo to inform the Sultan of his intention to open the Suez Canal.

The Porte has recently spoken in the most complimentary terms with regard to the assistance now being rendered to its cause by the Viceroy, adding an expression of regret for the loss of two Egyptian men-of-war in the Black Sea and the death of Admiral Hassan Pacha. To this the Viceroy replied that he had nothing left to desire so long as the Sultan's own valuable life was spared, and he was able to come to his assistance; adding, that he was now more ready than ever to make fresh sacrifices for the common cause. Then followed some remarks on the railway the Viceroy proposes making between Cairo and Suez, in which England takes a great interest; and, after alluding to the unfortunate condition of the national Exchequer, as left by the late Abbas Pacha, his Highness pointed out the advantages which might ensue from the formation of international financial companies for the execution of useful works in the Ottoman Empire – the making of the Suez Canal, for instance.

He added that he had no doubt of the Sultan's acquiescence in the two schemes, for a railway and a canal.

He thought it useless to enter into longer explanations, which he is, however, prepared to give if necessary, by forwarding all the documents in support of the scheme. Such an act of respectful courtesy, to which the conventions relating to the Government of Egypt do not strictly bind Mohammed Said, will doubtless be appreciated as it deserves at Constantinople, where the maintenance of the present friendly relations with the Viceroy is much desired.

My previsions on the subject of certain foreign susceptibilities have been soon enough realised. Influenced probably by the presence in Cairo of Mr Murray, late English Consul-General in Egypt and now Minister in Persia, who has too long carried on the old policy of antagonism and jealous rivalry between France and England, Mr Bruce has begun to make some opposition. For instance, he has told the Viceroy that he is in too much of a hurry about the Suez Canal affair. His Highness replied firmly that in a question of civilisation and progress he could not believe that he should meet with opposition from any European Power, but that if any foreign agent should presently have objections to make *on the part of his Government*, he should request that they be stated in writing, so that he might *draw up his document*.

The English mail is just going, so I cannot give you my ideas to-day about the formation of our company, in which the money kings of Paris and London will be able to make their profits for the common good, although it will not do to let them have their own way entirely. Subscription lists, open for a certain time, will allow of the public taking shares at par.

The survey of the isthmus is put off until the 24th, that the necessary preparations may be made. Canvass opinion in England. Heaven helps those who help themselves.

[. . .]

26 To the Viscount Stratford de Redcliffe

CONSTANTINOPLE, February 28, 1855
MY LORD, There are questions which, to be properly settled, should be frankly entered into, just as there are wounds which must be laid bare in order to be cured. The straightforward manner in which you received the remarks I made in the first instance on a subject, the importance of which I do not attempt to conceal, encourages me to submit to your appreciation a point of view which, I think, it would be useful to consider with regard to the Isthmus of Suez. The great influence which your

character and your long experience entitle you to exercise in the decisions of your Government in all questions concerning the East, renders it a matter of the highest importance, in my eyes, that your Excellency's opinion should be based on a full knowledge of the facts.

The results already obtained through the close alliance of France and England, prove sufficiently how beneficial it is that the two nations should be united in the interest of the balance of power in Europe and of civilisation. The future and the welfare of all nations depend, therefore, upon the perfect maintenance and preservation of a state of things which, to the everlasting credit of the Government by which it was established, can alone, with time, secure to humanity the blessings of progress and peace. Hence the necessity of getting rid beforehand of every cause of dissension, or even of coolness, between the two nations; hence, therefore, it becomes a matter of positive duty to seek in future contingencies what causes would be likely to arouse feelings of antagonism which are the growth of centuries and produce in either nation explosions against which the wisdom of Governments is powerless. Motives of hostile rivalry are gradually making way for that generous emulation from which grand results inevitably follow.

If the matter, as it stands, be looked at in a general manner, it is difficult to see any ground or motive for renewing a struggle which has cost so much bloodshed to the world. Could financial and commercial interests be a source of dissension between the two nations? But the general investment of British capital in French enterprises and the immense impulse given to international trade, create between them bonds of union which daily become closer. Can it be a matter of political interest, or of principle? But both nations have now one and the same object, one and the same ambition, viz., the triumph of right over might, of civilisation over barbarity. Can it be some petty jealousy connected with territorial aggrandisement? But it is now admitted by both that the world is large enough to satisfy the spirit of enterprise of either nation, that there are countries to be turned to account and human beings to be rescued from a state of barbarism; besides, if both flags keep together, the activity of one must profit by the conquests of the other.

Hence, at first sight, there is nothing in the general aspect of matters that would seem likely to affect our good understanding with England.

Yet, on closer inspection, a contingency becomes apparent, which, by allowing the most enlightened and moderate Governments to be influenced by popular prejudices and passions, might revive old enmities, thus compromising the alliance and its good fruit.

There is a spot in the world the free passage through which is directly connected with the political and commercial power of Great Britain, a spot which France, on the other hand, had, in days gone by, been ambitious to possess. This spot is Egypt, the direct route from Europe to India – Egypt, where Frenchmen have fought and bled.

It is unnecessary to dwell upon the motives which make it impossible that England should allow Egypt to pass into the hands of a rival Power without offering the most determined resistance; but what should also be taken into full account is that France, though not so directly interested, but acting under the influence of glorious traditions and of other feelings more instinctive than rational, and for that very reason most powerful in the case of an impressionable race, would not, on her side, allow England to assume the peaceful mastery of Egypt. It is clear that so long as the route to India through Egypt is open and safe, and that the state of the country guarantees easy and rapid communication, England will not voluntarily create for herself difficulties of the most serious nature for the sake of appropriating a territory which, to her, is only valuable as a means of transit.

It is equally evident that France, whose policy for the last fifty years has consisted in contributing to the prosperity of Egypt, both by means of advice and the co-operation of many Frenchmen distinguished in science, in matters of administration, and in all the arts of peace or of war, will not try to carry out there the ideas of another age, so long as England does not interfere.

But supposing that a crisis should occur such as those which have so often convulsed the East, that a circumstance should take place which would render it imperative for England to get a footing in Egypt in order to prevent another Power from stealing a march on her, can it be maintained for a moment that the alliance could possibly survive the complications which would result from such an event? And why should England be placed in such a position? Why should England think herself bound to be mistress of Egypt, even at the risk of breaking off her alliance with France? For the simple reason that Egypt is the shortest, the most direct, route from England to her Eastern possessions, that this route must always remain open to her, and that, as regards a matter of such vital interest, she can make no compromise. Thus, through the position which nature has assigned to her, Egypt may again become the subject of a conflict between France and England; so that this possibility of dissension would disappear if, by a providential event, the geographical conditions of the Old World were changed, and the route to India, instead of passing through the heart of Egypt, were to be brought back to the boundary, and, being open to all, were the sole privilege of no one. Well, this event, which must be within the views of Providence, is now in the power of man. It can be accomplished by human industry. It can be realised by piercing the Isthmus of Suez, an undertaking to which nature presents no obstacle, and in which available capital from England as well as from other countries will undoubtedly be invested. Let the isthmus be cut through, let the waves of the Mediterranean mingle with the waters of the Indian Ocean, let the railway be continued and finished, and Egypt, whilst acquiring more importance as a productive and commercial country, as a market and as a medium of transit generally, will lose her dangerous reputation as a means of uncertain and disputed communication. The possession of her territory being no longer a matter of interest to England, ceases to be the cause of a possible struggle between that Power and France; the union of the two nations is thenceforth assured for ever, and the world is saved from the misery which would be entailed by a quarrel between them.

This result offers such guarantees for the future that it will be sufficient to point to it, to secure for the undertaking by which it is to be obtained the sympathy and encouragement of those statesmen who are striving to place the Anglo-French alliance on an imperishable basis. You are one of those men, my Lord, and the part you take in the discussion of matters of the highest political moment, with which I am not familiar, is too important a one for me not to seek to make known to you my wishes.

In sending you, with my note of the day before yesterday, my papers relating to the Suez affair, my intention was to leave them at your disposal. I, therefore, beg your Excellency will keep them.
[. . .]

66   *Letter delivered by the Empress to the Emperor (Report of my visit to London)*

MY first act was to come to an arrangement with Mr Rendel, chief engineer for harbour works in England. This gentleman, who fully understands the importance which the construction of a canal through the Isthmus of Suez will be for his country, will devote his attention to the realisation of the scheme. He has agreed to join the commission of European engineers for examining the preliminary designs of the Viceroy's engineers, and will visit Egypt in the course of two months, in order to decide on the spot on the practicability of the scheme.

I next published in London a pamphlet in English, accompanied by all the documents relating to the scheme, and supported by the opinions of English travellers and *savants* who have written on the subject. This pamphlet has been sent to the members of both Houses of Parliament, to the papers and reviews, to the merchants and shipowners connected with Indian commerce in London, Liverpool, Manchester, Glasgow, etc. It was accompanied at the same time by a circular making known the proposal for submitting the question of its execution to the decision of European science, announcing the adherence of Mr Rendel, and pointing out that the two houses Baring Brothers and Rothschild are my London correspondents.

The *Times* of the 6th of August, in the money market article, after making a favourable digest of the pamphlet, thus expresses its opinion:

M. de Lesseps may be assured that the national belief in the special advantages which England derives from every circumstance tending to accelerate exchanges between different parts of the world, will be favourably disposed towards all his ideas.

The following are extracts from the answers which have been sent to me by the Peninsular and Oriental Steam Navigation Company and the East India Company:

1st   By order of the Directors of the Peninsular and Oriental Steam Navigation Company:

The importance of the results, which would be attained by connecting the Mediterranean to the Red Sea by a navigable canal is so evident that there can be no two opinions on the matter, and if the scheme is realised, this company will be greatly benefited by the important results to the commerce, not only of England but of the whole world.

2nd   By order of the Court of Directors of the East India Company:

With reference to the importance of the enterprise of piercing the Isthmus of Suez, I am directed to inform you that the Court takes the greatest interest in the success of such an enterprise, destined to facilitate the means of communication between this country and India.

The replies which are daily sent to me by English statesmen and politicians all express the same opinion, of which the *Times* is the medium. This paper must shortly publish a leading article on the question. Other papers are preparing articles which will leave no doubt as to the general feeling of the country.

The Indian papers, especially the *Bombay Gazette*, have expressed their sympathy with the construction of a canal through the Isthmus of Suez.

Source: Ferdinand De Lesseps (1805–94). *The Suez Canal: Letters and Documents Descriptive of Its Rise and Progress in 1854–56*, trans. N. D'Anvers. Pennsylvania: Scholarly Resources, 1976, pp. 1–7, 10–17, 36–8, 39–40, 90–4, 168–9. (Orig. pub. 1876).

Chapter Six

Spectacular Suez: The Gala Opening of the Suez Canal, 1869

"A whole world must be set in motion."
Auguste Mariette, Egyptologist

Introduction

The inauguration of the Suez Canal was a spectacular theatrical event, designed to display the canal as one of the world's more recent wonders, a feat envisioned by European genius and accomplished by European technology. Ismail Pasha, the Khedive of Egypt under whose administration the canal was completed, considered the Suez Canal Egypt's passage to Europe and the modern world. Hans Busch, a Verdi scholar, reports that Ismail Pasha proclaimed, "My country is no longer in Africa. I have made it part of Europe" (1978: 6). Ismail Pasha, who was educated in Paris and enamored of things European, was willing to pay any price to present Egypt as *the* cultural capital of the African continent. He instituted a museum for Egyptian antiquities, ordered the building of the Cairo Opera House, and funded the inauguration to celebrate his reign and Egypt's glorious future. Ismail Pasha, Ferdinand De Lesseps, and Auguste (Bey) Mariette, the famous archaeologist and Egyptologist who conceived the original outline for *Aïda*, similarly considered Egypt – its land, its architectural and cultural history – a stage, a site in which splendid and magnificent possibilities could be realized. Even the surrounding countryside was incorporated into the grand production; for example, the extant roadway from Cairo to the Pyramids was rushed to completion in six weeks to coincide with the Canal's opening. Historian Arnold Wilson reports that this feat was accomplished "by forced labour urged on by the lash" (1939: 40).

Ismail Pasha's economic confidence was understandable. The Civil War in the United States had enabled Egypt to corner the world's cotton market; Egyptian profits were considerable. The Pasha's plans for Egypt were as visionary and ambitious as De Lesseps' plans for the canal and Mariette's for the opera that would celebrate its existence. The Egyptian ruler expanded Egyptian commerce and industry and reformed his nation's courts, schools, and universities; his political desires and investments were, in part, influenced by friends like De Lesseps, who convinced Ismail Pasha that the Canal would revivify Egypt. The Canal was also a massive financial burden for the Egyptian people whose taxes and labor assisted its completion. Ismail Pasha's political designs bankrupted his country and jeopardized its future. The grave results of the high expenditures, however, were not in plain sight during the inaugural festivities. Verdi's opera illustrated that the Canal and its cultural constellations were indeed grand; a whole world *was* set in motion, as the Canal itself had changed the map of the political future.

MC

Additional Reading

Budden, Julian. *The Operas of Verdi, Volume Three: From Don Carlos to Falstaff.* New York, 1981.

Busch, Hans. *Verdi's Aïda: The History of an Opera in Letters and Documents.* Minneapolis, 1978.

Osborne, Charles. *Verdi: A Life in the Theatre.* London, 1987.

Phillips-Matz, Mary Jane. *Verdi: A Biography.* New York, 1993.

Said, Edward. *Culture and Imperialism.* New York, 1993.

Wilson, Arnold. *The Suez Canal: Its Past, Present, and Future.* London, 1939.

28   Giuseppe Verdi, et al.: Miscellaneous Correspondence (1870)

Auguste Mariette to Camille Du Locle

Boulaq, 27 April 1870

My dear friend,

I received your two letters. I expected M. Verdi's refusal, which will rather annoy the Viceroy. But try to see our viewpoint. If M. Gounod accepts, we would be very happy. With regard to Prince P., I think that there are some clouds involved and that the Viceroy would only hesitatingly enter into an agreement.

In the meantime I am sending you an outline. Don't be shocked by the fancy printing – I have no secretary. I wanted to have four sets of the manuscript copied out; that would have cost 100 francs. So I had four copies printed for 40 francs. This typographical luxury is, therefore, quite a bonus and the result of economy. Consequently regard the enclosed copy as the most modest of manuscripts.

I need not tell you that the editing is mine. If I have intervened, it is, in the first place, because of the Viceroy's order and, in the second place, because of my belief that I could give the work true local color, which is the indispensable condition for an opera of this kind. Indeed I repeat to you that what the Viceroy wants is a purely ancient and Egyptian opera. The sets will be based on historical accounts; the costumes will be designed after the bas-reliefs of Upper Egypt. No effort will be spared in this respect, and the *mise-en-scène* will be as splendid as one can imagine. You know the Viceroy does things in a grand style. This care for preserving local color in the *mise-en-scène* obliges us, by the same token, to preserve it in the outline itself. In fact, there is a special phraseology for this – a frame of mind, an inspired note which only a thorough acquaintance with Egypt can provide. It is in this capacity that I have intervened and continue to intervene.

Here, my dear friend, is where we stand.

Now if the outline suits you, if you agree to write the libretto, if you find a composer, this is what must be done. You must write me that the subject in question is so archaeologically Egyptian and Egyptological that you cannot write the libretto without an advisor at your side at all times and that my presence in Paris is furthermore indispensable for the sets and costumes. I ask no more of you. If

I could go to Paris this summer, my goal would be attained.

It goes without saying that I am not bringing any kind of personal vanity into this matter and that you can change, turn around, and improve the outline as you see fit.

I forgot to tell you that the Viceroy has read the outline, that he has completely approved it, and that I am sending it to you by his order.

Don't be alarmed by the title. *Aida* is an Egyptian name. Normally it would be *Aita*. But that name would be too harsh, and the singers would irresistibly soften it to *Aida*. Moreover I care no more for this name than for the other.

For the second scene of the second act and the chant of the priests there is in the *Ritual* a hymn to the sun which exudes poetry and local color. Perhaps it will inspire you.

I know my place, my dear friend, and I would be very happy if in my humble role I may have been able to show you from far away the road we must travel. For the rest I rely on your talent as a poet. With this I press your hand.

Auguste Mariette to Camille Du Locle

[Cairo,] 28 April [1870]

My dear friend,

This instant I have left H. H., the Viceroy, to whom I have given your letter.

I shall not hide from you the fact that H. H. is extremely annoyed and chagrined by the idea of forgoing the collaboration of M. Verdi whose talent he holds in the highest esteem.

Under the circumstances he makes the offer that rehearsals be held in Paris or in Milan, at the Maestro's choice; the artists of the Cairo Theatre would then receive the order to betake themselves wherever M. Verdi wishes. See if this plan might be agreeable. I have time to write you only these few words in order not to miss the mail.

P.S. One final word. If Maestro Verdi should not accept, H. H. asks you to knock at another door. [. . .] We are thinking of Gounod and even Wagner. If the latter should accept, he could do something grandiose.

Auguste Mariette to Camille Du Locle

Alexandria, 29 May 1870

My dear friend,

Since my mail from France ran after me to Cairo and caught up with me only in Alexandria, I received your letter containing Verdi's letter only yesterday.

I have not yet been able to see the Viceroy. But I have been authorized for a long time to tell you to go ahead. Everything will be arranged according to your wishes. The Viceroy is ready for anything, and rather extraordinary circumstances would be required to give you cause to complain about him. Therefore put the opera boldly in the works. The Viceroy will be enchanted with Verdi's acceptance. He was particularly eager that the opera should be written by him, since he is a great admirer of the Maestro.

The opera will be performed for the first time in Cairo in Italian. But I know the Viceroy would be very proud if thereafter the opera were performed in French at our foremost lyric theatre. On this point there is no difficulty whatsoever. To the contrary.

Nothing will be neglected here for the *mise-en-scène*, which the Viceroy wants to be as splendid and magnificent as possible. Everything will be made in Paris, sets and costumes.

As for me, I sincerely hope to leave here one of these days. As soon as I see the Viceroy, I shall bluntly pose the question of my true purpose. I am the one who did the outline; I am the one, of all his employees, who knows Upper Egypt best, as well as the question of costumes and sets. Consequently, I am the one he must send to France. I hope this argument will decide the matter. [. . .] If there is any news, I shall inform you by telegraph. P.S. The Viceroy is most anxious to have *Aida* performed in Cairo, at the latest during February of next year.

Camille Du Locle to Verdi

Paris, 31 May 1870

[. . .] I have requested from you, in complete confidence, the conditions you desire for the Egyptian business. They write and telegraph me without respite, asking me for these conditions; they declare themselves ready for everything. The Viceroy passionately wishes to conclude the affair. I have already been asked to take charge of the sets and costumes, etc., etc. Nothing is lacking but your yes and a good contract. [. . .]

Verdi to Camille Du Locle

St. Agata, 2 June 1870

Dear Du Locle,

Here I am at the Egyptian affair; and first of all I must set aside time to compose the opera, because this is work of the broadest proportions (as though it were for the *grande boutique*), and because the

Italian poet must first find the thoughts to put into the mouths of the characters and then fashion the verses from them. Assuming that I am able to finish all of this in time, here are the conditions:

1   I shall have the libretto done at my expense.
2   I shall send someone to Cairo, also at my expense, to conduct and direct the opera.
3   I shall send a copy of the score and the music for use only in the Kingdom of Egypt, retaining for myself the rights to the libretto and to the music in all other parts of the world.

In compensation, I shall be paid the sum of 150,000 francs, payable at the Rothschild Bank in Paris at the moment the score is delivered.

Here's a letter for you, as cut and dried as a promissory note. It's business, and you will forgive me, my dear Du Locle, if for now I don't digress to other things.

Auguste Mariette to Paul Draneht

Paris, 15 July 1870

My dear Bey,

I received your telegram, for which I thank you, and I hasten to send you the letter I have brought for you.

Since Verdi accepted the offer the Viceroy made to him, the opera (the outline of which you know) will be done. Now this business must be started.

It is toward this end that H. H., the Viceroy, has deigned to send me to France. The Viceroy wants the opera to retain its strictly Egyptian color, not only in the libretto but in the costumes and the sets; and I am here to attend to this essential point.

On my part I am not losing an hour. But it is a difficult thing. In the operas we already know, the task is not as great because one has the traditions to follow. But here everything must be created. Add to this the exotic quality of the *mise-en-scène*. It is in the costumes, above all, that we shall encounter difficulty. To create imaginary Egyptians as they are usually seen in the theatre is not difficult; and if nothing else were needed, I would not be involved. But to unite in proper measure the ancient costumes shown in the temples and the requirements of the modern stage constitutes a delicate task. A king may be quite handsome in granite with an enormous crown on his head. But when it comes to dressing one of flesh and bone and making him walk and sing . . . that becomes embarrassing and, it is to be feared, makes people laugh. In addition, the most consistent principle of Egyptian costume is the absence of beards – a principle observed even more because it was imposed by the religion. Now do you feel up to forcing all your people to cut off their beards? And from another point of view, can you see Naudin dressed as a Pharaoh with a short beard, like the Emperor Napoleon? Obviously the short beard will destroy all the effect and all the harmony of the costumes, no matter how exact we make them. So we must not ignore the fact that the job is difficult and that to mount an opera under the conditions the Viceroy demands is a task to be considered twice. On my part, I am putting my whole heart into it. As for you, I am counting on your arrival in Paris soon. In the meantime I am working vigorously. Verdi has promised to have the opera ready by the end of January. (The Viceroy expressly desires that.) But the costumers and scene painters have declared that they do not have a day to lose. Believe me . . . in order to follow the instructions the Viceroy has given me, to make a scholarly as well as a picturesque *mise-en-scène*, a whole world must be set in motion.

Verdi to Giuseppe Piroli

[St. Agata,] 16 July 1870

[. . .] I am busy. Guess! . . . Writing an opera for Cairo!!! Oof. I shall not go to stage it because I would be afraid of being mummified; but I shall send a copy of the score and retain the original for Ricordi.

I must tell you, however, that the contract has not yet been signed (and therefore do not talk about it for now); but since my conditions – and they were tough – have been accepted by telegram, it must be considered as done. If anyone had told me two years ago, You will write for Cairo, I would have considered him a fool; but now I see that I am the fool. [. . .]

Auguste Mariette to Paul Draneht

Paris, 19 July 1870

My dear Bey,

I received your two letters of 16 and 17 July at almost the same time and I am replying quickly.

You are perfectly correct to demand that you be informed of what is happening in regard to the progress of Verdi's opera; the letter from H. H. that I sent you was meant to keep you posted, and naturally I have nothing to add to it.

Actually a grand opera in the ancient Egyptian style was commissioned by H. H. from Verdi, who has agreed to undertake it. The only condition H. H. made, a condition *sine qua non*, is that the opera must be presented in Cairo at the end of next January. Moreover Verdi is already at work, since all the arrangements have been made with Verdi directly from Alexandria at the personal suggestion of H. H., the Viceroy.

With regard to the mission that now calls me to France, it has as its point of departure the Viceroy's desire to see the opera composed and executed in a strictly Egyptian style. According to the most formal orders that H. H. has given me, I must first place myself at the disposal of the composer and the librettist in order to supply these gentlemen with all the proper information to enlighten them about the local color to be given to the work. Second, I must also take charge of everything pertaining to the *mise-en-scène*, that is, the sets and the costumes. The sets and the costumes, according to H. H.'s orders, must be drawn and executed under my eyes; and for greater accuracy H. H. has directed me to choose the scene painter and the costumer whom I judge the most capable. [. . .] This, in short, is the goal of my mission here – a mission which, with your assistance, my dear Bey, I hope to fulfill to the satisfaction of H. H.

I am quite embarrassed to reply to your second letter on the subject of M. Zuccarelli. When I arrived in Paris you were not here; and since I had the instructions of H. H., I had to get in touch with the scene painters at once and begin the task. What would you have me do now? To find a pretext to put an end to the work already begun is impossible. The task is horribly intricate, and my attention is needed everywhere all the time. The subject is completely new; and at every moment one has to do, undo, and redo, so that I am beginning to believe that we shall only half succeed – even here in Paris with the world's foremost scene painters. I would have to go to Cairo, then, break off the proposals already exchanged, and, in a word, do in Egypt what the Viceroy directed me to come to Paris to do. You will understand that I do not undertake any extra responsibilities.

As for the credit of 250,000 francs that the Viceroy has sent you, it is intended to pay for the initial expenses incurred by the opera in France. If you wish more information on this subject, I shall (to the best of my knowledge) furnish it to you on your return here, which, I hope very much, will not be delayed any longer.

There, my dear Bey, is the information I have been able to furnish you. It is a question of mounting, of creating, a completely new opera. The task will be very difficult and bristling with obstacles caused by the novelty of the subject. But the honor your administration will derive from this will be all the greater. Therefore, I shall be happy to contribute to it to the extent of my abilities.

Auguste Mariette to Paul Draneht

Paris, 21 July 1870

My dear Bey,

I have this instant received your letter of 19 July.

There was no need for you to tell me the contents of the letter from H. H. that I sent you, because, for the good of the mission that I am performing here, H. H. deemed that I should know about it and even charged me to add some less urgent details, which I shall soon be able to communicate to you in person.

You are so right to call the work we are planning a colossal work. As I believe I told you there is really no tradition whatever to follow, and everything must be created. I am not embarrassed to also admit to you that I did not suspect the immensity of the details and that I am literally losing my mind.

Furthermore come to Paris as soon as possible. The two of us are not too many to carry this very heavy burden.

I take the opportunity, my dear Bey, to tell you that you may count on me completely. From now until the end of January, for our dear and illustrious master [the Viceroy], we have to achieve a work of consequence which, to a certain extent, will help to augment the renown Egypt has already acquired for herself. It is essential that we not produce a fiasco. Therefore, just as the Viceroy appealed to the most illustrious living composer, we must do everything possible to make the *mise-en-scène* worthy of this initial step. Until now I have neglected nothing to arrive at that result, and I have proceeded in my research without haste. I hope you will be pleased and that the opera, presented for the first time in Cairo this winter, will bring you great honor. As for myself, I declare in advance that with regard to the libretto and all artistic aspects of the work my name should not even be mentioned.

Source: This selection of Verdi letters and documents are from Hans Busch *Verdi's Aida: The History of An Opera in Letters and Documents.* Minneapolis: University of Minnesota Press, 1978, pp. 11–12, 18–19, 33–5.

Note

Giuseppe Verdi (1813–1901) was born the impoverished son of an Italian tavern-keeper and grocer. His youthful musical talents attracted the attention of Antonio Barezzi, a music amateur who paid for Verdi's education and served as his patron. Verdi was a well-known and success-ful composer by the time the Khedive contacted him to write *Aida*; his grand operas *Macbeth* (1847), *Rigoletto* (1851), *Il Trovatore* (1853), and *La Traviata* (1853) had already been written and produced. Verdi accepted the invitation to compose the opera for the Suez Canal's opening, but rejected the invitation to write the inaugural hymn for the opening. *Aida* debuted at the newly built Cairo Opera House two years after the inaugural opening on Christmas Eve, 1871.

29   Baron Samuel Selig de Kusel: *An Englishman's Recollections of Egypt 1863 to 1887* (1915)

During the year 1869 we were exceedingly busy; not only in connection with our regular line of steamers, but also owing to the fact that we had undertaken the pilgrim traffic, which was generally confined to tramp steamers; the great majority of pilgrims were bound for Morocco, Tripoli, and Tunis, returning home through Alexandria from Mecca, and we generally managed to put from four to five hundred aboard each vessel. The steamer would anchor just opposite the railway station at Gabbarí, and as the trains arrived the pilgrims were promptly put into large barges and towed alongside; a barrier was fixed up half-way across the steamer, and as the Arabs came aboard they had to pay their passage money before passing it. If I remember rightly the fare was about five or six dollars, and each pilgrim, when he paid his money, received a tally which he had to keep and deliver up at his destination as he left the ship. When most of them had paid and gone through to the other side of the barrier, at which sailors were always posted to prevent a rush, there invariably remained a certain number, both male and female, who pretended that they only possessed one or two dollars in the world, others would swear that they had not even a piastre left, and the scene became indescribable, as they refused to leave the ship, and commenced to scream and howl.

The first time I saw this I felt quite sorry for them; but in that I was alone, for our people thoroughly understood the pleasant little ways of pilgrims.

The stevedore, Hassan, who attended to all our steamers, had two stalwart negroes under him, who looked after and kept the pilgrims in order; their special duty, however, was to search those who refused to pay their fare, and these were generally seized, one at a time, and taken below, where they were stripped and searched thoroughly, the result being that money was found hidden in the most inexplicable places, generally more than enough to pay their passages. It was not only the men one had to treat in this way, for it was more often than not females who were the worst offenders, submitting to be stripped and searched, rather than pay up.

In the end there were usually a few who really had nothing, and these were allowed a free passage; however, the steamers were always detained several hours by these manœuvres.

By this time, having pretty well mastered Italian, I set to work to learn French, and having had a certain amount driven into me at school, before long I was able to converse fairly easily.

On November 16, 1869, the Suez Canal was formally opened; this great work had taken ten years to complete at a cost of about seventeen million sterling. It was my good fortune to be present, having had the honour to be invited as one of the guests of His Highness the Khedive. I left Alexandria on the 15th in one of the Rubattino steamers, which had come specially from Italy with a number of distinguished guests on board. As we steamed out of the harbour the French Imperial yacht *Aigle* was preparing to leave. I remember as we passed alongside seeing Her Majesty, the Empress Eugénie, standing on the bridge, surrounded by her suite, and I may safely say that all eyes were centred upon her.

The next day, Tuesday, November 16, we arrived at Port Said, where we found the harbour crowded with vessels, chiefly French, Italian, and Austrian, whilst outside were anchored five British men-of-war, *Lord Warden* (with Sir A. Milne's flag flying), *Royal Oak*, *Prince Consort*, *Caledonia*, *Bellerophon*, and Rapid despatch boats, two Austrian ironclads, and some Italian ships.

When the *Aigle* arrived at about eight o'clock in the morning, the fleet manned yards and fired a grand salute. She anchored alongside the Khedival yacht, *Mahroussah*, on the other side of which lay the Austrian Imperial yacht.

At three in the afternoon a benediction was pronounced by the Ulemas of the Mussulman religion, by the Coptic, Roman Catholic, and Greek clergy. A pavilion had been erected on the seashore for the purpose, the front of which was lined by Egyptian troops.

Other pavilions were erected for the Khedive and his royal guests, and as they were about a quarter of a mile away from the landing stage, quite a procession was formed. The Heir Apparent of Egypt led the way with the Princess of Holland, the Empress Eugénie on the arm of the Emperor of Austria, the Khedive Ismail and the Crown Prince of Prussia walking on each side, the Grand Duke Michael of Russia, the Prince of Holland, the Archduke Victor, brother of the Emperor of Austria, the Princes Augustus of Sweden, Amadeus of Savoy, and Louis of Hesse, following with a brilliant staff of French, Austrian, Italian, and Egyptian officers, amongst whom walked Monsieur de Lesseps and Colonel Staunton, the British Consul-General, and many other notable people.

After the religious ceremony, Monsignor Bauer, the Empress Eugénie's confessor, made a most eloquent speech.

Port Said that night, town as well as harbour, was brilliantly illuminated, a glorious moon adding to the splendour of this scene. The next day, Wednesday, November 17, at 8 a.m., the Suez Canal was opened formally, and a procession of about seventy steamers of various nationalities passed, headed by the Imperial yacht *Aigle* with the Empress of the French. The following were the names of the ships, none of which drew more than thirteen feet of water:

Austrian Imperial yacht, with Emperor of Austria; Prussian frigate with Crown Prince; Swedish yacht with Prince Oscar of Sweden; Russian warship with Grand Duke Michael; Russian Admiral's ship; Dutch gunboat with Prince and Princess of Holland; *Psyche*, English despatch boat with English Ambassador from Constantinople; Swedish vessel; *Peluse*, French Messageries Maritime steamer; *Rapid*, English gunboat; a French Messageries Maritime steamer; *Vulcan*, Austrian warship; *Forbin*, French gunboat; a French steamer; *Cambria*, English yacht with owner, Mr. Ashbury; *Dido*, English telegraph steamer; English steam yacht; Swedish vessel; British sloop-of-war; Messageries steamer; Austrian Lloyd steamer; *Hawk*, English steamer carrying to Suez the shore-end of the British Indian Telegraph; Russian merchant steamer; Messageries steamer; *Lynx*, English steamer; *Principe Tomaso* and *Principe Oddone*, Italian steamers; *Principe Aurades*, Italian steamer; Austrian steamers; *Scilla*, Italian war frigate; Austrian Lloyd steamer; *Chabin*, Egyptian Government steamer; *Fayoun*, Egyptian Government steamer; and these followed by about as many more.

The Imperial yacht *Aigle* and the Khedive's yacht after a passage of twelve hours arrived at Ismailia, the others followed later on.

As the Royal guests landed, they were conducted by the Khedive to the new palace, which he had had built specially for this occasion.

Shortly after this, the Empress Eugénie and the Emperor of Austria, on camels, accompanied by Monsieur de Lesseps on a white pony, rode past the Arab camp towards the desert, and on returning entered a small pony chaise, and drove for some time about the streets.

The guests of less importance had not been forgotten, and in different parts of the town large marquees had been erected, in which tables beautifully decorated awaited those who wished to eat or drink; every delicacy from all parts of the world had been imported, while wines of all kinds, and of the most recherché quality, were supplied to any guest who happened to pass by.

Waiters and attendants, dressed in the most gorgeous Khedival liveries, attended to the slightest wishes of all present.

I shall never forget the magnificence of the ball at the new Khedival palace that evening, for it was one of the most brilliant sights I have ever witnessed, especially the Royal procession, as it passed through the principal ball-room, on its way to a supper, which was in itself a thing to be long remembered.

On the following day, most of the Royal guests left Ismailia for Suez, but many of the others proceeded direct to Cairo by train, where some remained two or three weeks, sight-seeing, and enjoying themselves at the expense of the Khedive, even the carriages hired by them being paid for by Ismail, and so ended the fêtes given on the occasion of the opening of the Suez Canal. The expense to the Khedive must have been enormous.

The title of Khedive was granted to Ismail Pasha by the Sultan in 1867, since when it has been used by the latter as his official title; the word (pronounced as a dissyllable) is derived from Persian Khidiv and means sovereign, it is therefore a more dignified title than the former one of Vali – Viceroy.

Those people who have never travelled through this canal might be interested in the following details of this great work. On leaving Port Said, one crosses the Menzaleh lake, a shallow body of salt water, something like the Venetian lagoons, and then proceeds for about twenty-seven miles to El Kantarah, which was formerly the chief caravan station on the road from Egypt to Syria.

At Ismailia, one encounters another lake five miles in length, and this is the central point, or half-way home of the canal; at the time of the opening there were only a few houses there, but very soon afterwards a pleasant little town had sprung up with villas, shops, cafés, hotels, etc., and fine streets and squares.

Now there is a central railway station there from whence passengers can travel to Suez, Cairo, or Alexandria.

Besides this great navigable canal which shortens so splendidly the distance between Europe and the Far East, there is a fresh water canal, constructed on purpose to supply the population at various points on the line, this runs from the Nile to Ismailia on Temsah Lake, from Ismailia to Suez on the west side of the canal, and from Ismailia to Port Said. This last is not really a canal, like the first two sections, but consists of a large iron pipe through which the water is conveyed to the sundry stations.

When the canal was first started in 1859, it was very difficult to procure fresh water, as it had to be brought across Lake Menzaleh, from Damietta, in Arab boats, and it was only in 1863 that the iron pipe was laid down between Port Said and Ismailia. The great advantage of the canal is the shortening of the distance between Europe and the Far East. From London to Bombay by the Suez Canal it is about 6,300 miles, whilst by the Cape it is about 11,000 miles. From Marseilles to Bombay by the Cape it is 10,000 miles, and by the Suez Canal 4,600 miles. The steamers generally pass through the canal at the rate of 5 to 6 knots.

I might mention that, in 1875, the British Government purchased from the Khedive his shares in the canal, paying four million sterling for 176,602 shares, out of a total of 400,000, and they made a very good investment.

On November 25, 1869, the Austrian and German colony in Alexandria gave a ball to His Majesty the Emperor of Austria. It took place in the rooms of the Mohammed Ali Club, which were at that time on the first floor of a fine building, the ground floor of which was occupied by the Alexandria Bourse. I was present at this function and enjoyed it immensely.

[. . .] I remember meeting about this time a Captain George Hyde commanding the P. and O. steamer, *Pera*. He was a great favourite with most of the Anglo-Indians, and was a well-known celebrity throughout the service, his soubriquet in the P. and O. was "Magnificent George," and really he was a very fine, handsome man. He often gave little luncheons and dinners on board his vessel, and being rather a gourmet, he took care that they were really good. He had a smattering of Italian, of which he was very proud, airing it whenever an opportunity occurred, adding at the end of some very high-sounding sentence, "This is from Dante."

Sometimes he would write his menus in Italian, and one of the items generally found was "Nightingales' tongues, stewed in the dew of roses." His guests, of course, expected to see some marvellous culinary concoction; but when the dish appeared, it was only a dish of cream, with pieces of sponge cake floating about. However, his sparkling Moselle cup was a dream, and a boon on a hot summer's day. He, poor fellow, died some years ago at Lord's whilst watching a cricket match.

I was always very enthusiastic in regard to everything connected with music, and when it was announced that the Khedive Ismail Pasha had commissioned Verdi to write an opera, taking his subject from Egypt, all of us looked forward with considerable excitement to the first production, which took place at the Opera House in Cairo on December 24, 1871. Verdi was expected to come to Cairo to direct this first performance of "Aïda" himself; but, unfortunately, his horror and dread of the sea prevented him accepting Ismail Pasha's invitation. I went specially to Cairo in order to be present at what for me was a great event.

A most brilliant audience literally crowded the house; the Khedive with all the princes were there, and the Khedivah was present, and the Egyptian princesses were in the Royal Harem boxes, the fronts of which were covered in with thin lattice work, through which one could see, hazily, the forms of the ladies, with their diamonds and precious stones sparkling as they moved to and fro in the large royal box. All the Consul-Generals and their wives were present, the ministers and the Khedival staff officers in their brilliant uniforms, while in every box were many lovely women, resplendent with jewels. This premier performance of "Aïda" was simply perfect, and it was in the early hours of the morning that I left the theatre after an evening which, to me, had been divine.

The cast was as follows:

IL RE	Tommaso Costa	*Basso*
AMNERIS	Eleonora Grossi	*Mezzo-Soprano*
AÏDA	Antonietta Pozzoni	*Soprano*
RADAMES	Pietro Mongini	*Tenore*
RAMFS	Paolo Medini	*Basso*
AMONATIO	Francesca Steller	*Baritone*
UN MESSAGGIERO	Stecchi Bottordi	*Tenore*

The Conductor was Mæstro Bottesini, the famous violinist.

Source: Extracts from chapter 3 of Baron Samuel Selig de Kusel *An Englishman's Recollections of Egypt 1863 to 1887*. London: John Lane, 1915, pp. 73–80, 88–90.

Note

Baron de Kusel (Bey) (1848–?) was English Controller-General of Egyptian customs. His memoirs of Egypt span more than two and a half decades, and include observations on the building and opening of the Suez Canal and the eventual British occupation of Egypt.

Chapter Seven

The Battlefield of the Future:
The Canal and Its Consequences

Introduction

In the 1850s as Ferdinand De Lesseps tirelessly campaigned on behalf of *his* canal in the academies, civic halls, and geographical institutes of Europe, his plan aroused anxieties and excitement in equal measure. Shipping magnates, trading companies, captains of industry, commercial speculators, colonial administrators, and military leaders enthusiastically supported the Suez Canal plan because it would provide quicker passage to the East, thereby expanding and easing trade and providing the British navy with an emergency route in times of trouble, such as the recent Sepoy rebellion in India. Others, like the British Prime Minister, Lord Palmerston, who passionately lobbied against the building of the Canal, predicted that the new passage to India would be the cause of unrest for years to come. The Suez Canal would, in other words, further complicate the Eastern Question – the ongoing challenge to manage and control the Ottoman Empire (Turkey) and Russia – by adding the Egyptian Question to Britain's already complicated imperial agenda and raising the matter of how

control of the Suez Canal would be determined in times of peace and war and to whom authority over the Canal would be granted. In his study of the region, D. A. Cameron reports that a Monsieur (Ernest?) Renan responded to De Lesseps' Canal boosterism by warning the Frenchman and his audience that, "The isthmus cut becomes a straight, a battlefield . . . You have marked the field of the great battles of the future," words that would ring true for the remainder of the nineteenth century and into the twentieth, as the Suez Crisis of 1956 would demonstrate.

A grand canal across the isthmus had been envisioned in the days of the pharaohs; when Napoleon set his sights on Egypt in the eighteenth century, the plan for building the modern canal was conceived. Napoleon's designs on the region were part of his grand plan to seize the Indian colonial possessions from the British. In the 1840s Mehemet Ali, the Viceroy of Egypt, contemplated the building of a canal; however, the Egyptian leader shared Palmerston's spectral vision of such a project. The possibility of increased revenue for his government could not put to rest fears that a canal through the isthmus would attract global attention; he decided that the canal would jeopardize his nation's autonomy and well-being. Neither Mehemet Ali nor his successor, Abbas Pasha approved of the canal project. Abbas Pasha's successor, Mohammed Said Pasha, and his successor, Ismail Pasha eventually embraced the Frenchman's canal scheme.

In 1854, Mohammed Said Pasha granted De Lesseps a Concession for the construction of the canal; the Concession inaugurated the Compagnie Universelle du Canal Maritime de Suez, which was directed by De Lesseps. The Company was granted administrative control of the Suez Canal for a term of 99 years from the day of the Canal's opening; after the term's expiration, control of the Canal would revert to the Egyptian government. "The Original Firman of Concession" (1854) permitted the Company to extract from the mines and quarries belonging to the public, gave the Company uncultivated public lands and the use of private lands adjacent to the Suez Canal (with compensation to be determined by the Company), and granted the Company tax-free status. "The Chapter of Concession" (1856) virtually indentured the Egyptian *fellahs* (peasants) by promising that four-fifths of the workmen would be Egyptians. These extremely generous (or foolishly granted) gifts were made conditional to the Sultan's approval, which was eventually granted in 1866 after De Lesseps' sale of public subscriptions to the canal (1858). Pro-expansionist Prime Minister, Benjamin Disraeli would purchase 44 percent of these shares with four million pounds borrowed from the Rothschild's Bank in 1875, in an attempt to insure that Great Britain would hold the "key to India." The gifts granted to De Lesseps by Mohammed Said Pasha would later cripple the Egyptian economy. Ismail Pasha paid over two million pounds sterling to fulfill his predecessor's founder's shares, which was only a small portion of the duties paid to the Company to support the Suez Canal through to its completion in 1869. D. A. Cameron estimates that Mohammed Said Pasha's gift cost Egypt over sixteen million pounds sterling, an amount that cannot address the costs paid by the Egyptian people.

Once the Suez Canal was completed, the battles for its control began in earnest. The British journalistic essays on the Egyptian Question reflect the era's fiscal and political conservatism. The war in Crimea was a reminder of the possibility of political alliances between former competitors; however, the events of the past also highlighted the fragility and impermanence of such alliances. The Canal was sure to generate aggressive competition between the English and the French. Recent troubles in India were also ominous reminders of native

discontentment and unrest; the unrest in Ireland also made politicians and statesmen aware of the possibility of forthcoming and potentially troublesome land and home rule issues. For the bold celebrants of imperialism, like Prime Minister Disraeli and the Jingoes, the promises of increased capital and expanded commerce outweighed the logic of cautionary discourses. Whether Great Britain was to seize outright the Suez Canal, to build its own canal, or to buy-out the French and all other competitors, the Jingoes considered Egypt the Empire's predestined acquisition. In their eyes, Great Britain's military-naval strength and financial might made the Egyptian Question a moot one.

MC

Additional Reading

Anonymous. "The Canal Dilemma: Our True Route to India," *Blackwood's Edinburgh Magazine*, Sept. 1888: 271–82.

Avram, Berno. *The Evolution of the Suez Canal Status from 1869 to 1956: A Historio-Juridical Study*. Paris, 1958.

Baker, Benjamin and John Fowler. "A Sweet-Water Ship-Canal Through Egypt," *The Nineteenth Century*, Jan. 1883: 164–72.

Cameron, D. A. *Egypt in the Nineteenth Century, or Mehemet Ali and His Successors Until the British Occupation in 1882*. London, 1898.

Dicey, Edward. "Why Not Purchase the Suez Canal?" *The Nineteenth Century*, Aug. 1883: 189–205.

Dusany. "England and the Suez Canal," *The Nineteenth Century*, Dec. 1882: 839–60.

Magniac, C. "The Pretensions of M. De Lesseps," *The Nineteenth Century*, Jan. 1884: 13–27.

Obieta, Joseph A. *The International Status of the Suez Canal*. The Hague, 1960.

Schonfield, Hugh J. *The Suez Canal in Peace and War*. Coral Gables, FL, 1962. (British title: *The Suez Canal in World Affairs*, 1952).

Society of Comparative Legislation and International Law. *The Suez Canal: A Selection of Documents Relating to the International Status of the Suez Canal and the Position of the Suez Canal Company, November 30, 1854–July 26, 1965*. London, 1956; New York, 1956.

Films

George Arliss. *Disraeli* (1929).
Allan Dwan. *Suez* (1938).

30   Anonymous: "Latest – From the Sphinx" (1869)

Across the desert's sandy sea
   Though sorely battered brows I rear,
Still with my stony eyes I see,
   Still with my stony ears I hear.

"MOSÉ IN EGITTO!!!"

Plate 2   Cartoon from *Punch*, December 11, 1875.

Thousands of years this resting place
  Betwixt the Pyramids I hold,
And still their daily shadow trace,
  Broadening o'er me, blue and cold.

And many wonders have I known,
  And many a race and rule of men,
Since first upon the desert's zone
  I fixed my calm, unwinking ken.

'Neath these same orbs that still revolve
  Above my granite brows sedate,
I forged the riddles, which to solve
  Was fame, wherein to fail was fate.

But darker riddle never yet
  I framed for ŒDIPUS the wise,
Than those that to the world I set,
  Touching these things before my eyes.

What of this piercing of the sands?
  What of this union of the seas?
This grasp of unfamiliar hands,
  This blending of strange litanies?

Aves and Allah-hu's that flow
  From ulemas and monsignors –
These *feridjees* and *robes-fourreau*,
  These eunuchs and ambassadors –

This *pot-pourri* of East and West,
  Pillau and *potage à la bisque*; –
Circassian belles whom WORTH has drest,
  And Parisiennes *à l'odalisque*!

Riddles that need no Sphinx to put,
  But more than ŒDIPUS to read –
What good or ill from LESSEPS' cut
  Eastward and Westward shall proceed?

Whose loss or profit? War or peace?
  Sores healed, or old wounds oped anew?
Upon the loosing of the seas,
  Strife's bitter waters let loose too?

The Eastern question raised, at last?
  The Eastern question laid for aye?
Russian ambition fettered fast?
  Or feathered but for freer play?

The shattering of the Sultan's throne?
  Or the Khedivè's rise, to fall?
England and France, like hawks let flown?
  Or *Aigle* on perch and Bull in stall?

Answer in vain the Sphinx invites;
  A darkling veil the future hides:
We know what seas the work unites,
  Who knows what sovereigns it divides?

Source: "Punch," November 27, 1869, p. 210.

31   Anonymous: "The Sultan's Complaint" (1869)

"HERE's Ismail, regardless
  Of *meum* and *tuum*,
Thinks this Suez Canal
  Has made everything *suum*!

"Midst crown'd heads at Cairo,
  O'ercrows Stamboul's wassail!
Spends more than his Sovereign, –
  The impudent vassal!

"Then to make both ends meet
  His poor *fellaheen* pinches,
Fain to eke out his ell
  By the aid of their inches.

"But for each pound so squeezed
  He spends three times the money,
And the more bees he plunders
  The more he wants honey.

"In his greed for the golden eggs
  Kills off the ganders;
Drains *my* Egypt dry
  With the millions he squanders.

"Then when quite out-at-elbows,
  His pockets swept clean,
He at ten per cent borrows,
  While I pay fifteen!

"Now, thus to have pockets
  Sans fond as a sieve is,
And thus, without limit,
  Beg, borrow, and thieve, is
A Sultan's prerogative,
  Not a Khedivè's!"

Source: "Punch," December 18, 1869, p. 240.

32   "The Original Firman of Concession Granted by the Viceroy of Egypt Mohamed Said, to Ferdinand De Lesseps, 1854"

Our friend Monsieur Ferdinand de Lesseps, having called our attention to the advantages which would result to Egypt from the junction of the Mediterranean and Red Seas, by a navigable passage for large vessels, and having given us to understand the possibility of forming a company for this purpose composed of capitalists of all nations, we have accepted the arrangements which he has submitted to us, and by these presents grant him exclusive power for the establishment and direction of a Universal Company, for cutting through the Isthmus of Suez, and the construction of a canal between the two Seas, with authority to undertake or cause to be undertaken all the necessary works and erections, on condition that the Company shall previously indemnify all private persons in case of dispossession for the public benefit. And all within limits, upon the conditions and under the responsibilities, settled in the following Articles.

ART. 1   Monsieur Ferdinand de Lesseps shall form a company, the direction of which we confide to him, under the name of the Universal Suez Maritime Canal Company, for cutting through the Isthmus of Suez, the construction of a passage suitable for extensive navigation, the foundation or appropriation of two sufficient entrances, one from the Mediterranean and the other from the Red Sea, and the establishment of one or two ports.

ART. 2   The Director of the Company shall be always appointed by the Egyptian Government, and selected, as far as practicable, from the shareholders most interested in the undertaking.

ART. 3   The term of the grant is ninety-nine years, commencing from the day of the opening of the Canal of the two Seas.

ART. 4   The works shall be executed at the sole cost of the Company, and all the necessary land not belonging to private persons shall be granted to it free of cost. The fortifications which the Government shall think proper to establish shall not be at the cost of the Company.

ART. 5   The Egyptian Government shall receive from the Company annually fifteen per cent of the net profits shown by the balance sheet, without prejudice to the interest and dividends accruing from the shares which the Government reserves the right of taking upon its own account at this issue, and without any guarantee on its part either for the execution of the works or for the operations of the Company; the remainder of the net profits shall be divided as follows: Seventy-five per cent, to the benefit of the Company; ten per cent, to the benefit of the members instrumental in its foundation.

ART. 6   The Tariffs of dues for the passage of the Canal of Suez, to be agreed upon between the Company and the Viceroy of Egypt, and collected by the Company's agents, shall be always equal for all nations; no particular advantage can ever be stipulated for the exclusive benefit of any one country.

ART. 7   In case the Company should consider it necessary to connect the Nile by a navigable canal cut with the direct passage of the Isthmus, and in case the Maritime Canal should follow an indirect course, the Egyptian Government will give up to the Company the uncultivated lands belonging to the public domain, which shall be irrigated and cultivated at the expense of the Company, or by its instrumentality. The Company shall enjoy the said lands for ten years free of taxes, commencing from the day of the opening of the canal; during the remaining eighty nine years of the grant, the Company shall pay tithes to the Egyptian Government, after which period it cannot continue in possession of the lands above mentioned without paying to the said Government an impost equal to that appointed for lands of the same description.

ART. 8   To avoid all difficulty on the subject of the lands which are to be given up to the Company, a plan drawn by M. Linant Bey, our Engineer Commissioner attached to the Company, shall indicate the lands granted both for the line and the establishments of the Maritime Canal and for the alimentary canal from the Nile, as well as for the purpose of cultivation, conformably to the stipulations of Article 7.

It is moreover understood that all speculation is forbidden from the present time, upon the lands to be granted from the public domain, and that the land previously belonging to private persons and which the proprietors may hereafter wish to have irrigated by the waters of the alimentary canal, made at the cost of the Company, shall pay a rent of . . . per feddan cultivated (or a rent amicably settled between the Government and the Company).

ART. 9   The Company is further allowed to extract from the mines and quarries belonging to the public domain, any materials necessary for the work of the Canal and the erections connected therewith, without paying dues; it shall also enjoy the right of free entry for all machines and materials which it shall import from abroad for the purposes of carrying out this grant.

ART. 10   At the expiration of the concession the Egyptian Government will take the place of the Company, and enjoy all its rights without reserva-

tion, the said Government will enter into full possession of the Canal of the two Seas, and of all the
establishments connected therewith. The indemnity to be allowed the Company for the relinquish-
ment of its plant and movables shall be arranged by
amicable agreement or by arbitration.

ART. 11   The statutes of the Society shall be
moreover submitted to us by the Director of
the Company, and must have the sanction of our
approbation. Any modifications that may be
hereafter introduced must previously receive our
sanction. The said statutes shall set forth the names
of the founders, the list of whom we reserve to
ourselves the right of approving. This list shall
include those persons whose labours, studies, exertions or capital have previously contributed to the
execution of the grand undertaking of the Canal of
Suez.

ART. 12   Finally, we promise our true and
hearty co-operation and that of all the functionaries
of Egypt in facilitating the execution and carrying
out of the present powers.

Cairo, 30th of November 1854

Source: White Paper on the Nationalisation of the
Suez Maritime Canal Company. Cairo: (Ministry
for Foreign Affairs) Government Press, 1956, pp.
17–20.

---

33   Charter of Concession and Book of Charges for the Construction and Working of the Suez Grand Maritime Canal and Dependencies (1856)

We Mohammed Said–Pacha Vice-Roy of Egypt,

Considering our charter bearing date the 30th
November 1854, by which we have granted to our
friend M. Ferdinand de Lesseps exclusive power to
constitute and direct a Universal Company for cutting the Isthmus of Suez, opening a passage suitable for large vessels, forming or adapting two
sufficient entrances, one on the Mediterranean, the
other on the Red Sea, and establishing one or two
ports, as the case may be:

M. Ferdinand de Lesseps, having represented to
us that in order to constitute a company as above
described under the forms and conditions generally
adopted for companies of that nature, it is expedient to stipulate beforehand by a fuller and more
specific document, the burthens, obligations and

services to which that company will be subjected on
the one part, and the concessions, immunities,
and advantages to which it will be entitled, as also
the facilities which will be accorded to it for its
administration, on the other part:

Have decreed as follows the conditions of the
concession which is the subject matter of these
presents.

Charges

ART. 1   The Company founded by our friend M.
Ferdinand de Lesseps in virtue of our charter of the
30th November 1854, shall execute at its own
cost, risk and damage all the necessary works and
construction for the establishment of:

(1)   A canal navigable by large vessels between
Suez on the Red Sea, and the Gulf of Pelusium on
the Mediterranean;

(2)   A canal of irrigation adapted to the river
traffic of the Nile, joining that river to the above-
mentioned Maritime Canal;

(3)   Two branches for irrigation and supply,
striking out of the preceding Canal, and in the
direction respectively of Suez and Pelusium.

The works shall be completed within the period
of six years, unavoidable hinderances and delays
excepted.

ART. 2   The Company shall have the right to
execute the works they have undertaken, themselves and under their own management, or to
cause them to be executed by contractors by means
of public tender or private contract under penalties. In all cases, four-fifths of the workmen employed upon these works shall be Egyptians.

ART. 3   The Canal navigable by large vessels
shall be constructed of the depth and width fixed
by the scheme of the International Scientific
Commission.

Conformably with this scheme, it will commence at the port of Suez; it will pass through the
basin of the Amer Lakes and Lake Timsah, and will
debouche into the Mediterranean at whatever point
in the Gulf of Pelusium may be determined in the
final plans to be prepared by the engineers of the
Company.

ART. 4   The Canal of Irrigation adapted to the
river traffic, according to the terms of the said
scheme, shall commence in the vicinity of the city
of Cairo, follow the valley (Ouadée) of Tomilat,
(ancient land of Gessen), and will fall into the
Grand Maritime Canal at Lake Timsah.

ART. 5   The branches from the above Canal
shall strike out from it above the debouchure into
Lake Timsah, from which point they shall proceed,

on one side to Suez, and on the other to Pelusium, parallel to the Grand Maritime Canal.

ART. 6   Lake Timsah shall be converted into an inland harbour capable of receiving vessels of the highest tonnage.

The Company shall moreover be bound, if necessary; first, to construct a harbour of refuge at the entrance of the Maritime Canal into the Gulf of Pelusium; secondly, to improve the port and roadstead of Suez so that it shall equally afford a shelter to vessels.

ART. 7   The Maritime Canal, the ports connected therewith, as also the Junction Canal of the Nile and the branch Canals, shall be permanently maintained in good condition by the Company and at their expense.

ART. 8   The owners of contiguous lands desirous of irrigating their property by means of water-courses from the Company's canals shall obtain permission so to do in consideration of the payment of an indemnity or rent, the amount whereof shall be fixed according to Article 17 hereinafter recited.

ART. 9   We reserve the right of appointing at the official head quarters of the Company a special commissioner, whose salary they shall pay and who shall represent at the Board of Direction the rights and interests of the Egyptian Government in the execution of these presents.

If the principal office of the Company be established elsewhere than in Egypt, the Company shall be represented at Alexandria by a superior agent furnished with all necessary powers for securing the proper management of the concern and the relations of the Company with our Government.

Concessions

ART. 10   For the construction of the Canals and their dependencies mentioned in the foregoing articles, the Egyptian Government grants to the Company, free of impost or rent, the use and enjoyment of all lands not the property of individuals which may be found necessary.

It likewise grants to the Company the use and enjoyment of all uncultivated lands not the property of individuals which shall have been irrigated and cultivated by their care and at their expense, with these provisions:

(1)   The lands comprised under the latter head shall be free of impost during ten years, only to date from their being put in a productive condition.

(2)   That after that period, they shall be subject for the remainder of the term of concession, to the same obligations and imposts to which are sub-

jected under like circumstances, the land in other provinces of Egypt.

(3)   That the Company shall afterwards, themselves or through their agents, continue in the use and enjoyment of these lands and the water-courses necessary to their fertilisation, subject to payment to the Egyptian Government, of the imposts assessed upon lands under like conditions.

ART. 11   For determining the area and boundaries of the lands conceded to the Company under Article 10, reference is made to the plans hereunto annexed, in which plans the land conceded for the construction of the Canals and their dependencies free of impost or rent, conformably to Clause 1, is coloured black, and the land conceded for the purpose of cultivation, on paying certain duties conformably with Clause 2, is coloured blue.

All acts and deeds done subsequently to our charter of the 30th November, 1854, the effect of which would be to give to individuals as against the Company, either claims to compensation which were not then vested in the ownership of the lands, or claims to compensation more considerable than those which the owners could then justly advance, shall be considered void.

ART. 12   The Egyptian Government will deliver to the Company, should the case arise, all lands the property of private individuals, whereof possession shall be necessary for the execution of the works and the carrying into effect of the concession, subject to the payment of just compensation to the parties concerned.

Compensation for temporary occupation or definitive appropriation shall as far as possible be determined amicably; in case of disagreement the terms shall be fixed by a court of arbitration deciding summarily and composed of:

(1)   An arbitrator chosen by the Company;

(2)   An arbitrator chosen by the interested parties;

(3)   A third arbitrator appointed by us.

The decisions of the court of arbitration shall be executed without further process, and subject to no appeal.

ART. 13   The Egyptian Government grants to the leasing Company, for the whole period of the concession, the privilege of drawing from the mines and quarries belonging to the public domain, without paying duty, impost or compensation, all necessary materials for the construction and maintenance of the works and buildings of the undertaking. It moreover exempts the Company from all duties of customs, entrance dues and others, on the importation into Egypt of all machinery and materials whatsoever which they shall bring from foreign countries, for employment in the construction of the works or working the undertaking.

ART. 14   We solemnly declare for our part and that of our successors, subject to the ratification of His Imperial Majesty the Sultan, that the Grand Maritime Canal form Suez to Pelusium and the ports appertaining thereto, shall always remain open as a neutral passage to every merchant ship crossing from one sea to another, without any distinction, exclusion, or preference of persons or nationalities, on payment of the dues and observance of the regulations established by the Universal Company lessee for the use of the said Canal and its dependencies.

ART. 15   In pursuance of the principle laid down in the foregoing article, the Universal Company can in no case grant to any vessel, company, or individual, any advantages or favour not accorded to all other vessels, companies or individuals on the same conditions.

ART. 16   The term of the Company's existence is fixed at 99 years, reckoning from the completion of the works and the opening of the Maritime Canal to large vessels.

At the expiration of the said term, the Egyptian Government shall enter into possession of the Maritime Canal constructed by the Company, upon condition, in that event, of taking all the working stock and appliances and stores employed and provided for the naval department of the enterprise, and paying to the Company such amount for the same as shall be determined either amicably or by the decision of sworn appraisers.

Nevertheless, if the Company should retain the concession for a succession of terms of 99 years, the amount stipulated to be paid to the Egyptian Government by Article 18, hereinafter recited, shall be raised for the second term to 20 per cent, for the third term to 25 per cent, and so on augmenting at the rate of 5 per cent for each term, but so as never to exceed on the whole 35 per cent, of the net proceeds of the undertaking.

ART. 17   To indemnify the Company for the expenses of construction, maintenance and working, charged upon them by these presents, we authorize the Company henceforth, and during the whole term of their lease, as determined by clauses 1 and 3 of the preceding Article, to levy and receive for passage through and entrance into the canals and ports thereunto appertaining, tolls and charges for navigation, pilotage, towage to harbour dues, according to tariffs which they shall be at liberty to modify at all times, upon the following express conditions:

(1)   That these dues be collected, without exception or favour, from all ships under like conditions;

(2)   That the tariffs be published three months before they come into force, in the capitals and principal commercial ports of all nations whom it may concern;

(3)   That for the simple right of passage through the Canal, the maximum toll shall be 10 francs per measurement ton on ships and per head on passengers, and that the same shall never be exceeded.

The Company may also, for granting the privilege of establishing water-courses, upon the request of individuals by virtue of Article 8, receive dues, according to tariffs to be hereafter settled, proportionable to the quantity of water diverted and the extent of the lands irrigated.

ART. 18   Nevertheless, in consideration of the concessions of land and other advantages accorded to the Company by the preceding Articles, we reserve on behalf of the Egyptian Government a claim of 15 per cent, on the net profits of each year, according to the dividend settled and declared by the General Meeting of Shareholders.

ART. 19   The list of Foundation Members who have contributed by their exertions, professional labours, and capital to the realization of the undertaking before the establishment of the Company, shall be settled by us.

After the said payment to the Egyptian government, according to Article 18 above recited, there shall be divided out of the net annual profits of the undertaking, one share of 10 per cent, among the Foundation Members or their heirs or assigns.

ART. 20   Independently of the time necessary for the execution of the works, our friend and authorized agent, M. Ferdinand de Lesseps, shall preside over the direct the Company, as original founder, during ten years from the first day on which the term of concession for 99 years shall begin to run, by the terms of Article 10 above contained.

ART. 21   The Articles of Association hereunto annexed of the Company, established under the title of THE SUEZ MARITIME CANAL UNIVERSAL COMPANY, are hereby approved, and the present approval shall have force as an authority for its constitution in the form of Sociétés Anonymes, to date from the day when the entire capital of the Company shall be completely subscribed.

ART. 22   In witness of the interest which we feel in the success of the undertaking, we promise to the Company the loyal co-operation of the Egyptian Government; and we expressly, by these presents, call upon the functionaries and agents of all our administrative departments to give aid and protection at all times to the Company.

Our engineers, Linant Bey and Mougel Bey, whose services we place at the disposal of the Company for the direction and conduct of the works ordered by the said Company, shall have the superintendence of the workmen, and shall be charged with the enforcing of regulations respecting the execution of the works.

ART. 23 All provisions of our Charter of the 30th November 1854, and others which are inconsistent with the clauses and conditions of the present book of charged, which alone shall constitute the law in respect of the concession to which it applies, are hereby revoked.

Done at Alexandria, January 5, 1856.

Source: White Paper on the Nationalisation of the Suez Maritime Canal Company. Cairo: (Ministry for Foreign Affairs) Government Press, 1956, pp. 21–8.

---

34 "Agreement of February 22, 1866, Determining the Final Terms as Ratified by the Sublime Porte"

1 Abolition of Forced Labour from the Canal Works

ART. 1 Shall be entirely abolished, all reference in the Regulations dated July 20, 1856, pertaining to the employment of fellaheen in the works of the Suez Canal. In consequence, shall be considered null and void the provisions of Art. 2 of the Act of Concession dated January 5, 1856, which provides: "In all cases, four fifths of the workmen employed upon these works shall be Egyptian."

The Government of Egypt shall, in compensation for the abolition of the Regulations dated July 20, 1856, and the privileges involved thereon, pay the Company 38 million francs.

And henceforth, the Company shall, without any privileges or hindrance, employ the necessary workmen for the enterprise according to the common law.

2 Curtailing the Area of the Ceded Lands and Certain Privileges

ART. 2 The Company renounces the benefits of provisions of Arts. 7 and 8 of the Act of Concession dated November 30, 1854, as well as Arts. 11 and 12 of the Act dated January 5, 1856. The area of the lands capable of irrigation which had been ceded to the Company under the said 1854 and 1856 Acts and which was receded to the Government is fixed, by mutual agreement, at 63,000 hectares from which shall be deducted 3,000 hectares which form part of the site assigned for the requirements of the Martime Canal.

ART. 3 Since, as provided in Articles 7 and 8 of the 1854 Act of Concession and Articles 10, 11 and 12 of that of 1856, remain annulled, the compensation due to the Company from the Government of Egypt for the reclamation of these lands shall amount to 30 million francs, at the rate of 500 francs per hectare.

ART. 4 Considering the necessity of determining the area of lands required for the establishment of the maritime canal and its working under proper conditions as will insure the prosperity of the enterprise; that this area must not be limited to the space which will be materially occupied by the canal itself, by its free-boards and by the towing paths; considering that, to give full and complete satisfaction to working requirements, it is necessary that the Company shall be able to establish, within the proximity of the maritime canal, depots, warehouses, workshops and ports where their usefulness will be acknowledged, and, finally, appropriate habitations for the guardians, superintendents, workmen charged with maintenance work, and for all administration officials; that it is also appropriate that lands be annexed to the said habitations which might be cultivated as gardens to provide certain argricultural provisions in such places as are entirely deprived of these supplies.

And, finally, it is absolutely necessary that the Company shall have at its disposal sufficient lands for cultivation and establishment thereon of works intended to protect the maritime canal against invading sand and ensure its maintenance; but it should not be granted more than is necessary to amply meet the needs of the various works indicated above;

Considering that the Company can have no claim to obtain any areas of land whatsoever for speculation purposes, whether by putting it under cultivation, establishing buildings thereon or by sale to others when the population increase;

Being bound by these considerations in determining the boundaries of the lands lying along the length of the maritime canal whose possession shall be necessary, throughout the duration of the concession, for the establishment, working and maintenance of the canal, the Two Contracting Parties mutually agree that these lands be determined in conformity with the plans and tables drawn up, preconcerted, signed and appended to this effect by the present.

ART. 5   The Company shall return to the Government of Egypt the second part of the fresh water canal situated between El Wadi, Ismailia and Suez; just as it had already returned the first part of the said canal, lying between Cairo and El Wadi Domain under the agreement dated March 18, 1863.

The return of the second part of this canal is made under the following terms and conditions:

(1)   The Company undertakes to complete the remaining works to have El Wadi – Ismailia – Suez Canal comply with the dimensions agreed upon, and in a suitable condition for taking over;

(2)   The Government of Egypt shall take over the fresh-water canal, the technical constructions and the land dependent thereon as soon as the Company is in a position to deliver the canal according to the preceding conditions.

This delivery, which implies acknowledgement of receipt on the part of the Government of Egypt, shall take place contradictorily between Government engineers and those of the Company, and shall be recorded in a procès-verbal showing in detail the points where the state of the Canal departs from the conditions which it ought to have fulfilled.

(3)   As from the date of delivery, the Government of Egypt shall undertake the maintenance of the said Canal, i.e.:

I   To carry out during the proper time all plantation and cultivation work as well as the necessary fortifications to prevent the delapidation of the banks and the settling of sand; and to maintain feeding the Canal from the Zagazig canal until such feeding can be ensured directly from Cairo water intake.

II   To carry out the works pertaining to the part returned to it under the Agreement of March 8, 1863; and to connect this first part to the second at El Wadi junction point.

III   To ensure navigation during all the seasons by maintaining the canal water level at 2.50 metres during high Nile water, at 2 metres during middle water level and at 1 metre during lowest water level.

IV   Moreover, to supply the Company with 70,000 cubic metres of water daily for supplying the population living alongside the maritime canal, for watering the gardens, for driving the machinery designed for the maintenance of the maritime canal and machinery of industrial establishments connected with its working; for the irrigation of seed plots, sand hill plantations as well as other lands among the dependencies of the maritime canal which cannot be naturally irrigated; and, lastly, to supply vessels passing through the said Canal.

V   To carry out all the necessary clearing and other works so as to maintain the fresh-water canal and its technical constructions in good condition.

On this account, the Government of Egypt shall substitute the Company in all the charges and obligations that befall it as a result of insufficient maintenance; taking into account the condition on which the canal will be on delivery, and the delay necessary for carrying out such works as would have been demanded by that condition.

3   The Company is Subject to Egyptian Sovereignty and to Laws and Customs of the Country

ART. 9   The Maritime Canal shall remain under the Egyptian Police who will have free authority over it as is exercised elsewhere in the Egyptian territory, with a view to maintaining order and public security and ensuring the enforcement of the country's laws and regulations.

The Government of Egypt shall enjoy the right of passage across the Maritime Canal, where this passage is judged necessary, whether to insure its communications or free circulation for commerce and the public. The Company shall under no pretext whatsoever levy any charges or other dues.

ART. 10   The Government of Egypt shall occupy, within the boundaries of lands reserved as dependencies to the Maritime Canal, any position or strategic point which it judges necessary for the defence of the country. This occupation should not prejudice navigation, nor easements attached to the free-boards of the Canal.

ART. 11   The Government of Egypt may, under the same reservations, occupy for the use of its administrative services (post, customs, barracks, etc.) any available place it deems convenient; taking into account the exigencies of operating the services of the Company. In this case, the Government shall, where this is necessary, repay the Company the sums which this latter might have spent on the creation or appropriation of the lands which the Government proposes to dispose of. [. . .]

ART. 16   Since the Universal Company of the Maritime Suez Canal is an Egyptian Company, it remains subject to the laws and usages of the country. However, regarding its constitution as a Company and the relation of shareholders among themselves, it is – in virtue of a special convention – governed by the laws regulating joint stock companies. It has been agreed that all disputes resulting thereof will be submitted to arbiters in France for judgment and with appeals before the Imperial Court of Paris as being a superarbiter.

As regards the disputes that arise in Egypt between the Company and individuals of whatever nationality, these must be referred to Egyptian courts, and their procedure be subject to Egyptian law, usages and treaties.

As regards the disputes that may arise between the Company and the Egyptian Government, these must in like manner be referred to Egyptian judiciary and settled in accordance with Egyptian law.

Workers and other individuals subject to the administration of the Company will be tried before Egyptian courts and in accordance with Egyptian laws and treaties. This applies to all contraventions and disputes where either or both parties concerned would be Egyptian. Should all parties to the dispute be foreigners, the case will be subject to the established procedure.

All notifications addressed to the Company by any of the parties interested in Egypt will be valid when dispatch to the Company's Office at Alexandria.

4   The Canal is an Egyptian Public Domain

This is apparent from all the provisions of the Convention (1866) and, in particular from article 13:

ART. 13   In the interest of commerce, industry and the successful operation of the Canal, every individual shall have the right to settle down either alongside the Maritime Canal or within the villages set up along its course, provided permission is obtained from the Government beforehand, and being subject to the administrative and municipal regulations of the local authority as well as to laws, customs and taxes system of the country.

Shall be excepted, the free-boards, banks and towing paths which shall remain open for free circulation under the regulations governing their use.

This settling down is not permissible except in such places as declared by the Company's engineers as being unnecessary for the working of its services.

Beneficiaries shall repay the Company such sums as it might have spent in the creation or appropriation of these places.

The Object of the Concession

From the foregoing, it will be clearly seen that the Universal Suez Maritime Canal Company is a commercial company operating a public utility enterprise as determined in the act of concession.

The object of this concession forms the target of the company and the field of its activities as indicated in Article 2 of the company's organic law, which was approved by the Government of Egypt on January 5, 1856.

Article 2   The Object of this Company

(1)   The establishment of a canal navigable by large vessels between the Red Sea and the Mediterranean, from Suez to the Gulf of Pelusium.

(2)   Establishment of a canal of irrigation adapted to the river traffic of the Nile, joining the Nile to the maritime canal, from Cairo the Lake Timsah.

(3)   Establishment of two branches striking out of the preceding canal at its inlet into Lake Timsah and proceeding on one side to Suez, and on the other to Pelusium.

(4)   Utilisation of the said Canal and branches and other dependencies.

(5)   Utilisation of lands granted to the Company.

The above will be governed by the conditions and stipulations provided for in the two Firmans dated November 20, 1854 and January 5, 1856.

The first Firman grants M. Ferdinand de Lesseps exclusive power to establish and direct a company to carry out the above works in his capacity of being the original founder of the Company and its managing director. The second Firman grants the Company a concession to carry out the establishment of the above canals and dependencies under the provisions set therein with all the attendant costs, obligations, rights or privileges envisaged by the Government.

The Canal is an Egyptian Territory

The Canal is dug in Egyptian Public Domain. This is evidenced by the following provisions of Firman dated January 5, 1856:

ART. 10 For the construction of the Canals and their dependencies mentioned in the foregoing articles, the Egyptian Government grants to the Company, free of impost or rent, the use and enjoyment of all lands not the property of individuals which may be found necessary.

It likewise grants to the Company the use and enjoyment of all uncultivated lands not the property of individuals which shall have been irrigated and cultivated by their care and at their expense, with these provisoes:

(1) The lands comprised under the latter head shall be free of impost during ten years, only to date from their being put in a productive condition.

(2) That after that period, they shall be subject for the remainder of the term of concession, to the same obligations and imposts to which are subjected under like circumstances, the land in other provinces of Egypt.

(3) That the Company shall afterwards, themselves or through their agents, continue in the use and enjoyment of these lands and the water-courses necessary to their fertilisation, subject to payment to the Egyptian Government, of the imposts assessed upon lands under like conditions.

ART. 11 For determining the area and boundaries of the lands conceded to the Company under Article 10, reference is made to the plans hereunto annexed, in which plans the land conceded for the construction of the Canals and their dependencies free of impost or rent, conformably to Clause one is coloured black, and the land conceded for the purpose of cultivation, on paying certain duties conformably with Clause two is coloured blue.

All acts and deeds done subsequently to our charter of the 30th November, 1854, the effect of which would be to give to individuals as against the Company, either claims to compensation which were not then vested in the ownership of the lands, or claims to compensation more considerable than those which the owners could then justly advance, shall be considered void.

ART. 12 The Egyptian Government will deliver to the Company, should the case arise, all lands the property of private individuals, whereof possession shall be necessary for the execution of the works and the carrying into effect of the con-cession, subject to the payment of just compensation to the parties concerned.

Compensation for temporary occupation or definitive appropriation shall as far as possible be determined amicably; in case of disagreement the terms shall be fixed by a court of arbitration deciding summarily and composed of:

(1) An arbitrator chosen by the Company;
(2) An arbitrator chosen by the interested parties;
(3) A third arbitrator appointed by us.

The decisions of the court of arbitration shall be executed without further process, and subject to no appeal.

ART. 13 The Egyptian Government grants to the leasing Company, for the whole period of the concession, the privilege of drawing from the mines and quarries belonging to the public domain, without paying duty, impost or compensation, all necessary materials for the construction and maintenance of the works and buildings of the undertaking. It moreover exempts the Company from all duties of customs, entrance dues and others, on the importation into Egypt of all machinery and materials whatsoever which they shall bring from foreign countries, for employment in the construction of the works or working the undertaking.

ART. 16 The term of the Company's existence is fixed at 99 years, reckoning from the completion of the works and the opening of the Maritime Canal to large vessels.

At the expiration of the said term, the Egyptian Government shall enter into possession of the Maritime Canal constructed by the Company, upon condition, in that event, of taking all the working stock and appliances and stores employed and provided for the naval department of the enterprise, and paying to the Company such amount for the same as shall be determined either amicably or by the decision of sworn appraisers.

Nevertheless, if the Company should retain the concession for a succession of terms of 99 years, the amount stipulated to be paid to the Egyptian Government by Article 18, hereinafter recited, shall be raised for the second term to 20 per cent, for the third term to 25 per cent, and so on augmenting at the rate of 5 per cent for each term, but so as never to exceed on the whole 35 per cent of the net proceeds of the undertaking.

This is also evidenced by article 4 of the agreement dated February 22, 1866 which provides:

ART. 4 Considering the necessity of determining the area of lands required for the establishment of the Maritime Canal and its working under proper conditions as will insure the prosperity of the enterprise; that this area must not be limited to the space which will be materially occupied by the canal itself, by its free-boards and by the towing paths; considering that, to give full and complete satisfaction to working requirements, it is necessary that the Company shall be able to establish, within the proximity of the Maritime Canal, depots, warehouses, workshops and ports where their usefulness will be acknowledged, and, finally, appropriate habitations for the guardians, superintendents, workmen charged with maintenance work, and for all administration officials; that it is also appropriate that lands be annexed to the said habitations which might be cultivated as gardens to provide certain agricultural provisions in such places as are entirely deprived of these supplies.

And, finally, it is absolutely necessary that the Company shall have at its disposal sufficient lands for cultivation and establishment thereon of works intended to protect the Maritime Canal against invading sand and ensure its maintenance; but it should not be granted more than is necessary to amply meet the needs of the various works indicated above.

Considering that the Company can have no claim to obtain any areas of land whatsoever for speculation purposes, whether by putting it under cultivation, establishing building thereon or by sale to others when the population increase;

Being bound by these considerations in determining the boundaries of the lands lying along the length of the Maritime Canal whose possession shall be necessary, throughout the duration of the concession for the establishment, working and maintenance of the canal, the Two Contracting Parties, mutually agree that these lands be determined in conformity with the plans and tables drawn up, preconcerted, signed and appended to this effect by the present.

Source: White Paper on the Nationalisation of the Suez Maritime Canal Company. Cairo: (Ministry for Foreign Affairs) Government Press, 1956, pp 29–35, 39–42.

35 D. A. Cameron: *The Suez Canal* (1898)

THE story of the Suez Canal may be briefly told. In 1841 Lord Palmerston was blamed by some for having curtailed the independence of Egypt, yet his policy was justified by the inheritance of Mehemet Ali falling into the weaker hands of Abbas, Said, and Ismail. He continued loyal to that settlement till his death, in 1865. He was anxious for peace with the French empire, and, seeing that he could not effectually counteract the influence of M. de Lesseps without destroying the semi-independence guaranteed to the pashalik after Acre, he was obliged to let matters slowly take their course. He did not want a Suez Canal because he did not want an Egyptian Question, but he could not prevent it because the French were our allies in the Crimea, and because De Lesseps enjoyed high favour at the Imperial Court. All he could do was to delay the issue as long as possible, and he warned the French that a state of affairs might arise which would lead to complications. The French persisted in making the canal route to India, and thereby forced an English occupation only thirteen years after its completion. Indeed, as M. Renan said in his answer to the Academy speech of De Lesseps

The isthmus cut becomes a strait, a battle-field. A single Bosphorus has hitherto sufficed for the troubles of the world; you have created a second much more important one. In case of naval war it would be of supreme interest, the point for the occupation of which the whole world would struggle to be first. You have marked the field of the great battles of the future.

As early as 1796 Napoleon entertained the idea of a maritime canal from Suez, but his chief engineer, Lepère, stated that the Red Sea level was thirty feet above the Mediterranean. This error was rectified by another Frenchman, M. Linant de Bellefonds, who submitted his plans to De Lesseps, at that time French consul-general, in 1833.

"In 1840," M. Linant writes, "England and the East India Company wished for a canal. In 1841 I signed a contract to that effect with the Peninsular and Oriental Company, and in 1842 the Indian Government accepted my project with enthusiasm."

In 1847 a mixed commission, of which Robert Stephenson was a member, surveyed the isthmus with Linant, and agreed that there was no difference of level between the two seas. Mehemet Ali doubted whether the scheme would succeed, but (to his glory be it recorded) one of his last acts was to render the commissioners every official assistance. Nothing further was done till the accession of Said Pasha, and in November, 1854, M. de Lesseps obtained that viceroy's formal consent.

This promise was ratified in January, 1856, by a second Act of Concession. A lease was granted for ninety-nine years, to count from the opening of the canal. De Lesseps was to make also a fresh-water canal from Cairo to Ismailia, with branches north and south to Port Said and Suez. For this purpose he was given the lands necessary for buildings and works gratis and free from taxation; the lands, not private property, brought under cultivation gratis and free from taxation for ten years; the right to charge land-owners for fresh-water which he was bound to supply; all mines found on the company's lands, and the right to work State mines and quarries free of cost or tax; exemption from customs duties on imports for the service of the company; the whole enterprise to be completed, save for unavoidable delays, within six years. Native labour was to be employed to the extent of four-fifths, a special convention settling the terms on which the pasha was to supply relays of thousands of fellaheen diggers every three months. The tolls were fixed at ten francs per passenger and ten francs per ton of "capacity" – an ambiguous word, which led to trouble later on. The company was to be Egyptian, and subject to local jurisdiction. The profits were to be thus divided, after payment of five per cent interest to share-holders and five to reserve fund; namely, fifteen per cent to the Egyptian Government, ten per cent to founders, and seventy-five per cent to shareholders, directors, and staff. At the end of the lease the canal and its appurtenances were to revert to the Egyptian Government, the company retaining its material and stores.

Such was the princely gift of Said to De Lesseps when the enterprise began in 1858. The capital was fixed at 200 million francs (eight millions sterling) in twenty-pound shares, interest at five per cent. Owing, however, to sundry loans, the capital had risen to 458 million francs in 1887.

In 1855, while the concession was still doubtful, De Lesseps posed as the friend of England, of English free-trade and honesty. British honour, he said, forbad that we should oppose the canal on the selfish grounds that we should lose our monopoly round the Cape, and have to share the profits of transit through the Mediterranean. But on April 7th, 1856, after obtaining the concession, he wrote

I found Lord Palmerston just as he was in 1840, defiant and prejudiced against France and Egypt. He believed France had for a long time been carrying on a Machiavellian policy against England in Egypt, and he saw the result of this in the canal scheme. Then he persisted that it was impossible to make the canal, and that he knew better about it

than all the engineers of Europe, and their opinions would not shake his. Then he delivered a long tirade about the inconveniences which would result for Turkey and Egypt if the viceroy's demands were conceded by the sultan, and the enterprise carried out. He told me frankly that he opposed me. I listened, asking myself whether he was a maniac or a statesman. Not one of his arguments was worth a minute's serious consideration. I answered all his objections as he brought them forward; but, as I was arguing with one whose mind was already made up, I found it only waste of time to prolong the interview.

Again on April 21st he wrote

We now know the real motive of Lord Palmerston's opposition. He is afraid of assisting the development of Egypt's prosperity and power. I have suspected this a long time, and mentioned it to Said Pasha last year with reference to a despatch from a late governor-general of India, in which he stated that if England one day came into possession of Egypt, as she had done of India, she would be the mistress of the world.

The viceroy will see by my advice and conduct how desirous I am not to compromise him. *If I thought more of the canal than I do of him*, nothing would be easier than to give up the scheme into the hands of great capitalists who would quickly carry it out by absorbing him. *But I want him to remain master of the situation, and for the canal to be a means of consolidating and strengthening his political position.*

How did M. de Lesseps act up to this moral engagement? After Said, Ismail Pasha was in favour of the scheme, and paid up some two millions sterling due for 177,642 founder's shares subscribed for by his predecessor. In 1863 he referred an important question to the arbitration of Napoleon the Third, with the result that in July, 1864, the latter delivered an award for an indemnity of £3,360,000 to be paid by Ismail to the company, namely, £1,520,000 for the withdrawal of native forced labour, £1,200,000 for the resumption by the Egyptian Government of land bordering on the canal, except two hundred metres on either bank, and £640,000 for the fresh-water canal from Ismailia to Suez. This was paid off by 1869. Again, in 1866, the company obtained a further payment of over £300,000 for the cession of Wadi Tumilat (land of Goshen), which it had bought in 1861 for some £74,000. Altogether, Said Pasha's gift cost Egypt an ultimate total of more than sixteen millions sterling paid to the company before the canal was opened in 1869.

Meanwhile, how had the enterprise been prospering since 1858? Lord Palmerston was fully justified in predicting that, if made, the canal would be only a stagnant ditch. The Suez Canal, it must be remembered, was intended for sailing vessels. M. de Lesseps, when trying to raise money in England, said: "It is not your steamers that I am wooing, but your fleet of sailing ships now going round the Cape." He asserted that ordinary steamers, not men-of-war or mail-packets, could not afford to go to India under steam because of the great quantity of coal required. Palmerston had before his eyes the expedition of 1801, when Baird's ships were three months sailing from Bombay to Kosseir. Even at the present time it would take a fast clipper ship the better part of a month to beat up from Perim to Suez, because of the narrowness of the Red Sea. This difficulty was overcome by the invention of the compound engine for steamers, which saved nearly half the fuel, and enabled them to utilize the canal. In the opinion of Sir John Stokes, had the canal been opened in 1862 it would have been a financial failure, because the ships of that day could not have used it. Only the invention of the compound engine gave it a chance of success. Yet another factor must be mentioned – the extraordinary growth of our mercantile steam marine, owing to this invention before the canal was opened. Nevertheless, the enterprise was bankrupt. In 1871–72 its twenty-pound shares had fallen to seven, and no dividends could be paid. Then it was that England came to the rescue by persuading the Powers at the Constantinople Conference to allow the company a surtax of 40 per cent on the tolls. Combine these separate strokes of good luck derived from England, add the sixteen millions received from Ismail, and we see why the Suez Canal became a success.

Another point merits attention. Speaking in 1887, Sir John Stokes said

I have found on the part of the *Egyptian Government* a very deep-rooted opinion that the canal has injured Egypt from a national point of view. No doubt their large indemnities might lead to this impression, but the real injury arose from improvident sacrifice of the royalties, which amounted to 15 per cent of the net receipts. These profits were abandoned in 1880 to a French syndicate to cover a debt of £700,000. During the last seven years the syndicate has encashed £1,212,000, and, supposing the receipts did not increase, the company would pay to the syndicate 14 millions sterling up to 1968

for that trifling debt of £700,000. Probably the payment will be three times that amount. I think the Egyptian Government has no right to complain, for at the time of doing it they had already received £83,000 in five bad years, so that they must have known they had got a valuable property.

In this unanswerable and business-like statement Sir John Stokes lays bare the weak point of the case when he speaks of an "Egyptian Government." The only Government was the will of Said Pasha, or of Ismail, who pledged the future of Egypt; and it was this which Lord Palmerston feared when he predicted to De Lesseps the "inconveniences" which might arise later on. But what becomes of M. de Lesseps' promises made in April, 1856? *He* has neither made the khedive master of the situation, nor has he consolidated the power of the dynasty. On the contrary, he established for a time an autocracy of his own, aspiring to the rights and privileges of an independent maritime Power unknown to international law. When British ship owners protested against his high tariff for "capacité" of tonnage, he so prevaricated that on July 7th, 1874, Lord Derby wrote: "This is a specimen of M. de Lesseps' mode of representing facts." A display of force was threatened by Ismail, and the company accepted the inevitable, agreeing to charge on the net, and not on the gross tonnage of vessels.

But the climax was reached during the British expedition of 1882. By charter the company was Egyptian, and not French or "universal"; it could not be neutral so long as Turkey was neutral, it could not be "neutral" when the khedive was in danger from internal rebellion. For the first time, in repayment for the concession and sixteen millions sterling, there was an opportunity for the khedive to derive some personal benefit by turning Arabi's position at Kafr Dowàr, to become master of the situation, and consolidate his power, as De Lesseps promised in 1856. When, however, the British appeared at Port Said, in order to restore the dynasty, M. de Lesseps and his son Victor protested against their entering the canal. According to father and son, it was no longer an Egyptian, but a De Lesseps canal. Nevertheless, Admiral Hoskins smiled at these protests, and passed on to Ismailia, while M. Charles de Lesseps, at Paris, assuming the status of a maritime power, addressed a circular letter to the ambassadors, inveighing against the violation of his family canal. The French Government did not support him, and begged us to deal gently with a man who enjoyed so high a reputation as "le grand Français," and we were magnanimous. But though he failed to thwart us, M. de Lesseps made himself ridiculous. He telegraphed to Aràbi to leave his canal alone, adding, "Jamais les Anglais n'y pénétreront, jamais, jamais."

Again he insisted

Make no attempt to intercept *my* canal. *I* am there. Not a single English soldier shall disembark without being accompanied by a French soldier. *I* answer for everything."

Aràbi replied

Sincere thanks. Assurances consolatory, but not sufficient under the existing circumstances. The defence of Egypt requires the temporary destruction of the canal.

From an English point of view we cannot blame him. He was really a great Frenchman, a redoubtable foe, who believed in Egypt as a French appanage, and had worked for his country's interests there during fifty years. Then came the British occupation, and his life's work was undone in a moment. At the fatal crisis France abandoned him, as she had abandoned Dupleix, Labourdonnais, Montcalm, and other great Frenchmen, who fought us in the last century. "His" canal will remain as his monument, and the painful incidents of the enterprise will be forgotten by the admirers of his work.

His sin was against Egypt, the khedivial dynasty, the fellaheen. He turned the document of concession into a bond, and exacted the last drop of blood with his pound of flesh. However much, therefore, we may criticize the profuse expenditure of Said and of Ismail as against the fellaheen, we are bound to give them credit for their generosity towards Europe, especially when it is remembered that the canal ruined the railway transit for troops, mails, and passengers, a traffic which brought a large revenue into their treasury. If our commerce has benefited, our thanks are due to Said and Ismail, our pity for the fellaheen, whose taxes paid more than half the cost of the enterprise. If we apply the one weight and the one measure between Egypt and Europe, the glory of the Suez Canal belongs to the two viceroys, because they made a free gift to their own disadvantage, because they were ever the munificent patrons of De Lesseps, as Mehemet Ali was of the English Waghorn.

And now, having briefly sketched its past history, we may fairly ask what is likely to be the future of the canal? It may safely be answered that it is an instrument on behalf of peace. There is no historic precedent of such another artificial passage at so important a point on the earth's surface. It may be difficult to keep it open during the next naval war between great powers, and it may be very easy to close it by accident or design; the discussion of these alternatives can at present, therefore, be purely academical. On the other hand, as the value of the canal is yearly increasing for all the nations of Europe, anxiety for their commerce must assuredly act as a deterrent from war. This is more particularly the case as between England and France. The French people and the British Government are the chief shareholders, and two-thirds of the tonnage in transit is British. The two chief sufferers in revenue and commerce from the closing of the canal would be ourselves and the French. Thus it is to our mutual interests to make the canal a bond of alliance, the strength of which shall increase with the steady prosperity of De Lesseps' work. We cannot, however, become real allies if we remain ignorant of the past or shirk the problems of the future. What is most needed by Englishmen as a first step towards the peaceful solution of the "Egyptian Question" is an accurate study of the history of Egypt during the nineteenth century, our victories and defeats and drawn battles, whether in war or diplomacy. Then alone will they acknowledge the force of "accomplished facts," both in favour of England and against her, and fully realize that there is no more powerful argument working for peace in Europe than the commercial safety of the Suez Canal.

[. . .] If, now, we could regard this period of 1798–1882 from a distance – as it were a mediæval century of the Byzantine empire – the minor incidents fully described in the preceding chapters would be lost to view, and we should see merely the chief episodes and actors – Nelson and Napoleon, Mehemet's Ali's massacre of the Mamelukes, Ibrahim's victory at Konia, Napier at Acre, Waghorn's Overland Route, De Lesseps' Canal, the revolt of Aràbi, and Lord Wolseley's triumph at Tell-el-Kebir. These, again, would cluster into one fact, the long struggle between England and France for the control of the Egyptian route to India. Mehemet Ali, though a great man, was a "hero" but in a limited sphere, because the work of his life will not bear rigid and impartial criticism. England and her commercial policy in the East is the real plot of this Egyptian drama during the nineteenth century, and the Great Pasha has to be fitted into it as one of the leading characters, not English policy into the life of Mehemet Ali. For two generations, and more, Canning, Peel,

Palmerston, and Gladstone determined that there should not be an Egyptian Question. As Waghorn asserts, Canning discouraged Englishmen from setting at Alexandria; Palmerston promptly stifled the trouble by bombarding Acre and bringing the pasha to his knees; Beaconsfield, alive to the growing danger of the canal, bought up the shares offered for sale, and Gladstone was forced to intervene. Such is the British occupation – a logical sequence of Napoleon's expedition, dreaded by Mehemet Ali as early as 1814, prophesied by Kinglake in "Eôthen" in 1835, and forced upon us by Waghorn and De Lesseps.

What the future has in store for England in Egypt no man can tell, for it depends on the power of France, of Russia, and the fate of Constantinople. It is, above all, a naval question; and though at present we possess a certain supremacy in the Mediterranean, that would be modified by the establishment of a new Byzantine empire on the Bosphorus, with hostile arsenals at the Dardanelles, Smyrna, and Alexandretta. On the other hand, it must not be forgotten that the Red Sea is a continuation of the Canal, and that not Suez, but Perim and Aden, form the true strategic entrance from the south under British control. In 1827, at Navarino, England, France, and Russia defeated Turkey and Egypt. In 1833 Egypt invaded Turkey, the czar aided the sultan, while France and England effected a compromise. In 1840 England and Russia supported the sultan against France and Egypt. In 1882 France and Russia held aloof, and England began her military occupation. As early as Navarino Palmerston was on his guard against an alliance between Russia and France. Seventy years have passed, and such an alliance is now become a notorious fact.

In 1807 England was defeated by Mehemet Ali at El-Hamàd. In 1840 Palmerston assured Egypt to the pasha as an hereditary principality. In 1882 we restored the dynasty at Tell-el-Kebir. That our generosity has not been wasted is shown in the acts of the lamented Tewfik Pasha until his death, in 1892. A great burden had been thrown on that prince – a mad revolt of ignorant Arabs who had some just grievances that cried for reform, and a gigantic debt of nearly a hundred millions sterling due to foreign bondholders, who, as honest buyers in the open market, demanded the payment of their interest. Only England could restore the situation, because she alone possessed the two necessary qualities, supremacy at sea and supremacy in financial credit. No one knew better than Tewfik Pasha the vices of Ismail's Government which had led to the revolt of Aràbi. That *régime*, of course, could never return; but he also bore other facts in mind: he was the descendant of Mehemet Ali, and he owed his dynasty to the British. Loyalty to his ancestor prompted him to save the family name; loyalty to the British, to whom he owed his restoration, led him to cordially support the work of reform. He was like a man succeeding to a mortgaged estate in the hands of administrators; the military force and the financial credit needed for its rehabilitation belonged to England, and not to himself; he was paying the penalty for Ismail and Said, and he did so with a patient equanimity and self-denial deserving of the highest praise. Of Tewfik Pasha it may be said that he was a beloved and popular khedive, who, choosing the path of safety, succeeded in handing on the heritage to his eldest son.

India has been spoken of as the land of regrets. Egypt, on the other hand, is a land of promise, a country with a great future in the twentieth century. The Nile will have been opened up from Nyanza to the sea. We shall have railroads and steamers through the heart of the Soudan, the canal will revert to the State at the end of the concession in 1969, the public debt will have been reduced to moderate dimensions, and, for its size, the province of Egypt will have become the most valuable domain on the face of the globe. At present we are but on the threshold of this new era, and it behoves us as Englishmen, and the heirs of Nelson, to study its possibilities and to prepare for its development.

Source: D. A. Cameron *Egypt in the Nineteenth Century, or, Mehemet Ali and His Successors Until the British Occupation in 1882.* London: Smith, Elder and Co., 1898, pp 235–47, 272–6.

Note

Donald Andreas Cameron (b. 1856) had a distinguished diplomatic career as British Consul at Port Said, Suakin, and Bengazi. From 1889 to 1897 he served as a Judge of the Native Appeal Court in Cairo, and in 1905 was appointed Consul-General at Suez. He also published several books, including an Arabic-English vocabulary (1892).

Chapter Eight

The Occupation of Egypt:
The Arabi Uprising, 1881–1882

Introduction

"Egypt is ready still, nay desirous, to come to terms with England, to be fast friends with her, to protect her interests and keep her road to India, to be her ally. But she must keep within the limits of her jurisdiction." In these terms Arabi Pasha appealed to Prime Minister Gladstone on July 2, 1882, just days before the bombardment of Alexandria on 11 July. Arabi (1839–1911) who hailed from an Egyptian fellah, or peasant, background to become a colonel in the Egyptian Army, had led an army mutiny – or, as was also argued, a nationalist movement – against the Khedive Tawfiq and his British supporters on September 9 of the preceding year, and since January 1882 had been acting as Egypt's Minister of War. What was to become of Britain's jurisdiction? In June the London government had ordered General Wolseley and the British fleet to the area and threatened military action against the nationalist opposition. That threat was carried out in the July 11 bombardment of Alexandria; followed by the seizure of Ismailia on July 29, and then consummated in the devasting destruction of Egyptian forces at the battle of Tel al-Kebir on September 29. Arabi and his associates

were arrested, tried, and Arabi sentenced to exile in Ceylon. And with that the British formally occupied Egypt.

For Arabi and his followers, the Suez Canal had become part of the pilgrimage route to Mecca and Medina; for Britain, however, it had assumed significance as facilitating shortened sea-passage to India. In both cases, however, the Canal had burdened Egypt and the Egyptians with a colossal debt. Since Mohammad Ali's reign as Viceroy of Egypt from 1805 to 1848, and through his successors Ibrahim (1848), Abbas (1848–54), Said (1854–63), and Ismail (1863–79), Egypt's commitments to European interests in Egypt had been costly, including the financing of the Canal's building and the expenses of the ceremonies that celebrated its opening. Those costs were exacted through ever-increasing taxation, but the Egyptian economy continued to deteriorate, and in 1876 the French and the British took over, in name of the "Dual Control," the Khedive's Government. With the Dual Control, the "relationship of ruler and ruled was placed under the official notice of Europe" (Hourani, 1991: 275). Various investments were at stake in ensuring the stability and dependency of Egypt. Economically, European financial and commercial groups competed and cooperated with indigenous merchant and landowning classes towards increased participation in trading advantages, while the rural population and the impoverished inhabitants of the cities suffered under the mounting pressures of fiscal extraction. Politically, Britain and France were concerned to maintain their alliance against both Russia and the Ottoman Empire over control of the Mediterranean and the routes to the East.

Arabi's uprising, then, with its slogan "Egypt for the Egyptians," claimed to represent the interests of Egypt and the Egyptians in these contests. What then was to become of Britain's jurisdiction following the threat to the even then precarious status quo? Already in 1877, Gladstone had raised the question in his article, "Aggression on Egypt and Freedom in the East," arguing that "enlargements of the Empire are for us an evil fraught with serious, though possibly not immediate danger." But there were other members of his government, as well as public policy- and opinion-makers who insisted that direct intervention in Egyptian affairs, if not territorial occupation, was incumbent on an empire that needed to maintain both its suzerainty and its access to territory, trade, and expansion. If the occupationists would seem to have won the day in the immediate aftermath of the Arabi uprising, the debate continued. Should Britain restore order and withdraw quickly to its previous role of a "moral influence," or remain in Egypt to ensure reform following the restoration of order? How long, that is, would/should the occupation last? In the event, it continued until 1956 and the Suez Canal War, in which France, Britain and Israel sought to contest Abdel Nasser's nationalization of the waterway.

But if Britain was to assume control of Egypt, Arabi and his followers must first be dealt with. Arrested in fall 1882, the trial took place shortly thereafter. There were those in England and Egypt alike who clamored for Arabi's immediate and summary execution. Others would argue just as adamantly for the imperative of a "fair trial" and due process. It was perhaps not just the man, but his example that needed to be disposed of. For Lord Cromer (Sir Evelyn Baring), it was urgent to cancel the effects of such insubordination as Arabi's, asking in his memoirs, "at what point the sacred right of revolution begins or ends, . . . at what stage a disturber of the peace passes from a common rioter . . . to the rank of a leader of a political movement?" For Cromer, the Arabi uprising marked neither such a point nor such a stage, and, he would maintain, the British had practical experience in contending with "mutinies."Cromer, following his own assignment in the India Service,

had only recently taken over the Consul-Generalship of Egypt in September 1883. His admirers and detractors alike emphasize his administrative prowess and discipline in carrying out his politically mandated work – whether in India or Egypt. According to his colleague in the service, Lord Milner, for example, "It would be difficult to overestimate what the work of England in Egypt owes to the sagacity, fortitude, and patience of the British Minister" (1893: 438). Wilfrid Scawen Blunt, by contrast, had earned the reputation, as he himself proudly admits, of a "nonconformist conscience." A champion of Arabi and his cause of self-government for the Egyptians, Blunt challenged the attempt to criminalize the work of the national leader, and organized legal counsel through Mark Napier and A. M. Broadley to represent Arabi throughout his trial. As it happened, Arabi was not executed, but exiled to Ceylon – where Blunt would later visit him on the occasion of his visit to India in the interests of establishing an institute of Muslim higher education there – even as he championed the rescue mission to Gordon in Khartoum in 1885. Denied thereafter entry into British Egypt, Blunt's subsequent engagements as a "nonconformist conscience" would also include a period in Galway Jail in consequence of his support of Irish claims for Home Rule and self-government.

Meanwhile, the British did occupy Egypt, requiring further development of the attributes of the "Anglo-Egyptian official." As Cromer pointed out, "The efficient working of the administrative machine depends . . . mainly on choosing the right man for the right place." Many of those same officials, however, saw the "right place" for the "right men" as at "office, club and dinner." But the larger place, Egypt, representing for some the "key to India," for others "the Gate of the East," had for the time being become British Egypt.

BH

Additional Reading

Blunt, Wilfrid Scawen. *The Secret History of the English Occupation of Egypt.* London, 1907.
—. *India Under Ripon.* London, 1909.
—. *Gordon at Khartoum.* London, 1911.
—. *The Land War in Ireland.* London, 1913.
Broadley, A. M. *How We Defended Arabi and His Friends.* London, 1884.
Berque, Jacques. *Egypt: Imperialism and Revolution* (1967). Trans. Jean Stewart. London, 1972.
Cole, Juan. *Colonialism and Revolution in the Middle East: Social and Cultural Origins of Egypt's 'Urabi' Movement.* Princeton NJ, 1993.
Daniel, Norman. *Islam, Europe and Empire.* Edinburgh, 1966.

Farwell, Brian. "Wolseley Versus Arabi and the Queen, 1881–82," in *Queen Victoria's Little Wars* (1972). New York, 1985.

Hourani, Albert. *A History of the Arab Peoples*. Cambridge, MA, 1991.

Landes, David S. *Bankers and Pashas: International Finance and Economic Imperialism in Egypt* (1958). New York, 1969.

Lytton, The Earl of. *Wilfrid Scawen Blunt: A Memoir by his Grandson*. London, 1961.

Milner, Alfred. *England in Egypt*. London, 1893.

Mitchell, Timothy. *Colonising Egypt*. Cambridge, 1988.

Robinson, Ronald, and John Gallagher, with Alice Denny. *Africa and the Victorians: The Climax of Imperialism* (1961). New York, 1968.

36   Timeline of Significant Events

November 1869	Opening of the Suez Canal
1876	Dual Control established
1879	Ismail deposed and Tewfiq appointed as Khedive
September 9, 1881	Mutiny of the Egyptian Army
January 1882	Arabi appointed Minister for War
June 11, 1882	Riots in Alexandria
July 11, 1882	Bombardment of Alexandria
September 13, 1882	Battle of Tel el-Kebir
September 15, 1882	Cairo occupied by British troops; Arabi arrested
December 3, 1882	Arabi condemned to exile

37   The Government of Egypt 1805–1914

Viceroys of Egypt

Mohammed Ali	1805–48
Ibrahim Pasha (as Regent)	1848 (for four months only)
Abbas Pasha (grandson of Mohammed Ali)	1848–54
Said Pasha (third son of Mohammed Ali)	1854–63
Ismail Pasha (second son of Ibrahim Pasha and grandson of Mohammed Ali) (raised to dignity of Khedive)	1863–79

Khedives of Egypt

Ismail Pasha	Reigned 1863–79
Tewfik Pasha	Reigned 1879–92
Abbas Pasha	Reigned 1892–1914

British Protectorate proclaimed December 17, 1914

British Agents and Consuls-General to Egypt

General Stanton	1865–76
Lord Vivian	May 10, 1876–October 10, 1879
Sir Edward Malet	October 10, 1879–September 11, 1883
Lord Cromer	September 11, 1883–May 6, 1907
Sir Eldon Gorst	May 6, 1907–July 12, 1911
Lord Kitchener	September 1911–July 1914

38   Bob McGee: "De War in Egyp'" (1882)

Egyp' kickin' up er row –
  Pullin' on de trigger!
F-r-e-e-z-e, my honey, to de plow,
  Fotch er yell, ole nigger!
Cotton ain't gwine hab no show
  Whar de people's fightin';
Grass is gwinter to walk de row
  Sen' de crop er-kitin'.
Ebberbody on dis side
  Make er mighty tussle,
Take advantage ob de tide,
  Strain de bone and mussle!
Make ole Kit mule plum' de line,
  Keep old Pete er-prancin',
Set yer head ter cut er shine,
  Keep dem hoes er-dancin'!
Prices going up atter while –
  Make de nigger "fussy";
Make him feel so happy, chile,
  Oh, Lawdy, Lawdy, mussy!

Source: Puck, vol. XI, no. 284 (August 16), 1882, p. 379.

39   Lord Cromer: "The Mutiny of the Egyptian Army: January–September 1881"

SIR JOHN BOWRING wrote in 1840: "The situation of the Osmanlis in Egypt is remarkable; they exercise an extraordinary influence, possess most of the high offices of state, and, indeed, are the depositories of power throughout the country. . . . They are few, but they tyrannise; the Arabs are many, but obey."

After Sir John Bowring wrote these lines, the Egyptians, properly so called, gradually acquired a greater share in the administration of the country, but in 1881, as in 1840, the Turks were the "paramount rulers." In the army, however, the number and influence of the Turks sensibly diminished as time went on. During the reigns of Abbas, Said, and Ismail, the Egyptian element amongst the officers had increased to such an extent as to jeopardise the little that remained of the still dominant Turco-Circassian element.

The large number of officers who were placed on half-pay in 1878 were, for the most part, Egyptians. The discontent due to this cause was increased by the fact that, whilst great and in some degree successful efforts were made to improve the civil administration of the country, nothing was done to improve the condition of the army. The prevailing discontent eventually found expression in a petition addressed by certain officers of the army to Riaz Pasha on January 15, 1881.

Ahmed Arábi, an Egyptian of fellah origin, who was colonel of the 4th Regiment, soon took the lead in the movement which was thus begun. But the prime mover in the preparation of the petition was Colonel Ali Bey Fehmi, who commanded the 1st Regiment. His regiment had been the object of special attention on the part of the Khedive. It guarded the palace. For some time previously, however, there had been a marked cessation of friendly relations between the Khedive and Ali Bey Fehmi. In the East, to be in disgrace is to be in danger. Ali Bey Fehmi determined to strengthen his position by showing that the Egyptian portion of the army could no longer be treated with neglect, and that he himself could not with impunity be dismissed or exiled.

The petition set forth that the Minister of War, Osman Pasha Rifki, had treated the Egyptian officers of the army unjustly in the matter of promotions. He had behaved "as if they were his enemies, or as if God had sent him to venge His wrath on the Egyptians." Officers had been dismissed from the service without any legal inquiry. The petitioners, therefore, made two demands. The first was that the Minister of War should be removed, "as he was incompetent to hold such a high position." The second was that an inquiry should be held into the qualifications of those who had been promoted. "Nothing," it was said, "but merit and knowledge should entitle an officer to promotion, and in these respects we are far superior to those who have been promoted."

This petition was presented by the two Colonels in person to Riaz Pasha. Riaz Pasha was ignorant of military affairs, and had never interfered with the administration of the army, which he considered to be a prerogative of the Khedive. He endeavoured unsuccessfully to induce the Colonels to withdraw their petition, promising at the same time that inquiry should be made into their grievances. A fortnight was allowed to elapse, during which time further unsuccessful efforts were made in the same direction. In the meanwhile, the Colonels had learnt that their petition was viewed with disfavour by the Khedive and his Turkish surroundings. Riaz Pasha received a hint from the palace that the dilatory manner in which he was treating the question was calculated to throw some doubts on his loyalty. He determined, therefore, to provoke an immediate decision. The matter was discussed at a meeting of the Council of Ministers held under the presidency of the Khedive on January 30, from which Sir Auckland Colvin and M. de Blignières were most unwisely excluded. All idea of compromise was rejected. It was resolved to arrest the Colonels, and to try them by Court-martial. Subsequently, an inquiry would be made into their grievances. An order was drawn up and countersigned by the Khedive, summoning the Colonels to the Ministry of War on February 1.

One peculiarity of Egyptian official life is that no secrets are ever kept. The Colonels were immediately informed of the decision at which the Council of Ministers had arrived. Everything was, therefore, arranged for the action which followed. It was settled that, in the event of the Colonels not returning in two hours, the officers and men of their regiments should go to the Ministry of War and deliver them if they were under arrest. At the same time, a message was sent to Toura, about ten miles distant from Cairo, with a view to securing concerted action on the part of the regiment quartered there. This programme was faithfully executed. The Colonels were summoned to the Ministry of War on the pretext that certain arrangements had to be made for a procession which was to accompany one of the princesses on the occasion of her marriage. They obeyed the summons. On their arrival at the Ministry of War, they were arrested and placed on their trial. Whilst the trial was proceeding, the officers and men of their regiments arrived, and broke into the room where the Court was sitting. They treated the Minister of War roughly, destroyed the furniture, and delivered the Colonels, who then marched with their troops to the Khedive's palace, and demanded the dismissal of the Minister of War. The Ministers and other high functionaries soon gathered round the Khedive.

Some counselled resistance, but the practical difficulty presented itself that no force was available with which to resist. The only sign of fidelity given by any of the troops belonging to the Cairo garrison was that the regiment quartered at Abbassieh, two miles distant from the town, refused to join the mutineers, but the most their Turkish officers could do was to keep them where they were. They would not have defended the Khedive against the mutinous regiments. The regiment stationed at Toura marched to Cairo, according to previous arrangement, and insisted on continuing its march, although messengers were sent to dissuade the men from advancing after the obnoxious Minister had been dismissed.

Under these circumstances, resistance was impossible. After some hesitation, the Khedive sent for the Colonels and informed them that Osman Pasha Rifki was dismissed and Mahmoud Pasha Baroudi[1] named Minister of War in his place. This announcement was received with cheers. The troops dispersed and tranquillity was for the time being restored. The mutinous Colonels were allowed to remain in command of their regiments. They waited on the Khedive, asked his pardon for their past misconduct, and gave assurances of unalterable fidelity and loyalty to his person.

This was the second mutiny of the Egyptian Army. It had followed the same course as the first. It originated with legitimate grievances to which no attention was paid. The next stage was mutiny. The final result was complete submission to the will of the mutineers. The whole affair was mismanaged, and for this mismanagement the Khedive appears to have been largely responsible. Two courses were from the first open to the Khedive. Either he should have endeavoured to rally to his side a sufficient force to crush the mutineers, or, if that was impossible, he should have made terms with the officers before discontent developed into mutiny. Unfortunately, he adopted neither of these courses. The attempt to decoy the Colonels away from their troops and to punish them without any trustworthy force behind him to ensure effect being given to the decisions of the Court-martial, was probably the most unwise course which could have been adopted. Sir Edward Malet expressed his opinion that the officers were treated "in the way best calculated to destroy all confidence in the Khedive and his Government, although it was in harmony with the traditions of Oriental statesmanship."

1 Baroudi was the family name. He was also frequently called Mahmoud Pasha Sami.

The Egyptian officers and soldiers now learnt for the second time that they had only to assert themselves in order to obtain all they required. With this encouragement, they would not be slow to mutiny a third time, should the necessity for doing so arise.

For the moment, however, a truce was established between the Khedive and his mutinous officers; but suspicions and fears were rife on both sides. The Khedive and his Ministers were afraid to disband the disaffected regiments, or even to remove them from Cairo. The officers, on the other hand, although their victory had been complete, were fearful of the consequences of their own action. They mistrusted the Khedive and thought that, should an opportunity occur, the reluctant pardon which they had received would be cancelled, and that they would be visited with condign punishment. They felt even greater resentment against Riaz Pasha than against the Khedive, and began a series of intrigues with a view to bringing about a change of Ministry.

These intrigues were encouraged by Baron de Ring, the French Consul-General, who had frequent interviews with the mutinous Colonels. The action of Baron de Ring increased the difficulties of the situation. If, in addition to financial embarrassments, defective administration, and a mutinous army, there was to be superadded hostile intrigue on the part of the French Government, the position of the Egyptian Ministry would clearly become untenable. Riaz Pasha wished to resign, but was dissuaded from doing so. The Khedive eventually wrote to the President of the French Republic to complain of Baron de Ring's conduct. The result was that he was recalled. He left Egypt on February 28. The Khedive then summoned the principal officers of the army to the palace, and expressed the confidence he entertained in Riaz Pasha, of whom he spoke in eulogistic terms. Already the pay of the unemployed Egyptian officers had been increased, and a public declaration had been made by the Khedive to the effect that for the future every class of officer, whether Turk, Circassian, or Egyptian, would be treated on the same footing. These measures somewhat improved the position of the Ministry. When Sir Edward Malet left in May on a short leave, he "had reason to believe that confidence was being restored; that the officers had, in fact, nothing to fear from intrigue; that they were gradually relaxing measures for their own protection, and beginning to feel that the Khedive and the Ministers no longer aimed at their lives."

It is unnecessary to give the detailed history of the next few months. The officers still entertained a deep-rooted mistrust of the intentions of the Khedive and his Ministers. "The traditions of the days of Ismail Pasha," Sir Edward Malet wrote, "stalked like spectres across their paths." They thought that their lives were in danger. Insubordination increased daily. A Commission was appointed to inquire into the grievances of the army. Arabi Bey was one of its members. His language to the Minister of War was very disrespectful. In the month of July, an artilleryman was run over by a cart and killed in the streets of Alexandria. His comrades bore his dead body to the palace, and forced an entrance in defiance of the orders of their officers. They were tried and the ringleaders condemned to punishment. About the same time, nineteen officers brought against their Colonel (Abdul-Al). These charges formed the subject of inquiry. They were found to be groundless. The officers were in consequence dismissed from the active list of the army, but were shortly afterwards restored to their former positions by the Khedive. The Colonels were greatly offended. They believed that the Khedive's action had been taken with the intention of encouraging the insubordination of their junior officers towards them. About the same time, Mahmoud Pasha Baroudi, the Minister of War, who sympathised with the officers concerned in the mutiny of February 1, was dismissed, and the Khedive's brother-in-law, Daoud Pasha, was appointed in his place. This measure also caused great dissatisfaction.

Within the Ministerial circle, a good deal of dissension reigned. The relations between Riaz Pasha and M. de Blignières became strained. The Khedive's confidence in Riaz Pasha was impaired. It was whispered that His Highness favoured the return to power of Chérif Pasha.

It was clear that another crisis was not far off, but at the moment it was about to occur, the Government were hopeful that their main difficulties had been overcome. "At no period," Sir Edward Malet wrote, "since February 1 had the confidence of the Khedive and his Government been so complete as immediately before the outbreak of September 9. On the very eve, and on the morning itself of that day, Riaz Pasha assured those with whom he conversed that the Government were masters of the situation, and that the danger of a military movement had passed away. But, in fact, all the terrors of the Colonels for their personal safety had been again aroused. A story had got abroad that the Khedive had obtained a secret Fetwa, or decree from the Sheikh-ul-Islam, condemning them to

death for high treason. There was absolutely no foundation for this story, but it is currently believed, and at this moment the position of the Sheikh-ul-Islam is precarious in consequence of it. Spies were continually hovering about the residences of the Colonels, and on the night of the 8th September a man presented himself at the house of Arábi Bey, was refused admittance, and was afterwards followed and seen to return to the Prefecture of Police. There was no doubt in the mind of Arábi Bey that he was to be murdered; he left his house and went to that of the other Colonels, to whom a similar incident had just occurred. It is my belief that then only were measures taken for immediate action, that it was concerted and planned that night, as it was executed on the following day."

On September 9, the 3rd Regiment of Infantry, which was stationed at Cairo, was ordered to Alexandria. This order produced a mutiny. Arábi Bey, with 2500 men and 18 guns, marched to the square in front of the Abdin Palace. The Khedive was at the Ismailia Palace, distant about a quarter of a mile from Abdin. He did the wisest thing possible under the circumstances. He sent for Sir Auckland Colvin.

Sir Auckland Colvin was a member of the Indian Civil Service. In the hour of trial he did not belie the proud motto, *Mens aequa in arduis*, inscribed under the picture of Warren Hastings which hangs in the Calcutta Council Chamber. It is one which might fitly apply to the whole of that splendid body of Englishmen who compose the Indian Civil Service. The spirit of the Englishman rose high in the presence of danger. It was not the first time he had heard of mutiny. He knew how his own countrymen had met dangers of this sort. The example of Lawrence and Outram, of Nicholson and Edwards, pointed the way to the Indian Civilian. His duty was clear. He must endeavour at the risk of his own life to impart to the Khedive some portion of the spirit which animated his own imperial race. He spoke in no uncertain terms. "The Viceroy," he subsequently wrote, "asked my opinion on what should be done. I advised him to take the initiative. Two regiments in Cairo were said by Riaz Pasha to be faithful. I advised him to summon them to the Abdin Square, with all the military police available, to put himself at their head, and, when Arábi Bey arrived, personally to arrest him. He replied that Arábi Bey had with him the artillery and cavalry, and that they might fire. I said that they would not dare to, and that if he had the courage to take the initiative, and to expose himself personally, he might succeed in overcoming the mutineers. Otherwise, he was lost. Stone Pasha[2] warmly supported me. . . . While his carriage was coming Sir Charles Cookson[3] arrived, expressed to the Viceroy his concurrence in my views, and returned to the Agency to telegraph to his Government."

What followed may best be told in Sir Auckland Colvin's words. "I accompanied the Viceroy," he wrote, "in a separate carriage; the Ministers also, and some five or six native officers of rank, with Stone Pasha. We went first to the Abdin barracks, where the regiment of the guard turned out, and with the warmest protestations swore loyalty. Thence we drove to the Citadel, where the same occurred; but we learnt that this regiment, previous to our arrival, had been signalling to the regiment (Arábi Bey's) in the Abbassieh barrack. The Viceroy then announced his intention of going to the Abbassieh barrack. It was already 3.30; I urged him to return to the Abdin Square taking with him the Citadel Regiment, and when he arrived at the square to put himself at the head of that regiment, the regiment of the guard and the military police. He drove off, however, to Abbassieh. It was a long drive, and when we got there about 4 (the Ministers having left us at the Citadel and returned direct) we found Arábi Bey had marched with the regiment to Cairo. We followed, and on entering the town the Viceroy took a long *détour*, and arrived at the Abdin Palace by a side door. I jumped out of my carriage, and urged him on no account to remain in the palace, but to come into the square. He agreed at once, and we went together, followed at a considerable distance by four or five of his native officers, Stone Pasha, and one or two other European officers. The square was entirely occupied by soldiers drawn up round it, and keeping all spectators at a distance. The Viceroy advanced firmly into the square towards a little group of officers and men (some mounted) in the centre. I said to him, 'When Arábi Bey presents himself, tell him to give you his sword, and to give them the order to disperse. Then go the round of the square and address each regiment separately, and give them the order to disperse.' Arábi Bey approached on horse-back; the Viceroy called out to him to dismount. He did so, and came forward on foot, with several others and a guard with fixed bayonets, and saluted. I said to the Viceroy, 'Now is your moment.' He replied, 'We are between four fires.' I said, 'Have courage.'

He took counsel of a native officer on his left, and repeated to me: 'What can I do? We are between four fires. We shall be killed.' He then told Arábi Bey to sheathe his sword. The order was obeyed; and he then asked Arábi Bey what all this meant; Arábi Bey replied by enumerating three points, adding that the army had come there on the part of the Egyptian people to enforce them, and would not retire till they were conceded. The Viceroy turned to me and said, 'You hear what he says.' I replied that it was not fitting for the Viceroy to discuss questions of this kind with Colonels, and suggested to him to retire into the Palace of Abdin, leaving me to speak to the Colonels. He did so, and I remained for about an hour till the arrival of Sir Charles Cookson, explaining to them the gravity of the situation for themselves, and urging them to retire the troops while there was yet time."

The three points to which Sir Auckland Colvin alluded as constituting the demands of Arábi were: (1) that all the Ministers should be dismissed; (2) that a Parliament should be convoked; and, (3) that the strength of the army should be raised to 18,000 men.

Sir Charles Cookson then entered into negotiations with the mutineers. The Khedive consented to dismiss his Ministers on the understanding that the other points demanded by the officers should be left in suspense until reference could be made to the Porte. Arábi agreed to these terms. The question then arose of who should be President of the Council. One or two names were put forward by the Khedive, and rejected by Arábi and his followers. The Khedive then intimated that he would be prepared to nominate Chérif Pasha. This announcement "was received with loud and universal shouts of 'Long live the Khedive!' . . . Arábi Bey then asked to be allowed to see the Khedive and make his submission. This favour was granted to him and the other Colonels, and then the troops were drawn off in perfect quietness to their respective barracks."

Some difficulty was encountered in inducing Chérif Pasha to accept office. He objected to becoming Prime Minister as the nominee of a mutinous army. Sir Charles Cookson, M. Sienkiewicz (the French Consul-General), and Sir Auckland Colvin endeavoured to overcome this reluctance, which was in no degree feigned. They so far succeeded that Chérif Pasha consented to enter into negotiations with the leaders of the military movement. At first, there appeared but little prospect of an arrangement. Chérif Pasha asked that, on condition of his undertaking the government, and

---

2 An American officer in the Egyptian army.
3 Sir Charles Cookson was acting as Consul-General during the temporary absence of Sir Edward Malet.

guaranteeing the personal safety of the leaders of the movement, the mutinous regiments should withdraw to the posts assigned to them. The more violent amongst the officers had, however, got the upper hand. They did not fear Turkish intervention, the probability of which now began to be discussed. Indeed, there was some reason to suppose that the mutineers had received encouragement from Constantinople. Chérif Pasha's terms were rejected, and he declared that he would not undertake to form a Ministry.

Under these circumstances, the Khedive intimated that he was "ready to yield everything in order to save public security." Suddenly, however, on September 13, things took a turn for the better. The relief came from an unexpected quarter. Arábi had summoned to Cairo the members of the Chamber of Notables. When they arrived, "they proved more capable of appreciating the true situation than their military allies. Informed of the negotiations going on with Chérif Pasha, they in a body went to him, and entreated him to agree to form a Ministry, offering him their personal guarantee that, if he consented, the army should engage to absolute submission to his orders. The military leaders seem to have been more struck by this conduct than by all the previous representations made to them." Seeing that public opinion was not altogether with them, Arábi and his followers modified their tone. They tendered their "absolute submission to the authority of Chérif Pasha as the Khedive's Minister." They only made two conditions. One was that Mahmoud Pasha Sami should be reinstated in office. The second was that the Military Law recommended by the Commission, which had been recently sitting, should be put into immediate execution. "To both of these demands," Sir Charles Cookson wrote, "Chérif Pasha, most reluctantly, was compelled to yield, but as to the latter, he expressly reserved to himself the liberty of omitting the most important article, which proposed to raise the army to 18,000 men."

This incident was significant. It showed that there were two parties in opposition to the Khedive. These were, first, a mutinous army half-mad with fear of punishment, and secondly, a party, the offspring of Ismail Pasha's dalliance with constitutionalism, who had some vague national aspirations, and who, as representing the civil elements of society, shunned the idea of absolute military government. Under statesmanlike guidance, this tendency to separation between the two parties might perhaps have been turned to account. The main thing was to prevent amalgamation. If the national party were once made to believe that the only hope of realising its aspirations lay in seeking the aid of the soldiers, not only would the authority of the Khedive disappear altogether, but all hope of establishing a régime under which the army would be subordinate to the civil Government would have to be abandoned.

One of the many political apophthegms attributed to Prince Bismarck is the following: "La politique est l'art de s'accommoder aux circonstances et de tirer parti de tout, même de ce qui déplaît." It would have been wise for the Khedive at this moment to have acted on the principle set forth in this maxim. The military party and the national party were alike distasteful to him. The interests both of his dynasty and of his country pointed, however, to the necessity of conciliating the latter in order to keep in check the former of these two parties. Unfortunately, the Khedive did not possess sufficient political insight to grasp whatever opportunities the situation offered to him.

The new Ministry was nominated on September 14. Chérif Pasha was assured of the support of the British and French Governments. At his own request, he was further assured that "in case the army should show itself submissive and obedient, the Governments of England and France would interpose their good offices with the Sublime Porte in order to avert from Egypt an occupation by an Ottoman army." The usual exchange of letters took place between the Khedive and his Prime Minister setting forth the principles which were to guide the new Ministry. These letters contained only one remark which is noteworthy. Chérif Pasha was no friend to European interference in Egypt. But he had learnt that it might be productive of some good. His letter to the Khedive, therefore, contained the following passage: "The institution of the Control, at first criticised from different points of view, has greatly assisted towards the re-establishment of the finances, at the same time that it has been a real support for the Government of Your Highness. In this twofold capacity, it is important to maintain it as instituted by the Decree of November 15, 1879." To this, the Khedive replied as follows: "A perfect understanding between the Control and my Government is necessary; it must be maintained and strengthened."

The new Ministry, therefore, began work with such props from without as were possible under the circumstances. But for all that, it was clear that the real masters of the situation were the leaders of the mutinous army. Arábi had already treated on equal terms with the representatives of the Powers. He had issued a Circular on September

9 signed "Colonel Ahmed Arábi, representing the Egyptian army," in which he assured the Consuls-General that he and those acting in concert with him" would continue to protect the interests of all the subjects of friendly Powers." There could be no mistaking this language. It was that of a ruler who disposed of power to assert his will, and who intended to use his power with that object.

Yet, whilst Arábi was heading a mutiny against his Sovereign, and employing language which could only lawfully proceed from the Khedive or from one of his Ministers, there can be little doubt that his conduct was mainly guided by fear of the Khedive's resentment and vengeance. Sir Charles Cookson thought that the officers had "exclusively regarded their own safety and interest throughout the agitation." Sir Edward Malet entertained a similar opinion. Every word and deed of the mutineers showed, indeed, that fear was the predominating influence at work amongst them. In the Circular which Arábi addressed to the representatives of the Powers, he said: "Since the Khedive's return to Cairo, intrigues have been on the increase, while we have been threatened both openly and secretly; and they have culminated in an attempt to create disunion among the military, in order to facilitate the object in view, namely, to destroy and avenge themselves upon us. In this state of things, we consider it our duty to protect our lives and interests." Sir Edward Malet was informed by "a Musulman gentleman, who had had long and frequent conversations" with Arábi, that the latter thought that action had become absolutely necessary in self-defence. At a later period, Arábi said that he believed that a party of Circassians agreed together to kill him, as well as every native Egyptian holding a high appointment, on October 1, 1881. "We heard," he said, "that three iron boxes had been prepared into which to put us, so that we might be dropped into the Nile." Men in this frame of mind would probably not, at an early stage of the proceedings, have been uncontrollable. But, in order to control them, one condition was essential. They might have been treated with severity, or, if that was impossible or undesirable, with leniency, but in either case it was essential that they should be treated in a manner which would leave no doubt in their minds as to the good faith of their rulers. Moreover, the practices which until a recent period had existed in Egypt, notably the fate of Ismail Pasha's Finance Minister, the naturally suspicious character of Orientals, and their belief, which is often well founded, that some intrigue lies at the bottom of every action of the Government, should have rendered it clear to the Khedive that the slightest whisper imputing bad faith would be fatal to his reputation for loyalty. The utmost caution was, in fact, necessary. A bold, straightforward conduct, and a stern repression of all palace intrigues, might perhaps have quieted the fears of the officers. Riaz Pasha, although he may not have grasped the whole situation, had sufficiently statesmanlike instincts to appreciate the true nature of the danger. He warned the Khedive frequently not to do or say anything which could give rise to the least suspicion as to his intentions. It is improbable that the Khedive had any deliberate plan for wreaking vengeance on the mutineers. It is certain that his humane nature would have revolted at any idea of assassination, such as was attributed to him. At the same time, if he had considered himself sufficiently powerful to act, he would not improbably have made his displeasure felt in one form or another, in spite of the pardon which had been reluctantly wrung from him. Like Macbeth, he would not play false, but yet would wrongly win. It would be in harmony with the inconsistency even of an honest Oriental to pardon fully, and at the same time to make a mental reserve, which would enable him at some future time to act as though the pardon had only been partial. He allowed his surroundings, which almost always exercise a baneful influence in an Oriental court, to intrigue and to talk in a manner which was calculated to excite the fears and suspicions of the mutineers. Arábi, in his Circular to the Consuls-General, made special allusion to the intrigues of Yousuf Pasha Kemal, the Khedive's agent, and Ibrahim Aga, the Khedive's Tutunji (Pipe-bearer), who, he said, "had been sowing discord." National proclivities and foreign intrigue may, therefore, have had something to do with the mutiny of September 9, but there can be little doubt that the main cause was truly stated by Arábi. It was fear.

This was the third mutiny of the Egyptian army. On each occasion, the mutineers gained confidence in their strength. On each occasion, the submission of the Government was more complete than previously. The first mutiny was quelled by the sacrifice of an unpopular Minister (Nubar Pasha), whom the ruling Khedive did not wish to maintain in office. On the second occasion, the War Minister (Osman Pasha Rifki) was offered up to appease the mutineers. On the third occasion, the mutineers dictated their own terms at the point of the bayonet; they did not rest satisfied without a complete change of Ministry. "Things bad begun make strong themselves by ill." No remnant of military discipline was now left. The Khedive was shorn of all real authority. The smallest incident would suffice to show that the Ministers only held office on sufferance from the mutineers. No long time was to elapse before such an incident occurred.

Source: Lord Cromer *Modern Egypt*, vol. 1. London: Macmillan, 1908, pp. 175–93.

Note

Evelyn Baring, the first Earl of Cromer (1841–1917), a member of the Baring banking family, was Consul General in Egypt from 1883 to 1907. In 1872, as private secretary, he had accompanied his cousin, Lord Northbrook, who had been named Viceroy, to India. His experience in the sub-continent determined his negative attitude toward colonial peoples and their capacity for self-government, an attitude which would characterize his administration of Egypt as well. While this opinion earned him the admiration of many fellow members of the British foreign office, it was also challenged by critics – such as Wilfred Blunt – of British imperial policy. He retired from Egypt and administration following the Dinshawai incident in 1907 in which a British officer was killed and the Egyptian peasants accused of involvement in the incident brutally punished. On his return to England, he supported policies of free trade in the House of Lords.

40   Arabi Pasha: Appeal to Gladstone, *The Times*, July 2, 1882

To the Right Hon. W. E. Gladstone, MP
Alexandria, July 2, 1882
Sir, Our Prophet in his Koran has commanded us not to seek war nor to begin it. He had commanded us also, if war be waged against us, to resist, and under penalty of being ourselves as unbelievers to follow those who have assailed us with every weapon and without pity.

Hence England may rest assured that the first gun she fires on Egypt will absolve the Egyptians from all treaties, contracts, and conventions, that the control and debt will cease, that the property of Europeans will be confiscated, that the canals will be destroyed, the communications cut, and that use will be made of the religious zeal of Mahomedans to preach a holy war in Syria, in Arabia, and in India. Egypt is held by Mahomedans as the key of Mecca and Medina, and all are bound by their religious law to defend these holy places and the ways leading to them. Sermons on this subject have already been preached in the mosques of Damascus, and an agreement has been come to with the religious leaders of every land throughout the (Mahomedan) world. I repeat it again and again that the first blow struck at Egypt by England or her allies will cause blood to flow through the breadth of Asia and of Africa, the responsibility of which will be on the head of England.

The English Government has allowed itself to be deceived by its agents, who have cost their country its prestige in Egypt. England will be still worse advised if she attempts to regain what she has lost by the brute force of guns and bayonets.

On the other hand there are still more humane and friendly means to this end. Egypt is ready still, nay desirous, to come to terms with England, to be fast friends with her, to protect her interests and keep her road to India, to be her ally. But she must keep within the limits of her jurisdiction. If, however, she prefer to remain deceived and to boast and threaten us with her fleets and her Indian troops, it is hers to make the choice. Only let her not underrate, as she has done, the patriotism of the Egyptian people. Her representatives have not informed her of the change which has been wrought among us since the days of Ismail's tyranny. Nations in our modern age make sudden and gigantic strides in the path of progress.

England, in fine, may rest assured that we are determined to fight, to die martyrs for our country – as has been enjoined on us by our Prophet – or else to conquer and so live independently and happy. Happiness in either case is promised to us, and when a people is imbued with this belief their courage knows no bounds.

Ahmed Arabi

Note

The Times: The above letter was addressed by Arabi Pasha to Mr Gladstone a few days before the bombardment of Alexandria, but did not reach his hands until after that event. The letter unanswered: 25 July 1882, in the Lords, Hansard 272, col. 1669–70, and *Political Correspondence*, 23 July vol. 1, p. 404.

41   Wilfrid Scawen Blunt: "The Arabi Trial" (1907)

While these great events were happening on the Nile, I at my home at Crabbet spent the summer sadly enough. My sympathies were, of course, still all with the Egyptians, but I was cut off from every means of communication with them, and the war fever was running too strongly during the first weeks of the fighting for further words of mine to be of any avail. Publicly I held my peace. All that I could do was to prepare an "Apologia" of the National movement and of my own connection with if – for this was now being virulently attacked in the press – and wait the issue of the campaign.

Nevertheless, though in dire disgrace with the Government, I did not wholly lose touch with Downing Street. I saw Hamilton once or twice, and submitted proofs of my "Apologia" to him and Mr Gladstone before it was published, and this was counted to me by them for righteousness. It appeared in the September number of "The Nineteenth Century Review," and at a favourable moment when the first sparkle of military glory had faded, and reasonable people were beginning to ask themselves what after all we were fighting in Egypt about. Written from the heart even more than from the head, my pleading had a success far beyond expectation and, taken in connection with an anti-war tour embarked on in the provinces by Sir Wilfrid Lawson, Mr Seymour Keay and a few other genuine Radicals, touched at last what was called the "Nonconformist" conscience of the country and turned the tide of opinion distinctly in my favour. This encouraged me. About the same time, too, a letter reached me from General Gordon, dated "Cape Town, the 3rd of August," in which he avowed his sympathy with the cause I had been advocating, and which elated me not a little. It was as follows:

Cape Town, 3, 8, 82

MY DEAR MR BLUNT,

You say in "Times" you are going to publish an account of what passed between you and the Government. Kindly let me have a copy addressed as enclosed card. I have written a MS. bringing things down from Cave's mission to the taking of office by Cherif, it is called "Israel in Egypt," and shall follow it with a sequel, "The Exodus." I do not know whether I shall print it, for it is not right to rejoice over one's enemies. I mean *official* enemies. What a fearful mess Malet and Colvin have made, and one cannot help remarking the *finale* of all Dilke's, Colvin's, and Malet's secretiveness. Dilke, especially, in the House evaded every query on the plea that British interests would suffer. Poor thing. I firmly believe he knows no more of his policy than the Foreign Office porter did; he had none. Could things have ended worse if he had said everything? I think not. No more Control – no more employés drawing £373,000 a year – no more influence of Consuls-General, a nation hating us – no more Tewfik – no more interest – a bombarded town, Alexandria – these are the results of the grand secret diplomacy. Colvin will go off to India, Malet to

China – we shall know no more of them. All this because Controllers and Consuls-General would not let Notables see the Budget when Cherif was in office. As for Arabi, whatever may become of him individually, he will live for centuries in the people; they will never be "your obedient servants" again.

Believe me, yours sincerely,
C. G. Gordon

The value to me of this letter I saw at once was great, for, though out of favour with the Foreign Office, Gordon's name was one to conjure with in the popular mind, and especially with that "Nonconformist conscience" which, as I have said, was beginning now to support me, and consequently I knew with Gladstone; and it was on the text of it that I began a fresh correspondence with Hamilton. Mr Gladstone had stated in Parliament that I was the "one unfortunate exception," among Englishmen who knew Egypt, to the general approval of the war; and I sent him, through Hamilton, a copy of Gordon's letter, and at the same time invited his attention to accounts which had begun to appear in the newspapers of certain atrocities of vengeance which had been indulged in by Tewfik and his new Circassian Ministers at Alexandria on Nationalist prisoners made during the war. Torture had, it was related, been inflicted on Mahmud Fehmi, the engineer General, and the thumb-screw and kurbash were being used freely. I asked whether such was the state of things Mr Gladstone had sent troops to Egypt to re-establish. The letter brought a prompt and interesting answer, and one which proved of value to me a few days later when it came to my pleading that Arabi should not be done to death by the Khedive without fair trial.

10, Downing Street, Whitehall,
September 8th, 1882

I need hardly say that Mr Gladstone has been much exercised in his mind at the rumours about these "atrocities." I can call them by no other name. Immediate instructions were sent out to inquire into the truth of them, and to remonstrate strongly if they were confirmed. I am glad to say that, as far as our information at present goes, the statements appear to be unfounded. The strictest orders have been given for the humane treatment of the prisoners. There seems to be some doubt as to whether thumb-screwing was not inflicted on a spy in one case; and searching inquiries are to be instituted with peremptory demands of explanation and guarantees against recurrence. You may be quite sure that Mr Gladstone will denounce "Egyptian atrocities" as strongly as "Bulgarian atrocities."

I cannot help thinking that your and Chinese Gordon's opinion of Arabi would be somewhat modified if you had seen some of the documents I have read.

Some months ago (this, please, is quite private) certain inquiries were made about Chinese Gordon. He had suggestions to make about Ireland, and the result of these inquiries were, to the best of my recollection, that he was not clothed in the rightest of minds.

The last paragraph is historically curious. The proof Gordon had given Mr Gladstone's Government of his not being clothed in his right mind was that he had written, during a tour in western Ireland, to a member of the Government, Lord Northbrook, recommending a scheme of Land Purchase and, if I remember rightly, Home Rule as a cure for Irish evils.

I was thus once more in a position of semi-friendly intercourse with Downing Street and of some considerable influence in the country when the crowning glory of the war, the news of the great victory of Tel-el-Kebir, reached England, and soon after it of Arabi's being a prisoner in Drury Lowe's hands at Cairo. The completeness of the military success for the moment turned all English heads, and it was fortunate for me that I had had my say a fortnight before it came, for otherwise I should have been unable to make my voice heard, either with the public or at Downing Street, in the general shriek of triumph. It had the immediate result of confirming the Government in all its most violent views, and of once more turning Mr Gladstone's heart, which had been veering back a little to the Nationalists, to the hardness of a nether millstone. The danger now was that in order to justify to his own conscience the immense slaughter of half-armed peasants that had been made at Tel-el-Kebir, he would indulge in some conspicuous act of vengeance on Arabi, as the scapegoat of his own errors. His only excuse for all this military brutality was the fiction that he was dealing with a military desperado, a man outlawed by his crimes, and, as such, unentitled to any consideration either as a patriot or even the recognized General of a civilized army. I have reason to know that if Arabi had been captured on the field at Tel-el-Kebir, it was Wolseley's intention to give him the short benefit of a drum-head court martial, which means shooting on the spot, and that it was only the intervention of Sir John Adye, a General much older in years and in length of service than Wolseley, that prevented it later – Adye having represented to Wolseley the disgrace there would be to the British

army if the regular commander of an armed force, whom it had needed 30,000 troops to subdue, should not receive the honourable treatment universally accorded to prisoners of war. At home, too, I equally know that Bright, in indignant protest, gave his mind on the same point personally to Gladstone. It must not, however, at all be supposed that anything but the overwhelming pressure of public opinion brought to bear, as I will presently describe, frustrated the determination of our Government, one way or other, to make Arabi pay forfeit for their own political crime with his life. Mr Gladstone was as much resolved on this as was Lord Granville, or any of the Whig lords in his Cabinet. To explain how their hands were forced in the direction of humanity I must go into detail.

The capitulation of Cairo and Arabi's surrender to Drury Lowe were announced in the "Times" of the 16th, and with it a telegram from its Alexandria correspondent, Moberley Bell, who represented the Anglo-Khedivial official view, demanding "exemplary punishment" on eleven of the National leaders, whom he named, including Arabi. I knew that this could only mean mischief resolved on of the gravest kind, and I consequently telegraphed at once to Button, asking him what the position in official circles was. His first answer was reassuring. "I can't think there is the least danger of their shooting anybody. You should, however, take immediate steps to appeal for merciful treatment." Two hours later, however, a second message from him came. "I don't like official tone with regard to your friends. Write me privately such a letter as I can show to my chief." By his "chief" he, of course, meant Chenery, the "Times" editor, with whom, as I have said, he was on very intimate terms. I consequently wrote at once to Hamilton:

"I cannot think there should be any danger of death for the prisoners taken at Cairo, but should there be, I trust you will let me know in time, as I have certain suggestions to make regarding the extreme difficulty of obtaining them a fair trial just now, and other matters."

To this it is significant that I received no answer for two days, and then an off-hand one, to the effect that Hamilton was about to leave London for the country, "and so would be a bad person to depend upon for any intimation such as I wished." But I was not thus to be put off, and passing beyond Hamilton, I wrote once more direct to Mr Gladstone. I did this after consultation with Button and with Broadley, whom I met at his house on the afternoon of the 19th. We decided that the latter would be the man for our purpose, and that the best chance of saving Arabi's and the other prisoners' lives would be for me to take Broadley out with me at once and produce him as their legal defender. Button, who knew the ins and outs of most affairs, was certain there was no time to lose, and we half engaged Broadley at a fee of £300, afterwards increased to £800 with refreshers. In the meantime Button rendered the cause a great service in the immediate crisis by managing that it should be announced next morning in the "Times" that Arabi and his companions were not to be executed without the consent of the English Government, and that they were to be defended by efficient counsel. Of course, we had not a shadow of authority to go upon for this statement, but the "Times" having announced it made it very difficult, later, for the Government to go back upon a humane decision so publicly attributed to them.

My letter to Mr Gladstone, sent in the same evening, was as follows:

Sept. 19, 1882

My DEAR SIR,

Now that the military resistance of the Egyptians is at an end, and Arabi and their chief leaders have surrendered to Her Majesty's forces, I venture once more to address you in the interests of justice no less than of those whom the fortune of war has thus suddenly thrown into your hands. It would seem to be contemplated that a Court Martial should assemble shortly to try and judge the military leaders for rebellion, and, in the case of some of these, and of civilians, a civil tribunal to inquire into their alleged connection with certain violent proceedings. If this should be the truth, I would earnestly beg your attention to certain circumstances of the case which seem to demand careful consideration.

1   The members of the proposed Court Martial, if Egyptians and appointed by the Khedive, can hardly be free agents or uninfluenced in their feelings towards the prisoners. They would be chosen from among the few officers who espoused the Khedive's cause, and would of necessity be partisans.

2   Even were this not the case, native false witness is so common in Egypt, and the falsification of Arabic documents so easy, that little reliance could be placed upon the testimony adduced. The latter would need to be submitted to experts before being accepted with any certainty.

3   Native evidence, if favourable to the prisoners, will be given under fear. There will be a strong inducement to withhold it, and as strong an inducement in the desire of Court favour to offer evidence unfavourable. The experts charged with examining documents will, if natives, be equally subject to these influences.

4   The evidence of Europeans settled in Egypt, though given without fear of consequences, may be expected to be strongly coloured by resentment. These Europeans are, it would seem, themselves in some measure parties to the suit. They will many of them have lost property or have been injured in their trade during the late troubles or have personal insults to avenge. The vindictive tone of the English in Egypt is every day apparent in their letters published by the English Press.

5   It will be insufficient, if full justice for the prisoners is to be secured, that the ordinary form of Her Majesty's representative being present through a dragoman or otherwise, at the proceedings, should be the only one observed. Political feeling has probably run too high at Cairo during the last six months for quite impartial observation.

6   Should English officers, as it may be hoped will be the case, be added to the native members of the Court Martial, they will be ignorant or nearly ignorant of the language spoken by the prisoners, and will be unable themselves to examine the documents or cross-examine the witnesses. They will necessarily be in the hands of their interpreters, who, if unchecked, may alter or distort the words used to the detriment of the prisoners. *Nearly* all the dragomens of the Consulates are Levantine Christians violently hostile to the Mussulman Arabs, while it may safely be affirmed that there are no Englishmen in Egypt both fully competent and quite unbiassed who could be secured in this capacity. Arabic is a language little known among our officials, and their connection with the late troubles is too recent to have left them politically calm.

It would seem, therefore, that unless special steps are taken there is grave danger of a miscarriage of justice in the trial.

To remedy this evil as far as possible I have decided, at my own charge and that of some of my friends, to secure the services of a competent English counsel for the principal prisoners, and to proceed with him to Cairo to collect evidence for the defence. I shall also take with me the Rev. Mr Sabunji as interpreter, and watch the proceedings on behalf of the prisoners. My knowledge of Arabic is too imperfect for me to act alone, but Mr Sabunji is a friend of the chief prisoners, and is eminently capable of speaking for them. He knows English, French, Turkish, and Italian well, and is probably the first Arabic scholar now living. The prisoners have full confidence in him, and I believe also that they have full confidence in me. Thus alone, perhaps, they will obtain, what I submit they are entitled to, a full, a fair, and – to some extent – even a friendly hearing.

In conclusion, it may not be unnecessary that I should promise you that while thus engaged I, and those with me, would scrupulously avoid all interference with contemporary politics. I shall esteem it a favour if I can be informed at as early a date as possible what will be the exact nature of the trial and what the principal charges made. I hope, too, that every facility will be afforded me and those with me in Egypt to prosecute our task, and I cannot doubt that your personal sense of justice will approve it.

I am, &c., Wilfrid Scawen Blunt

This letter, which I knew it would be difficult for Mr Gladstone to answer with a refusal, especially after his recent assurances about "Egyptian atrocities" and "Bulgarian atrocities," I sent at once to Downing Street, having previously called there and seen Hamilton, to whom I explained my plan. He did not, however, give me much encouragement, as his answer to a further note I sent him next morning proves. My note was that I was writing to Arabi, and to ask him how the letter should be sent, and expressing a hope to have an answer from his Chief before Friday, the next mail day. Hamilton's answer suggests procrastination:

Your letter, I am sorry to say, just missed the bag last night. It reached me about three minutes too late; but in any case I don't think you must count on a very immediate reply. Mr Gladstone is moving about, and moreover will most likely have to consult some one before he gives an answer. I am absolutely ignorant myself as to questions which your intended proceedings may raise; and therefore I have no business to hazard an opinion. But is it not open to doubt whether according to international law or prescription a man can be defended by foreign counsel? I am equally ignorant about the delivery of letters to prisoners of war; but I should presume that no communication could reach Arabi except through and with the permission of the Khedive and our Commander-in-Chief. In any case Malet will probably be your best means of communication.

According to this suggestion I wrote a letter to Arabi telling him of our plans of legal defence and

enclosed it, with a draft of the letter, to Malet, and for more precaution sent both by hand to the Foreign Office, to be forwarded, with a note to Lord Tenterden commending it to his care. By a singular accident, however, both note and letter were returned to me with the message that His Lordship had died suddenly that morning, and I was obliged, as the mail was starting, to send it by the same hand, Button's servant Mitchell, to Walmer Castle where Lord Granville was, and it was only just in time. In the sequel it will be seen that the packet, though despatched to Cairo, was not delivered farther than into Malet's hands and then with the instruction that my letter to Arabi should be returned to me. Malet's official letter to me performing this duty is sufficient evidence, if any were needed, to show how far the Government was from co-operating at all with me in my design of getting the prisoners a fair trial. It is very formal and unmistakable:

Cairo, Oct. 4, 1882

SIR,

Acting under instructions from Her Majesty's Principal Secretary of State I return you herewith the letter for Arabi Pasha which you sent to me to be forwarded in your letter of the 22nd ultimo.

I am, etc., Edward B. Malet.

My letter to Arabi had been as follows:
To My Honourable Friend H. E. Ahmed Pasha Arabi

May God preserve you in adversity as in good fortune.

As a soldier and a patriot you will have understood the reasons which have prevented me from writing to you or sending you any message during the late unhappy war. Now, however, that the war is over, I hope to show you that our friendship has not been one of words only. It seems probable that you will be brought to trial, either for rebellion or on some other charge, the nature of which I yet hardly know, and that, unless you are strongly and skilfully defended, you run much risk of being precipitately condemned. I have therefore resolved, with your approval, to come to Cairo to help you with such evidence as I can give, and to bring with me an honest and learned English advocate to conduct your defence; and I have informed the English Government of my intention. I beg you, therefore, without delay, to authorize me to act for you in this matter – for your formal assent is necessary; and it would be well if you would at once send me a telegram, and also a written letter, to authorize me to engage counsel in your name. Several liberal-minded Englishmen of high position will join me in defraying all the expenses of your case. You may also count upon me, personally, to see, during your captivity, that your family is not left in want. And so may God give you courage to endure the evil with the good.

Wilfrid Scawen Blunt
Sep. 22, 1882, Crabbet Park,
Threebridges, Sussex

Gladstone's answer, which came sooner than I expected, shows as little disposition to favour any idea of a fair trial as was that of the Foreign Office. It came in this form from Hamilton:

10 Downing Street, Sept. 22, 1882
Mr Gladstone has read the letter which you have addressed to him about Arabi's trial and your proposal to employ English counsel. All that he can say at the present moment is that he will bring your request under the notice of Lord Granville with whom he will consult, but that he cannot hold out any assurance that it will admit of being complied with.

This was very plain discouragement, though short of a direct refusal, and a few words added by Hamilton in a separate note were even more so: "I confess," he says, "that the more I think of it the greater is the number of difficulties which present themselves to my mind involved by such a proposal as yours. You will, I presume, hear further on the subject in a day or two but not from me, because I am off as you know."

I was left, therefore, still in doubt while the situation was daily becoming more critical. I dared not leave for Egypt without having received a definite answer, for I knew that at Cairo I should be powerless, if unarmed with any Government authority, and should probably not even be allowed to see the prisoners, while Broadley, tired of waiting, had gone back to Tunis. The Parliamentary session was over and every one was leaving London, the work of the Ministers being left to Under-Secretaries; and all business practically at a standstill. Meanwhile the question of Arabi's death was being keenly debated in the Press, and all the Jingo papers were clamouring for his execution, only here and there a feeble voice being raised in protest. Sir Wilfrid Lawson's Egyptian Committee, which had done such good work during the summer, had become silent, and from Lawson himself I received just then a most desponding letter: "I greatly doubt," he said, "whether they will allow Arabi to have anything like a *fair* trial. They know well

enough that if they do it will end in their own condemnation, and 'Statesmen' are too crafty to be led into anything of that sort. At any rate you are right in *trying* to get fair play for him." All I could do was to stay on in London and still worry Downing Street for an answer and go on prompting the "Times." Therefore, after waiting five more days, I wrote again to Gladstone for a definite answer, the situation having become to the last degree critical at Cairo.

Sept. 27, 1882
I wrote to you about ten days ago, stating my intention of engaging competent English counsel for Arabi Pasha and the other chief Egyptian prisoners in case they should be brought to trial, and of going myself to Cairo to procure evidence for them and watch the proceedings; and I begged you to give me early notice of any decision that might be come to regarding them.

Your reply, through Mr Hamilton, though giving me no assurance that English counsel would be allowed, seemed to suggest that my proposal would be considered; and I accordingly retained, provisionally, a barrister of eminence to act for the prisoners, should it be decided they should be thus defended. In view also of the legal necessity of gaining the prisoners' consent to the arrangement, I wrote, under cover to Sir Edward Malet, to Arabi Pasha, begging his authorization of my thus defending him, a letter to which I have as yet received no answer; nor have I received any further communication from yourself or from Lord Granville, to whom you informed me the matter would be referred.

Now, however, I see it reported in the "Times," from Cairo, that a Military Court to try all offenders will be named no later than to-morrow, the paragraph being as follows:

"The Military Court to try all offenders will be named to-morrow. The Khedive, Sherif, and Riaz all insist strongly on the absolute necessity of the capital punishment of the prime offenders, an opinion from which there are few, if any, dissentients. Sherif, whose gentleness of character is well known, said to me to-day: 'It is not because I have a feeling of spite against any of them, but because it is absolutely necessary for the security of all who wish to live in the country. An English expedition is an excellent thing, but neither you nor we want it repeated every twelve months.'"[1]

If this statement is true it would seem to confirm my worst suspicions as to the foregone decision of

1 Telegram from Moberly Bell.

the Khedive's advisers to take the prisoners' lives, and to justify all my arguments as to the improbability of their obtaining a fair trial. I therefore venture once more to urge a proper legal defence being granted them, such as I have suggested; and, in any case, to beg that you will relieve me of further doubt and, if it must be so, responsibility in the matter, by stating clearly whether English counsel will be allowed or refused in the case of Arabi Pasha and the chief prisoners, and whether proper facilities can be promised me in Egypt of communicating with the prisoners, and obtaining them competent interpretation.

In the present state of official feeling at Cairo, it would be manifestly impossible for me, and those I have proposed to take with me, to work effectually for the prisoners without special diplomatic protection and even assistance.

The urgency of the case must be my excuse with you for begging an immediate answer.

This last letter, however, never reached its destination. Gladstone had left London, and Horace Seymour, his secretary in charge of his correspondence, under cover to whom I had sent it, handed it on, whether by order or not I do not know, to the Foreign Office. "Mr. Gladstone," he explained, "is out of Town, so upon receipt of your letter yesterday I sent the further communication which you addressed to him straight to the Foreign Office. . . . I did so because he had placed your former letter in Lord Granville's hands, as Hamilton informed you, and also because I gathered from your note that this would meet your wish and save time. I understand that you will shortly receive an official reply from Lord Granville conveying to you the view of the Government on the matters to which you refer." Gladstone, therefore, had shifted his responsibility of saying "yes" or "no" on to Granville, and Granville being of course also out of town it was left for the Foreign Office clerks to deal with according to their ways. In spite of Seymour's promise that the view of the Government would shortly be conveyed to me, all the answer I received was one signed "Julian Pauncefote," stating that Mr Gladstone had referred my two letters of the 19th and 27th to Lord Granville, and that Lord Granville regretted that he did not feel justified in entering into correspondence with me on the subject. It was thus that Gladstone, who had made up his mind that Arabi should be executed no less than had the Foreign Office, finally evaded the responsibility with which I had sought to bind him. I give the incident in detail as an illustration of official craft no less than as one of historical importance.

This "Pauncefote" reply decided us to waste no more time. In consultation with Button and with Lord De la Warr, who had come to London and had been working to get an answer from Lord Granville on independent lines, and who now offered to share with me the costs of the trial if we could secure one (a promise which I may note Lord De la Warr failed to redeem), it was agreed that we should telegraph at once to Broadley at Tunis to hold himself in readiness to proceed to Egypt, and that in the meanwhile we should send out to Cairo by that very night's mail the first briefless barrister we could lay our hands on as Broadley's junior till his arrival, and be on the spot to act as circumstances should suggest. Lord Granville had not agreed, nor had he at that time the least intention of agreeing, to the appearance of English counsel on behalf of the prisoners. But the "Times," as we have seen, had already committed the Government to a statement that Arabi was not to be executed without its consent, and that he was to be defended by efficient counsel; and this they had not had the face publicly to disavow. And now Button's influence was so great with Chenery that he was confident he could again force Lord Granville's hand in the matter of English counsel through the insistence of the "Times" on a fair trial.

All that day, therefore, we searched the Inns of Court, which were almost empty, it being holiday time, and it was only at the last moment that we were fortunate enough to light upon the man we wanted. This was Mark Napier, than whom we could not have found a better agent for our purpose, a resourceful and determined fighter with a good knowledge of the law and one difficult to rebuff. He had the immense advantage, too, through his being the son of a former British Ambassador, of understanding the common usages and ways of diplomacy as also of speaking French fluently, a very necessary qualification at Cairo. Having agreed to go he received our short instructions, which were that he was to go straight to Malet and say that he had arrived as Arabi's counsel, and insist on seeing his client. This was all he could hope at present to achieve, and if he could do this he would do much. If Malet should refuse he was to protest and take advantage of every opening given him to emphasize the refusal. Above all he was to keep us constantly informed by telegram of what was going on, while we on our side would fight the battle no less energetically at the Foreign Office and in the Press. Mark, as I have said, had the great advantage of having had a diplomatic training and so could not be imposed upon by the prestige and mystery with which diplomacy is invested for outsiders, and which gives it so much of its strength. We could not possibly have lit upon a better man. He started, as proposed, that night by the Brindisi mail, taking with him a cipher code and two or three letters of introduction. That, with a hand-bag, was all his luggage.

As to myself, De la Warr, who knew the temper of the Foreign Office and their personal rage against me, was very insistent that I should not go to Cairo and to this I assented. At Cairo I should have been only watched by spies, possibly arrested and sent home, while here I could continue far more effectively the Press campaign which, of course, could only really win our battle. Button that very night managed a new master-stroke in the "Times." De la Warr had succeeded in getting from Granville an assurance that all reasonable opportunities would be given by the Khedive for the defence. This assurance was of course illusory as far as a really fair trial went, as the only legal assistance procurable at the time by the prisoners at Cairo was that of the various Levantine lawyers who practised in the international Courts, and these could be no better depended upon than were the terror-stricken native lawyers themselves to serve their clients honestly by telling the whole truth, though a defence of this perfunctory kind would be sufficient to serve our Government's purpose of being able, without risk of a conflict with English popular opinion, to ratify the intended sentences of death. It was intended to have the trial in the Egyptian Court over in a couple of days, and having proved "rebellion," to proceed at once to execution; and English counsel would, no doubt, have been ruled out of the proceedings as a preposterous intervention of foreigners with no legal status in the country.

Granville's words to De la Warr had been no more than this: "I have no reason to doubt that the Khedive, with whom the proper authority rests, will give all reasonable opportunities for Arabi's defence which may not involve any extraordinary or unnecessary delay, and it devolves on the prisoners and their friends to take such measures as they may think fit on their own responsibility." This Button cleverly reproduced next morning in the "Times" as follows: "Lord Granville has written that every reasonable facility will be afforded the prisoners in Egypt and their friends for obtaining counsel for their defence. Mr. Broadley has therefore been telegraphed to go at once to Cairo." It is clear from Lord Granville's angry expostulation with Lord De la Warr (see Blue Book) how little intention he had of having his words thus interpreted. But, once published in the "Times,"

he could not with any decency back out of the position; and thus by a very simple device we again forced his hand and this time on a point which, in the event, gained for us the whole battle.[2]

Nevertheless, we were very nearly being tricked out of our fair trial after all, and a singularly ugly circumstance of the position in our eyes was the sudden reappearance, just then at Cairo, of Colvin, the man of all others most interested, after the Khedive, in preventing publicity. The Foreign Office object clearly now was to hurry on the trial, so as to get it over before Broadley should have time to arrive, for Tunis was and still is without any direct communication with Egypt, and it was probable that ten days would elapse before he could be there. Of Napier's sending they had no knowledge. Orders, therefore, were at once given as a first step that Arabi should be transferred from the safe keeping of the British Army to the ill-custody of the Khedivial police, where communication with the outside world would be effectually barred for him without the English Government incurring thereby any odium. This was done on the 4th of October, two days before Napier's arrival; and the trial was fixed for the 14th, while Broadley did not succeed in reaching Cairo till the 18th. Nothing but Napier's unexpected appearance at the English Agency disarranged the concerted plan.

A further step taken to hasten the end and make an English defence difficult was to select the French criminal military code for use in the court martial, a form which under an unscrupulous government gives great advantages to the prosecution. According to it a full interrogatory of prisoner and witnesses is permitted before these have seen counsel and they are thus easily intimidated, if they take a courageous attitude, from repeating their evidence at the trial. Thus both Arabi and others of his fellow prisoners were during the interval between the interrogatory and the day fixed for trial secretly visited by a number of the Khedive's eunuchs, who brutally assaulted and ill-treated them in their cells with a view of "breaking their spirit." Lastly, the Egyptian Government were permitted to declare

2 I have been recently asked to explain that the true reason why the "Times" so strongly supported us in our attempt at this critical juncture to obtain for Arabi a fair trial was the Macchiavellian one of forcing the British Government to undertake responsibilities which would entail their assumption of full authority in Egypt. I heard, however, nothing of this at the time, and I prefer still to believe that it was a generous impulse more worthy of the "Times's" better tradition and of Chenery's excellent heart.

that no counsel should be allowed to plead except in Arabic, thus excluding those we were sending to the prisoners help. These particulars were telegraphed me by Napier soon after his arrival and made us anxious.

All that the English Government had done in some measure to protect the prisoners from the Khedive's unregulated violence was to appoint two Englishmen who had a knowledge of Arabic to be present at the proceedings. These by a great stroke of good fortune were both honest and humane men, and, as it happened, old friends of my own, Sir Charles Wilson, whom I had travelled with in 1881 from Aleppo to Smyrna (not to be confounded with Sir C. Rivers Wilson), and Ardern Beaman, whom I had known at Damascus, and who now was Malet's official interpreter at the Agency. Both these men had been favourably impressed by Arabi's dignified bearing during the days of his detention as English prisoner of war, and now willingly gave Napier what little private help they could.

With Malet himself Napier succeeded at least so far as to get his status and that of the solicitor Eve, whom he had fortunately found at Cairo, recognized as legal representatives of Arabi's friends, though he could not obtain from him any definite promise or more than a vague assurance that English counsel would be allowed to represent Arabi himself. His applications to see his client were constantly put off by Malet by referring him to Riaz Pasha, the Khedivial Minister of the Interior, who as constantly refused, and in the meanwhile the trial was being pushed forward with all haste, so that it was clear to Napier that he was being played with and that the trial would be over before the question of the admissibility of English counsel had been plainly decided.

Things were standing thus when on the 12th of October I received a sudden warning from De la Warr, who was still in communication with the Foreign Office: "From what I hear, unless vigorous steps are taken, Arabi's life is in great danger. You have probably received information from Mr Napier." With this ill news I rushed off immediately to Button's rooms and there fortunately found him, and as all his information tallied with mine we agreed that a supreme appeal must be made to the public, and that the Foreign Office must be directly and strongly attacked and Gladstone compromised and forced into a declaration of policy. I consequently sat down and wrote a final letter to Gladstone, in which I spared nothing in my anger of accusation against Granville and was careful to insist on his own connection with the matter, and

his early sympathies with the Nationalist leader, and, without troubling ourselves to ask for an answer in Downing Street, Button "plumped" it into next morning's "Times," Chenery generously giving it full prominence and directing attention to it in a leading article. He had ascertained that the intention of the Government was that the trial should commence on Saturday, that sentence should be pronounced on Monday, and that Arabi's execution should instantly follow. It was already Friday, so we only had three days (one of them a Sunday when no newspapers are published) in which to rouse English feeling against this *coup de Jarnac*. Fortunately it was enough. I believe it was on this occasion that Bright, learning from my letter how things stood, went down to Gladstone and told him personally and plainly that he would be disgraced through all history as a renegade from his humaner principles if he allowed the perpetration of so great a crime. Be this as it may, the Foreign Office capitulated to us there and then, and, admitting our plea of the necessity of a fair trial, gave instructions to Malet to withdraw his opposition and treat the counsel sent to Arabi favourably. The following telegram from Napier announces our success: "Granville has directed Malet to require that Arabi shall be defended by English counsel. Proceedings expected to be lengthy."

I have thought it necessary to go into very minute detail in narrating these early phases of Arabi's trial, because in this way only is it possible to refute the false and absurd legend that has sprung up in Egypt to the effect that there was from the first some secret understanding between Gladstone and Arabi that his life should be spared. I can vouch for it, and the documents I have quoted in large measure prove it, that so far from having any sentiment of pity for, or understanding with, the "arch rebel," Gladstone had joined with Granville in the design to secure his death, through the Khedive's willing agency, by a trial which should be one merely of form and should disturb no questions, as the surest and speediest method of securing silence and a justification for their own huge moral errors of the last six months in Egypt. It was no qualm of conscience that prevented Gladstone from carrying it through to the end, only the sudden voice of the English public that at the last moment frightened him and warned him that it was dangerous for his reputation to go on with the full plan. This is the plain truth of the matter, whatever glosses Mr Gladstone's apologists may put on it to save his humane credit or whatever may be imagined about it by French political writers desirous of finding an explanation for a leniency shown to Arabi after the war, which has seemed to them inexplicable except on the supposition of some deep anterior intrigue between the English Prime Minister and the leader of the Egyptian rebellion.

This supreme point of danger past, it was not altogether difficult to foresee that the trial could hardly now end otherwise than negatively. A fair trial in open court with the Khedivial rubbish heap turned up with an English pitchfork and ransacked for forgotten crimes was a thought not to be contemplated by Tewfik without terror, while for the British Government as well there would be revelations destructive of the theory of past events constructed on the basis of official lies and their own necessity of finding excuses for their violence. The Sultan, too, had to be safeguarded from untimely revelations. The danger for the prisoners' lives was not over, but there seemed fair prospect of the thing ending in a compromise if we could not gain an acquittal. The changed state of things at Cairo is announced by Napier as early as the 16th October; and I will give the rest of my story of the trial mainly in the form of telegrams and letters.

Napier to Blunt, Oct. 16th
It is believed the Egyptian Government will try to quash the trial altogether, and that the chief prisoners will be directed to leave the country. I have not sufficient facts at my command to form a judgment on this point, but I think it not unlikely.

And again from Broadley, just arrived at Cairo:

Broadley to Blunt, Oct. 20th
Borelli Bey, the Government prosecutor, admitted frankly that the Egyptian Government had no law or procedure to go by, but suggested we should agree as to a procedure. He admitted the members of the Court were dummies and incompetent. He hoped I should smooth the Sultan and let down Tewfik as *doucement* as possible.

Napier to Blunt, Oct. 20th
I think now, we can guarantee a clean breast of the whole facts. It is as much as the Khedive's throne is worth to allow the trial to proceed.

The chief danger we had to face was a desire, not yet extinct at the Foreign Office, still by hook or crook, to establish some criminal charge against Arabi which should justify his death. Chenery writes to me 21st October: "Among important people there is a strong feeling against him [Arabi] on the alleged ground that he was concerned with,

or connived at, the massacre in Alexandria. The matter will almost certainly come up at the trial." This danger, however, did not at Cairo seem a pressing one, and certainly it was one that the prosecution was least likely to touch, the Khedive himself being there the culprit. Nothing is more noticeable in the interrogatories than the pains taken by the members of the Court to avoid questions tending in that direction and the absence on that point of all evidence which could incriminate any one. It was one, however, of great political importance to our Government that it should be proved against Arabi, for on it they had based the whole of their wilful insistence in forcing on a conflict, and without it their *moral* excuse for intervention fell flatly to the ground. The same might be said in regard to another absurd plea, insisted upon personally by Gladstone, that there had been an abuse of the white flag during the evacuation of Alexandria, a supposition which he had caught hold of in one of his speeches and made a special crime of, though in truth withdrawal of troops while a white flag is flying is permitted according to all the usages of war. Otherwise the coast seemed clear enough of danger, for it was evident that the British public would no longer allow our Government to sanction Arabi's death for mere political reasons.

Meanwhile at Cairo things were going prosperously. On the 22nd Broadley and Napier were admitted to Arabi's cell and speedily found in what he could tell them the groundwork of a strong defence. Arabi's attitude in prison was a perfectly dignified one, for whatever may have been his lack of physical courage, he had moral courage to a high degree, and his demeanour contrasted favourably with that of the large majority of those who had been arrested with him and did not fail to impress all that saw him. Without the smallest hesitation he wrote down in the next few days a general history of the whole of the political affairs in which he had been mixed, and in a form which was frank and convincing. No less outspoken was he in denouncing the ill-treatment he had received since he had been transferred to his present prison from those scoundrels, the Khedive's eunuchs, who had been sent at night by their master to assault and insult him. Not a few of the prisoners had been thus shamefully treated; yet by a singular lack of moral courage the greater number dared not put into plain words a crime, personally implicating the cowardly tyrant who had been replaced as master over them. Nothing is more lamentable in the depositions than the slavish attitude assumed by nearly all the deponents towards the Khedive's person, hated as he had been by them and despised not a month before. A more important event still was the recovery from their concealment of Arabi's most important papers, which had been hidden in his house and which he now directed should be sought out and placed in Broadley's hand. It was with great difficulty that his son and wife in their terror could be brought to allow the search – for they, too, had been "visited" by the Khedive's servants – but at last the precious documents were secured and brought to Broadley by Arabi's servant already mentioned, Mohammed Sid Ahmed. They proved of supreme value – including as they did the letters written by order of the Sultan to Arabi and others of a like compromising kind. The news of the discovery struck panic into the Palace and there seemed every chance that the trial would be abandoned.

Napier writing to me October 30th says: "The fact is I believe we are masters now, and that the Khedive and his crew would be glad to sneak out of the trial with as little delay as possible. The fidelity of Arabi's servant and the constancy of his wife enabled us to recover all his papers but one. They are now in a safe deposited in Beamen's room at the Consulate. . . . The Government cannot face our defence. They will offer a compromise, banishment with all property reserved. What better could be got? . . . This question will probably soon have to be considered."

It will be understood that the changed aspect of affairs at Cairo found its echo, and more than its echo, in the London Press. Cairo was full of newspaper correspondents, and Broadley, who was a past master in the arts of journalism, soon had them mostly on his side. His hospitality (at my expense) was lavish, and the "chicken and champagne" were not spared. Malet and Colvin, supreme in old days, were now quite unable to stem the torrent of news, and revelation followed revelation all destructive of the theory they had imposed on the Government, that Arabi and the army had been alone in opposing the English demands and that the National movement had been less than a universal one. Colvin was now become discredited at the Foreign Office as a false guide, and Malet's incapacity was at last fully recognized. Lord Granville, furious at our success, and seeing the political situation in Egypt drifting into a hopeless muddle, did what was probably his wisest course in submitting the whole matter to Lord Dufferin for a settlement. I had early notice from Button of this new move and that Dufferin's first business on arriving at Cairo would be to bring about a compromise of the trial. My letter of instructions to Broadley in view of the new situation thus created is worth inserting here:

Blunt to Broadley, Nov. 2, 1882

I wish to state over again my ideas and hopes in undertaking Arabi's defence and that of his companions, which if they are realized will repay me for the cost even though larger than I had originally thought probable. Of course the main object was to save the prisoners' lives, and that I think we may consider already accomplished, for public opinion has declared itself in England, and, the preliminary investigation having so entirely failed in the matter of the June riots and the burning of Alexandria, no evidence that now could be produced, and no verdict given by the judges could any longer place them in jeopardy. Since your arrival, however, and through your skill and good fortune, a flush of trumps has come into our hands: Instead of Arabi's papers being locked up in the Foreign Office they are in our possession, and, as you tell me to-day, our defence is perfect while we hold such a commanding position over the enemy that we can fairly dictate them terms. We cannot, therefore, be content with anything less than an honourable acquittal or the abandonment of the trial. At present the latter seems the most probable. Lord Dufferin has been ordered to Egypt; the Premier yesterday threw out a feeler for a compromise, and from everything I hear proposals will shortly be made for some arrangement of the affair by which the scandal and discredit of an exposure will be avoided. It depends, therefore, entirely on us to save not only Arabi's life but his honour and his freedom, and also I believe the lives and freedom of all the political prisoners inculpated with him.

I believe a strong attempt will be made by Lord Dufferin to get Arabi to agree to a detention in the Andaman Islands, or some part of the British Empire where he would remain a political prisoner treated with kindness but not suffered to be at large. I believe also he will endeavour to get from him a cession of his papers. Neither of these attempts must be allowed to succeed, and all proposals including them must be rejected. It is no business of ours to save the Sultan's or the Khedive's honour nor to save Lord Granville from embarrassment, and I shall consider our failure a great one if we do not get far more. I think Arabi should, in the first place, state that he demands a trial in order to clear his honour, and especially to demonstrate the innocence of those who acted with him during the war, viz., the whole nation, or, if not brought to trial, that the charges against them should be withdrawn as well as against himself. There should, in fact, be a general amnesty, also he should retain his papers, though probably he might give an understanding that they should not be published for a term of years. We cannot, under the circumstances, object absolutely to exile, because I suppose it would be argued the Khedive could exile him by decree, but even this I should make a matter of favour, because the Constitution of February, 1882 (which I hope you have closely studied, and which is a most valuable document from the fact of its having been confirmed by the Sultan as well as granted by the Khedive) forbids such exiling. Still the point would have to be conceded. We should, however, refuse anything like imprisonment. The Khedive might exile him from Egypt, and the Sultan from the Ottoman Empire, but neither would have a right to fix the place or nature of his abode beyond them.

Nor could the English Government, having handed Arabi to the Khedive for trial, let him be taken back untried to be dealt with as a criminal by England. The English Government has recognized this by refusing so to take him back. Still less could it imprison him if so taken without trial. It is, therefore, clear that unless tried and convicted he must leave Egypt a free man. Nor can he legally be deprived in Egypt of his rank and pay. But I should suppose that he will agree to retiring with military rank only, and a small maintenance to save him from actual poverty and the necessity of working with his hands. I think these terms would be dignified, and they are terms we can insist upon. Otherwise I urge the necessity of a defence tooth and nail, and I sincerely trust that you will not listen to any proposal which may be made of a *pro forma* trial and letting the Khedive down *doucement* [gently], as Borelli proposed. There should either be a real honest exposure of *all* the facts, or an honourable withdrawal of *all* the charges. I trust in you to co-operate with me fully in obtaining this result, without regard for the feelings of Consuls or Ambassadors or Viceroys. They are nothing to us, and our client's honour and cause are everything. Your diplomatic skill is, I have no doubt, a match for Lord Dufferin's, and it will be a great game to win. You have made Malet do what you wanted, and so you will make Dufferin do. If you achieve this we will not talk more about the fee. I enclose a letter of introduction to Lord Dufferin.

The following from Mr. Beaman, Malet's official interpreter, and a witness of unimpeachable authority, is of the highest historical importance. Beaman had been in charge of the Agency at Cairo during the last weeks before the bombardment, and being a good Arabic scholar knew more of the true state of affairs than any one employed there. He had been appointed a few days before the date of his letter to superintend, on Malet's part, the trial:

> Beaman to Blunt, Cairo, Nov. 6, 1882
> [. . .] This is our last day before the adjournment. . . . The Palace people here are in a great stew at the advent of Lord Dufferin, who arrives to-morrow. Broadley's arrival has been an agony to them, but this is the last blow. I believe Dufferin is a man who will quickly see through our friend Tewfik, and as I hear that his ears are open to everybody the temporary Embassy will be better informed, I expect, than the Agency has ever been. I had a great deal of intercourse with natives before the bombardment of all classes and parties, and knew the whole of the game from the four sides, English, Turkish, Arabi, and Tewfik. They were each quite distinct. As I could not have given my authorities, and as people would not have accepted my word for things I could have told, I kept my information for myself, but I have given some good hints to Sir Charles Wilson, who now has a fairer idea of the Egyptian question than any of our officials here. He is an extremely cautious man, with a great share of shrewdness and true judgment which he does not allow to be warped. Through him I have been able to get facts to Malet which I should never have told Malet himself. I think now that Malet has quite lost any respect he could ever have had for the Khedive. Throughout our proceedings he has acted with the greatest fairness to us, although dead against his own interests. . . . You know how deeply he was pledged to the Khedive, and it is quite bitter enough a cup to him to see his idol come down from the card house which is breaking up. . . . I think the Ibrahim Agha business alone is quite enough to show the Khedive in his true colours. I heard the whole story direct from the Palace, how the *titunji*, the Khedive's pipe bearer, had kissed the Khedive's hand, asked permission to spit in the faces of the prisoners, and it was on this that Sir Charles Wilson made inquiry and found it all true. Nevertheless, because it was evident that the Khedive had a very dirty piece of linen to be washed in the business, it was left alone. I suggested when all the witnesses swore falsely that the oath of triple divorce should be administered to them, and Sir Charles Wilson was in favour of it too, but it was hushed up. His Highness's own family now no longer pretend to deny it among themselves. And this is the man for whom we came to Egypt.

If I was not bound by my position here not to advise Broadley, I could give him hints enough for his cross-examination to turn out the Khedive tomorrow. I hope it will come out nevertheless. The first man to be got rid of is Riaz. He is playing the very devil through Egypt. The other day he said: "The Egyptians are serpents and the way to prevent serpents from propagating is to crush them under foot. So will I crush the Egyptians." And he is doing it.

Matters stood thus in the first week of November, the date of Lord Dufferin's arrival at Cairo. It was a fortunate circumstance for us who were defending the cause of justice in England that Parliament that year happened to be holding an autumn session. It brought to our aid in the House of Commons several Members of first rate fighting value – Churchill, Wolff, Gorst, Lawson, Labouchere, besides Robert Bourke, Lord John Manners, W. J. Evelyn, and the present Lord Wemyss, of the regular Tory opposition, with two or three Irish Members. Percy Wyndham, to his credit, was the only Tory who had voted with the minority of twenty-one against the war.

Source: Wilfred Scawen Blunt. *The Secret History of the English Occupation of Egypt.* London: T. Fisher Unwen, 1907, pp. 426–59.

Note

What Disraeli called "peace with honour," Blunt referred to as "peace with plunder." Blunt (1840–1922) was a close friend and defender of Ahmed Arabi, whom he had met during his first visit to Egypt. Blunt's interest in Egyptian affairs continued throughout his life, and he maintained a residence there as well as an attachment to Arabian horses and poetry. His wife, Anne Blunt, shared his commitments. He was also a committed critic in print and practice of Britain's imperial policies generally, and eventually became a member of parliament. The four volumes of his diaries describe his activism relating to Egypt, India, the Sudan, and Ireland.

42   Thomas Cook and Son: Daily Itinerary of the Twenty Days' Voyage – Cairo to Aswan and Back, $340.75 (1929–30)

Passengers are respectfully requested to read carefully the following Itineraries, from which they will gather information as to the approximate time of arrival at and departure from each of the stopping stations, and the arrangements for sightseeing. In order to avoid confusion and unnecessary trouble on the river banks, passengers must not leave the steamer until the dragoman or manager has announced that the donkeys are ready, intimation of which will be given by sounding the gong or ringing the bell.

First Day (Wednesday)   The steamer sails punctually at 10 a.m. from the landing stage of Thos. Cook & Son, Ltd., above the Kasr-el-Nil Bridge. The first impression of the Nile is a delightful one, for Cairo, viewed from a river steamer, is a very different place from the bustling town just left. Stately palaces on either bank, countless minarets of mosques, the noble Mokkattam hills and the Citadel at their foot form a fitting introduction to the beauties of the Nile, whilst the three great pyramids of Giza rise in stately dignity over the western plain.

The Tura quarries, whence the stone for the Pyramids was hewn, and Helwan, famous for its sulphur baths, are passed, the steamer arriving at Bedrechen soon after lunch. Here donkeys will be in readiness for the ride to the site of ancient Memphis.

It is difficult to imagine that one of the most famous capitals of antiquity once stood where now is but a picturesque grove of palm trees. Yet all that remains in view is a beautiful alabaster Sphinx and two colossal statues of Rameses II. An hour's ride further on, however, lies the vast Necropolis, in itself sufficient proof of the extent of the ancient city, which tells more of the life of its inhabitants than any ruin could do. The Step Pyramid of Sakkara, the tomb of King Zoser, is more ancient than the Pyramids of Giza. Early in 1925 a statue of Zoser was discovered bearing an inscription which confirms the view that this was his place of burial. Excavations now being made have revealed the proto-doric columns of Zoser's time shown in the illustration overleaf. The Serapeum is the Tomb of the Sacred Bulls, and the Tombs of Ti and Ptah-Hetep, wealthy citizens of ancient Memphis, offer in their mural decorations realistic representations of life in Egypt over 5,000 years ago.

Ample time is allowed for visiting, and after an hour's ride the steamer is reached about 5 p.m. The steamer will proceed south to the neighbourhood of Ayat (56 miles from Cairo).

Second Day (Thursday)   Leaving Ayat at daylight, the steamer passes Beni Suef, the first town of importance to be seen, and the "Gebel el-Teyr" or Bird Mountain, a precipitous cliff rising sheer out of the water. Tradition relates that all the birds of Egypt assemble here once a year, and, when departing, leave one solitary bird on guard until the following year. Upon the summit stands a Coptic convent. The boat will anchor for the night near Minia (157 miles from Cairo).

Third Day (Friday)   The steamer arrives at Beni Hassan in the morning, and an excursion is made to the grotto of Speos Artemedos and to the rock tombs, a ride of about forty minutes. Architecturally these tombs are of great interest, as are the scenes painted on the walls, representing carpenters, boat builders, bakers and others at work, and a company of merchants from the East bringing wares for sale in Egypt. The tombs of Ameni Amenamah and Khnum-Hotep will be visited.

Half an hour's ride brings the passengers to the steamer, which will proceed as far as Manfalut for the night (224 miles from Cairo).

Fourth Day (Saturday)   Asyut is reached during the morning, after passing through the Barrage lock. This Barrage is designed to hold up the river level during the spring and summer months and ensure delivery of water into the Ibrahimia Canal during low Nile. The Canal, commencing at Asyut, is nearly 200 miles long and supplies middle Egypt and the Faiyum with water.

Donkeys will be in readiness for half an hour's ride through the town to the foot of the mountain to visit the tomb of Hapzefai, Prince of the Nome in the reign of Usertesen I., and the tomb of Kheti. It is well worth climbing to the top of the mountain, whence one of the finest views of the Nile valley is obtained.

The principal of the American college at Asyut extends a cordial invitation to passengers to visit the boys' college (a few minutes' walk or ride from the steamer) and the girls' school in the town (250 miles from Cairo).

Fifth Day (Sunday)   The steamer leaves Asyut at daybreak. Early risers should not miss the delightful views over the Nile valley after sunrise. For a couple of hours the delicate tints on the lofty sandstone cliffs, the broad fields of clover or corn at their feet, the clusters of mud hut and palm tree that form the native villages, and the broad bosom of the river itself, form an irresistible appeal to the lover of colour, whilst the first low rays of the sun strike the white sails of the picturesque "gyassas" or the whitewashed wall of some villa nestling on the river bank.

This will be a restful day as the steamer proceeds southward. The entire life of Egypt is found on or near the banks of the river, whilst picturesque sailing boats, laden with the produce of the land, are met at every bend. The steamer will anchor for the night near Girga (343 miles from Cairo).

Sixth Day (Monday)   Leaving early in the morning, Baliana, the starting point for visiting Abydos, is passed. The visit to this beautiful temple is postponed until the return journey, as the ruins are so grand and magnificent that they lose none of their charm and novelty even after Karnak has been seen. The steamer, therefore, continues the voyage, passing through the beautiful gorge of Abu Shusha, and the new Nag-Hamadi Barrage now in course of construction.

One item of interest illustrating the customs of Egyptian life occurs shortly after passing the Nag-Hamadi bridge. A small boat shoots out from the bank and slips alongside, and into this is dropped a bag of alms from the ship's crew. The occupants of the boat are the descendants of Sheikh Selim, who, it is said, sat stark naked on the bank at this spot for 53 years. He was believed to possess great powers in assisting navigation and every craft passing upstream gave alms for his support. He died in 1891, but his family still collects toll from every boat. His tomb will be seen on the bank.

The steamer will probably reach Dendera that evening (417 miles from Cairo).

Seventh Day (Tuesday)   It is but half an hour's ride from the steamer to the temple of Dendera. This wonderfully preserved temple is probably but little older than the beginning of the Christian era. It is dedicated to Hathor, the Egyptian Venus, and is closely associated with the beautiful Cleopatra. The famous portraits of Cleopatra and her son Cæsarion are on the end wall of the exterior. The famous Zodiac of Dendera, now in the Bibliothèque Nationale in Paris, was taken from the shrine of Osiris on the temple roof. A duplicate will be seen in the original position.

On returning from the temple, the voyage is continued; towards sunset the massive pylons of Karnak come into view, followed soon after by the colonnades of the Temple of Luxor, close to which the steamer is moored.

It is small wonder that the ancient Egyptians chose this site for their capital of Thebes. On both sides of the river the precipitous limestone cliffs retreat into the distance, leaving a broad and fertile plain, which no doubt then, as now, offered a pleasing prospect of prosperity. They could hardly have selected a more picturesque spot, and to this day the charm of Luxor is only rivalled by that pearl of Egypt, Aswan.

The steamer remains at Luxor for three days (460 miles from Cairo).

Eighth Day (Wednesday)   The morning is devoted to a visit to the great temples at Karnak, notably the Temple of Chonsu and the great Temple of Amen, justly considered one of the wonders of the world. The great Hypostyle Hall, although only a fragment of this colossal temple, covers an area equal to that of Notre Dame at Paris. It consists of 134 columns ranged in a space of 6,000 square yards, and for pure impressiveness is only equalled by the great Temple of Abu Simbel. The effect is particularly fine by moonlight.

The great Temple of Luxor is visited after tea.

Ninth Day (Thursday)   After an early breakfast the river is crossed in small boats to the western bank, where donkeys will be waiting for a ride of half an hour to the Temple of Kurna, and thence in about forty minutes to the Tombs of the Kings. The principal tombs are readily accessible, and are lighted by electricity. The walls are covered with exquisite paintings depicting the deceased king, accompanied by the sun-god, sailing through the underworld at night, finally rising with the sun to a new life in the next world. The tombs of Rameses IX, Rameses VI, and Seti I, in which the reliefs surpass all others in beauty of execution and even rival those of Abydos, are visited.

Passengers will then go over the Libyan Chain, commanding a glorious view over the Nile valley, descending near the "Chalet Hatasu," a rest house erected by Thos. Cook & Son, expressly for the use of travellers under their arrangements. Here lunch will be served. The terrace temple of Queen Hatasu is then visited, and on the way back to the river the Rameseum and the famous Colossi of Memnon are passed, the steamer being reached about 4.30 p.m.

Tenth Day (Friday)   After crossing the river again, it is half an hour's donkey ride to the Rameseum – the great Temple of Rameses the

Great – after visiting which another short ride brings us to the small temple of Deir-el-Medina (the judgment hall of Osiris), and to the temple of Medinet-Haboo, which was the palace and great temple of Rameses III, containing also a small temple of Thotmes III.

The tombs of Queen Nefertari, the beautiful wife of Rameses II, and Prince Amon-her-Khopshaf, the young son of Rameses III, will also be visited.

Lunch is taken on the return to the steamer.

Eleventh Day (Saturday)   The steamer leaves Luxor early in the morning, and passes the Barrage of Isna by means of a lock. This Barrage was constructed in 1906–9 to regulate the irrigation of the province of Qena. Isna is reached about 10 a.m. and a visit is paid to the temple, which is only a short walk from the river side. This temple is of the Ptolemaic period, but so far only the vestibule has been excavated, the remainder being completely buried under the town.

The steamer leaves again about 11 a.m., proceeding as far as Edfu, where the Temple of Horus stands in almost perfect preservation. This temple is, in fact, practically complete, and, by comparison, enables one to visualize the wonderful monuments at Karnak and Thebes. An ascent to the summit of the pylon is recommended, the view being exceptionally attractive, not only over the temple itself but also over the whole countryside.

Ample time is allowed for inspection, after which the steamer may proceed further south.

Twelfth Day (Sunday)   The voyage is resumed early in the morning, passing through the gorge of Silsila, with its vast quarries, bearing the cartouches of Egyptian kings back for several thousand years. At Komombo a stay is made for about an hour to visit the temple, which stands in a commanding position on the bank of the river. This temple is duplex, and in that respect unique. One shrine is dedicated to Sebek, the evil deity, and the other to Amen, the representative of God as personified in the Sun. Many of the paintings are as brilliant now as when first produced. One item of interest which should not be missed amongst the mural decorations, is a representation of surgical instruments in use at the time. It is a surprising revelation that many of them can be recognized as identical with the instruments used at the present day.

As the steamer approaches Aswan the scenery undergoes a complete change. Vegetation ceases in places and the desert often extends down to the river banks. The sandstone cliffs have disappeared and huge granite rocks abound, even in the middle of the stream. As a rule the steamer arrives at Aswan after lunch.

There is no doubt that Aswan is the most delightful spot in Egypt. Situated at the foot of the First Cataract, where the Nile is dotted with innumerable islands and rocks, surrounded on all sides by the desert, equipped with excellent hotels and a centre for novel and interesting excursions, this picturesque little town offers all that can be desired by the traveller in search of health-giving pleasure.

Special mention must be made of the Cataract Hotel, which, like Aswan itself, has a charm and individuality differing from everything else in Egypt.

Aswan is 595 miles from Cairo by river.

Thirteenth Day (Monday)　After an early breakfast, donkeys will be taken for a twenty minutes' ride to the granite quarries, where lies an unfinished obelisk of colossal dimensions, still undetached from the living rock. Another forty minutes' ride and the Temple of Philæ comes into view. Small boats are taken to visit this beautiful temple, but it should be pointed out that November and December are the best months for the visit, as afterwards the level of the water above the dam is raised and the temple thereby partly submerged.

The boats then sail down stream to the great Aswan dam, constructed in 1898–1902, the largest of its kind and one of the most impressive sights in Egypt. The dam will be crossed by trolley, and lunch is usually served in the picturesque chalet, overlooking the dam, with the reservoir above and the cataract below.

The dam is again crossed by trolley, and the donkeys are remounted for the ride back to the steamer by a different route.

Passangers for Abu Simbel and the Second Cataract sail from the Dam to the "Thebes" near Philæ.

Fourteenth Day (Tuesday)　Small boats will be taken to visit the Island of Elephantine, including the famous Nilometer and the museum. The town of Aswan and its bazaars will also prove of great interest, and the view from the terrace of the Cataract Hotel should not be missed.

All passengers who take any interest in Egyptian antiquities should visit the painted tombs of Mechu, Ben and Se-Renpu, situated on the western side of Aswan, which were opened out at the expense of Lord (then Sir Francis) Grenfell. They could be visited in the evening, but we strongly advise that they should be seen before breakfast in the morning, when the sun shines straight into the tombs, and shows out the colouring most distinctly.

Fifteenth Day (Wednesday)　The steamer leaves Aswan early in the morning and steams straight through to Luxor, which is usually reached the same evening.

Sixteenth Day (Thursday)　The morning is spent at Luxor in order to give those who wish an opportunity of revisiting any of the monuments.

The steamer leaves Luxor at 11 a.m. and will proceed as far as Nag-Hamadi.

Seventeenth Day (Friday)　Baliana is reached after breakfast, and donkeys are taken for a one and a half hours' ride to the magnificent ruins at Abydos. The wonderful temple of Seti I is the apotheosis of ancient Egyptian art. It differs from all other temples in having seven sanctuaries instead of one, whilst the workmanship of the inscriptions and reliefs is incomparable. Here is the famous "Tablet of Abydos" – a list of seventy-six kings of Egypt, beginning with Mena, the first king of Egypt, the most wonderful genealogical record in the world.

Luncheon is taken in the temple itself, after which a visit is paid to the temple of Rameses II.

The steamer may proceed further north that evening.

Eighteenth Day (Saturday)　Asyut is usually reached about noon and after a short stay the steamer will pass through the lock and proceed north.

Nineteenth Day (Sunday)　The voyage is continued northwards, passing Minia, "Gebel-el-Teyr" and Beni Suef.

Twentieth Day (Monday)　Passing Wasta in the early morning, the Pyramid of Meidun, or the "false pyramid," comes into view, and Cairo is normally reached in the afternoon.

Passengers may remain on board the steamer until after breakfast on Tuesday morning, if they wish to do so.

Notes on the Return Voyage from Aswan

On the downward voyage the steamers stop for sightseeing at Luxor, Baliana (for Abydos), and Asyut. As the half-day stoppage at Luxor is simply to enable those who wish to see a second time any particular object they are interested in, no fixed programme will be announced, and passengers are requested to inform the dragoman or the Manager the night before what they specially wish to see, so that arrangements may be made for donkeys and guides.

Any passengers wishing to visit the western suburb of Thebes on the downward voyage must leave early in the morning to ensure being back in time for the steamer, which leaves at 11.0 a.m.

Should the steamer, through any unforeseen circumstances, not arrive at Luxor until the morning after leaving Aswan, it must nevertheless leave again at 11.0 a.m., to ensure the necessary time at Abydos.

Hints on Outfit

Passengers' Mail, etc.

Our advice to travellers is: "Come out to Egypt and the Nile just as you would travel anywhere else in Spring or Autumn." Among the articles of real use are helmets, good wideawakes, "Terai," or other shady hats; these can be obtained in Cairo. For ladies, some suitable dress, such as the divided skirt, is also desirable for donkey riding. No one need be afraid of great heat during the Nile voyage on board a steamer; on the contrary, a warm rug, shawl, or a good overcoat should be taken, as the mornings and evenings are cool, and even during the day, when steaming against the wind, it is sometimes cold. Strong walking shoes are essential for sightseeing, and a seat stick is invaluable.

Letters and Telegrams

The Cairo Postal Administrations have established an office on our premises for dealing with all mail matter addressed through Thos. Cook & Son, Ltd. Letters, etc., should be addressed: (Name), care of Thos. Cook & Son, Ltd., Cairo. They will be re-forwarded by special mail-bag to the steamers up river, Telegrams to passengers should be addressed: (Name), care of Cook, Cairo. They can be retransmitted up river.

Letters for Europe and America may be posted at any station where the steamer stops, and they will be dispatched by first mail to destination.

Telegrams can be dispatched to any part of the world from all important places on the river.

Passports

The traveller must hold a valid passport bearing visa(s) of a Consular representative in the United Kingdom for the country or countries to or through which he is proceeding. He must be careful to see that the endorsement and visas fully cover the period and route, as neglect of this may involve him in serious difficulties. Passports are obtainable through any of our Offices.

Money

The Travellers' Cheques issued by us in denominations of £5, £10, £20, in sterling or dollars, will be found a convenient form in which to carry funds in the Orient and elsewhere. Besides being cashed at our Offices in Lower Egypt and in Palestine, payment of them can be obtained at Luxor, Aswan and Khartoum at current rate of exchange. They are also issued at the Cairo, Alexandria and Jerusalem Offices. We undertake the remittance of money by cheque and telegram between our principal Offices.

Guide Books

Cook's Handbook for Egypt and the Sudan, by Sir E. A. Wallis Budge, M. A., Keeper of the Egyptian and Assyrian Antiquities in the British Museum. A new and revised edition (1925). Price 20/–.

Cook's Handbook for Palestine and Syria, by Roy Elston, new edition (1929), revised by H. C. Luke, B.Litt., M. A., Late Assistant-Governor of Jerusalem, with an appendix on the historical interest of the Sites and Monuments of Palestine by Professor J Garstang, M. A., B.Litt., D. Sc. (Oxon.), Director of the British School of Archæology in Jerusalem, Director of the Department of Antiquities in Palestine. Price 10/6.

Cook's Handbook for Jerusalem and Judea (1924). Price 4/–.

Laundry

Passengers on the Nile steamers may utilize the facilities afforded by the hotels at Luxor and Aswan for laundry purposes. The same facilities are afforded by the hotels in Palestine.

Hotels

Hotel accommodation may be secured before leaving for Egypt through any of our Offices, at any class of hotel, from single bedrooms to suites of apartments on any floor, with whatever aspect may be desired. *En pension* terms are also arranged for an extended stay.

Baggage Insurance

All travellers are strongly advised to make use of Cook's system of baggage insurance, particulars of which can be obtained at any Office.

Special Notice

Thos. Cook & Son and/or Thos. Cook & Son, Ltd, give notice that the arrangements shown in this Programme, excepting such as apply strictly to their Steamers and Dahabeahs, are made by them in their capacity as Agents only. All tickets and coupons are issued by them, and all arrangements for transport or conveyance or for hotel accommodation, are made by them as Agents upon the express condition that they shall not be liable for any injury, damage, loss, accident, delay or irregularity which may be occasioned either by reason of any defect in any vehicle, or through the acts or default of any company or person engaged in conveying the passenger or in carrying out the arrangements of the tour(s), or otherwise in connection there-

with, or of any hotel proprietor or servant. Such conveying, etc., is subject to the laws of the Country where the conveyance, etc., is provided.

Baggage is at "owner's risk" throughout the tour(s) unless insured. Small articles, coats, wraps, umbrellas and other hand baggage are entirely under the care of the passenger, who is cautioned against the risk attached to these being left in conveyances when sightseeing.

Thos. Cook & Son and/or Thos. Cook & Son, Ltd, accept no responsibility for losses or additional expense due to delays or changes in train, steamer or other services, sickness, weather, strikes, war, quarantine, or other causes. All such losses or expenses will have to be borne by the passenger.

Source: Programme of Arrangements for Visiting Egypt, the Nile, Sudan, Palestine and Syria. New York: Thomas Cook and Son. 1929–30 Season, pp. 21–31, 47–8.

Note

Thomas Cook (1808–92) was a significant innovator of the "conducted tour" in the nineteenth century. The first excursion that he offered was between Leicester and Longborough in 1841, on a special train bound for a temperance meeting. Cook also ran outings to the Great Exhibition in 1851 [see Part V]. In 1856, Thomas Cook altered his first railway tour of Europe; in the 1860s the company, now trading as Thomas Cook and Son, began tours to the USA.

Part III

The Great Game

Chapter Nine

The Indian Rebellion of 1857–1858

Introduction

"Anyone who tries to tell the story of Cawnpore must subsist on a sometimes sparse diet of questionable dispositions, muddled accounts, dubious journals, and narratives of shell-shocked survivors with axes to grind" (Ward 1996: 555). For these and other reasons, unequivocal representation of the Rebellion or Sepoy Uprising is, perhaps, an impossible endeavor. Ambiguities and contradictions are evident from the very start, as the descriptions of the events of 1857–8 are referred to variously as a military mutiny, a national revolt, and a native rebellion or uprising. Were the events the outcome of Indian backwardness and native superstition, or were they the result of native treachery, sinister plotting, and insurgence? In the days and months after the events, politicians in the

British Parliament argued and debated these questions in an attempt to determine whether the rebellious actions were confined to the military or, more gravely, whether they were, as Benjamin Disraeli inquired, "a reflex of the national mind" Were the Sepoys' actions "mere barbaric movements" or something greater and less containable? Was the Rebellion an extraordinary event or did the explosion of violence foreshadow the end of empire?

Some historians suggest that the Company's administrative and legislative policies were one of the primary causes for the violent rebellion; for example, the adoption restrictions implemented by Lord Dalhousie, Governor-General of India (1847–56), challenged native rulers' system of inheritance. Indian adoption policies guaranteed Indian rulers an heir in the case of the death or murder of the inheritor of the estate; childless couples, like the Raja and Rani of Jhansi, also utilized this tradition.

Lord Dalhousie perfected an existing administrative policy that gave the Company the right to refuse an adopted son as the new ruler of a native state. The Company would declare the throne "lapsed," in other words, vacant, and would then annex the ruler's property and place it under Company "protection" (ownership) and administrative rule.

Other historians discount the Company's political and administrative policies and native reactions to them as significant factors in the Rebellion. The activities of Missionary Societies and rumors of their attempts at widespread conversion are pointed to as cause for native unrest. Some also suggest that the Rebellion was provoked by native rulers who were primarily concerned about their waning wealth and power; these rulers are alleged to have duped the masses and utilized India's criminal element in the attempt to regain control of their territories. Their "call to arms" was believed to have been disseminated across the land with the use of seditiously encoded chapatties, an Indian bread. Still other accounts blame the revolt on Indian "superstition" – a general description of Indian religious beliefs and practices – the Indian and Muslim soldiers' "hysterical" aversion to the pig and cow fat reputedly required to grease the cartridges of their Enfield rifles.

The Rebellion caused a flurry of responses and interpretations and created an explosion of visual and narrative representations. But Government response to the events was swift and decisive: the Company's rule over India would come to an end. For political, practical and economic reasons, a "better" system of government had to be implemented.

MC

Additional Reading

Anonymous (William Jonah Shepard). *The Guilty Men of 1857: Failure of England's Great Mission to India* (1879). Delhi, 1987.

Bond, Ruskin. *A Flight of Pigeons* (juvenile literature). Bombay, 1980.

Chaudhuri, Sashi Bhusan. *English Historical Writings on the Indian Mutiny, 1857–59*. Calcutta, 1979.

Dhutt, Utpal. *The Great Rebellion 1857* (play). Calcutta, 1986.

Farell, J. G. *The Siege of Krishnapur* (novel). London, 1973.

Hilton, Richard. *The Indian Mutiny: A Centenary History*. London, 1957.

Hutchinson, David. *Annals of the Indian Rebellion*. London, 1974.

Sengupta, Kaylan Kumar. *Recent Writings on the Revolt of 1857: A Survey*. New Delhi, 1975.

Ward, Andrew. *Our Bones Are Scattered: The Cawnpore Massacres and the Indian Mutiny of 1857*. New York, 1996.

Films

J. Lee Thompson. *Flame Over India* (1950).

Satyajit Ray. *The Chess Players*. Urdu title: *Shatraaj Ke Khiladi* (1977).

Shyam Benegal. *Junoon*. English titles: *The Possessed*, and *A Flight of Pigeons* (1978).

43   Timeline of Significant Events

1857	May 2	Rebellion of the 7th Irregulars at Lucknow
	May 10	Rebellion at Meerut
	May 11	Rebels take Delhi
	June 5	Rebellion at Cawnpore
	June 30	Siege at Lucknow
	July 5	Victory of Sepoy army at Shahganj near Agra
	July 7	Havelock marches to Cawnpore
	July 16	First Battle of Cawnpore
	August 13	Defeat of Kunwar Singh at Jagdishpur
	September 21	King of Delhi surrenders to Hodson
	November 17	Relief of Lucknow by Sir Colin Campbell
	December 6	British reclaim Cawnpore
1858	March 20	Canning's Oudh Proclamation
	March 21	Final relief at Lucknow
	June 1	Tatya Tope and the Rani of Jhansi seize Gwalior
	June 17	Death of the Rani of Jhansi
	August 2	Transfer of the British East India Company to the Crown
	November 1	Queen Victoria's Proclamation
1859	July	Lord Canning declared first Viceroy of India

44   Rulers and Rebels: Major Figures in the Indian Rebellion

Rulers

Lord Dalhousie   James Andrew Broun Ramsay (1812–60); 10th Earl of Dalhousie, Governor-

General of India (1847–56). Dalhousie was recognized as the maker of modern India. His famous and infamous policies of annexation were cited as one of the primary causes of the unrest in India. Dalhousie implemented the Doctrine of Lapse, the policy under which Indian lands and kingdoms were seized and put under British control. "Lapsed" territories were those allegedly lacking a legitimate heir. Dalhousie refused to recognize the Indian rulers' practice of adopting a male child to guarantee an heir to the throne. Dalhousie's aggressive annexation policies seized Satara (1848), Punjab (1849), Jhansi (1854), Nagpur (1854), and Oudh (Oude) in 1856. Oudh was seized against a living ruler's will, based on Dalhousie's accusations of "native" misgovernment. Dalhousie planned the expansion of the Indian railway and telegraph systems; promoted the completion of the Grand Trunk Road; promoted the education of girls; suppressed the practices of infanticide and human sacrifice; and centralized the postal system. However, his annexation policies, and the Indian responses to them, are central to understanding Dalhousie's Indian career.

Sir Colin Campbell ("Old Careful") (1792–1863);   Commander-in-Chief of the British forces during the Indian Rebellion. Campbell was born in Glasgow, Scotland, the son of a carpenter. He served in the War of 1812 against the United States and in the Opium War in China in 1842. Campbell's rise in the military was a slow one, despite his distinguished service in both of those wars; his humble origins are suspected of having affected his career advancement. Campbell was eventually knighted for his service in the Second Sikh War (1848–9). He was appointed Commander-in-Chief at the outbreak of the Rebellion. Campbell acquired his nickname as the result of his military caution and careful protection of the men under his leadership; he was both criticized and praised for these attributes. Campbell was raised to the peerage in 1858 for his service and leadership during the Rebellion. He was buried at Westminster Abbey.

General Henry Havelock (Sir Henry); (1795–1857).   General Havelock first distinguished himself while serving in the First Anglo-Burmese War (1824–6), and later, during the First Afghan War (1839–42). He was promoted in 1843 while serving as an interpreter during the first Gwalior Campaign. Havelock also served under Sir James Outram during the Persian Expedition in 1857; he was called to India at the outbreak of the Rebellion.

General Havelock fought against Nana Sahib at Lucknow, which he reclaimed upon his fourth attempt. Havelock was rewarded with a knighthood (the Order of the Bath) for rescuing Lucknow and was promoted to Major-General; however, he died from dysentery before learning of his promotion.

John Laird Mair Lawrence, First Baron ("Savior of the Punjab"); (1811–79).   Lawrence first served in India as an assistant judge in Delhi; he maintained this position for 19 years. During these years, Lawrence was renowned for his opposition to the talukdas (tax collectors) and their mistreatment of the peasantry; his sympathy for the common people would later become the cause of a rift between Lawrence and his older brother, Henry Lawrence, the President of the Board of Administration in the Punjab. At age 35, Lawrence was appointed to the newly annexed Jullundur region as a reward for his service during the First Sikh War (1845–6). Lawrence's nickname paid tribute to the judge's economic, social, and political reforms in the region; he established courts and police posts, and suppressed female infanticide and sati. Lawrence was made a baronet and Knight of the Grand Cross of Bath for successfully negotiating a treaty with the Afghan ruler Dost Mohammad Khan. He was later appointed Viceroy and Governor-General (1864). While serving in this capacity, Lawrence supported Indian education, but resisted the appointment of Indians to high positions in the Civil Service.

Sir Henry Montgomery Lawrence; (1806–1857).   Henry Lawrence was a distinguished soldier and administrator who was placed in charge of Ferozepur in the Punjab (1839). Lawrence would later be appointed resident of Lahore (1846). He was knighted in 1848 for his reform activities (sati, forced labor, infanticide) and for his suppression of mutinies in Kangra and the Kasmir. A specialist in Indian and Oriental Languages (Urdu, Hindi, Persian), Henry Lawrence was appointed President of the Board of Administration in the Punjab (1849). During this period of service, he and his brother John Lawrence, the finance supervisor of the region, quarreled over financial reforms. John favored the peasants, while Henry championed the Sikh aristocracy. The brothers' disagreement caused the younger John to request a transfer out of the region. In 1857, Henry Lawrence was assigned to Oudh. He was mortally wounded at the siege of Lucknow and died before learning that he had been appointed provisional Governor-General.

Viscount Canning ("Clemency Canning"), Charles John, 1st Earl, (1812–63); Governor-General of

India (1857); first Viceroy of India (1858). Viscount Canning began his career as a statesman serving as a member of parliament in 1836. He later served as undersecretary for foreign affairs in Sir Robert Peel's Cabinet (1841). While serving as Governor-General of India, Canning refused to succumb to the public cries of bloodletting and widespread vengeance against the Indians during and after the Rebellion. He was vilified by some for being cowardly and traitorous. His July 1858 policy of conciliation and his insistence on calm and reasonable justice for the Indian rebels and citizens earned him his nickname. Canning became the first Viceroy of India when the British East India Company was turned over to the Crown. He was given an earldom in 1859.

Rebels

Lakshmi Bai, Maharani   b. November 19, 1835, at Varanasi, Uttar Pradesh; daughter of Shri Moropant Tambe and widow of Raja Gangadhar Rao. Her original name was Manikarnika. Became regent of Jhansi State after the death of her husband in 1835. The British refused to recognise her or her adopted son, Damodar Rao. Took up arms against the British seizure of her State. Attacked the British forces and drove them out of Jhansi in June 1857. Inflicted further defeats on the British at Mauranipur and Barwasagar and became the most powerful rebel leader of the 1857 revolt. Her army was further strengthened when the rulers of Banpur and Shahgarh in Bundelkhand became her allies. Fought valiantly against the attacks by the British forces under Sir Hugh Rose. The battle lasted about two weeks and she had to escape to Kalpi due to British pressure. She was joined at Kalpi by the forces of Rao Sahib and Tatya Tope. Their combined army fought bitter battles at Koonch and Kalpi. Due to adverse circumstances, she had to proceed to Gwalior. Set up the Peshwa's authority at that place. Pursued by the British troops, she decided to have a showdown. Personally commanded her forces wearing male attire. Fought against the superior British forces with great courage and bravery, but was mortally wounded in the battle at Kotah-ki-Sarai in Gwalior on June 18, 1858. Her body was cremated by her soldiers in the nearby garden of Baba Ganga Das, now known as Phool Bagh. After independence, a memorial was constructed at the spot to perpetuate the memory of her heroic deeds and martyrdom.

Nana Saheb alias *Dhondu Pant* Resident of Bithoor, near Kanpur, Uttar Pradesh; s. of Shri Madhav Rao Narayan Bhat. Adopted by Peshwa Baji Rao II in 1827; Inherited the title and estates bequeathed by the Peshwa in a written testament of 1841. Made a futile appeal to the Court of Directors of the East India Company against the decision of the Governor-General-in-Council to discontinue the grant of a pension of Rs. 8 lakhs to him. Participated in the Great Revolt of 1857 as one of the principal leaders of the revolutionary forces. Defeated the British forces, declared himself the Peshwa and assumed control of the revolutionary government at Kanpur. Reorganised the civil and military administration with the assistance of a Council of Advisers which included Bala Saheb, Baba Bhat, Azimullah Khan and Tatya Tope. Took part in many encounters with the British troops and fought for every inch of the ground during the battle of Kanpur before the British commander, General Havelock, could enter the city on July 17, 1857. Reorganised his army and marched to Avadh where his troops caused severe harrassment to Havelock's force. Sent two envoys to Chandernagore, a French possession in Bengal, to negotiate and conclude an alliance with the French Emperor, Napoleon III. Proceeded to Kalpi to take charge of the Avadh forces. Launched an attack to recapture Kanpur in December 1857, but could not succeed although his troops surrounded the city in a semi-circle. Proclaimed as the Peshwa in June 1858 by Lakshmi Bai, the patriotic Rani of Jhansi, who led her army against the British at Gwalior. Facing heavy odds, he was forced to retreat. The British troops pursued him for the next six months after the defeat of his forces in quick succession. Escaped into Nepal and is believed to have died of fever on September 24, 1859, in the Dang district of Nepal.

Kunwar Singh b. about 1782 at v. Jagdishpur, Distt. Shahabad, Bihar; Eldest son of Shri Sahibzada Singh; Owner of the large Jagdishpur Estate which he developed and expanded. The management of his estate was taken over by the British as he faced financial difficulties caused by family litigation. Took a very prominent part in the Great Revolt of 1857 as the principal leader of the anti-British forces in eastern India. Joined the revolutionary forces as they reached Arrah on July 26, 1857. Proclaimed himself to be the ruler of Shahabad. Entered into correspondence with other rebel leaders like Nana Saheb and persuaded other chiefs in Bihar to revolt. Defeated the British forces at Arrah, but failed to stop their advance. Dislodged from Jagdishpur, he marched towards Mirzapur and threatened Rewa and part of Allahabad district from a position of vantage.

Moved to Banda where the Nawab had already identified himself with the rebel cause. Went to Kalpi on Nana Saheb's invitation to participate in the assault on Kanpur. Visited Lucknow, where he was warmly received by Birjis Qadr, invested with a high position of honour and granted a *firman* for taking over Azamgarh. Occupied the town after defeating the British forces. Decided to return to his ruined home in Jagdishpur as he saw no chance of retaining Azamgarh against the superior British forces. Fought a series of heroic and brilliant rear-guard actions during the withdrawal. While crossing the Ganga river, he lost one of his hands which was shattered by a cannon ball. Returned to Shahabad with hardly two thousand battle-weary and ill-armed men. Led another attack on the British forces and inflicted a crushing defeat on them on April 23, 1858. Expired on the following day as a result of the severe wounds received during the battles. The deeds of valour performed by this brave 75-year-old patriot have been the subject of song and legend.

Tatya Tope alias *Ram Chandra Pandurang*   b. 1814 at v. Gola, Maharashtra; s. of Shri Pandurang Bhat; Follower of Nana Sahib alias Dhondupant, who rose to be a General in the latter's army and one of the most important and eminent figures of the Great Revolt of 1857. Organised the rebel forces and planned the strategy of war against the British with great brilliance. Fought against the British army at several places in Uttar Pradesh and Madhya Pradesh, performing great military feats. Captured the towns of Charkhari and Gwalior and inflicted heavy losses on the British. After losing Gwalior to the British, he launched a successful guerilla campaign against the British forces in the Sagar and Narbada regions and in Khandesh and Rajasthan. The British forces failed to subdue him for more than a year. He was, however, betrayed into the hands of the British by his trusted associate Man Singh, Chief of Narwar, while asleep in his camp in the Paron forest. Captured by the British and taken to Sipri. Tried by a military court and executed on the gallows on April 18, 1859.

Tula Ram, Rao   Resident of Rewari, Distt. Gurgaon, Haryana; Chieftan of Rewari and successor to the jagir of his grand-father, Rao Tej Singh. Played a prominent part in the Great Revolt against British rule in 1857. Took up arms against the British and fought a brief engagement on October 7, 1857, against the British troops near the fort of Rampura. Shortly afterwards, a big battle against

the British forces was fought by his army at Nasibpur near Narnaul and he was at the point of defeating the British force under Colonel Gerrard when the pro-British Naga Sadhus of Galta (Jai pur) and the Sikh army from Jind, Kapurthala and Patiala came to their rescue. Ordered a retreat and escaped. The leaders of the Great Revolt met at Kalpi to consider the situation and decided to depute Rao Tula Ram as the head of a mission to seek foreign help. Rao Tula Ram led the mission consisting of Ram Pandit (Shalig Ram Tripathi), Tara Singh and Nathwa Ram Mali. They went out of India in disguise aboard a ship from Bombay. Visited Iran to negotiate with the Russian Ambassador in Teheran through the good offices of the Iranian Government. Met Amir Dost Mohammad Khan of Afghanistan at Kandahar. The mission reached Kabul for further negotiations with Dost Mohammad's son, Amir Sher Ali Khan. Fell ill due to the rigors of the journey and died at Kabul on September 8, 1862. The Afghan Government gave him a State funeral and his body was cremated outside the Delhi Gate in Kabul, where a small memorial was also erected.

Source: The biographies of the Indian rebels are from vol. 3 of *The Who's Who of Indian Martyrs*, 3 vols. P. N. Chopra, Chief Editor. New Delhi: Ministry of Education and Youth Services, Government of India, 1969–73, pp. 81, 105–6, 98–9, 43–4, 146–7.

---

45   Anonymous: "How to Make an Indian Pickle" (1857)

ENTRUST the selection of materials and the whole management of affairs to a commercial company, like (for instance) the East India Company. Allow them to make use of as much corruption as they please. Throw in various green things, such as incompetent judges, cruel tax-gatherers, and overbearing military officers. Stir up the above with a large Spoon of the ELLENBOROUGH pattern. Mix the above with native superstitions, and by no means spare the official sauce. Allow the above quietly to ferment for several years without taking any notice of how matters are going on. When you come to look into the state of things, you will find that you have as fine an Indian Pickle as you could wish. You need not trouble yourself about the jars, for they will be supplied to you afterwards, gratis. For further particulars, inquire of the great Indian Pickle Warehouse, in Leadenham Street. NB No pickle is genuine, unless there is the mark of "JOHN COM-PANY" plainly visible on the face of it.

Source: Punch, August 15, 1857.

Note

The "Indian Pickle" poem highlights many of the charges of corruption and unfair governmental practices leveled against the East India Company, which is directly blamed for being the primary cause of the unrest in India. The "Ellenborough" remark refers to Viscount (Edward Law) Ellenborough, who was President of the Board of Control for India for brief periods in 1834–5 and 1841. Ellenborough was appointed Governor-General of India in 1841; he served in this capacity until 1844. Ellenborough fell out of favor with Company directors when he reportedly became influenced by Sir Charles Napier. Napier's suspicions about the Indian rulers in Sindh led to war in the region (February to March 1843) and the annexation of Sindh. After a subsequent war broke out in Gwalior (1844), Ellenborough was recalled from India. Upon his return to England, however, he was made an earl and viscount. Ellenborough would later be called upon to draft a new policy for the government of India after the Rebellion in 1858; his hostility toward the newly appointed Viceroy (Charles John) Canning hastened the end of his political career.

46 "Proclamation to the People of Oude on its Annexation, February 1856"

By a treaty concluded in the year 1801, the Honourable East India Company engaged to protect the Sovereign of Oude against every foreign and domestic enemy, while the Sovereign of Oude, upon his part, bound himself to establish "such a system of administration, to be carried into effect by his own officers, as should be conducive to the prosperity of his subjects, and calculated to secure the lives and property of the inhabitants." The obligations which the treaty imposed upon the Honourable East India Company have been observed by it for more than half a century, faithfully, constantly, and completely.

In all that time, though the British Government has itself been engaged in frequent wars, no foreign foe has ever set his foot on the soil of Oude; no rebellion has ever threatened the stability of its throne; British troops have been stationed in close promixity to the king's person, and their aid has never been withheld whenever his power was wrongfully defied.

On the other hand, one chief and vital stipulation of the treaty has been wholly disregarded by

every successive ruler of Oude, and the pledge which was given for the establishment of such a system of administration as should secure the lives and property of the people of Oude, and be conducive to their prosperity, has, from first to last, been deliberately and systematically violated.

By reason of this violation of the compact made, the British Government might, long since, have justly declared the treaty void, and might have withdrawn its protection from the rulers of Oude. But it has hitherto been reluctant to have recourse to measures which would be fatal to the power and authority of a royal race who, whatever their faults towards their own subjects, have ever been faithful and true to their friendship with the English nation.

Nevertheless, the British Government has not failed to labour, during all that time, earnestly and perseveringly, for the deliverance of the people of Oude from the grievous oppression and misrule under which they have suffered.

Many years have passed since the Governor-General, Lord William Bentinck, perceiving that every previous endeavour to ameliorate the condition of the people of Oude had been thwarted or evaded, made formal declaration to the court of Lucknow, that it would become necessary that he should proceed to assume the direct management of the Oude territories.

The words and the menace which were then employed by Lord William Bentinck were, eight years ago, repeated in person by Lord Hardinge to the king. The sovereign of Oude was, on that day, solemnly bid remember that, whatever might now happen, "it would be manifest to all the world" that he "had received a friendly and timely warning."

But the friendly intentions of the British Government have been wholly defeated by the obstinacy, or incapacity, or apathy of the viziers and kings of Oude. Disinterested counsel and indignant censure, alternating, through more than fifty years, with repeated warning, remonstrance, and threats, have all proved ineffectual and vain.

The chief condition of the treaty remains unfulfilled, the promises of the king rest unperformed, and the people of Oude are still the victims of incompetence, corruption, and tyranny, without remedy or hope of relief. It is notorious throughout the land that the king, like most of his predecessors, takes no real share in the direction of public affairs.

The powers of government throughout his dominions are for the most part abandoned to worthless favourites of the court, or to violent and corrupt men, unfit for their duties and unworthy of trust.

The collectors of the revenue hold away over their districts with uncontrolled authority, extorting the utmost payment from the people, without reference to past or present engagements.

The king's troops, with rare exceptions undisciplined and disorganized, and defrauded of their pay by those to whom it is entrusted, are permitted to plunder the villages for their own support, so that they have become a lasting scourge to the country they are employed to protect.

Gangs of freebooters infest the districts. Law and justice are unknown. Armed violence and bloodshed are daily events; and life and property are nowhere secure for an hour.

The time has come when the British Government can no longer tolerate in Oude these evils and abuses, which its position under the treaty serves indirectly to sustain, or continue to the sovereign that protection which alone upholds the power whereby such evils are inflicted.

Fifty years of sad experience have proved that the treaty of 1801 has wholly failed to secure the happiness and prosperity of Oude, and have conclusively shown that no effectual security can be had for the release of the people of that country from the grievous oppression they have long endured, unless the exclusive administration of the territories of Oude shall be permanently transferred to the British Government.

To that end it has been declared, by the special authority and consent of the Honourable Court of Directors, that the treaty of 1801, disregarded and violated by each succeeding sovereign of Oude, is henceforth wholly null and void.

His Majesty Wajid Alee Shah was invited to enter into a new engagement whereby the government of the territories of Oude should be vested, exclusively and for ever, in the Honourable East India Company; while ample provision should be made for the dignity, affluence, and honour of the king and of his family.

But his Majesty the King refused to enter into the amicable agreement which was offered for his acceptance.

Inasmuch, then, as his Majesty Wajid Alee Shah, in common with all his predecessors, has refused or evaded, or neglected to fulfil the obligations of the treaty of 1801, whereby he was bound to establish within his dominions such a system of administration as should be conducive to the prosperity and happiness of his subjects; and inasmuch as the treaty he thereby violated has been declared to be null and void; and inasmuch as his Majesty has refused to enter into other agreements which were offered to him in lieu of such treaty; and

inasmuch as the terms of that treaty, if it had been still maintained in force, forbade the employment of British officers in Oude, without which no efficient system of administration could be established there, it is manifest to all that the British Government had but one alternative before it.

Either it must altogether desert the people of Oude, and deliver them up helpless to oppression and tyranny, which acting under the restriction of the treaty it has already too long appeared to countenance; or it must put forth its own great power on behalf of a people for whose happiness it, more than fifty years ago, engaged to interpose, and must at once assume to itself the exclusive and permanent administration of the territories of Oude.

The British Government has had no hesitation in choosing the latter alternative.

Wherefore, proclamation is hereby made that the Government of the territories of Oude is henceforth vested, exclusively and for ever, in the Honourable East India Company.

All Amils, Nazims, Chuckledars, and other servants of the Durbar; all officers, civil and military; the soldiers of the State; and all the inhabitants of Oude, are required to surrender, henceforth, implicit and exclusive obedience to the officers of the British Government.

If any officer of the Durbar – Jageerdar, Zemindar, or other person – shall refuse to render such obedience, if he shall withhold the payment of revenue, or shall otherwise dispute or defy the authority of the British Government, he shall be declared a rebel, his person shall be seized, and his jageers or lands shall be confiscated to the State.

To those who shall, immediately and quietly, submit themselves to the authority of the British Government, whether Amils or public officers, Jageerdars, Zemindars, or other inhabitants of Oude, full assurance is hereby given of protection, consideration, and favour.

The revenue of the districts shall be determined on a fair and settled basis.

The gradual improvement of the Oude territories shall be steadily pursued.

Justice shall be measured out with an equal hand.

Protection shall be given to life and property; and every man shall enjoy, henceforth, his just rights, without fear of molestation.

Source: J. J. MacLeod Innes. *Lucknow and Oude in the Mutiny.* London: A. D. Innes and Co, 1895, pp 314–16.

Note

The "Proclamation to the People of Oude" contains the East India Company's rationalization for its annexation of the Bengal region. The Company is presented as the rescuing party whose gentle and superior government will ensure happiness and protect the Indian people from unjust and exorbitant indigenous practices. The document presents the Company as a humanizing enterprise whose primary concern is civilizing India: the East India Company's trading interests and mercantile mission are not referred to in the announcement.

47 Rani Lakshmi Bai: Two Letters to the Marquis of Dalhousie (1853, 1854)

Letter 1

Translation of a Kureeta [Persian letter] from Her Highness the Lakshme Bai the widow of Gungadhur Rao the late Maharajah of Jhansi to the address of the Marquis of Dalhousie the Most Noble the Governor General of India, 3rd December 1853.

After Compliments –

The services rendered by Sheo Rao Bhao, the father of my late husband, to the British government before its authority in this part of the Country was established are recorded with other State Documents and have been amply rewarded by the unceasing flow of benefits which his family have derived from the acknowledged favour and protection of such a mighty power.

The concluding article of the Treaty with my late husband signed by Colonel Sleeman in 1842 guarantees to the Jhansi Government the continued existence of all the benefits claimable by virtue of a former treaty made with Ramchand Row in 1817 not specifically cancelled by the terms of the new agreement then made.

This treaty was declaredly made in consideration of the very respectable character borne by the late Subhadar Sheo Rao Bhow and his uniform and faithful attachment to the British Government and in deference to his wish expressed before his death that the principality of Jhansi might be confirmed in perpetuity to his grandson Ramchand Rao.

As the means of effecting this and with the view to confirming the fidelity and attachment to the Government of Jhansi the second article acknowledges and constitutes Rao Ramchand his heirs and successors hereditary rulers of the territory enjoyed by the late Sheo Rao Bhow thereby meaning that any party who he adopted as his son to perform the

funeral rites over his body, necessary to ensure beatitude in a future world, would be acknowledged by the British Government as his successor and one through whom the name and interests of the family might be preserved.

The Hindu Shastras inculcate the doctrine that the libation offered to the manes of a deceased parent are as efficacious when performed by an adopted as by a real son and the custom of adoption is accordingly found prevalent in every part of Hindostan. My husband therefore, upon the morning of the 19th November last, sent for Dewan Nara Sing, Rao Appa, Lalla Lahori Mull, and Lalla Futteh Chund the Ministers and myself and told us to consult with the Shastra and elect a duly qualified child from his own "Gote" clan to succeed him as ruler of Jhansi, as he found himself getting worse and the medicines doing him no good.

Ramchand Baba was in consequence summoned, when at his recommendation out of several children of the Gote it was agreed that Anund Rao, a boy of five years of age the son of Bashdeva, was the best qualified for the purpose. My husband then ordered the Shastri to perform the rites of adoption. The next morning Benaik Rao Pandit performed the Saukalpa when Bashdeva the father of Anund Rao having poured water on my husband's hands with the usual ceremonies the boy was named Damodhur Rao Gungadhur when the ceremony was completed.

The Ministers by order of the Raja wrote to Major Ellis who was encamped at Sayer, 6 Cos from Jhansi, and to Major Martin, the officer Commanding the Station, requesting their attendance at the Palace with the view of bearing witness to what had been done. These two Gentlemen came to the Palace at 10 a.m. the next morning, the 20th November, when my husband delivered a letter to Major Ellis requesting him to obtain the sanction of Government to the adoption which was read over in their presence, when Major Ellis promised that he would make known his wishes to your Lordship.

The next day, Monday the 21st November, my husband expired; the different funeral rites required to be performed by a son have all been discharged by Anund Rao styled Damodhur Rao Gungadhur.

My late husband before his death made the boy over to the protection and favour of the British government – and as the adoption made by Parakshata (the late Rajah of Datia), that of Bala Rao (the last Chief of Jaloun) and that of Tej Singh (the last Raja of Urcha) have all been sanctioned by your Lordship – the more strongly as the term "dawana" (perpetuity) made use of in the Treaty of the Jhansi State is not mentioned in theirs.

Letter 2

Translation of a Khureeta from Her Highness the Lackmee Bau the widow of Gunghadhur Rao late Maharajah of Jhansi to the address of the Marquis of Dalhousie the Most Honourable the Governor General of India, dated Jhansi, 16th February 1854.

After Compliments –

Distress at recent affliction when I addressed your Lordship upon the 3rd December last had prevented my entering as fully as I ought to have done into the circumstances of the adoption made by my late husband, an omission which I now beg leave to supply.

It was the good fortune of Sheo Rao Bhao, the father of my late husband, to be the first of the chiefs in this part of the country who tendered their allegiance to the British Government, which he improved by subsequent exertions in inducing them to follow his example; at which Lord Lake was so pleased that he directed him to submit a paper of requests as to the manner in which the interests of himself and family could be best served. In obedience to these orders a paper, Wajib ul urz ["record of rights"], containing seven different articles, was submitted, thro' Captain John Baillie, the Political Agent for Bundlecund, which were all sanctioned by order of the Most Noble the Governor General of India. Sheo Rao Bhao having omitted to define certain requests in the Wajib ul urz, which he was anxious to make, and having in the mean time had an opportunity of rendering further services, His Lordship entered into a new agreement, for the purpose of rectifying this omission, and thereby becoming an additional pledge of fidelity and attachment on his part to the Government. The new agreement consisted of nine articles, in which the benefits of two new articles were added to those already derivable from the seven articles of the Wajib ul urz, and having been duly signed and sealed by the Governor General, was delivered to him by Captain John Baillie, at Kotra.

In the 6th article of the Wajib ul urz, Sheo Rao Bhao reports that the Rajas of Urcha, Duttia, Chanderi, and other neighbouring States, are ready to tender their allegiance to the British Government, provided the different places then in their possession was [sic] confirmed to them, and prepared to pay their accustomed tribute to the British Government. Upon which an order was passed, to the effect that any chief who imitated his example

in showing obedience and attachment to the British cause should be confirmed in possession of all the advantages then belonging to them; moreover, that other marks of friendship might be expected from service in such a cause.

It was from the same desire to reward past services like these that the British Government entered into a treaty, in 1817, with Rao Ram Chundra Rao, the grandson of Sheo Rao Bhao, the second article of which acknowledges Rao Ram Chundra, his heirs and successors, as hereditary rulers in perpetuity of the Jhansi principality, and guaranteed its protection to them from foreign aggression.

During the Burmese war in 1824, Rao Ram Chundra Rao advanced upwards of 70,000 rupees to banjarahs [suppliers] employed in carrying grain to the troops in Burmah. Mr Ainslie reported his having done so in favourable terms to the Governor General, who ordered the money to be repaid; but Rao Ram Chundra Rao having declined repayment on the grounds that he was an ally of the British Government, and that the interests of the two States were identical, the Governor General was pleased to send him a dress of honour, with a complimentary Khareeta, thanking him for his services upon the occasion. I regret to say that this Khareeta has been mislaid, and would esteem it a favour if your Lordship would kindly order my being furnished with a copy of it.

Shortly afterwards, during the siege of Bharutapoor, the city Kalpi, in the British Territory, being threatened with an attack from Nannay Pandit, at the time in the rebellion against Jaloun, Mr Ainslie, the agent, called upon Bhikraji Nana, Kamdar of Jhansi during the minority, to dispatch troops with the utmost expedition to Kalpi, with a view to protect the Kooneh district from plunder; in consequence of which, Bhikraji Nana made immediate arrangements for sending off 2 guns, 4,000 sowars, [cavalry] and 1,000 foot soldiers, to Kalpi, and which arrived in time to save Kalpi from being plundered, and proved the means of restoring general confidence to the people in the Kooneh district. Copies of letters from Mr Ainslie to Ram Chundra Rao, the minor Rajah, and Bhakaji, his kamdar, thanking them for their services on this emergent occasion, are submitted with the view of showing that Jhansi state was always foremost in the field when opportunity occurred for displaying its loyalty to the Paramount Power.

When Lord William Bentinck was at Jhansi in 1832, he visited Rao Ram Chunder Rao in the fort on the evening of the 19th December, and conferred upon him the title Maharaj Dhiraj Fidwi Badshah Janujah Englistan [King of Kings, Faithful to the Emperor of England], Maharajah Ram

Chunder Rao Bahadur, ordering him to have it engraved on his seal, investing him at the same time with the insignia of the Nakara and Chonar, with permission to adopt the British flag, telling him, in open durbar, that of all the chiefs of Budelkund, his uncle, Sheo Rao Bhao, had done the best service, and that the honours now conferred were the reward of his meritorious services to the British Government. On arrival at Saugur, his Lordship was further pleased to send him a complimentary letter in English, having a gold-leaf border, dated 20th December 1832, copy of which is forwarded, repeating what he had stated in Durbar, and adding, that the letter then issued would serve ever afterwards as a patent of his rank and authority.

Raghonath Rao, who succeeded his nephew, Ram Chundra Rao, in 1835, died in 1838, when the right of my husband to the succession was acknowledged; but owing to the State being in debt at the time, it was placed under the superintendence of Captain D. Ross for a period of three years, at the expiration of which it was restored to him, with an agreement on his part by which he ceded Duboh, Talgong, and other districts, valued at 255,891 Jhansi rupees, as payment towards a legion to be employed for the purpose of coercing any of his turbulent feudatories who might set his authority at defiance; and one on Colonel Sleeman's part, dated 1st January 1843, confirming to the Jhansi State all of the advantages guaranteed to it by virtue of former treaties.

It cannot be denied that the terms Warisan [wārişan], "heirs", and Janishnian [jānishin], "successors", made use of in the second article of the treaty with Ram Chundra Rao, refer to different parties; the term Warisan being confined in meaning to natural or collateral heirs, while Janishnian, on the contrary, refers to the party adopted as heir and successor to the estate, in the event of their being no natural or collateral heir entitled to the succession. Treaties are studied with the utmost care before ratification; and it is not to be supposed that the term Janishnian used in contradistinction to Warisan was introduced in an important document of this kind, of the authority almost of a revelation from Heaven, without a precise understanding of its meaning, the advantages of which are further explained by the clause declaring the gift then made to have been one in perpetuity to the family. It was with this understanding of the terms of the treaty that my husband, the day before his death, summoned Major Ellis and Captain Martin, the officer commanding the station, to the palace, and with his dying breath, in full Durbar, made over Anand Rao, his adopted son, to the care and protection of the British Government, delivering at the same time a kharita, or testament, further declaratory of his wishes on this solemn occasion for communication to your Lordship.

I take the liberty of enclosing a list of some of the precedents which have occurred in Bundlecund in which the right of the native chief or his widow to adopt a successor to the guddi [throne], in default of natural heirs, has been sanctioned; and as it is the firm reliance which they feel in the integrity and justice of the British Government which enables them to pass their days in peace and quietness, without other care than how to prove their loyalty, venture to express a hope that the widow of the son of Sheo Rao Bhao will not be considered undeserving of that favour and compassion which others similarly situated have been declared entitled to.

Source: Michael Fisher (ed.). *The Politics of the British Annexation of India.* Delhi: Oxford University Press, 1993, pp. 252-9.

Note

Rani Lakshmi Bai (The Rani of Jhansi; 1835–58) became the ruler of Jhansi State after her husband, the Raja's death in 1853. After numerous unsuccessful legal and diplomatic appeals to Company administrators and British politicians and statesmen, the Rani militarily rebelled against the annexation of her kingdom. Her beauty and military daring along with her adoption of male attire on the battlefield, captured the imagination of the Indians and British. The Rani fought alongside Rao Sahib and Tatya Tope. She was mortally wounded at the battle of Gwalior in June of 1858.

For a book-length study on the Rani of Jhansi, see Joyce Lebra-Chapman's *The Rani of Jhansi: A Study in Female Heroism.* Honolulu: University of Hawaii Press, 1986.

48   John William Kaye: *The History of the Sepoy War in India* (1880)

The Chupatties (1857)

[It is stated that Mr Ford, Magistrate and Collector of Goorgaon, was the first to call the attention of the Government of the North-Western Provinces to this subject. His letter, addressed, in official course, to the Commissioner of Delhi, is appended:]

"Goorgaon Magistracy, February 19, 1857

"SIR, – I have the honour to inform you that a signal has passed through numbers of the villages of this district, the purport of which has not yet transpired.

The Chowkeydars of the villages bordering on those belonging to Mutra have received small baked cakes of atta, with orders to distribute them generally through this district.

A Chowkeydar, upon receiving one of these cakes, has had five or six more prepared, and thus they have passed from village to village; so quickly has the order been executed, that village after village has been served with this notice.

This day, cakes of this description have arrived and been distributed in the villages about Goorgaon, and an idea has been industriously circulated that Government has given the order.

W. FORD, Magistrate

To Simon Fraser, Esq.,
Commissioner, Delhi.

[In the course of the trial of the King of Delhi great pains were taken to extract from the witnesses, both European and Native, some explanation of the "Chupatty mystery"; but nothing satisfactory was elicited. The following opinions, however, were recorded:]

*From the Evidence of Jat Mall, News-writer
to the Lieutenant-Governor*

Q   Did you ever hear of the circulation of chupatties about the country some months before the outbreak; and if so, what was supposed to be the meaning of this?

A   Yes, I did hear of the circumstance. Some people said that it was a propitiatory observance to avert some impending calamity; others, that they were circulated by the Government to signify that the population throughout the country would be compelled to use the same food as the Christians, and thus be deprived of their religion; while others, again, said that the chupatties were circulated to make it known that Government was determined to force Christianity on the country by interfering with their food, and intimation of it was thus given that they might be prepared to resist the attempt.

Q   Is sending such articles about the country a custom among the Hindoos or Mussulmans; and would the meaning be at once understood without any accompanying explanation?

A   No, it is not by any means a custom; I am fifty years old, and never heard of such a thing before.

Q   Did you ever hear that any message was sent with the chupatties?

A   No; I never heard of any.

Q   Were these chupatties chiefly circulated by Mahomedans or Hindoos?

A   They were circulated indiscriminately, without reference to either religion, among the peasantry of the country.

The Bone-Dust Story (1857)

[The following translations from Native letters and papers show how general was the belief among the Sepoys in all parts of the country that the Government had mixed ground bones with the flour, and purposed to compel or to delude them to eat it:]

Translation of an Anonymous Petition sent, in March, 1857, to Major Matthews, commanding the 43rd Regiment at Barrackpore

"The representation of the whole station is this, that we will not give up our religion. We serve for honour and religion; if we lose our religion, the Hindoo and Mahomedan religions will be destroyed. If we live, what shall we do? You are the masters of the country. The Lord Sahib has given orders, which he has received from the Company, to all commanding officers to destroy the religion of the country. We know this, as all things are being bought up by Government. The officers in the Salt Department mix up bones with the salt. The officer in charge of the ghee mixes up fat with it; this is well known. These are two matters. The third is this: that the Sahib in charge of the sugar burns up bones and mixes them in the syrup the sugar is made of; this is well known – all know it. The fourth is this: that in the country the Burra Sahibs have ordered the Rajahs, Thakurs, Zemindars, Mahajans, and Ryots, all to eat together, and English bread has been sent to them; this is well known. And this is another affair, that throughout the country the wives of respectable men, in fact, all classes of Hindoos, on becoming widows, are to be married again; this is known. Therefore we consider ourselves as killed. You all obey the orders of the Company, which we all know. But a king, or any other one who acts unjustly, does not remain.

With reference to the Sepoys, they are your servants; but, to destroy their caste, a council assembled and decided to give them muskets and cartridges made up with greased paper to bite; this is also evident. We wish to represent this to the General, that we do not approve of the new musket and cartridge; the Sepoys cannot use them. You are the masters of the country; if you will give us all our discharge we will go away. The Native officers, Soubahdars, Jemadars, are all good in the whole Brigade, except two, whose faces are like pigs: the Soubahdar Major of the 70th Regiment, who is a Christian, and Thakur Misser, Jemadar of the 43rd Regiment Light Infantry.

Whoever gets this letter must read it to the Major as it is written. If he is a Hindoo and does not, his crime will be equal to the slaughter of a lakh of cows; and if a Mussulman, as though he had eaten pig; and if a European, must read it to the Native officers, and if he does not, his going to church will be of no use, and be a crime. Thakur Misser has lost his religion. Chattrees are not to respect him. Brahmins are not to salute or bless him. If they do, their crime will be equal to the slaughter of a lakh of cows. He is the son of a Chumar. The Brahmin who hears this is not to feed him; if he does, his crime will be equal to the murdering of a lakh of Brahmins or cows.

May this letter be given to Major Matthews. Any one who gets it is to give it, if he does not, and is a Hindoo, his crime will be as the slaughter of a lakh of cows; and if a Mussulman, as if he had eaten pig; and if he is an officer he must give it.

Final Orders to the Musketry Schools (1857)

The Adjutant-General of the Army to Major-General Hearsey

Adjutant-General's Office, Simlah, April 13, 1857 "Sir, – Referring to the telegraph message from this office dated the 23rd ultimo (and your acknowledgments of the 25th idem), communicating the Commander-in-Chief's orders to postpone the target practice of the Native soldiers at the Rifle Depot at Dum-Dum, pending further instructions from this Department, I am now desired to request you will be good enough to inform the officer commanding at Dum-Dum, and through him the Depot authorities concerned, that the course of instruction is to be completed by the Native details, and that their target practice is to be commenced as soon as practicable after the Government General Order disbanding the Nineteenth Regiment of Native Infantry has been read to the troops at the station, including the detachments of Native regiments at the Depot.

2   The grease for the cartridge is to be any unobjectionable mixture which may be suited for the purpose, to be provided by selected parties comprising all castes concerned, and is to be applied by the men themselves.

3   The paper of which the cartridges are constructed having been proved by chemical test, and otherwise, to be perfectly free from grease, and in all respects unobjectionable; and all possible grounds for objection in regard to the biting of the cartridge, and the nature of the grease to be used, having been removed, it is not anticipated that the men will hesitate to perform the target practice; but, in the event of any such unexpected result, the Commander-in-Chief desires that their officers may be instructed to reason calmly with them, pointing out the utter groundlessness for any objection to the use of the cartridges now that biting the end has been dispensed with, and the provision and application of the necessary greasing material has been left to themselves; and, further, to assure them that any one who shall molest or taunt them on return to their corps, shall be visited with severe punishment.

4   The officer commanding the Depot will be held responsible that the above directions respecting the greasing mixture, and those recently issued in regard to the new mode of loading, are strictly observed.

5   If, notwithstanding all these precautions and considerate measures, any disinclination to use the cartridges shall be manifested, the parties demurring are to be warned calmly and patiently, but firmly, that a persistence in such unjustifiable conduct will be viewed as disobedience of orders and insubordination, and treated accordingly, and in the event of any individuals after such warning obstinately refusing to fire, the officer commanding at Dum-Dum will at once place such parties in arrest or confinement, according to the rank of the offenders, and cause them to be tried by Court-Martial.

6   If, however, the entire Depot shall combinedly refuse to fire, which is very improbable, the Commander-in-Chief, under such circumstances, empowers you to place all the Native officers in arrest pending his Excellency's further orders, which you will immediately apply for; to deprive the non-commissioned officers and Sepoys of their arms and accoutrements, and to pay them up and summarily discharge them on the spot, excepting, of course, any ringleaders in these latter grades or parties whose refusal may be accompanied by insolence or insubordination, who are to be placed under arrest or confinement, in view of their being arraigned before a District or General Court-Martial, as the case may require.

7   This communication is to be considered purely confidential, and his Excellency relies implicitly on your carrying out the instructions

it contains with the utmost caution and discretion.

> I have the honour to be, Sir,
> Your most obedient, servant, C. CHESTER,
> Col. Adjt-Gen. of the Army

Source: John William Kaye. *The History of the Sepoy War in India, 1857–1858*. London: Longmans, Green, and Co., 1880, pp. 630–1, 632–3, 639–41 (orig. pub. 1864–76).

Note

John William Kaye (1814–76) served in the Bengal Artillery and later became secretary of the India Office (1858–74). He was knighted in 1871.

49   Act no. XIV of 1857 on the Punishment of Soldiers under Company Rule

WHEREAS it is necessary to make further provision for the trial and punishment of persons who endeavour to excite mutiny and sedition among the Forces of the East India Company, and also for the trial of offences against the State: It is enacted as follows:

I   Whoever intentionally seduces or endeavours to seduce any Officer or Soldier in the service or pay of the East India Company from his allegiance to the British Government or his duty to the East India Company, or intentionally excites or stirs up, or endeavours to excite or stir up, any such Officer or Soldier, or any Officer or Soldier serving in any part of the British Territories in India in aid of the Troops of the British Government, to commit any act of mutiny or sedition; and whoever intentionally causes, or endeavours to cause, any other person to commit any such offence – shall be liable upon conviction to the punishment of death, or to the punishment of transportation for life, or of imprisonment with hard labour for any term not exceeding fourteen years; and shall forfeit all his property and effects of every description.

II   Whoever, shall knowingly harbour or conceal any person who shall have been guilty of any offence mentioned in the preceding section, shall be liable to imprisonment, with or without hard labour, for any term not exceeding seven years, and shall also be liable to fine.

III   It shall be lawful for the Governor-General of India in Council, from time to time, by Order in Council, to empower every General or other Officer having the command of Troops in the Service of Her Majesty or of the East India Company, or any of such General or other Officers, to appoint General Courts-Martial for the trial of any person or persons charged with having committed an offence punishable by this Act or by Section I or Section II of Act XI of 1857, and also to confirm and carry into effect any sentence of such Court-Martial.

IV   Any General Court-Martial, which may be appointed under the authority of this Act, shall be appointed by the Senior Officer on the spot, and shall consist of not less than five Commissioned Officers, the number to be fixed by the General or other Officer appointing the Court-Martial. The Order in Council may direct that a General Court-Martial to be appointed under the provisions of this Act shall consist wholly of European Commissioned Officers or wholly of Native Commissioned Officers, or partly of European Commissioned Officers, and partly of Native Commissioned Officers; and in such case the Officer appointing the Court-Martial shall determine whether the same shall consist wholly of European Officers or wholly of Native Officers, or partly of European Officers and partly of Native Officers.

V   Sentence of death or other punishment to which the offender is liable by law, may be given by such Court-Martial, if a majority of the members present concur in the sentence; and any such sentence may be confirmed by, and carried into effect immediately or otherwise by order of, the Officer by whom the Court-Martial shall have been appointed, or, in case of his absence, by the Senior Officer on the spot.

VI   It shall be lawful for the Governor-General in Council to countermand or alter any Order in Council which may be issued under the authority of this Act.

VII   It shall be lawful for the Governor-General in Council, or for the Executive Government of any Presidency or place, or for any person or persons whom the Governor-General in Council may authorise so to do, from time to time to issue a Commission for the trial of all or any persons or person charged with having committed within any district described in the Commission, whether such district shall or shall not have been proclaimed to be in a state of rebellion, any offence punishable by Sections I and II of Act XI of 1857, or by this Act, or any other crime against the State, or murder, arson, robbery, or other heinous crime against person or property.

VIII   The Commissioner or Commissioner authorised by any such Commission, may hold a Court in any part of the district mentioned in the Commission, and may there try any person for any of the said crimes committed within any part thereof, it being the intention of this Act that the district mentioned in the Commission shall, for the purpose of trial and punishment of any of the said offences, be deemed one district.

IX   Any Court held under the Commission shall have power, without the attendance or futwa of a Law Officer, or the assistance of Assessors, to pass upon every person convicted before the Court of any of the aforesaid crimes any sentence warranted by law for such crime; and the judgment of such Court shall be final and conclusive; and the said Court shall not be subordinate to the Sudder or other Court.

X   If a Commission be issued under the authority of this Act, any Magistrate or other Officer having power to commit for trial within the district described in the Commission may commit persons charged with any of the aforesaid crimes within such district for trial before a Court to be held under this Act.

XI   Nothing in this Act shall extend to the trial or punishment of any of Her Majesty's natural born subjects born in Europe, or of the children of such subjects.

XII   This Act shall not extend to the trial or punishment of any person for any offence for which he is liable to be tried by the Articles of War.

XIII   The word "Soldier" shall include every person subject to any Articles of War.

XIV   This Act shall continue in force for one year.

Source: John William Kaye. *The History of the Sepoy War in India, 1857–1858* (1880). London: Longmans, Green, and Co., 1896, pp. 661–4.

---

50   Alfred, Lord Tennyson: "The Defence of Lucknow" (1879)

I

BANNER of England, not for a season, O banner of
   Britain, hast thou
Floated in conquering battle or flapt to the
   battle-cry!
Never with mightier glory than when we had rear'd
   thee on high
Flying at top of the roofs in the ghastly siege of
   Lucknow –
Shot thro' the staff or the halyard, but ever we
   raised thee anew,
And ever upon the topmost roof our banner of
   England blew.

II

Frail were the works that defended the hold that we
   held with our lives –
Women and children among us, God help them,
   our children and wives!
Hold it we might – and for fifteen days or for
   twenty at most.
"Never surrender, I charge you, but every man die
   at his post!"
Voice of the dead whom we loved, our Lawrence
   the best of the brave;
Cold were his brows when we kiss'd him – we laid
   him that night in his grave.
"Every man die at his post!" and there hail'd on our
   houses and halls
Death from their rifle-bullets, and death from their
   cannon-balls,
Death in our innermost-chamber, and death at our
   slight barricade,
Death while we stood with the musket, and death
   while we stoopt to the spade,
Death to the dying, and wounds to the wounded,
   for often there fell,
Striking the hospital wall, crashing thro' it, their
   shot and their shell,
Death – for their spies were among us, their marksmen were told of our best,
So that the brute bullet broke thro' the brain that
   could think for the rest;
Bullets would sing by our foreheads, and bullets
   would rain at our feet –
Fire from ten thousand at once of the rebels that
   girdled us round –
Death at the glimpse of a finger from over the
   breadth of a street,
Death from the heights of the mosque and the
   palace, and death in the ground!
Mine? yes, a mine! Countermine! down, down! and
   creep thro' the hole!
Keep the revolver in hand! you can bear him – the
   murderous mole!
Quiet, ah! quiet – wait till the point of the pickaxe
   be thro'!

Click with the pick, coming nearer and nearer again
  than before –
Now let it speak, and you fire, and the dark pioneer
  is no more;
And ever upon the topmost roof our banner of
  England blew!

III

Ay, but the foe sprung his mine many times, and it
  chanced on a day
Soon as the blast of that underground thunder-clap
  echo'd away,
Dark thro' the smoke and the sulphur like so many
  fiends in their hell –
Cannon-shot, musket-shot, volley on volley, and
  yell upon yell –
Fiercely on all the defences our myriad enemy fell.
What have they done? where is it? Out yonder.
  Guard the Redan!
Storm at the Water-gate! storm at the Bailey-gate!
  storm, and it ran
Surging and awaying all round us, as ocean on
  every side
Plunges and heaves at a bank that is daily drown'd
  by the tide –
So many thousands that, if they be bold enough,
  who shall escape?
Kill or be kill'd, live or die, they, shall know we are
  soldiers and men!
Ready! take aim at their leaders – their masses are
  gapp'd with our grape –
Backward they reel like the wave, like the wave
  flinging forward again,
Flying and foil'd at the last by the handful they
  could not subdue;
And ever upon the topmost roof our banner of
  England blew.

IV

Handful of men as we were, we were English in
  heart and in limb,
Strong with the strength of the race to command,
  to obey, to endure,
Each of us fought as if hope for the garrison hung
  but on him;
Still – could we watch at all points? we were every
  day fewer and fewer.
There was a whisper among us, but only a whisper
  that past;
"Children and wives – if the tigers leap into the
  fold unawares –
Every man die at his post – and the foe may outlive
  us at last –

Better to fall by the hands that they love, than to
  fall into theirs!"
Roar upon roar in a moment two mines by the
  enemy sprung
Clove into perilous chasms our walls and our poor
  palisades.
Rifleman, true is your heart, but be sure that your
  hand be as true!
Sharp is the fire of assault, better aimed are your
  flank fusillades –
Twice do we hurl them to earth from the ladders to
  which they had clung,
Twice from the ditch where they shelter we drive
  them with hand-grenades;
And ever upon the topmost roof our banner of
  England blew.

V

Then on another wild morning another wild earthquake out-tore
Clean from our lines of defence ten or twelve good
  paces or more.
Rifleman, high on the roof, hidden there from the
  light of the sun –
One has leapt up on the breach, crying out: "Follow me, follow me! –"
Mark him – he falls! then another, and *him* too, and
  down goes he.
Had they been bold enough then, who can tell but
  the traitors had won?
Boardings and rafters and doors – an embrasure!
  make way for the gun!
Now double-charge it with grape! It is charged and
  we fire, and they run.
Praise to our Indian brothers, and let the dark face
  have his due!
Thanks to the kindly dark faces who fought with
  us, faithful and few,
Fought with the bravest among us, and drove
  them, and smote them, and slew,
That ever upon the topmost roof our banner in
  India blew.

VI

Men will forget what we suffer and not what we do.
  We can fight!
But to be soldier all day, and be sentinel all thro'
  the night –
Ever the mine and assault, our sallies, their lying
  alarms,
Bugles and drums in the darkness, and shoutings
  and soundings to arms,
Ever the labor of fifty that had to be done by five,

Ever the marvel among us that one should be left alive,

Ever the day with its traitorous death from the loopholes around,

Ever the night with its coffinless corpse to be laid in the ground,

Heat like the mouth of a hell, or a deluge of cataract skies,

Stench of old offal decaying, and infinite torment of flies,

Thoughts of the breezes of May blowing over an English field,

Cholera, scurvy, and fever, the wound that *would* not be heal'd,

Lopping away of the limb by the pitiful-pitiless knife, –

Torture and trouble in vain, – for it never could save us a life.

Valor of delicate women who tended the hospital bed,

Horror of women in travail among the dying and dead,

Grief for our perishing children, and never a moment for grief.

Toil and ineffable weariness, faltering hopes of relief,

Havelock baffled, or beaten, or butcher'd for all that we knew –

Then day and night, day and night, coming down on the still-shatter'd walls

Millions of musket-bullets, and thousands of cannon-balls –

But ever upon the topmost roof our banner of England blew.

VII

Hark cannonade, fusillade! is it true what was told by the scout,

Outram and Havelock breaking their way through the fell mutineers?

Surely the pibroch of Europe is ringing again in our ears!

All on a sudden the garrison utter a jubilant shout,

Havelock's glorious Highlanders answer with conquering cheers,

Sick from the hospital echo then, women and children come out,

Blessing the wholesome white faces of Havelock's good fusileers,

Kissing the war-harden'd hand of the Highlander wet with their tears!

Dance to the pibroch! – saved! we are saved! – is it you? is it you?

Saved by the valor of Havelock, saved by the blessing of heaven!

"Hold it for fifteen days!" we have held it for eighty-seven!

And ever aloft on the palace roof the old banner of England blew.

Source: Alfred, Lord Tennyson. *Ballads and Other Poems.* Boston: James R Osgood and Co., 1880, pp. 470–2.

---

51   A. Dashe: Letter on Measures to Suppress the Mutiny in Kiyalpore District (1858)

From A. DASHE, Collector and Magistrate of Kiyalpore, to R. TAPE, Esq., Commissioner and Superintendent of Kwâbabad

Dated 11th May 1858

SIR, In reply to your No. 103 of the 20th April requesting me to report on the course of the Mutiny in my district, the measures taken to suppress it, and its effects, if any, on the judicial, executive, and financial work under my charge, I have the honour to enclose a brief statement, which for convenience' sake I have drafted under the usual headings of the annual report which I was unable to send in till last week. I regret the delay, but the pressure of work in the English office due to the revising of forfeiture and pension lists made it unavoidable. I have the honour, etc., etc.,

A. DASHE, Coll. and Magte

Introductory Remarks   So far as my district is concerned, the late disturbances have simply been a military mutiny. At no time could they be truthfully called a rebellion. In the outlying posts, indeed, the people knew little or nothing of what was going on around them, and even in the towns resistance was not thought of until the prospect of any immediate suppression of the mutiny disappeared.

The small force of soldiers in my district of course followed the example of their brethren. Nothing else could be expected from our position midway between two large cantonments; indeed the continuous stream of mutinous troops which passed up and down the main road during the summer had a decidedly bad effect.

I commenced to disperse the disturbers of the public peace on the 21st May. These were largely escaped felons from the Meerut jail; and the fact that they were quite indiscriminate in their lawlessness enabled me to rally most of the well-doing people on my side. I hanged a few of the offenders, and having enlisted a small corps with the aid of some native gentlemen (whose names I append for reference), sent it out under charge of my assistant (I myself being forced throughout the whole business to remain at headquarters and keep a grip on things) to put down some Goojurs and other predatory tribes who took occasion to resort to their ancestral habits of life.

No real opposition, however, was ever met with; but in June (after our failure to take Delhi by a *coup de main* became known) there was an organised attempt to seize the Treasury. Fortunately I had some twenty or thirty of my new levy in headquarters at the time, so that the attempt failed and I was able to bring one or two of the ringleaders (one, I regret to say, a man of considerable importance in my district) to justice.

I subsequently made several applications to the nearest cantonment for a few European soldiers to escort my treasure – some two lakhs – to safer quarters. But this, unfortunately, could not be granted to me, so I had to keep a strong guard of men over the money, who might have been more useful elsewhere.

Until the fall of Delhi matters remained much the same. Isolated bands of marauders ravaged portions of my district, often, I regret to say, escaping before punishment could be meted out to them. The general feeling was one of disquiet and alarm to both Europeans and natives. My table attendant, for instance, absented himself from dinner one day, sending a substitute to do his work, under the belief that I had given orders for a general slaughter of Mahommedans that evening. I had done nothing of the kind.

After the fall of Delhi, as you are aware, the mutinous fugitives, some fifty or sixty thousand strong, marched southwards in a compact body and caused us much alarm. But after camping on the outskirts of my district for a few days, they suddenly disappeared. I am told they dispersed during one night, each to his own home. Anyhow they literally melted away, and the public mind seemed to become aware that the contest was over, and that the struggle to subvert British rule had ignominiously failed. Matters therefore assumed a normal aspect, but I believe that there is more shame, sorrow, and regret in the hearts of many than we shall probably ever have full cognisance of, and that it will take years for the one race to regain its confidence, the other its self-respect.

Civil Judicature   The courts were temporarily suspended for a week or two; after that original work went on much as usual, but the appellate work suffered. There was an indisposition both to institute and hear appeals, possibly due to the total eclipse of the higher appellate courts. I myself had little leisure for civil cases.

Criminal Justice   There has been far less crime than usual during the past year. Possibly because much of it had necessarily to be treated summarily and so did not come on the record. I am inclined to believe, however, that petty offences really are fewer when serious crime is being properly dealt with.

Police   The less said about the behaviour of the police the better. The force simply melted away; but as it was always inefficient its absence had little effect. Save, perhaps, in a failure to bring up those trivial offences mentioned in the last para.

Jails   The jail was happily preserved throughout; for the addition of four or five hundred felons to the bad characters of my district might have complicated matters. I was peculiarly fortunate in this, since I learn that only nine out of the forty-three jails in the Province were so held.

Revenue (Sub-head, Land)   The arrears under this head are less than usual, and there seems no reason to apprehend serious loss to Government.

(Opium)   There has, I regret to say, been considerable detriment to our revenue under this head, due to the fact that the smuggling of the drug is extremely easy, owing to its small bulk, and that the demand was greater than usual.

(Stamps)   The revenue here shows an increase of Rs.72,000. I am unable to account for this, unless the prevailing uncertainty made the public mind incline towards what security it could compass in the matter of bonds, agreements, etc.

(Salt and Customs)   This department shows a very creditable record. My subordinates, with the help of a few volunteers, were able to maintain the Customs line throughout the whole disturbances.

Its value as a preventative of roving lawlessness cannot be overestimated. Four hundred and eighty-two smugglers were punished, and the Customs brought in Rs.33,770 more than in '56. But the work done by this handful of isolated European patrols – with only a few natives under them – to the cause of law and order, cannot be estimated in money.

Education   The higher education went on as usual. Primary instruction suffered. Female schools disappeared altogether.

Public Works   Many things combined to stop anything like a vigorous prosecution of new public works, and those in hand were greatly retarded.

Post-Office   The work in this department suffered occasional lapses owing to the murder of solitary runners by lawless ruffians, but the service continued fairly efficient. An attempt was made, by the confiscation of sepoys' letters, to discover if any organised plan of attack or resistance was in circulation, but nothing incriminatory was found, the correspondence consisting chiefly of love-letters.

Financial   At one time the necessary cash for the pay of establishment ran short, but this was met by bills upon native bankers, who have since been repaid.

Hospitals   The dispensaries were in full working order throughout the year, and the number of cases treated – especially for wounds and hurts, many of them grievous – above the average.

Health and Population   Both were normal, and the supply of food grains ample. Markets strong, and well supplied throughout. Some grain stores were burnt, some plundered; but, as a rule, if A robbed B, B in his turn robbed C. So the matter adjusted itself. In many cases also, the booty was restored amicably when it became evident that Government could hold its own.

Agriculture   Notwithstanding the violence of contest, the many instances of plundered and burnt villages, the necessary impressment of labour and cattle, and the licence of mutineers consorting with felons, agricultural interests did not suffer. Ploughing and sowing went on steadily, and the land was well covered with a full winter crop.

General Remarks   Beyond these plundered and burnt villages, which are still somewhat of an eye-sore, though they are recovering themselves rapidly, the only result of the Mutiny to be observed in my district is that money seems scarcer, and so that cultivators have to pay a higher rate of interest on loans.

There are, of course, some empty chairs in the district durbar. I append a list of their late occupants also, and suggest that the vacancies might be filled from the other list, as some of those gentlemen who helped to raise the levy have not yet got chairs.

In regard to future punishments, however, I venture to suggest that orders should be issued limiting the period during which mutineers can be brought to justice. If some such check on malicious accusation be not laid down we shall have a fine crop of false cases, perjuries, etc., since the late disturbances have, naturally, caused a good many family differences. In view of this also, I believe it would be safest, in the event of such accusations in the future, to punish the whole village to which the alleged mutineer belongs by a heavy fine rather than to single out individuals as examples. In a case like the present it is extremely difficult to measure the exact proportion of guilt attachable to each member of the community, and, even with the very greatest care, I find it is not always possible to hang the right man. And this is a difficulty which will increase as time goes on.

Source: Flora Annie Steele. *On the Face of the Waters* (novel). London: William Heineman, 1897, Appendix A, pp. 426–9.

Chapter Ten

The Game: The Afghan Wars

Introduction

The war fought in Afghanistan, along the northwest frontier of British India from 1839 to 1842, was the first of what have been called "Victoria's little wars." From that time (Victoria took the throne in 1837) until her death in 1901, not a single year elapsed that did not see the British fighting some war or skirmish across the reach of its imperial dominion: against Sikhs, Zulus or Ashantis, in the Crimea, in Burma, defending its opium trade in China, quelling nationalist uprisings in Egypt or the Sudan, or dispelling the aspirations of the Boers in South Africa in the interest of its own imperial prospects. The First Afghan War, however, resulted in a catastrophic rout and massacre of the British forces and their attendants from Kabul. Where would British rule in India begin – and where would it end?

Britain, Russia and Persia were all competing for influence, if not control, over the rugged mountainous tribal territories of Central Asia, but it was the protracted struggle between the first two powers, culminating in the Anglo-Russian Convention of 1907, that eventually came to be called the "great game." The term was coined by one Captain Arthur Connolly in 1842 while he was serving as a scout for the British in the region and seeking alliances with the ruling Emir, but it acquired its

popular currency through Rudyard Kipling's novel *Kim* (1901). For the English, in Calcutta and in London, the debate was between a "forward policy" and a "back to the Indus" position. Where should the line be drawn? and of what would that line be designed? Lord Auckland, Governor-General in India in 1838, determined that it was imperative that a British force alone would succeed in removing one Afghan ruler (Dost Muhammad) and replacing him with another (Shah Shuja) in Kabul. His chief adviser William Macnaghten concurred, and so it happened in the First Afghan War. But the newly placed leader was less than content with the continued British cantonment in his territory, and at the end of 1841, through bitter fighting, the British were forced to retreat. Of the 16,000 British who departed in early January 1842, only one, the surgeon William Brydon, reached Jellalabad. The diary of Lady Sale, the wife of Sir Robert Sale, the garrison's second-in-command, tells the story of the cantonment and its retreat, and the desperate stories of death, capture, and defeat.

For the next half century, decades that included the Second Afghan War from 1879 to 1882, the British continued to debate the promises of a "forward policy" versus the practicalities of drawing the line at the Indus. The mountain passes – of which the most famous would be the Khyber, but also the Baroghil, the Kilik, the Mustagh, the Karakoram, and the Saser – continued, however, to provide the treacherous setting for surveys, surveillances, skirmishes, and imperial insecurities, as well as the scenarios for such intrepid travellers, scouts and imperial agents as Frederick Burnaby and Francis Younghusband, and the schooling grounds of Kipling's young Kimball O'Hara in the "great game." And while the Anglo–Russian Convention of 1907 did bring a cessation to the play, it was by no means an end to the "game."

BH

Additional Reading

Barth, Frederik. *The Last Wali of Swat.* Oslo and New York, 1985.
Eyre, Lieut. Vincent. *The Military Operations at Cabul.* London, 1843.
Fraser, George Macdonald. *Flashman.* London, 1969.
French, Patrick. *Younghusband: The Last Great Imperial Adventurer* (1994). London, 1995.
Henty, G.A. *For Name and Fame, or Through Afghan Passes.* London, 189?.
Hopkirk, Peter. *The Great Game: The Struggle for Empire in Central Asia* (1990). New York, 1994.
Kaye, John William. *History of the War in Afghanistan* (2 vols). London, 1851.
Keay, John. *The Gilgit Game: The Explorers of the Western Himalayas 1865–95.* London, 1979.
Rashid, Ahmed. *The Resurgence of Central Asia; Islam or Nationalism?.* London and New Jersey, 1994.

Films

Henry Hathaway. *Lives of a Bengal Lancer* (1935).
George Stevens. *Gunga Din* (1939).
Victor Saville. *Kim* (1950).
J. Lee-Thompson. *Northwest Frontier* (1959).
John Huston. *The Man Who Would Be King* (1975).
John Davies. *Kim* (1984).

52   Rudyard Kipling: Description of Mahbub Ali (1901)

But Kim did not suspect that Mahbub Ali, known as one of the best horse-dealers in the Punjab, a wealthy and enterprising trader, whose caravans penetrated far and far into the Back of Beyond, was registered in one of the locked books of the Indian Survey Department as C.25.1B. Twice or thrice yearly C.25 would send in a little story, baldly told but most interesting, and generally – it was checked by the statements of R.17 and M.4 – quite true. It concerned all manner of out-of-the-way mountain principalities, explorers of nationalities other than English, and the gun-trade – was, in brief, a small portion of that vast mass of "information received" on which the Indian Government acts. But, recently, five confederated Kings, who had no business to confederate, had been informed by a kindly

Northern Power that there was a leakage of news from their territories into British India. So those Kings' prime ministers were seriously annoyed and took steps, after the Oriental fashion. They suspected, among many others, the bullying, red-bearded horse-dealer whose caravans ploughed through their fastnesses belly deep in snow. At least, his caravan that season had been ambushed and shot at twice on the way down, when Mahbub's men accounted for three strange ruffians who might, or might not, have been hired for the job. Therefore Mahbub had avoided halting at the insalubrious city of Peshawur, and had come through without stop to Lahore, where, knowing his country-people, he anticipated curious developments.

> *Source:* Rudyard   Kipling.   *Kim*   London: Macmillan 1901, chap. 1.

Note

Mahbub Ali was an Afghan horse trader and a participant in the "great game" on the side of England in Kipling's novel. It is Mahbub Ali who first draws Kim into the "game," when he gives him a coded message to deliver to Colonel Creighton.

53   Lt. Gen. Sir George Macmunn: "Mahbub Ali," from "Some Kipling Origins" (1927)

If you turn into the Sultan Serai at Lahore you will pass under an ancient gateway into the particular part of the serai or travellers' rest frequented by Afghan traders, horse-traders for choice, where used to sit the sons of Mahbub Ali, the Afghan horse-dealer of "Kim" fame. There were three of them: Wazir Khan, a typical old Afghan; the elder brother, fat old Afzul Khan; and the youngest, Aslam, now the sole survivor. Rows of horses are tethered in the yard or under the arched recesses of the serai walls. They used to export the horses of Central Asia, Turcomani, Badakshani, and Kandahari, and would again but for the Amir of Kabul, who of late years has forbidden export. In some pitch-dark stable, perhaps underground, thin horses would be gobbling chopped green food the day long, to put soft deceptive flesh on their none too good bones; getting fat as butter in the process, so that you can hardly feel where the missing rib should be, and taking the fancy of some buyer who likes his horses round. Now and again the

Turcomani horses would fight, heels and teeth, till some groom would read the riot act, emphasising his admonishings with blows from a tent-peg.

But young Aslam, who is now old Aslam, quarrelled with his brothers in the serai, and split the business as Mahbub Ali knew he would, and lives elsewhere. Now mark the generations and the process of evolution. Mahbub Ali's father was an honourable Kabuli horse thief in a gentlemanly way, who had espoused the British fortunes in 1839 in the "great adventure" of those days, which was then called the "great game," no less an undertaking than the crossing of the foreign Punjab and the penetration of Afghanistan. When the British left the land, then he left the land, lest a halter be his guerdon and six feet of Afghan soil his patrimony. Mahbub Ali of "Kim" and his sons were horse-dealers of Lahore pure and simple, and purveyed polo ponies to all and sundry, and mules and horses for the cavalry. I once asked Mr James Daly of Liffey Bank outside Dublin if he was a Home Ruler, a foolish question. "Sorr," said he, "I am a harse dealer," and much the same answer would Mahbub Ali have given if you touched on Kabul politics. "*Kabul ki bat mut pucho, sahib*" – "Don't even ask, sir, of affairs in Kabul." Now again watch the process of evolution. Young Aslam sent his son to Cambridge to take a veterinary degree and make a speciality of trading in screws, but the lad would not do a day's work at the Varsity, and sits at home in Lahore in ease demanding more money of his father, *en route* from clogs to clogs. Young Aslam, who is now old Aslam, sometimes comes and sees me, and tells me of it sorrowfully, and tries to sell me the "best horse in India," which the remounts had foolishly sold out of the stud, during the process, while bemoaning the fallen family of Mahbub Ali.

But in the Sultan *Serai*, though none of the sons of Mahbub Ali hold sway, horse-dealers are still in occupation with the bundles of Bokhara carpets that have come down on camels through the Khaiber and still the "Persian pussy-cats spit on the bales." – It was in this same *Serai* among the Persian pussy-cats and the screaming Turcomanis and the Afghans drinking coffee that MacIntosh and Jelaluddin, the whiskified objectionable who had once been a fellow of his college, passed away.

PUNCH, OR THE LONDON CHARIVARI.—November 30, 1878.

"SAVE ME FROM MY FRIENDS!"

"IF AT THIS MOMENT IT HAS BEEN DECIDED TO INVADE THE AMEER'S TERRITORY, WE ARE ACTING IN PURSUANCE OF A POLICY WHICH *IN ITS INTENTION* HAS BEEN UNIFORMLY *FRIENDLY* TO AFGHANISTAN."—*Times*, Nov. 21.

Plate 3   Cartoon from *Punch*, November 30, 1878.

Source: *Blackwood's Magazine*, vol. CCXXII, no. MCCCXLII (July 1927), pp. 153–4.

54   George N. Curzon: *Russia in Central Asia in 1889 and the Anglo-Russian Question* (1889)

Whilst, however, I have confessed that in entering upon her Central Asian career, I believe Russia to have been actuated by no far-seeing policy, and in pursuing it to have been driven largely by the impulse of natural forces, I am not the less convinced that her presence there is a serious menace to India, and that she is prepared to turn it for her own purposes to the most profitable account. She is like a man who has tumbled quite naturally, but very much to his own surprise, into the inheritance of a wealthy relative, of whom he never heard, but of whom he was the unknowing heir; and who is not deterred by the adventitious source of his fortune from turning it to the most selfish advantage. Russia finds herself in a position in Central Asia where she can both benefit herself by opening up the material and industrial resources of a continent, and attack at his most vulnerable point the formidable adversary whose traditional policy is hostile to the fulfilment of what she describes as her national aspirations in Europe. I do not suppose that a single man in Russia, with the exception of a few speculative theorists and here and there a giddy subaltern, ever dreams seriously of the conquest of India. To anyone, Russian or English, who has even superficially studied the question, the project is too preposterous to be entertained. It would be an achievement compared with which the acquisition of India by a trading company – in itself one of the phenomena of history – would be reduced to child's play; it would involve the most terrible and lingering war that the world has ever seen; and it could only be effected by a loss, most unlikely to occur, and more serious in its effects upon the human race than that of India itself, namely, the loss of the fibre of the British people. To those who solicit more practical considerations it may be pointed out that, with all the advantages of transport which she now enjoys, Russia would still be confronted with the difficulty of supplies, a difficulty great enough, as I have shown, even in the earlier stages of conflict in Afghanistan, but increasing in geometrical progression with every mile that she advanced beyond Balkh or Herat; and that

the recent extension and fortification of the British frontier in Pishin and Beluchistan will supply her with sufficient preliminary nuts to crack before she ever dips her hand into the rich garner of Hindostan. On the day that a Russian army starts forth from Balkh for the passes of the Hindu Kush, or marches out of the southern gate of Herat *en route* for Kandahar, with reason may the British commander repeat the triumphant exclamation of Cromwell (according to Bishop Burnet) at Dunbar, "Now hath the Lord delivered them into my hand!"

But though neither Russian statesmen nor Russian generals are foolish enough to dream of the conquest of India, they do most seriously contemplate the invasion of India; and that with a very definite purpose which many of them are candid enough to avow. The Parthian retreated, fighting, with his eye turned backward. The Russian advances, fighting, with his mind's eye turned in the same direction. His object is not Calcutta, but Constantinople; not the Ganges, but the Golden Horn. He believes that the keys of the Bosphorus are more likely to be won on the banks of the Helmund than on the heights of Plevna. To keep England quiet in Europe by keeping her employed in Asia, that, briefly put, is the sum and substance of Russian policy. Sooner than that England should intervene to thwart another San Stefano, or again protect with her guns a vanquished Stamboul, Herat must be seized by a *coup de main*, and General Annenkoff's cars must be loaded with armed men. I asked a distinguished Russian diplomatist under what circumstances his Government would feel itself justified in violating the Afghan frontier, so solemnly settled a year and a half ago, and challenging a conflict with England in the East. His reply was very distinct. "Upon the occurrence of either of two contingencies," he said; "if you tamper with the Russian dominions north of the Oxus; or if you interfere with the realisation of our national aims in Europe." It requires no Daniel to interpret the last named handwriting on the wall.

[. . .] It would be an error, however, to suppose that schemes for striking at India through Afghanistan are the emanation of military brains alone, or are to be attributed to the mingled tedium and irresponsibility of garrison life in the steppes. Statecraft is at least as much interested as generalship in the solution of the problem; and behind the more daring spirits who manufacture opportunities or execute designs upon the frontier, are cooler heads and more sagacious brains in the public offices upon the Neva, whose voice, particularly under the existing *régime*, possesses at least an equal share in the decision. The present head of the Asiatic Department of the Foreign Office at St Petersburg (a post which may be compared to our Secretaryship of State for India) is M. Zinovieff, who was formerly Russian Minister at Teheran, and is profoundly versed in the Central Asian Question. It is interesting, therefore, to have from his pen, as typical of the most distinguished civilian opinion among the bureaucracy, the admission that military necessities or frontier security were not the only motives that led Russia across the Caspian; and that statesmen as well as soldiers see in Afghanistan (the country outside the legitimate sphere of Russian influence) a fair field for the exercise of their abilities. In a despatch to the Minister for Foreign Affairs, sent from Teheran in March 1881, upon the policy of retaining the Akhal-Tekke oasis after the fall of Geok Tepe, M. Zinovieff expressed himself with much candour as follows:

It must not be forgotten that one of the causes which urged us to operations eastward of the Caspian Sea was the necessity for making an impression upon England, and checking her attempts against us in Central Asia. This was the consideration that produced our expedition in 1878 to Khwaja Kala. We then became convinced of the policy of subduing the Tekkes. It is impossible to believe that in the future the same necessity will not again arise. . . . Voluntarily to give up the dearly-bought successes of our present expedition would be all the more foolish since there is at present a most important Central Asian Question as yet unsettled – viz. the future of Afghanistan. . . . Even though Gladstone's Ministry is opposed to a policy of interference or incorporation, the English Conservatives, in the event of their return to power, will not find it impossible to discover sufficient reasons for the pacification of Afghanistan, in order to realise their political programme, which is to push the dominions and power of England to the uttermost, and to diminish the importance of Russia in Central Asia. Our advanced post at the northeast extremity of Khorasan, united as it is with our base on the Caspian by good lines of communication, will doubtless compel the English to be more circumspect in their ambitious schemes, as all the roads to the east and south-east are now open to us.

In deploying this chain of evidence, I have been announcing no new discovery; but, on the contrary, have recapitulated facts for the most part familiar to every student of the question: facts which render it impossible for anyone to deny that there is an Anglo-Russian Question of incalculable seriousness and vast proportions; facts, moreover, which, by the resistless force of their own accumulation, have made so deep an impression upon the public mind in this country that there is now but one opinion as to the lessons which they inculcate, and but one voice as to the duty that they impose. The school of politicians who described anxiety at Russia's advance upon India as "old women's fears," have closed the doors of their discredited academy. The policy of "masterly inactivity" meets with a hundred contemptuous critics for a single honest champion; and but a few voices, feebly bleating in the wilderness, still proclaim the unshaken security of the Indus Valley Frontier. No more significant proof of the *volte-face* which has been forced upon English opinion can be given, than that it was under a Liberal Prime Minister, himself the author of the memorable phrase above quoted, that this country was brought nearer to war with Russia in Central Asia than it has been at any time since the Crimean War; that it was by a Liberal Administration that a credit of eleven millions sterling for Imperial defence was demanded, and by a Liberal Viceroy of India that Beluchistan was annexed, the Amir of Afghanistan subsidised, and an advanced British frontier pushed forward into Quetta and Pishin. Russia may congratulate or commiserate herself upon having been convicted out of the mouth of her own witnesses.

It will have been noticed that what may be described as the mainspring of Skobeleff's policy was the employment of such seditious or insurgent elements as might be found open to anti-British appeals in India. And here, accordingly, I am brought in contact with a cardinal misconception underlying, and to a great extent vitiating, every Russian argument bearing upon invasion – namely, the deeply-rooted conviction, which has been betrayed by every Russian who has written upon the subject, and which was expressed to me by every Russian with whom I conversed about it, that the British rule in India is one of odious and incredible tyranny, that the majority of the Indian people are plunged in bitter affliction, and that the smallest spark falling in this magazine of combustibles must produce an explosion that will blow the British authority to atoms. It is useless to point out to the Russian that his belief is scarcely compatible with the fact that over 270,000,000 of this dangerous material are held in tranquil subjection by a force of 70,000 white soldiers, associated with a native army of double that number – or in other words, that there is only one armed man in India to every 1,300 of the population; whereas in Russian Turkestan and Transcaspia 45,000 men are required to control a native population of less than two and a-half millions, or at the rate of one armed man to every fifty of the native peoples. These calculations fail to disturb what is to his mind an *a priori* certainty, independent of reasoning, and based on an imperious confidence both in the popularity of Russia and in the hatred inspired by England.

[. . .] A firm belief in the destiny of Russia as the heaven-sent emancipator of distressed nationalities, and of peoples groaning under British misrule, is a factor in the situation which it is difficult to say whether an Englishman should regard with greater serenity or regret. On the one hand, he feels that in precise proportion to the magnitude of the illusion will be the recoil that must ensue upon its collapse. I repeat what is the testimony of those who have spent a life-time in India and know it best, when I say that whatever charges may plausibly or even fairly be brought against British administration in that country, whatever the discontent that may be lurking among native peoples, and however great the hopes that are habitually associated with change, there is no desire, and there would be no conspiracy for such a change as would substitute the mastery of Russia for that of Great Britain, and replace a dominion which, for all its austerity or its pride, has uniformly been characterised by public spirit, integrity, and justice, by one that has never, either in Europe or Asia, purged itself of the canker of corruption, coarseness, and self-seeking. Quite recently I read in the leading organ of the native party in India, and the strongest advocate of the Congress movement, the significant admission, "The princes and people of India look with positive dread upon Russian rule."

Source: George N. Curzon. *Russia in Central Asia in 1889 and the Anglo-Russian Question.* London: Frank Cass and Company, 1889, pp. 319–22, 331–5, 338.

55   Richard Issaq Bruce: "Lord Roberts's Speech, 1898"

THE last great contribution to the controversy on the Forward Policy was the debate on March 7, 1898, in the House of Lords on Lord Roberts's speech on the subject of British relations with the neighbouring tribes on the North-Western Frontier of India, and the military operations undertaken against them in 1897–98. Probably there is no means by which I could forward the object I have at heart better than by helping to keep before the public the opinions of the great statesmen who took the leading part in that debate, and the conclusions to be drawn from them.

I will not dwell on those parts showing how materially the Forward Policy bears on the great Imperial problems of the most effectual means of checking the advance of Russia, or the nature our relations should take with regard to Afghanistan, but will confine my remarks more particularly to showing how it affects the pacification of our Border-land, the civilisation of the tribes themselves, the bringing of them into line with ourselves, and identifying their interests with our own in the great scheme for the defence, strengthening, and consolidation of our frontier up to the boundary of our ally, the Amir of Afghanistan, as defined under the Durand Agreement. Lord Roberts – after calling attention to the papers presented to Parliament on the subject, and urging that it should not be regarded as a party question – spoke thus about the Forward Policy:

So great has been the divergence of opinion expressed on this question by men whose long connection with India gives them a claim to be listened to, it is no wonder that the public are puzzled with regard to it, and that statesmen should hesitate to commit themselves to any line of action until the subject has been thoroughly thrashed out, and the right course to pursue has been made clear to them and to the nation generally. This divergence of opinion among so-called experts, and which is apparently so unaccountable, is easily explained by the fact that those who oppose what has come to be known as the "Forward Policy" steadily ignore or treat as chimerical the reason which makes the carrying out of that policy essential if we are to retain our hold over India. The Forward Policy – in other words, *the policy of endeavouring to extend our influence over, and establish law and order on, that part of the Border where anarchy, murder, and robbery up to the present time have reigned supreme,* a policy which has been attended with the happiest results in Beluchistan and on the Gilgit frontier – is necessitated by the incontrovertible fact that a great Military Power is now within striking distance of our Indian possessions, and in immediate contact with a State for the integrity of which we have made ourselves responsible. Some forty years ago the policy of non-interference with the tribes, so long as they did not trouble us, may have been wise and prudent, though selfish and not altogether worthy of a great civilising Power. But during that period circumstances have completely changed, and what was wise and prudent then is most unwise and imprudent now. At that time Russia's nearest outpost was one thousand miles away; her presence in Asia was unheeded by, if not unknown to, the people of India; and we had no powerful reason for anxiety as to whether the two hundred thousand warriors on our Border would fight for us or against us.

Russia Our Neighbour

To-day Russia is our near neighbour; her every movement is watched with the keenest interest from Peshawar to Cape Comorin; she is in a position to enter Afghanistan whenever it may seem to her convenient or desirable so to do; and the chance of her being able to attack us is discussed in every bazaar in India. We are bound in honour, bound by a solemn promise made seventeen years ago, to protect Afghanistan, and between us and that nation are these two hundred thousand fighting men, who may either make the fulfilment of that promise easy or else most difficult if not impossible; for, if we should have to subdue these two hundred thousand warriors before going to the assistance of Afghanistan, any army we could put into the field would be used up before we could reach that country. Throughout the last Afghan war so persistently were we harassed by the tribesmen that the greater number of the troops employed were occupied in keeping open the lines of communication. On the Peshawar-Cabul line alone between eleven thousand and twelve thousand men were required, and, as I told the Viceroy at the time, had there been anything like combination or organisation among the tribes that number would have had to be doubled. The all-important question, therefore, that we have to consider is by what means can we ensure that this enormous military strength may be used for us, and not against us. The opponents of the Forward Policy tell us that this can only be done by continuing the system tried for nearly half a century of letting the tribesmen alone, no matter what atrocities they commit, so long as they do not interfere with us, and, when their conduct necessitates punishment, recurring to the punitive expeditions which have already cost us such a vast expenditure in blood and money, and inflicted such cruel misery on the innocent families of the delinquents. Burning houses and destroying crops, necessary and justifiable as such measures may be, unless followed up by some form of authority or jurisdiction, mean starvation for many of the women and children of the enemy, and for us a rich harvest of hatred and revenge in more daring acts of outrage so soon as the tribesmen recover from their temporary check.

The Forward Policy

The advocates of the Forward Policy, on the other hand, contend that the system they recommend, and which has also been tried, but with far different results, on the southern and northern frontiers, is the only one which will enable us to gain the confidence and secure the allegiance of the wild and lawless, but brave and manly, inhabitants of the central section of the Border, who have so clearly proved by the part they have taken in the late disturbances the absolute failure of the policy of non-interference. For so completely was the policy of non-interference tried with the bordermen, especially with the Afridis, that their country was until the other day a *terra incognita* to us; and so anxious were we to avoid giving them the slightest cause for suspicion that we wished to interfere with their independence that the political officer in the Khyber, who also commanded the Khyber Rifles and was responsible for the pass being kept open, was absolutely prohibited from going to the right or left of the narrow road which leads through the pass, and the only British officer who ever ventured to enter Afridiland before Sir William Lockhart's force went there was punished by being removed from his appointment. We gave the Afridis large sums for permitting kafilas to go backwards and forwards once a week through the Khyber Pass for trading purposes, and we paid them an annual subsidy for allowing us to make use of the shortest route between Peshawar and Kohat, which runs for a short distance through a corner of their land, and which they closed against us whenever it pleased them to do so, greatly to our inconvenience and annoyance. Is it possible for non-interference to be carried further? The recent very serious rising, which is still not altogether suppressed, as well as most of the frontier troubles of late years, have not been caused, as is so frequently stated, by the Forward Policy, but by that policy not having been pushed far enough; by our refusing to recognise the responsibilities of our position with regard to India and Afghanistan; and by the half-hearted manner in which we have carried on our dealings with the tribesmen. Not, in fact, by what we have done, but by what we have left undone. The Forward Policy must, in my opinion, be gradually and judiciously but steadily pursued until we obtain political control over the robber-haunted No-man's Land which lies on our immediate frontier, where every man's dwelling is a miniature fortress, fortified against his neighbour, and must be continued until our influence is felt up to the boundary of our ally, the ruler of Afghanistan. When the responsibility for the defence of the North-West Frontier devolved on me as Commander-in-Chief in India I never contemplated any defence being possible along the frontier, as marked on our maps by a thin red line – the haphazard frontier inherited by us from the Sikhs – which did well enough so long as we had only to guard against tribal depredations. A frontier more than one thousand miles in length, with a belt of huge mountains in its front, inhabited by thousands of warlike men, over whom neither we nor any other Power had control, and with a wide, impassable river in its rear, seemed to me then, as it does now, an impossible frontier, and one on which no scheme for the defence of India could be safely based.

The Essentials of Defence

For that defence it is evident that we must have the command of the most important of the roads which run through those mountains, and, to use a favourite expression of the great Duke of Wellington's, "we must be able to see the other side of the hill"; for, unless we know for certain what is going on there, it will be impossible to prevent an enemy from making use of them, and debauching on the plains of India when and where he pleases. So satisfied was I as to the weakness and unfitness of our present frontier, that I pointed out to the Government of which I had the honour to be a member that money would be thrown away on fortifications and entrenched positions along such a line, and that, after securing the safety of the two most advanced arsenals, Queita and Rawul Pindi, we should devote ourselves to improving and extending our frontier roads and, so far as financial considerations would permit, our railway communications, to enable the field army to advance whenever a further movement might be required. I never ceased, at the same time, to reiterate that roads and railways could not be made through a hostile country, and that we should do all in our power to enter into closer and more friendly relations with those tribes through whose lands the roads and railways would have to run. This course will assuredly be forced on us, whether we like it or not, in the interests of civilisation and by circumstances over which we have very little control. It is a great satisfaction, therefore, to know that whereever it has been thoroughly carried out it has

proved eminently successful. In support of this statement I would invite attention to the fact that throughout the present unusual frontier excitement not a shot has been fired in that part of Beluchistan which is under our control, or in Chitral, where British officers are in direct communication with the tribes and where our boundary is practically coterminous with Afghanistan. And, as your lordships will doubtless remember, when disturbances broke out in Chitral in the beginning of 1895 the very men who had most strenuously opposed us in Hunza Nagar three years before actually volunteered to serve under our officers, whom they had learned to know and to trust, and a body of levies drawn from these robber hordes did excellent service for us on that occasion. I trust you will not be persuaded to believe that the tribesmen would fight for us if left to themselves. Why should they? They would have nothing to fear from us and nothing to gain by siding with us, for we should have nothing to offer them in return; while they would be induced to fight against us by the prestige which an advancing force always carries with it, and by promises, which would be freely given, that they should be sharers in the plunder of the riches of India. The question we are discussing is, believe me, of vital importance to our future in India, for the attitude, not only of the Border tribes, but of the whole Afghan nation, will depend on the character of our frontier policy. If we are able to convince them that we have the will and the power to protect them, and are determined to let no other nation interfere with them, we may confidently reckon on their throwing in their lot with us. But this desirable result, my lords, can only be brought about by extending our influence over the tribes in the centre of our frontier, as it has been extended over the people of Chitral and Beluchistan, and by letting the Afghans see that we are prepared to go to their assistance should occasion arise.

Sir R. Sandeman's Policy

I would point out that the Forward Policy has not been simply a military subjugation; for, although at times force has had to be resorted to to keep the tribesmen in order, the conquest on the north and south has been largely a peaceful conquest. If anyone doubts this statement I would ask him to read the Life of Sir Robert Sandeman, one of the greatest frontier administrators – the very embodiment of the Forward Policy. With very little fighting Beluchistan – an immense tract of mountain and desert country, and inhabited by clans as wild and restless as any on our frontier – was rescued by that practical Border officer from a condition of absolute chaos, and turned into what is now a peaceful and prosperous province, where our officers move about freely escorted by the tribesmen themselves, and are everywhere met by signs of confidence and respect. Sir Robert Sandeman used to describe his policy as one of "peace and goodwill," and that it certainly was. In 1885 Sir Charles Aitchison, Lieutenant-Governor of the Punjab, one of the great Lord Lawrence's most devoted followers; and who as Foreign Secretary in India had been a steady adherent of the policy of "masterly inactivity," wrote to the then Viceroy, the Earl of Dufferin, in the following words: "Sandeman is doing noble work at Quetta. He knows personally all the heads of the tribes and all the leading men, and has great influence over them. The people are rapidly settling down and learning respect for law and order. I believe the change between Quetta now and Quetta five years ago is greater than between the India of to-day and the India as I knew it before the Mutiny, and that is saying a good deal. For this we have mainly to thank Robert Sandeman, whose personal influence is something marvellous. Cultivation is rapidly spreading on the Quetta plateau, and villages with foliage are springing up all round the cantonment. . . . I cannot speak too highly of the work he is doing. It is noble pioneer work." It is this same system of tribal management that has been so successfully introduced on the Gilgit frontier, where law and order have taken the place of raids, brigandage, and the horrors of the slave trade. The occupation of Gilgit and Chitral and the successful Hunzanagar expedition brought about this desirable change, by which numbers of unhappy people who had passed long years in slavery have been restored to their homes. When the expense and loss of life involved in the Chitral expedition are dwelt on, and we are urged to withdraw our troops, these facts should not be forgotten. Moreover, the evacuation of a country which has been the scene of warlike operations is not, as some people imagine, always an advantage to the inhabitants. When Dost Mahomed Khan was allowed to return to Kabul as Amir he made short work of everyone who had helped us during the first Afghan war. Yakub Khan, in the few months he was ruler after the Treaty of Gandamak, showed that he had every intention of following his grandfather's example, and all who assisted us in Afghanistan in 1879–80 have either been made away with or are obliged to live as exiles in our territory. In considering the question of what advantage we are to gain from the series of extremely difficult operations which have

been so successfully carried out by the distinguished officer in charge, General Sir William Lockhart – an officer in whom the country may have every confidence – and by the loyal and brave soldiers, native as well as British, serving under his command, we must bear in mind that our present frontier position is not due to any desire on the part of the rulers of India to acquire territory or subjugate races for our own aggrandisement.

Our Present Frontier Position

We have been constrained to press on, partly by the action of the tribesmen themselves, who have made it impossible for our fellow-subjects to live at peace with them as neighbours, partly by the advance of Russia, and partly at the special request of the Amir of Afghanistan, who, when we objected to his interfering with recalcitrant tribesmen, justly remarked that it would be impossible to maintain peace on his side of the Border unless these men were brought either under his or our control. So anxious was the Government of India not to be drawn on that in some instances positions taken up were abandoned, only to be, of necessity, re-occupied later on; and each successive Viceroy, Liberal and Conservative alike, has been compelled to move forward whether he wished it or not. When we left Candahar in the early days of the Marquis of Ripon's Viceroyalty it was intended to fall back to Jacobabad, if not to the Indus; but with all the will in the world to follow this course it was found impossible to do so, and we were obliged to remain at Quetta, because a further retrograde movement would have endangered the safety of Sind and the Lower Derajat. So nearly, however, was the retirement to Jacobabad carried into effect that the railway which was being laid through the Bolan Pass was taken up, and the material sent to Bombay, only to be brought back again and re-laid at considerable additional expense before the noble Marquis left India. This measure had only just been determined on when the aggressive action of Russia on the northern boundary of Afghanistan necessitated the railway being extended to Chaman, and sufficient material stored there to carry it on to Candahar, if occasion should require.

After describing the humiliating results of our retirement from Kurram, and consequent breach of our promise and obligations to the Kurram tribes and people, he continued:

It is sometimes urged as a reason against our endeavouring to get control over the inhabitants in the central part of the frontier that they are more difficult to deal with than the people of Beluchistan. Beluchis, no doubt, are less fanatical than Pathans, but they are just as warlike, and were just as much given to pillaging and murdering as their more northern neighbours; moreover, a great number of the inhabitants of Beluchistan are Pathans, while in Gilgit and Chitral the character- istics of the people are infinitely more Pathan than Beluch. The truth is that Pathans – robbers and murderers though they may be, because they know no better – are fine, gallant fellows, and, like Orientals everywhere, are responsive to vigorous and sympathetic treatment, as we know from our experience of those of them who have served in our ranks. If our present operations are followed up by an Administrator of the Sandeman stamp being placed in political charge of the frontier tribes; by the occupation of some commanding position in Afridiland which will ensure our having the control of the Khyber Pass, and will form a much-needed sanatorium for the fever-stricken garrisons in the Peshawar Valley, by giving the tribesmen employ- ment on such roads and railways as may be needed for our requirements; and if we make our influence felt in establishing law and order without inter- fering with their habits, customs, or religion, the Afridis, and in time the rest of the Border tribes, will settle down and become, not only peaceful neighbours, but as brave and loyal soldiers in our service as the Sikhs, Goorkhas, and other warlike races who have fought against us, have proved themselves to be. It is impossible to doubt this when we call to mind the recent splendid behaviour of the Khyber Rifles, who, even after having been deprived in a most incomprehensible manner of the support of their British officer at the time when that support was most needed, defended Lundi-Kotal against their own kith and kin until overcome by numbers, when they retired to Jamrud, and have since been fighting alongside our regular troops.

Lord Roberts here reviewed the reasons why we cannot disregard the advance of Russia, and pointed out the error of those who contend that she could not again raise up serious com- plications for us in Afghanistan, and why it is specially incumbent on us to be prepared for such contingencies, and, while the times are fa- vourable, to set our frontier in order. His lordship further explained why it was not his business to discuss the question from a financial point of view, and wound up his stirring appear in the following words:

I conceive it to be my duty, as one who has had peculiar opportunities of making himself acquainted with our position on the North-West Frontier of India, to lay before you as clearly as I am able to do the reasons for the policy I advocate, and which seems to me to be the only policy that can ensure the safety of India. And it is for you and the nation to decide on the course to be followed. I can only venture to express my firm conviction that, whatever may be the cost of the measures I propose, the cost, to say nothing of the danger to the Empire, will be infinitely greater if we allow matters to drift until we are obliged, in order to resist aggression in Afghanistan, to hurriedly mobi- lise a sufficient force to subdue the hostile tribes through whose country we should have to pass before we could reach those strategical positions which it is essential we should be able to occupy without delay if we do not intend India – that brightest jewel in Great Britain's Crown – to pass out of our safe keeping.

Lord Roberts was followed in the debate by the Earl of Onslow, Under-Secretary of State for India, and it can hardly be said that he seriously contested the fundamental principles held by Lord Roberts. The following portions of his lordship's speech are those which I think have the most direct bearing on the question at issue; and they further show the policy the Government of India had resolved to adopt, for the time being at all events. His lordship remarked:

If I understand the proposal of the noble lord to- night, it is that we should assume political control of what he calls "the robber-haunted No-man's Land" between India and Afghanistan, that we should take up our boundary so as to be coterminous with that of the Amir of Afghanistan, take control of all the roads which lie between the two countries, and construct railways to the fron- tier of the Amir's territory. Now, my lords, I do not for a moment wish to differ from the noble lord when he says that it is most desirable that we should have roadways and railways up to the fron- tier of Afghanistan, but I think the noble lord will agree with me that that can be accomplished on one condition, and one condition only – namely, that we should place these tribes through whose terri- tories these roads and railways would pass under the subjection of the Government of India. There is one feature in the speech of the noble lord which I welcome. There was no attempt to suggest that the military operations which have recently been carried on on the North-West Frontier were due to the action of one party or another party in the State. There has been a good deal too much in the recent controversies we have listened to on this subject of trying to attach blame to one set of her Majesty's Ministers or another. I welcome in the noble lord's speech a contribution towards the attempt to solve a most difficult question, one which has been a perennial embarrassment to successive Governments of India. The noble lord did not suggest to us by what means he would proceed to the subjugation of these independent tribes on the frontier. No doubt it is a fascinating picture to draw that we should occupy the great plateau of the Tirah, standing as it does at considerable elevation above the level of the sea and in marked difference to Peshawar and our cantonments lower down the valley. But though the Tirah commands some of the principal passes, like the Khyber, the Bolan, and the Kohat, it does not command the whole of our North-West Frontier. That frontier is a thousand miles in length. It is obvious that even if we adopted the noble lord's suggestion, and established a sanatorium at Tirah, we should still have a large extent of frontier with which we should have to deal in a different way. [. . .]

The noble lord compared the nature of the Beluchis and the Pathans, but I venture to think that the nature of these tribes is essentially different, as is also their system. Among the Beluchis there is a head man of the tribe, and once his consent is obtained to a proposal you have the consent of the whole tribe. That is not so with the Pathans; indeed, there is a system of government among them with which we are not wholly unacquainted in this country. I believe they enjoy what is known there as Party government, and that in no country, not even in France, are such rapid changes made as among those who administer the affairs of their tribes. But when he says we should endeavour to cultivate more friendly relations with the frontier tribes, that is a very different thing, for his first proposal was that we should occupy that territory and take political control there. The Pathans are not wild animals that you have to seek out in their lairs, or to stalk like deer in the Highlands. They come down and mix with their fellow-subjects in India, and thousands of them spend months among them on the other side of the Indus. They have relations with us that are entirely friendly, and even now when we have been engaged in what some may call bitter warfare with them – though I do not think they would do so – they send down their women to Peshawar to be looked after by the ladies there, satisfied that they would be well treated and cared for, and they have no hesitation in handing their letters to our people for safe delivery. Does that not show a full confidence in our declaration that we will leave them in entire occupation of their country and that we have no desire to interfere with their tribal customs? [. . .]

I had the advantage in 1894 of being present at a solemn durbar held by Lord Elgin, in which he made a speech addressed not only to our fellow-subjects there, but to all representatives there from the confines of India and Afghanistan. He said: "It is our aim and ambition so to regulate our relations with the brave frontier tribes of the North-West Border as at the same time to secure peace and security of life and property, on which all our Treaty obligations, and the dictates of humanity, compel us to insist, and to leave to them the entire occupation of their country, with the fullest measure of autonomy and the most complete liberty to follow their internal affairs and tribal customs." When this was translated I thought there was a look on the face of the people which showed that it fell on no unwilling ears. That declaration is the policy of her Majesty's Government, and a despatch to which the noble lord has referred lays down that it is the policy of the Government to avoid any extension of administrative control over the tribes, but at the same time the Government recognise the necessity of acting in absolute fulfilment of those responsibilities in which we have concurred. Those responsibilities are that we must protect our own Borders and those who dwell on the Borders in British India. We must fulfil the solemn engagements we entered into with Afghanistan, and with the view of carrying out that policy the Secretary of State has laid down that the roads and communications necessary for that purpose must be preserved and that posts must be established. But in the establishment of these posts a great deal of limitation is placed in the despatches. Those who have followed the operations on the North-West Frontier will have observed that many of the posts which have been attacked were not sufficiently defensible, and the Viceroy has been enjoined to limit the establishment of posts on the frontiers outside our own Border to those which are sufficiently defensible, and which can promptly and immediately repel attack. He has also been enjoined to weight financial considerations. Not only must the posts established be desirable, but the gain of them established must be commensurate with their expense.

After referring to the arrangements with the Afridis for the safety of the Khyber Pass, and the reasons why in the late imbroglio the officer commanding the Khyber Rifles had been withdrawn and no troops had been sent to their relief, his lordship continued:

The noble lord has referred to the question of the appointment of a Frontier Commission, but not in great detail, and also to Sir R. Sandeman – and nobody ever served the Crown with greater distinction and success. But I would ask him if he can point at this moment to anyone who has fulfilled the conditions which Sir R. Sandeman fulfilled, and on whom all eyes are concentrated as a man who ought to be appointed. Until he can, I think that is a question which may remain slumbering. I think that in the history of every country, in the history of England, and in the history of Europe, there have been many cases where mountain tribes have maintained their independence and resisted civilisation for a long time. In almost every one of these instances these populations and these mountaineers have ultimately had to accept the civilisation which had been brought to their doors, and had been absorbed in the great States that have grown up round them. I do not think any one of us would predict any other destiny for the barbarous tribes of our North-West Frontier. The time when this should be accomplished seems to be in the hands of destiny. Whether it should be accelerated lies very much with the Government of India and the Government of this country. I submit that the moment is not opportune for hurrying on this question. The sacrifice of treasure and men involved is not commensurate with the objects. The rapid advance of Russia was referred to by the noble and gallant lord, but I am not going to follow him in that part of his speech. In the past gigantic strides have been made by Russia towards our frontier in India, but at the present moment, however, whatever may happen in the future, Russia seems to be intent on other parts of her empire. The Trans-Continental Railway requires her attention more than Afghanistan. The present moment is not one which has any special reason why we should make advances as rapidly as has been desired by the noble lord. I would rather wish that the matter should be allowed to remain in the condition in which it now is. Let us go on cultivating these friendly relations with the frontier tribes, and do not let us attempt to administer their territory or to obtain greater control over their tribal customs.

The Present Position

The position in which we now stand may be summed up in a very few words. What we have done is to dispel the delusion which seems to be entertained by these tribes that there is any part of their territory inaccessible to us should we choose to go there. We have proved our sincerity that we do not desire to occupy any part of their territory. The terms we have given them are leniency themselves. Just as a Bank of England note is currency in all parts of the world because there is no reason to suppose that the Bank will not carry out the obligations printed on the note, so it is known that the declarations that we would avenge any attempt at inroad upon our own territory is equally certain to be accomplished, and that once accomplished we shall return to the solemn undertaking that we have made in the declaration which I have read to your lordships, that we have no other wish than to cultivate the friendship and goodwill of our neighbours who live on the North-West Frontier of our Indian territory.

The Earl of Northbrook, without giving his own views as to the general results of the Foward Policy, expressed his acquiescence in the present attitude of the Government of India, chiefly on the grounds that "he could not help thinking" that the recent troubles on the frontier were produced by a suspicion that an encroachment on the independence of the tribesmen was intended, and commended the principle that there should be "no interference with them and no permanent control."

If the cause of the recent troubles was either the apprehension of the tribes as to their independence being tampered with, or of our intervention and control, why did the troubles not extend to Beluchistan proper – to Zhob and Bori, to Wana, the Mahsud country, and to Kurram, where intervention and control was and is an essential factor in the policy pursued? No, believe me, if such apprehensions existed and were due to a Forward Policy, it was not to that policy carried out on the conciliatory lines which proved successful under the Sandeman system; which could, indeed, hardly be deprecated by Lord Northbrook, who proved to be himself one of the chief pioneers of the forward movement in deputing Sandeman on his missions of friendly intervention to the Beluchistan tribes and to Quetta, in 1876–77, and at a later period by establishing a British political officer at Gilgit, the two most forward posts on our North and North-Western Frontiers.

Indeed it might be inferred from the Under-Secretary's most flattering reference to Sir Robert Sandeman's work, and pointed question as to whether at the present time any possible officer could be found to take up his mantle, that he also approved of the Sandeman Forward Policy. But in an important Imperial question like this so intimately affecting the well-being of the frontier, if the thing is the right thing to be done and our duty is plain, it is contrary to the usage and tradition of the British nation that it should remain long undone, either for want of a capable man to carry it out or on account of the cost it might entail.

Lord Northbrook struck a very useful key in reminding us that an important point which should not be lost sight of in the determination of our tribal policy is the using of these Border lands as a recruiting ground for our Indian army. This I believe to be another factor the benefits of which cannot be fully attained or utilised without the extension of our control over the tracts in question. But I shall have another word to add on this subject before I close these Memoirs.

Lord Lansdowne expressed his concurrence in the opinion of Lord Roberts, and as he gave his views fully in his customary clear and straightforward, and to my mind unanswerable, way, I will quote his words nearly at length. His lordship said:

He could not help thinking that those who had listened to the speech of the noble and gallant lord must have felt that the account which he had given of the so-called Forward Policy differed very widely indeed from that which had been presented to the public in the Press and on the platform during the past few months. They had been constantly told that the Government of India had been captured by a little clique of military gentlemen inspired with a desire for wide schemes of annexation, and inspired above all things with a thirst for medals. He could not help thinking that the Under-Secretary had scarcely apprehended the meaning which his noble and gallant friend intended to convey to the House. He (Lord Lansdowne) certainly did not understand him to suggest that what he described as his Forward Policy should be applied in anything but a gradual and most cautious manner. There was no suggestion of an immediate occupation of tribal country, or any immediate advance of boundary in the direction of Afghanistan. In point of fact, he gathered what his noble and gallant friend would advocate was very much what was advocated by the Under-Secretary himself, who told the House how the result of recent operations had been to dispel the delusion of the inaccessibility of the tribes, and that, that result having been achieved, he was in favour of being more friendly with the tribes. That was the policy of the despatch, and that, he ventured to say, was the policy of every sensible person who had ever considered this matter. He (Lord Lansdowne) had protested against the exaggerated descriptions of the Forward Policy which had been placed before the country of late. All of them know that the policy of Lord Lawrence, excellent though it was in its day, was one which had been left far behind, and by far the most numerous and largest strides had been taken by the party opposite. What was perfectly obvious was that the advance of Russia to the very gates of Persia and Afghanistan and our own advance to points very far beyond the line of the Indus, and, above all, engagements we had entered into with the Amir, rendered it out of the question that the old policy of Lord Lawrence should be resorted to in the present day. Another thing had, he thought, further accentuated the difference between the old order of things and the order of things in the present day, and that was the conclusion of the Durand agreement. He knew it had been held that one of the results of the Durand Agreement had been to create a feeling of unrest among the tribes. There might be some truth in that assertion, but on the other hand he was convinced that the Durand Agreement was the greatest step for a long time in the direction of placing our relations with the tribes on one hand and the Amir on the other on a satisfactory footing. During those discussions they constantly heard it said that it was desirable to exercise an influence of some kind over those tribes. He doubted if any single speech had been made or any single despatch written in which that expression "influence" did not occur. He wanted to know what it was they meant when they talked in that way of the tribes. The word was wanting in precision, and they were more likely to arrive at its meaning if they considered what it did not mean. He rather thought that even within our own hearts we carried the plan of extending our provincial administration a little too far. The tribesmen were lawless and rough people and did not understand technicalities and formalities, but valued the substance of justice more than its form. They were not grateful to us for giving them an elaborate code of laws with the right of appealing to a Court hundreds of miles from their homes. The result of this was not advantageous to our own officers, but made them depend rather too much on mere technicalities and forms instead of looking to the substantial justice and effectiveness of their administration. He was therefore by no means in favour of bringing the frontiers outside our limits within the scope of our administration. Influence did not mean mere abstention. In private life we could not influence our neighbours by pretending to be unaware of their presence, and if occasionally they varied the procedure by violent assault, they might arrive at some kind of influence, but it would not be what the noble lord called "friendly influence," which was what he desired over the tribes. And much as they might wish to maintain the attitude of pure abstention facts would not allow us to do so. Fancy pictures were sometimes drawn which looked as if we had nothing to do with what happened on the other side of the Border. But that was not so. The tribes frequented our territory, and moved backwards and forwards between the plains and the hills, so that we could not ignore their existence.

Thus there was forced on us not a policy of abstention, but a policy of abstention qualified by very severe police methods. Those familiar with India knew the kind of circle round which events travelled. They had months, perhaps years, of lawlessness and misconduct, but the authorities put their blind eye to the telescope; but at last, the raids becoming too numerous, a fine was imposed, which was paid by the most respectable members of the tribes. If it was unpaid then they had a blockade, which injured the laborious and hardworking portion of the community, and then came an expedition, the result being that the troops go away leaving behind them a legacy of hatred and contempt, hatred for the injuries we had done them and contempt because we could not maintain the advantage we had gained. Was such a policy dignified and worthy of a Great Power? Was it an economical policy judging from the large sums spent on it? And he asked whether we could be surprised that, there should have grown up in India a school of public men who, without harbouring sinister designs on the independence of the tribes, desired to see something more worthy of such a Power as ours. He noticed the Leader of the Opposition quoted from a book written by Mr Thorburn on the subject, which he recommended to his hearers. Mr Thorburn said that "to teach the hill tribes a lasting lesson a severe loss must be inflicted on them, by the wholesale destruction of available property such as towers, houses, crops, &c., while territory must be annexed and leading men or families blotted out by deportation if the work is to be thorough or endurable." He certainly was not prepared to go as far as that. He believed there were many men in India who were weary of a frontier policy of that kind, and desired to substitute a better policy. If such a feeling was entertained, it was a feeling which originated, not with ambitious soldiers, but with a great many of our best and most intelligent officers and civilian officials, who were

convinced it was within our power to manage the tribes on a different principle. The policy which he understood to be advocated by Lord G. Hamilton's despatch was a policy of control over the tribes within our sphere of influence coupled with the minimum of interference with their domestic affairs. To talk of tribal independence was a little misleading. There could be no complete independence in the case of people who had not the power of transferring their allegiance in any direction they pleased. That power was not given to the frontier tribes, and it was better, therefore, not to speak of them as independent. That condition of qualified independence was very common all through the Borders of India. The small frontier tribes were not strong enough to stand alone. They knew they must lean on some stronger Power, and in the case of the tribes in question he took it that it was our intention they should lean on us and not on any other Power. But if that policy was to have any success, he held strongly – and he found nothing in the despatch inconsistent with it – that we must show the tribes that they had something to hope as well as something to fear from us. That, he took it, was the essence of the policy advocated by the noble and gallant lord, and that was the policy which was indicated in the despatch, in which he found that, even in the case of the Afridi tribes, who had most defied our authority, the Government of India was instructed that it was, if possible, to enlist their good will and secure their assistance in maintaining the road through the Khyber Pass. With regard to roads and railways, the noble lord in the matter of railways was always a little ahead of the Indian Government. He desired to see certain strategic lines made, but the Government thought they would be very expensive and bring in little or no return. The case of roads stood on different footing. That the main arterial roads were to be left open was not denied, but in the case of subsidiary roads it was not so clear, though he did not think any money was better spent on the frontier than in encouraging tribes of their own free will to make and improve roads, which were great civilisers. As to the question of posts, there the policy of the despatch was quite clear. The Government desired to see as few military posts as possible, and those placed in the strongest and most carefully selected positions. The tendency was to concentrate the posts, but there must be some posts to guard the roads. With regard to the question of the frontier officers by whom the tribal affairs were to be regulated, he was in entire agreement with the noble and gallant lord. Sir R. Sandeman's policy was signally successful in Beluchistan. The tribes differed a great deal in organisation and qualities, and where one tribe was found to be peaceful another was warlike. He believed it was possible to administer the frontier in a better manner than by reverting to the old system of inflicting severe punishment on the tribes and then withdrawing altogether from intercourse with them. Among the qualities which distinguished the race to which we belonged stood out conspicuously those qualities of self-reliance and broad sympathy which had enabled us all over the world to win over to ourselves men belonging to races less civilised than our own.

The concurrent opinions of Lord Roberts and the Marquis of Lansdowne should be of themselves sufficient for my purpose, as few will venture to assert that they are not the two greatest living authorities on the subject; but what if I can add to them the agreement of two of the greatest, if not the two greatest, statesmen; which may I think be gathered from the following words of the Duke of Devonshire, speaking for himself and for Lord Salisbury:

The Duke of Devonshire said that, like his noble friend, he very much regretted the absence of the Prime Minister, but he could assure his noble friend that if the Prime Minister had been present there would have been no divergence of opinion between him and the Secretary of State for War. He did not know on what foundation his noble friend formed the inference that there was a divergence of views between the India Office and the Secretary for War, unless it was that the Secretary for War spoke with great respect of the very able speech which had been delivered by the noble and gallant lord on the cross benches, and pointed out that if it was an exposition of what was called the Forward Policy it was an exposition very different indeed from some they had been accustomed to hear. He had some difficulty in understanding what was the divergence which his noble friend opposite found between the speech of the Secretary for War and the despatch of the Secretary for India. His noble friend the Secretary for War had explained that it was not possible at the present time, after all that had happened, to revert to that policy which was associated with the name of Lord Lawrence in respect to the frontier tribes. That principle is also fully admitted in the despatch of the Secretary of State for India. It was impossible at the present time to revert to what used to be called the aloof policy, and refuse to have anything to do with these tribes unless on occasions when it was thought necessary to have recourse to punitive expeditions. At

the conclusion of his observations his noble friend opposite said that he believed the true manner of dealing with these tribes was to cultivate friendly relations with them. There was not a word in the speech of his noble friend the Secretary of State for War which inculcated any other policy. It was admitted by the late Government of India and by the present Government of India that our responsibilities towards these tribes had very greatly increased, and that the system that might have been the best to pursue a few years ago was one which could be no longer pursued. His noble friend opposite said that the Forward Policy was a policy which had led to Afghan wars in the past. He (the Duke of Devonshire) saw no indication of a reversion to that policy. Nothing that had been said by Lord Roberts himself to-night, still less anything that had been said by the Secretary of State for War, could have conveyed to the mind of anyone the idea that any reversion to that policy was intended. That was a policy of aggression on independent tribes. On what independent tribes did we now desire to lay a hand? The only question now was how were friendly relations to be maintained with a certain number of tribes which everyone had admitted we had brought into closer relationship than formerly was the case. The Secretary for War said we could not deal with them exactly on the same principles as used to be adopted, and he (the Duke of Devonshire) failed to see that his noble friend opposite in his very vague references to the cultivation of friendly relations had indicated any other policy. His noble friend was absolutely mistaken in supposing that if the Prime Minister were present tonight he would have given the slightest shadow of confirmation to the inference which his noble friend had drawn that there was any diversity of opinion between the two departments on this subject. He had heard no word from the Secretary for War to-night which departed in the slightest degree from the principle laid down by Lord Salisbury in his speech in the debate on the Address.

All alike agree that it is essential we should continue to exercise influence over the tribes, all concur that we must bring them under our "friendly influence," but those of what may be called the "aloof policy" say this must be done without intervention and without permanent control. Lord Lansdowne went to the root of the matter when he asked the pertinent question what this influence meant, and when he dissipated the mischievous delusion of the independence of the tribes. The fact is the two things are incompatible, as without intervention and control no friendly influence of any value can be extended. Hence the phrase is a misleading one.

As pointed out by Lord Lansdowne, they are not independent as they cannot transfer their "allegiance," and we have bound them in their engagements with us not to transgress the boundary of our friend and ally the Amir. The only "friendly influence" of value to our Government is that which is founded on respect for the Suzerain power and on mutual intercourse and reciprocal relations, their country being open for us to come and go in, as ours is to them.

As long as there is a *purdah* or screen in their country the Mullahs and other evil-disposed factions will hatch all manner of intrigues and villainies behind it, and we can never really know what goes on or prevent it, while the tribe at large regard it as an infallible sign of weakness on our part, see that they can utilise it to evade their engagements, and despise us accordingly. They will take our arms, and take our money and arm themselves, without our having one substantial guarantee that they will not turn them on ourselves in the day of our difficulty.

Many years ago, when Sandeman and I were first tackling the Marris and Bugtis, I wrote about these tribes:

Independence means bloodshed, desolation, risk, and danger in every shape and form, and in the interests of peace and civilisation it is absolutely essential that they be brought under some paramount Power. If the Amir or the Khan of Khelat claim tribes as their own, they should admit and act up to their responsibilities and keep them in order. If they are under no rule, the sooner they are brought under one the better it will be for themselves and all concerned.

The only title to independence they have is that of the pirate or highway robber, having cut themselves adrift from all wholesome governing authority, thereby obtaining a license to cut throats and murder and plunder their neighbours.

There is a natural instinct in the minds of these men that this spurious independence is not permanent, and it is only the evil-doers, who make plunder and bloodshed pay, who resist being brought again under a sovereign authority. The chiefs and men of position who possess landed property and a stake in the country look on the state of affairs as unwholesome, and regard the intervention which restores the country to a healthy condition with gratitude. Nothing has done more mischief than the encouragement of the theory that these tribes

are independent, or tends so much to keep them outside the pale of civilisation.

Many years' subsequent work among the tribes has only confirmed me in the opinion I then expressed. The Marris and Bugtis have now got a healthy independence and are a strength instead of a weakness to our frontier, but what I wrote about them in 1884 is equally true about the Mahsud Waziris to-day.

But there is yet another authority I must quote, and perhaps the most important of all, as with him may rest the practical decision as to whether for the next few years our policy is to be Forward, Backward, or the Slumbering Policy – I refer to the present Viceroy, Lord Curzon of Kedleston.

Not long since he, then the Hon. George Curzon, MP, wrote an able letter to the "Times" advocating the retention of Chitral. Space does not permit my quoting the whole of it here, but I will refer to those parts which apply with equal if not greater force to other parts of our frontier, and to Waziristan in particular. In referring to the value of the tribal levies he wrote:

As regards the loyalty and fighting capacity of the tribesmen. Sir James Lyall threw doubt on the probable behaviour of the Hunza and Puniali levies in the recent campaign. We now know that it was largely owing to their gallantry that Colonel Kelly was able to make his famous march which raised the siege of Chitral Fort. What these men who were fighting against us in 1892 have done as our allies in 1895, the Chitralis, who belong to a milder race, will be ready to do in an even less period.

In alluding to the arguments of the advocates of retreat he wrote:

Even, however, if these contentions were sound, it can easily be shown that they cover but a small portion of the ground. Why is it that retreat from Chitral at this moment would be so unwise? The reasons are as follows:

Russia has, by the Pamir Convention concluded with Great Britain, just come into possession of three-fourths of the whole territory known as the Pamirs, and of a position which brings her down to the main stream of the Oxus. Locally this involves a great extension of her military and political prestige. If at the very same moment that she is thus permitted to advance up to the Hindu Kush on the north, Great Britain voluntarily retires from a position which for ten years she has occupied on the south, but one interpretation will be placed upon this coincidence by the natives of those regions. They do not understand high diplomacy, and they do not read the letters of retired Governors and Generals in the "Times." But with one alphabet they are perfectly familiar, and its two symbols are Forward and Backward. They will say that Russia is the winning and Great Britain the receding Power.

By our arrangements with the Amir of Afghanistan – of his belief in the binding nature of which his many conversations with me at Kabul, no less than the presence of his son in this country, have given convincing proof – we have practically guaranteed the integrity of his dominions as delimited by ourselves with the Russians. Now, Afghanistan includes Badakhshan; and the Indian watch-tower for Badakhshan is Chitral. If ever we should be called upon to fulfil our obligations in that quarter, it would be a deplorable mishap if we were found to have previously surrendered the obvious base of action.

The danger to India from a hostile authority in Chitral is not that of military occupation by a declared enemy alone. It is the danger that arises from clandestine influence and intrigue. A native ruler in Chitral who was in secret alliance with, and was, perhaps, subsidised by, another Power would be a more formidable thorn in the side of the British than would be several sotnias of Cossacks on the Dorah Pass. We cannot afford to have upon our flank such a gratuitous source of trouble. And yet if we retire from Chitral we positively encourage it. Retreat will further involve the suffering, if not the sacrifice, of all those who have stood by us in the recent campaign. [. . .]

The solution of the problem appears to be in the retaining of the British Political Agent in Chitral with a sufficient escort to insure his safety and command respect; the recognition as Mehtar of some member of the old reigning family other than the despicable youth who murdered his brother, the late Nizam-ul-Mulk; and, lastly, the keeping open of the direct road to Chitral through Dir by the occupation of military posts along it, and the formation of levies under the control of British officers. Under such a system the military strength of these frontier States would be trained and controlled by British officers; new recruiting grounds for the ranks of the Indian army would be available to the Government of India; roads would be opened up, and the entire frontier made accessible for military purposes, and a flow of trade between the settled districts of India and the remote valleys of the Hindu Kush created. As has happened all over India, the incessant strife of tribe against tribe, of one prince against another, would be put a stop to; an air of security would gradually settle down over these turbulent districts; half the men who have hitherto thought of little else than fighting each other or anybody who attempts to intrude upon them would be tilling their fields as peaceably as the once turbulent men of the Punjab or tribes of Beluchistan are now, and the rest would be fighting as sturdily for the Government of India as that Government's formerly redoubtable foes, the Sikhs, have recently done in the defence of Chitral. All this will not be effected without effort and without temporary checks and difficulties, but there is nothing inherently impossible in it; it is the same kind of work as has been done over and over again in the history of India. . . .

Those of my readers who have had the patience to follow me through these Memoirs – the account of the occupation of Fort Sandeman, and connected opening of the Gomal Pass; the occupation of Jandola, Kajuri-Kach, and Sarwekai, with troops, at the request of the Mahsud Maliks, for the control of hostile and marauding factions; the consequent murder of three of the Maliks; the occupation of Wana at the spontaneous and earnest request of the Wana Waziris; and the opening of the Tochi valley on the invitation of the Dawaris and Derwesh-Khels – will recognise that if we are bound by our obligations not to forsake the Chitralis, and not to forsake the Nawabs of Dir and Nawagai, our engagements and obligations binding us to Waziristan are still stronger; and our own direct advantages from its retention greater in the latter case than those set forth by Mr. Curzon in the former. And again, in a letter to Lady Sandeman referring to Sir Robert Sandeman's valuable work as accomplished in the occupation of Zhob and the opening of the Gomal, Mr. Curzon wrote:

Beluchistan and the frontier fringe as far as the Zhob valley and Gomal Pass are a standing monument to his system. This consisted in reconciling conflicting local interests under the common ægis of Great Britain; in employing the tribes as custodians of the highways and guardians of the peace in their own districts; in paying them for what they did well (and conversely in fining them for transgression), in encouraging commerce and traffic by the lightening or abolition of tolls and the security of means of communication; in the protection, rather than diminution of tribal and clan independence, subject only to the over-lordship of the British raj; in a word, in a policy not of spasmodic and retributive interference, but of steady and unfaltering conciliation.

To one who so thoroughly understood the Sandeman methods, and appreciated the policy so successfully inaugurated in Waziristan by the opening of the Gomal Pass through the co-operation of the Waziri Maliks, both Mahsud and Derwesh-Khel, we may in confidence look to pressing on systematically to completion the good work until the whole of Waziristan is linked up with Beluchistan in a uniform and civilising policy, with its powerful and warlike tribes ranged on the side of the British Government. We cannot afford to lose time, for if we continue to slumber on, the next imbroglio with Russia or Afghanistan may give us a rude awakening and cause us to pay dearly for lost opportunities.

Sir Robert Sandeman himself wrote:

The Waziri, Mando-Khel, Sherani, and other tribes do not in any great degree differ from the tribes of this Agency, and some do not differ at all. Where difference of race has existed, we have found human nature the same and amenable to like influences. We have made a commencement with the Waziris, and having placed our hands to the plough let us avoid nerveless vacillation and maintain a firm continuity of action. Let us not think of turning back, but let us carry to a successful conclusion what has been begun. If we knit the frontier tribes into our Imperial system in time of peace, and make their interests ours, they will certainly not oppose us in time of war, and as long as we are able and ready to hold our own, we can certainly depend on their being on our side.

For Government to allow matters to stagnate is tantamount to suspending the best education of their frontier civil officers, while at the same time it renders them powerless to prevent affairs drifting into complications which bring about those very punitive expeditions so universally condemned, and which the Government themselves avow it to be their chief object to prevent.

Source: Richard Issaq Bruce. *The Forward Policy and Its Results.* London and New York: Longmans, Green and Company 1900, pp. 324–50.

56 The Anglo-Russian Convention, August 31, 1907

Agreement concerning Persia

The Governments of Great Britain and Russia having mutually engaged to respect the integrity and independence of Persia, and sincerely desiring the preservation of order throughout that country and its peaceful development, as well as the permanent establishment of equal advantages for the trade and industry of all other nations;

Considering that each of them has, for geographical and economic reasons, a special interest in the maintenance of peace and order in certain provinces of Persia adjoining, or in the neighbourhood of, the Russian frontier on the one hand, and the frontiers of Afghanistan and Baluchistan on the other hand; and being desirous of avoiding all cause of conflict between their respective interests in the above-mentioned provinces of Persia;

Have agreed on the following terms:

I

Great Britain engages not to seek for herself, and not to support in favour of British subjects, or in favour of the subjects of third Powers, any Concessions of a political or commercial nature – such as Concessions for railways, banks, telegraphs, roads, transport, insurance, &c. – beyond a line starting from Kasr-i-Shirin, passing through Isfahan, Yezd, Kakhk, and ending at a point on the Persian frontier at the intersection of the Russian and Afghan frontiers, and not to oppose, directly or indirectly, demands for similar Concessions in this region which are supported by the Russian Government. It is understood that the above-mentioned places are included in the region in which Great Britain engages not to seek the Concessions referred to.

II

Russia, on her part, engages not to seek for herself and not to support, in favour of Russian subjects, or in favour of the subjects of third Powers, any Concessions of a political or commercial nature – such as Concessions for railways, banks, telegraphs, roads, transport, insurance, &c. – beyond a line going from the Afghan frontier by way of Gazik, Birjand, Kerman, and ending at Bunder Abbas, and not to oppose, directly or indirectly, demands for similar Concessions in this region which are supported by the British Government. It is understood that the above-mentioned places are included in the region in which Russia engages not to seek the Concessions referred to.

III

Russia, on her part, engages not to oppose, without previous arrangement with Great Britain, the grant of any Concessions whatever to British subjects in the regions of Persia situated between the lines mentioned in Articles I and II.

Great Britain undertakes a similar engagement as regards the grant of Concessions to Russian subjects in the same regions of Persia.

All Concessions existing at present in the regions indicated in Articles I and II are maintained.

IV

It is understood that the revenues of all the Persian customs, with the exception of those of Farsistan and of the Persian Gulf, revenues guaranteeing the amortization and the interest of the loans concluded by the Government of the Shah with the "Banque d'Escompte et des Prêts de Perse" up to the date of the signature of the present Agreement, shall be devoted to the same purpose as in the past.

It is equally understood that the revenues of the Persian customs of Farsistan and of the Persian Gulf, as well as those of the fisheries on the Persian shore of the Caspian Sea and those of the Posts and Telegraphs, shall be devoted, as in the past, to the service of the loans concluded by the Government of the Shah with the Imperial Bank of Persia up to the date of the signature of the present Agreement.

V

In the event of irregularities occurring in the amortization or the payment of the interest of the Persian loans concluded with the "Banque d'Escompte et des Prêts de Perse" and with the Imperial Bank of Persia up to the date of the signature of the present Agreement, and in the event of the necessity arising for Russia to establish control over the sources of revenue guaranteeing the regular service of the loans concluded with the first-named bank, and situated in the region mentioned in Article II of the present Agreement, or for Great Britain to establish control over the sources of revenue

guaranteeing the regular service of the loans concluded with the second-named bank, and situated in the region mentioned in Article I of the present Agreement, the British and Russian Governments undertake to enter beforehand into a friendly exchange of ideas with a view to determine, in agreement with each other, the measures of control in question and to avoid all interference which would not be in conformity with the principles governing the present Agreement.

Convention concerning Afghanistan

The High Contracting Parties, in order to ensure perfect security on their respective frontiers in Central Asia and to maintain in these regions a solid and lasting peace, have concluded the following Convention:

Article I

His Britannic Majesty's Government declare that they have no intention of changing the political status of Afghanistan.

His Britannic Majesty's Government further engage to exercise their influence in Afghanistan only in a pacific sense, and they will not themselves take, nor encourage Afghanistan to take, any measures threatening Russia.

The Russian Government, on their part, declare that they recognize Afghanistan as outside the sphere of Russian influence, and they engage that all their political relations with Afghanistan shall be conducted through the intermediary of His Britannic Majesty's Government; they further engage not to send any Agents into Afghanistan.

Article II

The Government of His Britannic Majesty having declared in the Treaty signed at Kabul on the 21st March, 1905, that they recognize the Agreement and the engagements concluded with the late Ameer Abdur Rahman, and that they have no intention of interfering in the internal government of Afghan territory, Great Britain engages neither to annex nor to occupy in contravention of that Treaty any portion of Afghanistan or to interfere in the internal administration of the country, provided that the Ameer fulfils the engagements already contracted by him towards His Britannic Majesty's Government under the above-mentioned Treaty.

Article III

The Russian and Afghan authorities, specially designated for the purpose on the frontier or in the frontier provinces, may establish direct relations with each other for the settlement of local questions of a non-political character.

Article IV

His Britannic Majesty's Government and the Russian Government affirm their adherence to the principle of equality of commercial opportunity in Afghanistan, and they agree that any facilities which may have been, or shall be hereafter, obtained for British and British-Indian trade and traders, shall be equally enjoyed by Russian trade and traders. Should the progress of trade establish the necessity for Commercial Agents, the two Governments will agree as to what measures shall be taken, due regard, of course, being had to the Ameer's sovereign rights.

Article V

The present arrangements will only come into force when His Britannic Majesty's Government shall have notified to the Russian Government the consent of the Ameer to the terms stipulated above.

Agreement concerning Thibet

The Governments of Great Britain and Russia recognizing the suzerain rights of China in Thibet, and considering the fact that Great Britain, by reason of her geographical position, has a special interest in the maintenance of the *status quo* in the external relations of Thibet, have made the following Agreement:

Article I

The two High Contracting Parties engage to respect the territorial integrity of Thibet and to abstain from all interference in its internal administration.

Article II

In conformity with the admitted principle of the suzerainty of China over Thibet, Great Britain and Russia engage not to enter into negotiations with Thibet except through the intermediary of the Chinese Government. This engagement does not exclude the direct relations between British Commercial Agents and the Thibetan authorities provided for in Article V of the Convention between Great Britain and Thibet of the 7th September, 1904, and confirmed by the Convention between Great Britain and China of the 27th April, 1906; nor does it modify the engagements entered into by Great Britain and China in Article I of the said Convention of 1906.

It is clearly understood that Buddhists, subjects of Great Britain or of Russia, may enter into direct relations on strictly religious matters with the Dalai Lama and the other repesentatives of Bhuddhism in Thibet; the Governments of Great Britain and Russia engage, so far as they are concerned, not to allow those relations to infringe the stipulations of the present Agreement.

Article III

The British and Russian Governments respectively engage not to send Representatives to Lassa.

Article IV

The two High Contracting Parties engage neither to seek nor to obtain, whether for themselves or their subjects, any Concessions for railways, roads, telegraphs, and mines, or other rights in Thibet.

Article V

The two Governments agree that no part of the revenues of Thibet, whether in kind or in cash, shall be pledged or assigned to Great Britain or Russia or to any of their subjects.

Annex to the Agreement between Great Britain and Russia concerning Thibet

Great Britain reaffirms the Declaration, signed by his Excellency the Viceroy and Governor-General of India and appended to the ratification of the Convention of the 7th September, 1904, to the effect that the occupation of the Chumbi Valley by British forces shall cease after the payment of three annual instalments of the indemnity of 2,500,000 rupees, provided that the trade marts mentioned in Article II of that Convention have been effectively opened for three years, and that in the meantime the Thibetan authorities have faithfully complied in all respects with the terms of the said

Convention of 1904. It is clearly understood that if the occupation of the Chumbi Valley by the British forces has, for any reason, not been terminated at the time anticipated in the above Declaration, the British and Russian Governments will enter upon a friendly exchange of views on this subject.

Source: C. H. Philips et al. (eds). *The Evolution of India and Pakistan, 1857–1947. Select Documents.* London: Oxford University Press, 1962, pp. 483–7.

Chapter Eleven

The Game and Its Rules: Governing the Subcontinent

Introduction

In 1858, following directly from out of the crisis of the Indian Rebellion, responsibility for the government of India passed from the charge of the Company to that of the Crown. According to the Government of India Act decreed on August 2, 1858, "India shall be governed by and in the name of Her Majesty, and all rights in relation to any terriories which might have been exercised by the said Company if this Act had not been passed shall and may be exercised by and in the name of Her Majesty as rights incidental to the Government of India." In September the Company issued its last instructions to its servants and handed over their trust to the Queen: "Let Her Majesty appreciate the gift – let her take the vast country and the teeming millions of India under Her direct control; but let Her not forget the great corporation from which she has received them nor the lessons to be learnt from its success" (*Cambridge History of India*, 1922: 212). Victoria's proclamation then was delivered on November 1: "When, by the blessing of Providence, internal tranquillity shall be restored, it is our earnest desire to stimulate the peaceful industry of India, to promote the works of public utility and improvement, and to administer its government for the benefit of all our subjects resident therein."

The problem of famine, for example, plagued India throughout the nineteenth century and into the twentieth; historians, economists, administrators, and statesmen have offered various explanations for the country's continual cycles of agricultural distress. These explanations included blaming Indians for their fiscal irresponsibility and high debt; some suggested that the Indian ryots (peasants or farmers) recklessly borrowed to fund unnecessary and expensive "superstitious" religious or social ceremonies. Others blamed the agricultural farmers' financial problems on unscrupulous native moneylenders or general indolence. Some historians and scientists too have attributed India's famine problems to the irregularity of monsoon seasons and to the man-made problems created by colonization itself. When the East India Company – and later, the Crown administration – colonized and ruled India, it disrupted the indigenous economic, cultural, and agricultural traditions. The native textile industry, for example, was severely crippled by the importation of cheaper fabrics produced in Britain's textile industries. Native cottage industries were destroyed and growing numbers of people became newly dependent on the fragile agricultural economy.

Many of the issues that had divided political positions and public opinion under the Company's rule persisted under the Crown's supervision as well, in significant part as these contentions distinguished between rule by conquest and rule by consent. In India, according to Macaulay's minute, Indians were being "anglicized," and the Civil Service "Indianized." In 1853, competitive examinations had been introduced in England as part of the entrance requirements to the ICS, and admission to the Company's college at Haileybury was opened to all natural-born subjects of Her Majesty, whether European, Indian, or of mixed race. The

Indian Army was subject to similar changes, although the still fresh memories of the Rebellion would continue to affect discussions, debate and decisions concerning the capacity of Indians for self-government. The Ilbert Bill of 1883, which allowed Indian magistrates to sit in judgement over Europeans, provoked a crisis of dissension over the augmented role of Indians in the government of India. Meanwhile, as in the cases of thuggee and sati, and despite the general policy of non-interference in Indian customs and traditions, it was women once again who provided the pretext for such intervention, with the legislation concerning polygamy and child-marriage at the end of the century.

MC and BH

Additional reading

Allen, Charles (ed.). *Plain Tales from the Raj*. London, 1975.
Arnold, David. *Famine: Social Crisis and Historical Change*. Oxford, 1988.
Bayly, C. A. (gen. ed.). *The Raj: India and the British 1600–1947*. London, 1990.
Blair, Charles. *Indian Famines: Their Historical, Financial, and Other Aspects* (1874). New Delhi, 1986.
The Cambridge History of India, vol. 6, *The Indian Empire 1858–1918*, ed. H. H. Dodwell. Cambridge, 1922.
Cohn, Bernard S. "Representing Authority in Colonial India," in Eric Hobsbawm and Terence Ranger (eds), *The Invention of Tradition*. Cambridge, 1983.
Dufferin, Lord and Ava, Lady Dufferin. *Our Viceregal Life in India 1884–1888* (2 vols). London, n.d.
Farrell, J. G. *The Hill Station: An Unfinished Novel*, 1981.
Grewal, Inderpal. *Home and Harem: Nation, Gender, Empire and the Cultures of Travel*. Durham and London, 1996.
Hirschmann, Edwin. *'White Mutiny': The Ilbert Bill Crisis in India and Genesis of the Indian National Congress*. New Delhi, 1980.
Jhabvala, Ruth Prawer. *Heat and Dust*. London, 1975.
Kennedy, Dane. *The Magic Mountains: Hill Stations and the British Raj*. Berkeley, 1977.
McAlpin, Michelle Burge. *Subject to Famine: Food Crises and Economic Change in Western India, 1860–1920*. Princeton, 1983.
Morris, Jan. *Stones of Empire: The Buildings of British India*. Oxford, 1882.
Seavoy, Ronald E. *Famine in Peasant Societies*. New York, 1986.
Sen, Amartya. *Poverty and Famines: An Essay on Entitlement and Deprivation*. Oxford, 1981.
Scott, Paul. *The Raj Quartet*. New York and London, 1976.
Srivastava, Hari Shanker. *The History of Indian Famines and Development of Famine Policy, 1858–1918*. Agra, 1968.
Stokes, Eric. *The English Utilitarians and India*. Oxford, 1959.
Wilson, Angus. *The Strange Ride of Rudyard Kipling: His Life and Works* (1977). London, 1994.

Woodruff, Philip. *The Men Who Ruled India: The Guardians*. New York, 1954.

Films

Zoltan Korda and Robert Flaherty. *Elephant Boy* (1936).
Zoltan Korda and André de Toth. *Jungle Book* (1942).
Wolfgang Reitheman. *Jungle Book* (cartoon) (1967).
James Ivory. *Heat and Dust* (1983).
David Lean. *A Passage to India* (1984).

57 Rudyard Kipling: Refrain from "The Ballad of East and West" (1889)

O, East is East, and West is West, and never the twain shall meet,
Till Earth and Sky stand presently at God's great judgment Seat;
But there is neither East nor West, Border, nor Breed, nor Birth,
When two strong men stand face to face, though they come from the ends of the earth!

Source: Rudyard Kipling. *Barrack Room Ballads.* London: Methuen, 1892.

---

58 The Government of India Act, August 2, 1858

II India shall be governed by and in the name of Her Majesty, and all rights in relation to any territories which might have been exercised by the said Company if this Act had not been passed shall and may be exercised by and in the name of Her Majesty as rights incidental to the Government of India; [. . .]

III Save as herein otherwise provided, one of Her Majesty's Principal Secretaries of State shall have and perform all such or the like powers and duties in anywise relating to the government or revenues of India, and all such or the like powers over all officers appointed or continued under this Act, as might or should have been exercised or performed by the East India Company, or by the Court of Directors or Court of Proprietors of the said Company, either alone or by the direction or with the sanction or approbation of the Commissioners for the affairs of India in relation to such government or revenues, and the officers and servants of the said Company respectively, and also all such powers as might have been exercised by the said Commissioners alone; [. . .]

VI In case Her Majesty be pleased to appoint a fifth Principal Secretary of State, there shall be paid out of the revenues of India to such Principal Secretary of State and to his Under Secretaries respectively the like yearly salaries as may for the time being be paid to any other of such Secretaries of State and his Under Secretaries respectively.

VII For the purposes of this Act a council shall be established, to consist of fifteen members, and to be styled the Council of India; and henceforth the Council in India now bearing that name shall be styled the Council of the Governor General of India.

VIII Within fourteen days after the passing of this Act the Court of Directors of the East India Company shall, from among the Persons then being Directors of the said Company or having been theretofore such Directors, elect Seven Persons to be with the Persons to be appointed by Her Majesty as hereinafter mentioned the First Members of the Council under this Act, and the names of the Persons so elected by the Court of Directors shall be forthwith, after such election, certified to the Board of Commissioners for the Affairs of *India*, under the Seal of the Said Company, and it shall be lawful for Her Majesty, by warrant under Her Royal Sign Manual, within thirty days after the passing of this Act, to appoint to be members of such Council Eight Persons: Provided always, that if the Court of Directors of the *East India* Company shall refuse or shall for such fourteen days neglect to make such Election of such Seven Persons, and to certify the names of such Persons as aforesaid, it shall be lawful for Her Majesty, by warrant under Her Royal Sign Manual, within thirty days after the expiration of such fourteen days, to appoint from among the said Directors Seven Persons to make up the full Number of the said Council: Provided also, that if any Person being or having been such Director, and elected or appointed as aforesaid, shall refuse to accept the office, it shall be lawful for Her Majesty, by warrant under Her Royal Sign Manual, to appoint in the Place of every Person so refusing some other Person to be a Member of the Council, but so that Nine Members of the Council at the least shall be Persons qualified as hereinafter mentioned.

IX Every vacancy happening from time to time among the members of the Council appointed by Her Majesty, not being members so appointed by reason of the refusal or neglect of the Court of Directors or the refusal to accept office hereinbefore mentioned, shall be filled up by Her Majesty, by warrant under Her Royal Sign Manual, and every other vacancy shall be filled up by the Council by election made at a meeting to be held for that purpose.

X   The major part of the persons to be elected by the Court of Directors, and the major part of the persons to be first appointed by Her Majesty after the passing of this Act, to be members of the Council, shall be persons who have served or resided in India for ten years at the least, and (excepting in the case of late and present Directors and officers on the Home establishment of the East India Company who shall have so served or resided) shall not have last left India more than ten years next preceding the date of their appointment; and no person other than a person so qualified shall be appointed or elected to fill any vacancy in the Council unless at the time of the appointment or election nine at the least of the continuing members of the Council be persons qualified as aforesaid.

XI   Every member of the Council appointed or elected under this Act shall hold his office during good behaviour; provided that it shall be lawful for Her Majesty to remove any such member from his office upon an address of both Houses of Parliament.

XII   No member of the Council appointed or elected under this Act shall be capable of sitting or voting in Parliament.

XIX   The Council shall, under the direction of the Secretary of State, and subject to the provisions of this Act, conduct the business transacted in the United Kingdom in relation to the Government of India and the correspondence with India, but every order or communication sent to India shall be signed by one of the Principal Secretaries of State: and, save as expressly provided by this Act, every order in the United Kingdom in relation to the Government of India under the Act shall be signed by such Secretary of State: and all despatches from Governments and Presidencies in India, and other despatches from India, which if this Act had not been passed should have been addressed to the Court of Directors or to their Secret Committee, shall be addressed to such Secretary of State.

XX   It shall be lawful for the Secretary of State to divide the Council into committees for the more convenient transaction of business, and from time to time to re-arrange such committees, and to direct what departments of the business in relation to the Government of India under this Act shall be under such committees respectively, and generally to direct the manner in which all such business shall be transacted.

XXIII   At any meeting of the Council at which the Secretary of State is present, if there be a difference of opinion on any question other than the question of the election of a member of Council, or other than any question with regard to which a majority of the votes at a meeting is hereinafter declared to be necessary, the determination of the Secretary of State shall be final; [. . .]

XXVI   Provided, that where it appears to the Secretary of State that the despatch of any communication, or the making of any order, not being an order for which a majority of the votes at a meeting is hereby made necessary, is urgently required, the communication may be sent or order given notwithstanding the same may not have been submitted to a meeting of the Council or deposited for seven days as aforesaid, the urgent reasons for sending or making the same being recorded by the Secretary of State, and notice thereof being given to every member of the Council, except in the cases hereinafter mentioned.

XXVII   Provided also, that any order, not being an order for which a majority of votes at a meeting is hereby made necessary, which might, if this Act had not been passed, have been sent by the Commissioners for the affairs of India through the Secret Committee of the Court of Directors to Governments or Presidencies in India, or to the officers or servants of the said Company, may, after the commencement of this Act, be sent to such Governments or Presidencies, or to any officer or servant in India, by the Secretary of State without having been submitted to a meeting, or deposited for the perusal of the members of the Council, and without the reasons being recorded or notice thereof given as aforesaid.

XXVIII   Any despatches to Great Britain which might if this Act had not been passed have been addressed to the Secret Committee of the Court of Directors, may be marked 'secret' by the authorities sending the same, and such despatches shall not be communicated to the members of the Council, unless the Secretary of State shall so think fit and direct.

XXIX   The appointments of Governor-General of India, fourth ordinary member of the Council of the Governor-General of India, and Governors of Presidencies in India, now made by the Court of Directors with the approbation of Her Majesty, and the appointments of Advocate-General for the several Presidencies now made with the approbation of the Commissioners for the affairs of India, shall be made by Her Majesty by warrant under Her Royal Sign Manual; the appointments of the ordinary members of the Council of the Governor-General of India, except the fourth ordinary member, and the appointments of the Members of Council of the several Presidencies, shall be made by the Secretary of State in Council, with the concurrence of a majority of members present at a meeting; the appointments of the Lieutenant-Governors of provinces or territories shall be made by the Governor-General of India, subject to the approbation of Her Majesty; and all such appointments shall be subject to the qualifications now by law affecting such offices respectively.

XXX   All appointments to offices, commands, and employments in India, and all promotions, which by law or under any regulations, usage, or custom, are now made by any authority in India, shall continue to be made in India by the like authority, and subject to the qualifications, conditions, and restrictions now affecting such appointments respectively; but the Secretary of State in Council, with the concurrence of a majority of members present at a meeting, shall have the like power to make regulations for the division and distribution of patronage and power of nomination among the several authorities in India, and the like power of restoring to their stations, offices, or employments, officers and servants suspended or removed by any authority in India as might have been exercised by the said Court of Directors, with the approbation of the Commissioners for the affairs of India, if this Act had not been passed.

XXXII   With all convenient speed after the passing of this Act, Regulations shall be made by the Secretary of State in Council, with the Advice and Assistance of the Commissioner for the time being acting in execution of Her Majesty's Order in Council of Twenty-first May one thousand eight hundred and fifty-five, 'for regulating the Admission of Persons to the Civil Service of the Crown', for admitting all Persons being natural-born subjects of Her Majesty (and of such age and qualification as may be prescribed in their behalf) who may be desirous of becoming candidates for Appointment to the Civil Service of India to be examined as candidates accordingly, and for prescribing the branches of knowledge in which such candidates shall be examined, and generally for regulating and conducting such examinations under the superintendence of the said last-mentioned Commissioners, or of the Persons for the time being entrusted with the carrying out of such Regulations as may be from time to time established by Her Majesty for Examination, certificate or other test of fitness in relation to appointments to junior situations in the Civil Service of the Crown, and the candidates who may be certified by the said Commissioners or other Persons as aforesaid to be enlisted under such Regulations shall be recommended for appointments according to the order of their proficiency as shown by such examinations, and such Persons only as shall have been so certified as aforesaid shall be appointed or admitted to the Civil Service of India by the Secretary of State in Council: Provided always, that all Regulations to be made by the said Secretary of State in Council under this Act shall be laid before Parliament within fourteen days after the making thereof, if Parliament be sitting, and, if Parliament be not sitting, then within fourteen days of the next meeting thereof.

XXXIII   All appointments to cadetships, naval and military, and all admissions to service not herein otherwise provided for, shall be vested in Her Majesty; and the names of persons to be from time to time recommended for such cadetships and service shall be submitted to Her Majesty by the Secretary of State.

XLI   The expenditure of the revenues of India, both in India and elsewhere, shall be subject to the control of the Secretary of State in Council, and no grant or appropriation of any part of such revenues, or of any other property coming into the possession of the Secretary of State in Council by virtue of this Act, shall be made without the concurrence of a majority of votes at a meeting of the Council.

LIII   The Secretary of State in Council shall, within the first fourteen days during which Parliament may be sitting next after the first day of May in every year, lay before both Houses of Parliament an account for the financial year preceding that last completed of the annual produce of the revenues of India, distinguishing the same under the respective heads thereof, at each of the several Presidencies or Governments, and of all the annual receipts and disbursements at home and abroad on account of the Government of India, distinguishing the same under the respective heads thereof, together with the latest estimate of the same for the last financial year, and also the amount of the debts chargeable on the revenues of India, with the rates of interest they respectively carry, and the annual amount of such interest, the state of the effects and credits at each Presidency or Government, and in England or elsewhere, applicable to the purposes of the Government of India, according to the latest advices which have been received thereof, and also a list of the establishment of the Secretary of State in Council, and the salaries and allowances payable in respect thereof; and if any new or increased salaries or pensions of fifty pounds a year or upwards have been granted or created within any year, the particulars thereof shall be specially stated and explained at the foot of the acount of such year; and such account shall be accompanied by a statement prepared from detailed reports from each Presidency and district in India in such form as shall best exhibit the moral and material progress and condition of India in each such Presidency.

LV   Except for preventing or repelling actual invasion of Her Majesty's Indian possessions, or under other sudden and urgent necessity, the revenues of India shall not, without the consent of both Houses of Parliament, be applicable to defray the expenses of any military operation carried on beyond the external frontiers of such possessions by Her Majesty's forces charged upon such revenues.

Source: C. H. Philips, et al. (eds). *The Evolution of India and Pakistan, 1857–1947. Select Documents.* London: Oxford University Press, 1962, pp. 5–9.

---

59   Queen Victoria's Proclamation, November 1, 1858

And we, reposing especial trust and confidence in the loyalty, ability, and judgment of our right trusty and well-beloved cousin and councillor, Charles John Viscount Canning, do hereby constitute and appoint him, the said Viscount Canning, to be our first Viceroy and Governor-General in and over our said territories, and to administer the government thereof in our name, and generally to act in our name and on our behalf, subject to such orders and regulations as he shall, from time to time, receive from us through one of our Principal Secretaries of State.

And we do hereby confirm in their several offices, civil and military, all persons now employed in the service of the Honourable East India Company, subject to our future pleasure, and to such laws and regulations as may hereafter be enacted.

We hereby announce to the native Princes of India that all treaties and engagements made with them by or under the authority of the Honourable East India Company are by us accepted, and will be scrupulously maintained, and we look for the like observance on their part.

We desire no extension of our present territorial possessions; and, while we will permit no aggression upon our dominions or our rights to be attempted with impunity, we shall sanction to encroachment on those of others. We shall respect the rights, dignity and honour of native Princes as our own; and we desire that they, as well as our own subjects, should enjoy that prosperity and that social advancement which can only be secured by internal peace and good government.

We hold ourselves bound to the natives of our Indian territories by the same obligations of duty which bind us to all our other subjects, and those obligations, by the blessing of Almighty God, we shall faithfully and conscientiously fulfil.

Firmly relying ourselves on the truth of Christianity, and acknowledging with gratitude the solace of religion, we disclaim alike the right and the desire to impose our convictions on any of our subjects. We declare it to be our royal will and pleasure that none be in anywise favoured, none molested or disquieted, by reason of their religious faith or observances, but that all shall alike enjoy the equal and impartial protection of the law; and we do strictly charge and enjoin all those who may be in authority under us that they abstain from all interference with the religious belief or worship of any of our subjects on pain of our highest displeasure.

And it is our further will that, so far as may be, our subjects, of whatever race or creed, be freely and impartially admitted to offices in our service, the duties of which they may be qualified, by their education, ability, and integrity, duly to discharge.

We know, and respect, the feelings of attachment with which the natives of India regard the lands inherited by them from their ancestors, and we desire to protect them in all rights connected therewith, subject to the equitable demands of the State; and we will that generally, in framing and administering the law, due regard be paid to the ancient rights, usages, and customs of India. [. . .]

Our clemency will be extended to all offenders, save and except those who have been, or shall be, convicted of having directly taken part in the murder of British subjects. With regard to such the demands of justice forbid the exercise of mercy. [. . .]

When, by the blessing of Providence, internal tranquillity shall be restored, it is our earnest desire to stimulate the peaceful industry of India, to promote works of public utility and improvement, and to administer its government for the benefit of all our subjects resident therein. In their prosperity will be our strength; in their contentment our security, and in their gratitude our best reward. And may the God of all power grant to us, and to those in authority under us, strength to carry out these our wishes for the good of our people.

Source: C. H. Philips, et al. (eds). *The Evolution of India and Pakistan, 1857–1947. Select Documents*. London: Oxford University Press, 1962, pp. 10–11.

60 Resolution of the Government of India on Famine Policy, September 22, 1868

[. . .] 5   In proceeding to consider the manner in which the Government should act if severe scarcity arises, His Excellency in Council would first most earnestly impress upon all persons in authority the necessity for not permitting the smallest interference with the ordinary operations of trade during the continuance of the scarcity. On this subject the following extract from a paper drawn up in 1861 by Mr. J. Strachey, then Collector of Moradabad, may be regarded as expressing the views of the Government of India at the present time:

There is one other point connected with this part of the question to which it is desirable to refer. The Government has already publicly expressed its disapproval of all interference by its officers with the object of reducing the price of food. I believe that orders still more strong and explicit would be useful. Unfortunately, public education in these matters is at a miserably low ebb. In times of difficulty, like the present, almost every Magistrate is constantly urged, both by Englishmen and by Natives, to interfere, in some way or other, for the purpose of cheapening food, or of rendering it easier of access to the consumers. Reports frequently become prevalent that in some part of the country such interference has been actually practised. Whether these reports be true or false, they are extremely mischievous. The determination of Government to allow no such interference ought to be so notorious that reports of this kind shall obtain no credence. These rumours are the more readily believed, because they fall in with the general idea of what is proper and probable. The mere suspicion of any interference of the kind is sufficient to check the speculations of the corn-merchants, and it cannot be doubted that this is a cause which often, in this country, has the effect of stopping the exportation of grain from distant markets.

It cannot be too clearly borne in mind that in time of extreme famine, when it is impossible to

supply the deficiency of food by importation, the main safeguard against general starvation is the reduction of consumption, and that this can only be effectually brought about by a rise of prices. The grain-dealer, therefore, while he works for his own personal advantage by raising the price of food as it becomes scarce, is in fact providing the means of securing the community against the extremity of famine, and his action, so far from being, as it is too often ignorantly described to be, that of a public enemy, is much more that of a public benefactor.

Source: C. H. Philips, et al. (eds). *The Evolution of India and Pakistan, 1857–1947. Select Documents*. London: Oxford University Press 1962, p. 668.

61 Lord Lytton: Minute on Famine Policy, August 12, 1877

[. . .] 5   The policy of the Government of India, as declared after previous famines, was to give all possible facilities for the transport of grain to distressed districts; to abstain from interference with the grain trade, so long as that trade was active; to give relief wages to the destitute who would labor on useful public works; to relieve gratuitously, under trustworthy supervision, the helpless poor, when the pressure of famine became extreme; and to avert death from starvation by the employment of all means practically open to the resources of the State and the exertions of its officers; but to discharge this duty at the lowest cost compatible with the preservation of human life from wholesale destruction. In the autumn of 1876, no general instructions were issued by the Government of India for the management of serious and widespread famine, nor until November was it certain, from the reports received by the Supreme Government, that positive famine was impending in the Madras districts. [. . .]

11   In regard to the main object of relief operations, viz., the saving of human life, much, but not complete, success has been attained. In some tracts relief operations began too late; at centres of population, like Madras and Bangalore, and on some of the roads leading to such centres, starvation deaths have occurred; the death-rate from cholera, dysentry, and such like diseases has greatly increased over large areas. But, on the whole, the worst evils of famine have, so far, been successfully averted over the vast tracts visited by failure of

crops. According to the standard of mortality during the Orissa famine, from three to five millions of people must have died of famine in Southern India during the year 1877 if the guaranteed railways had not existed, and if Government had incurred no outlay on relief operations. Nothing of this sort has occurred; and on this result the Governments, and the local officers, who have exerted themselves admirably, deserve the acknowledgments of the Government of India. I fear, however, it may hereafter be found that over large tracts relief operations were, for considerable periods, conducted without sufficient system, and without due regard to economy. [. . .]

18   When harvests fail in an Indian province, considerable old stocks of food are left in the hands of the land-holding and mercantile classes: but these stocks are often held back from sale. Markets have, therefore, to be supplied with grain imported from a distance. I consider that, except under most peculiar and exceptional circumstances, the function of supplying the demand for imported grain can be best, and, indeed, alone, discharged by private trade; and that private trade should be left to do its work in this respect with as little interference from Government as practicable. The Government and its officers should, however, give all possible information, and should give, where necessary, additional facilities, to private trade. Early and correct information as to prices and means of carriage should be published. The carrying power of railways and canals, leading into the famine tracts, should be reinforced; tolls and other restraints on free inter-communication should be removed; roads into the interior should be improved and kept in order; rates of railway or other carriage might be reduced; and, in cases of extreme necessity, temporary railways, or tramways, might be laid from main railway lines into populous tracts, whereto means of communication failed, or were insufficient. These will, indeed, be the most useful of all works, if we have to meet another year of famine. Grain required by Government for alms to the helpless poor, or for labourers on relief-works, or for any tract where supplies were deficient, should be obtained through the trade, at or near the local markets, and should not be imported from a distance by Government itself. Experience has shown that Government operations in the grain market disorganise and paralyse private trade, to an extent out of all proportion to the operations themselves. Moreover, where the carrying power of a country by rail, canal, or cart, is limited, and is fully utilised, Government grain importations must necessarily displace a corresponding quantity of privately imported grain. My view, therefore, is

that, under no circumstances, which are likely to occur, ought the Government itself to engage in the business of importing grain. Free and abundant private trade cannot co-exist with Government importation. Absolute non-interference with the operations of private commercial enterprise must be the foundation of our present famine policy. Trade towards the famine country from Bengal and Northern and Central India is at present active; and there is every reason to believe that the Indian sources of supply are still considerable. But even if these should fail, the interference of the Government would be a ruinous error. It could only have the effect of decreasing the total amount of food available, and thus aggravating the catastrophe. I am confident that more food, whether from abroad or elsewhere, will reach Madras, if we leave private enterprise to itself, than if we paralyse it by Government competition. These remarks refer to the famine we are now dealing with. I do not, of course, intend to assert that famines cannot occur, in which Government interference for the importation of food may not be absolutely necessary. Indeed, the Orissa famine was one of those cases.

Source: C. H. Philips, et al. (eds). *The Evolution of India and Pakistan, 1857–1947. Select Documents.* London: Oxford University Press 1962, pp. 669–70.

Note

Lord (Edward) Robert Bulwer Lytton (1876–1891) was a diplomat, colonial administrator, and poet. He was appointed Governor-General of India by Prime Minister Benjamin Disraeli in 1875; he later became Viceroy of India (1876–80). Lytton's attempts to suppress by force the Russian influence in Afghanistan led to the Second Afghan War (1878–80). Lytton's career was distinguished by his famine relief measures, the abolition of customs barriers, and the decentralization of the colony's financial system; he is also remembered for having reserved one-sixth of Civil Service appointments for Indians.

62   Govt of India to Govt of Bengal: Letter on the Suppression of Polygamy in Bengal, August 8, 1866

Your letters dated the 5th of April and the 12th of June having been considered by the Governor General in Council with care the which is due to the high importance of the question to which they relate, I am directed to communicate the following remarks. [. . .]

2   Your letter dated the 5th of April encloses copy of a Memorial "recently presented to the Lieutenant Governor by the Maharajah of Burdwan, and nearly 21,000 other Hindoos of Bengal, praying for the enactment of a law to prevent the abuses attending the practice of polygamy among the Hindoos; and the Lieutenant Governor requests the authority of the Governor General for the introduction into the Bengal Council of a measure "for the prevention of polygamy among Hindoos in Bengal, except under certain specified circumstances." The Lieutenant Governor adds that it is his intention to take as the basis of his measure a draft Bill which was prepared about three years ago by Rajah Deonarain Sing; and in another part of your letter the scope of the proposed measure is further indicated by the statement that, "as regards Bengal, there is ample evidence to show that the feeling of the great bulk of the intelligent and thinking portion of the Hindoo community is strongly in favor of bringing the practice of polygamy strictly within the limits prescribed by ancient Hindoo law."

3   The letter of the 12th June forwards, in continuation of the previous letter, a petition from certain inhabitants of the Mymensing District, praying "for the suppression of polygamy".

4   The Governor General in Council does not doubt that the great bulk of the intelligent and thinking portion of the Hindoo community in Bengal would be found in favor of some measure for repressing the special abuses which in Bengal have been engrafted on the liberty accorded by the Hindoo law to marry more than one wife, and His Excellency in Council cordially commends and sympathises with the feeling which the present movement among this class indicates. But the Governor General in Council is obliged to say that there is nothing to show that the people generally even in Bengal are prepared, and that in his judgement they are not in fact prepared, for so great a change either as the complete suppression of polygamy, which evidently is in the minds of some of the Memorialists, or for the strict limitation of polygamy which is contemplated by the Lieutenant Governor. It must be remembered that polygamy, as it exists in India, is a social and religious institution prevalent to a great extent throughout the whole country, and the Governor General in Council doubts whether the great difficulty of dealing with the subject in India, or even in Bengal, has been fully considered. As regards the latter Province there is nothing in the papers before Government which, in the opinion of the Governor General in Council, would lead a calm and unbiased enquirer to the conclusion that a large majority of even the more enlightened people of the Province will be found to be heartily against polygamy, apart from the special abuses practised by the Coolin Brahmins. Few certainly, if any, of the Mahomedans would be found of this way of thinking, and probably a good many Hindoos would also be found opposed to any interference by the British Government with this part of their system. This would of course be still more the case beyond Bengal, in the other Provinces of British India. For it is not a few scattered individuals only who advocate and practise polygamy, but the largest proportion of all classes, Hindoo and Mahomedan, who are in a position to maintain a plurality of wives. The practise is indeed closely interwoven with the social condition of the people throughout Asia.

5   There is the further difficulty in adopting any such measure as that devised by Rajah Deonarain Sing that, whereas the institution of polygamy does not at present derive any force or validity from our laws, it would by such a measure be distinctly recognized and regulated under restrictions imposed by English legislation. The Lieutenant Governor treats this objection as "of little weight," arguing that the existence and legality of polygamy have been recently admitted by the Indian Legislature in the Native Converts' Marriage Dissolution Act. It seems, however, to the Governor General in Council that there is the greatest possible difference between a law which, in providing for the dissolution under certain circumstances of the marriage of one who has ceased to be a Hindoo, simply deals with the possible fact of his having, as a Hindoo, married more than one wife, and a law which would have for its express object the regulation of polygamy among the Hindoo people generally. [. . .]

9   But the Governor General in Council, while not regarding this ground of objection so lightly as the Lieutenant Governor does, would yet by no means press it so far as to shut out all recourse to legislation for the suppression of the great and peculiar evil which is represented in the papers submitted by the Lieutenant Governor as being practised specially in the Province of Bengal by the Coolin Brahmins. On the contrary, His Excellency in Council will be most happy to take into consideration any measure which, after full deliberation, the Lieutenant Governor may think fit to recommend for the purpose of putting a stop to the custom which has grown up among that class of Hindoos, provided that it does not at the same time affect the general liberty which is now possessed by all Hindoos to take more than one wife, or, on the other hand, give the express sanction of English

legislation to that feature of the Hindoo system. With this object, it seems desirable that the Lieutenant Governor should further consult some of the ablest of the leading Native gentlemen in Bengal, and with their assistance carefully mature the plan which they would recommend for adoption.

Source: C. H. Philips, et al. (eds). *The Evolution of India and Pakistan, 1857–1947. Select Documents.* London: Oxford University Press, 1962, pp. 729–31.

63 A. O. Hume: The Congress and the Age of Consent Bill, January 25, 1891

Sir, I desire to say a few words about the Age of Consent Bill, the more so that the *Englishman* appears to be hopelessly muddled as to the position of parties where this measure is concerned.

The *Englishman* practically announces, as if it were a novel discovery of his own, that people who are opposed to the raising of the age of consent, are unworthy to enjoy those privileges for which the Congress has been praying. But this is exactly what four-fifths of the Congress party throughout India have been saying, and, for my part, if I had not been able to satisfy myself that the great majority of the party, taking the empire as a whole, was favourable to the change, I would have resigned the General Secretaryship and washed my hands of the entire party. I will do anything and everything for India, serve her as the humblest servant, but it must be *per fas* and not *per nefas*.

As a fact the Congress party, as a party, are grieved that any wing of theirs, however small, should have placed itself in opposition to this much needed reform, for which we, *the great majority of the Congress party, memorialized Government from our Social Conference at Bombay only one year ago.*

In Calcutta certain most objectionable social customs obtain, which I defy any decent, educated Bengali gentleman to defend. This raising of the age of consent will interfere with these regrettable customs. [. . .]

Again, a few, who hate these customs, and will not tolerate them in their own houses, yet oppose the Bill because, say they, these are social and *quasi*-religious customs, with which the legislature should not interfere, but should leave to be dealt with by the growing good sense and good feeling of the community. Now *Suttee* and *Thuggee* were both

social and *quasi*-religious customs, and by a parity of reasoning the legislature ought not to have interfered with *them.*

But, say they, these latter involved a palpable crime against the community, and it seems impossible to drive into their heads that the social custom that leads to the violation of girls under 12 years of age, premature conception, and degeneracy of offspring, is equally a palpable crime [. . .]

Besides these two small classes of respectable opponents of the measure, there is a considerable rabble, of more or less noisy denouncers of the Bill, who seek to pose as upholders of Hinduism, and make capital for themselves, our of antagonism to this measure. [. . .]

Lastly, I wish to make it clear that this opposition to the Bill is almost exclusively confined to Lower Bengal. Elsewhere for one man who would vote against it, ten would vote for it. No doubt the great majority of these are perfectly indifferent to the matter, because in all the best families, everywhere but in Lower Bengal, no one ever dreams of allowing marriages to be *consummated* before the girls attain the age of 12 years *at least.*

[. . .] As it is, even in Calcutta, a memorial in favour of the Bill is in progress of signature, *and will be signed by all who respect themselves and really have at heart the credit of their nation,* and I can only recommend the respectable members of the opposition to look ahead, a little, and try and realise the comments that their own grandsons will make upon their conduct. [. . .]

A. O. Hume

PS – I write this, of course, in my private capacity, and not as General Secretary to the Congress.

Source: C. H. Philips, et al. (eds.). *The Evolution of India and Pakistan, 1857–1947. Select Documents.* London: Oxford University Press, 1962, pp. 729–31.

64 Lord Lansdowne: Speech on the Age of Consent Bill, March 19, 1891

[. . .] The opposition which it has encountered has proceeded from three quarters. There is, in the first place, the general suspicion which has been occasioned in the public mind from the fact that the Government of India has determined to legislate upon a subject which, although it does not immediately affect the marriage law of any section of the community, has an indirect bearing upon the social

usages of one of those sections. To the more ignorant portion of the public, an appeal has been made
upon the ground that its religion is threatened by
the action of the Government of India; and this
statement has probably been enough to cause uneasiness to many who are entirely unaware of the
real scope of the Bill, who do not read the discussions which take place in Council, or even those
which are to be found in the columns of the newspapers, and who are ready, upon the mere affirma-
tion of the framers of hostile resolutions, or the
conveners of public meetings, summoned under
the circumstances so well described by the Hon'ble
Mr. Nugent, to testify their alarm, and their
conviction that their spiritual welfare is seriously
threatened. Of the opposition which we have encountered from this quarter, all I have to say is that
I hope and believe that it will be of a transient
character, and that the Hindu community, and
even the most unenlightened section of it, will in
time find out that its religion is not endangered by
what we are about to do. Although we cannot blame
the credulous listeners who are led to believe assertions of this kind, made on apparently good authority, we have, I think, a right to complain of those
who are reckless enough to disseminate such statements and, upon so slender a pretext, to fan the
embers of a dangerous agitation. [. . .]

The main volume of the opposition with which
the Bill has met has, however, originated not so
much in sources of this kind as in the belief, apparently entertained by many devout Hindus, that the
new law will involve a direct interference with a
specific religious observance. We are told that the
Hindu religion requires the consummation of marriage immediately upon the attainment of puberty
by the wife; that puberty is not unfrequently attained prior to the age of twelve; that, if in such
cases the marriage is consummated, the person who
so consummates it will find himself an offender
against the Penal Code, owing to the performance
of an act which his religion requires him not to
leave unperformed. Such interference on the part
of the British Government is, we are told, in direct
opposition to the terms of the Queen's Proclamation; and this argument has been largely, and I
must say most unscrupulously, used for the purpose of discrediting the Bill, and imputing a breach
of faith to the Government which has introduced
it. Now, with regard to this contention, let me say
at once that no Government of India has yet admitted, and that no Government of India will, I hope,
ever be found to admit, that the Queen's Proclamation, to which this appeal is made, is capable of any
such interpretation as that which has been placed

upon it by those who used this argument. If that
interpretation is to cover the case now under discussion, we must read the Queen's Proclamation as
a contract that, whenever the requirements of public morality, or of the public welfare, moral or material, are found to be in conflict with the alleged
requirements of any of the various religions prevailing in this country, religion is to prevail, and
considerations affecting public health, public morality, and the general comfort and convenience of
the Queen's subjects are to become of no account.
The contention is, on the face of it, a preposterous
one. Such a contract would have been absolutely
retrograde and out of place in the great charter
issued in 1858 by one of the most humane and
enlightened sovereigns who has ever ruled over the
nations of the earth.

I will venture to say that, in the eyes of every
reasonable man or woman, the pledges contained in
the Queen's Proclamation must be read with a twofold reservation, upon which the Government has
always acted, and which was not specified in the
letter of the contract simply because it had always
been acted upon and was perfectly obvious and well
understood. The first of these reservations is this,
that, in all cases where demands preferred in the
name of religion would lead to practices inconsistent with individual safety and the public peace, and
condemned by every system of law and morality in
the world, it is religion, and not morality, which
must give way. It has already been pointed out that
this reservation has been invariably insisted upon,
and examples have been adduced in which, from
time to time, the Government of India has intervened in order to prohibit certain acts, which unquestionably had the sanction of religion, upon the
ground that those acts were opposed to the general
interests of society. The precedents afforded by our
legislation against infanticide, against the immolation of widows, and against the immunities enjoyed
by Brahmins, have been appropriately cited in illustration of this argument. Every one of these
enactments were, if we are to accept the narrow
interpretation of the Queen's Proclamation, acts of
"interference with the religious belief or worship"
of the Queen's subjects from which those in authority under the Queen were charged to abstain on
pain of Her highest displeasure.

[. . .] What I have said seems to lead inevitably
to the second of the two reservations of which I
spoke a moment ago. It is this: that in all cases
where there is a conflict between the interests of
morality and those of religion, the Legislature is
bound to distinguish, if it can, between essentials
and nonessentials, between the great fundamental

principles of the religion concerned and the subsidiary beliefs and accretionary dogmas which have accidentally grown up around them. In the case of the Hindu religion, such a discrimination is especially needful, and one of the first questions which we have to ask ourselves is, assuming that the practice with which our proposed legislation will interfere is a practice supported by religious sanctions, whether those sanctions are of first-rate importance, and absolutely obligatory, or whether they are of minor importance, and binding only in a slight degree.

Now, I venture to affirm that the discussion which has taken place has established beyond controversy that the particular religious observance which we are urged to respect is, in the first place, a local observance, and one far from being universally recognized by those who profess the Hindu faith. It is a practice which is, in the main, peculiar to the Province of Bengal, and which is followed only in a portion of that Province and only by certain classes with that portion. It will not be contended that devout Hinduism is not to be found outside the restricted area, but the Hindus of other parts of India do not share the alarm with which this Bill is regarded in Bengal. In the next place, it is admitted that the religious sanctions, by which the practice is supported, are of the weakest kind. The elaborate statement recently published by Dr Bhandarkar, of the Dekkhan College at Poona, who is admitted to be one of the highest extant authorities upon questions of Hindu religious law, makes it perfectly clear that the precepts upon which the practice in question rests may be regarded as permissive only. It is conceded on all hands that, under certain circumstances, the consummation of the marriage may lawfully be postponed, and that, even where it is not lawfully postponed, the omission of the necessary act is an offence which may be expiated by the slenderest and most insignificant penalties. It was stated a few days ago by Mr Javerilal Umiashankar Yajnik, in the eloquent speech delivered by him at the meeting recently held at Bombay, that it might be said, without exaggeration, of the eighteen millions of the Hindu population to whom he was referring, that the bulk of them not only did not perform the *Garbhadhan* ceremony, but even the name of it is not known to them. Look, again, at the evidence which we have received from His Highness the Maharaja of Jeypore with regard to the manner in which these questions are regarded by the Chiefs and Sardars of Rajputana, who are well described in Rao Bahadur Kanti Chunder Mookerjee's admirable letter as "rigid and orthodox Hindus", and far from likely to break the laws of their religion without compunc

tion. Look, also, at the outspoken utterances of such men as our hon'ble colleague Mr Nulkar, as Mr Telang, as His Highness the Maharaja of Travancore, as His Highness the Maharaja of Vizianagram, as Mr Justice Muttusami Aiyar of Madras, and, even in Bengal, of such men as His Highness the Maharaja of Bettiah, His Highness the Maharaja of Durbhanga, or, in Calcutta itself, as Raja Durga Churn Law, lately our colleague in the Legislative Council, as Babu P. C. Mozoomdar, whose note upon the subject deserves the most attentive study, and as Dr Rash Behary Ghose, the eminent pleader, who has stated that, within his knowledge, the *Garbhadhan* ceremony is admittedly not observed in many respectable Hindu families, and is not unfrequently more honoured in the breach than in the observance. I cannot, in the face of the evidence of such men as these, accept, without a protest, the statement of our hon'ble colleague Sir Romesh Chunder Mitter, whose absence from the Council I deeply regret, that we are "forcing this reform upon an unwilling people." To them, and to many more who have raised their voices in support of the measure, I desire to offer a public acknowledgment of the service which they have rendered. I feel convinced that the time is not far off when their fellow-citizens, without exception, will recognize that such men as these, rather than they who have so noisily, and so thoughtlessly, repeated the parrot cry "our religion is in danger," are the true leaders of the public opinion in this country.

[. . .] I will pass for a moment to the third great objection which has been raised against the measure. It is the objection founded upon the anticipation that it will lead to inquisitorial action by the police, to prosecutions instituted from vindictive motives, and to criminal investigations into family matters of the most domestic and private character. Of this objection I will say that, whatever may be our opinions with regard to some of the arguments which have been brought forward against the Bill, there can be no doubt as to the perfect sincerity with which this argument has been urged upon us. The apprehension, considering the conditions under which a great part of the population of this country lead their lives, is a perfectly natural one: we should, if we were situated as they are, probably entertain a similar apprehension ourselves. I would, however, in the first place, entreat the public to be cautious how, in this or in any other case, it allows itself to be too much influenced by arguments founded upon the possibility that a new law is likely to be abused in this manner. If the Government of India had been deterred from legislating whenever it could be told that its legislation would place in the hands of the police, or of private persons, a weapon which they might use in an improper manner, many of our most useful enactments would never have found their way into the Code. Now, as far as bonà fide prosecutions are concerned the assumption that there will be frequent prosecutions under the new section is obviously based on the anticipation that the law will be frequently broken. I am sanguine enough to believe that this expectation will not be fulfilled. It is an expectation upon which the frequently expressed belief that the new law will be a dead letter is a somewhat remarkable commentary. Our proposals, moreover, already command a very large measure of public support, and I do not doubt that, in the end, Native opinion, which has always ended by supporting the law in cases of this kind, will end by supporting it in this instance also. When once it has become established that that which is, I believe, already regarded by a majority of the people of this country as a moral offence, and which our hon'ble colleague Sir Romesh Chunder Mitter himself stigmatizes as a vice, and as a pernicious custom, is also an offence which will render those who commit it, or those who abet it, liable to penal consequences, the offence will, I venture to think, become one of rare occurrence. I may observe, in passing, that it was mainly in deference to the apprehensions of which I have spoken that we found ourselves unable to accept the well-intentioned proposal that we should insert in the Bill, as an alternative for the limit of age which we have adopted, the attainment of puberty by the girl. This proposal, which seemed to us open to objection upon other grounds was certainly open to criticism, for the reason that its adoption might have led to investigations far more inquisitorial, and far more repugnant to family sentiment, than any which are likely to take place under the Bill as it stands.

It is, however, contended that the tendency of the Bill will be to encourage proceedings which are not instituted bonà fide, but from malicious motives, and in order to bring disgrace upon the family of the accursed, and a moving picture has been drawn of the anguish and humiliation which such proceedings will occasion, of the outrage to which an innocent woman might be exposed before the question of fact could be satisfactorily disposed of, and of the public scandal which would be created if things which usually *sub lodice teguntur* are allowed to be openly discussed in a public Court of Justice. The argument is one which I can assure the Council, the Government of India has most anxiously considered. We have, I think, shown our sense of the necessity of guarding against these risks by making the offence a non-cognizable one, and thereby increasing the difficulties in the way of

vexatious prosecutions. We have also agreed to add to the measure a clause preventing all but District Magistrates from dealing with cases in which husband and wife are concerned, and precluding any police officer below the rank of Inspector from making, or taking part in, the investigation, when one has been directed by the Magistrate.

Source: C. H. Philips, et al. (eds) *The Evolution of India and Pakistan, 1857–1947. Select Documents.* London: Oxford University Press, 1962, pp. 736–40.

65 The Age of Consent Act, March 19, 1891

An Act to amend the Indian Penal Code and the Code of Criminal Procedure, 1882.

WHEREAS it is expedient to amend the Indian Penal Code and the Code of Criminal Procedure, 1882; It is hereby enacted as follows:

Indian Penal Code

1 In section 373 of the Indian Penal Code, in the clause marked Fifthly and in the Exception, the word "twelve" shall be substituted for the word "ten".

Code of Criminal Procedure, 1882

2 After section 560 of the Code of Criminal Procedure, 1882, the following shall be added, namely:
  "561 (1) Notwithstanding anything in this Code, no Magistrate except a Chief Presidency Magistrate or District Magistrate shall

(a) take cognizance of the offence of rape where the sexual intercourse was by a man with his wife, or
(b) committ the man for trial for the offence;

  (2) And, notwithstanding anything in this Code, if a Chief Presidency Magistrate or District Magistrate deems it necessary to direct an investigation by a Police-officer with respect to such an offence as is referred to in sub-section (1) of this section, no Police-officer of a rank below that of Police Inspector shall be employed either to make, or to take part in, the investigation."
  3 In Schedule II to the said Code, for the entry respecting section 376 of the Indian Penal Code, the following shall be substituted, namely:

Column 1	Column 2	Column 3	Column 4
	Rape –		
	If the sexual intercourse was by a man with his own wife.	Shall not arrest without warrant.	Summons.
	In any other case.	May arrest without warrant.	Warrant.

Column 5	Column 6	Column 7	Column 8
Rape – Bailable	Not compoundable.	Transportation for life, or imprisonment of either description for 10 years, and fine.	Court of Session.
Not bailable	Ditto.	Ditto.	Ditto.

Source: C. H. Philips et al. (eds) *The Evolution of India and Pakistan, 1857–1947. Select Documents.* London: Oxford University Press, 1962, pp. 740–1.

66   The Ilbert Bill (1883)

A BILL to AMEND the CODE of CRIMINAL PROCEDURE, 1882, so far as it relates to the exercise of JURISDICTION over EUROPEAN BRITISH SUBJECTS.

WHEREAS it is expedient to amend the Code of Criminal Procedure, 1882, so far as it relates to the exercise of jurisdiction of European British subjects: It is hereby enacted as follows:

1   For the last clause of section 22, the following shall be substituted:

may, by notification in the official gazette, appoint such persons as he or it thinks fit, who, being
(a)   members of the Covenanted Civil Service,
(b)   members of the native Civil Service constituted under the Statute 33 Vict. cap. 3,
(c)   assistant commissioners in non-regulation provinces, or
(d)   cantonment magistrates, invested with the powers of a magistrate of the first class, to be justices of the peace within and for the territories mentioned in the notification.

2   In section 25, after the words "British India" the following shall be inserted:

sessions judges and district magistrates are justices of the peace within and for the whole of the territories administered by the Local Government under which they are serving.

3   In section 443, the words "and an European British subject" shall be omitted.

4   For section 444, the following shall be substituted:

444. An assistant sessions judge shall not exercise jurisdiction over an European British subject, unless he has held the office of assistant sessions judge for at least three years, and has been specially empowered in this behalf by the Local Government.

5   Section 450 and the last sixteen words of section 459 are hereby repealed.

6   (1) In this Act "section" means section of the Code of Criminal Procedure, 1882.
    (2) All references to that code made in enactments heretofore passed or hereafter to be passed shall be read as if made to that Code as amended by this act.

7   Nothing in this Act shall affect the validity of any appointment made before the passing of this Act.

Statement of Objects and Reasons

SHORTLY after the Code of Criminal Procedure, Act X of 1882, was passed, the question was raised whether the provisions of that Code which limit the jurisdiction over European British subjects outside the Presidency towns to judicial officers who are themselves European British subjects should not be modified. It was thought anomalous that, while, natives of India were admitted to the Covenanted Civil Service and held competent to discharge the highest judicial duties, they should be deemed incompetent to be justices of the peace and to exercise jurisdiction over European British subjects outside the Presidency towns.

2   After consulting the local Governments, the Government of India has arrived at the conclusion

that the time has come for modifying the existing law and removing the present bar upon the investment of native magistrates in the interior with powers over European British subjects. The Government of India has accordingly decided to settle the question of jurisdiction over European British subjects in such a way as to remove from the Code, at once and completely, every judicial disqualification which is based merely on race distinctions.

3   With this object the present Bill has been prepared. In section one, it amends section 22 of the Code, which provides that only European British subjects can be appointed justices of the peace, and gives the Government power to appoint to that office such persons as it thinks fit belonging to the following classes:

(a)   Members of the Covenanted Civil Service;
(b)   Members of the Native Civil Service constituted by the rules made under the Statute 33 Vic., cap. 3;
(c)   Assistant Commissioners in Non-Regulation Provinces; or
(d)   Cantonment magistrates,

and being persons invested with the powers of a magistrate of the first class.

4   The Bill then in section two amends section 25 of the Code, and makes all sessions judges and district magistrates *ex officio* justices of the peace.

5   Section three repeals so much of section 443 of the Code as limits jurisdiction over European British subjects outside the Presidency towns to magistrates who are themselves European British subjects.

6   Section four repeals the similar provision of section 444 of the Code with regard to sessions judges.

7   Lastly, section five repeals section 450 of the Code, which provides for the case where the sessions judge of the division within which the offence is ordinarily triable is not an European British subject. The same section of the Bill also repeals so much of section 459 of the Code as provides that that section shall not be deemed to confer on magistrates and sessions judges outside the Presidency towns, not being European British subjects, jurisdiction over European British subjects.

The 30th January 1883   C. P. ILBERT

Source: Edwin Hirschmann. *White Mutiny: The Ilbert Bill Crisis in India and Genesis of the Indian National Congress.* New Delhi: Heritage, 1980, pp. 294–6.

Note

The Ilbert Bill, passed in 1883, aroused considerable controversy among both English and Indians by its provisions allowing Indian magistrates to sit in judgment on Europeans.

Sir Courtenay Peregrine Ilbert (1841–1924), was called to the Bar in 1869 and later worked as an advisor to the Indian National Congress over the adoption of the Indian parliamentary system.

67   C. P. Ilbert: On the Principles and Purposes of the Ilbert Bill of 1883

[. . .] As to the object at which we ought to aim, there will be no difference of opinion. It is simply the effectual and impartial administration of justice, and as to the facts with which we have to deal, no one who has studied the statistics and reports of the cases involving charges against European British subjects can fail to be struck with two things, first, that as compared with the great mass of ordinary criminal business they are exceptionally rare, and secondly, that they are exceptionally troublesome and difficult. To what conclusion do these two peculiarities point? They appear to me to show that, in the interests of the effectual and impartial administration of justice it is not necessary, and that, in the same interests it is not desirable, to clothe all Magistrates indiscriminately with the power of dealing with these cases. As we are justified in excluding from the jurisdiction of interior Magistrates as such the cognisance of the graver classes of offences, so we should be justified in excluding from their jurisdiction the cognisance of a class of offences the trial of which, from the circumstances under which they are ordinarily committed, presents features of exceptional difficulty . . . the further question which we have to determine is how this class is to be defined. My answer is that the line ought to be drawn with reference to the presumable fitness of the Magistrate, and with reference to that alone, and that we ought not to base any difference which we may think fit to make between particular classes of Magistrates, on race distinctions which are as invidious as they are unnecessary.

These are the principles by which we have been guided in framing the proposals which I am now asking leave to lay before the Council. We are of opinion that the time has come when the settlement which was arrived at in 1872 may with safety, and ought in justice to be reconsidered; we are of opinion that if this question is reopened it ought to be settled on a permanent and stable foundation; and finally we are of opinion that no change in the law can be satisfactory or stable which fails to remove at once and completely from the Code every judicial disqualification which is based merely on race distinctions.

Source: C. H. Philips, et al. (eds). *The Evolution of India and Pakistan, 1857–1947. Select Documents.* London: Oxford University Press, 1962, pp. 121–2.

68   *The Times*: Editorial on Opposition to the Ilbert Bill, February 26, 1883

The telegram from our Calcutta Correspondent which we print this morning shows that increased familiarity with the Criminal Jurisdiction Bill only intensifies the distrust with which it is regarded by the European community in India. That feeling found its earliest and, perhaps, its strongest expression in Bengal, but it is evident that it exists in equal force wherever there are European capitalists or residents to be affected by the new scheme. The newspapers are filled with articles and letters protesting against the proposed change, and our Correspondent testifies to the widespread and intense indignation it has evoked. The Bengal Chamber of Commerce has passed a resolution declaring its unqualified disapproval and its intention to oppose the measure by every means in its power. A requisition signed by all the leading non-official Europeans in Calcutta has been presented to the Sheriff, asking him to call a public meeting in order that the sense of the European community may be formally taken and made known to the Indian Government and to Parliament. A large and influential meeting at Madras has resolved that the Bill demands the concerted opposition of the European community throughout India, is an unnecessary sacrifice of a highly-prized right to ideal legislation, and will seriously check the introduction of European capital into India. The planters of Assam protest indignantly against the Bill, as calculated seriously to injure existing interests and to stop the progress of the province, besides reviving the antagonism of race which was happily disappearing. The indigo planters of Behar and the tea-growers of Darjeeling join in the general outcry, while despatches from every centre of European activity testify to the universality of the opposition excited by this unfortunate measure. It is, of course, more difficult to obtain conclusive evidence as to the drift of official opinion. Official propriety requires that it should be expressed with caution, and stronger motives are not wanting to prevent excessive candour. But officials are also private citizens, permitting themselves greater freedom in that capacity, and our Correspondent affirms that, with obvious exceptions, they agree, as is, indeed, to be expected, with the general opinion of the non-official Europeans. Those who take their stand upon some abstract theory or sentiment may, of course, exclaim *fiat justitia* after the magnificent manner of sentimentalists everywhere, but practical politicians will agree with us in thinking that the universal opinion of the European community cannot be thus lightly disposed of. We do not govern India exclusively through the Civil Service. Every man who plants tea or indigo or cinchona, who exports wheat, or who runs a mill, is part of an agency for the development of India which is the necessary complement of the machinery of government. Without European capital and enterprise the Government of India might mark time, but it could not advance. Therefore, the opinion of the mercantile community is entitled as a mere matter of statesmanship to serious consideration, and ought not to be disregarded, except for some very cogent reason.

69   Memorial of the Eurasian and Anglo-Indian Association to the Governor General in Council, March 8, 1883

That your memorialists have become aware of the desire of the Legislature to be informed of public feeling, in all classes concerned, in regard to a proposed change in the criminal law relating to the subjection of European British subjects to certain Native magistrates in the Mufassil; and that, as loyal subjects, many of whom personally possess the status of European British subjects under the law, your memorialists submit for consideration the following objections which they hold against the change. [. . .]

2   That it is a wise maxim of British statesmanship that legislation, and more especially important legislation, should wait upon necessity; and that no pressing necessity has been made out for this change in the Statement of Objects and Reasons which has been given to the country.

3   That, in the absence of such necessity, the grounds advanced for the change are, that "it was thought anomalous that, while Natives of India were admitted to the Covenanted Civil Service, and held competent to discharge the highest judicial duties, they should be deemed incompetent to be justices of the peace, and to exercise jurisdiction over Europeans outside the Presidency towns"; and that the "Government of India had accordingly decided to settle the question of jurisdiction over European British subjects in such a way as to remove from the Code, at once and completely, every judicial disqualification which is based merely on race distinctions." [. . .]

5   That in the opinion of the European and Anglo-Indian community, the concessions to native prejudice made in connexion with the administration of justice, such as the exemption of the Native gentry and ladies from attendance as witnesses in our law courts, represent greater anomalies than any involved in the right of European British subjects to be tried by their peers. To such concessions the European community have never demurred; and they feel that, on this very account, the only right which they themselves have hitherto enjoyed should remain untouched.

6   That, without presuming to assert that the Indian Legislature has no strict legal power to enact that European British subjects may be tried by Native judicial officers, your memorialists respectfully submit that a great constitutional difficulty underlies the proposed legislation. That during the many centuries through which the English people struggled for liberty and for the complete and practical attainment of the right of trial by one's peers, the possibility of the spectacle of an Englishman being tried by anybody but an Englishman was not and could not have been contemplated. That such a possibility has now arisen, not only in India, but in several of the dependencies and colonies belonging to the British Empire, such as Cape Colony, Natal, New Zealand, and the West Indies. That, without denying the many virtues and merits of the Natives of India and of these other countries, it cannot be contended that they are the peers or equals of Englishmen. That the trial of an Englishman by a Native of any of these dependencies, that is to say,

the trial of an Englishman by one who is not his peer, is an infringement of a great constitutional right. That your memorialists respectfully, but confidently, submit that the Parliament of Great Britain and Ireland is the only Legislature which ought to deal with so momentous a trespass on the principle which is the foundation of English constitutional law.

Source: C. H. Philips et al. (eds). *The Evolution of India and Pakistan, 1857–1947. Select Documents.* London: Oxford University Press, 1962, pp. 123–4.

70   J. Gibbs: Letter to Lord Ripon, April 17, 1883

I have been able to get very thorough information as to the origin of the opposition. [. . .]

The Bar have been very sore about the reduction of the judges' pay . . . and were only too glad of an opportunity to do Govt. an injury if they could – and the idea of an opposition to the Bill was started in the Bar library by some of the English Barristers. Communications were entered into with the Englishman's office(?) and circulars in the shape of letters were sent to the planters . . . up country suggesting they oppose the Bill . . . they took the bait and urged their correspondents and agents here to move in the matter and hence the opposition took firm hold . . . the delay between the 2 and 19 Feb. when the fiercer opposition broke out is accounted for by the time it took to communicate with up country and get replies before the matter could be prominently(?) mooted in Calcutta . . . it acquired force by morning and its climax was reached on 28 Feb. at the Town Hall.

Source: C. H. Philips, et al. (eds). *The Evolution of India and Pakistan, 1857–1947. Select Documents.* London: Oxford University Press, 1962, p. 124.

Chapter Twelve

The Game Board: Getting To and Around India

Introduction

Before the opening of the Suez Canal in 1869, the sea voyage from England to India could take as long as half a year. To be sure, there were those travellers like Frederick Burnaby who, for reasons of the "game," would proceed overland on "horseback through Asia Minor," but the larger part of the entrants to the Raj in the subcontinent took pleasure in the passage to India through the Canal. Not only transportation had been improved with the new technologies of steam, but communication as well, by way of the submarine telegraph cables that were laid in the 1860s and 1870s, consolidating the network of interactivity and intervention between Britain and her empire in the East.

And just as the passage to India was facilitated by the technological advances, so too were the connections across the subcontinent. Between 1845 and 1875, nearly 100 million pounds had been invested in railway construction in India. By 1902, British India had nearly 26,000 miles of railroads (more even than the rest of Asia put together, and over three times as much as Africa) (see Headrick,

1981). As Karl Marx wrote in one of his dispatches to the *New York Daily Tribune*, "I know that the English millocracy intend to endow India with railways with the exclusive view of extracting at diminished expenses the Cotton and other raw materials for their manufactures. But when you have once introduced machinery into the locomotion of a country, which posesses iron and coals, you are unable to withold it from its fabrication. You cannot maintain a net of railways over an immense country without introducing all those industrial processes necessary to meet the immediate and current wants of railway locomotion, and out of which there must grow the application of machinery to those branches of industry not immediately connected with railways. The railway system will therefore become, in India, truly the forerunner of modern industry. . . . Modern industry, resulting from the railway system, will dissolve the hereditary divisions of labor, upon which rest the Indian castes, those decisive impediments to Indian progress and Indian power" (August 8, 1853).

Not just the division of labor was affected by the railways, however, but the social distinctions as well. Whereas the Grand Trunk Road, so vividly described in Kipling's *Kim* and stretching between Calcutta and the Khyber Pass, mixed its travellers without regard to class, caste or ethnicity, travel by train required tickets, and tickets also determined carriage by social rank and status, thus dividing British and Indian. Between 1861 and 1862, 61,000 first class passengers, 299,820 second class, and 6,477,055 third class travellers, had journeyed the 700 miles of track that had been laid at the time (Satow and Desmond). The railways in India serviced multiple interests: from providing work for engineers, to providing food to famine stricken areas, to provisioning the picnic in the Malabar Hills hosted by Aziz for Adela and Mrs Moore in Forster's *A Passage to India*. Who would run them, and what commercial stakes were to be engaged? If once the East India Company had managed the transportation to India, the new railway ventures were rerouting the connections with and within, the subcontinent, but the control of the enterprise remained in the hands of the London overseers: "Of the 50,000 holders of Indian railroad shares in 1868, only 400 were Indian because shares could only be traded in London" (Headrick, 1981: 188).

BH

Additional Reading

Headrick, Daniel R. *The Tools of Empire: Technology and European Imperialism in the Nineteenth Century*. New York and Oxford, 1981.
——. *The Tentacles of Progress: Technology Transfer in the Age of Imperialism 1850–1940*. New York and Oxford, 1988.
——. *The Invisible Weapon: Telecommunications and International Politics 1851–1945*. New York and Oxford, 1991.
Macleod, Roy and Deepak Kumar (eds). *Technology and the Raj: Western Technology and Technical Transfers to India 1700–1947*. New Delhi and London, 1995.
Theroux, Paul. *The Great Railway Bazaar*. New York, 1975.
Withey, Lynne. *Grand Tours and Cook's Tours: A History of Leisure Travel 1750–1915*. New York, 1997.

Film

Michael Anderson. *Around the World in Eighty Days* (1956).

71   Col. Henry Yule and A. C. Burnell: Definitions of "bungalow," "dawk bungalow," and "Sahib" (1886)

BUNGALOW, s. H. and Mahr. *banglā*. The most usual class of house occupied by Europeans in the interior of India: being on one story, and covered by a pyramidal roof, which in the normal bungalow is of thatch, but may be of tiles without impairing its title to be called a *bungalow*. Most of the houses of officers in Indian cantonments are of this character. In reference to the style of the house, *bungalow* is sometimes employed in contradistinction to the (usually more pretentious) *pucka house*; by which latter term is implied a masonry house with a terraced roof. A *bungalow* may also be a small building of the type which we have described, but of temporary material, in a garden, on a terraced roof for sleeping in, etc., etc. The word has also been adopted by the French in the East, and by Europeans generally in Ceylon, China, Japan, and the coast of Africa.

Wilson writes the word *bānglā*, giving it as a Bengālī word, and as probably derived from *Banga*, Bengal. This is fundamentally the etymology mentioned by Bp. Heber in his *Journal* (see below), and that etymology is corroborated by our first quotation, from a native historian, as well as by that from F. Buchanan. It is to be remembered that in Hindustan proper the adjective "of or belonging to Bengal" is constantly pronounced as *bangālā* or *banglā*. Thus one of the eras used in E. India is distinguished as the *Banglā* era. The probability is that, when Europeans began to build houses of this character in Behar and Upper India, these were called *Banghā* or "Bengal-fashion" houses; that the name was adopted by the Europeans themselves and their followers, and so was brought back to Bengal itself, as well as carried to other parts of India. ["In Bengal, and notably in the districts near Calcutta, native houses to this day are divided into *ath-chala*, *chau-chala*, and *Bangala*, or eight-roofed, four-roofed, and Bengali, or common huts. The first term does not imply that the house has eight coverings, but that the roof has four distinct sides with four more projections, so as to cover a verandah all round the house, which is square. The *Bangala*, or Bengali house, or *bungalow* has a sloping roof on two sides and two gable ends. Doubtless the term was taken up by the first settlers in Bengal from the native style of edifice, was materially improved, and was thence carried to other parts of India. It is not necessary to assume, that the first bungalows were created in Behar." (*Saturday Rev.*, 17th April 1886, in a review of the first ed. of this book).]

A. H. 1041 = A. D. 1633   "Under the rule of the Bengalis (*daralul-i-Bangālāyān*) a party of Frank merchants, who are inhabitants of Sundíp, came trading to Sátgánw. One kog above that place they occupied some ground on the banks of the estuary.

Under the pretence that a building was necessary for their transactions in buying and selling, they created several houses in the Bengálí style." – *Bádsháhuáma*, in *Flliol*, vii. 31.

c.1680 In the tracing of an old Dutch chart in the India Office, which may be assigned to about this date, as it has no indication of Calcutta, we find at Hoogly: "*Ougli . . . Hollantza Logia . . .* Bangelaer of Speelhuys," i.e. "Hoogly . . . Dutch Factory . . . Bungalow, or Pleasure-house."

1711 "*Mr. Herring, the Pilot's, Directions for bringing of Ships down the River of Hughley.*

"From *Gull Gat* all along the *Hughley* Shore until below the *New Chancy* almost as far as the *Dutch* Bungelow lies a Sand. . . ." – *Thornton, The English Pilot*, Pt. III. p. 54.

1711 "*Natty* Bungelo or *Nedds* Bangalla River lies in this Reach (Tanna) on the Larboard side . . ." – Ibid. 56. The place in the chart is *Nedds* Bengalla, and seems to have been near the present Akra on the Hoogly.

1747 "Nabob's Camp near the Hedge of the Bounds, building a Bangallaa, raising Mudd Walls round the Camp, making Gun Carriages, &c. . . . (Pagodas) 55 : 10 : 73." – *Acrt. of Extraordinary Charges* . . . January, at *Fort St. David, MS. Records in India Office.*

1758 "I was talking with my friends in Dr. Fullerton's bangla when news came of Ram Narain's being defeated." – *Seir Mutaqheria*, ii. 103.

1780 "To be Sold or Let, A Commodious Bungalo and out Houses . . . situated on the Road leading from the Hospital to the Burying Ground, and directly opposite to the Avenue in front of Sir Elijah Impey's House. . . ." – *The India Gazelle*, Dec. 23.

1781–83 "Bungelows are buildings in India, generally raised on a base of brick, one, two, or three feet from the ground, and consist of only one story: the plan of them usually is a large room in the center for an eating and sitting room, and rooms at each corner for sleeping; the whole is covered with one general thatch, which comes low to each side; the spaces between the angle rooms are *viranders* or open porticoes . . . sometimes the center *viranders* at each end are converted into rooms." – *Hodges, Travels*, 146.

1784 "To be let at Chinsurah . . . That large and commodious House. . . . The outbuildings are – a warehouse and two large *bottle-connahs*, 6 store-rooms, a cook-room, and a garden, with a bungalow near the house." – *Cal. Gazettè*, in *Seton-Karr*, i. 40.

1787 "At Barraokpore many of the Bungalows much damaged, though none entirely destroyed." – Ibid. p. 213.

1793 ". . . the bungalo, or Summer-house. . . ." – *Dirom*, 211.

"For Sale, a Bungalo situated between the two Tombstones, in the Island of Coulaba." – *Bombay Courier*, Jan. 12.

1794 "The candid critic will not however expect the parched plains of India, or bungaloes in the land-winds, will hardly tempt the Aonian maids wont to disport on the banks of Tiber and Thames. . . ." – *Hugh Boyd*, 170.

1809 "We came to a small bungalo or garden-house, at the point of the hill, from which there is, I think, the finest view I ever saw." – *Maria Graham*, 10.

c.1810 "The style of private edifices that is proper and peculiar to Bengal consists of a hut with a pont roof constructed of two sloping sides which meet in a ridge forming the segment of a circle. . . . This kind of hut, it is said, from being peculiar to Bengal, is called by the natives Banggolo, a name which has been somewhat altered by Europeans, and applied by them to all their buildings in the cottage style, although none of them have the proper shape, and many of them are excellent brick houses." – *Buchanan's Dinagepore* (in *Eastern India*, ii. 922).

1817 "*The Yorŭ-bangala* is made like two thatched houses or bangalas, placed side by side. . . . These temples are dedicated to different gods, but are not now frequently seen in Bengal." – *Ward's Hindoos*, Bk. II. ch. i.

c.1818 "As soon as the sun is down we will go over to the Captain's bungalow." – *Mrs Sherwood Stories*, etc., ed. 1873, p. 1. The original editions of this book contain an engraving of "The Captain's Bungalow at Cawnpore" (*c*.1811–12), which shows that no material change has occurred in the character of such dwellings down to the present time.

1824 "The house itself of Barrackpore . . . barely accommodates Lord Amherst's own family; and his aides-de-camp and visitors sleep in bungalows built at some little distance from it in the Park. Bungalow, a corruption of Bengalee, is the general name in this country for any structure in the cottage style, and only of one floor. Some of these are spacious and comfortable dwellings. . . ." – *Heber*, ed. 1844, i. 33.

1872 "L'emplacement du bungalou avait été choisi avec un soin tout particulier." – *Rev. des Deux Mondes*, tom., xcviii. 930.

1875 "The little groups of officers dispersed to their respective bungalows to dress and breakfast." – *The Dilemma*, ch. i.

[In Oudh the name was specially applied to Fyzabad.

[1858 "Fyzabad . . . was founded by the first rulers of the reigning family, and called for some time Bungalow, from a bungalow which they built on the verge of the stream." – *Sleeman, Journey through the Kingdom of Oudh*, i. 137.]

BUNGALOW, DAWK, s. A rest-house for the accommodation of travellers, formerly maintained (and still to a reduced extent) by the paternal care of the Government of India. The *matériel* of the accommodation was humble enough, but comprised the things essential for the weary traveller – shelter, a bed and table, a bathroom, and a servant furnishing food at a very moderate cost. On principal lines of thoroughfare these bungalows were at a distance of 10 to 15 miles apart, so that it was possible for a traveller to make his journey by marches without carrying a tent. On some less frequented roads they were 40 or 50 miles apart, adapted to a night's run in a palankin.

1853 "Dâk-bungalows have been described by some Oriental travellers as the 'Inns of India.' Playful satirists!" *Oakfield*, ii. 17.

1866 "The Dawk Bungalow; or, Is his Appointment Pucka!" – By *G. O. Trevelyan*, in *Fraser's Magazine*, vol. 73, p. 215.

1878 "I am inclined to think the value of life to a dak bungalow fowl must be very trifling." – *In my Indian Garden*, 11.

SAHIB, s. The title by which, all over India, European gentlemen, and it may be said Europeans generally, are addressed, and spoken of, when no disrespect is intended, by natives. It is also the general title (at least where Hindustani or Persian is used) which is affixed to the name or office of a European, corresponding thus rather to *Monsieur* than to Mr. For *Colonel Ṣāḥib, Collector, Ṣāḥib, Lord Ṣāḥib*, and even *Sergeant Ṣāḥib* are thus used, as well as the general vocative *Ṣāḥib*, I; 'Sir!' In other Hind. use the word is equivalént to 'Master'; and, it is occasionally used as, a specific title both among Hindus and Musulmans, e.g. *Appa, Ṣāḥib, Tipū Ṣāḥib*; and generically is affixed to the titles of men of rank when indicated by those titles, as *Khān Ṣāḥib, Nawāb Ṣāḥib, Rāja Ṣāḥib*. The word is Arabic, and originally means 'a companion'; (sometimes a companion of Mahommed). [In the *Arabian Nights* it is the title of a Wazīr (*Burton*, i. 218).]

1673 ". . . To which the subtle Heathen replied, Sahab (i.e. Sir), why will you do more than the Creator meant?" – *Fryer*, 417.

1689 "Thus the distracted Husband in his *Indian* English confest, *English fashion*, Sab, best fashion, have one Wife best for one Husband." – *Ovington*, 326.

1853 "He was told that a 'Sahib' wanted to speak with him." – *Oakfield*, ii. 252.

1878 ". . . forty Elephants and five Sahibs with guns and innumerable followers." – *Life in the Mofussil*, i. 194.

Source: Col. Henry Yule and A. C. Burnell. *Hobson-Iobson: A Glossary of Colloquial Anglo-Indian Words and Phrases.* New Delhi: Munshiram Manoharlal, 1994, pp. 128, 129, 781–2 (Orig. pub. 1886).

72 George Francklin Atkinson: *Curry and Rice on Forty Plates* (1859)

WHAT varied opinions we constantly hear
    Of our rich Oriental Possessions;
What a jumble of notions, distorted and queer,
    Form an Englishman's "Indian impressions!"

First a sun, fierce and glaring, that scorches and bakes;
    Palankeens, perspiration, and worry:
Mosquitoes, thugs, cocoa-nuts, Brahmins, and snakes,
    With elephants, tigers, and Curry.

Then, Juggernat, punkahs, tanks, buffaloes, forts,
    With bangles, mosques, nautches, and dhingees;
A mixture of temples, Mahometans, ghats,
    With scorpions, Hindoos, and Feringhees.

Then jungles, fakeers, dancing-girls, prickly heat,
    Shawls, idols, durbars, brandy-pawny;
Rupees, clever jugglers, dust-storms, slipper'd feet,
    Rainy season, and mulligatawny.

Hot winds, holy monkeys, tall minarets, Rice,
    With crocodiles, ryots or farmers;
Himalayas, fat baboos, with paunches and pice,
    So airily clad in pyjamas.

With Rajahs – But stop, I must really desist,
    And let each one enjoy his opinions,
Whilst I show in what style Anglo-Indians exist
    In her Majesty's Eastern dominions.

Preface

GENTLE READER,
    Before you can be landed on the sunny shores of Ind, a tedious voyage must be overcome; so, in like manner, before you are transported into the scenes depicted in the following pages, a preliminary voy-

age, in the way of a Preface, has to be encountered. Allow me, then, to improve the occasion by a few sober words of exhortation, that I may dissipate at once and for ever some of those fallacious opinions and crude notions that you persist in entertaining regarding that land called "India."

Allow me, first, to impress upon you this geographical fact, that India is about the size of all Europe; and, moreover, that the British possessions are subdivided into distinct governments, each a kingdom in itself; and that Bengal, Madras, and Bombay are as different and far more disconnected than are England, Ireland, and Scotland; so that that eccentricidea, that floats so persistently in your imagination, of jumping to the conclusion that because dear Charley is going to India, he must infallibly meet dear Willy, who is already there, is slightly illogical; for dear Willy, if I mistake not, belongs to the Bengal Presidency, and is stationed at the very North-west boundary of the empire, at the foot of the Himalayas, close to Cashmere; while dear Charley is bound for Madras, and you may probably hear from him at Cape Comorin, when there will be *only* the trifling intervening distance of some 2,000 miles between them.

You might equally well hope that your travelling cousin Alex, who is going to fish in Norway, must be sure to see your dear cousin Maria, who is scrambling about the ruins of the Parthenon; or that because the aforesaid migratory Alex is going to St. Petersburg, he will need a letter of introduction to General Friskhimoff, the Military Governor of Eastern Siberia.

Secondly, let me remind you that, while there are numerous races with a different creed, caste, and language, so there are customs and manners peculiar to each: and this variety is not confined to the natives; for the habits and customs of social life among the English in India likewise present their petty diversities; and the "Qui Hye" of Bengal, the "Mull" of Madras, and the "Duck" of Bombay, adhere to and defend their own customs with jealous warmth of feeling; so that in the following pages, it must be explained, the scenes are drawn to exhibit the customs of society on the Bengal side, as it was necessary throughout to adhere to some one character of people among whom the English were located; but they are such as are common to the whole of India, judging from personal experience in the three Presidencies. And this brings me to the last point upon which I would wish to say a few words.

Among mankind, the perfect individual affords no scope for the exercise of humour. Perfection has nothing comic in it whatsoever; and it is only as

perfection is deviated from that the victim becomes the object of wit or a shaft for ridicule: just as a sound and well-constructed wheel, that revolves smoothly on its axle, has nothing in it to excite, observation; but when that wheel rotates in a grotesque fashion, symptomatic of immediate aberration from its axle, and, moreover, rattles profusely, it then becomes an object of attraction, and is apt to create a smile.

Those, then, of my readers, who imagine that I have singled out the faults and absurdities of our race, will, perhaps, accept as my reason for so doing, that my object was not to illustrate perfection, but to afford amusement, by dwelling upon the sunny side of Indian life, after all the narratives of horror that have of late fallen upon the English ear; but I wish it to be distinctly known that no living mortals have been taken as models for the pictures here drawn, and that if there are any sensitive beings who will fit the cap on their own heads, I can only say that it is their own doing, and not mine.

And now, having brought you so far on your voyage, with the comforting assurance that you are not the persons "so cruelly handed up," let me land you in the East, where you will receive a warm welcome most assuredly. That you may experience a pleasant time of it during your visit at "Our Station," I indulge a hope; and if in the Plates of "Curry and Rice," now set before you, the flavour is found to be a little too spicy and a little too pungent, and, to many perhaps, a thought too hot, remember that it is the nature of Curry to be so. Trusting, however, that it will prove to be a dish to your liking, and leaving you alone to partake of it, and I hope enjoy it, I wish you a Merry Christmas and a Happy New Year!

THE CHALET, LINDFIELD   G. F. ATKINSON
December

Our Station

"Our Station" rejoices in the euphonious appellation of Kabob: it is situated in the plains of Dekchy, in the province of Bobarchy. Far from the busy haunts of a civilized world, and the traffickings of men, and plunged in the wild retirement of a luxuriant jungle, smiles Kabob, "the loveliest village of the plain," basking beneath the rays of the orient sun. Oh! If there be a paradise upon earth, I suspect it must be this!

The general aspect of Kabob is obtrusively prepossessing; it is bounded on the north and east by a mountainous range of – flaming brick-kilns, whilst on the south and west it is embraced in the tortuous sinuosities of a circumambient ravine populous with pigs. But Kabob – and the truth must be told outright – Kabob is not regarded in the light of being the most attractive station in India. Popular prejudice protests against its secluded locality, and malignant slander whispers, in no faint accents, that a hotter and duller hole is not to be discovered by the most enterprising and enthusiastic tropical traveller,

Remote, unfriended, melancholy, slow.

To be sure, and we must confess it, Kabob is not the capital of the province; the councillors of the kingdom, the great men and the mighty men, do not reside here, nor do the high Church dignitaries, nor any military magnate, not even a general. Then, again, it is not situated on the banks of the holy Gunga; its solitary temple is not reflected in the bosom of that sacred and budgerow-bearing river; nor, again, do its stately dwellings and lofty palm-trees grace the skirts of the Grand Portmanteau Road that intersects the Northern Empire. Steamers do not furrow the waters that flow by its sunburnt banks, dropping as they pass their timely offerings of Allsop and of Bass; nor does the shrill whistle and intermittent puff of the locomotive "molest its ancient solitary reign." But what of that? Have not the works of the Great Lohar Railroad been commenced upon? Have not the great capitalists of Kabob – the princes, the governors, the captains, the judges, and all the rest of them – taken shares? and does not every one know that in twenty years' time the line will be open, and that Kabob will then be within one hundred and fifty miles only of the nearest point on the line? Ha! Ha! What can scandal say then? – Kabob will be isolated no more – benighted no longer. We see it all; the once dim future is now a very meridian blaze of brightness. We see with a distinct vision consignments of bitter beer pouring into our rugged highways. No longer shall the anxious bullock yield his last breath in glorious but unavailing efforts to drag the much-expected load of six dozen chests. The wild tracks shall no longer be made known by the whitened bones which there unburied shine, and tell the startling tale of supplies for British mouths from Briton's isle drawn ruthlessly over many a hundred miles of bleak expanse.

Away with melancholy, then! For Kabob, let me tell you, will be, moreover, a thoroughfare to the lands of the West, when the Great Lohar line is open. Visions haunt me of travellers thronging to our portals – blue-eyed young maidens fresh from dear England; and blear-eyed old Indians, belivered and bedevilled, on their way to England.

Visions of claret and Allsop, of choicest delicacies hermetically sealed – all at a reduced tariff. O Kabob! Enviable Kabob, what greatness is in store for thee!

But let us stray through thy sandy meadows and grass-grown streets, fair Kabob! and tell of all thy architectural splendours – thy accumulated glories of whitewash and of thatch – thy mud-built edifices and thy mud-built cottages – thy mud-built enclosure-walls, in all their mud-begotten majesty!

Ah! There is the parade-ground; there, on that bare and barren plain, do our dusky Trojans learn the art of war; there the embryo hero rises from the pristine performance of the goose-step to a full knowledge of brigade manoeuvres. In order that Kabob may enjoy the full benefit of the westerly breezes – which in summer, let me tell you, blow with summary and unquenchable fury, but which, nevertheless, are highly appreciated – "Our Station," as usual, faces the west. On the eastern side, then, of the Parade are the "Lines." First, is a row of apparently magnified sentry-boxes, commonly called Bells of Arms, which appellation denotes their object. In rear of these are the huts for the native troops – small mud-wall tenements roofed with thatch, amidst rows of sickly plantains.

Immediately behind these are the domiciles for the officers, in two or more lines, – each dwelling, commonly yclept a bungalow, in its own peculiar territory, which varies in dimensions, as orthodoxy had originally designed it, under the fond but fanciful delusion that subalterns had small and field officers great requirements. These bungalows, you observe, look like exaggerated beehives, perched upon mile-stones, – a judicious combination of mud, whitewash, and thatch. Stop; we will go into one presently; let us now see only the outer life of Kabob. There, that square whitewashed edifice, with an excrescence at one end, looking for all the world like an extinguisher on a three-dozen chest! What is it? You may well ask. It is the church! A regular protestant building protesting against everything architectural, aesthetic, ornamental, or useful; designed and built according to a Government prescription. Next to it is our assembly-room and theatre; just beyond you see the hospitals; then comes the racket-court, and to the left is the well-stocked burial-ground. This is the course, where the live splendour of Kabob resort when shades of evening close-upon us. There is the band-stand, and this is the station bath. On the extreme right are the barracks, for you must know that Europeans man the guns of our battery that is quartered here. That is the artillery-mess, and opposite lives Stickerdoss, who sells Europe goods, and can accommodate you with anything, from a baby's bottle to a bolster.

Now we must turn to the left, and verging from the confines of the military cantonment, we plunge into territory that is under civil sway. These are the civil lines; those flat-roofed edifices in the Brummagem Tuscan order, all pillars, plaster, and peagreen paint, are the courts of law; this shed is the treasury, and those men guarding it are Our Magistrate's own peculiars. This piece of ground, with its five cabbages, three peach-trees, and patch of onions, is the Government Botanical Garden; and, on your right and left, those wide-verandahed habitations are the dwelling-places of the civilians.

And now, as the sun is getting piping hot, let us gallop home; and after breakfast we will make a day of it, and you shall be introduced to all the beauty and fashion of "Our Station."

Our Judge

I must introduce you to Turmeric; he is "Our Judge" – a tremendous dignitary! Right at the top of the social tree of Our Station, but so desperately absorbed with his official duties, that we see but little of him; his judicial soul being so saturated with appeals, criminal cases, decrees, circular orders, and the like, that when we do meet, the theme of his discourse is so potently flavoured with law, we are overwhelmed with references to Act 95 of 17, Regulation 11 of 78, or some such frightful numbers, which are about as intelligible to us as the hieroglyphics of Nineveh. Who cares for Act 95 of 17, I should like to know?

There you see him in his court – niggers – ten thousand pardons! no, not niggers, I mean natives – sons of the soil – Orientals – Asiatics, are his source of happiness; and there, penned up in that stifling enclosure from "rosy morn, to stewy eve," does he vegetate, surrounded by his jabbering myrmidons. In external man "Our Judge" is suggestive of a boiled bamboo, and in his style of apparel there is presumptive evidence of its being home-made. It is clear that he is no longer – as when a gay Lothario at Calcutta – heedful of the vanities of dress, for he is addicted to the white jacket of a bygone cycle, and appears to encourage the hiatus that exists between it and its nether continuations; these invariably fail to extend to the vicinity of his shoes, which, built after an ancient model, are prodigal in bows.

For thirty and two years uninterruptedly has "Our Judge" been parboiling in India, nor can he be persuaded to turn his steps to old England, of which country his notions are somewhat opaque. I have a faint idea he hopes to get into Council, and prefers an official life for his declining day, to idleness in obscure retirement. To him, modern England has no luring attractiveness; in his estimation, life in London involves a residence in small, dark rooms; and that to stare out of window at the rain, is one's only solace and delight: whilst a country life consists in vegetating with cows and corn, in ignoble obscurity. These, coupled with the necessary perquisites of colds, coughs, umbrellas, sore throats, chilblains, draughts, chest complaints, and such-like, disincline "Our Judge" from returning to the land of his fathers. In private life "Our Judge" is musical; he operates upon the violoncello, and a great adept at the fiddle and the bow is "Our Judge". What our musical *soirées* would be without him is a problem that remains to be solved, for the violoncello, accompanied by its rightful owner, is invariably to be found at every party – a regular standing dish! Turmeric himself gives ornamental tea-parties for the furtherance of harmony on a large, and enjoyment on a small scale; for who could be such a heathen as even to whisper during the perpetration of a piece of Mozart's some five and forty pages in length, even if silence was not enforced by the fair Mrs Turmeric, whose admonition, conveyed in terrible frowns, combined with telegraphic signals of a manual nature, is wonderfully efficacious as an antidote to loquacity.

Mrs Turmeric play? Not she; she has as much idea of a piano as of the sackbut, psaltery, dulcimer, or any other kind of musical instrument. Turmeric, Mrs Capsicum, Cheeny, and Pullow form the standing quartette, and great are the practisings which periodically occur; and if Pullow was only a little less asthmatic, and Mrs Capsicum would not pound so much, or Turmeric plunge down to such awful depths with his bass at inappropriate periods, the effect would be transcendentally sweet. As it is; Pullow swears that Turmeric never keeps time, Cheeny, as he lights his parting cheroot, vows that Mother Capsy puts him out with her confounded "one, two, three, four – one, two, three, four," that she counts out aloud; and Turmeric gets all abroad with his quavers, at Cheeny interpolating unjustifiable variations on his violin, and gets so confused that he begins alluding to Regulation 54 of 99 on the spot; while, as for Mrs Capsicum, she tells me, in strict confidence, that odious Major Pullow never will let her finish a bar, but poo-poos of most unpremeditatedly, as if he couldn't help it.

But it all tends to promote sociability, which Turmeric loves in his quiet way. He is hospitable to a degree; his house, never without its visitors, is a perfect travellers' home, and, moreover, his table, which is often spread, is by no means a *terra incog.* to subalterns, to whom he gives a friendly welcome. Altogether, "Our Judge" is decidedly popular, and his departure from Kabob would be much felt by every one at "Our Station."

Our Judge's Wife

But you really must call upon Mrs Turmeric! She is the *Burra Beebee*, the great lady of Kabob; and I am inclined to think she is not entirely unconscious of the dignity of her state in life; for when Lord Tamarind, on his Eastern travels, passed through Kabob, and handed Mrs Chutney in to dinner, great was the indignation in the Turmeric bosom. I would recommend your not alluding to the peerage, or you will infallibly be inflicted with a detailed narrative of the entire proceeding. Mrs Turmeric is a victim to grief. The world, it would appear, wages a continual warfare with her, and all belonging to her – the greatest grievance being on the state of the Civil Service; and she bewails loudly at the cruelty of her husband not being a Commissioner, and avers that it was a most unjustifiable act of aggression that he was superseded, when he ought to be one of the *Suddur*, or, at any rate, the Resident of Horsepore, or Governor-General's Agent at Salaamabad – and, between ourselves, I suspect she imagines he ought to be Governor-General himself.

A regular perambulating civil-service compendium is Mrs Turmeric! Just hear how she Jeremiahs at the slowness of promotion. "Only think," says she, "Hulwer Sone has got into the *Suddur*, he has been popped over the heads of eleven of his seniors; Johnny Kullum goes home, Mr. Kydy has got the Judgeship of Seeipore, and Charley Dufter is to be Collector of Croquetabad. Only think, Pitty Patty, quite a boy, not thirteen years in the service, is to be Commissioner in Hulwer Sone's place – and Mr. Lafarfer is appointed Civil Auditor – what will the Shelgums say to this job? – Shelgum, who didn't go home last year, expecting to get into the *Suddur*, and Mrs S. just come out from England with all her finery, going to cut such a dash at Atushpore, will have all her silks and satins and feathers destroyed at that wretched Junglabad (and serve her right – what business had she to go to court!); and all this because Pitty Patty must be provided for; and only think, the Bonus scheme will be knocked on the head; for that odious Currer Row, and Pusund Ney, and others, will not subscribe; and there's Johnny Walah offers to go if we will only pay up 15,000 rupees and land him in Bond-street; and there never was such a good step as that. And then

the annuity business – they want Turmeric to pay Heaven knows how many thousand rupees, because those foolish young boys at college will marry so soon, get such large families, and then die off, leaving us to support the awful arrears to the fund, which cannot exist under such pressure from without."

Such are Mrs Turmeric's official griefs. She has some also of a domestic nature. "Now this is really too bad," she says; "you see Mrs McGhee, the Chutneys, Dr Goley, and ourselves, form a Mutton Club, and we kill a sheep in turn; and it is quite shocking to see the scraggy stuff they send – just like half-starved kid; and then they take my beautiful sheep, that have been three years on grain; and what's more, when they do give a party, it is sure to be on Mrs Turmeric's killing-day.' I really must speak to Mrs Chutney; I don't believe she gives a particle of grain all the year round; and as for Mrs McGhee, she wants to palm off her nasty grass-fed sheep as the best flock in the club."

But, with all her afflictions, the portly frame of "Our Judge's Wife" appears to thrive. It is currently reported that old Turmeric's generous hospitality goes sadly against her grain, and that her abilities as a household financier and domestic manager are exquisitely unique, personally supervising with a detective's skill the operations of the kitchen, and not scorning to assist in the manipulation of puddings, pastry, and the like. She is judicious in her selection of a ham, and has a keen eye for a turkey; and from her frequent allusions to a continental wine-merchant, we are led to infer that the champagne is not a decoction of gooseberries. Mirrich, who knows everything, positively asseverates that the liquids are purchased from that villain Stickerdoss; that they have been fished out of the Ganges, and subsequently bought at auction. This I suspect must be an erroneous impression; for if you send your slave to appropriate clandestinely the Judge's private bottle, you'll find it to be of a peculiarly good vintage. Garlic, who was at the coffee-shop this morning (and a shockingly libellous fellow he is, no one can possibly believe him), takes his affidavit that he often sees Mrs Turmeric walloping the turkeys, and chevying the fowls, to make them lay eggs; he declares he has seen her in her verandah larruping the goatman with her slipper, because there appeared a deficit in the milk-pail; and Chabook, her coachman, came howling out of the compound-gate the other day with a cuff on his head, for having suggested the propriety of dispensing a little more grain to the horses. Between ourselves, old Capsicum declares that Mrs Turmeric's sheep are as lean as her husband, and a good deal more tough.

But Mrs Turmeric is a good old soul, and she would be positively miserable without a grievance, and if all things went absolutely smooth; but if she would let off the steam without the addition of the whistle, the explosive matter would escape without its being so generally known throughout the length and breadth of "Our Station."

Our Spins

Loveliness! That characteristic of British women, is but faintly exemplified among those at "Our Station," who recreate in the appellation of "Spins."

Barbara McGhee is a Spin; but in the popular eye she is regarded as impracticable. We discern in the bud what she will be in the flower; safely may we predicate that she will eventually resemble her mamma in human architecture.

The bachelor mind, on matrimonial thoughts intent, pictures to itself the object of adoration as ever remaining the same delicate, pretty being that she now is. But to have such a dip into futurity as is demonstrated by Barbara's mamma, especially as silly Mrs McGhee persists in affirming that she was once exactly like Barbara, is a prospect quite sufficient to whirl-away every project of a holy alliance. Moreover, who could possibly encounter the appalling prospect of having Mrs McGhee plunging into the retirement of one's domestic hearth.

Next on our roster is Letitia Goley, sister to our civil surgeon, rather antique, but cleverish; a child of sentiment, the victim of tender sensibilities, and with a nose suggestive of a cricket-ball! Nine-and-twenty are the summers she has seen; with a few thousand rupees of her own, and a temper to match, she is decidedly eligible. She calls herself a brunette, and prides herself on her Spanish descent, which is about true, considering the Grandmamma Goley was indigenous, and powerfully tinctured with the blood of a Hindoo. It is currently reported that to "claim her hand unnumbered suitors came," but that she prefers the state of single-blessedness. She views matrimony in a sentimental light, and imgines that when love becomes a duty it must cease to be interesting; that wedlock would instantly blast the tendrils of affection, and sound a knell to expiring joy. We admire her doctrine, and – allow her to remain single!

But Letitia is fond of society, and of small talk; goes to every party, and wears mittens. We have registered a small vow to eschew all partners (either temporarily in the dance, or for life) who wear mits. Damp digits are far from indispensable qualifica-

tions in a wife, and moist knuckles are anything but conductive to the heart's affections. But Letty is highly accomplished: she is a poet, perpetrates sonnets, which Herr Guttler, the band-master, sets to music. Her most brilliant composition was a heart-rending duet, commencing,

What are those vile knaves saying,
Sinner, the whole day long?

Then she warbles, too; sings a duet with Mrs Chutney, all about a bank whereon something grows; but whether in time, or out of time, or what time has to do with it, beyond that it is very wild, is exceedingly dubious: then somebody dances with delight, and wonderful is the quivering and quavering at the word "dances." However, the novelty of the song is charming.

Next, we have Bella Clove, with plenty of head, and scarcity of brain; a great adept at slang, and all giggle and gums. Rising sixteen, she has the skittishness of a two-year-old, and will soon entangle some amorous ensign by her rolick and rattle, backed up as it is with those bright hazel eyes, that twinkle so attractively, and that merry laugh. Bella is daughter of Clove of ours, who imported her last cold weather; and very little does she trouble her papa in the chaperoning line; for Bella scorns attendance; rattles all about the cantonment on that little Arab of hers; scampers round the racecourse in the morning with the young ensigns; gallops at full speed down the Mall with a similar escort, to the intense horror of poor Mrs Dhurrter, who drives out in her buggy by herself, and whose horse, startled by the rushing tramp of hoofs, forthwith plays insanely the part of a dancing dervish, and bucking about in the shafts, which are as rigid as maypoles, sets her bobbing about on her cushion like a parched pea, fluctuating indiscriminately between the hood and the splash board, to the infinite delight of Miss Bella, who shrieks with laughter as she rides away to the band. And there she trots about among the carriages – chaffs the Colonel, promises to teach him the polka, upon which he retaliates that he has, fortunately, got a wife, and has no idea of being churned into matrimony. When away she goes, and asks old Guttler why he plays such stupid tunes, and begs he will always drop those horrid operatic airs, and give polkas, waltzes, and gallops instead; then she engages herself for every dance for the next ball, whenever such a contingency should chance to occur; and when the company disperse, the last departure, and the last voice we hear, are those of the merry Bella Clove.

Then we have Carry Cinnamon, who lives with Mrs Chutney, the best and brightest of the bunch. If the crazy, susceptible ensign are allured by the rattling Bella, a perfect swarm of admirers hover round the Chutneys' carriage at the band, basking in the fair smiles, and thrilling under the pensive glances of those large blue eyes. No, not a really good feature does Carry possess, and yet,

With a wild violet grace and sweetness born,

she wins all hearts; for she is so gentle and so pleasing; admirably educated, plays nicely on the piano and harp; has not much voice, but great taste; never affects Italian, although she does understand it; but she will sing you a simple ballad if you really wish it; and I am much mistaken if you would not like to hear it again.

Popular rumour announces that she has rejected many a good offer, as she declines to give her hand where her heart cannot follow. But such a combination, it is pretty well acknowledged, is capable, at last, of being realized; in which case we shall have cause to lament the loss of the most attractive Spin of "Our Station."

Our Nuwab

Among the magnates of "Our Station" – and I had almost been so unthankful as to omit him in this faithful record – is that Oriental potentate, the Nuwab of Kabob. Imbued with much generosity, and impregnated with a taste for English sports and pastimes, the Nuwab is a character of considerable appreciation among us. Where he picked up his predilections for our race has not transpired, nor is it a matter for the display of any anxiety; suffice it to know that the Nuwab is game for anything, from a pool of billiards to giving a ball to the Station.

That is the Nuwab's palace, if you can call that accumulation of tattered buildings of brick and mud and plaster a palace. But let us introduce you to him, let us drive up to his house. There he is, bedecked in gold-embroidered velvet, with a velvet-and-gold turban; pearls depend from his ears, and patent-leather shoes encompass his feet, which are clothed in stockings; across his shoulders is a Cashmere shawl, and he smokes his hookah, waiting till his equipage is ready.

But look at his sporting turn-out; an old English drag, imported by General Bamboo, and with which the old general "stuck" the Nuwab when he went home. And, by the way, you should examine the Palace: it is a perfect refuge for the destitute –

destitute articles, for which no purchasers could be found when their owners left Kabob, and of which the benevolent Nuwab relieved them; articles that an unaccomplished Oriental would find great use for; such as pianos by the dozen – desperate creations, that make the tips of your fingers tingle to touch; harps, babies' cots, four-post bedsteads, ladies' wardrobes, marble-topped round tables, and the like. Then there are carriages *ad infinitum* – veritable arks, with gigantic springs, and violently yellow in complexion; lofty mail phaetons, with hoods, once down, no power on earth could cause to be put up again; and billiard-tables, with caverns for pockets, and a prevailing irregularity of surface, engendered by the curling up of the wood. But the Nuwab shrugs his shoulders, smiles, and knows full well that his asylum is stocked, not from any absolute necessity for the things that are to be found therein, but from sheer feelings of charity to relieve the oppressed of their superfluous furniture.

See, the Nuwab, who knows it is sporting to drive four-in-hand, and so thoroughly English, retains the fashion, but somewhat Orientalizes it; for, instead of handling the ribbons himself, he squats cross-legged on his velvet cushion, which is spread on the roof, and there, while his Jehu,

With whistling thong,
Urges at speed his prancing team along,

the Nuwab puffs away at his hookah; occasionally roused, however, by the urgent necessity that frequently arises of having to hold on tight, as the team, taking the Jehu where they like, whirl suddenly round some sharp turning. But note the putting-to; would it not convulse a genuine English Jarvie to behold? First the Jehu gains his seat, next come the leaders, who are duly installed, and their reins unite them to the whip; then are the wheelers brought to the scratch, and with much rearing and plunging, much lying down on the pole and other extravagant physical contortions, the steeds are announced to be ready. The Nuwab surmounts the roof by means of a ladder; he crosses his legs; the reins have entangled themselves in the Jehu's palm; the horse-keepers suspend their chirrupings and remonstrances; the near leader, a ginger-coloured brute with a stiltish style of leg, and the off wheeler, a cream-colour with the pinkiest of eyes, stand on their respective hind legs, receive the maledictions and the cudgellings of the bystanders, spring forward, and away they all go.

With this equipage our Nuwab occasionally comes to the Band, where he dismounts and talks to the ladies, whom he invites to a nautch at his own mansion.

And now, let us drop in to his palace on such an occasion. The guests arrive, and are installed in velvet-cushioned chairs, and otto of roses is handed round with dried fruits and sweetmeats. Then come the dancing-girls, gyrating on their heels, ogling and leering, and shaking their uplifted palms, with other idiotic contortions, indicative, in the Eastern eye, of grace and dignity of motion. But "Our Nuwab" invites us to supper; and there we find tables groaning with the productions of Sticker Doss's Europe shop, for which "Our Nuwab" has given unlimited orders. But liberality and redundancy have been more considered than appropriateness of assortment. Lobsters and "tart fruits" commingle, while truffled sausages and sugared almonds share mutually the same dish. Nor is it for want of crockery, as dishes and plates, and vessels even of the most domestic character, grace the board, side by side with silver plate and glittering ormoulu, to the unsmotherable amusement of the guests.

But the wines and beer have been properly cooled, and, considering they came from Sticker Doss's, are not so bad. We have great fun, and the laughter is prodigious; the Nuwab, who, as a strict Hindoo, sits complacently a looker-on, joining in our mirth, but urging us to partake with greater courage; which, indeed, it needs, for the table slaves of his highness are not adepts at Christian cookery, and trifling irregularities grate the senses. The salad indicates the presence of cod-liver oil, and we have faint suspicions that "Day & Martin" has been introduced as a sauce.

But the Nuwab is in blissful unconsciousness of it all, and we drink his health in three times three, which gratifies him intensely. Then we adjourn to witness the fireworks, and a troop of fifty pariah-dogs let loose, each with a lighted squib at his tail, is pronounced to be great sport. The Nuwab is pleasantness itself. He offers the loan of his elephants at any time, and hopes we will join him on his next shooting expedition; promises to show us his new rifle, which his old friend Bamboo has sent him as a present from England; and then, with a cordial shake of the hand, he wishes us good night, and expresses (in Hindustani, for he cannot speak English) a hope that he may often be gratified by having the happiness of affording such gaiety as is in his power to the residents of "Our Station."

Our Departure for Home

And so everything comes to an end. Even the long, the lingering, the dreary, and the tedious hours of an Indian day must have a close – even that fiery sun, which shot up in the vaulted arch at such a small hour, and which seems to loiter on its way, does at last take a downward journey, and sink to its repose – even on the sultriest of nights, when one wooes the balmy, but which will not be won, the dog that bays the moon does at last hold his peace, the jackal does eventually cease from his lamentations, the cricket from its chirrups, the bull-frogs from their croakings, and the kids from their bleatings; and though "the lingering hours prolong the night," yet even they have an ending, and the morning gun does at last boom upon the ear.

Even the reader, the gentle reader to whom we fervently hope the preceding pages have acted as the above dispellers of sleep, and who has been kept awake till now – even the reader must come to the last page and the last picture; and, to crown all, even the ten long weary years of the exile in Ind, which by the immutable laws of the empire, immutable as the laws of the Medes and the Persians, he must pass under its fiery sun before he can return to the fatherland – even those ten long years do come to a close, and we find ourselves revelling in the unutterable joy of being permitted to tear ourselves away even from the lovely station of Kabob, that lies so sweetly in the plains of Dekchy, in the province of Bobarchy, and wing our way homeward from this land of the East, from this clime of the sun, to that better land,

That pale, that white-faced shore,
Whose foot spurns back the Ocean's roaring tide,
And coops from other lands her islanders.

And are we not in a dream – in a magnificent dream? Are we, in sober reality, to exchange the scorched and sunburnt plains of the lovely Kabob for the green fields sprinkled with great white sheep? Is the cracked gong to jar no longer on the ear, but be exchanged for the soothing chimes of the far church bells? Are the screeching brats of "India's supple sons" to give place to the rosy-cheeked children, the personification of health and merriment? Are our pale cheeks to feel the balmy air of an English winter's day, and our fingers to feel benumbed with the frost? Are we to taste once more of the real "roast-beef of old England," and our plate be gratified with really fresh oysters and porter? Are we to hear our mother-tongue popularly spoken, and our eyes to be gladdened with the sight of faces that are not dusky, but that are rosy and fresh? Verily, we are; and, in unmitigated transports of delight, we resolve upon disposing of our worldly chattels, and making instant preparations for departure.

Great and many have been the longings for the possession of our choicest Arab; many an eye has looked covetously upon our irreproachable turn-out; that slapping mare that trots her fourteen in the hour, and that buggy so singularly adapted for a young and blushing bride, and which the blandishments of friend Cheeny could in no wise inveigle from us; that superlatively delicious easy-chair; that immaculate spring couch; those lamps, those bookcases, those flower-vases, and the like. But we resolutely refuse to sell, and prefer to have an auction at our dwelling, when, under the presiding direction of Blades – the comic Blades – who is our auctioneer, a general clearance is made. Then we make straight for the office of the Kabob Tatoo Traction Company; but inasmuch as the behaviour of the equine species had in no wise improved, and as the rival company had expended its ammunition of tattoos, we resolve to charter a vehicle to be propelled by the bipeds of the East, who in the long run – and a very good long run too – prove to be as fleet as the quadrupeds, and vastly more tractable.

Then are our stores laid in for our lengthened journey, above a thousand miles by land, before the many thousand miles at sea have to be encountered. We bid adieus – and painful adieus – to the good, kind friends who have helped to cheer full many a lingering hour during our sojourn in Kabob; and if we have a regret at "going home," it is that in all human probability we may perhaps never meet again those happy faces that ever smiled a welcome as we approached; and that although, in our future peregrinations in the West, we may make many an acquaintance – ay, and perhaps an occasional friend – we have no hopes of ever meeting with a recurrence of such friendships as we established and enjoyed in the East. But we are getting horribly sentimental; and the second bugle has sounded, and we are engaged to take our farewell dinner at the mess, which we accordingly do. The claret, more diligently cooled than ever, and the sparkling Moselle, assist to

Speed the light convival hour.

We drown dull care in the rosy bowl, and all that sort of thing; and eventually do we tear ourselves away, fling ourselves horizontally on the cushions of our vehicle, light our cheroot, quaff our last "peg," have our hand wrung cordially, nay, violently – our torch is lit, the team moves on, and a parting cheer vibrates in the air as we pass through the compound-gate. Then do we sedulously devote ourselves to the wooing of the balmy. The team breaks into a trot, and we whirl along; but gentle sleep sheds oblivion upon us just as emerging on the barren plain, we take our final departure from "Our Station."

Source: George Francklin Atkinson. *Curry and Rice on Forty Plates: or The Ingredients of Social Life at "Our Station" in India.* London: Day and Son, (1859), Epigraph, Preface and pp. 17–18, 21–2, 25–6, 73–4, 125–6, 169–70.

Note

George Francklin Atkinson (1822–59) was born in Calcutta and served in the Bengal Engineers. As well as writing an account of the British campaign in India 1857–8, he also published watercolours of India and humorous sketches of life in the Raj.

73   Report of the Indian Famine Commission, 1880

[. . .] 12   With a view to the more systematic and consistent development of a system of railways which may give the greatest attainable security to the country as a whole, we consider that it is expedient to frame a scheme for the distribution among the several provinces of the total sum which can be provided for this class of works, based on a consideration of the already existing lines, and of the lines of traffic on which it is expedient to construct new railways, as well as on the general resources of each province and its liability to suffer from drought.

13   Each province should be required to draw out a scheme for the application of the funds allotted to it extending over a series of some years, and after making provision for bringing into harmony the schemes for adjacent provinces, the several Governments should be left to carry out the lines in the order and on the general plan agreed upon, the principle of provincial financial responsibility being as far as practicable applied in the manner already explained in an earlier part of our Report. In this manner we might anticipate that before another 25 years has passed away there will be no district and no important town in British India, with the exception of the mountain districts, to which railway communication will not be extended.

Source: The Evolution of India and Pakistan: 1858 to 1947: Select Documents. Edited by C. H. Philips et al. London: Oxford University Press 1962, pp. 701–2.

74   Select Committee Report on East India Railway Communication, 1884

[. . .] 20   Your Committee have given the most careful consideration to the arguments thus summarized, and they consider the evidence in favour of a more rapid extension of railway communication to be conclusive.

21   With regard to the question of gauge, your Committee are of opinion that all the leading trunk lines, with their principal feeders, should be on the broad gauge, the metre being as a rule confined to tracts of country where that system is already in successful operation, and to local lines where the traffic is likely to be so light, that cheapness of construction more than counterbalances the undoubted disadvantage of break of gauge. The witnesses, with singular unanimity, General Strachey and Mr. Rendel being the only exceptions, attached great importance to the avoidance of breaks of gauge.

22   In considering the means by which a more rapid extension of railway communication may be accomplished, your Committee have given great attention to the merits of State operations, as compared with construction and working by the means of companies; and they are of opinion that it is desirable to employ both agencies. State operations are according to the present practice limited to the strength of the Public Works Department, the permanent staff of which it is not desirable to increase, for reasons given before the Select Committee of 1878–79, which reasons your Committee fully endorse. On the one hand, money can be raised more cheaply by the State, on the other construction and working by companies does not necessarily involve any increase of the staff of the Public Works Department, and it relieves the Government of India of a somewhat onerous charge; besides which, the emulation between quasi-private enterprise and Government working tends to promote economical construction and management.

23   Your Committee think that the time may come when new railways will be made in India by unassisted private enterprise, and that this should be kept in view in all contracts made by the State, so that nothing should be done to prejudice a change of system which improved financial results of Indian railways, and greater consequent confidence on the part of the investing public might justify. Your Committee are confirmed in this belief by an examination of the last year's railway

accounts, which show clearly that, irrespective of loss by exchange, which is a matter really outside the consideration of loss or profit on any particular line, the return on the whole railway investment of India was 5.68 per cent. [. . .]

28   Your Committee are of opinion that the technical distinction which has been hitherto made between protective and productive lines cannot be maintained. They recommend, therefore, that railways, needed for protection from famine or for the development of the country, be made as required, whether they be technically considered protective or productive. Your Committee do not approve of the entire removal of the existing check upon the construction of unremunerative railways, as suggested by the Indian Government. The evidence even of their own witnesses has been against this revolution of policy. Your Committee are strongly of opinion that the bulk of the lines made should be self-supporting. [. . .]

34   In making the recommendations contained in this Report, your Committee wish most emphatically to endorse the declaration of the Government of India, made by Major Conway-Gordon and Mr. Westland, that the proposed extension of railways should not involve additional taxation.

Source: The Evolution of India and Pakistan: 1858 to 1947: Select Documents. Edited by C. H. Philips et al. London: Oxford University Press 1962, pp. 702–3.

75   Thomas Robertson: Report on the Administration and Working of Indian Railways, 1903

[. . .] 74   I have so far considered the administration of railways in India as a whole, but it may not be out of place for me to make some observations on the question of the merits of State versus Company management.

75   I may state at once that I cannot say I have noticed any very marked superiority in practical management in the Company-worked railways over those worked by the State, or vice versa; but different countries have different circumstances to deal with.

In India, the objections to State management appear to me to be:

(i)   The difficulty in which the Government must often find themselves through having to adjudicate in disputes or differences in which they themselves are really one of the interested parties.

As an instance of this, the treatment of the Southern Punjab railway may be quoted. The Company were unable to obtain redress for their grievances against the North-Western State railway, and finally had to appeal to arbitration, which resulted in the Cripps award against the State railway.

(ii)   The danger that the interests of the State railway may be sacrificed to serve some object, political or otherwise, which it is desired to attain, or because it is less difficult to yield to the other party's demand than to resist it.

As an instance of this, the Southern Punjab railway may again be quoted. The interests of the North-Western State railway were to no small extent sacrificed to secure the early construction of the Southern Punjab railway by a Company.

(iii)   The danger that something necessary in the interests of some other railway or the public may be withheld because it may be regarded as being in some way injurious to the interests of the State railway. The general good is liable to be sacrificed for the benefit of the individual.

As an instance, the dispute between the Bengal and North-Western and the Oudh and Rohilkhand State railways over the metre-gauge link may be quoted.

(iv)   The difficulty of working the railway on strictly commercial principles when a part of the staff is pensionable and is not confined to one railway.

In 1881, when the idea was conceived of working the State railways on strictly commercial lines, it was decided to employ no more men on the pensionable establishment, either in the superior or subordinate branches, of the Traffic, Locomotive and Stores Departments. These Departments have since been recruited accordingly, but the Engineering and Accounts Departments still retain the pensionable service, and the officers of these Departments, instead of being confined to one railway, are eligible for service all over India. The commercial success of an undertaking depends on continuity of service in its servants. Pensionable service does not necessarily mean indifference to the interests of the em-

ployer, but non-pensionable service ensures greater zeal as a general rule in a commercial undertaking.

(v)   The danger that continuity of policy will be absent from the management of the property.

As an example, the case of the Eastern Bengal State railway may be mentioned. In the five years 1898 to 1902, there were no less than seven changes in the Manager of the railway. . . .

The changes were numerous in the case of the departmental officers also, but here they were due to leave vacancies and were not generally of a nature to disturb continuity of policy.

I have enquired to what extent constant changes in the administrative head of the railway have occurred on Company-worked railways, but I have been unable to find any parallel case. Changes there frequently are, but not of the kind which occurred on the Eastern Bengal State railway, or of the kind to which exception can very well be taken.

(vi)   The very great difficulty of differentiating between the Railway Department and the other Departments of the State, and of treating the business of the railway as a purely commercial undertaking, and of regulating the salaries of its servants by the same considerations as govern skilled labour in similar undertakings managed by Companies instead of by a standard which may be suitable enough for officers in other Departments of the State, but which is quite inapplicable in the case of men managing large commercial enterprises.

As an example, the Manager of the North Western railway, who controls 3,750 miles of line, receives a salary of Rs. 2,500 a month. The Managers of the other State lines until recently only received Rs. 1,600 a month, and now only draw, one Rs. 2,000 and one Rs. 1,800. The Agents of the neighbouring Company-worked lines receive Rs. 3,000 a month for managing railways nearly 1,000 miles shorter. Similarly, the Chief Traffic Officer of the North Western received Rs. 1,600 a month, and of the other State-worked railways only Rs. 1,350 a month, while those of the Company-worked railways referred to receive not less than Rs. 2,000.

The same remarks apply to all the other Departments.

(vii)   The great difficulty experienced in getting rid of inefficient men, whether superior or subordinate, pensionable or non-pensionable.

   The same difficulty is experienced by all Departments of the State, but its evil effects are felt in a greater degree in a Department which is expected to be worked as a commercial undertaking.

(viii)   The difficulty of ignoring the claims of seniority when there is nothing special against a man, but when it is well known that he would not be the best selection for an appointment, and another his junior, would perhaps be much more suitable.

   This is a difficulty common to all Departments and the remedy is not an easy one so long as the choice is limited to the servants of the State.

(ix)   Lastly, the absence of that healthy and beneficial control which a strong and judicious Board of Directors is capable of exercising.

   A body of men who have a personal interest in, and responsibility for, the welfare of the business entrusted to them, their dividends depending on their proper conduct of it, must necessarily have a more powerful influence for good than any system of control which lacks personal responsibility for results.

76   On the other hand, the advantages of, or perhaps it would be more correct to say the reasons necessitating, direct State management have been represented as follows:

(i)   That it is very important for military reasons that the Government should have absolute control of the North-Western State railway at all times.

   This is a question of high policy which falls outside my province, but I would remark that the officers managing Company-worked lines are drawn from the same class and nationality as those managing the State-worked railways, and, in an emergency, the former could be relied upon to be as patriotic and loyal as the latter. Further, in times of military necessity it would always be possible for the Government to take over all railways as was done in South Africa.

(ii)   That the State lines are needed for the training of Military Officers in railway duties.

   It has not been found necessary to have State railways in England for this purpose.

(iii)   That the State lines are needed as a training ground for the supervising staff in the offices of the Government of India and of the Consulting Engineers; and it has been stated that the State railway training is so good that the Companies select their Agents from among the State railway officers.

   Speaking generally, I have not found that Company-trained officers are inferior to State railway officers, and I am of the opinion that, if the field for selection of officers for the higher railway appointments under the Government were widened and made to embrace all railways in India instead of only the State railways, the Government administration would be strengthened, not weakened.

(iv)   That the State-worked railways afford an excellent opportunity to the Government of holding them up as object lessons to all other railways of the best practice in railway management. If they were ever used in this way the argument would be a very strong one for their being worked as State Railways; but I am of opinion that the retention of the North-Western State railway alone would be sufficient for this purpose.

77   From the foregoing it would appear that the disadvantages of direct State-management outweigh any advantages which it may possess. But it will probably also be seen that the majority of these disadvantages are not due to State-management per se, but to the system of working some railways through Companies and some directly by the State; and that if the duality of system were eliminated, most of the objections in direct State-management would disappear.

   It would seem clear, therefore, that the two systems should not both be in operation in India, and that the Government should either work all the railways as State railways, or lease them all to Companies to work. The latter, I consider, would on the whole be the best course for India, as, in the first place, the Government would then be in a much stronger position to watch the interests of the country and to hold the scales evenly between contesting parties than they are at present, on account of having so large a personal share in the direct management of some of the railways, and, in the second place, the public would have the benefits resulting from healthy competition between bodies independent of each other and who were each anxious to increase their business as much as possible.

78   If it is decided to transfer all State lines to Companies to work, provision should be made in

the contracts for the Companies to take over all the existing State railway staff on their present terms of service.

If it is decided to retain State railways, I am of opinion that the scale of pay of heads of Departments and others is inadequate and that these should be brought more into line with those prevailing on the neighbouring Company-worked railways.

Source: The Evolution of India and Pakistan: 1858 to 1947: Select Documents. Edited by C. H. Philips et al. London: Oxford University Press 1962, pp. 703–7.

76   Lord Curzon: Minute on the Railways, October 1, 1903

[. . .] 34   There are two further and conspicuous advantages in this scheme to which I must draw attention. One of the severest and justest criticisms against our existing system of Railway Administration has been its indifference to the commercial aspect of railway development; and it was one of the vulnerable points of my earlier plan that, while it provided for the management of railways in their technical and even administrative aspect by experts, it left the above criticism unanswered, and furnished no machinery by which the growing demands of the public for a commercial handling of railway problems could be met. Not even the creation of a Railway Board will be a guarantee for reform in this respect, since technical knowledge and authority must always be in the ascendant upon it. At the same time there are a large number of questions of railway policy, connected with tariffs, freights, the classification of goods, the movement or congestion of traffic, and the like, . . . in which commercial interests are involved, and which it is desirable that Government should consider and decide, not exclusively from the railway point of view. I would place these in charge of the Member for Commerce and Industry. The Railway Board would be in frequent contact with him for this branch of their work, and he would thus naturally take his place as their representative on Council, for any work that might require to be brought before it.

Source: The Evolution of India and Pakistan: 1858 to 1947: Select Documents. Edited by C. H. Philips et al. London: Oxford University Press 1962, p. 707.

77   W. S. Caine: *Picturesque India: A Handbook for European Travellers* (1898)

Introduction

IT has been a difficult task to compress into a single book even the superficial information necessary to enable a would-be traveller to a vast country like India, to decide where he will go, what he would like to see, or how much he can accomplish in a given time, and my success can at best be only partial and comparative. I have not crowded my pages with a single sentence which I thought unnecessary. It will be found that I endeavour, by constant references, to embrace some very valuable standard books on special subjects, which every intelligent traveller in India will do well to have always with him, notably those written by Mr Fergusson on Indian Architecture and by Sir George Birdwood on Indian Art. The best popular handbooks on Indian History, Ethnology, Sociology and Politics, which the traveller can take with him, are "India, Past and Present," by Mr James Samuelson, Sir W. W. Hunter's "Indian Empire," the "Statistical Abstract," and "Moral and Material Progress of India," published annually by the India Office; "India," by Sir John Strachey, and "The Annual Report of the Indian National Congress," which may be obtained at Palace Chambers, Westminster, from the British Congress Committee. The following is a brief list of useful standard works on India, which may be obtained through any bookseller: –

General

The Imperial Gazetteer of India.   14 volumes.   By Sir W. W. Hunter, K.C.S.I.
The Indian Empire; its history, people and products; a condensation into one volume of the Statistical survey of India.   Sir W. W. Hunter, K.C.S.I.
History of India.   Hindu and Muhammedan periods.   Mount Stuart Elphinstone.
India Revisited.   Sir E. Arnold, K.C.I.E.
Modern India.   Sir George Campbell.
Geography of British India.   G. Smith.
India.   Sir John Strachey.
A Brief History of the Indian People.   Sir W. W. Hunter, K.C.S.I.
England's Work in India.   Sir W. W. Hunter, K.C.S.I.
History of the Indian Mutiny.   Col. G. B. Malleson.

New India.   H. S. Cotton.
India; past and present.   J. Samuelson.
Industrial Arts of India.   Sir George Birdwood.
India for the Indians – and England.   Wm. Digby,
   C.I.E.

Archæology

History of Indian and Eastern Architecture.   J.
   Fergusson.
Essays on Indian Antiquities.   Jas. Prinsep.

Religion

India, what it can teach us.   Max Müller.
The Religions of India.   A. Barth.
The faith and progress of the Brahmo-Somaj.   P. C.
   Mozoomdar
Religious thought and life in India.   Sir Monier
   Williams.
Sketch of the Religious Sects of the Hindus.   H. H.
   Wilson.
Indian Caste.   Dr. J. Wilson.
The Light of Asia.   Sir Edwin Arnold.
Buddhism.   T. W. Rhys Davids.
The Indian Mussalmans.   Sir W. W. Hunter,
   K.C.S.I.
The Parsis, their history and religion.   Framji
   Dhosabhai.
Missionary Conference Reports – published in Cal-
   cutta at intervals.
History of Protestant Missions in India.   Sherring.

Barth's "Religions of India," Fergusson's "Indian Architecture," Sir George Birdwood's "Industrial Arts of India," and Sir W. W. Hunter's
"Indian Empire," are, in my judgment, the four
most valuable books the ordinary tourist can read
before he goes, and take with him as trusty companions on his journey. Messrs Thacker & Co. of
Bombay, Calcutta, and Newgate Street, London,
and Newman & Co. Lim. of Calcutta, keep in stock
every standard book on India, and travellers will be
able to select from their shelves many guides and
handbooks, local and general, as well as works on
the Fauna and Flora, the customs and religions of
the peoples of India, its history, geography, Etc.,
Etc.

Very few travellers will care to visit India during
the hot or rainy seasons, and the climate is so eq-
uable during what is called the "cold season," (from
the end of October to the middle of March), that
very little information on the subject of outfit is
needful. The traveller who intends to confine himself to the north of a line drawn from Bombay to
Calcutta, will find ordinary summer clothing, as
worn in England, all that is necessary, with a light
and heavy overcoat. It is best to wear flannel underclothing, and, indeed, I wear nothing but flannel all
over India. My own outfit is always a very simple
one, and I have found it amply sufficient during
each of the four winters I spent in India.

Shoes	2 pair of brown canvas shoes.
	1 " light walking boots.
	1 " dress shoes.
	1 " slippers.
	1 " thin brown canvas leggings for riding.
Socks	12 pair new merino.
Shirts	6 white dress shirts.
	4 thin flannel with collars attached.
	4 thick " " " "
Collars	1 dozen white linen.
Drawers.	6 very thin, all wool.
	4 medium " "

Sleeping dress   6 pairs flannel pyjamas.
12 woven cholera belts.
2 suits of dark grey flannel, carefully made by a
   good tailor. Coats made to wear without waistcoat
   if desired.
1 suit of warm tweed, for the voyage and Northern
   India.
1 morning coat and waistcoat of thin black cloth.
1 pair thin grey tweed trousers.
1 dress suit of light cloth.
1 grey alpaca dust coat, without lining.
1 light overcoat.
1 medium ulster.
1 good felt wide-awake hat.
2 light silk caps for railway and ship.
6 towels.
6 pillow-slips.
Handkerchiefs and small sundries to suit my own
tastes and habits.
A white umbrella.
An air cushion.

With this outfit, any gentleman can go with comfort to any place written about in this book. Of
course, if the traveller intends to hunt, fish and
shoot, or do anything exceptional, he must fit himself out for it without my help.

Washing can be done at short notice everywhere
in India, so that there is no need to overburden
oneself with underclothing. A necessary part of
every traveller's baggage is a bedding kit, for use in
railway carriages, and at Dak bungalows and even
at some hotels, which only provide bedsteads. This
kit is best obtained in Bombay, but two pairs of

really good blankets and a woollen travelling rug will be found of service, and should be brought from England.

The sun-hats, which are the universal wear in India, are best purchased in Bombay.

Umbrellas should be white, as it never rains in the cold season, and the sun is often fierce during the day.

The tradesmen in the large cities of India are quite as good as they are at home, and no difficulty will be experienced in supplementing my list. If any time is to be spent in Southern India, half-a-dozen suits of white cotton will be desirable, but these can be got better and cheaper in India than at home.

A lady, who has spent a winter travelling in India, writes to me as follows:

It is unnecessary for ladies travelling in India to burden themselves with a large quantity of luggage. It is desirable to take a variety of morning and evening dresses, such as would be worn at home in spring or summer weather. On the voyage, and in the Northern parts of India, warm dresses, jackets, and wraps are needed. A plentiful supply of underclothing, both warm and cool, will be required, especially on the voyage, when it is impossible to get any washing done. Elaborate trimmings on underclothing will fare badly in India, where the washermen treat such things with ruinous roughness.

Dust cloaks and gauze veils are indispensable for the hot and dusty provinces in India, and a thin riding-habit will often be found useful. The dresses for wearing on ship-board should be good and well made. These should include a comfortable serge or stuff gown, and one of thin silk or foulard. Thin beige, serge or cotton skirts, with silk or cotton blouses, make good wear both for the voyages and for India.

No one "dresses for dinner" on board ship, though a little change is generally made from the attire of the morning.

Hats or caps are always worn on deck, generally of the deerstalker order, and a comfortable warm hood for wear on deck in the evening will be found very welcome. A good rug, ulster, warm jacket and Shetland wrap will be required, both for the voyage, and for the cold evenings and mornings in the North-West Provinces and the Punjab.

There is a "baggage day," once or twice a week during the voyage, when portmanteaus in the luggage room may be got at and opened, so that warm garments worn in the Bay of Biscay and the Mediterranean may be exchanged for thinner clothing for the Red Sea, and *vice versâ* on the way home; the cabins, therefore, need not be unreasonably crowded with trunks.

A large hanging pocket with several divisions will be found useful in the state-room.

Ladies will of course make up their list of toilet necessaries and other travelling comforts to suit their own requirements, but I recommend as articles that will often be found very useful, either on the voyage or in India: a rubber hot-water bottle, and folding bath, Rimmel's vinegar, Pears' soap, a travelling Etna or small "afternoon tea" basket, Keating's powder, some towels, sheets and pillowcases, a pair of good Jaeger blankets, and a large air-cushion.

Silk or "Anglo-Indian" underclothing is very safe and pleasant for use in India, and to avoid risk of chills, it is a wise precaution to wear one of those woven belts of wool, known to the outfitters by the unnecessarily alarming name of "Cholera belts."

Hospitality in India is boundless and universal, and it is well to have one or two good evening dresses of some material that will suffer least from package. Of course travellers are not expected to be as smart as other folk.

Pith or other sun-hats should be bought in Bombay after arrival; the double awnings of the steamer render them quite unnecessary on the voyage.

In addition to any parasol or sunshade, a strong, double-lined, white umbrella will be found useful as a protection from the sun, which is always fierce in the middle of the day, as well as two pair of blue or tinted spectacles.

White canvas shoes will be pleasant both for deck use and travel in the country, and a pair of thick, woollen socks will be useful, to pull over the shoes when visiting mosques, and other holy places, where the shoes must be either removed, or covered by an appearance of removal.

To most travellers, the first thought in deciding on a journey is: What will it cost? This question will be completely answered by a shilling handbook published by Messrs Thos. Cook & Sons, Ludgate Circus, London, the well-known excursion agents, who have branch offices in Bombay and Calcutta, and who are giving very close attention to the development of Indian business. In this little volume, sixteen different tours in India are quoted, which will give a general idea of the cost of Railway journeys. It also contains the fullest information with regard to every detail of Indian travel.

The fares of the various steamship companies to India and back are as follows:

Peninsular & Oriental Co., to Bombay, Karachi or Madras, or Calcutta, or Ceylon, and BACK to London:

For three months: 1st Class £90; 2nd Class £55.
For six months: 1st Class £100; 2nd Class £60.
Extra via Brindisi: 1st Class £12; 2nd Class £6.

"Clan" line, or "Hall" line, Liverpool to Bombay and back, available for six months:

1st Class only, £85 10s. £5 extra to Calcutta.

British India Co., London to Calcutta and back:

1st Class, £94 10s; 2nd Class, £57 12s.

I advise all travellers to go by the P. & O. Co.'s steamers. The other lines are very comfortable and well-managed, but the slight extra cost by P. & O. is fully compensated for by speed and general comfort. I write with the experience of fifteen voyages in this line. The second class accommodation is exceedingly comfortable, and in these days of depreciated rupees, is eagerly resorted to by officers in the army and their families, and missionaries.

The following round tour will be found to include the greater part of India, and is quite as much as ought to be undertaken by the most energetic traveller in the most extended tour possible during the cold season.

From Bombay to Jabalpur, Allahabad, Mirzapur, Patna, Calcutta, Darjiling and back to Calcutta, Benares, Lucknow, Cawnpur, Agra, Aligarh, Delhi, Umballa, Amritsar, Lahore, Peshawar, Multan, Rewari, Ulwar, Jaipur, Ajmir, Mt. Abu, Ahmedabad, Baroda, and back to Bombay. Bombay to Puna, Bijapur, Haidarabad, Raichur, Madras, Bangalore, Mysore, Utakamand, Trichinopoli, Madura, Tinnivelli, Tanjore, Madras, and back to Bombay. The first-class railway fares for the whole of this tour amount to about 720 Rupees; second class, 380 Rupees; third class 100 Rupees.

If it is intended to include Burma and Ceylon some of these places will have to be omitted. An alternative route in that case would be Bombay, Baroda, Ahmedabad, Abu, Jaipur, Delhi, Amritsar, Lahore, Agra, Cawnpore, Lucknow, Benares, Calcutta, Darjiling, steamer from Calcutta to Rungoon, Mandalay, Bhamo, and the Irrawady river, steamer from Raugoon to Madras, Tanjore, Trichinopoly, Madura, Tuticorin, steamer to Colombo, Kandy and Newaraliya, home direct from Colombo.

Tickets for the whole of these, or any other round tour upon which the traveller chooses to settle, are issued at short notice by Thomas Cook & Sons, whose entire Indian business, including that of banking, is very efficiently managed. Their Bombay office is a model of prompt and courteous business arrangement.

It is necessary to engage a travelling servant, for it is not the custom in many Indian hotels, or in any of the Dak bungalows, to provide service. A first-rate servant may be had for 30 Rupees per month, and a good, useful fellow as low as 15 Rupees. An allowance of 30 Rupees more will suffice for their food. So that 50 to 60 Rupees per month will be an ample estimate for the cost of a personal attendant. He will pay porters, stamps for letters, telegrams, tips, cabs, and such like, which will amount to 20 Rupees a month, will take railway tickets, and look after luggage arrangements. Thos. Cook & Sons, Bombay, will provide this servant, if written to before-hand.

It will thus be seen that about 350 Rupees will suffice for wages, food and third class fare for a personal attendant on a four months' tour in India.

The usual charge for hotels is 5 to 7 Rupees each day, for four meals and a bed-room. Carriages, except in large cities, may be hired for 3 or 4 Rupees a day. I find it easy to travel with comfort in India for 12 Rupees a day, outside railway fares.

It will be seen by these figures, that the actual cost of a tour in India of four months, with the passage out and home by P. & O. steamer, need not, with a little economy, exceed £300, and may be done luxuriously for £500.

Return ticket London to Bombay, First Class, £100

Railway Fares for self, say	720 rupees	
" for servant	110 "	
Wages and food of servant	250 "	
Hotel expenses for four months	750 "	2800 Rupees
Carriages	470 "	
Petty expenses	500 "	
2,800 rupees at 15 to £1 = say £200		

£50 may be added if Burma is to be included. Economical persons who can travel second class, which is very comfortable both in the P. & O. steamers and on Indian railways, and who can despise the luxury of a travelling servant, can face a four months' journey through India, including passage out and home, with £200. Second class fares are one-half, and third class one-eighth that charged for first. On every train there is a third class compartment reserved for Europeans.

Railway travelling in India is very comfortable. All first and second class carriages are convertible at night into sleeping berths, and have good lavatories. There are excellent meals to be obtained at regular intervals at the various refreshment rooms. At most junctions, and at many minor stations even, there are waiting-rooms, with bedsteads for the use of travellers. Although all the railway companies lag sadly behind European and American enterprise, they do a great deal for the comfort of long-journey passengers. It is impossible to speak too highly of the universal civility and kindness of Indian station-masters. Adventurous travellers, alighting at road-side stations for remote places of interest, who have written a day or two beforehand to the station-master, will find whatever resources the place possesses ready for his use. It may be that he wants a shakedown for the night in the station, a country cart to visit some out-of-the-way antiquity, or at some more important place, a bed at the Dak Bungalow, and some conveyance to take him there from the station; whatever it may be, let him write beforehand to the station-master, and if it is to be had at all, it will be duly provided.

In case of illness, however slight, an English doctor should be consulted. There is no place in India, likely to be visited by the ordinary tourist, from which an English doctor is far distant. If travellers are subject to any infirmity, they should not depend upon the drugs available in India, but take out medicine from England, made up specially under the prescription of their own medical man. The compressed drugs of Messrs. Burroughs, Wellcome & Co., Snow Hill Buildings, London, E.C., are thoroughly reliable. I showed some of them, that I had taken with me round the world; and afterwards to India and back, to a distinguished physician, who, after careful examination, pronounced them as good as ever. They were then three years old. A whole medicine-chest of these compressed drugs can be packed into a small cigar-box.

The best railway guide for India is "Newman's Indian Bradshaw," which may be purchased from Thos. Cook & Son, or Stanford's, 55, Charing Cross.

A little care is necessary with regard to diet. An experienced medical officer in India, whom I once had occasion to consult, summed up the question of diet in these words: "Never eat twice cooked food, butter your own toast, and avoid alcohol." The exhortation about toast will be understood in a moment by any one who has seen a native cook do it with a greasy old rag. Drinking water is not always good, but soda-water is cheap and universal, and excellent tea may be had at every important railway station. It is not wise to purchase fruit indiscriminately at small roadside stations, except oranges, bananas, and such other fruit as have an outside rind to be removed.

There are of course districts in India full of intense interest to the traveller, such as Kashmir, Nepal, Orissa, Travancore and Assam, which I have hardly referred to in this book, for the excellent reason that I have had no experience of them, or knowledge beyond that which I have acquired from books. This volume, as I have already said, is only intended as a help to travellers in visiting the more beaten tracks of this vast country. Trübners, of Ludgate Hill, or Thacker & Co., Newgate Street, London, have upon their shelves a great variety of books, a selection from which will enable anyone to inform himself fully with regard to Remoter India.

It will be observed that I have given much information, necessarily condensed, with regard to Christian Missions in India; I have generally selected those stations to be found in cities where the traveller is likely to remain a few days. Most missionaries welcome with cordiality any traveller who is really interested in missionary enterprise, and they are always delighted to show their schools and other institutions, or give every possible information on the social customs and native institutions of the communities among whom they labour. These gentlemen are generally men of culture, thoroughly in earnest in their efforts to improve and elevate their people, and are charming companions to those travellers who can appreciate their work and who do not scoff. I think any book professing to be a guide or help to the traveller in India would not be complete without at any rate indicating those mission stations worthy of his attention. My information on this subject may be relied upon, as it has in every case been supplied to me by missionaries on the spot. The best work is no doubt being done in remote places in rural Bengal, Orissa, Travancore, or among the wild hill tribes and Aborigines. My book does not reach these districts. Every ten years there is published in Calcutta "Baddeley's Directory of Missionaries," which gives a complete statistical return of every mission in British and Native India. Many of the missionaries whose names I have mentioned may not now be at the stations quoted, as some of the societies move their men about very much.

The politician will find India a country of vast unsolved problems which are now being discussed with much acuteness by educated Indians.

The Indian National Congress of representative men from all over India, called into existence more than twelve years ago, meets every year between Christmas and New Year's day, at some capital of a province or other central place, for the discussion of such constitutional reforms as they think ripe and urgent. Their chief demand is for some scheme of representation which shall at any rate admit educated Indians to a due and reasonable share in the legislation and administration of their own country.

The Congress meets at different centres each year. European visitors are always made very welcome, and seats in the best portion of the auditorium are reserved for them. Apart from its political interest, the spectacle is impressive and remarkable, being an assemblage of three or four thousand persons gathered together from every part of Inda, all attired in the characteristic dress of their districts. The report of every year's Congress has been printed in a volume of 150 or 200 pages, which may be obtained, with other kindred literature, from the offices of its British Committee, Palace Chambers, Westminster, London, S.W.

The aspirations of the Congress are strongly opposed by many Anglo-Indians and an influential section of Indian Society, of whom the late Sir Syed Ahmed of Aligarh was the chosen leader and mouthpiece. They have not any agency in England, like the Congress party, but their views have been expressed in numerous pamphlets, which can be got through any of the Indian booksellers in London already mentioned.

It will greatly increase the interest which an English traveller must feel in his Indian fellow subjects, to have some surface knowledge at any rate of those social and political problems which are exciting them from time to time. Those who pass through India visiting only Anglo-Indians, can learn but little of the inner life and aspirations of the Native Indian. I shall myself be glad to give letters of introduction to native gentlemen, to any English traveller who really wishes to get below the surface.

It will also give me much pleasure at any time, to answer special enquiries, within reasonable limits, from any traveller who intends visiting India.

I have, wherever I have felt enough confidence to do so, named the best hotels. None of the Indian hotels are first-rate. They are as a rule furnished as a speculation by some wealthy native, and leased to a caterer. Their management continually changes, and it is better, before going up country from Bombay, to call at Thos. Cook & Son's offices, and get a list of the best managed hotels from them. By constant enquiry from travellers and from other sources of information they manage to keep up a list, which is really the only safe hotel guide in India. Newman's Indian Bradshaw also contains a fairly trustworthy list of hotels and clubs. G. F. Kellner & Co., who are the "Spiers and Pond" of Northern India, have a good many hotels at the railway stations, which are all clean and well managed. It is always well in the case of both hotels and Dak bungalows, to order rooms beforehand, stating hour of arrival, and ordering conveyance from the station.

One of the many small annoyances of travel, is the general unwieldiness of guide-books. My own custom for many years has been to take my guidebook to a binder, and have it cut up in thin volumes of about 50 or 100 pages, bound in limp cloth or Morocco. I advise my readers to treat this book in the same fashion, of course ordering a fresh copy at once for their own library shelves.

I have not thought it convenient to allocate the towns to their respective provinces. It will be found that I have arranged them along the respective trunk lines and their branches. The contents of each chapter, and a very full index will enable the reader to turn at once to any point of attraction. An excellent and comprehensive map of India is published by Edward Stanford, folded in portable case. I have adopted Sir Wm. Hunter's spelling throughout my book, as it is now the recognised standard.

Source: W. S. Caine. *Picturesque India: A Handbook for European Travellers.* London. George Routledge and Sons, 1898, pp. xxxiii–xl.

Note

William Sproston Caine (1842–1903) served for many years as an MP and was a passionate supporter of the temperance movement. He campaigned for Indian self-government during 1895–6 and served on the Royal Commission on Administration of the Indian Expenditure.

Part IV

The Scramble for Africa

Chapter Thirteen

From Berlin to Fashoda: 1885–1898

It was in 1868, when nine years old or thereabouts, that while looking at a map of Africa of the time and putting my finger on the blank space then representing the unsolved mystery of that continent, I said to myself with absolute assurance and an amazing audacity which are no longer in my character now:
"When I grow up I shall go *there*."
Joseph Conrad. *A Personal Record.* 1913

Deal table in the middle, plain chairs all around the walls, on one end a large shining map, marked with all the colours of a rainbow. There was a vast amount of red – good to see at any time, because one knows that some real work is done there, a deuce of a lot of blue, a little green, smears of orange, and, on the East Coast, a purple patch, to show where the jolly pioneers of progress drink the jolly lager-beer.
Joseph Conrad. *Heart of Darkness.* 1898/99

Introduction

Conrad's Marlow was meeting with representatives of the Company in Brussels, engaging to pursue their enterprises in Africa, when he observed the colors of that map, colors that had redesigned the map's "blank space" identified by his author as a child. Red marked the spaces claimed by England, blue those of the French, orange stood for the Portuguese, and purple for the Germans. Much of the kaleidoscopic design had been drawn by the European participants in the Berlin Conference convened by Bismarck in November 1884 and concluded in February 1885. But the "scramble for

Africa" was not only a variegated collage, it was also a struggle between black and white.

Early in the century, Hegel's *Philosophy of History* had excluded the African continent from all existing historical processes: "Africa proper, as far as History goes back," he wrote in the introduction, "has remained – for all purposes of connection with the rest of the World – shut up; it is the Gold-land compressed within itself – the land of childhood, which lying beyond the day of self-conscious history, is enveloped in the dark mantle of Night." The German philosopher concludes his abbreviated discussion of Africa: "What we properly understand by Africa, is the Unhistorical, Undeveloped Spirit, still involved in the conditions of mere nature, and which had to be presented here only as on the threshold of the World's History." Hegel's displacement of Africa from the world-historical map draws on hues for its outlines and contours to be sure, but imposes on the diagrammatic sketch two other paradigms as well, those of child/adult and night/day, and instantiates the cultural grounds for a narrative of development that will significantly overdetermine Europe's imperial and imperious relations – and the rationales for her territorial claims – with Africa for the next two centuries.

"Civilization, Christianity, and Commerce," according to the legendary David Livingstone, were the bases for the European "mission" across Africa. And each of those agendas would have its respective, if not always respectable, proponents: precipitous explorers, zealous missionaries, and opportunistic traders cum administrators. The English occasionally referred to their empire as a "civilizing mission," which the French in turn translated as "la mission civilisatrice." Africa and its African inhabitants must be taught to "grow up," to enter "history," but on European terms. Race then would provide an important additional legitimization to that mission, from the scientific theories of Darwin to their revisions into social Darwinism. The imperial project was, in that regard, a white and black one; the other colors on Marlow's map came from the political and economic competitions among the European powers themselves for control of the resources of the continent. It was, as Conrad maintained, "not a pretty thing when you look into it too much." For Conrad, and his spokesperson, "What redeems it is the idea only."

The "idea," however, was not necessarily any more coherent – or pretty or redemptive – than the mottled map; Germans competing with Portuguese, Italians with Belgians, and the French against the British, and each against the other – and the African peoples. From the Suez Canal to the Cape of Good Hope, from the Congo River to the Nile, administrators like Rhodes and Lugard, adventurers such as Stanley and Leopold II, soldiers like Gordon and Kitchener, competed in the interests of their national governments in claiming personal status and states' rights. The General Act of the Conference of Berlin, signed on February 26, 1885, was written to adjudicate such disputes, of trade, territory, spheres of influence, and the use of "spirituous liquors," but the persistent altercations and tendentious ambitions would be fought out repeatedly in the last decades of the imperial century: at Khartoum, at Omdurman, along the Congo River, in the Transvaal. Crises were continuous, but the statesmanly "conference" of Berlin among the European nations might be said to have culminated in the "incident at Fashoda," and the fateful meeting between Jean-Baptiste Marchand the French career diplomat and the English General Sir Herbert Kitchener. It had been Marchand's plan to proceed east across Africa to confront the English as they moved south from Egypt through the Sudan. If the English, in Rhodes's formulation, designed to map Africa along the "Cape to Cairo" axis, the French would redraw the lines from the Congo to the Nile, from the Atlantic Ocean to the Red Sea. But it didn't happen that way. And the "incident at Fashoda," on September 19, 1898, when the French expedition led across Africa by Major Jean-Baptiste Marchand was met by British forces under General H. H. Kitchener and finally forced to withdraw, culminated in a capitulation of French claims to British demands. A century later, however, the map of Africa, albeit colored differently following decolonization, remains drawn along much the same lines as those determined at the Berlin Conference of 1885.

BH

Additional Reading

Boahen, A. Adu (ed.). *General History of Africa, Vol VII, Africa Under Colonial Domination.* London, Paris, and Berkeley, 1990.

Bull, Bartle. *Safari: A Chronicle of Adventure.* London, 1988.

Davidson, Basil. *The Black Man's Burden: Africa and the Curse of the Nation State.* New York, 1992.

Davidson, Basil. *The Search for Africa: History, Culture, Politics.* New York, 1994.

Lewis, David Levering. *The Race to Fashoda: European Colonialism and African Resistance in the Scramble for Africa.* New York, 1987.

Pakenham, Thomas. *The Scramble for Africa: White Man's Conquest of the Dark Continent From 1876 to 1912.* New York, 1991.

Robinson, Ronald and John Gallagher, with Alice Denny. *Africa and the Victorians: The Climax of Imperialism* (1961). New York, 1968.

David Livingstone and the Victorian Encounter with Africa. London: National Portrait Gallery, 1996.

Film

Cy Endfield. *Zulu* (1964).

78 Timeline of Significant Events

1807	Slave trade abolished throughout the British Empire
1810	Saartje Bartman ("The Hottentot Venus") on exhibit in Europe
1834	Slavery abolished throughout the British Empire
1848	Slavery abolished throughout the French colonies
1849–50	David Livingstone's first expedition
1870–1	Diamond rush to Kimberley
1871	Charles Darwin publishes *The Descent of Man*
April 18, 1874	David Livingstone buried in Westminster Abbey

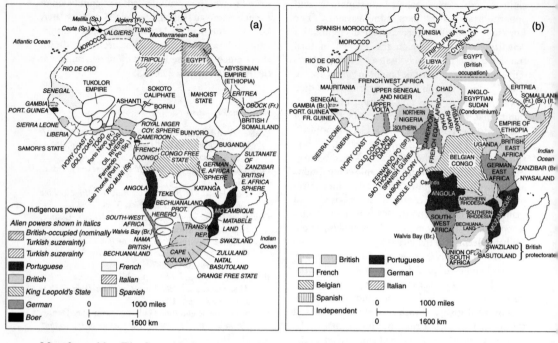

Map 2a and b   The Scramble for Africa, (a) 1886 and (b) 1912.

1876	Stanley travels down the Congo River
1883	Stanley plants the Belgian flag over Stanley Falls
1884–5	Berlin Conference
1885	H. Rider Haggard publishes *King Solomon's Mines*
1885	Relief expedition to Gordon in Khartoum
1886	Gold rush to the Witwatersrand
September 1, 1898	Kitchener defeats Mahdist forces at Omdurman
September 19, 1898	Incident at Fashoda
1898	*Heart of Darkness* published in *Blackwood Magazine*
1889–1902	Anglo–Boer War
1902	Death of Cecil Rhodes
1904	Creation of the Congo Reform Association

79   G. W. F. Hegel: "Africa" (1822)

[. . .] In accordance with these data we may now consider the three portions of the globe with which History is concerned, and here the three characteristic principles manifest themselves in a more or less striking manner: Africa has for its leading classical feature the Upland, Asia the contrast of river regions with the Upland, Europe the mingling of these several elements.

Africa must be divided into three parts: one is that which lies south of the desert of Sahara – Africa proper – the Upland almost entirely unknown to us, with narrow coast-tracts along the sea; the second is that to the north of the desert – European Africa (if we may so call it) – a coastland; the third is the river region of the Nile, the only valley-land of Africa, and which is in connection with Asia.

Africa proper, as far as History goes back, has

remained – for all purposes of connection with the rest of the World – shut up; it is the Gold-land compressed within itself – the land of childhood, which lying beyond the day of self-conscious history, is enveloped in the dark mantle of Night. Its isolated character originates, not merely in its tropical nature, but essentially in its geographical condition. The triangle which it forms (if we take the West Coast – which in the Gulf of Guinea makes a strongly indented angle – for one side, and in the same way the East Coast to Cape Gardafu for another) is on two sides so constituted for the most part, as to have a very narrow Coast Tract, habitable only in a few isolated spots. Next to this towards the interior, follows to almost the same extent, a girdle of marsh land with the most luxuriant vegetation, the especial home of ravenous beasts, snakes of all kinds – a border tract whose atmosphere is poisonous to Europeans. This border constitutes the base of a cincture of high mountains, which are only at distant intervals traversed by streams, and where they are so, in such a way as to form no means of union with the interior; for the interruption occurs but seldom below the upper part of the mountain ranges, and only in individual narrow channels, where are frequently found innavigable waterfalls and torrents crossing each other in wild confusion. During the three or three and a half centuries that the Europeans have known this border-land and have taken places in it into their possession, they have only here and there (and that but for a short time) passed these mountains, and have nowhere settled down beyond them. The land surrounded by these mountains is an unknown Upland, from which on the other hand the Negroes have seldom made their way through. In the sixteenth century occurred at many very distant points, outbreaks of terrible hordes which rushed down upon the more peaceful inhabitants of the declivities. Whether any internal movement had taken place, or if so, of what character, we do not know. What we do know of these hordes, is the contrast between their conduct in their wars and forays themselves – which exhibited the most reckless inhumanity and disgusting barbarism – and the fact that afterwards, when their rage was spent, in the calm time of peace, they showed themselves mild and well disposed towards the Europeans, when they became acquainted with them. This holds good of the Fullahs and of the Mandingo tribes, who inhabit the mountain terraces of the Senegal and Gambia. The second portion of Africa is the river district of the Nile – Egypt; which was adapted to become a mighty centre of independent civilization, and therefore is as isolated and singular in Africa as Africa itself appears in relation to the other parts of the world. The northern part of Africa, which may be specially called that of the *coast-territory* (for Egypt has been frequently driven back on itself, by the Mediterranean) lies on the Mediterranean and the Atlantic; a magnificent territory, on which Carthage once lay – the site of the modern Morocco, Algiers, Tunis, and Tripoli. This part was to be – *must* be attached to Europe: the French have lately made a successful effort in this direction: like Hither-Asia, it looks Europewards. Here in their turn have Carthaginians, Romans, and Byzantines, Mussulmans, Arabians, had their abode, and the interests of Europe have always striven to get a footing in it.

The peculiarly African character is difficult to comprehend, for the very reason that in reference to it, we must quite give up the principle which naturally accompanies all *our* ideas – the category of Universality. In Negro life the characteristic point is the fact that consciousness has not yet attained to the realization of any substantial objective existence – as for example, God, or Law – in which the interest of man's volition is involved and in which he realizes his own being. This distinction between himself as an individual and the universality of his essential being, the African in the uniform, undeveloped oneness of his existence has not yet attained; so that the Knowledge of an absolute Being, an Other and a Higher than his individual self, is entirely wanting. The Negro, as already observed, exhibits the natural man in his completely wild and untamed state. We must lay aside all thought of reverence and morality – all that we call feeling – if we would rightly comprehend him; there is nothing harmonious with humanity to be found in this type of character. The copious and circumstantial accounts of Missionaries completely confirm this, and Mahommedanism appears to be the only thing which in any way brings the Negroes within the range of culture. The Mahommedans too understand better than the Europeans, how to penetrate into the interior of the country. The grade of culture which the Negroes occupy may be more nearly appreciated by considering the aspect which *Religion* presents among them. That which forms the basis of religious conceptions is the consciousness on the part of man of a Higher Power – even though this is conceived only as a *vis naturæ* – in relation to which he feels himself a weaker, humbler being. Religion begins with the consciousness that there is something higher than man. But even Herodotus called the Negroes sorcerers: now in *Sorcery* we have not the idea of a God, of a moral faith; it exhibits man as the highest power, regarding him as alone occupying a position of command over the power of Nature. We have here therefore nothing to do with a spiritual adoration of God, nor with an empire of Right. God thunders, but is not on that account recognized as God. For the soul of man, God must be more than a thunderer, whereas among the Negroes this is not the case. Although they are necessarily conscious of dependence upon nature – for they need the beneficial influence of storm, rain, cessation of the rainy period, and so on – yet this does not conduct them to the consciousness of a Higher Power: it is they who command the elements, and this they call "magic." The Kings have a class of ministers through whom they command elemental changes, and every place possesses such magicians, who perform special ceremonies, with all sorts of gesticulations, dances, uproar, and shouting, and in the midst of this confusion commence their incantations. The second element in their religion, consists in their giving an outward form to this supernatural power – projecting their hidden might into the world of phenomena by means of images. What they conceive of as the power in question, is therefore nothing really objective, having a substantial being and different from themselves, but the first thing that comes in their way. This, taken quite indiscriminately, they exalt to the dignity of a "Genius"; it may be an animal, a tree, a stone, or a wooden figure. This is their *Fetich* – a word to which the Portuguese first gave currency, and which is derived from *feitizo*, magic. Here, in the Fetich, a kind of objective independence as contrasted with the arbitrary fancy of the individual seems to manifest itself; but as the objectivity is nothing other than the fancy of the individual projecting itself into space, the human individuality remains master of the image it has adopted. If any mischance occurs which the Fetich has not averted, if rain is suspended, if there is a failure in the crops, they bind and beat or destroy the Fetich and so get rid of it, making another immediately, and thus holding it in their own power. Such a Fetich has no independence as an object of religious worship; still less has it æsthetic independence as a work of art; it is merely a creation that expresses the arbitrary choice of its maker, and which always remains in his hands. In short there is no relation of dependence in this religion. There is however one feature that points to something beyond – the *Worship of the Dead* – in which their deceased forefathers and ancestors are regarded by them as a power influencing the living. Their idea in the matter is that these ancestors exercise vengeance and inflict upon man various injuries – exactly in the sense in which this

was supposed of witches in the Middle Ages. Yet the power of the dead is not held superior to that of the living, for the Negroes command the dead and lay spells upon them. Thus the power in question remains substantially always in bondage to the living subject. Death itself is looked upon by the Negroes as no universal natural law, even this, they think, proceeds from evil-disposed magicians. In this doctrine is certainly involved the elevation of man over Nature; to such a degree that the chance volition of man is superior to the merely natural – that he looks upon this as an instrument to which he does not pay the compliment of treating it in a way conditioned by itself, but which he commands.

But from the fact that man is regarded as the Highest, it follows that he has no respect for himself; for only with the consciousness of a Higher Being does he reach a point of view which inspires him with real reverence. For if arbitrary choice is the absolute, the only substantial objectivity that is realized, the mind cannot in such be conscious of any Universality. The Negroes indulge, therefore, that perfect *contempt* for humanity, which in its bearing on Justice and Morality is the fundamental characteristic of the race. They have moreover no knowledge of the immortality of the soul, although spectres are supposed to appear. The undervaluing of humanity among them reaches an incredible degree of intensity. Tyranny is regarded as no wrong, and cannibalism is looked upon as quite customary and proper. Among us instinct deters from it, if we can speak of instinct at all as appertaining to man. But with the Negro this is not the case, and the devouring of human flesh is altogether consonant with the general principles of the African race; to the sensual Negro, human flesh is but an object of sense – mere flesh. At the death of a King hundreds are killed and eaten; prisoners are butchered and their flesh sold in the markets; the victor is accustomed to eat the heart of his slain foe. When magical rites are performed, it frequently happens that the sorcerer kills the first that comes in his way and divides his body among the bystanders. Another characteristic fact in reference to the Negroes is Slavery. Negroes are enslaved by Europeans and sold to America. Bad as this may be, their lot in their own land is even worse, since there a slavery quite as absolute exists; for it is the essential principle of slavery, that man has not yet attained a consciousness of his freedom, and consequently sinks down to a mere Thing – an object of no value. Among the Negroes moral sentiments are quite weak, or more strictly speaking, non-existent. Parents sell their children, and conversely children their parents, as either has the opportunity.

Through the pervading influence of slavery all those bonds of moral regard which we cherish towards each other disappear, and it does not occur to the Negro mind to expect from others what we are enabled to claim. The polygamy of the Negroes has frequently for its object the having many children, to be sold, every one of them, into slavery; and very often naïve complaints on this score are heard, as for instance in the case of a Negro in London, who lamented that he was now quite a poor man because he had already sold all his relations. In the contempt of humanity displayed by the Negroes, it is not so much a despising of death as a want of regard for life that forms the characteristic feature. To this want of regard for life must be ascribed the great courage, supported by enormous bodily strength, exhibited by the Negroes, who allow themselves to be shot down by thousands in war with Europeans. Life has a value only when it has something valuable as its object.

Turning our attention in the next place to the category of *political constitution*, we shall see that the entire nature of this race is such as to preclude the existence of any such arrangement. The standpoint of humanity at this grade is mere sensuous volition with energy of will; since universal spiritual laws (for example, that of the morality of the Family) cannot be recognized here. Universality exists only as arbitrary subjective choice. The political bond can therefore not possess such a character as that free laws should unite the community. There is absolutely no bond, no restraint upon that arbitrary volition. Nothing but external force can hold the State together for a moment. A ruler stands at the head, for sensuous barbarism can only be restrained by despotic power. But since the subjects are of equally violent temper with their master, they keep him on the other hand within limits. Under the chief there are many other chiefs with whom the former, whom we will call the King, takes counsel, and whose consent he must seek to gain, if he wishes to undertake a war or impose a tax. In this relation he can exercise more or less authority, and by fraud or force can on occasion put this or that chieftain out of the way. Besides this the Kings have other specified prerogatives. Among the Ashantees the King inherits all the property left by his subjects at their death. In other places all unmarried women belong to the King, and whoever wishes a wife, must buy her from him. If the Negroes are discontented with their King they depose and kill him. In Dahomey, when they are thus displeased, the custom is to send parrots' eggs to the King, as a sign of dissatisfaction with his government. Sometimes also a deputation is sent,

which intimates to him, that the burden of government must have been very troublesome to him, and that he had better rest a little. The King then thanks his subjects, goes into his apartments, and has himself strangled by the women. Tradition alleges that in former times a state composed of women made itself famous by its conquests: it was a state at whose head was a woman. She is said to have pounded her own son in a mortar, to have besmeared herself with the blood, and to have had the blood of pounded children constantly at hand. She is said to have driven away or put to death all the males, and commanded the death of all male children. These furies destroyed everything in the neighborhood, and were driven to constant plunderings, because they did not cultivate the land. Captives in war were taken as husbands; pregnant women had to betake themselves outside the encampment; and if they had born a son, put him out of the way. This infamous state, the report goes on to say, subsequently disappeared. Accompanying the King we constantly find in Negro States, the executioner, whose office is regarded as of the highest consideration, and by whose hands, the King, though he makes use of him for putting suspected persons to death, may himself suffer death, if the grandees desire it. Fanaticism, which, notwithstanding the yielding disposition of the Negro in other respects, can be excited, surpasses, when roused, all belief. An English traveller states that when a war is determined on in Ashantee, solemn ceremonies precede it: among other things the bones of the King's mother are laved with human blood. As a prelude to the war, the King ordains an onslaught upon his own metropolis, as if to excite the due degree of frenzy. The King sent word to the English Hutchinson: "Christian, take care, and watch well over your family. The messenger of death has drawn his sword and will strike the neck of many Ashantees; when the drum sounds it is the death signal for multitudes. Come to the King, if you can, and fear nothing for yourself." The drum beat, and a terrible carnage was begun; all who came in the way of the frenzied Negroes in the streets were stabbed. On such occasions the King has all whom he suspects killed, and the deed then assumes the character of a sacred act. Every idea thrown into the mind of the Negro is caught up and realized with the whole energy of his will; but this realization involves a wholesale destruction. These people continue long at rest, but suddenly their passions ferment, and then they are quite beside themselves. The destruction which is the consequence of their excitement, is caused by the fact that it is no positive idea, no thought which produces these commotions – a physical rather than a spiritual enthusiasm. In Dahomey, when the King dies, the bonds of society are loosed; in his palace begins indiscriminate havoc and disorganization. All the wives of the King (in Dahomey their number is exactly 3,333) are massacred, and through the whole town plunder and carnage run riot. The wives of the King regard this their death as a necessity; they go richly attired to meet it. The authorities have to hasten to proclaim the new governor, simply to put a stop to massacre.

From these various traits it is manifest that want of self-control distinguishes the character of the Negroes. This condition is capable of no development or culture, and as we see them at this day, such have they always been. The only essential connection that has existed and continued between the Negroes and the Europeans is that of slavery. In this the Negroes see nothing unbecoming them, and the English who have done most for abolishing the slave-trade and slavery, are treated by the Negroes themselves as enemies. For it is a point of first importance with the Kings to sell their captured enemies, or even their own subjects; and viewed in the light of such facts, we may conclude *slavery* to have been the occasion of the increase of human feeling among the Negroes. The doctrine which we deduce from this condition of slavery among the Negroes, and which constitutes the only side of the question that has an interest for our inquiry, is that which we deduce from the Idea: viz. that the "Natural condition" itself is one of absolute and thorough injustice – contravention of the Right and Just. Every intermediate grade between this and the realization of a rational State retains – as might be expected – elements and aspects of injustice; therefore we find slavery even in the Greek and Roman States, as we do serfdom down to the latest times. But thus existing in a State, slavery is itself a phase of advance from the merely isolated sensual existence – a phase of education – a mode of becoming participant in a higher morality and the culture connected with it. Slavery is in and for itself *injustice*, for the essence of humanity is *Freedom*; but for this man must be matured. The gradual abolition of slavery is therefore wiser and more equitable than its sudden removal.

At this point we leave Africa, not to mention it again. For it is no historical part of the World; it has no movement or development to exhibit. Historical movements in it – that is in its northern part – belong to the Asiatic or European World. Carthage displayed there an important transitory phase of civilization; but, as a Phœnician colony, it belongs to Asia. Egypt will be considered in reference to the passage of the human mind from its Eastern to its Western phase, but it does not belong to the African Spirit. What we properly understand by Africa, is the Unhistorical, Undeveloped Spirit, still involved in the conditions of mere nature, and which had to be presented here only as on the threshold of the World's History.

> *Source:* G. W. F. Hegel *The Philosophy of History*, trans. J. Sibree (1899). New York: Dover Publications, 1956, pp. 91–9 (Orig. pub. 1822).

80   General Act of the Conference of Berlin, Signed February 26, 1885

Chapter I   Declaration relative to Freedom of Trade in the Basin of the Congo, its Mouths and circumjacent Regions, with other Provisions connected therewith

Article 1

The trade of all nations shall enjoy complete freedom –

1   In all the regions forming the basin of the Congo and its outlets. This basin is bounded by the watersheds (or mountain ridges) of the adjacent basins, namely, in particular, those of the Niari, the Ogowé, the Schari, and the Nile, on the north; by the eastern watershed line of the affluents of Lake Tanganyika on the east; and by the watersheds of the basins of the Zambesi and the Logé on the south. It therefore comprises all the regions watered by the Congo and its affluents, including Lake Tanganyika, with its eastern tributaries.

2   In the maritime zone extending along the Atlantic Ocean from the parallel situated in 2° 30' of south latitude to the mouth of the Logé.

The northern boundary will follow the parallel situated in 2° 30' from the coast to the point where it meets the geographical basin of the Congo, avoiding the basin of the Ogowé, to which the provisions of the present Act do not apply.

The southern boundary will follow the course of the Logé to its source, and thence pass eastwards till it joins the geographical basin of the Congo.

3   In the zone stretching eastwards from the Congo Basin as above defined, to the Indian Ocean from 5 degrees of north latitude to the mouth of the Zambesi in the south, from which point the line of

demarcation will ascend the Zambesi to 5 miles above its confluence with the Shiré, and then follow the watershed between the affluents of Lake Nyassa and those of the Zambesi, till at last it reaches the watershed between the waters of the Zambesi and the Congo.

It is expressly recognized that in extending the principle of free trade to this eastern zone, the Conference Powers only undertake engagements for themselves, and that in the territories belonging to an independent Sovereign State this principle shall only be applicable in so far as it is approved by such State. But the Powers agree to use their good offices with the Governments established on the African shore of the Indian Ocean for the purpose of obtaining such approval, and in any case of securing the most favourable conditions to the transit (traffic) of all nations.

Article 2

All flags, without distinction of nationality, shall have free access to the whole of the coast-line of the territories above enumerated, to the rivers there running into the sea, to all the waters of the Congo and its affluents, including the lakes, and to all the ports situate on the banks of these waters, as well as to all canals which may in future be constructed with intent to unite the watercourses or lakes within the entire area of the territories described in Article 1. Those trading under such flags may engage in all sorts of transport, and carry on the coasting trade by sea and river, as well as boat traffic, on the same footing as if they were subjects.

Article 3

Wares, of whatever origin, imported into these regions, under whatsoever flag, by sea or river, or overland, shall be subject to no other taxes than such as may be levied as fair compensation for expenditure in the interests of trade, and which for this reason must be equally borne by the subjects themselves and by foreigners of all nationalities. All differential dues on vessels, as well as on merchandize, are forbidden.

Article 4

Merchandize imported into these regions shall remain free from import and transit dues.

The Powers reserve to themselves to determine after the lapse of twenty years whether this freedom of import shall be retained or not.

Article 5

No Power which exercises or shall exercise sovereign rights in the above-mentioned regions shall be allowed to grant therein a monopoly or favour of any kind in matters of trade.

Foreigners, without distinction, shall enjoy protection of their persons and property, as well as the right of acquiring and transferring movable and immovable possessions; and national rights and treatment in the exercise of their professions.

Article 6 – Provisions relative to Protection of the Natives, of Missionaries and Travellers, as well as relative to Religious Liberty

All the Powers exercising sovereign rights or influence in the aforesaid territories bind themselves to watch over the preservation of the native tribes, and to care for the improvement of the conditions of their moral and material well-being, and to help in suppressing slavery, and especially the Slave Trade. They shall, without distinction of creed or nation, protect and favour all religious, scientific, or charitable institutions, and undertakings created and organized for the above ends, or which aim at instructing the natives and bringing home to them the blessings of civilization.

Christian missionaries, scientists, and explorers, with their followers, property, and collections, shall likewise be the objects of especial protection.

Freedom of conscience and religious toleration are expressly guaranteed to the natives, no less than to subjects and to foreigners. The free and public exercise of all forms of Divine worship, and the right to build edifices for religious purposes, and to organize religious Missions belonging to all creeds, shall not be limited or fettered in any way whatsoever.

Article 7 – Postal Régime

The Convention of the Universal Postal Union, as revised at Paris the 1st June, 1878, shall be applied to the Conventional basin of the Congo.

The Powers who therein do or shall exercise rights of sovereignty or Protectorate engage, as soon as circumstances permit them, to take the measures necessary for the carrying out of the preceding provision.

Article 8 – Right of Surveillance vested in the International Navigation Commission of the Congo

In all parts of the territory had in view by the present Declaration, where no Power shall exercise rights of sovereignty or Protectorate, the International Navigation Commission of the Congo, instituted in virtue of Article 17, shall be charged with supervising the application of the principles proclaimed and perpetuated ("consacrés") by this Declaration.

In all cases of difference arising relative to the application of the principles established by the present Declaration, the Governments concerned may agree to appeal to the good offices of the International Commission, by submitting to it an examination of the facts which shall have occasioned these differences.

Chapter II   Declaration relative to the Slave Trade

Article 9

Seeing that trading in slaves is forbidden in conformity with the principles of international law as recognized by the Signatory Powers, and seeing also that the operations, which, by sea or land, furnish slaves to trade, ought likewise to be regarded as forbidden, the Powers which do or shall exercise sovereign rights or influence in the territories forming the Conventional basin of the Congo, declare that these territories may not serve as a market or means of transit for the trade in slaves, of whatever race they may be. Each of the Powers binds itself to employ all the means at its disposal for putting an end to this trade and for punishing those who engage in it.

Chapter III   Declaration relative to the Neutrality of the Territories comprised in the Conventional Basin of the Congo

Article 10

In order to give a new guarantee of security to trade and industry, and to encourage, by the maintenance of peace, the development of civilization in the countries mentioned in Article 1, and placed under the free trade system, the High Signatory Parties to the present Act, and those who shall hereafter adopt it, bind themselves to respect the neutrality of the territories, or portions of territories, belonging to the said countries, comprising therein the territorial waters, so long as the Powers which exercise or shall exercise the rights of sovereignty or Protectorate over those territories, using their option of proclaiming themselves neutral, shall fulfil the duties which neutrality requires.

Article 11

In case a Power exercising rights of sovereignty or Protectorate in the countries mentioned in Article 1, and placed under the free trade system, shall be involved in a war, then the High Signatory Parties to the present Act, and those who shall hereafter adopt it, bind themselves to lend their good offices in order that the territories belonging to this Power and comprised in the Conventional free trade zone shall, by the common consent of this Power and of the other belligerent or belligerents, be placed during the war under the rule of neutrality, and considered as belonging to a non-belligerent State, the belligerents thenceforth abstaining from extending hostilities to the territories thus neutralized, and from using them as a base for warlike operations.

Article 12

In case a serious disagreement originating on the subject of, or in the limits of, the territories mentioned in Article 1 and placed under the free trade system, shall arise between any Signatory Powers of the present Act, or the Powers which may become parties to it, these Powers bind themselves, before appealing to arms, to have recourse to the mediation of one or more of the friendly Powers.

In a similar case the same Powers reserve to themselves the option of having recourse to arbitration.

Chapter IV   Act of Navigation for the Congo

Article 13

The navigation of the Congo, without excepting any of its branches or outlets, is, and shall remain, free for the merchant-ships of all nations equally, whether carrying cargo or ballast, for the transport of goods or passengers. It shall be regulated by the provisions of this Act of Navigation, and by the Rules to be made in pursuance thereof.

In the exercise of this navigation the subjects and flags of all nations shall in all respects be treated on a footing of perfect equality, not only for the direct navigation from the open sea to the inland ports of the Congo and *vice versa*, but also for the great and small coasting trade, and for boat traffic on the course of the river.

Consequently, on all the course and mouths of the Congo there will be no distinction made between the subjects of Riverain States and those of non-Riverain States, and no exclusive privilege of navigation will be conceded to Companies, Corporations, or private persons whatsoever.

These provisions are recognized by the Signatory Powers as becoming henceforth a part of international law.

Article 14

The navigation of the Congo shall not be subject to any restriction or obligation which is not expressly stipulated by the present Act. It shall not be exposed to any landing dues, to any station or depot tax, or to any charge for breaking bulk, or for compulsory entry into port.

In all the extent of the Congo the ships and goods in process of transit on the river shall be submitted to no transit dues, whatever their starting-place or destination.

There shall be levied no maritime or river toll based on the mere fact of navigation, nor any tax on goods aboard of ships. There shall only be levied taxes or duties having the character of an equivalent for services rendered to navigation itself, to wit:

1   Harbour dues on certain local establishments, such as wharves, warehouses, &c., if actually used.

The Tariff of such dues shall be framed according to the cost of constructing and maintaining the said local establishments; and it will be applied without regard to whence vessels come or what they are loaded with.

2   Pilot dues for those stretches of the river where it may be necessary to establish properly-qualified pilots.

The Tariff of these dues shall be fixed and calculated in proportion to the service rendered.

3   Charges raised to cover technical and administrative expenses incurred in the general interest of navigation, including lighthouse, beacon, and buoy duties.

The last-mentioned dues shall be based on the tonnage of vessels as shown by the ship's papers, and in accordance with the Rules adopted on the Lower Danube.

The Tariffs by which the various dues and taxes enumerated in the three preceding paragraphs shall be levied, shall not involve any differential treatment, and shall be officially published at each port.

The Powers reserve to themselves to consider, after the lapse of five years, whether it may be necessary to revise, by common accord, the above-mentioned Tariffs.

Article 15

The affluents of the Congo shall in all respects be subject to the same Rules as the river of which they are tributaries.

And the same Rules shall apply to the streams and rivers as well as the lakes and canals in the territories defined in paragraphs 2 and 3 of Article 1.

At the same time the powers of the International Commission of the Congo will not extend to the said rivers, streams, lakes, and canals, unless with the assent of the States under whose sovereignty they are placed. It is well understood, also, that with regard to the territories mentioned in paragraph 3 of Article 1, the consent of the Sovereign States owning these territories is reserved.

Article 16

The roads, railways, or lateral canals which may be constructed with the special object of obviating the innavigability or correcting the imperfection of the river route on certain sections of the course of the Congo, its affluents, and other water-ways placed under a similar system, as laid down in Article 15, shall be considered in their quality of means of communication as dependencies of this river, and as equally open to the traffic of all nations.

And, as on the river itself, so there shall be collected on these roads, railways, and canals only tolls calculated on the cost of construction, maintenance, and management, and on the profits due to the promoters.

As regards the Tariff of these tolls, strangers and the natives of the respective territories shall be treated on a footing of perfect equality.

Article 17

There is instituted an International Commission, charged with the execution of the provisions of the present Act of Navigation.

The Signatory Powers of this Act, as well as those who may subsequently adhere to it, may always be represented on the said Commission, each by one Delegate. But no Delegate shall have more than one vote at his disposal, even in the case of his representing several Governments.

This Delegate will be directly paid by his Government. As for the various agents and employés of the International Commission, their remuneration shall be charged to the amount of the dues colected in conformity with paragraphs 2 and 3 of Article 14.

The particulars of the said remuneration, as well as the number, grade, and powers of the agents and employés, shall be entered in the returns to be sent yearly to the Governments represented on the International Commission.

Article 18

The members of the International Commission, as well as its appointed agents, are invested with the privilege of inviolability in the exercise of their functions. The same guarantee shall apply to the offices and archives of the Commission.

Article 19

The International Commission for the Navigation of the Congo shall be constituted as soon as five of the Signatory Powers of the present General Act shall have appointed their Delegates. And pending the constitution of the Commission the nomination of these Delegates shall be notified to the Imperial Government of Germany, which will see to it that the necessary steps are taken to summon the meeting of the Commission.

The Commission will at once draw up navigation, river police, pilot, and quarantine Rules.

These Rules, as well as the Tariffs to be framed by the Commission, shall, before coming into force, be submitted for approval to the Powers represented on the Commission. The Powers interested will have to communicate their views with as little delay as possible.

Any infringements of these Rules will be checked by the agents of the International Commission wherever it exercises direct authority, and elsewhere by the Riverain Power.

In the case of an abuse of power, or of an act of injustice, on the part of any agent or employé of the International Commission, the individual who considers himself to be aggrieved in his person or rights may apply to the Consular Agent of his country. The latter will examine his complaint, and if he finds it *prima facie* reasonable, he will then be entitled to bring it before the Commission. At his instance then, the Commission, represented by at least three of its members, shall, in conjunction with him, inquire into the conduct of its agent or employé. Should the Consular Agent look upon the decision of the Commission as raising questions of law ("objections de droit"), he will report on the subject to his Government, which may then have recourse to the Powers represented on the Com-

mission, and invite them to agree as to the instructions to be given to the Commission.

Article 20

The International Commission of the Congo, charged in terms of Article 17 with the execution of the present Act of Navigation, shall in particular have power –

1   To decide what works are necessary to assure the navigability of the Congo in accordance with the needs of international trade.

On those sections of the river where no Power exercises sovereign rights, the International Commission will itself take the necessary measures for assuring the navigability of the river.

On those sections of the river held by a Sovereign Power the International Commission will concert its action ("s'entendra") with the riparian authorities.

2   To fix the pilot tariff and that of the general navigation dues as provided for by paragraphs 2 and 3 of Article 14.

The Tariffs mentioned in the first paragraph of Article 14 shall be framed by the territorial authorities within the limits prescribed in the said Article.

The levying of the various dues shall be seen to by the international or territorial authorities on whose behalf they are established.

3   To administer the revenue arising from the application of the preceding paragraph (2).

4   To superintend the quarantine establishment created in virtue of Article 24.

5   To appoint officials for the general service of navigation, and also its own proper employés.

It will be for the territorial authorities to appoint Sub-Inspectors on sections of the river occupied by a Power, and for the International Commission to do so on the other sections.

The Riverain Power will notify to the International Commission the appointment of Sub-Inspectors, and this Power will undertake the payment of their salaries.

In the exercise of its functions, as above defined and limited, the International Commission will be independent of the territorial authorities.

Article 21

In the accomplishment of its task the International Commission may, if need be, have recourse to the war-vessels of the Signatory Powers of this Act, and of those who may in future accede to it, under reserve, however, of the instructions which may be given to the Commanders of these vessels by their respective Governments.

Article 22

The war-vessels of the Signatory Powers of this Act that may enter the Congo are exempt from payment of the navigation dues provided for in paragraph 3 of Article 14; but unless their intervention has been called for by the International Commission or its agents, in terms of the preceding Article, they shall be liable to the payment of the pilot or harbour dues which may eventually be established.

Article 23

With the view of providing for the technical and administrative expenses which it may incur, the International Commission created by Article 17 may, in its own name, negotiate loans to be exclusively guaranteed by the revenues raised by the said Commission.

The decisions of the Commission dealing with the conclusion of a loan must be come to by a majority of two-thirds. It is understood that the Governments represented on the Commission shall not in any case be held as assuming any guarantee, or as contracting any engagement or joint liability ("solidarité") with respect to the said loans, unless under special Conventions concluded by them to this effect.

The revenue yielded by the dues specified in paragraph 3 of Article 14 shall bear, as a first charge, the payment of the interest and sinking fund of the said loans, according to agreement with the lenders.

Article 24

At the mouth of the Congo there shall be founded, either on the initiative of the Riverain Powers, or by the intervention of the International Commission, a quarantine establishment for the control of vessels passing out of as well as into the river.

Later on the Powers will decide whether and on what conditions a sanitary control shall be exercised over vessels engaged in the navigation of the river itself.

Article 25

The provisions of the present Act of Navigation shall remain in force in time of war. Consequently all nations, whether neutral or belligerent, shall be always free, for the purposes of trade, to navigate the Congo, its branches, affluents, and mouths, as well as the territorial waters fronting the embouchure of the river.

Traffic will similarly remain free, despite a state of war, on the roads, railways, lakes, and canals mentioned in Articles 15 and 16.

There will be no exception to this principle, except in so far as concerns the transport of articles intended for a belligerent, and in virtue of the law of nations regarded as contraband of war.

All the works and establishments created in pursuance of the present Act, especially the tax-collecting offices and their treasuries, as well as the permanent service staff of these establishments, shall enjoy the benefits of neutrality ("placés sous le régime de la neutralité"), and shall, therefore, be respected and protected by belligerents.

Chapter V   Act of Navigation for the Niger

Article 26

The navigation of the Niger, without excepting any of its branches and outlets, is and shall remain entirely free for the merchant-ships of all nations equally, whether with cargo or ballast, for the transportation of goods and passengers. It shall be regulated by the provisions of this Act of Navigation, and by the rules to be made in pursuance of this Act.

In the exercise of this navigation the subjects and flags of all nations shall be treated, in all circumstances, on a footing of perfect equality, not only for the direct navigation from the open sea to the inland ports of the Niger, and *vice versa*, but for the great and small coasting trade, and for boat trade on the course of the river.

Consequently, on all the course and mouths of the Niger there will be no distinction made between the subjects of the Riverain States and those of non-Riverain States; and no exclusive privilege of navigation will be conceded to Companies, Corporations, or private persons.

These provisions are recognized by the Signatory Powers as forming henceforth a part of international law.

Article 27

The navigation of the Niger shall not be subject to any restriction or obligation based merely on the fact of navigation.

It shall not be exposed to any obligation in regard to landing-station or depôt, or for breaking bulk, or for compulsory entry into port.

In all the extent of the Niger the ships and goods in process of transit on the river shall be submitted to no transit dues, whatever their starting-place or destination.

No maritime or river toll shall be levied based on the sole fact of navigation, nor any tax on goods on board of ships. There shall only be collected taxes or duties which shall be an equivalent for services rendered to navigation itself. The Tariff of these taxes or duties shall not warrant any differential treatment.

Article 28

The affluents of the Niger shall be in all respects subject to the same rules as the river of which they are tributaries.

Article 29

The roads, railways, or lateral canals which may be constructed with the special object of obviating the innavigability or correcting the imperfections of the river route on certain sections of the course of the Niger, its affluents, branches, and outlets, shall be considered, in their quality of means of communication, as dependencies of this river, and as equally open to the traffic of all nations.

And, as on the river itself, so there shall be collected on these roads, railways, and canals only tolls calculated on the cost of construction, maintenance, and management, and on the profits due to the promoters.

As regards the Tariff of these tolls, strangers and the natives of the respective territories shall be treated on a footing of perfect equality.

Article 30

Great Britain undertakes to apply the principles of freedom of navigation enunciated in Articles 26, 27, 28, and 29 on so much of the waters of the Niger, its affluents, branches, and outlets, as are or may be under her sovereignty or protection.

The rules which she may establish for the safety and control of navigation shall be drawn up in a way to facilitate, as far as possible, the circulation of merchant-ships.

It is understood that nothing in these obligations shall be interpreted as hindering Great Britain from making any rules of navigation whatever which shall not be contrary to the spirit of these engagements.

Great Britain undertakes to protect foreign merchants and all the trading nationalities on all those portions of the Niger which are or may be under her sovereignty or protection as if they were her own subjects, provided always that such merchants conform to the rules which are or shall be made in virtue of the foregoing.

Article 31

France accepts, under the same reservations, and in identical terms, the obligations undertaken in the preceding Articles in respect of so much of the waters of the Niger, its affluents, branches, and outlets, as are or may be under her sovereignty or protection.

Article 32

Each of the other Signatory Powers binds itself in the same way in case it should ever exercise in the future rights of sovereignty or protection over any portion of the waters of the Niger, its affluents, branches, or outlets.

Article 33

The arrangements of the present Act of Navigation will remain in force in time of war. Consequently, the navigation of all neutral or belligerent nations will be in all time free for the usages of commerce on the Niger, its branches, its affluents, its mouths, and outlets, as well as on the territorial waters opposite the mouths and outlets of that river.

The traffic will remain equally free in spite of a state of war on the roads, railways, and canals mentioned in Article 29.

There will be an exception to this principle only in that which relates to the transport of articles destined for a belligerent, and considered, in virtue of the law of nations, as articles of contraband of war.

Chapter VI   Declaration relative to the essential Conditions to be observed in order that new Occupations on the Coasts of the African Continent may be held to be effective

Article 34

Any Power which henceforth takes possession of a tract of land on the coasts of the African Continent outside of its present possessions, or which, being hitherto without such possessions, shall acquire them, as well as the Power which assumes a Protectorate there, shall accompany the respective act with a notification thereof, addressed to the other Signatory Powers of the present Act, in order to enable them, if need be, to make good any claims of their own.

Article 35

The Signatory Powers of the present Act recognize the obligation to insure the establishment of authority in the regions occupied by them on the coasts of the African Continent sufficient to protect existing rights, and, as the case may be, freedom of trade and of transit under the conditions agreed upon.

Chapter VII   General Dispositions

Article 36

The Signatory Powers of the present General Act reserve to themselves to introduce into it subsequently, and by common accord, such modifications and improvements as experience may show to be expedient.

Article 37

The Powers who have not signed the present General Act shall be free to adhere to its provisions by a separate instrument.

The adhesion of each Power shall be notified in diplomatic form to the Government of the German Empire, and by it in turn to all the other Signatory or adhering Powers.

Such adhesion shall carry with it full acceptance of all the obligations as well as admission to all the advantages stipulated by the present General Act.

Article 38

The present General Act shall be ratified with as little delay as possible, the same in no case to exceed a year.

It will come into force for each Power from the date of its ratification by that Power.

Meanwhile, the Signatory Powers of the present General Act bind themselves not to take any steps contrary to its provisions.

Each Power will address its ratification to the Government of the German Empire, by which notice of the fact will be given to all the other Signatory Powers of the present Act.

The ratifications of all the Powers will be deposited in the archives of the Government of the German Empire. When all the ratifications shall have been sent in, there will be drawn up a Deposit Act,

in the shape of a Protocol, to be signed by the Representatives of all the Powers which have taken part in the Conference of Berlin, and of which a certified copy will be sent to each of those Powers.

Source: Henry Wellington Wack. *The Story of the Congo Free State.* New York and London: G. P. Putnam's Sons, 1905, pp. 302–16.

81   Chapter VI of the General Act of the Brussels Conference, July 2, 1890

Restrictive Measures Concerning the Traffic in Spirituous Liquors

Article XC

Justly anxious about the moral and material consequences which the abuse of spirituous liquors entails on the native populations, the Signatory Powers have agreed to apply the provisions of Articles XCI, XCII, and XCIII within a zone extending from the 20th degree north latitude to the 22nd degree south latitude, and bounded by the Atlantic Ocean on the west and by the Indian Ocean on the east, with its dependencies, comprising the islands adjacent to the mainland, up to 100 sea miles from the shore.

Article XCI

In the districts of this zone where it shall be ascertained that, either on account of religious belief or from other motives, the use of distilled liquors does not exist or has not been developed, the Powers shall prohibit their importation. The manufacture of distilled liquors there shall be equally prohibited.

Each Power shall determine the limits of the zone of prohibition of alcoholic liquors in its possessions or Protectorates, and shall be bound to notify the limits thereof to the other Powers within the space of six months. The above prohibition can only be suspended in the case of limited quantities destined for the consumption of the non-native population and imported under the régime and conditions determined by each Government.

Article XCII

The Powers having possessions or exercising protectorates in the region of the zone which are not

PUNCH, OR THE LONDON CHARIVARI.—APRIL 21, 1894.

THE BLACK BABY.

MR. BULL. "WHAT, ANOTHER!!—WELL, I SUPPOSE I MUST TAKE IT IN!!!"

Plate 4   Cartoon from *Punch*, April 21, 1894.

placed under the action of the prohibition, and into which alcoholic liquors are at present either freely imported or pay an import duty of less than 15 fr. per hectolitre at 50 degrees Centigrade, undertake to levy on these alcoholic liquors an import duty of 15 fr. per hectolitre at 50 degrees Centigrade for three years after the present General Act comes into force. At the expiration of this period the duty may be increased to 25 fr. during a fresh period of three years. At the end of the sixth year it shall be submitted to revision, taking as a basis the average results produced by these Tariffs, for the purpose of then fixing, if possible, a minimum duty throughout the whole extent of the zone where the prohibition referred to in Article XCI is not in force.

The Powers have the right of maintaining and increasing the duties beyond the minimum fixed by the present Article in those regions where they already possess that right.

Article XCIII

The distilled liquors manufactured in the regions referred to in Article XCII, and intended for inland consumption, shall be subject to an excise duty.

This excise duty, the collection of which the Powers undertake to insure as far as possible, shall not be lower than the minimum import duty fixed by Article XCII.

Article XCIV

Signatory Powers having in Africa possessions contiguous to the zone specified in Article XC undertake to adopt the necessary measures for preventing the introduction of spirituous liquors within the territories of the said zone by their inland frontiers.

Article XCV

The Powers shall communicate to each other, through the Office at Brussels, and according to the terms of Chapter V, information relating to the traffic in alcoholic liquors within their respective territories.

Declaration Annexed to the General Act of the Brussels Conference, signed July 2, 1890

The Powers assembled in Conference at Brussels, who have ratified the General Act of Berlin of the 26th February, 1885, or who have acceded thereto.

After having drawn up and signed in concert, in the General Act of this day, a collection of meas-

ures intended to put an end to the Slave Traffic by land as well as by sea, and to improve the moral and material conditions of existence of native races.

Taking into consideration that the execution of the provisions which they have adopted with this object imposes on some of them who have possessions or Protectorates in the conventional basin of the Congo, obligations which absolutely demand new resources to meet them.

Have agreed to make the following Declaration:

The Signatories or acceding Powers who have possessions or Protectorates in the said Conventional basin of the Congo shall be able, so far as authority is required to this end, to establish duties upon imported goods, the scale of which shall not exceed a rate equivalent to 10 per cent *ad valorem* at the port of entry, always excepting spirituous liquors, which are regulated by the provisions of Chapter VI of the General Act of this day.

After the signing of the said General Act, negotiations shall be opened between the Powers who have ratified the General Act of Berlin or who have acceded to it, in order to draw up, within a maximum limit of the 10 per cent *ad valorem*, the system of Customs Regulations to be established in the conventional basin of the Congo.

Nevertheless it is understood:

1 That no differential treatment or transit duty shall be established;
2 That in applying the Customs Regulations which are to be agreed upon, each Power will undertake to simplify formalities as much as possible, and to facilitate trade operations;
3 That the arrangement resulting from the proposed negotiations shall remain in force for fifteen years from the signing of the present Declaration.

At the expiration of this term, and failing a fresh Agreement, the Contracting Powers will return to the conditions provided for by Article IV of the General Act of Berlin, retaining the power of imposing duties up to a maximum of 10 per cent, upon goods imported into the conventional basin of the Congo.

The ratifications of the present Declaration shall be exchanged at the same time as those of the General Act of this day.

Convention Respecting Liquors in Africa, signed at Brussels, November 3, 1906

Article I

From the coming into force of the present Convention, the import duties on spirituous liquors shall be raised, throughout the zone where there does not exist the system of total prohibition provided by Article XCI of the General Act of Brussels to the rate of 100 fr. the hectolitre at 50 degrees Centigrade.

It is understood, however, as far as Erythrea is concerned, that this duty may be at the rate of 70 fr. only the hectolitre at 50 degrees Centigrade, the surplus being represented in a general and permanent manner by the total of the other duties of that Colony.

The import duty shall be augmented proportionally for each degree above 50 degrees Centigrade. It may be diminished proportionally for each degree below 50 degrees Centigrade.

The Powers retain the right of maintaining and increasing the duty beyond the minimum fixed by the present Article in the regions in which they now possess that right.

Article II

In accordance with Article XCIII of the General Act of Brussels, distilled drinks made in the districts mentioned in Article XCII of the said General Act, and intended for consumption, shall pay an excise duty.

This excise duty, the collection of which the Powers undertake to ensure as far as is possible, shall not be lower than the minimum import duty fixed by Article I of the present Convention.

It is understood, however, as far as Angola is concerned, that the Portuguese Government shall be able, with a view to effecting the gradual and complete transformation of the distilleries into sugar factories, to deduct from the money raised by the duty of 100 fr. a sum of 30 fr., which shall be given to the producers on condition that they effect such transformation under Government control.

If the Portuguese Government make use of this facility, the number of distilleries working and the capacity for production of each one of them must not exceed the number and capacity certified on the 31st October, 1906.

Article III

The provisions of the present Convention are to hold good for a period of ten years.

At the end of this period, the import duty fixed in Article I shall be submitted to revision, taking as a basis the results produced by the preceding rate.

Each of the Contracting Powers shall, however, have the option of calling for such a revision at the end of the eighth year.

Such Powers as shall make use of this option must notify their intention six months before the date of expiry to the other Powers through the intermediary of the Belgian Government, who shall undertake to convoke the Conference within the six months above mentioned.

Article IV

It is understood that the Powers who signed the General Act of Brussels or who have acceded to it, and who are not represented at the present Conference, preserve the right of acceding to the present Convention.

Article V

The present Convention shall be ratified, and the ratifications shall be deposited at the Ministry for Foreign Affairs at Brussels within the shortest possible period, and such period shall not in any case exceed one year.

A certified copy of the *procés-verbal* of deposit shall be addressed by the Belgian Government to all the Powers interested.

Article VI

The present Convention shall come into force in all the possessions of the Contracting Powers situated in the zone defined by Article XC of the General Act of Brussels on the 30th day after the date of the termination of the *procés-verbal* of deposit mentioned in the preceding Article.

From that date, the Convention regulating the question of spirituous liquors in Africa, signed at Brussels on the 8th June, 1899, shall cease to have effect.

Declaration Modifying Paragraph 5 of the Declaration Annexed to the General Act
SIGNED AT BRUSSELS JULY 2, 1890, SIGNED AT BRUSSELS JUNE 15, 1910

The Powers which have ratified or acceded to the Berlin General Act of the 26th February, 1885, have agreed to make the following Declaration:

In modification of paragraph 5 of the Declaration annexed to the Brussels General Act of the 2nd July, 1890, the Powers which signed that Act or acceded thereto, and which have possessions or protectorates in the Conventional Basin of the Congo, are authorised, so far as such authorisation is necessary, to impose therein upon imported arms and munitions duties exceeding the maximum limit of 10 per cent, of the value at the port of importation, fixed by the aforesaid Declaration.

The present Declaration shall be ratified and the Ratifications shall be deposited at the Ministry for Foreign Affairs at Brussels within a period of one year or sooner if possible.

It shall come into force on thirty days after the date on which the Protocol recording such deposit shall have been closed.

General Act of the Conference of Berlin. Signed 26 February 1885.

Source: Henry Wellington Wack. *The Story of the Congo Free State.* New York and London: G. P. Putnam's Sons, 1905, pp. 317–22.

Chapter Fourteen

The Mission and Its Missionaries

Introduction

Representations of Africa and Africans frequently reflect the invention of racial categories and depict the refinement of extremely flexible systems of classification based on questionable forms of "evidence." The exemplary standards of beauty, morality, intelligence, and of physical and political strength were fundamentally Aryan; the savage races represented the depths to which humanity, if not racially pure or careful, could sink. Africa, typically described as the Dark Continent, became the absolute measure of scientific, moral, and biological difference. The black body and skin were pointed to as the primary evidence that the African was a thing apart, a "human fossil," an infantile specimen; the frequently parodied African languages and orally-based societies were further evidence of the continent's cultural simplicity. The African's blackness also became the metaphor for many of the empire's undesirable or unruly subjects: women, the working classes, rebellious Indians, Boers, the Irish, even European colonial competitors were visually and verbally depicted as irrational, unchangeable, impulsive, under-developed savages – a designation which frequently rationalized domination and legitimized aggressive and disciplinary scientific, administrative, and legislative regimes.

Although missionary activity in African began under the direction of Portugal's Prince Henry in the fifteenth century, the missionary enterprise vastly expanded in the eighteenth and nineteenth centuries. The brutal realities of slavery inspired British evangelists to campaign for the cessation of the British slave trade (abolished in 1807); the end of Great Britain's sinful trade in bodies led to the expansion of what was referred to as legitimate commerce. Missionary-explorers like David Livingstone wanted to uplift Africa by means of commercialization and Christian conversion; political economists and theorists, represented here by Count Gobineau and Walter Bagehot, speculated about the dangers and opportunities involved in such an endeavor. The missionaries' work on behalf of African "development" was depicted as generous endeavor, one that would save the Africans from spiritual darkness and debasement. Western emissaries would encourage the Africans to evolve and join the ranks of the civilized races and nations. The missionaries' rhetoric combined idealistic discourses of enlightenment and salvation with aggressive militaristic jingoism; the Christian mission was a war on heathenism and barbarism and an enterprise that was believed to benefit both African subjects and their European "saviors."

MC

Additional Reading

Beidelman, T. O. *Colonial Evangelism: A Socio-Historical Study of an East African Mission at the Grassroots.* Bloomington, 1982.

Berman, Edward H. *African Reactions to Missionary Education.* New York, 1975.

Biddiss, Michael D. *Father of Racist Ideology: The Social and Political Though of Count Gobineau.* New York, 1970.

Bowler, Peter J. *Charles Darwin: The Man and His Influence*. Oxford, 1990.

Brenman, Jan (ed.). *Imperial Monkey Business: Racial Supremacy in Social Darwinist Theory and Colonial Practice*. Amsterdam, 1980.

Carroll, Joseph. *Evolution and Literary Theory*. New York, 1995.

Darwin, Charles. *The Origin of the Species*. London, 1859.

——. *The Descent of Man*. London, 1871.

Groves, C. P. The *Planting of Christianity in Africa* 4 vols. London, 1948–58.

Hughes, Rev. W. *Dark Africa and the Way Out: A Scheme for Civilizing and Evangelizing the Dark Continent*. London, 1892.

Murray, Jocelyn. *Proclaim the Good News: A Short History of the Church Missionary Society*. London, 1985.

Renan, Ernest. *The Future of Science* (1893).

Spencer, Herbert. *Principles of Sociology* (1906).

Stanley, Henry M. *How I Found Livingstone: Travels and Discoveries in Central Africa*. New York, 1872.

Films

Zoltan Korda. *Sanders of the River* (1935).

Henry King. *Stanley and Livingstone* (1939).

Franklin J Schaffner. *Planet of the Apes* (1968).

Richard Loucraine. *The Missionary* (1983).

John Greyson. *Zero Patience* (1993).

Philip Haas. *Angels and Insects* (1995).

82   Count J. A. Gobineau: "Influence of Christianity upon Moral and Intellectual Diversity of Races" (1856)

BY the foregoing observations, two facts seem to me clearly established: first, that there are branches of the human family incapable of spontaneous civilization, so long as they remain unmixed; and, secondly, that this innate incapacity cannot be overcome by external agencies, however powerful in their nature. It now remains to speak of the civilizing influence of Christianity, a subject which, on account of its extensive bearing, I have reserved for the last, in my consideration of the instruments of civilization.

The first question that suggests itself to the thinking mind, is a startling one. If some races are so vastly inferior in all respects, can they comprehend the truths of the gospel, or are they forever to be debarred from the blessing of salvation?

In answer, I unhesitatingly declare my firm conviction, that the pale of salvation is open to them all, and that all are endowed with equal capacity to enter it. Writers are not wanting who have asserted a contrary opinion. They dare to contradict the sacred promise of the Gospel, and deny the peculiar characteristic of our faith, which consists in its accessibility to all men. According to them, religions are confined within geographical limits which they cannot transgress. But the Christian religion knows no degrees of latitude or longitude. There is scarcely a nation, or a tribe, among whom it has not made converts. Statistics – imperfect, no doubt, but, as far as they go, reliable – show them in great numbers in the remotest parts of the globe: nomad Mongols, in the steppes of Asia, savage hunters in the table-lands of the Andes; dark-hued natives of an African clime; persecuted in China; tortured in Madagascar; perishing under the lash in Japan.

But this universal capacity of receiving the light of the gospel must not be confounded, as is so often done, with a faculty of entirely different character, that of social improvement. This latter consists in being able to conceive new wants, which, being supplied, give rise to others, and gradually produce that perfection of the social and political system which we call civilization. While the former belongs equally to all races, whatever may be their disparity in other respects, the latter is of a purely intellectual character, and the prerogative of certain privileged groups, to the partial or even total exclusion of others.

With regard to Christianity, intellectual deficiencies cannot be a hindrance to a race. Our religion addresses itself to the lowly and simple, even in preference to the great and wise of this earth. Intellect and learning are not necessary to salvation. The most brilliant lights of our church were not always found among the body of the learned. The glorious martyrs, whom we venerate even above the skilful and erudite defender of the dogma, or the eloquent panegyrist of the faith, were men who sprang from the masses of the people; men, distinguished neither for worldly learning, nor brilliant talents, but for the simple virtues of their lives, their unwavering faith, their self-devotion. It is exactly in this that consists one great superiority of our religion over the most elaborate and ingenious systems devised by philosophers, that it is intelligible to the humblest capacity as well as to the highest. The poor Esquimaux of Labrador may be as good and as pure a Christian as the most learned prelate in Europe.

But we now come to an error which, in its various phases, has led to serious consequences. The utilitarian tendency of our age renders us prone to seek, even in things sacred, a character of material usefulness. We ascribe to the influence of Christianity a certain order of things, which we call *Christian civilization*.

To what political or social condition this term

can be fitly applied, I confess myself unable to conceive. There certainly is a Pagan, a Brahmin, and Buddhistic, a Judaic civilization. There have been, and still are, societies so intimately connected with a more or less exclusive theological formula, that the civilizations peculiar to them, can only be designated by the name of their creed. In such societies, religion is the sole source of all political forms, all civil and social legislation; the groundwork of the whole civilization. This union of religious and temporal institutions, we find in the history of every nation of antiquity. Each country had its own peculiar divinity, which exercised a more or less direct influence in the government, and from which laws and civilization were said to be immediately derived. It was only when paganism began to wane, that the politicians of Rome imagined a separation of temporal and religious power, by attempting a fusion of the different forms of worship, and proclaiming the dogma of legal toleration. When paganism was in its youth and vigor, each city had its Jupiter, Mercury, or Venus, and the local deity recognized neither in this world nor the next any but compatriots.

But, with Christianity, it is otherwise. It chooses no particular people, prescribes no form of government, no social system. It interferes not in temporal matters, has naught to do with the material world, "its kingdom is of another." Provided it succeeds in changing the interior man, external circumstances are of no import. If the convert fervently embraces the faith, and in all his actions tries to observe its prescriptions, it inquires not about the built of his dwelling, the cut of his garments, or the materials of which they are composed, his daily occupations, the regulations of his government, the degree of despotism, or of freedom, which pervades his political institutions. It leaves the Chinese in his robes, the Esquimaux in his seal-skins; the former to his rice, the latter to his fish-oil; and who would dare to assert that the prayers of both may not breathe as pure a faith as those of the *civilized* European? No mode of existence can attract its preference, none, however humble, its disdain. It attacks no form of government, no social institution; prescribes none, because it has adopted none. It teaches not the art of promoting worldly comforts, it teaches to despise them. What, then, can we call a Christian civilization? Had Christ, or his disciples, prescribed, or even recommended any particular political or social forms, the term would then be applicable. But his law may be observed under all – of whatever nature – and is therefore superior to them all. It is justly and truly called the *Catholic*, or Universal.

And has Christianity, then, no civilizing influence? I shall be asked. Undoubtedly; and a very great one. Its precepts elevate and purify the soul, and, by their purely spiritual nature, disengage the mind from worldly things, and expand its powers. In a merely human point of view, the material benefits it confers on its followers are inestimable. It softens the manners, and facilitates the intercourse between man and his fellow-man; it mitigates violence, and weans him from corrosive vices. It is, therefore, a powerful promoter of his worldly interests. But it only expands the mind in proportion to the susceptibility of the mind for being expanded. It does not give intellect, or confer talents, though it may exalt both, and render them more useful. It does not create new capacities, though it fosters and develops those it finds. Where the capacities of an individual, or a race, are such as to admit an improvement in the mode of existence, it tends to produce it; where such capacities are not already, it does not give them. As it belongs to no particular civilization, it does not compel a nation to change its own. In fine, as it does not level all individuals to the same intellectual standard, so it does not raise all races to the same rank in the political assemblage of the nations of the earth. It is wrong, therefore, to consider the equal aptitude of all races for the true religion, as a proof of their intellectual equality. Though having embraced it, they will still display the same characteristic differences, and divergent or even opposite tendencies. A few examples will suffice to set my idea in a clearer light.

The major portion of the Indian tribes of South America have, for centuries, been received within the pale of the church, yet the European civilization, with which they are in constant contact, has never become their own. The Cherokees, in the northern part of the same continent, have nearly all been converted by the Methodist missionaries. At this I am not surprised, but I should be greatly so, if these tribes, without mixing with the whites, were ever to form one of the States, and exercise any influence in Congress. The Moravians and Danish Lutheran missionaries in Labrador and Greenland, have opened the eyes of the Esquimaux to the light of religion; but their neophytes have remained in the same social condition in which they vegetated before. A still more forcible illustration is afforded by the Laplanders of Sweden, who have not emerged from the state of barbarism of their ancestors, though the doctrine of salvation was preached to them, and believed by them, centuries ago.

I sincerely believe that all these peoples may

produce, and, perhaps, already have produced, persons remarkable for piety and pure morals; but I do not expect ever to see among them learned theologians, great statesmen, able military leaders, profound mathematicians, or distinguished artists; – any of those superior minds, whose number and perpetual succession are the cause of power in a preponderating race; much less those rare geniuses whose meteor-like appearance is productive of permanent good only when their countrymen are so constituted as to be able to understand them, and to advance under their direction. We cannot, therefore, call Christianity a promoter of civilization in the narrow and purely material sense of some writers.

Many of my readers, while admitting my observations in the main to be correct, will object that the modifying influence of religion upon the manners must produce a corresponding modification of the institutions, and finally in the whole social system. The propagators of the gospel, they will say, are almost always – though not necessarily – from a nation superior in civilization to the one they visit. In their personal intercourse, therefore, with their neophytes, the latter cannot but acquire new notions of material well-being. Even the political system may be greatly influenced by the relations between instructor and pupil. The missionary, while he provides for the spiritual welfare of his flock, will not either neglect their material wants. By his teaching and example, the savage will learn how to provide against famine, by tilling the soil. This improvement in his condition once effected, he will soon be led to build himself a better dwelling, and to practise some of the simpler useful arts. Gradually, and by careful training, he may acquire sufficient taste for things purely intellectual, to learn the alphabet, or even, as in the ease of the Cherokees, to invent one himself. In course of time, if the missionaries' labors are crowned with success, they may, perhaps, so firmly implant their manners and mode of living among this formerly savage tribe, that the traveller will find among them well-cultivated fields, numerous flocks, and, like these same Cherokees, and the Creeks on the southern banks of the Arkansas, black slaves to work on their plantations.

Let us see how far facts correspond with this plausible argument. I shall select the two nations which are cited as being the furthest advanced in European civilization, and their example will, it seems to me, demonstrate beyond a doubt, how impossible it is for any race to pursue a career in which their own nature has not placed them.

The Cherokees and Creeks are said to be the remnants or descendants of the Alleghanian Race, the supposed builders of those great monuments of which we still find traces in the Mississippi Valley. If this be the case, these two nations may lay claim to a natural superiority over the other tribes of North America.

Deprived of their hereditary dominions by the American government, they were forced – under a treaty of transplantation – to emigrate to regions selected for them by the latter. There they were placed under the superintendence of the Minister of War, and of Protestant missionaries, who finally succeeded in persuading them to embrace the mode of life they now lead. Mr Prichard, my authority for these facts, and who derives them himself from the great work of Mr Gallatin, asserts that, while all the other Indian tribes are continually diminishing, these are steadily increasing in numbers. As a proof of this, he alleges that when Adair visited the Cherokee tribes, in 1762, the number of their warriors was estimated at 2,300; at present, their total population amounts to 15,000 souls, including about 1,200 negroes in their possession. When we consider that their schools, as well as churches, are directed by white missionaries; that the greater number of these missionaries – being Protestants – are probably married and have children and servants also white, besides, very likely, a sort of retinue of clerks and other European employees; – the increase of the aboriginal population becomes extremely doubtful, while it is easy to conceive the pressure of the white race upon its pupils. Surrounded on all sides by the power of the United States, incommensurable to their imagination; converted to the religion of their masters, which they have, I think, sincerely embraced; treated kingly and judiciously by their spiritual guides; and exposed to the alternation of working or of starving in their contracted territory – I can understand that it was possible to make them tillers of the earth.

It would be underrating the intelligence of the humblest, meanest specimen of our kind, to express surprise at such a result, when we see that, by dexterously and patiently acting upon the passions and wants of animals, we succeed in teaching them what their own instincts would never have taught them. Every village fair is filled with animals which are trained to perform the oddest tricks, and is it to be wondered at that men submitted to a rigorous system of training, and deprived of the means of escaping from it, should, in the end, be made to perform certain mechanical functions of civilized life; functions which, even in the savage state, they are capable of understanding, though they have not the will to practise them? This were placing human beings lower in the scale of creation than the learned pig [. . .] Such exultation on the part of the believers in the equality of races is little flattering to those who excite it.

I am aware that this exaggeration of the intellectual capacity of certain races is in a great measure provoked by the notions of some very learned and distinguished men, who pretend that between the lowest races of men, and the highest of apes there was but a shade of distinction. So gross an insult to the dignity of man, I indignantly reject. Certainly, in my estimation, the different races are very unequally endowed, both physically and mentally; but I should be loath to think that in any, even in the most degraded, the unmistakable line of demarcation between man and brute were effaced. I recognize no link of gradation which would connect man mentally with the brute creation.

But does it follow, that because the lowest of the human species is still unmistakably human, that all of that species are capable of the same development? Take a Bushman, the most hideous and stupid of human families, and by careful training you may teach him, or if he is already adult, his son, to learn and practise a handicraft, even one that requires a certain degree of intelligence. But are we warranted thence to conclude that the nation to which this individual belongs, is susceptible of adopting our civilization? There is a vast difference between mechanically practising handicrafts and arts, the products of an advanced civilization, and that civilization itself. Let us suppose that the Cherokee tribes were suddenly cut off from all connection with the American government, the traveller, a few years hence, would find among them very unexpected and singular institutions, resulting from their mixture with the whites, but partaking only feebly of the character of European civilization.

We often hear of negroes proficient in music, negroes who are clerks in counting-rooms, who can read, write, talk like the whites. We admire, and conclude that the negroes are capable of everything that whites are. Notwithstanding this admiration and these hasty conclusions, we express surprise at the contrast of Sclavonian [Slavonic] civilization with ours. We aver that the Russian, Polish, Servish [Serbian] nations, are civilized only at the surface, that none but the higher classes are in possession of our ideas, and this, thanks to their intermixture with the English, French, and German stock; that the masses, on the contrary, evince a hopeless inaptitude for participating in the forward movement of Western Europe, although

these masses have been Christians for centuries, many of them while our ancestors were heathens. Are the negroes, then, more closely allied to our race than the Sclavonic nations? On the one hand, we assert the intellectual equality of the white and black races; on the other, a disparity among subdivisions of our own race.

There is a vast difference between imitation and comprehension. The imitation of a civilization does not necessarily imply an eradication of the hereditary instincts. A nation can be said to have adopted a civilization, only when it has the power to progress in it unprompted, and without guidance. Instead of extolling the intelligence of savages in handling a plough, after being shown; in spelling and reading, after they have been taught; let a single example be alleged of a tribe in any of the numerous countries in contact with Europeans, which, with our religion, has also made the ideas, institutions, and manners of a European nation so completely its own, that the whole social and political machinery moves forward as easily and naturally as in our States. Let an example be alleged of an extra-European nation, among whom the art of printing produces effects analogous to those it produces among us; where new applications of our discoveries are attempted; where our systems of philosophy give birth to new systems; where our arts and sciences flourish.

But, no; I will be more moderate in my demands. I shall not ask of that nation to adopt, together with our faith, all in which consists our individuality. I shall suppose that it rejects it totally, and chooses one entirely different, adapted to its peculiar genius and circumstances. When the eyes of that nation open to the truths of the Gospel, it perceives that its earthly course is as encumbered and wretched as its spiritual life had hitherto been. It now begins the work of improvement, collects its ideas, which had hitherto remained fruitless, examines the notions of others, transforms them, and adapts them to its peculiar circumstances; in fact, erects, by its own power, a social and political system, a civilization, however humble. Where is there such a nation? The entire records of all history may be searched in vain for a single instance of a nation which, together with Christianity, adopted European civilization, or which – by the same grand change in its religious ideas – was led to form a civilization of its own, if it did not possess one already before.

On the contrary, I will show, in every part of the world, ethnical characteristics not in the least effaced by the adoption of Christianity. The Christian Mongol and Tartar tribes lead the same erratic life as their unconverted brethren, and are as distinct from the Russian of the same religion, who tills the soil, or plies his trade in their midst, as they were centuries ago. Nay, the very hostilities of race survive the adoption of a common religion, as we have already pointed out in a preceding chapter. The Christian religion, then, does not equalize the intellectual disparities of races.

> Source: Chapter VII of Count J. A. Gobineau, *The Moral and Intellectual Diversity of Races, with Particular Reference to Their Respective Influence in the Civil and Political History of Mankind.* Philadelphia: J. B. Lippincott and Co., 1856, pp. 215–33.

Note

Count Arthur Gobineau (1816–82) was an aristocrat, novelist, and Orientalist. For a brief time, he was employed as the Secretary to Alexis de Tocqueville during his term as Foreign Minister of France (1849). Gobineau's theory of racial determinism was, in part, developed in response to the fervent republicanism and socialism that were influencing French, British, and European politics and culture; his investment in the idea of a strict social, class and caste hierarchy informed his Orientalist interpretations and pseudo-scientific racial and anthropological theories. Ironically, the passionate defender of aristocratic order and Aryan privilege was born on Bastille Day. Gobineau's works include the novels *The Pleiads* (1874) and *The Crimson Handkerchief* (1872); he is also known for his *History of the Persians* (1869), and the influential *Essay on the Inequality of Human Races* (4 vols, 1853–5) – the work that would impress Richard Wagner, Friedrich Nietzsche, Houston Stewart Chamberlain, and Adolf Hitler.

83 Walter Bagehot: "Nation-Making" (1869)

In still ruder ages the religion of savages is a thing too feeble to create a schism or to found a community. We are dealing with people capable of history when we speak of great ideas, not with prehistoric flint-men or the present savages. But though under very different forms, the same essential causes – the imitation of preferred characters and the elimination of detested characters – were at work in the oldest times, and are at work among rude men now. Strong as the propensity to imitation is among civilized men, we must conceive it as an impulse of which their minds have been partially denuded. Like the far-seeing sight, the infallible hearing, the magical scent of the savage, it is a half-lost power. It

was strongest in ancient times, and *is* strongest in uncivilized regions.

This extreme propensity to imitation is one great reason of the amazing sameness which every observer notices in savage nations. When you have seen one Fuegian, you have seen all Fuegians – one Tasmanian, all Tasmanians. The higher savages, as the New Zealanders, are less uniform; they have more of the varied and compact structure of civilized nations, because in other respects they are more civilized. They have greater mental capacity – larger stores of inward thought. But much of the same monotonous nature clings to them too. A savage tribe resembles a herd of gregarious beasts; where the leader goes they go too; they copy blindly his habits, and thus soon become that which he already is. For not only the tendency, but also the power to imitate is stronger in savages than civilized men. Savages copy quicker, and they copy better. Children, in the same way, are born mimics; they cannot help imitating what comes before them. There is nothing in their minds to resist the propensity to copy. Every educated man has a large inward supply of ideas to which he can retire, and in which he can escape from or alleviate unpleasant outward objects. But a savage or a child has no resource. The external movements before it are its very life; it lives by what it sees and hears. Uneducated people in civilized nations have vestiges of the same condition. If you send a housemaid and a philosopher to a foreign country of which neither knows the language, the chances are that the housemaid will catch it before the philosopher. He has something else to do; he can live in his own thoughts. But unless she can imitate the utterances, she is lost; she has no life till she can join in the chatter of the kitchen. The propensity to mimicry, and the power of mimicry, are mostly strongest in those who have least abstract minds. The most wonderful examples of imitation in the world are perhaps the imitations of civilized men by savages in the use of martial weapons. They learn the *knack*, as sportsmen call it, with inconceivable rapidity. A North American Indian – an Australian even – can shoot as well as any white man. Here the motive is at its maximum, as well as the innate power. Every savage cares more for the power of killing than for any other power.

The persecuting tendency of all savages, and, indeed, of all ignorant people, is even more striking than their imitative tendency. No barbarian can bear to see one of his nation deviate from the old barbarous customs and usages of their tribe. Very commonly all the tribe would expect a punishment from the gods if any one of them refrained from what was old, or began what was new. In modern times and in cultivated countries we regard each person as responsible only for his own actions, and do not believe, or think of believing, that the misconduct of others can bring guilt on them. Guilt to us is an individual taint consequent on choice and cleaving to the chooser. But in early ages the act of one member of the tribe is conceived to make all the tribe impious, to offend its peculiar god, to expose all the tribe to penalties from heaven. There is no "limited liability" in the political notions of that time. The early tribe or nation is a religious partnership, on which a rash member by a sudden impiety may bring utter ruin. If the state is conceived thus, toleration becomes wicked. A permitted deviation from the transmitted ordinances becomes simple folly. It is a sacrifice of the happiness of the greatest number. It is allowing one individual, for a moment's pleasure or a stupid whim, to bring terrible and irretrievable calamity upon all. No one will ever understand even Athenian history who forgets this idea of the old world, though Athens was, in comparison with others, a rational and sceptical place, ready for new views, and free from old prejudices. When the street statues of Hermes were mutilated, all the Athenians were frightened and furious; they thought that they should *all* be ruined because some *one* had mutilated a god's image and so offended him. Almost every detail of life in the classical times – the times when real history opens – was invested with a religious sanction; a sacred ritual regulated human action; whether it was called "law" or not, much of it was older than the word "law"; it was part of an ancient usage conceived as emanating from a superhuman authority, and not to be transgressed without risk of punishment by more than mortal power. There was such a *solidarité* then between citizens that each might be led to persecute the other for fear of harm to himself.

It may be said that these two tendencies of the early world – that to persecution and that to imitation – must conflict; that the imitative impulse would lead men to copy what is new, and that persecution by traditional habit would prevent their copying it. But in practice the two tendencies co-operate. There is a strong tendency to copy the most common thing, and that common thing is the old habit. Daily imitation is far oftenest a conservative force, for the most frequent models are ancient. Of course, however, something new is necessary for every man and for every nation. We may wish, if we please, that tomorrow shall be like today, but it will not be like it. New forces will impinge upon us; new wind, new rain, and the light of another sun; and we must alter to meet them. But

the persecuting habit and the imitative combine to ensure that the new thing shall be in the old fashion; it must be an alteration, but it shall contain as little of variety as possible. The imitative impulse tends to this, because men most easily imitate what their minds are best prepared for – what is like the old, yet with the inevitable minimum of alteration; what throws them least out of the old path, and puzzles least their minds. The doctrine of development means this – that in unavoidable changes men like the new doctrine which is most of a "preservative addition" to their old doctrines. The imitative and the persecuting tendencies make all change in early nations a king of selective conservatism, for the most part keeping what is old, but annexing some new but like practice – an additional turret in the old style.

It is this process of adding suitable things and rejecting discordant things which has raised those scenes of strange manners which in every part of the world puzzle the civilized men who come upon them first. Like the old head-dress of mountain villages, they make the traveller think not so much whether they are good or whether they are bad as wonder how anyone could have come to think of them; to regard them as "monstrosities," which only some wild abnormal intellect could have hit upon. And wild and abnormal indeed would be that intellect if it were a single one at all. But in fact such manners are the growth of ages, like Roman law or the British Constitution. No one man – no one generation – could have thought of them – only a series of generations trained in the habits of the last and wanting something akin to such habits could have devised them. Savages *pet* their favourite habits, so to say, and preserve them as they do their favourite animals; ages are required, but at last a national character is formed by the confluence of congenial attractions and accordant detestations.

Another cause helps. In early states of civilization there is a great mortality of infant life, and this is a kind of selection in itself – the child most fit to be a good Spartan is most likely to survive a Spartan childhood. The habits of the tribe are enforced on the child; if he is able to catch and copy them he lives; if he cannot he dies. The imitation which assimilates early nations continues through life, but it begins with suitable forms and acts on picked specimens. I suppose, too, that there is a kind of parental selection operating in the same way and probably tending to keep alive the same individuals. Those children which gratified their fathers and mothers most would be most tenderly treated by them, and have the best chance to live, and as a rough rule their favourites would be the children of most "promise"; that is to say, those who seemed most likely to be a credit to the tribe according to the leading tribal manners and the existing tribal tastes. The most gratifying child would be the best looked after, and the most gratifying would be the best specimen of the standard then and there raised up.

Even so, I think there will be a disinclination to attribute so marked, fixed, almost physical a thing as national character to causes so evanescent as the imitation of appreciated habit and the persecution of detested habit. But, after all, national character is but a name for a collection of habits more or less universal. And this imitation and this persecution in long generations have vast physical effects. The mind of the parent (as we speak) passes somehow to the body of the child. The transmitted "something" is more affected by habits than it is by anything else. In time an ingrained type is sure to be formed, and sure to be passed on if only the causes I have specified be fully in action and without impediment.

As I have said, I am not explaining the origin of races, but of nations, or, if you like, of tribes. I fully admit that no imitation of predominant manner, or prohibitions of detested manners, will of themselves account for the broadest contrasts of human nature. Such means would no more make a Negro out of a Brahmin, or a red man out of an Englishman, than washing would change the spots of a leopard or the colour of an Ethiopian. Some more potent causes must co-operate, or we should not have these enormous diversities. The minor causes I deal with made Greek to differ from Greek, but they did not make the Greek race. We cannot precisely mark the limit, but a limit there clearly is.

If we look at the earliest monuments of the human race, we find these race-characters as decided as the race-characters now. The earliest paintings or sculptures we anywhere have give us the present contrasts of dissimilar types as strongly as present observation. Within historical memory no such differences have been created as those between Negro and Greek, between Papuan and red Indian, between Eskimos and Goth. We start with cardinal diversities; we trace only minor modifications, and we only see minor modifications. And it is very hard to see how any number of such modifications could change man as he is in one race-type to man as he is in some other. Of this there are but two explanations; *one*, that these great types were originally separate creations, as they stand – that the Negro was made so, and the Greek made so. But this easy hypothesis of special creation has been tried so often, and has broken down so very often, that in no case, probably, do any great number of careful inquirers very firmly believe it. They may

accept it provisionally, as the best hypothesis at present, but they feel about it as they cannot help feeling as to an army which has always been beaten; however strong it seems, they think it will be beaten again. What the other explanation is exactly I cannot pretend to say. Possibly as yet the data for a confident opinion are not before us. But by far the most plausible suggestion is that of Mr Wallace, that these race-marks are living records of a time when the intellect of man was not as able as it is now to adapt his life and habits to change of region; that consequently early mortality in the first wanderers was beyond conception great; that only those (so to say) haphazard individuals throve who were born with a protected nature – that is, a nature suited to the climate and the country, fitted to use its advantages, shielded from its natural diseases. According to Mr Wallace, the Negro is the remnant of the one variety of man who without more adaptiveness than then existed could live in interior Africa. Immigrants died off till they produced him or something like him, and so of the Eskimos or the American.

Any protective habit also struck out in such a time would have a far greater effect than it could afterwards. A gregarious tribe, whose leader was in some imitable respects adapted to the struggle for life, and which copied its leader, would have an enormous advantage in the struggle for life. It would be sure to win and live, for it would be coherent and adapted, whereas, in comparison, competing tribes would be incoherent and unadapted. And I suppose that in early times, when those bodies did not already contain the records and the traces of endless generations, any new habit would more easily fix its mark on the heritable element, and would be transmitted more easily and more certainly. In such an age, man being softer and more pliable, deeper race-marks would be more easily inscribed and would be more likely to continue legible.

But I have no pretence to speak on such matters; this paper, as I have so often explained, deals with nation-making and not with race-making. I assume a world of marked varieties of man, and only want to show how less marked contrasts would probably and naturally arise in each. Given large homogeneous populations, some Negro, some Mongolian, some Aryan, I have tried to prove how small contrasting groups would certainly spring up within each – some to last and some to perish. These are the eddies in each race-stream which vary its surface, and are sure to last till some new force changes the current. These minor varieties, too, would be infinitely compounded, not only with those of the same race, but with those of others. Since the beginning of man, stream has been a thousand times poured into stream – quick into sluggish, dark into pale – and eddies and waters have taken new shapes and new colours, affected by what went before, but not resembling it. And then on the fresh mass the old forces of composition and elimination again begin to act, and create over the new surface another world. "Motley was the wear" of the world when Herodotus first looked on it and described it to us, and thus, as it seems to me, were its varying colours produced.

If it be thought that I have made out that these forces of imitation and elimination be the main ones, or even at all powerful ones, in the formation of national character, it will follow that the effect of ordinary agencies upon that character will be more easy to understand than it often seems and is put down in books. We get a notion that a change of government or a change of climate acts equally on the mass of a nation, and so are we puzzled – at least, I have been puzzled – to conceive how it acts. But such changes do not at first act equally on all people in the nation. On many, for a very long time, they do not act at all. But they bring out new qualities, and advertise the effects of new habits. A change of climate, say from a depressing to an invigorating one, so acts. Everybody feels it a little, but the most active feel it exceedingly. They labour and prosper, and their prosperity invites imitation. Just so with the contrary change, from an animating to a relaxing place – the naturally lazy look so happy as they do nothing that the naturally active are corrupted. The effect of any considerable change on a nation is thus an intensifying and accumulating effect. With its maximum power it acts on some prepared and congenial individuals; in them it is seen to produce attractive results, and then the habits creating those results are copied far and wide. And, as I believe, it is in this simple but not quite obvious way that the process of progress and of degradation may generally be seen to run.

Source: Walter Bagehot *Physics and Politics, or, Thoughts on the Application of the Principles of "Natural Selection" and "Inheritance" to Political Society* (1869). New York: Alfred A Knopf, 1948, pp. 104–15.

Note

Walter Bagehot (1826–77) was a journalist, literary critic, and economist; he became the editor of *The Economist* in 1860. Bagehot's best known works include, *The English Constitution* (1867) and *Lombard Street: A Description of the Money Market* (1892). His collection of *Biographical*

Studies (1895) includes essays on the Reform Act of 1832, Sir Robert Peel, Gladstone and Disraeli, William Cobden, and Lord Palmerston.

84 William Booth: *Salvation Army Songs* (1880s)

Soldiers Praying

GOD bless our Army brave,
  Soon shall our colours wave
    O'er land and sea.
Clothe us with righteousness,
Our faithful soldiers bless,
And crown with great success
  Our Army brave.
The "blood and fire" bestow,
Go with us when we go
  To fight for Thee.
Still with our Army stay,
Drive sin and fear away,
Give victory day by day
  On Israel's side.
God bless our General,
Our Officers as well –
  God bless them all.
Oh, give us power to fight,
To put all hell to flight,
Let victory still delight
  Our Army brave.

O THOU God of every nation,
  We now for Thy blessing call;
Fit us for full consecration,
  Let the fire from heaven fall;
Bless our Army! With Thy power baptise us all.
  Fill us with Thy Holy Spirit,
    Make our soldiers white as snow;
  Save the world through Jesus' merit,
    Satan's kingdom overthrow!
Bless our Army! Send us where we ought to go!
  Give us all more holy living,
    Fill us with abundant power;
  Give The Army more thanksgiving;
    Greater victories every hour.
Bless our Army! Be our Rock, our Shield, our Tower.
  Bless our General, bless our Leaders,
    Bless our Officers as well!
  Bless Headquarters – bless our Soldiers;
    Bless the foes of sin and hell!
Bless our Army! We will all Thy goodness tell.

War

JESUS, give Thy blood-washed Army
  Universal liberty;

Keep us fighting, waiting calmly
  For a world-wide jubilee.
Hallelujah! We shall have the victory.
    Thou hast bound brave hearts together,
      Clothed us with the Spirit's might,
    Made us warriors for ever,
      Sent us in the field to fight;
In The Army We will serve Thee day and night.
  'Neath Thy sceptre foes are bending,
    And Thy name makes devils fly;
  Christless kingdoms Thou art rending,
    And Thy blood doth sin destroy;
For Thy glory We will fight until we die.
    Lift up valleys, cast down mountains,
      Make all evil natures good;
    Wash the world in Calvary's fountain,
      Send a great salvation flood;
All the nations We shall win with fire and blood.

A WORLD in rebellion our Jesus defied,
His soldiers they faltered, for others
  He cried;
Just then our dear Saviour the blood and fire waved,
And said He'd ne'er furl it, till all men were saved.
Saving the world through the blood of the Lamb.
We care not though foes may be crowding our track.
All earth, hell, and devils shall ne'er keep us [back;
King Jesus is leading, we trust in His might,
So down with the wrong, and up with the right.
Heaven born is our purpose, the wide world our
  field,
We hold a commission by Jesus' blood sealed;
How sacred our duty, how honoured our post,
We follow our Captain, to bring home the lost.
If ready for battle with me take your stand,
If ready to suffer in this cause so grand,
If ready for conquest, dark millions to win,
Then fix every bayonet and help me to sing.

ONWARD! upward! blood-washed soldier;
  Turn not back, nor sheathe thy sword,
Let its blade be sharp for conquest,
  In the battle for the Lord.
    To arms, to arms, ye brave;
    See, see the standard wave!
    March on, march on, the trumpet sounds.
      To victory or death.
From the great white throne eternal
  God Himself is looking down;
He it is who now commands thee –
  Take the cross and win the crown!
Onward! upward! doing, daring
  All for Him who died for thee;
Face the foe, and meet with boldness
  Danger, whatsoe'er it be.
From the battlements of glory

Holy ones are looking down;
Thou canst almost hear them shouting,
  "On! let no one take thy crown!"
Onward! till thy course is finished,
  Like the ransomed ones before;
Keep the faith through persecution,
  Never give the battle o'er.
Onward! upward! till, victorious,
  Thou shalt lay thine armour down,
And thy loving Saviour bids thee
  At His hand receive thy crown.

Songs of Victory

SALVATION soldiers, full of fire,
  From battle never stay;
Keep up the fire, keep aiming higher,
  Make ready, fire away!
    With The Army we will go,
    To the world our colours show,
    Never, never fear the foe,
      But fire away!
      Fire away! fire away!
      Fire away! fire away!
    With the gospel gun we will fire away!
      Mighty victories have been won
      With the great salvation gun!
      Stand your ground and fire away!
Salvation soldiers, every hour
  King Jesus we'll obey;
He loads our guns with saving power;
  In faith we'll fire away!
Salvation soldiers bound for heaven,
  Keep fighting night and day;
Use every gun that God has given –
  Make ready! fire away!

HARK, hark, my soul, what warlike songs are
  swelling
  Through all the land and on from door to door;
How grand the truths those burning strains are
  telling
  Of that great war till sin shall be no more.
    Salvation Army, Army of God,
    Onward to conquer the world with fire and
    blood.
Onward we go, the world shall hear our singing,
  Come, guilty souls, for Jesus bids you come;
And through the dark its echoes, loudly ringing,
  Shall lead the wretched, lost, and wandering
  home.
Far, far away, like thunder grandly pealing,
  We'll send the call for mercy full and free,
And burdened souls by thousands humbly
  kneeling,
  Shall bend, dear Lord, their rebel necks to Thee,

Conquerors at last, though the fight be long and
    dreary,
       Bright day shall dawn and sin's dark night
         [be past:
Our battles end in saving sinners weary,
    And Satan's kingdom down shall fall at last.

WE are sweeping through the land,
    With the sword of God in hand;
We are watching, and we're praying while we fight,
    On the wings of love we'll fly,
    To the souls about to die,
And we'll force them to behold the precious light.
    With the conquering Son of God,
    Who has washed us in His blood,
    Dangers braving, sinners saving,
    We are sweeping through the land.
    Oh, the blessed Lord of Light,
    We will serve Him with our might,
And His arm shall bring salvation to the poor;
    They shall lean upon His breast,
    Know the sweetness of His rest,
Of His pardon He the vilest will assure.
    We are sweeping on to win
    Perfect victory over sin,
And we'll shout the Saviour's praises evermore;
    When the strife on earth is done,
    And some million souls we've won,
We'll rejoin our conquering comrades gone before,
    Burst are all our prison bars,
    And we'll shine in heaven like stars,
For we'll conquer 'neath our blessed Lord's
    command.
    See, salvation's morning breaks,
    And our country now awakes,
The Salvation Army's sweeping through the land.

Source: William Booth *Salvation Army Songs.*
London: Salvation Publishing and Supplies,
1880s, song nos 507, 508, 510, 529, 535, 561, 564,
574.

Note

Methodist minister "General" William Booth (1829–
1912) began his missionary career with the establishment
of The Christian Mission in London's East End; that
organization would later become the Salvation Army.
Booth published a series of missionary instructional
books, including *Salvation Soldiery: A Series of Addresses
on the Requirements of Jesus Christ's Service* (1883), *Salvation Music* (1883), and *How to Make the Children into
Saints and Soldiers of Jesus Christ* (1888). He was succeeded as head of the Salvation Army by his eldest son,
Bramwell Booth; his other children also committed their
lives to missionary work.

85   David Livingstone: Cambridge Lecture No. 1 (1858)

DELIVERED before the University of Cambridge, in
the Senate-House, on Friday, 4th December, 1857.
Dr Philpott, Master of St Catharine's College,
Vice-Chancellor, in the chair. The building was
crowded to excess with all ranks of the University
and their friends. The reception was so enthusiastic
that literally there were volley after volley of
cheers. The Vice-Chancellor introduced Dr
Livingstone to the meeting, who spoke nearly as
follows:

When I went to Africa about seventeen years ago I
resolved to acquire an accurate knowledge of the
native tongues; and as I continued, while there, to
speak generally in the African languages, the result
is that I am not now very fluent in my own; but if
you will excuse my imperfections under that head,
I will endeavour to give you as clear an idea of
Africa as I can. If you look at the map of Africa you
will discover the shortness of the coast-line, which
is in consequence of the absence of deep indenta-
tions of the sea. This is one reason why the interior
of Africa has remained so long unknown to the rest
of the world. Another reason is the unhealthiness of
the coast, which seems to have reacted upon the
disposition of the people, for they are very un-
kindly, and opposed to Europeans passing through
their country. In the southern part of Africa lies the
great Kalahari desert, not so called as being a mere
sandy plain, devoid of vegetation: such a desert
I never saw until I got between Suez and Cairo.
Kalahari is called a desert because it contains no
streams, and water is obtained only from deep
wells. The reason why so little rain falls on this
extensive plain, is, because the winds prevailing
over the greater part of the interior country are
easterly, with a little southing. The moisture taken
up by the atmosphere from the Indian Ocean is
deposited on the eastern hilly slope; and when the
moving mass of air reaches its greatest elevation, it
is then on the verge of the great valley, or, as in the
case of the Kalahari, the great heated inland plains
there meeting with the rarefied air of that hot, dry
surface, the ascending heat gives it greater capacity
for retaining all its remaining humidity, and few
showers can be given to the middle and western
lands in consequence of the increased hygrometric
power. The people living there, not knowing the
physical reasons why they have so little rain, are in
the habit of sending to the mountains on the east
for rain-makers, in whose power of making rain

they have a firm belief. They say the people in those mountains have plenty of rain, and therefore must possess a medicine for making it. This faith in rain-making is a remarkable feature in the people in the country, and they have a good deal to say in favour of it. If you say you do not believe that these medicines have any power upon the clouds, they reply that that is just the way people talk about what they do not understand. They take a bulb, pound it, and administer an infusion of it to a sheep: in a short time the sheep dies in convulsions, and then they ask, Has not the medicine power? I do not think our friends of the homœopathic "persuasion" have much more to say than that. The common argument known to all those tribes is this – "God loves you white men better than us: He made you first, and did not make us pretty like you: He made us afterwards, and does not love us as He loves you. He gave you clothing, and horses and waggons, and guns and powder, and that Book, which you are always talking about. He gave us only two things – cattle and a knowledge of certain medicines by which we can make rain. We do not despise the things that you have; we only wish that we had them too; we do not despise that Book of yours, although we do not understand it: so you ought not to despise our knowledge of rain-making, although you do not understand it." You cannot convince them that they have no power to make rain. As it is with the homœopathist, so it is with the rain-maker – you might argue your tongue out of joint, and would convince neither.

I went into that country for the purpose of teaching the doctrines of our holy religion, and settled with the tribes on the border of the Kalahari desert. These tribes were those of the Bakwains, Bushmen and Bakalahari. Sechele is the chief of the former. On the occasion of the first religious service held, he asked me if he could put some questions on the subject of Christianity, since such was the custom of their country when any new subject was introduced to their notice. I said, "By all means." He then inquired "If my forefathers knew of a future judgment?" I said, "Yes"; and began to describe the scene of the great white throne, and HIM who should sit on it, from whose face the heavens shall flee away, and be no more seen; interrupting he said, "You startle me, these words make all my bones to shake, I have no more strength in me. You have been talking about a future judgment, and many terrible things, of which we know nothing," repeating, "Did your forefathers know of these things?" I again replied in the affirmative. The chief said, "All my forefathers have passed away into darkness, without knowing anything of what

was to befall them; how is it that your forefathers, knowing all these things, did not send word to my forefathers sooner?" This was rather a poser; but I explained the geographical difficulties, and said it was only after we had begun to send the knowledge of Christ to Cape Colony and other parts of the country, to which we had access, that we came to them; that it was their duty to receive what Europeans had now obtained the power to offer them; and that the time would come when the whole world would receive the knowledge of Christ, because Christ had promised that all the earth should be covered with a knowledge of Himself. The chief pointed to the Kalahari desert, and said, "Will you ever get beyond that with your Gospel? We, who are more accustomed to thirst than you are, cannot cross that desert; how can you?" I stated my belief in the promise of Christ; and in a few years afterwards that chief was the man who enabled me to cross that desert; and not only so, but he himself preached the Gospel to tribes beyond it. In some years, more rain than usual falls in the desert, and then there is a large crop of water-melons. When this occurred, the desert might be crossed: in 1852, a gentleman crossed it, and his oxen existed on the fluid contained in the melons for twenty-two days. In crossing the desert, different sorts of country are met with; up to 20th south latitude, there is a comparatively dry and arid country, and you might travel for four days, as I have done, without a single drop of water for the oxen. Water for the travellers themselves was always carried in the waggons, the usual mode of travelling south of the 20th degree of latitude being by ox-waggon. For four days, upon several occasions, we had not a drop of water for the oxen; but beyond 20th south latitude, going to the north, we travelled to Loanda, 1,500 miles, without carrying water for a single day. The country in the southern part of Africa is a kind of oblong basin, stretching north and south, bounded on all sides by old schist rocks. The waters of this central basin find an exit through a fissure into the river Zambesi, flowing to the east, the basin itself being covered with a layer of calcareous tufa.

My object in going into the country south of the desert was to instruct the natives in a knowledge of Christianity, but many circumstances prevented my living amongst them more than seven years, amongst which were considerations arising out of the slave system carried on by the Dutch Boers. I resolved to go into the country beyond, and soon found that, for the purposes of commerce, it was necessary to have a path to the sea. I might have gone on instructing the natives in religion, but as civilization and Christianity must go on together, I was obliged to find a path to the sea, in order that I should not sink to the level of the natives. The chief was overjoyed at the suggestion, and furnished me with twenty-seven men, and canoes, and provisions, and presents for the tribes through whose country we had to pass. We might have taken a shorter path to the sea than that to the north, and then to the west, by which we went; but along the country by the shorter route, there is an insect called the tsetse, whose bite is fatal to horses, oxen, and dogs, but not to men or donkeys. You seem to think there is a connexion between the two. The habitat of that insect is along the shorter route to the sea. The bite of it is fatal to domestic animals, not immediately, but certainly in the course of two or three months; the animal grows leaner and leaner, and gradually dies of emaciation: a horse belonging to Gordon Cumming died of a bite five or six months after it was bitten.

On account of this insect, I resolved to go to the north, and then westwards to the Portuguese settlement of Loanda. Along the course of the river which we passed, game was so abundant that there was no difficulty in supplying the wants of my whole party: antelopes were so tame that they might be shot from the canoe. But beyond 14 degrees of south latitude the natives had guns, and had themselves destroyed the game, so that I and my party had to live on charity. The people, however, in that central region were friendly and hospitable: but they had nothing but vegetable productions: the most abundant was the cassava, which, however nice when made into tapioca pudding, resembles in its more primitive condition nothing so much as a mess of laundress's starch. There was a desire in the various villages through which we passed to have intercourse with us, and kindness and hospitality were shown us; but when we got near the Portuguese settlement of Angola the case was changed, and payment was demanded for every thing. But I had nothing to pay with. Now the people had been in the habit of trading with the slavers, and so they said I might give one of my men in payment for what I wanted. When I shewed them that I could not do this, they looked upon me as an interloper, and I was sometimes in danger of being murdered.

As we neared the coast, the name of England was recognized, and we got on with ease. Upon one occasion, when I was passing through the parts visited by slave-traders, a chief who wished to shew me some kindness offered me a slave-girl: upon explaining that I had a little girl of my own, whom I should not like my own chief to give to a black man, the chief thought I was displeased with the size of the girl, and sent me one a head taller. By

this and other means I convinced my men of my opposition to the principle of slavery; and when we arrived at Loanda I took them on board a British vessel, where I took a pride in showing them that those countrymen of mine and those guns were there for the purpose of putting down the slave-trade. They were convinced from what they saw of the honesty of Englishmen's intentions; and the hearty reception they met with from the sailors made them say to me, "We see they are your countrymen, for they have hearts like you." On the journey, the men had always looked forward to reaching the coast: they had seen Manchester prints and other articles imported therefrom, and they could not believe they were made by mortal hands. On reaching the sea, they thought that they had come to the end of the world. They said, "We marched along with our father, thinking the world was a large plain without limit; but all at once the land said 'I am finished, there is no more of me'"; and they called themselves the true old men – the true ancients – having gone to the end of the world. On reaching Loanda, they commenced trading in firewood, and also engaged themselves at sixpence a day in unloading coals, brought by a steamer for the supply of the cruiser lying there to watch the slave-vessels. On their return, they told their people "we worked for a whole moon, carrying away the stones that burn." By the time they were ready to go back to their own country, each had secured a large bundle of goods. On the way back, however, fever detained them, and their goods were all gone, leaving them on their return home, as poor as when they started.

I had gone towards the coast for the purpose of finding a direct path to the sea, but on going through the country we found forests so dense that the sun had not much influence on the ground, which was covered with yellow mosses, and all the trees with white lichens. Amongst these forests were little streams, each having its source in a bog; in fact nearly all the rivers in that country commence in bogs. Finding it impossible to travel here in a wheel conveyance, I left my waggon behind, and I believe it is standing in perfect safety, where I last saw it, at the present moment. The only other means of conveyance we had was ox-back, by no means a comfortable mode of travelling. I therefore came back to discover another route to the coast by means of the river Zambesi.

The same system of inundation that distinguishes the Nile, is also effected by this river, and the valley of the Barotse is exceedingly like the valley of the Nile between Cairo and Alexandria. The inundations of the Zambesi, however, cause no muddy sediment like those of the Nile, and, only that there are no snow-mountains, would convey the impression that the inundations were the result of the melting of snow from adjoining hills. The face of the country presents no such features, but elevated plains, so level that rain-water stands for months together upon them. The water does not flow off, but gradually soaks into the soil, and then oozes out in bogs, in which all the rivers take their rise. They have two rainy seasons in the year, and consequently two periods of inundation. The reason why the water remains so clear is this; the country is covered by such a mass of vegetation that the water flows over the grass, etc. without disturbing the soil beneath.

There is a large central district containing a large lake formed by the course of the Zambesi, to explore which would be well worthy of the attention of any individual wishing to distinguish himself.

Having got down amongst the people in the middle of the country, and having made known to my friend the chief my desire to have a path for civilization and commerce on the east, he again furnished me with means to pursue my researches eastward; and, to shew how disposed the natives were to aid me in my expedition, I had 114 men to accompany me to the east, whilst those who had travelled to the west with me only amounted to 27. I carried with me thirty tusks of ivory; and, on leaving my waggon to set forth on my journey, two warriors of the country offered a heifer a-piece to the man who should slay any one who molested it. Having proceeded about a hundred miles, I found myself short of ammunition, and despatched an emissary back to the chief to procure more percussion caps from a box I had in my waggon. Not understanding the lock, the chief took a hatchet and split the lid open, to get what was wanted; and notwithstanding the insecure state in which it remained, I found, on returning two years after, that its contents were precisely as I left them. Such honesty is rare even in civilised Christian England, as I know from experience; for I sent a box of fossils to Dr Buckland, which, after arriving safely in England, was stolen from some railway, being probably mistaken for plate.

I could not make my friend the chief understand that I was poor: I had a quantity or sugar, and while it lasted the chief would favour me with his company to coffee; when it was gone, I told the chief how it was produced from the cane, which grew in central Africa, but as they had no means of extracting the saccharine matter, he requested me to procure a sugar mill. When I told him I was poor, the chief then informed me that all the ivory in the country was at my disposal, and he accordingly loaded me with tusks, ten of which on arriving at the coast I spent in purchasing clothing for my followers; the rest were left at Quillimane, that the impression should not be produced in the country that they had been stolen in case of my non-return.

Englishmen are very apt to form their opinion of Africans from the elegant figures in tobacconists' shops: I scarcely think such are fair specimens of the African. I think at the same time, that the African women would be much handsomer than they are if they would only let themselves alone: though unfortunately that is a failing by no means peculiar to African ladies; but they are, by nature, not particularly goodlooking, and seem to take all the pains they can to make themselves worse. The people of one tribe knock out all their upper front teeth, and when they laugh are perfectly hideous. Another tribe of the Londa country file all their front teeth to a point, like cats' teeth, and when they grin put one in mind of alligators: many of the women are comely, but spoil their beauty by such unnatural means. Another tribe has a custom of piercing the cartilage of the nose, and inserting a bit of reed, which spreads it out, and makes them very disagreeable looking: others tie their hair, or rather wool, into basket-work, resembling the tonsorial decorations of the ancient Egyptians; others, again, dress their hair with a hoop around it, so as to resemble the gloria round the head of the Virgin; rather a different application of the hoop to that of English ladies!

The people of central Africa have religious ideas stronger than those of the Caffres and other southern nations, who talk much of God but pray seldom. They pray to departed relatives, by whom they imagine illnesses are sent to punish them for any neglect on their part. Evidences of the Portuguese Jesuit missionary operations are still extant, and are carefully preserved by the natives: one tribe can all read and write, which is ascribable to the teaching of the Jesuits: their only books are, however, histories of saints, and miracles effected by the parings of saintly toe-nails, and suchlike nonsense: but, surely, if such an impression has once been produced, it might be hoped that the efforts of Protestant missionaries, who would leave the Bible with these poor people, would not be less abiding.

In a commercial point of view communication with this country is desirable. Angola is wonderfully fertile, producing every kind of tropical plant in rank luxuriance. Passing on to the valley of Quango, the stalk of the grass was as thick as a quill, and towered above my head, although I was mounted on my ox; cotton is produced in great abundance, though merely woven into common cloth; bananas and pine-apples grow in great luxuriance; but the people having no maritime communication, these advantages are almost lost. The country on the other side is not quite so fertile, but in addition to indigo, cotton, and sugar-cane, produces a fibrous substance, which I am assured is stronger than flax.

The Zambesi has not been thought much of as a river by Europeans, not appearing very large at its mouth; but on going up it for about seventy miles, it is enormous. The first three hundred miles might be navigated without obstacle: then there is a rapid, and near it a coal-field of large extent. The elevated sides of the basin, which form the most important feature of the country, are far different in climate to the country nearer the sea, or even the centre. Here the grass is short, and the Angola goat, which could not live in the centre, had been seen on the east highland by Mr Moffat.

My desire is to open a path to this district, that civilization, commerce, and Christianity might find their way there. I consider that we made a great mistake, when we carried commerce into India, in being ashamed of our Christianity; as a matter of common sense and good policy, it is always best to appear in one's true character. In travelling through Africa, I might have imitated certain Portuguese, and have passed for a chief; but I never attempted anything of the sort, although endeavouring always to keep to the lessons of cleanliness rigidly instilled by my mother long ago; the consequence was that the natives respected me for that quality, though remaining dirty themselves.

I had a pass from the Portuguese consul, and on arriving at their settlement, I was asked what I was. I said, "A missionary, and a doctor too." They asked, "Are you a doctor of medicine?" – "Yes." – "Are you not a doctor of mathematics too?" – "No." – "And yet you can take longitudes and latitudes." – Then they asked me about my moustache; and I simply said I wore it, because men had moustaches to wear, and ladies had not. They could not understand either, why a sacerdote [priest] should have a wife and four children; and many a joke took place upon that subject. I used to say, "Is it not better to have children with than without a wife?" Englishmen of education always command respect, without any adventitious aid. A Portuguese governor left for Angola, giving out that he was going to keep a large establishment, and taking with him quantities of crockery, and about five hundred waistcoats; but when he arrived in Africa, he made a "deal" of them. Educated Englishmen seldom descend to that sort of thing.

A prospect is now before us of opening Africa for commerce and the Gospel. Providence has been preparing the way, for even before I proceeded to the Central basin it had been conquered and rendered safe by a chief named Sebituane, and the language of the Bechuanas made the fashionable tongue, and that was one of the languages into which Mr Moffat had translated the Scriptures. Sebituane also discovered Lake Ngami some time previous to my explorations in that part. In going back to that country my object is to open up traffic along the banks of the Zambesi, and also to preach the Gospel. The natives of Central Africa are very desirous of trading, but their only traffic is at present in slaves, of which the poorer people have an unmitigated horror; it is therefore most desirable to encourage the former principle, and thus open a way for the consumption of free productions, and the introduction of Christianity and commerce. By encouraging the native propensity for trade, the advantages that might be derived in a commercial point of view are incalculable; nor should we lose sight of the inestimable blessings it is in our power to bestow upon the unenlightened African, by giving him the light of Christianity. Those two pioneers of civilization – Christianity and commerce – should ever be inseparable; and Englishmen should be warned by the fruits of neglecting that principle as exemplified in the result of the management of Indian affairs. By trading with Africa, also, we should at length be independent of slave labour, and thus discountenance practices so obnoxious to every Englishman.

Though the natives are not absolutely anxious to receive the Gospel, they are open to Christian influences. Among the Bechuanas the Gospel was well received. These people think it a crime to shed a tear, but I have seen some of them weep at the recollection of their sins when God had opened their hearts to Christianity and repentance. It is true that missionaries have difficulties to encounter; but what great enterprise was ever accomplished without difficulty? It is deplorable to think that one of the noblest of our missionary societies, the Church Missionary Society, is compelled to send to Germany for missionaries, whilst other societies are amply supplied. Let this stain be wiped off. The sort of men who are wanted for missionaries are such as I see before me – men of education, standing, enterprise, zeal, and piety, It is a mistake to suppose that *any one*, as long as he is pious, will do for this office. Pioneers in every thing should be the ablest and best qualified men, not those of small ability and education. This remark especially applies to the first teachers of Christian truth in regions which may never have before been blest with the name and Gospel of Jesus Christ. In the early ages the monasteries were the schools of Europe, and the monks were not ashamed to hold the plough. The missionaries now take the place of those noble men, and we should not hesitate to give up the small luxuries of life in order to carry knowledge and truth to them that are in darkness. I hope that many of those whom I now address will embrace that honourable career. Education has been given us from above for the purpose of bringing to the benighted the knowledge of a Saviour. If you knew the satisfaction of performing such a duty, as well as the gratitude to God which the missionary must always feel, in being chosen for so noble, so sacred a calling, you would have no hesitation in embracing it.

For my own part, I have never ceased to rejoice that God has appointed me to such an office. People talk of the sacrifice I have made in spending so much of my life in Africa. Can that be called a sacrifice which is simply paid back as a small part of a great debt owing to our God, which we can never repay? – Is that a sacrifice which brings its own blest reward in healthful activity, the consciousness of doing good, peace of mind, and a bright hope of a glorious destiny hereafter? – Away with the word in such a view, and with such a thought! It is emphatically no sacrifice. Say rather it is privilege. Anxiety, sickness, suffering, or danger, now and then, with a foregoing of the common conveniences and charities of this life, may make us pause, and cause the spirit to waver, and the soul to sink, but let this only be for a moment. All these are nothing when compared with the glory which shall hereafter be revealed in, and for, us. I never made a sacrifice. Of this we ought not to talk, when we remember the great sacrifice which HE made who left His Father's throne on high to give Himself for us; "Who being the brightness of that Father's glory, and the express image of His person, and upholding all things by the word of His power, when He had by Himself purged our sins, sat down on the right hand of the majesty on high."

English people are treated with respect; and the missionary can earn his living by his gun – a course not open to a country curate. I would rather be a poor missionary than a poor curate.

Then there is the pleasant prospect of returning home and seeing the agreeable faces of his countrywomen again. I suppose I present a pretty contrast to you. At Cairo we met a party of young English people, whose faces were quite a contrast to the skinny, withered ones of those who had spent the latter years of their life in a tropical clime: they were the first rosy cheeks I had seen for sixteen years; you can hardly tell how pleasant it is to see the blooming cheeks of young ladies before me, after an absence of sixteen years from such delightful objects of contemplation. There is also the pleasure of the welcome home, and I heartily thank you for the welcome you have given me on the present occasion; but there is also the hope of the welcome words of our Lord, "Well done, good and faithful servant."

I beg to direct your attention to Africa; I know that in a few years I shall be cut off in that country, which is now open; do not let it be shut again! I go back to Africa to try to make an open path for commerce and Christianity; do you carry out the work which I have begun. I LEAVE IT WITH YOU!

Source: Rev. William Monk (ed.). *Dr. Livingstone's Cambridge Lectures.* Cambridge: Deighton, Bell and Co., 1858, pp. 1–24.

Note

David Livingstone (1813–73) was ordained by the London Missionary Society in 1840. His explorations in Africa became internationally renowned due the uncertainty of his fate in Africa. Henry Morton Stanley's recovery of Livingstone provided the nineteenth-century audience with one of its most sensational rescue narratives. Livingstone's travel and adventure narratives include his *African Journal. 1853–56, Missionary Travels* (1857), *Explorations in Africa* (1872), and *The Last Journals of David Livingstone* (1875). Upon his demise, Livingstone was buried in Westminster Abbey.

Chapter Fifteen

The Administrators: Lugard and Rhodes

Introduction

Frederick Lugard who was born at Fort Saint George in Madras, India in January 1858, the year after the Indian Rebellion, considered himself a gentlemanly imperialist and modern pioneer. He knew well what he described as the terror and thrill of warfare, having served during the Afghan Wars (1879), the Suakin (Sudan) Campaign (1885), the Burma Wars (1886), and the Nyasa Campaign against Arab slave-traders (1888–9). After his active military service, Lugard accepted a series of jobs for African Charter Companies, including the imperial British East Africa Company (1889), the Royal Niger Company (1894–5), and the diamond prospecting British West Charterland Company (1896–7). He distinguished himself by successfully negotiating treaties that would rout the French and German competitors and expand Britain's African territories. Lugard described the plot of the "Old African Life" as "battle, murder, sudden death." He was a reluctant, but efficient warrior who believed in "civilization by applied science," which for him involved the development and efficient management of human and material resources, the eradication of disease, the implementation of fair trade, and annexation by legitimate treaty. He developed administrative policies that would rely on cooperation with native rulers and recognition of African traditions and cultural and political hierarchies. Lugard maintained a lifelong interest in African languages. He died in 1945.

MC

Cecil Rhodes was born in 1853, and at the age of seventeen he went to South Africa, where, even while completing a degree at Oriel College, Oxford, he built up a successful diamond business. The De Beers Mining Company, which he formed in 1880, won the amalgamation struggle against strenuous opposition by the supporters of another, freer, kind of trade. And Rhodes went on to launch Goldfields of South Africa in 1887, and to establish the British South Africa Company in 1889 – capitalizing all the while on the discovery of diamonds in South Africa in 1867 and of gold in the 1870s, and continuing the chartered company. He served in the Cape Parliament, and as Prime Minister there from 1890 till 1896 when he was forced to resign following the ill-fated raid against the Afrikaners in the Transvaal led by his close friend and longtime intimate Dr L. S. Jameson in 1895. A public figure, financier and politician with territorial designs, Rhodes's reputation has lived on into the late twentieth century in the naming of Rhodesia (now Zimbabwe) which he claimed to have made his own, following his campaigns in Matabele and Mashona lands. It was there too that he asked to be buried. He died in 1902, the year that saw as well the end of the Anglo–Boer War. Rhodes's "last will and testament" – edited and executed by his publicist friend W. T. Stead of the *Review of Reviews* – summarizes well the legacy he hoped to leave: his property in Rhodesia where he would be interred; the preservation of Groote Schuur, his residence by Table Mountain in the Cape Colony; and the Rhodes scholarships at Oxford for the continued "education of young colonists."

BH

THE RHODES COLOSSUS

STRIDING FROM CAPE TOWN TO CAIRO.

Plate 5 Cartoon from *Punch*, December 10, 1892.

Additional Reading

Lugard
Asiegbu, Johnson U. J. *Nigeria and Its British Invaders, 1851–1920: A Thematic Documentary History*. New York, 1984.
Callaway, Helen. *Gender, Culture, and Empire: European Women in Colonial Nigeria*. Basingstoke, 1987.
Hertslet, Edward. *The Map of Africa by Treaty*, 3 vols. London, 1909.
Kingsley, Mary, *West African Studies*. London, 1901.
Lugard, Frederick. *The Diaries of Lord Lugard*. Margery Perham and Mary Bull (eds). Evanston, 1959–63.
——. *The Rise of Our East African Empire: Early Efforts in Nyasaland and Uganda*. London, 1893.
Mockler-Ferryman, Augustus. *British Nigeria: A Geographical and Historical Description of the British Possessions Adjacent to the Niger River*. London, 1902.
Panter-Brick, Keith, (ed.). *Soldiers and Oil: The Political Transformation of Nigeria*. London, 1978.
Shaw, Flora Louisa (Lugard). *A Tropical Dependency: An Outline of the Ancient History of the Western Sudan with an Account of the Modern Settlement of Nigeria*. London, 1905.

Rhodes
Ally, Russell. *Gold and Empire: The Bank of England and South Africa's Gold Producers 1886–1926*. Johannesburg, 1994.
Galbraith, John S. *Crown and Charter: The Early Years of the British South Africa Company*. Berkeley and Los Angeles, 1974.
Haggard, H. Rider. *King Solomon's Mines*. London, 1885.
Millin, Sarah Gertrude. *Rhodes*. London, 1933.
Plomer, William. *Cecil Rhodes*. London, 1933.
Wheatcroft, Geoffrey. *The Randlords: The Men Who Made South Africa* (1985). London, 1993.

Films
Berthold Viertet. *Rhodes of Africa* (1936).
Robert Stevenson. *King Solomon's Mines* (1937).
Compton Bennett and Andrew Marton. *King Solomon's Mines* (1950).
J. Lee Thompson. *King Solomon's Mines* (1985).
Alvin Rakoff. *King Solomon's Treasure* (1977).

86   Frederick Lugard: "The Dual Mandate in British Tropical Africa" (1922)

Introduction

AFRICA has been justly termed "the Dark Continent," for the secrets of its peoples, its lakes, and mountains and rivers, have remained undisclosed not merely to modern civilisation, but through all the ages of which history has any record. There are many regions in Asia – in Persia, Assyria, Arabia, and Western China – in which modern explorers have claimed to have made discoveries. But all these countries were the seats of ancient civilisations, some of them highly developed, and exploration was concerned rather with piecing together chapters of past history than in discovery. The penetration into the interior of Africa, on the other hand, may as truly be described as discovery as that of America by Columbus.

The Muscat Arabs from Zanzibar were pioneers in the exploration of the region of the great lakes and the Congo basin, while in Western Africa the zeal of the Moslem Arabs and Berbers led them across the Sahara. Here indeed a great empire, famed for its culture, boasted a fragmentary history dating back to the eighth or ninth centuries; but in this or any other part of tropical Africa, from the frontiers of Egypt to the Zambesi, there are no traces of antecedent civilisations – no monuments or buried cities – like those of the prehistoric civilisations of Asia and South America.

That portion of the north of Africa which is included in the temperate zone, and contiguous to Europe, had been the home of the most ancient civilisations, first of Egypt, dating back to perhaps 4,000 BC, and later of the Phœnicians. But Egypt had penetrated no further south than Ethiopia, while the Carthagenians (though they had trade routes with the interior) for the most part confined their efforts to the establishment of colonies on the coast. We read of one or two expeditions to the interior both by Pharaoh Necho and by Carthage, but they were barren of results. So were the expeditions of the Greeks, who founded their first colony at Cyrene 1,000 years before Christ, and of the Romans, who later incorporated all North Africa as a Roman province.

Accurate knowledge even of the coast-line, and the establishment of European settlements upon it, dates only from the fifteenth century – synchronising with the discovery of America. The outlet for commerce and the new fields which this great discovery – together with the development of India – afforded to adventurous pioneers, diverted for some three centuries or more the tide of exploration which might otherwise have set towards Africa. The voyages of Da Gama and others in the fifteenth century had, however, already produced one very notable result. Hitherto the gateway which led to the great unknown interior had been situated in the north. Access to Timbuktu was by caravan across the desert from Tripoli or Algeria. The sea route discovered by Da Gama disclosed a back door, which was henceforth to become the principal entrance. As modern railways have rendered the desert route obsolete, they may in the not distant future restore it.

Thus the interior of Africa remained unknown. It appeared on the map as a great blank space, with a fringe of names all round its coasts, till Livingstone, Barth, and others began its systematic exploration about seventy years ago. For thirty or forty years tropical Africa remained a field for adventurous and sensational exploration, and it was not till 1885 – when the Berlin Act was passed – that the modern development of Africa began to assume definite and recognised form.

What, then, were the causes which led to the opening up of Africa, a continent which all the preceding ages of the world's history had left untouched, though it lay close to the homes of the early civilisations in Europe and Asia – a continent containing a fifth of the earth's land surface and a ninth of its population?

The dominant cause of Africa's isolation was, no doubt, that the world had not hitherto had urgent need of its products, and that its warlike tribes were able to repel unwelcome visitors armed but little better than themselves. Even when the economic pressure caused by the rapidly increasing population of Europe began to exert its inevitable influence, in driving men to seek for new markets and fresh supplies of food and raw material, the discovery of America, and the new fields for commerce in India, more than met the demand for several centuries. It was not until the great industrial revival which followed the Civil War in America that America began herself to compete in the world's markets, and to utilise her own resources primarily for the needs of her own industry.

One of the more immediate causes which led to the opening up of Africa was the Franco-Prussian War of 1870. Crippled by her defeat, France proclaimed by the mouth of her principal statesmen and writers – just as she is doing to-day – that it was to Greater France beyond the seas, and especially in West and North-West Africa, that she must look for rehabilitation. At that time, moreover, colonisation in tropical Africa was believed to be both possible and desirable. Germany, on the other hand, found herself with a great and increasing industrial population in urgent need of raw materials and additional food supplies. Not content with the wholly unrestricted market offered by British colonies, where Germans were welcomed, and exercised every privilege equally with their British rivals, she not unnaturally desired to have colonies of her own. We have since learnt that she had other motives – the creation of naval bases and world-wide wireless stations, and the raising of negro armies for world conquest.

Humanitarian motives – the desire to suppress the slave-trade, etc. – also played their part, but it was the rivalry of these two great Continental Powers which was the immediate cause of the modern "partition of Africa." By the Berlin Act of 1885, and the Brussels Act of 1892, Europe and America endeavoured in some feeble way to safeguard the interests of the natives – but these Acts were practically ineffective for their purpose. The one thing they did succeed in effecting was the restriction of the import of arms of precision to the natives, theoretically as a check to the slave-trade, but with the practical result of rendering the African more powerless than ever to resist conquest by Europeans.

England was unwillingly forced into the competition. On the one hand her colonies on the West Coast demanded some effort, to save them from being cut off from all access to the interior by hostile foreign tariffs, and becoming mere coast enclaves. Her vital interests in India, on the other hand, compelled her to protect her route thither – Egypt, the Suez Canal, and the eastern shores of Africa. The essential interests of Egypt, for which she had become responsible, demanded the protection of the Nile sources.

For a decade and more the "scramble" went on till it was brought to a close by the conventions with France of 1898 and 1899, and the Fashoda incident of the latter year. Germany had secured large colonies in East, West, and South Africa, at the expense of prior British claims, but we recognised her right to a place in the tropical sun. France added largely to her territory in West and Central Africa, and annexed the great island of Madagascar.

It was towards the close of this period of rivalry that Mr Joseph Chamberlain became Colonial Secretary, and for the first time in our history a policy of progress and development found favour at Whitehall. The colonies were encouraged to raise loans, supported if necessary by Imperial credit, for the development of their resources, and had it not been for the South African War this policy would, I know, have been carried much further. During the twelve years which elapsed between the South African and the recent world war, great progress was made in the construction of roads and railways, and the opening up of waterways, – for the material development of Africa may be summed up in the one word "transport."

Though we may perhaps at times entertain a lingering regret for the passing of the picturesque methods of the past, we must admit that the locomotive is a substantial improvement on head-borne transport, and the motor-van is more efficient than the camel. The advent of Europeans has brought the mind and methods of Europe to bear on the native of Africa for good or for ill, and the seclusion of ages must perforce give place to modern ideas. Material development is accompanied by education and progress.

The condition of Africa when Europe entered the continent, which Isaiah so graphically describes as "the land shadowing with wings, which is beyond the rivers of Ethiopia . . . a people scattered and peeled," was deplorable. On the East Coast, Arabs and half-castes were engaged in a lucrative trade in slaves for export to Arabia and to Turkish possessions. In the west, powerful armies of Moslem States depopulated large districts in their raids for slaves. Europe had failed to realise that throughout the length and breadth of Africa inter-tribal war was an ever-present condition of native life, and that extermination and slavery were practised by African tribes upon each other.

It was the task of civilisation to put an end to slavery, to establish Courts of Law, to inculcate in the natives a sense of individual responsibility, of liberty, and of justice, and to teach their rulers how to apply these principles; above all, to see to it that the system of education should be such as to produce happiness and progress. I am confident that the verdict of history will award high praise to the efforts and the achievements of Great Britain in the discharge of these great responsibilities. For, in my belief, under no other rule – be it of his own uncontrolled potentates, or of aliens – does the African enjoy such a measure of freedom and of impartial justice, or a more sympathetic treatment, and for that reason I am a profound believer in the British Empire and its mission in Africa.

In brief, we may say that the eighteenth century was chiefly remarkable for the acquisition of large and almost uninhabited portions of the earth, situated in the temperate zone. The nineteenth century saw the development of these great colonies into nations enjoying self-government. Its closing decade witnessed the dawning recognition of the vital importance of the tropics to civilisation, and the "discovery" and acquisition of large non-colonisable areas in tropical Africa – no longer regarded as picturesque appanages of Empire, but as essential to the very existence of the races of the temperate climes.

To the twentieth century belongs the heritage of the tropics and the task of their development. Two decades have already passed and wonderful progress has been made, not only in the improvement of the quality and quantity of the material output, by scientific research, by organised method, and by the expenditure of capital, but also in methods of administration for the welfare of the subject races, education, free labour, taxation, and other similar problems.

A comparative study of the methods by which these various problems – administrative and economic – have been approached in the several tropical dependencies of the Empire and by other nations would form a fascinating study and a useful guide, but the racial differences between Asiatics and Africans are so great (as my own experience in India and China have taught me) that methods applicable to the one may be quite misplaced with the other. The tropical dependencies in Africa, on the other hand, offer almost identical problems.

"No serious attempt," says Mr Kidd, "has so far been made to set forth the principles which should underlie our future relations with the tropical regions of the world. . . . Nowhere is there to be found any whole-hearted or consistent attempt either to justify the political relations which already exist, or to define the principles of any relations which ought to exist in the future." The following pages have been written in the hope that an experience, with short intervals, of forty years in the tropics, and of over thirty in responsible positions in Africa, may enable me to make some useful contribution to the study of these subjects. During the first half of these thirty years it was my privilege to assist in some degree in bringing under British control portions of Nyasaland, East Africa, Uganda, and Nigeria, where the difficulties of the pioneer had to be encountered. During the second fifteen it has been my good fortune to be entrusted with the development of Nigeria, and with the aid of capable colleagues to lay the foundations of a system of administration upon which others may build. I shall endeavour to describe the difficulties encountered, the methods used, and the results obtained in administration – which forms the most important part of our task in Africa.

It is, moreover, also of great moment that the British democracy, faced with problems which portend great changes in our social organisation, should understand the relation which our overseas dependencies bear to the economic well-being of this country – how vital to our industrial life are the products of the tropics, and its markets for our manufactures. It is indeed essential that democracy should take an intelligent and well-informed interest in questions which affect the Empire of which it is the inheritor and trustee. [. . .]

Some General Principles of Administration

THE British Empire, as General Smuts has well said, has only one mission – for liberty and self-development on no standardised lines, so that all may feel that their interests and religion are safe under the British flag. Such liberty and self-development can be best secured to the native population by leaving them free to manage their own affairs through their own rulers, proportionately to their degree of advancement, under the guidance of the British staff, and subject to the laws and policy of the administration.

But apart from the administration of native affairs the local Government has to preserve law and order, to develop the trade and communications of the country, and to protect the interests of the merchants and others who are engaged in the development of its commercial and mineral resources. What, then, are the functions of the British staff, and how can the machinery of Government be most efficiently constituted for the discharge of its duties in those countries in Africa which fall under British control?

The staff must necessarily be limited in numbers, for if the best class of men are to be attracted to a service which often involves separation from family and a strain on health, they must be offered adequate salaries and inducements in the way of leave, housing, medical aid – or their equivalents in money – for their maintenance in health and comfort while serving abroad, and this forms a heavy charge on the revenues. Policy and economy alike demand restriction in numbers, but the best that England can supply.

Obviously a consideration of the machinery of British administration in the tropics involves a review of its relations to the home Government on the one hand, and of its local constitution and functions on the other. I will take the latter first.

The Government is constituted on the analogy of the British Government in England. The Governor represents the King, but combines the functions of the Prime Minister as head of the Executive. The Councils bear a certain resemblance to the Home Cabinet and Parliament, while the detailed work of the administration is carried out by a staff which may be roughly divided into the administrative, the judicial, and the departmental branches.

The administrative branch is concerned with the supervision of the native administration and the general direction of policy; with education, and the collection and control of direct taxes, which involve assessment and close relations with the native population; with legislation and the administration of justice in courts other than the Supreme Court; and with the direct government and welfare of the non-native section of the population.

The departmental staff is charged with duties in connection with transport, communications, and buildings (railways, marine, and public works); with the development of natural resources (mines, collieries, forestry, agriculture, and geology); with the auxiliary services of government (medical, secretarial, accounting, posts and telegraphs, surveys, etc.); and the collection of customs duties.

The task of the administrative branch is to foster that sympathy, mutual understanding, and co-operation between the Government and the people, without which, as Sir C. Ilbert has observed, no Government is really stable and efficient. Its aim is to promote progress in civilisation and justice, and to create conditions under which individual enterprise may most advantageously develop the natural resources of the country. The task of the departments, on the other hand, is to maintain the Government machine in a state of efficiency, and to afford direct assistance in material development. Their motto is efficiency and economy. The two branches work together, and their duties overlap and are interdependent in every sphere. The efficient discharge of those duties in combination constitutes the white man's title to control.

There are in my estimation two vital principles which characterise the growth of a wise administration – they are Decentralisation and Continuity. Though, as Lord Morley said of India, "perfectly efficient administration has an inevitable tendency to over-centralisation," it is a tendency to be combated. It has indeed been said that the whole art of administration consists in judicious and progressive delegation, and there is much truth in the dictum, provided that delegation of duties be accompanied by public responsibility. This is not applicable to the head of the Government alone or in particular, but to every single officer, from the Governor to the foreman of a gang of daily labourers. The man who is charged with the accomplishment of any task, and has the ability and discrimination to select the most capable of those who are subordinate to him, and to trust them with ever-increasing responsibility, up to the limits of their capacity, will be rewarded not only with confidence and loyalty, but he will get more work done, and better done, than the man who tries to keep too much in his own hands, and is slow to recognise merit, originality, and efficiency in others. His sphere of work becomes a training school, and he is able to recommend his best men for promotion to greater responsibility than he himself can confer. The Governor who delegates to his Lieut.-Governors, Residents, and heads of departments the widest powers compatible with his own direct responsibility to the Crown, will witness the most rapid progress.

But delegation to an individual who is not equal to the responsibility obviously means disaster, and it is therefore often advisable to entrust extended powers to the individual rather than to incorporate them as a part of the duties of his office. His successor, who must obviously have less experience, and may or may not be his equal in ability, will not then automatically enjoy the same latitude, until he has proved his capacity in the higher office.

Increased latitude to the individual is not, however, inconsistent with increased delegation of duties to the office, more especially in the administrative branch of the service, where posts must of necessity grow in importance as the country as a whole develops. It is a frequent ground of criticism that the Colonial Office has been somewhat backward in appreciating the value of this principle in these young and rapidly-growing dependencies.

The Governor, by delegating work to others, would seem to lighten his own task, but in point of fact the more he delegates the more he will find to do in co-ordinating the progress of the whole. Moreover, in order to have a right appreciation of the abilities, and of the personal character of each principal administrative officer and head of department, he must be in close personal touch with them, and make absolutely clear to them the essential features of his policy. He must be the directing brain, and leave the execution to others. The task he undertakes is no light one, and if he should be called on to create an administration *ab ovo*, or to lay down new lines of policy in an old one, the work may become more than the time at his command suffices for, and the personal touch with his officers may temporarily suffer from the insistent demands of his office, until he is able gradually to delegate to those in whom he has confidence.

In applying the principle of decentralisation it is very essential to maintain a strong central co-ordinating authority, in order to avoid centrifugal tendencies, and the multiplication of units without a sufficiently cohesive bond. I shall revert to this point when discussing the grouping of colonies.

There are in British tropical Africa several blocks of territory under separate administrations which are contiguous to each other, and the question arises whether it would be more advantageous that they should be placed under a single directing authority, with a single fiscal system, a common railway policy, and identical laws – more especially if one controls the coast area, and the other has no access to the seaboard. Such a process would, of course, be in no way opposed to decentralisation of the machinery of Government. Amalgamation (that is, unification) and federation are both natural processes of evolution, as we have seen in the United States, in Canada, Australia, and South Africa, and more recently in Nigeria. The French have gone even further, and placed colonies widely separated from each other under a central authority. I will deal here only with the question of amalgamation. The federation or grouping of colonies raises a separate issue, which I shall discuss later.

Where one administration comprises the coast area, and collects the customs dues (which have hitherto formed the bulk of the revenue in most African dependencies), while another forms its hinterland, the latter must either establish an inland fiscal frontier, or share the duties collected by its neighbour. The former expedient adds to the cost of all imports – already enhanced by the inherent expense of long and costly transport services (involving a slower turnover of commercial capital), – and is obviously opposed to the progress of trade and development, apart from the heavy cost of the administration of an effective customs and preventive service. The latter course is rendered most difficult by the impossibility of arriving at a division of the customs revenue which will not be resented by both. Imported goods which have paid duty on the coast pass into the hands of native middlemen, and their ultimate destination, by a thousand byways of trade, may be in the hinterland; or the exportable produce for which they are bartered may originate in the interior territory. It is clearly impossible to discriminate with any accuracy in such circumstances between the value and volume of the trade properly belonging to each administration. The Liverpool Chamber of Commerce in July 1893 made strong representations in this sense to Lord Rosebery regarding Nigeria. The French Governor-General, M. Roume, referring to the fiscal reorganisation of the French West African colonies, observed that "it was not right to continue to allow the coast colonies alone to benefit by trade, a large proportion of which was destined for the interior," and Senegal had to make a subsidy to its hinterland.

A hinterland Government has not only to bear heavy transport charges from and to the coast on its imports and exports, but upon it falls the burden of frontier defence. In order to balance its budget it will probably have to depend on a grant from Parliament, paid by the British taxpayer, while the coast Government may have a surplus revenue. A grant-in-aid involves control by the Imperial Treasury – a department which knows nothing of local needs, and is solely concerned in reducing the charges – and the dual control of two departments of State is inimical to all progress.

With an increase of material prosperity, new and disturbing factors arise. An interior administration depends largely for its development on railways and improved waterways, for which capital is required – but loans are not permissible while as yet a country depends on an Imperial grant. Even if sufficient revenue for its needs were raised by taxation, payment of taxes must be largely made in kind, which can only be realised by conveying it to the coast. Some small part may be sold to merchants for cash, but they will not establish themselves, unless means of transport are available.

The organisation and control of railways, waterways, and telegraph lines traversing both territories must of necessity be in the hands of a central administration. It would obviously be inadvisable for one administration to treat the other as foreign territory, and to conclude railway and postal conventions with it in order to exercise separate control over its own section. Increased cost of administration, obstacles to trade, unnecessary accounting, and the certainty of friction must result. A comprehensive and far-sighted railway policy, to which the efforts of both would be consistently devoted, becomes impossible.

When legislation pursues two different channels, differences in policy in regard to native administration, the courts of law, and other vital matters are bound to arise, and it is obviously inadvisable that contiguous communities should be under different systems of taxation, and different penal codes. The evil is accentuated by the fact that the frontiers between the two – often fixed at a time when their geography and ethnology were almost unknown, by lines of latitude and longitude instead of by distinctive natural features – must inevitably intersect tribal boundaries. It goes without saying that a single co-ordinated effort will achieve more for the permanent good of a country than the separate efforts of two administrators, not focussed on a common objective.

Such conditions were applicable to Nigeria, and are still probably applicable to Kenya and Uganda. They were fully described by me in a Memo. dated May 1905; but the amalgamation of Nigeria, though supported by the Governors of the coastal administrations, was not decided upon till 1912, when Mr Harcourt charged me with the task. To administer such enormous territories as East Africa or Nigeria as a single unit, decentralisation is more than ever necessary, but how it can best be effected is not an easy problem.

In the administrative branch the chain of responsibility from the most junior grade to the head of the Government – the District Officer, the Resident of a Province, the Lieut.-Governor – is easily forged, but the departments offer a more difficult problem. If on the one hand each department is under a single head, responsible to the Governor, the tendency is towards a highly-centralised Government, in which the Lieut.-Governors are deprived of initiative and financial control, and there is a danger lest their instructions to the local representative of the department may conflict with those of the departmental head. The Lieut.-Governor for all practical purposes ceases to frame his own budget. On the other hand, the duplication of departmental heads in each area under a Lieut.-Governor involves extra cost, and some loss of technical efficiency and co-ordination. There are, moreover, a number of departments whose functions are indivisible, and they must remain under the direct control of the central authority – such as the judicial, railway, military, etc.

The scheme of amalgamation adopted in Nigeria was designed to involve as little dislocation of existing conditions as possible, while providing for the introduction later of such further changes as were either foreseen, but not immediately necessary, or might be suggested by future experience. They would then be rather in the nature of natural evolution than of reversal. There are twenty-one provinces in Nigeria – exclusive of the Mandate territory in the Cameruns and of the colony proper – each with an average area of 16,000 square miles, and a population of 800,000. To invest each Resident of a province with large powers of autonomy, or at the least to create half a dozen Lieut.-Governorships, would not be a measure of decentralisation but the reverse, for the work arising from each of the separate units – as well as from all the departments – would be centralised in the hands of the Governor. The truest principle of decentralisation was to make the area placed under a Lieut.-Governor so large and important that the officer appointed to its charge could relieve the Governor of all the routine functions of administration, leaving him to direct the general policy, initiate legislation, and control those departments which must necessarily be centralised.

The old northern and southern divisions of Nigeria were retained intact (the colony being a separate entity), and placed under Lieut.-Governors, pending the unification of the laws, the judicial system, and the general policy. It was thought that when the fundamental divergencies in these should have been removed, it would be possible (should the experience gained point in that direction) to create a third Lieut.-Governorship, or to make other changes. The task of amalgamating and re-enacting the statute-books of the two administrations was one which would necessarily take some time.

The difficulty regarding the decentralisation of the departments to which I have alluded was dealt with in the following way. A central secretariat (which would naturally later become the principal secretariat of Nigeria) was set up, while Lieut.-Governors retained their own secretariats. The departments which I have described as necessarily indivisible remained under the Governor and the Central Secretary. The other large departments, such as the Medical and Public Works, were retained in each unit as fully organised entities, and their receipts and expenditure were included in the Lieut.-Governor's budget, but they were placed under the general supervision of an officer senior to both the departmental heads, who, without interfering with the Lieut.-Governor's control, preserved uniformity and technical efficiency, and acted as adviser to Government. Minor departments, such as Police, Education, etc., whose spheres of action do not overlap, remained separate in each unit. Departmental promotion was in all cases to be determined by a common roster.

In fiscal matters the whole of Nigeria became a single entity. All revenue was paid into the common Treasury (a "central" department), and each Lieut.-Governor and the heads of the central departments framed and submitted his own estimates to the Governor, who personally examined them with him, and assigned such funds for new works or for departmental expansion as the requirements of the country as a whole permitted. I shall describe more fully the functions and powers of the Lieut.-Governor and other officers in the next chapter. It suffices to note here that the methods by which it was sought to secure effective decentralisation were (a) by the delegation of executive, financial, and administrative powers to Lieut.-Governors who would exercise responsibility and initiative, and not be merely Deputy-Governors with no executive powers of their own; (b) the administration of native affairs, being regarded not merely as a department, but as the most important duty of the administration, the Resident of a Province was as far as possible relieved of all other administrative duties, in order that he might devote his undivided

time and thought to this work; (c) the authority of its head over a department was unfettered, and subject only to the control of the Governor or Lieut.-Governor, as the case might be. This scheme of amalgamation was adopted in the particular circumstances then existing in Nigeria; and its general principles would of course require adaptation if applied elsewhere, and will require modification to the changing conditions of the development of Nigeria itself. [. . .]

The second of the two principles which I have described as vital in African administration is Continuity, and this, like Decentralisation, is applicable to every department and to every officer, however junior, but above all to those officers who represent the Government in its relations with the native population. The annually recurrent absence on leave, which withdraws each officer in West Africa from his post for about a third of his time, the occasional invalidings and deaths, and the constant changes rendered unavoidable of late years by a depleted and inadequate staff, have made it extremely difficult to preserve in that part of Africa any continuity whatever. The African is slow to give his confidence. He is suspicious and reticent with a newcomer, eager to resuscitate old land disputes – perhaps of half a century's standing – in the hope that the new officer in his ignorance may reverse the decision of his predecessor. The time of an officer is wasted in picking up the tangled threads and informing himself of the conditions of his new post. By the time he has acquired the necessary knowledge, and has learnt the character of the people he has to deal with, and won their confidence, his leave becomes due, and if on his return he is posted elsewhere, not only is progress arrested but retrogression may result.

It is also essential that each officer should be at pains to keep full and accurate records of all important matters, especially of any conversation with native chiefs, in which any pledge or promise, implied or explicit, has been made. It is not enough that official correspondence should be filed – a summary of each subject should be made and decisions recorded and brought up to date, so that a newcomer may be able rapidly to put himself *au courant*. The higher the post occupied by an officer, the more important does the principle become.

It is especially important that the decisions of the Governor should be fully recorded in writing, and not merely by an initial of acquiescence or a verbal order. This involves heavy office work, but it is work which cannot be neglected if misunderstandings are to be avoided and continuity preserved. The very detailed instructions regarding the duties of each newly-created department which were issued when the administration of Northern Nigeria was first inaugurated, served a very useful purpose in maintaining continuity of policy, till superseded on amalgamation by briefer general orders.

In the sphere of administration there are obviously many subjects – education, taxation, slavery and labour, native courts, land tenure, etc. – in which uniformity and continuity of policy is impossible in so large a country, unless explicit instructions are issued for guidance. By a perusal of the periodical reports of Residents, the Governor could inform himself of the difficulties which presented themselves in the varying circumstances of each province, and think out the best way in which they could be met, and could note where misunderstandings or mistakes had been made. By these means a series of Memoranda were compiled, and constantly revised as new problems came to light, and as progress rendered the earlier instructions obsolete. They formed the reference book and authority of the Resident and his staff.

In a country so vast, which included communities in all stages of development, and differing from each other profoundly in their customs and traditions, it was the declared policy of Government that each should develop on its own lines; but this in no way lessens the need for uniformity in the broad principles of policy, or in their application where the conditions are similar. It was the aim of these Memoranda to preserve this continuity and uniformity of principle and policy. Newcomers, by studying them, could make themselves fully acquainted with the nature of the task before them, the problems to be dealt with, and the attitude of Government towards each of those problems. Senior officers were spared the labour and loss of time involved in frequent iteration, when noting any misunderstanding or ignorance in the reports of their subordinates, by simply inviting attention to the pertinent paragraph of the Memorandum. Subversive policies cannot gradually creep in, and any change must be deliberately inaugurated by the formal cancellation of the particular instructions in the Memoranda. Though the preparation of the Memoranda involves considerable labour, they result in an eventual saving in the time both of the Governor and of senior officers. They are the embodiment of the experience of the most capable officers, co-ordinated by the head of the Government, who has access to the reports and is familiar with circumstances of all. When any point of particular difficulty presents itself where opinions are in conflict, and the information insufficient to form a clear judgment on the principles involved, the Governor may perhaps cause a précis to be circulated before a final decision is reached. The little volume of "Political Memoranda" has been of much use in Nigeria. It deals solely with the actual problems of practical administration.

The Statute Book, the Regulations and Orders made under the laws, the General Orders, and the Governor's Memoranda on administrative subjects, contain between them in a readily accessible and compact form the whole structural policy of the Administration, and constitute the "Laws and Usages" of the country. Had such a quartette existed, revised decennially since the earliest origin of our Indian Empire and of our Crown colonies, they would have formed valuable material for the history of the Empire. In Africa we are laying foundations. The superstructure may vary in its details, some of which may perhaps be ill-designed, but the stability of the edifice is unaffected. You may pull down and re-erect cupolas, but you cannot alter the design of the foundations without first destroying all that has been erected upon them.

Important as it is that the British Staff, so long as they are efficient, should remain in the same posts without more interruption than is necessary for the preservation of health, and the prevention of ennui or "staleness," it is of still greater importance that continuity should be maintained in the case of an efficient Governor, who directs the policy of the whole country. For in a rapidly-progressing country policy and legislation are developed from day to day, Regulations and Orders in Council for the carrying out of laws are matters of daily consideration; and in spite of every effort to decentralise and to delegate powers, the Governor has to deal daily with large numbers of Minute papers, each calling for a considered judgment on some problem of sufficient importance for reference to him.

It is above all important that he should be present towards the close of the year, when the estimates are framed in which the programme of material progress – railways, roads, buildings – and increases of staff, etc., are settled. These months, and the first quarter of the new year, are far more important from an administrative and business point of view than the remaining months, which form the rainy season in the tropics north of the Equator. The accounts are completed; annual reports from all departments begin to come in, and must be reviewed; and the yearly report to the Secretary of State, for which they form material, must be compiled. Communications are no longer impeded by washouts, or roads too soft from rain to carry vehicles, and the season permits of travel and inspection. In order always to be present at this season, a Governor in West Africa must take his leave either after eight or after about seventeen months in the country, and so make his absence coincide with the rainy season. By which arrangement will continuity be best preserved?

The seventeen months' tour of service involves a heavy strain. The Governor's absence on completing it would extend over a period of about $6\frac{1}{2}$ months, including voyages, thus seriously encroaching on the working season. During so long a period many matters of first-class importance must be decided without awaiting his return, new legislation must be put through, and even questions of policy may be affected. By so long an absence continuity is seriously sacrificed. Another hand must guide the helm, or there must be a period of stagnation and delay. Important questions await his return, and leave him but little time to read up all that has transpired during his long absence, so that he finds himself wasting precious time in the hopeless endeavour to overtake arrears at a moment of exceptional pressure, or dealing with questions with which he is perforce imperfectly acquainted.

The eight months' period of residential service offers less disadvantage in these respects, and is already applicable to the judges in Nigeria. But even an absence of four months in each year (including voyages) is a distressing break in continuity, if the Governor during this period is wholly detached from his work. It was, however, found necessary by Lord Cromer – though the climate of Cairo or Alexandria is better than that of West Africa, – and I believe he attributed much of his success to his annual holiday. The Governor-General of the Sudan also takes an annual leave, bringing home with him during the rainy season many of his senior officers, and transacting much business for his Government during his time in England. During the absence of Lord Cromer, or Sir R. Wingate, the *locum tenens* could not initiate any new policy or legislation. This was the Foreign Office solution of the problem. The Niger Chartered Company had found it no less necessary for their highest officers (the Agent-General and Chief Justice) to come home yearly, though in their case the administration was directed from London.

After six years' experience in West Africa, during which an exceptionally robust constitution enabled me to adopt the sixteen to eighteen months' period of foreign service, and so to avoid absence at the essential period of the year, I realised very fully its disadvantages, and submitted to Mr Lyttelton, then Secretary of State for the Colonies, a proposal by which I hoped that this lack of conti-

nuity might be overcome, and at the same time a closer touch assured between the Governor and the Secretary of State and commercial interests in England. The proposal was seen by Mr Chamberlain, who had recently left the Colonial Office, and he was inclined to approve it. The principle was also approved by Lord Cromer and other statesmen. Mr Lyttelton declared his intention of giving it a trial in Nigeria.

In brief, I suggested that "the Governor-General (of an amalgamated Nigeria) should spend six months of each year in Africa, and six in England, being on duty and not on leave while at home ... whether in England or in Africa he would remain the sole working head of the administration." The scheme was not cordially accepted by the permanent officials, and did not at that time take effect; but when in 1912 I was invited by Mr (now Lord) Harcourt to undertake the amalgamation of the two Nigerias, he agreed to adopt it on the basis of seven months' residence abroad and five months' absence, including voyages – which I think is better than six and six. With rapid sea passages it might even be eight and four months.

The scheme was in operation for some years, and I doubt whether the task of amalgamation, with the added difficulties of the war, could have been satisfactorily carried through without it. Arrangements had been made so that the rôle of the permanent officials at the Colonial Office should in no way be interfered with by the presence of the Governor, while his residence in England for four months during the rains each year involved an absence from Nigeria no longer, though more frequent, than the normal period of leave. He was in point of fact more closely in touch with his deputy than if he had been travelling in a distant part of Nigeria. His deputy in Africa was vested with full powers to deal with any emergency which might arise, and to carry on routine work.

It was hoped that the arrangement would have beneficial results in relieving the Governor for a period in each year, when he could best be spared, of the burden of routine work, and enable him to devote time to the study of larger problems, and to maintain a close touch with commercial interests in England. For the latter reason it was welcomed by the merchants. It was anticipated also that the Governor's presence in England – not on leave but on duty – might, if duly utilised, prove of value to the home authorities, and minimise despatch-writing.

Under the normal Colonial Office system, the Governor when on leave was rarely consulted, except on a matter of very exceptional importance, and was at liberty to leave England if he desired.

No doubt it was the kindly intention that he should have complete rest. The Acting-Governor was vested with full powers, and for the time being entirely superseded the Governor, and was alone recognised by the Colonial Office. Since the Governor did not see the despatches sent to or received from his Government, he lost all touch, and on his return he had a heavy task to overtake arrears and possess himself of what had transpired in his absence. The Foreign Office, as Lord Lansdowne told the House of Lords, like the French Government, has a different tradition.

Experience did not lessen the hostility of the permanent officials to the scheme. It was, they considered, contrary to all precedent, and even to constitutional usage. This could not indeed be gainsaid, but the experiment could be, and was, legalised like other experiments in Empire Administration, by Letters Patent and Royal instructions. The apprehensions of the permanent officials were not unnatural, for the presence of the Governor at the Colonial Office seemed to threaten the anonymity of the Secretary of State, from which they derived the powers so absolutely essential to the working of the Colonial Office system. [. . .] but in so far as this scheme is concerned, no interference with the functions of the permanent officials was ever contemplated, or alleged while it was in operation. The Governor, though working in close relation with the department, was not part of it, and had no claim to see the Office Minutes.

The primary object of the scheme, as I have explained, was to promote a true continuity of responsibility and control, in lieu of a continuity which was not real. That there is a tendency on the part of an Acting-Governor, vested with the fullest powers, to inaugurate policies of his own, had been the experience of more than one West African colony. It may not go so far as the reversal of legislation – which could be vetoed by the Secretary of State – and it may even be due to misunderstanding rather than to deliberate intention, but the result is equally deplorable.

The practicability of the principle of continuous responsibility of the Governor when absent from his post, and of his annual return to England, must, of course, depend largely on the distance of the colony and the time taken in sea voyages. It is adapted only to a group of colonies under a Governor-General – and the two Nigerias, in size, population, and wealth, might be said to represent such a group – and to colonies within a comparatively short sea voyage of England. A scheme which has been found feasible for West Africa, Egypt, and the Sudan would not be suitable for the Straits Settle-

ments, Ceylon, or Mauritius, unless aviation introduces new possibilities in the future. The French system in West Africa – which I shall presently describe – is not dissimilar.

British public opinion is in favour of trusting the "Man on the Spot," who represents the King, and is held responsible by the nation. If trouble occurs through the action of his deputy, it is the Governor's policy which is blamed. He should therefore have the same control over his deputy when he is in London as he would have were he absent in some distant part of the protectorate, where for all practical administrative purposes he would be less in touch than when in London. But the scheme, as Mr Churchill wittily said, involves an enlarged definition of the "Spot," due to the rapid means of transport and communications which steam and telegraphy have introduced, in order to give effect to the essential principle – control by the man who is held responsible.

No project can, however, be successfully carried out to which one party is consistently opposed, and the scheme has been abandoned, – nor should I have devoted so much space to it were it not that its revival – possibly in some modified form – would certainly in my view be desirable, if the proposal to "group" colonies [. . .] were adopted.

How, then, in the meantime can continuity of responsibility and co-operation best be preserved? It has been said that continuity is maintained by the permanency of the officials at the Colonial Office, whose rôle it is to oppose subversive policy by a new Governor based on insufficient experience, or the assumption of too wide powers by an Acting-Governor. This is, of course, an essential function of the Colonial Office under the present system – a function which, as we have seen, the Foreign Office had been accused of failing to perform in Uganda. The duty of acting as a drag on the wheels may indeed preserve continuity, but it is not necessarily a continuity of progress, and may even produce an attitude of mind tolerant of delays, and hostile to new lines of thought.

If it were made manifest to a Governor on leave that his presence and assistance is welcomed at the Colonial Office; if he saw all correspondence with the Acting-Governor, and were informed of all proposed changes; if the atmosphere of secrecy were exchanged for one of absolute frankness, not only by the seniors but by the juniors of the Office, and he were consulted in matters regarding his sphere of work, and invited to Conferences and Committees; if his period of leave were invariably to coincide with the rainy season – either annually with an absence of three to four months only, or (since conditions in West Africa now admit of longer residence) every alternate year, with a total absence not exceeding six months (say, from mid-March to mid-September); and finally, if the powers of the Acting-Governor were strictly curtailed, and the continuous responsibility of the Governor were officially recognised – much might be done not only to promote continuity, but also to forward the best interests of the country.

In the latter direction clear rules should be laid down and published. The initiation of legislation, the approval of important leases, and the appropriation of any considerable sums unprovided in the estimates, should be reserved to the Governor. His deputy should have no power to cancel or alter existing Regulations, General Orders, or Governor's instructions, or to issue any instructions contrary to these in letter or spirit, or incompatible with the general policy in regard to the native administration. He should not alter the boundaries of provinces, depose or appoint chiefs of the highest rank, alter the permanent distribution of the military forces, or give pledges to merchants or missionaries which involve important principles, without prior reference to the Governor.

The prosperity of a colony, and the welfare of its population, must obviously depend very largely on the character and energy of its Governor. It is therefore of the first importance that the best men should be selected for these posts, and that during their tenure of office the Secretary of State should have frequent opportunities of judging of their ability and sustained energy and enthusiasm.

The work and character of a Governor cannot be gauged by his popularity, or by the hearsay evidence of juniors, or of those whose pecuniary interests may have been affected by measures needed for the good of the country, for they are necessarily inadequately informed. Unpopularity arising from questions of public policy may indeed be a proof of strength of character and of a disinterested sense of duty.

It is manifest that when the right man is in the right place, it is to the benefit of the country that his tenure of office should be prolonged; but in order to avoid the retention of a man who has not come up to the expectations formed of him, or who, though thoroughly capable, is unsuited to the particular post, the period of Governorship should be limited as now to six years (though earlier transfers could, of course, be made), and the extension of this term should carry with it an increase of emoluments, so that the Governor may not suffer in pocket or status, and the extension may be regarded as a recognition of merit. There is a widespread feeling in the senior ranks of the service – the bitterness of which is probably not appreciated in Downing Street – that present methods provide no safeguard against inefficiency, and no guarantee for the selection of the best men.

A Governor is often a married man with a family. In the conditions hitherto prevailing in Africa, except in the eastern Highlands, he must be separated from the latter, even if his wife (probably no longer young) is able to accompany him. The best men, therefore, are apt to look for promotion to a colony which does not necessitate such separations. It is only within the last dozen years that Governors have remained for their full period of office in West Africa. Formerly they rarely remained for more than three years. Continuity again suffers, for Governors appointed from the eastern colonies (as so many have been in West Africa) have much to learn and unlearn before they become familiar with African conditions and African character – so essentially different from those of the East.

In the self-governing colonies limitation of tenure of office has special advantages. Continuity is maintained, not by the Governor-General, but by his ministers. Past controversies are buried with the advent of a new Governor, and the progress of democratic institutions in the Mother Country, and her relations towards the colony, are more accurately represented. The new Governor is, in fact, more up-to-date as the representative of the feelings and changes in Great Britain. In the tropical dependencies the case is otherwise. Personality counts for so much with native races that the departure of a man who has gained their confidence may set the clock back and delay progress – and the same may be said of material development. Given the right man, the longer he stays the better, provided he retains his energy and enthusiasm – as results have proved in Egypt and elsewhere. On the other hand, as decentralisation proceeds, the force of these arguments decreases. Continuity of method and policy is better assured, and the "new blood" which the Colonial Office constantly endeavours to infuse into the colonies has its advantages in bringing new ideas and new experience, and in preventing an administration from becoming limited in its channels of progress under the continued control of the same man.

Continuity may therefore suffer in three ways: first, by the short tenure of his post by a Governor; secondly, by his long absence on leave; and thirdly, by the indefinite powers given to his temporary deputy.

It may be said that as Faith, Hope, and Charity are to the Christian creed, so are Decentralisation,

Co-operation, and Continuity to African Administration – and the greatest of these is Continuity.

Source: Frederick Lugard. *The Dual Mandate in Tropical Africa* (1922). Hamden, CT: Archon Books, 1968. Introduction, pp. 1–7 and chap. V, pp. 94–113.

87   Olive Schreiner: *Trooper Peter Halket of Mashonaland* (1897)

All men made money when they came to South Africa, – Barney Barnato, Rhodes – they all made money out of the country, eight millions, twelve millions, twenty-six millions, forty millions; why should not he!

Peter Halket started suddenly and listened. But it was only the wind coming up the kopje like a great wheezy beast creeping upwards; and he looked back into the fire.

He considered his business prospects. When he had served his time as volunteer he would have a large piece of land given him, and the Mashonas and Matabeles would have all their land taken away from them in time, and the Chartered Company would pass a law that they had to work for the white men; and he, Peter Halket, would make them work for him. He would make money.

Then he reflected on what he should do with the land if it were no good and he could not make anything out of it. Then, he should have to start a syndicate; called the Peter Halket Gold, or the Peter Halket Iron-mining, or some such name, Syndicate. Peter Halket was not very clear as to how it ought to be started; but he felt certain that he and some other men would have to take shares. They would not have to pay for them. And then they would get some big man in London to take shares. He need not pay for them; they would give them to him; and then the company would be floated. No one would have to pay anything; it was just the name – "The Peter Halket Gold Mining Company, Limited". It would float in London; and people there who didn't know the country would buy the shares; *they* would have to give ready money for them, of course; perhaps fifteen pounds a share when they were up! – Peter Halket's eyes blinked as he looked into the fire. – And then, when the market was up, he, Peter Halket, would sell out all his shares. If he gave himself only six thousand and sold them each for ten pounds, then he,

Peter Halket, would have sixty thousand pounds! And then he would start another company, and another.

Peter Halket struck his knee softly with his hand.

That was the great thing – "Always sell out at the right time." That point Peter Halket was very clear on. He had heard it so often discussed. Give some shares to men with big names, and sell out: they can sell out too at the right time.

Peter Halket stroked his knee thoughtfully.

And then the other people, that bought the shares for cash! Well, they could sell out too; they could *all* sell out!

Then Peter Halket's mind got a little hazy. The matter was getting too difficult for him, like a rule of three sum at school when he could not see the relation between the two first terms and the third. Well, if they didn't like to sell out at the right time, it was their own faults. Why didn't they? He, Peter Halket, did not feel responsible for them. Everyone knew that you had to sell out at the right time. If they didn't choose to sell out at the right time, well, they didn't. *It's the shares that you sell, not the shares you keep, that make the money.*

But if they *couldn't* sell them?

Here Peter Halket hesitated. – Well, the British government would have to buy them, if they were so bad no one else would; and then no one would lose. "The British Government can't let British shareholders suffer." He'd heard that often enough. The British taxpayer would have to pay for the Chartered Company, for the soldiers, and all the other things, if *it* couldn't, and take over the shares if it went smash, because there were lords and dukes and princes connected with it. And why shouldn't they pay for *his* company? He would have a lord in it too!

Peter Halket looked into the fire completely absorbed in his calculations. – Peter Halket, Esq., Director of the Peter Halket Gold Mining Company, Limited. Then, when he had got thousands, Peter Halket, Esq., M.P. Then, when he had millions, Sir Peter Halket, Privy Councillor!

He reflected deeply, looking into the blaze. If you had five or six millions you could go where you liked and do what you liked. You could go to Sandringham. You could marry anyone. No one would ask what your mother had been; it wouldn't matter.

A curious dull sinking sensation came over Peter Halket; and he drew in his broad leathern belt two holes tighter.

Even if you had only two millions you could have a cook and a valet, to go with you when you went into the veld or to the wars; and you could have as much champagne and other things as you liked. At that moment that seemed to Peter more important than going to Sandringham.

He took out his flask of Cape Smoke, and drew a tiny draught from it.

Other men had come to South Africa with nothing, and had made everything! Why should not he?

He stuck small branches under the two great logs, and a glorious flame burst out. Then he listened again intently. The wind was falling and the night was becoming very still. It was a quarter to twelve now. His back ached, and he would have liked to lie down; but he dared not, for fear he should drop asleep. He leaned forward with his hands between his crossed knees, and watched the blaze he had made.

Then, after a while, Peter Halket's thoughts became less clear: they became at last, rather, a chain of disconnected pictures, painting themselves in irrelevant order on his brain, than a line of connected ideas. Now, as he looked into the crackling blaze, it seemed to be one of the fires they had made to burn the natives' grain by, and they were throwing in all they could not carry away: then, he seemed to see his mother's fat ducks waddling down the little path with the green grass on each side. Then, he seemed to see his huts where he lived with the prospectors, and the native women who used to live with him; and he wondered where the women were. Then – he saw the skull of an old Mashona blown off at the top, the hands still moving. He heard the loud cry of the native women and children as they turned the maxims on to the kraal; and then he heard the dynamite explode that blew up a cave. Then again he was working a maxim gun, but it seemed to him it was more like the reaping machine he used to work in England, and that what was going down before it was not yellow corn, but black men's heads; and he thought when he looked back they lay behind him in rows, like the corn in sheaves.

Source: Olive Schreiner. *Trooper Peter Halket of Mashonaland.* Chapter 1, pp. 32–6. (Orig. pub. 1897.)

Note

Olive Schreiner (1855–1920) is perhaps best known for her novel *The Story of an African Farm* (1883) and her essay *Woman and Labour* (1911), as well as her association with Havelock Ellis in London. But she was an ardent critic of British designs on her native South Africa, as a result of which she broke off her friendship with Rhodes. With her husband, Samuel Cron Cronwright, she also

wrote *The Political Situation* (1896), which anticipates the outbreak of the second Boer War in 1899.

Her 1897 novel told the story of young Peter Halket, a British soldier in the service of Rhodes's Chartered Company in Mashonaland. The narrative relays an anti-imperialist perspective as the fledgling recruit is obliged to come to terms with the differences between his entrepreneurial aspirations and the means–such as shooting prisoners–toward achieving those ends.

88   Cecil John Rhodes: Last Will and Testament (1902)

THE sixth and last Will and Testament of Cecil John Rhodes is dated July 1st, 1899. To this are appended various codicils, the last of which was dated March, 1902, when he was on his deathbed.

The full text of the Will and its Codicils will only be published when the Will is proved in South Africa.

The following are the substantive passages of the Will so far as they have as yet been given to the public.

The Will begins:

I am a natural-born British subject and I now declare that I have adopted and acquired and hereby adopt and acquire and intend to retain Rhodesia as my domicile.

1   His Burial Place in the Matoppos

I admire the grandeur and loneliness of the Matoppos in Rhodesia and therefore I desire to be buried in the Matoppos on the hill which I used to visit and which I called the "View of the World" in a square to be cut in the rock on the top of the hill covered with a plain brass plate with these words thereon – "Here lie the remains of Cecil John Rhodes" and accordingly I direct my Executors at the expense of my estate to take all steps and do all things necessary or proper to give effect to this my desire and afterwards to keep my grave in order at the expense of the Matoppos and Bulawayo Fund hereinafter mentioned.

I direct my Trustees on the hill aforesaid to erect or complete the monument to the men who fell in the first Matabele War at Shangani in Rhodesia the bas-reliefs for which are being made by Mr John Tweed and I desire the said hill to be preserved as a burial-place but no person is to be buried there unless the Government for the time being of Rhodesia until the various states of South Africa or any of them shall have been federated and after such federation the Federal Government by a vote of two-thirds of its governing body says that he or she has deserved well of his or her country.

2 His Property in Rhodesia

I give free of all duty whatsoever my landed property near Bulawayo in Matabeleland Rhodesia and my landed property at or near Inyanga near Salisbury in Mashonaland Rhodesia to my Trustees hereinbefore named Upon trust that my Trustees shall in such manner as in their uncontrolled discretion they shall think fit cultivate the same respectively for the instruction of the people of Rhodesia.

I give free of all duty whatsoever to my Trustees hereinbefore named such a sum of money as they shall carefully ascertain and in their uncontrolled discretion consider ample and sufficient by its investments to yield income amounting to the sum of £4,000 sterling per annum and not less and I direct my Trustees to invest the same sum and the said sum and the investments for the time being representing it I hereinafer refer to as "the Matoppos and Bulawayo fund." And I direct that my Trustees shall for ever apply in such manner as in their uncontrolled discretion they shall think fit the income of the Matoppos and Bulawayo Fund in preserving protecting maintaining adorning and beautifying the said burial-place and hill and their surroundings and shall for ever apply in such manner as in their uncontrolled discretion they shall think fit the balance of the income of the Matoppos and Bulawayo Fund and any rents and profits of my said landed properties near Bulawayo in the cultivation as aforesaid of such property. And in particular I direct my Trustees that a portion of my Sauerdale property a part of my said landed property near Bulawayo be planted with every possible tree and be made and preserved and maintained as a Park for the people of Bulawayo and that they complete the dam at my Westacre property if it is not completed at my death and make a short railway line from Bulawayo to Westacre so that the people of Bulawayo may enjoy the glory of the Matoppos from Saturday to Monday.

I give free of all duty whatsoever to my Trustees hereinbefore named such a sum of money as they shall carefully ascertain and in their uncontrolled discretion consider ample and sufficient by its investments to yield income amounting to the sum of £2,000 sterling per annum and not less and I direct my Trustees to invest the same sum and the said sum and the investments for the time being representing it I hereinafter refer to as "the Inyanga Fund." And I direct that my Trustees shall for ever apply in such manner as in their absolute discretion they shall think fit the income of the Inyanga Fund and any rents and profits of my said landed property at or near Inyanga in the cultivation of such property and in particular I direct that with regard to such property irrigation should be the first object of my Trustees.

For the guidance of my Trustees I wish to record that in the cultivation of my said landed properties I include such things as experimental farming, forestry, market and other gardening and fruit farming, irrigation and the teaching of any of those things and establishing and maintaining an Agricultural College.

3 Groote Schuur

I give my property following that is to say my residence known as "De Groote Schuur" situate near Mowbray in the Cape Division in the said Colony together with all furniture plate and other articles contained therein at the time of my death and all other land belonging to me situated under Table Mountain including my property known as "Mosterts" to my Trustees hereinbefore named upon and subject to the conditions following (that is to say):

(i)   The said property (excepting any furniture or like articles which have become useless) shall not nor shall any portion thereof at any time be sold let or otherwise alienated.

(ii)   No buildings for suburban residences shall at any time be erected on the said property and any buildings which may be erected thereon shall be used exclusively for public purposes and shall be in a style of architecture similar to or in harmony with my said residence.

(iii)   The said residence and its gardens and grounds shall be retained for a residence for the Prime Minister for the time being of the said Federal Government of the States of South Africa to which I have referred in clause 6 hereof my intention being to provide a suitable official residence for the First Minister in that Government befitting the dignity of his position and until there shall be such a Federal Government may be used as a park for the people.

(iv)   The grave of the late Jan Hendrik Hofmeyr upon the said property shall be protected and access be permitted thereto at all reasonable times by any member of the Hofmeyr family for the purpose of inspection or maintenance.

I give to my Trustees hereinbefore named such a sum of money as they shall carefully ascertain and in their uncontrolled discretion consider to be ample and sufficient to yield income amounting to the sum of one thousand pounds sterling per annum and not less upon trust that such income shall be applied and expended for the purpose following (that is to say) –

(i)   On and for keeping and maintaining for the use of the Prime Minister for the time being of the said Federal Government of at least two carriage horses one or more carriages and sufficient stable servants.

(ii) On and for keeping and maintaining in good order the flower and kitchen gardens appertaining to the said residence.

(iii) On and for the payment of the wages or earnings including board and lodging of two competent men servants to be housed kept and employed in domestic service in the said residence.

(iv) On and for the improvement repair renewal and insurance of the said residence furniture plate and other articles.

I direct that subject to the conditions and trusts hereinbefore contained the said Federal Government shall from the time it shall be constituted have the management administration and control of the said devise and legacy and that my Trustees shall as soon as may be thereafter vest and pay the devise and legacy given by the two last preceding clauses hereof in and to such Government if a corporate body capable of accepting and holding the same or if not then in some suitable corporate body so capable named by such Government and that in the meantime my Trustees shall in their uncontrolled discretion manage administer and control the said devise and legacy.

4   Bequests to Oriel College, Oxford

I give the sum of £100,000 free of all duty whatsoever to my old college Oriel College in the University of Oxford and I direct that the receipt of the Bursar or other proper officer of the College shall be a complete discharge for that legacy and inasmuch as I gather that the erection of an extension of High Street of the College buildings would cost about £22,500 and that the loss to the College revenue caused by pulling down of houses to make room for the said new College buildings would be about £250 per annum I direct that the sum of £40,000 part of the said sum of £100,000

shall be applied in the first place in the erection of the said new College buildings and that the remainder of such sum of £40,000 shall be held as a fund by the income whereof the aforesaid loss to the College revenue shall so far as possible be made good.

And inasmuch as I gather that there is a deficiency in the College revenue of some £1,500 per annum whereby the Fellowships are impoverished and the status of the College is lowered I direct that the sum of £40,000 further part of the sum of £100,000 shall be held as a fund by the income whereof the income of such of the resident Fellows of the College as work for the honour and dignity of the College shall be increased.

And I further direct that the sum of £10,000 further part of the said sum of £100,000 shall be held as a fund by the income whereof the dignity and comfort of the High Table may be maintained by which means the dignity and comfort of the resident Fellows may be increased.

And I further direct that the sum of £10,000 the remainder of the said sum of £100,000 shall be held as a repair fund the income whereof shall be expended in maintaining and repairing the College buildings.

And finally as the College authorities live secluded from the world and so are like children as to commercial matters I would advise them to consult my Trustees as to the investment of these various funds for they would receive great help and assistance from the advice of my Trustees in such matters and I direct that any investment made pursuant to such advice shall whatsoever it may be be an authorized investment for the money applied in making it.

5   The Scholarships at Oxford

Whereas I consider that the education of young Colonists at one of the Universities in the United Kingdom is of great advantage to them for giving breadth to their views for their instruction in life and manners and for instilling into their minds the advantage to the Colonies as well as to the United Kingdom of the retention of the unity of the Empire.

And whereas in the case of young Colonists studying at a University in the United Kingdom I attach very great importance to the University having a residential system such as is in force at the Universities of Oxford and Cambridge for without it those students are at the most critical period of their lives left without any supervision.

And whereas there are at the present time 50 or more students from South Africa studying at the University of Edinburgh many of whom are attracted there by its excellent medical school and I should like to establish some of the Scholarships hereinafter mentioned in that University but owing to its not having such a residential system as aforesaid I feel obliged to refrain from doing so. And whereas my own University the University of Oxford has such a system and I suggest that it should try and extend its scope so as if possible to make its medical school at least as good as that at the University of Edinburgh.

And whereas I also desire to encourage and foster an appreciation of the advantages which I implicitly believe will result from the union of the English-speaking peoples throughout the world and to encourage in the students from the United States of North America who will benefit from the American Scholarships to be established for the

reason above given at the University of Oxford under this my Will an attachment to the country from which they have sprung but without I hope withdrawing them or their sympathies from the land of their adoption or birth.

Now therefore I direct my Trustees as soon as may be after my death and either simultaneously or gradually as they shall find convenient and if gradually then in such order as they shall think fit to establish for male students the Scholarships hereinafter directed to be established each of which shall be of the yearly value of £300 and be tenable at any College in the University of Oxford for three consecutive academical years.

I direct my Trustees to establish certain Scholarships and these Scholarships I sometimes hereinafter refer to as "the Colonial Scholarships."

The appropriation of the Colonial Scholarships and the numbers to be annually filled up shall be in accordance with the following table:

	Total No. Appropriated		To be tenable by Students of or from	No. of scholarships to be filled up in each year
South Africa	24	9	Rhodesia	3 and no more
		3	The South African College School in the Colony of the Cape of Good Hope	1 and no more
		3	The Stellenbosch College School in the same Colony	1 and no more
		3	The Diocesan College School of Rondebosch in the same Colony	1 and no more
		3	St. Andrew's College School Grahamstown	1 and no more
		3	The Colony of Natal in the same Colony	1 and no more
Australasia	21	3	The Colony of New South Wales	1 and no more
		3	The Colony of Victoria	1 and no more
		3	The Colony of South Australia	1 and no more
		3	The Colony of Queensland	1 and no more
		3	The Colony of Western Australia	1 and no more
		3	The Colony of Tasmania	1 and no more
		3	The Colony of New Zealand	1 and no more
Canada	6	3	The Province of Ontario in the Dominion of Canada	1 and no more
		3	The Province of Quebec in the Dominion of Canada	1 and no more
Atlantic Islands	6	3	The Colony of Island of Newfoundland and its Dependencies	1 and no more
		3	The Colony or Islands of the Bermudas	1 and no more
West Indies	3	3	The Colony or Island of Jamaica	1 and no more
Total	60			20

I further direct my Trustees to establish additional Scholarships sufficient in number for the appropriation in the next following clause hereof directed and those Scholarships I sometimes hereinafter refer to as "the American Scholarships."

I appropriate two of the American Scholarships to each of the present States and Territories of the United States of North America. Provided that if any of the said Territories shall in my lifetime be admitted as a State the Scholarships appropriated to such Territory shall be appropriated to such State and that my Trustees may in their uncontrolled discretion withhold for such time as they shall think fit the appropriation of Scholarships to any Territory.

I direct that of the two Scholarships appropriated to a State or Territory not more than one shall be filled up in any year so that at no time shall more than two Scholarships be held for the same State or Territory.

By Codicil executed in South Africa Mr Rhodes after stating that the German Emperor had made instruction in English compulsory in German schools establishes fifteen Scholarships at Oxford (five in each of the first three years after his death) of £250 each tenable for three years for students of German birth to be nominated by the German Emperor for "a good understanding between England Germany and the United States of America will secure the peace of the world and educational relations form the strongest tie."

My desire being that the students who shall be elected to the Scholarships shall not be merely bookworms I direct that in the election of a student to a Scholarship regard shall be had to

(i)   his literary and scholastic attainments
(ii)   his fondness of and success in manly outdoor sports such as cricket football and the like
(iii)   his qualities of manhood truth courage devotion to duty sympathy for the protection of the weak kindliness unselfishness and fellowship

and

(iv)   his exhibition during school days of moral force of character and of instincts to lead and to take an interest in his school-mates for those latter attributes will be likely in after-life to guide him to esteem the performance of public duty as his highest aim.

As mere suggestions for the guidance of those who will have the choice of students for the Scholarships I record that (i) my ideal qualified student would combine these four qualifications in the proportions of three-tenths for the first two-tenths for the second three-tenths for the third and two-tenths for the fourth qualification so that according to my ideas if the maximum number of marks for any Scholarship were 200 they would be apportioned as follows – 60 to each of the first and third qualifications and 40 to each of the second and fourth qualifications (ii) the marks for the several qualifications would be awarded independently as follows (that is to say) the marks for the first qualification by examination for the second and third qualifications respectively by ballot by the fellow-students of the candidates and for the fourth qualification by the head master of the candidate's school and (iii) the results of the awards (that is to say the marks obtained by each candidate for each qualification) would be sent as soon as possible for consideration to the Trustees or to some person or persons appointed to receive the same and the person or persons so appointed would ascertain by averaging the marks in blocks of 20 marks each of all candidates the best ideal qualified students.

No student shall be qualified or disqualified for election to a Scholarship on account of his race or religious opinions.

Except in the cases of the four schools hereinbefore mentioned the election to Scholarships shall be by the Trustees after such (if any) consultation as they shall think fit with the Minister having the control of education in such Colony, Province, State or Territory.

A qualified student who has been elected as aforesaid shall within six calendar months after his election or as soon thereafter as he can be admitted into residence or within such extended time as my Trustees shall allow commence residence as an undergraduate at some college in the University of Oxford.

The scholarships shall be payable to him from the time when he shall commence such residence.

I desire that the Scholars holding the scholarships shall be distributed amongst the Colleges of the University of Oxford and not resort in undue numbers to one or more Colleges only.

Notwithstanding anything hereinbefore contained my Trustees may in their uncontrolled discretion suspend for such time as they shall think fit or remove any Scholar from his Scholarship.

In order that the Scholars past and present may have opportunities of meeting and discussing their experiences and prospects I desire that my Trustees shall annually give a dinner to the past and present Scholars able and willing to attend at which I hope my Trustees or some of them will be able to be present and to which they will I hope from time to time invite as guests persons who have shown sympathy with the views expressed by me in this my Will.

6   The Dalham Hall Estate

The Dalham Hall Estate[1] is by Codicil dated January 18th 1902 strictly settled on Colonel Francis Rhodes and his heirs male with remainder to Captain Ernest Frederick Rhodes and his heirs male.

The Codicil contains the following clause:

Whereas I feel that it is the essence of a proper life that very man should during some substantial period thereof have some definite occupation and I object to an expectant heir developing into what I call a "loafer."

And whereas the rental of the Dalham Hall Estate is not more than sufficient for the maintenance of the estate and my experience is that one of the things making for the strength of England is the ownership of country estates which could maintain the dignity and comfort of the head of the family but that this position has been absolutely ruined by the practice of creating charges upon the estates either for younger children or for the payment of debts whereby the estates become insufficient to maintain the head of the family in dignity and comfort.

And whereas I humbly believe that one of the secrets of England's strength has been the existence of a class termed "the country landlords" who devote their efforts to the maintenance of those on their own property. And whereas this is my own experience. Now therefore I direct that if any person who under the limitations hereinbefore contained shall become entitled as tenant for life or as tenant in tail male by purchase to the possession or to the receipt of the rents and profits of the Dalham Hall Estate shall attempt to assign charge or incumber his interest in the Dalham Hall Estate or any part thereof or shall do or permit any act or thing or any event shall happen by or in consequence of which he would cease to be entitled to such interest if the same were given to him absolutely or if any such person as aforesaid (excepting in this case my said brothers Francis Rhodes and Ernest Frederick Rhodes) (i) shall not when he shall become so entitled as aforesaid have been for at least ten consecutive years engaged in some profession or business or (ii) if not then engaged in

some profession or business and (such profession or business not being that of the Army) not then also a member of some militia or volunteer corps shall not within one year after becoming so entitled as aforesaid or (being an infant) within one year after attaining the age of twenty-one years whichever shall last happen unless in any case prevented by death become engaged in some profession or business and (such profession or business not being that of the Army) also become a member of some militia or volunteer corps or (iii) shall discontinue to be engaged in any profession or business before he shall have been engaged for ten consecutive years in some profession or business then and in every such case and forthwith if such person shall be tenant for life then his estate for life shall absolutely determine and if tenant in tail male then his estate in tail male shall absolutely determine and the Dalham Hall Estate shall but subject to estates if any prior to the estate of such person immediately go to the person next in remainder under the limitations hereinbefore contained in the same manner as if in the case of a person whose estate for life is so made to determine that person were dead or in the case of a person whose estate in tail male is so made to determine were dead and there were a general failure of issue of that person inheritable to the estate which is so made to determine.

Provided that the determination of an estate for life shall not prejudice or effect any contingent remainders expectant thereon and that after such determination the Dalham Hall Estate shall but subject to estates if any prior as aforesaid remain to the use of the Trustees appointed by my said Will and the Codicil thereto dated the 11th day of October 1901 during the residue of the life of the person whose estate for life so determines upon trust during the residue of the life of that person to pay the rents and profits of the Dalham Hall Estate to or present the same to be received by the person or persons for the time being entitled under the limitations hereinbefore contained to the first vested estate in remainder expectant on the death of that person.

After various private dispositions Mr Rhodes in his original will left the residue of his real and personal estate to the Earl of Rosebery, Earl Grey, Alfred Beit, William Thomas Stead, Lewis Lloyd Michell and Bourchier Francis Hawksley absolutely as joint tenants.

The same persons were also appointed executors and trustees.

In a Codicil dated January, 1901, Mr Rhodes directed that the name of W. T. Stead should be removed from the list of his executors.

---

1 Dalham Hall Estate was purchased by Mr Rhodes the year before his death. It is situate in Suffolk, not far from Newmarket, and is 3,475 acres in extent.

In a second Codicil dated October, 1901, Mr Rhodes added the name of Lord Milner to the list of joint tenants, executors and trustees.

In a third Codicil, dated March, 1902, Mr Rhodes appointed Dr. Jameson as one of his trustees, with all the rights of other trustees.

Source: Cecil John Rhodes. *The Last Will and Testament*. Edited by W. T. Stead. London: Review of Reviews Office, 1902, pp. 3–49.

Chapter Sixteen

Crises of Empire-Making: Khartoum, South Africa, and the Congo

Introduction

Even as European imperial control of the African continent and its peoples expanded and was consolidated, it was continually confronted with challenges and crises. From the Anglo-Egyptian Sudan, to southern Africa, to the Congo, indigenous resistance to empire would find supporters in the metropolitan capitals.

Gordon at Khartoum

In late 1883, General Gordon was about to enter King Leopold's service in the Congo, when, abruptly, he was called upon by his own country to embark on a mission to the Sudan. Whether Gordon was the most appropriate choice for such a task was much debated, no less than were the parameters of the mission itself. There was an uprising underway in the Sudan, led by the Mahdi; British interests were at stake; and British and Egyptian lives were at risk. An earlier mission in 1883, led by Colonel Hicks, had met with devastating disaster and death. What was Gordon to do? But how did Gordon understand his orders? And just what were those orders? Evacuation of the city? Defense of the city? The establishment of an orderly government there? Or, as is imputed by some critics to Gordon, was he himself set on nothing less than the determination to "smash the Mahdi"? If there had been a question as to the sending of

Gordon to Khartoum at all, there was even more consternated debate over the decision to rescue him, to send a relief expedition to his aid. For Gordon, it was the second such expedition, his mission, he maintained, having been the first sent in assistance to the city and its inhabitants. In any case, in August 1884, Lord Wolseley was given the orders to pursue such an endeavor of relief – "At last." But Wolseley and his forces arrived "Too late." Khartoum fell to the Mahdist forces in early February 1885 and the Mahdi received the head of Gordon as not the least of the evidence of his success and Britain's catastrophic failure to pursue its imperial policy through the congested corridors of political cavil and public outcry. The Mahdi himself outlived Gordon by only a few months, but it would be more than a decade before Britain retrieved its place of prominence in the Sudan, when General Kitchener's army defeated the Mahdist forces at Omdurman in 1898. From Omdurman, Kitchener, in pursuit of his own illustrious colonial career, would travel south, to join the Anglo-Boer War in South Africa.

The Anglo-Boer War

Fought for nearly three years, from 1899 to 1902, the Anglo-Boer War is perhaps the last of the major imperial wars. As the nineteenth century turned into the twentieth, global powers would prepare instead for world war. In the meantime, the Boer War – variously known as the Anglo-Boer War and the South African War – cost more than £200 million, and the lives of some 22,000 British, 25,000 Boers, and 12,000 Africans. While prosecuted in the name of the British empire in southern Africa, the war effort served no less the interests of international capital and monopoly trade. The war provided as well the extended occasion for a discussion of the controversial concomitants of imperialism, domestic support, foreign interventions, and the settlement of scores, both topographic and demographic. From parliamentary speeches, to poetic renditions, political cartoons, and popular reviews in journals and music halls, the archive of debate was voluminous – and involved such literary luminaries as Rudyard Kipling, Arthur Conan Doyle, and Olive Schreiner, and popularizers like H. Rider Haggard and G. A. Henty. No less significant were the criticisms of the British war practices, from treatment of prisoners of war, the use of dum-dum bullets (explicitly banned by the Hague Convention of

July 1899, to which Great Britain was a signatory), and concentrations camps for women and children. When the war ended, in 1902, the questions still remained of whether South Africa would be joined by a "closer union" – or bound together through federated allegiances.

The Congo Reform Association

Despite early, if sporadic, reports from missionaries and traders, the various accounts of the inhumanity of Leopold's sway over the Congo and its indigenous inhabitants were largely dismissed in European political circles and dispelled by Leopold's own protestations to the benevolence of his African regime and its select representatives. Then, in 1903, Roger Casement submitted his *Congo Report* to the British Parliament. In 1903, following upon concern at Leopold's monopolization of commerce in the region and the obstructions to the "free trade" of other European enterprises, Casement was commissioned by the British Foreign Office to carry out a fact-finding trip up the Congo River. The report that he eventually presented was perhaps more than even his contractors had anticipated, containing as it did appalling narratives and eye-witness accounts of abuse and atrocity rampant in the Congo Free State.

In 1904, then, Casement and E. D. Morel formed the Congo Reform Association. Morel, a Frenchman resident in England, had long been involved in the efforts to right the wrongs being perpetrated in the Congo Free State, working in significant part with H. R. Fox Bourne and the Aborigines Protection Society. Morel's account of *King Leopold's Rule in Africa* (1904) is a passionate denunciation of the state of affairs in the Congo at the time, and expresses as well the frustation of reformers at the persistent recalcitrance of politicians and public opinion alike to recognize the "horrors" being committed there. It was necessary, he determined, to organize a movement that would systematically appeal to and mobilize public indignation and political action. *The History of the Congo Reform Movement*, a work which Morel began in 1910, tells the story of that movement, its strategies of information gathering, modes of presentation, and tactics of appeal that were undertaken in order to challenge Leopold's hold over the territory and peoples of the Congo Free State, a hold which Arthur Conan Doyle would decry in 1905 as nothing less than the "crime of the Congo."

BH

Additional Reading (Gordon at Khartoum)

Allen, B. M. *Gordon and the Sudan*. London, 1931.
Doyle, Arthur Conan. *The Tragedy of the Korosko*. London, 1898.
Farwell, Byron. "The Sudan I: Heroes in Distress," and "The Sudan II: Too Late!," *Queen Victoria's Little Wars* (1972). New York, 1985.
Henty, G. A. *The Dash for Khartoum: A Tale of the Nile Expedition*. London, 1890s.
Holt, P. M. *The Mahdist State in the Sudan*. Oxford, 1958.
Mason, A. E. W. *The Four Feathers*. London, 1901.
Robson, Brian. *Fuzzy-Wuzzy: The Campaigns in the Eastern Sudan 1884–1885*. Tunbridge Wells, 1993.
Wingate, Francis Reginald. *Mahdism and the Egyptian Sudan*. London, 1898.
Wingate, Sir Ronald. *Wingate of the Sudan*. London, 1955.
Zulfo, Ismat Hasan. *Karari: The Sudanese Account of the Battle of Omdurman*. London, 1980.

Films

Ernest Schoedsack and Lothar Mendes. *The Four Feathers* (1929).
Zoltan Korda. *The Four Feathers* (1939).
Terence Young and Zoltan Korda. *Storm Over the Nile* (1955) (remake of the 1939 film).
Basil Dearden. *Khartoum* (1966).
Don Sharp. *The Four Feathers* (1978).

Additional Reading (The Anglo-Boer War)

Amery, L. S. (ed.). *The Times History of the War in South Africa* (7 vols). London, 1900–1909.
Churchill, Winston. *London to Ladysmith via Pretoria*. London, 1900.
Doyle, Arthur Conan. *The Great Boer War*. London, 1900.
First, Ruth and Ann Scott. *Olive Schreiner*. London, 1980.
Greenwall, Ryno. *Artists and Illustrators of the Anglo-Boer War*. Vlaeberg (SA), 1992.
Hobhouse, Emily. *Boer War Letters*, ed. Rykie Van Reenen. Capetown and Pretoria, 1984.
Haggard, H. Rider. *King Solomon's Mines*. London, 1885.
MacBride, Maud Gonne. *A Servant of the Queen*, 1938.
Pakenham, Thomas. *The Boer War* (1979). New York, 1992.
Plaatje, Sol. *Mafeking Diary: A Black Man's View of a White Man's War*, ed. John Comaroff. London, 1990.
Roberts, Brian. *Those Bloody Women: Three Heroines of the Boer War*. London, 1991.
Schreiner, Olive. *Thoughts on South Africa*. 1901.
——. *The Story of an African Farm*. 1883.
——. *Trooper Peter Halket of Mashonaland*. 1897.
Schreiner, Olive and C. S. Cronwright Schreiner. *The Political Situation*. 1896.
South African Conciliation Committee. *Salient Facts from the Camps' Blue Books: the Official Report on the Concentration Camps*. n.d.

Spies, S. B. *Methods of Barbarism? Roberts and Kitchener and Civilians in the Boer Republics January 1900–May 1902*. Cape Town and Pretoria, 1977.
Smith, M. Van Wyck. *Drummer Hodge: The Poetry of the Anglo-Boer War (1899–1902)*. Oxford, 1978.
Witton, Lieut. George. *Scapegoats of the Empire: The True Story of Breaker Morant's Bushveldt Carbineers*. 1907.

Films

Richard Attenborough. *Young Winston* (1972).
Bruce Beresford. *Breaker Morant* (1980).

Additional reading (Congo Reform Association)

Anstey, Roger. *King Leopold's Legacy: the Congo under Belgian Rule 1908–1960*. London, 1966.
Casement, Roger. *The Black Diaries*, ed. by Peter Singleton-Gates and Maurice Girodias. London, 1959.
Cocks, F. Seymour. *E. D. Morel: the Man and His Work*. London, 1920.
Conrad, Joseph. *Heart of Darkness*. London, 1898/9.
Gide, Andre. *Travels in the Congo* (1927/8), trans. Dorothy Bussy. Harmondsworth, 1986.
Inglis, Brian. *Roger Casement* (1973). Belfast, 1993.
Keith, A. Berriedale. *The Belgian Congo and the Berlin Act*. Oxford, 1919.
Morel, E. D. *Great Britain and the Congo*. London, 1909.

Films

Jack Cardiff. *Dark of the Sun* (1968).
Francis Ford Coppola. *Apocalypse Now* (1979).
Frank Marshall. *Congo* (1995).
Leon Gast. *When We Were Kings* (1996).

89   General Gordon: Journal at Khartoum (September–October 1885)

September 10   Colonel Stewart, MM. Power and Herbin, left during the night for Dongola, *via* Berber.

Spy came in from south front, and one from Halfeyeh reports Arabs will not attack, but will continue the blockade.

Sent off two sets of telegrams by a spy, who will go to Shendy.

Yesterday, when the messenger went out to deliver my answer to the Arabs, in response to Mahdi's letter, though he had a white flag, they fired on him, and tried to capture him. They use the white flag, and find it respected by us, and that we let their men go back. They chain any men we send to them.

It is wonderful how the people of the town, who have every possible facility to leave the city, cling to it, and how, indeed, there are hundreds who flock in, though it is an open secret we have neither money nor food. Somehow this makes me feel confident in the future, for it is seldom that an impulse such as this acts on each member of a disintegrated mass without there being some reason for it, which those who act have no idea of, but which is a sort of instinct. Truly I do not think one could inflict a greater punishment on an inhabitant of Kartoum than to force him to go to the Arabs.

Halfeyeh reports that Faki Mustapha, who was in command of the Arabs on the west or left bank of the White Nile, wishes to join the Government. He is informed we are glad of it, but wish him to remain quiet, and to take no active part till he sees how the scales of the balance go; if we rise, then he can act, if we fall he is not to compromise himself; but what we ask him is to send up our spies, which he can do without risk. The same advice was given to the people of Shendy, who wished to issue out and attack Berber.

The runaways of Tuti[1] wish to come back, which is allowed.

The "matches" used for the mines are all finished, and we are obliged to go back to powder hose, and unite the mines in families of ten.

Rows on rows of wire entanglement are being placed around the lines. General Gordon's horse was captured by the Arabs in the defeat of El foun; the other staff horse got a cut on the head, but is now all right.

The Mahdi is still at Rahad.[2] The answer to his letter (*vide* Colonel Stewart's journal) was sent open, so that the Arab leaders could read its contents.

With respect to letters written to the Mahdi and to the Arab chiefs, commenting on the apostacy of Europeans, they may, and are, no doubt, hard, but it is not a small thing for a European, for fear of death, to deny our faith; it was not so in old times, and it should not be regarded as if it was taking off one coat, and putting on another. If the Christian faith is a myth, then let men throw it off, but it is mean and dishonourable to do so merely to save one's life if one believes it is the true faith. What can be more strong than these words, "He who denies Me on earth I will deny in heaven." The old martyrs regarded men as their enemies, who tried to prevent them avowing their faith. In the time of Queens Mary and Elizabeth, what men we had, and then it was for less than here, for it was mainly the

1 Tuti is an island at the junction of the White and Blue Nile.
2 Near El Obeyed and about 200 miles from Kartoum.

question of the Mass, while here it is the question of the denial of our Lord and of his passion. It is perhaps as well to omit this, if this journal is published, for no man has a right to judge another. Politically and morally, however, it is better for us not to have anything to do with the apostate Europeans in the Arab camp. Treachery never succeeds, and, however matters may end, it is better to fall with clean hands, than to be mixed up with dubious acts and dubious men. Maybe it is better for us to fall with honour, than to gain the victory with dishonour, and in this view the Ulemas of the town are agreed; they will have nought to do with the proposals of treachery.

No doubt the letters to the Arabs will make the Arab chiefs work on the Europeans with them, to take an active part against us, by saying to those Europeans, "You are cast out"; but the Arabs will never trust them really, so they can do little against us.

We had a regular gaol delivery to-day, letting out some fifty, and are sending to the Arabs about nine prisoners whom it is not advisable to keep in the town. A donkey quietly grazing near the north fort, exploded one of the mines there (an iron alembic which belonged to the time of Mahomet Ali, and had been used for the reduction of gold; it held some 10 lbs. of powder); the donkey, angry and surprised, walked off unhurt! These alembics are [. . .] braced by iron straps together. It is extraordinary that after a good deal of rain, and three months' exposure, the domestic matchbox should have retained its vitality.

The school here is most interesting, as the scholars get a certain ration. It is always full, viz., two hundred. Each boy has a wooden board, on which his lesson is written, and on visiting it the object of each boy is to be called out to read his lesson, which they do with a swaying motion of body, and in a sing-song way, like the Jews do at the wailing place at Jerusalem and in their synagogues, from which we may infer this was the ancient way of worship, for the lessons are always from the Koran. Little black doves with no pretension to any nose, and not more than two feet high, push forward to say the first ten letters of the alphabet, which is all they know.

We have completed the census [. . .] and have 34,000 people in the town. [. . .]

The Relief Expedition

I altogether *decline* the imputation that the projected expedition has come to *relieve me*. It has *come to SAVE OUR NATIONAL HONOUR in extricating the gar-*

risons, etc., from a position our action in Egypt has placed these garrisons. I was relief expedition No. 1. They are *relief expedition No. 2.* As for myself I could make good my retreat at any moment if I wished. Now realise what would happen if this *first relief expedition* was to bolt and the steamers fell into the hands of the Mahdi: *this second relief expedition* (for the honour of England engaged in extricating garrisons) would be somewhat hampered. We the *first* and *second* expeditions are equally engaged for the honour of England. This is fair logic. *I came up to extricate the garrisons and failed. Earle comes up to extricate garrisons and (I hope) succeeds. Earle does not come to extricate me.* The extrication of the garrisons was supposed to affect our "national honour." If Earle succeeds the "national honour" thanks him and I hope rewards him, but it is altogether independent of me, who for failing incurs its blame. I am not the *rescued lamb,* and I will not be.

I hope the officers and men of Her Majesty's forces will be considerate to the Egyptian soldiers and sailors; *they do not understand English,* but as they have done some good service, I hope they will be kindly treated. They are a trying lot, as I well know, but if it were not for them, our soldiers would have to tramp many a weary sandy mile. It is one of my joys that I never have to see Great Britain again. I hope to get out of this affair, and either go to the Congo, *via* Equatorial Province, or by Brussels. At any rate I shall never have to undergo the worries I underwent during the week I was in England this year. I say this in order that those who may have to do with me may know how very determined a man's will must be who does not wish (and indeed *will not ever*) go back to England again, and to whom continuance in Her Majesty's Service, except for the honour of it, is a matter of indifference.

I am now going to be egotistic, but it will save a mint of trouble, and I may be pardoned, considering the circumstances. By being so I may save myself what I should much regret, a quarrel.

My idea is to induce Her Majesty's Government to undertake the extrication of all people or garrisons, now hemmed in or captive, and that if this is not their programme, then to resign my commission and do what I can to attain it (the object). As long as a man remains in Her Majesty's Service he is bound to obey the orders of his superiors, but if he resigns he cannot be held as insubordinate if he disobeys. Of course it may turn on the question of whether once having entered the service of Her Majesty's Army, one is free to leave it at one's will. But we officers are not like the private soldiers

engaged for a term of years, and perhaps one may risk dismissal if the cause is worthy of it – which, I think, the question of abandoning the garrisons is.

I say this, because I should be sorry for Lord Wolseley to advance from Dongola without fully knowing my views. If Her Majesty's Government are going to abandon the garrisons, then do not advance. I say nothing of evacuating the country, I merely maintain that if we do so, every one in the Soudan, captive or hemmed in, ought to have the option and power of retreat. Having given them that option and power, I have nothing more to say, and I would not care whether the country is evacuated or not.

It is a miserable country, but it is joined to Egypt, and to my idea it would be difficult to divorce the two.

I will end these egotistical remarks by saying that no persuasion will induce me to change my views; and that as to force, it is out of the question, for I have the people with me – at any rate of the towns which hold out. Therefore, if Her Majesty's forces are not prepared to relieve the whole of the garrisons, the General should consider whether it is worth coming up – in his place, *if not so prepared,* I would not do so. I do not dictate, but I say what every gentleman in Her Majesty's Army would agree to – that it would be *mean (coûte que coûte)* to leave men who (though they may not come up to our ideas as heroes) have stuck to me, though a *Christian dog in their eyes,* through great difficulties, and thus force them to surrender to those who have not conquered them, and to do that at the bidding of a foreign Power, to save one's own skin. Why the black sluts would stone me if they thought I meditated such action. Stewart knows all this and used to groan over perversity.

September 30 The Arabs fired seven shells last night at 9 p.m. which fell inside the lines, but did no harm. To-day being Bairam, they fired four rounds in their camp – a salute I suppose.

The spy who came in yesterday, says the report is rife that Seyd Mahomet Osman's men have entered Katarif.

The three steamers will leave here to-day for Shendy at 4 p.m.

[. . .] I believe that a good recruitment of blacks and Chinese would give England all the troops she wants for expeditions, mixed with one-sixth English. As for those wretched Sepoys, they are useless. I would garrison India with Chinese and blacks, with one-sixth English, and no army could stand against us. The Chinese in Shanghai had the greatest contempt for the Bombay Sepoys, and used to knock them about. Beloochees and Sikhs are a different class. I have the greatest contempt for the pure Indian Sepoys. Chinese, or blacks, or Goorkas, or Belochees are far better. The moment he (the pure Sepoy) is off parade, he puts off all uniform that connects him with Her Majesty's Government, and puts on his dish-clout. I hate these snake-like creatures. Any man accustomed to judge by faces sees that they hate us.

I would back the Mussulmans of India against the lot of those snakes. India, to me, is not an advantage; it accustoms our men to a style of life which they cannot keep up in England; it deteriorates our women. If we kept the sea-coast, it is all that we want. It is the centre of all petty intrigue, while if our energy were devoted elsewhere, it would produce tenfold. India sways all our policy to our detriment. Lord Cardwell replied (when I asked him the question as to the benefit we got from India), "*that we could not get out of it*," and I suppose that is the answer that must be given.

October 13   Cavalry sortie this morning from Bourré; captured fifteen slaves and killed thirteen men who resisted. This sortie was under Abdoul Hamid, the Sandjak of the Shaggyeh. We lost none.

The Arabs on Omdurman side have spread out their huts in a semicircle (but at a considerable distance) around Omdurman, on the left bank.

Shaggyeh from Halfeyeh will be in the North Fort to-day. The Arabs off South Front, near the White Nile, fired musketry against the lines, but did no harm.

Last night cavalry Shaggyeh captured three men who were going off to Sheikh el Obeyed from Halfeyeh; they had their arms with them. I have let them go again.

No definite news yet of the arrival of the Mahdi at Omdurman. The Mahdi will be furious with this cavalry sortie; it will be disagreeable news to him on his arrival here.

A man from the Arabs has come in to Omdurman with two letters; it is too late to see them to-night. By telegraph I hear that the man brought two letters for the Commandant at Omdurman from Faki Mustapha, saying the Mahdi was coming the day after to-morrow, and inviting him to submit; so I have told them to send the man off again.

We are a wonderful people; it was never our Government which made us a great nation; our Government has been ever the drag on our wheels. It is, of course, on the cards that Kartoum is taken under the nose of the expeditionary force, which will be *just too late*.

The expeditionary force will perhaps think it necessary to retake it; but that will be of no use, and will cause loss of life uselessly on both sides. It had far better quietly return, with its tail between its legs; for once Kartoum is taken, it matters little if the Opposition say "You gave up Kartoum," or "You gave up Kartoum, Sennaar," etc., etc., the sun will have set, people will not care much for the satellites.

> *Source:* A. Egmout Halle (ed.). *The Journals of Major-General C. B. Gordon, C. B. at Kartoum.* London: K. Paul, Trench and Co., 1885, pp. 3–7, 111–15, 189–91.

90   Queen Victoria: Letters to Mary Gordon (1885)

Osborne, 17 Feb. 1885

Dear Miss Gordon,

How shall I write to you, or how shall I attempt to express *what I feel*! To *think* of your dear, noble, heroic Brother, who served his Country and his Queen so truly, so heroically, with a self-sacrifice so edifying to the World, not having been rescued. That the promises of support were not fulfilled – which I so frequently and constantly pressed on those who asked him to go – is to me *grief inexpressible*! indeed, it has made me ill! My heart bleeds for you, his Sister, who have gone through so many anxieties on his account, and who loved the dear Brother as he deserved to be. You are all so good and trustful, and have such strong faith, that you will be sustained even now, when *real* absolute evidence of your dear Brother's death does not exist – but I fear there cannot be much doubt of it. Some day I hope to see you again, to tell you all I cannot express. My daughter Beatrice, who has felt quite as I do, wishes me to express her deepest sympathy with you. I hear so many expressions of sorrow and sympathy from *abroad*: from my eldest daughter, the Crown Princess, and from my Cousin, the King of the Belgians, – the very warmest. Would you express to your other Sisters and your elder Brother my true sympathy, and what I do so keenly feel, the *stain* left upon England for your dear Brother's cruel, though heroic, fate!

Ever, Dear Miss Gordon,
Yours sincerely and sympathizingly V. R. I.

WINDSOR CASTLE, March 16, 1885
Dear Miss Gordon,

It is most kind and good of you to give me this precious Bible,[1] and I only hope that you are not depriving yourself and family of such a treasure, if you have no other. May I ask you, during how many years your dear heroic Brother had it with him? I shall have a case made for it with an inscription, and place it in the Library here, with your letter and the touching extract from his last to you. I have ordered, as you know, a Marble Bust of your dear Brother to be placed in the Corridor here, where so many Busts and Pictures of our greatest Generals and Statesmen are, and hope that you will see it before it is finished, to give your opinion as to the likeness.

Believe me always, yours very sincerely,
VICTORIA R. I.

Source: Letters of General C. G. Gordon to His Sister Mary Gordon, ed. Mary Gordon. London and New York: Macmillan, 1890, pp. xv–xvi.

---

91   Lytton Strachey: "The End of General Gordon" (1921)

Gordon's last great adventure, like his first, was occasioned by a religious revolt. At the very moment when, apparently for ever, he was shaking the dust of Egypt from his feet, Mohammed Ahmed was starting upon his extraordinary career in the Sudan. The time was propitious for revolutions. The effete Egyptian Empire was hovering upon the verge of collapse. The enormous territories of the Sudan were seething with discontent. Gordon's administration had, by its very vigour, only helped to precipitate the inevitable disaster. His attacks upon the slave-trade, his establishment of a government monopoly in ivory, his hostility to the Egyptian officials, had been so many shocks, shaking to its foundations the whole rickety ma-

chine. The result of all his efforts had been, on the one hand, to fill the most powerful classes in the community – the dealers in slaves and ivory – with a hatred of the government, and on the other to awaken among the mass of the inhabitants a new perception of the dishonesty and incompetence of their Egyptian masters. When, after Gordon's removal, the rule of the Pashas once more asserted itself over the Sudan, a general combustion became inevitable: the first spark would set off the blaze. Just then it happened that Mohammed Ahmed, the son of an insignificant priest in Dongola, having quarrelled with the Sheikh from whom he was receiving religious instruction, set up as an independent preacher, with his headquarters at Abba Island, on the Nile, a hundred and fifty miles above Khartoum. Like Hong-siu-tsuen, he began as a religious reformer, and ended as a rebel king. It was his mission, he declared, to purge the true Faith of its worldliness and corruptions, to lead the followers of the Prophet into the paths of chastity, simplicity, and holiness; with the puritanical zeal of a Calvin, he denounced junketings and merry-makings, songs and dances, lewd living and all the delights of the flesh. He fell into trances, he saw visions, he saw the Prophet and Jesus, and the Angel Izrail accompanying him and watching over him for ever. He prophesied, and performed miracles, and his fame spread through the land.

There is an ancient tradition in the Mohammedan world, telling of a mysterious being, the last in succession of the twelve holy Imams, who, untouched by death and withdrawn into the recesses of a mountain, was destined, at the appointed hour, to come forth again among men. His title was the Mahdi, the guide; some believed that he would be the forerunner of the Messiah; others that he would be Christ himself. Already various Mahdis had made their appearance; several had been highly successful, and two, in mediæval times, had founded dynasties in Egypt. But who could tell whether all these were not impostors? Might not the twelfth Imam be still waiting, in mystical concealment, ready to emerge, at any moment, at the bidding of God? There were signs by which the true Mahdi might be recognised – unmistakable signs, if one could but read them aright. He must be of the family of the prophet; he must possess miraculous powers of no common kind; and his person must be overflowing with a peculiar sanctity. The pious dwellers beside those distant waters, where holy men by dint of a constant repetition of one of the ninety-nine names of God, secured the protection of guardian angels, and where groups of devotees, shaking their heads with

---

1 The Bible here referred to was one used by my Brother for many years, and was his constant companion when at Gravesend, Galatz, and during his first sojourn in the Soudan; it was then so worn out that he gave it to me. Hearing that the Queen would like to see it, I forwarded it to Windsor Castle, and subsequently offered it to Her Majesty, who was graciously pleased to accept it. The Bible is now placed in the South Corridor in the private apartments, enclosed in an enamel and crystal case, called the "St George's Casket," where it lies open on a white satin cushion, with a marble bust of General Gordon on a pedestal beside it.

a violence which would unseat the reason of less athletic worshippers, attained to an extraordinary beatitude, heard with awe of the young preacher whose saintliness was almost more than mortal and whose miracles brought amazement to the mind. Was he not also of the family of the prophet? He himself had said so; and who would disbelieve the holy man? When he appeared in person, every doubt was swept away. There was a strange splendour in his presence, an overpowering passion in the torrent of his speech. Great was the wickedness of the people, and great was their punishment! Surely their miseries were a visible sign of the wrath of the Lord. They had sinned, and the cruel tax-gatherers had come among them, and the corrupt governors, and all the oppressions of the Egyptians. Yet these things, too, should have an end. The Lord would raise up his chosen deliverer: the hearts of the people would be purified, and their enemies would be laid low. The accursed Egyptian would be driven from the land. Let the faithful take heart and make ready. How soon might not the long-predestined hour strike, when the twelfth Imam, the guide, the Mahdi, would reveal himself to the World? In that hour, the righteous would triumph and the guilty be laid low for ever. Such was the teaching of Mahommed Ahmed. A band of enthusiastic disciples gathered round him, eagerly waiting for the revelation which would crown their hopes. At last, the moment came. One evening, at Abba Island, taking aside the foremost of his followers, the Master whispered the portentous news. He was the Mahdi.

[. . .] That Mr Gladstone's motives and ambitions were not merely those of a hunter after popularity was never shown more clearly than in that part of his career which, more than any other, has been emphasised by his enemies – his conduct towards General Gordon. He had been originally opposed to Gordon's appointment, but he had consented to it partly, perhaps, owing to the persuasion that its purpose did not extend beyond the making of a "report." Gordon once gone, events had taken their own course; the policy of the Government began to slide, automatically, down a slope at the bottom of which lay the conquest of the Sudan and the annexation of Egypt. Sir Gerald Graham's bloody victories awoke Mr Gladstone to the true condition of affairs; he recognised the road he was on and its destination; but there was still time to turn back. It was he who had insisted upon the withdrawal of the English army from the Eastern Sudan. The imperialists were sadly disappointed. They had supposed that the old lion had gone to sleep, and suddenly he had come out of

his lair, and was roaring. All their hopes now centred upon Khartoum. General Gordon was cut off; he was surrounded, he was in danger; he must be relieved. A British force must be sent to save him. But Mr Gladstone was not to be caught napping a second time. When the agitation rose, when popular sentiment was deeply stirred, when the country, the Press, the sovereign herself, declared that the national honour was involved with the fate of General Gordon, Mr Gladstone remained immovable. Others might picture the triumphant rescue of a Christian hero from the clutches of heathen savages; before *his* eyes was the vision of battle, murder, and sudden death, the horrors of defeat and victory, the slaughter and the anguish of thousands, the violence of military domination, the enslavement of a people. The invasion of the Sudan, he had flashed out in the House of Commons, would be a war of conquest against a people struggling to be free. "Yes, those people are struggling to be free, and they are rightly struggling to be free." Mr Gladstone – it was one of his old-fashioned simplicities – believed in liberty. If, indeed, it should turn out to be the fact that General Gordon was in serious danger, then, no doubt, it would be necessary to send a relief expedition to Khartoum. But he could see no sufficient reason to believe that it was the fact. Communications, it was true, had been interrupted between Khartoum and Cairo but no news was not necessarily bad news, and the little information that had come through from General Gordon seemed to indicate that he could hold out for months. So his agile mind worked, spinning its familiar web of possibilities and contingencies and fine distinctions. General Gordon, he was convinced, might be hemmed in, but he was not surrounded. Surely, it was the duty of the Government to take no rash step, but to consider and to esquire and, when it acted, to act upon reasonable conviction. And then, there was another question. If it was true – and he believed it was true – that General Gordon's line of retreat was open, why did not General Gordon use it? Perhaps he might be unable to withdraw the Egyptian garrison, but it was not for the sake of the Egyptian garrison that the relief expedition was proposed; it was simply and solely to secure the personal safety of General Gordon. And General Gordon had it in his power to secure his personal safety himself; and he refused to do so; he lingered on in Khartoum, deliberately, wilfully, in defiance of the obvious wishes of his superiors. Oh! it was perfectly clear what General Gordon was doing: he was trying to force the hand of the English Government. He was hoping that if he remained long enough at

Khartoum he would oblige the English Government to send an army into the Sudan which should smash up the Mahdi. That, then, was General Gordon's calculation! Well, General Gordon would learn that he had made a mistake. Who was he that he should dare to imagine that he could impose his will upon Mr. Gladstone? The old man's eyes glared. If it came to a struggle between them – well, they should see! As the weeks passed, the strange situation grew tenser. It was like some silent deadly game of bluff. And who knows what was passing in the obscure depths of that terrifying spirit? What mysterious mixture of remorse, rage and jealousy? Who was it that was ultimately responsible for sending General Gordon to Khartoum? But then, what did that matter? Why did not the man come back? He was a Christian hero, was he? Were there no other Christian heroes in the world? A Christian hero! Let him wait till the Mahdi's ring was really round him, till the Mahdi's spear was really about to fall! That would be the test of heroism! If he slipped back then, with his tail between his legs –! The world would judge.

Source: Lytton Strachey. *Eminent Victorians.* New York: Harcourt, Brace and World, 1921, pp. 265–7, 301–4.

---

92 Olive Schreiner: *An English-South African's View of the Situation* (1899)

If it be asked, why at this especial moment we feel it incumbent on us not to maintain silence, and what that is which compels our action and speech, the answer may be given in one word – WAR!

The air of South Africa is

Heavy with Rumours;

inconceivable, improbable, we refuse to believe them; yet again and again they return.

There are some things the mind refuses seriously to entertain, as the man who has long loved and revered his mother would refuse to accept the assertion of the first passer-by that there was any possibility of her raising up her hand to strike his wife or destroy his child. But much repetition may at last awaken doubt, and the man may begin to look out anxiously for further evidence.

We English South Africans are stunned; we are amazed; we say there can be no truth in it. Yet we begin to ask ourselves, "What means this unwonted tread of armed and hired soldiers on South African soil? Why are they here?" And the only answer that comes back to us, however remote and seemingly impossible, is – WAR!

To-night we laugh at it, and to-morrow when we rise up it stands before us again, the ghastly doubt – war – ! war, and in South Africa! War – between white men and white! *War!* – Why? – Whence is the cause? – For whom? – For what? – And the question gains no answer.

We fall to considering, who gains by war?

Has our race in Africa and our race in England interests so diverse that any calamity so cataclysmic can fall upon us as war! Is any position possible that could make necessary that mother and daughter must rise up in one horrible embrace, and rend, if it be possible, each other's vitals? . . . Believing it impossible we fall to considering who is it gains by war?

There is peace to-day in the land; the two great white races, day by day, hour by hour, are blending their blood, and both are mixing with the stranger. No day passes but from the veins of some Dutch South African woman the English South African man's child is being fed; not a week passes but the birth cry of the English South African woman's child gives voice to the Dutchman's offspring; not an hour passes but on farm and in town and village Dutch hearts are winding about English,

And English about Dutch.

If the Angel of Death should spread his wings across the land and strike dead in one night every man and woman and child of either the Dutch or the English blood, leaving the other alive, the land would be a land of mourning. There would be not one household nor the heart of an African born man or woman that would not be weary with grief. We should weep the friends of our childhood, the companions of our early life, our grand-children, our kindred, the souls who have loved us and whom we have loved. In destroying the one race he would have isolated the other. Time, the great healer of all differences, is blending us into a great mutual people, and love is moving faster than time. It is no growing hatred between Dutch and English South African born men and women that calls for war. On the lips of our babes we salute both races daily.

Then we look round through the political world, and we ask ourselves what great and terrible and sudden crime has been committed, what reckless slaughter and torture of the innocents that blood can alone wash out blood? And we find the blood.

And still we look, asking what great and terrible difference has suddenly arisen, so mighty that the human intellect cannot solve it by means of peace, that the highest and noblest diplomacy falls powerless before it, and the wisdom and justice of humanity cannot reach it, save by the mother's drawing a sword and planting it in the heart of the daughter.

We can find none. And again, we ask ourselves,

Who Gains by War?

What is it for? Who is there that desires it? Do men shed streams of human blood as children cut off poppy heads to see the white juice flow?

Not England! She has a great young nation's heart to lose. She has a cable of fellowship which stretches across the seas to rupture. She has treaties to violate. She has the great traditions of her past to part with. Whoever plays to win, she loses.

Not Africa! The great young nation, quickening to-day to its first consciousness of life, to be torn and rent, and bear upon its limbs into its fully ripened manhood the marks of the wounds – wounds from a mother's hands?

Not the great woman whose eighty years to-night, who would carry with her to her grave the remembrance of the longest reign and the purest; who would have that when the nations gather round her bier the whisper should go round, "That was a mother's hand; it struck no child."

Not the brave English soldier; there are no laurels for him here. The dying lad with hands fresh from the plough; the old man tottering to the grave, who seizes up the gun to die with it; the simple farmer who as he falls hears yet his wife's last whisper, "For freedom and our land!" and dies hearing it – these men can bind no laurels on a soldier's brow! They may be shot, not conquered – fame rests with men. Go, gallant soldiers, and defend the shores of that small island that we love; there are no laurels for you here!

Who Gains by War?

Not we the Africans, whose hearts are knit to England. We love all. Each hired soldier's bullet that strikes down a South African does more; it finds a billet here in our hearts. It takes one African's life – in another it kills that which will never live again.

Who Gains by War?

There are some who *think* they gain! In the background we catch sight of misty figures; we know the old tread; we hear the rustle of paper passing from hand to hand, and we know the fall of gold; it is an old familiar sound in Africa; we know it now! There are some who *think* they gain! Will they gain?

But it may be said, "What matter who goads England on, or in whose cause she undertakes war against Africans; this at least is certain that she can win. We have the ships, we have the men, we have the money."

We answer, "Yes, might generally conquers – for a time at least." The greatest empire upon earth, on which the sun never sets, with its five hundred million subjects may rise up in its full majesty of power and glory, and crush those thirty thousand farmers. It may not be a victory, but at least it will be a slaughter. We ought to win. We have the ships, we have the men, and we have the money. May there not be something else we need? The Swiss had it when they fought with Austria; the three hundred had it at Thermopylæ though not a man was saved; it goes to make a victory. Is it worth fighting if we have not got it?

I suppose there is no man who to-day loves his country who has not perceived that in the life of the nation, as in the life of the individual, the hour of external success may be the hour of irrevocable failure, and that the hour of death, whether to nations or individuals, is often the hour of immortality. When William the Silent, with his little band of Dutchmen, rose up to face the whole empire of Spain, I think there is no man who does not recognise that the hour of their greatest victory was not when they had conquered Spain, and hurled backward the greatest empire of the world to meet its slow, imperial death; it was the hour when that little band stood alone with the waters over their homes,

Facing Death and Despair,

and stood facing it. It is that hour that has made Holland immortal, and her history the property of all human hearts.

It may be said, "But what has England to fear in a campaign with a country like Africa? Can she not send out a hundred thousand or a hundred and fifty thousand men and walk over the land? She can sweep it by mere numbers." We answer yes – she might do it. Might generally conquers; not always. I have seen a little *meer-kat* attacked by a mastiff, the first joint of whose leg it did not reach. I have seen it taken in the dog's mouth, so that hardly any part of it was visible, and thought the creature was dead. But it fastened its tiny teeth inside the dog's throat, and the mastiff dropped it, and mauled and wounded and covered with gore and saliva, I saw it creep back to its hole in the red African earth. But might generally conquers, and there is no doubt that England might send out sixty or a hundred thousand hired soldiers to South Africa, and they could bombard our towns and destroy our villages; they could shoot down men in the prime of life, and old men and boys, till there was hardly a kopje in the country without its stain of blood, and the Karoo bushes grew up greener on the spot where men from the midlands who had come to help their fellows fell, never to go home. I suppose it would be quite possible for the soldiers to shoot all male South Africans who appeared in arms against them. It might not be easy, a great many might fall, but a great Empire could always import more to take their places; *we* could not import more, because it would be our husbands and sons and fathers who were falling, and when they were done we could not produce more. Then the war would be over. There would not be a house in Africa – where African-born men and women lived – without its mourners, from Sea Point to the Limpopo; but South Africa would be pacified – as Cromwell pacified Ireland three centuries ago, and she has been being pacified ever since! As Virginia was pacified in 1677: its handful of men and women in defence of their freedom were soon silenced by hired soldiers. "I care that for the power of England," said "a notorious and wicked rebel" called Sarah Drummond, as she took a small stick and broke it and lay it on the ground. A few months later her husband and all the men with him were made prisoners, and the war was over. "I am glad to see you," said Berkely, the English Governor, "I have long wished to meet you; you will be hanged in half an hour!" and he was hanged and twenty-one others with him, and Virginia was pacified. But a few generations later in that State of Virginia was born George Washington, and on the 19th of April, 1775, was fought the battle of Lexington – "Where once the embattled farmers stood, and fired a shot, heard round the world," – and the greatest crime and the greatest folly of England's career was completed. England acknowledges it now. A hundred or a hundred and fifty thousand imported soldiers might walk over South Africa: it would not be an easy walk, but it could be done. Then from east and

west and north and south would come men of pure English blood to stand beside the boys they had played with at school and the friends they had loved; and a great despairing cry would rise from the heart of Africa. But we are still few. When the war was over the imported soldiers might leave the land – not all. Some must be left to keep the remaining people down. There would be quiet in the land. South Africa would rise up silently, and count her dead, and bury them. She would know the places where she found them. South Africa would be peaceful. There would be silence, the silence of a long exhaustion – but not peace! Have the dead no voices? In a thousand farmhouses black-robed women would hold memory of the count, and outside under African stones would lie the African men to whom South African women gave birth under our blue sky. There would be a silence, but no peace.

You say that all the fighting men in arms might have been shot. Yes, but what of the women? If there were left but five thousand pregnant South African born women, and all the rest of their people destroyed, those women would breed up again a race like to the first.

Oh, Lion Heart of the North,

do you not recognise your own lineage in these whelps of the South, who cannot live if they are not free?

The grandchildren and great-grandchildren of the men who lay under the stones (who will not be English then nor Dutch, but only Africans), will say as they pass those heaps, "There lie our fathers, or great-grandfathers, who died in the first great war of independence," and the descendants of the men who lay there will be the aristocracy of Africa. Men will count back to them and say: My father or my great-grandfather lay in one of those graves. We shall know no more of Dutch or English then; we shall know only the great African people. And *we*? We, the South Africans of to-day, who are still English, who have been proud to do the smallest good so that it might bring honour to England, who have vowed our vows on the honour of Englishmen, and by the faith of Englishmen, What of us?

What of us? We, too, have had our vision of Empire. We have seen as in a dream the Empire of England as a great banyan tree; silently with the falling of the dew and the dropping of the rain it has extended itself; its branches have dropped down and rooted themselves in the earth; in it all the fowl of heaven have taken refuge, and under its shade all the beast of the field have lain down to rest. Can we change it for an upas tree, whose leaves distil poison and which spells death to those who have lain down in peace under its shadow?

You have no right to take our dream from us; you have no right to kill our faith! Of all the sins England will sin if she makes war on South Africa, the greatest will be towards us.

Of what importance is honour and faith we have given her? You say, we are but few! Yes, we are few; but all the gold of Witwatersrand would not buy one throb of that love and devotion we have given her.

Do not think that when imported soldiers walk across South African plains to take the lives of South African men and women that it is only African sand and African bushes that are cracking beneath their tread; at each step they are breaking the fibres, invisible as air but strong as steel, which bind the hearts of South Africans to England. Once broken they can never be made whole again; they are living things; broken they will be dead. Each bullet which a soldier sends to the heart of a South African to take his life wakes up another who did not know he was an African. You will not kill us with your Lee-Metfords; you will make us. There are men who do not know they love a Dutchman, but the first three hundred that fall, they will know it.

Do not say, "But you are English, you have nothing to fear; we have no war with you!" There are hundreds of us, men and women who have loved England; we would have given our lives for her; but rather than strike down one South African man fighting for freedom, we would take this right hand and hold it in the fire, till nothing was left of it but a charred and blackened bone.

I know of no more graphic image in the history of the world than

The Figure of Franklin

when he stood before the Lords of Council in England, giving evidence, striving, fighting to save America for England. Browbeaten, flouted, jeered at by the courtiers, his words hurled back at him, as lies, he stood there fighting for England. England recognises now that it was he who tried to save an empire for her, and that the men who flouted and browbeat him lost it. There is nothing more pathetic than the way in which Americans who loved England, Washington and Franklin, strove to keep the maiden vessel moored close to the mother's side, bound by the bonds of love and sympathy, that alone could bind them. Their hands were beaten down, bruised and bleeding, wounded by the very men they came to save till they let go the mother ship and drifted away on their own great imperial course across the seas of time.

England knows now what those men strove to do for her, and the names of Washington and Franklin will ever stand high in honour where the English tongue is spoken; the names of Hutchinson, and North, and Grafton are not forgotten also; it might be well for them if they were!

Do not say to us: "You Englishmen, when the war is over, you can wrap the mantle of our imperial glory round you and walk about boasting that the victory is yours."

We could never wrap that mantle round us again. We have worn it with pride. We could never wear it then. There would be blood upon it, and the blood would be our brothers'.

We put it to the men of England. In that day where should we be found – we who have to maintain English honour in the South? Judge for us, and by your judgment we will abide. Remember, we are Englishmen!

Looking around to-day along the somewhat overclouded horizon of South African life, one figure strikes the eye, new to the circle of our existence here; and we eye it with something of that hope and sympathy with which a man is bound to view the new and unknown, which may be of vast possible good and beauty. What have we in this man, who represents English honour and English wisdom in South Africa? To a certain extent we know.

We have a man honourable in the relations of personal life, loyal to friend, and above all charm of gold; wise with the knowledge of books and men; a man who could not violate a promise or strike in the dark. This we know we have, and it is much to know this; but what have we more?

The man of whom South Africa has need to-day to sustain England's honour and her empire of the future is a man who must possess more than the knowledge and wisdom of the intellect.

When a woman rules the household with none but the children of her own body in it, her task is easy; let her obey nature, and she will not fail. But the woman who finds herself in a large, strange household, where children and step-children are blended, and where all have passed the stage of childhood and have entered on that stage of adolescence where coercion can no more avail, but where sympathy and comprehension are the more needed, that woman has need of large and rare qualities springing more from the heart than from the head. She who can win the love of her strange household in its adolescence will keep its loyalty and sympathy when adult years are reached, and will be rich indeed.

There have been Englishmen in Africa who had those qualities. Will

This New Englishman of Ours

evince them and save an empire for England and heal South Africa's wounds? Are we asking too much when we turn our eyes with hope to him?

Further off also, across the sea, we look with hope. The last of the race of great statesmen was not put into the ground with the old man of Hawarden; the great breed of Chatham and Burke is not extinct; the hour must surely bring forth the man.

We look further, yet with confidence, from the individual to the great heart of England, the people. The great fierce freedom-loving heart of England is not dead yet. Under a thin veneer of gold we still hear it beat. Behind the shrivelled and puny English Hyde, who cries only "gold," rises the great English Jekyll, who cries louder yet "Justice and honour." We appeal to him; history shall not repeat itself.

Nearer home, we turn to one whom all South Africa are proud of, and we would say to Paul Kruger, "Great old man, first but not last of South Africa's great line of rulers, you have shown us you could fight for freedom; show us you can win peace. On the foot of that great statue which in the future the men and women of South Africa will raise to you let this stand written, 'This man loved freedom, and fought for it; but his heart was large; he could forget injuries and deal generously.'"

And to our fellow Dutch South Africans, whom we have learnt to love so much during the time of stress and danger, we would say: "Brothers, you have shown the world that you know how to fight, show it you know how to govern; forget the past; in that Great Book which you have taken for your guide in life, turn to Leviticus, and read there in the 19th chapter, 34th verse; Be strong, be fearless, be patient. We would say to you in the words of the wise dead President of the Free State which have become the symbol of South Africa, 'Wacht een bietje, alles zal recht kom.'" (Wait a little, all will come right.)

On our great African flag let us emblazon these words, never to take them down, 'FREEDOM, JUSTICE, LOVE"; great are the two first, but without the last they are not complete.

Source: Olive Schreiner. *An English-South African's View of the Situation.* London: Hazell, Watson, and Viney, Ltd, 1899, pp. 75–96.

93 Emily Hobhouse: "Report of a Visit to the Camps of Women and Children in the Cape and Orange River Colonies" (1901)

As I have been acting as your delegate in South Africa I am anxious to submit to you without delay some account of the Camps in which the women and children are concentrated, and to put before you the need for further effort on their behalf. By the kind permission of Lord Milner and Lord Kitchener I have been enabled to visit a certain number of these Camps, investigate the needs of the people and arrange for the partial administration of the Fund with which you entrusted me.

Considering the changing condition of the Camps, it is hardly possible to draw up an ordinary conventional report. It would seem better to place before you what was written down day by day, as it was seen and as it happened. Here and there footnotes point out alterations or improvements of later date. By this means some faint picture may be presented to your minds of what is being undergone by the weaker members of two whole countries. Some suggestions are appended which, if adopted, would go far, in my opinion, to alleviate the conditions of life in the Camps during the months or years they may be maintained. – I have, etc.,

E. HOBHOUSE

January 22nd

"I had a splendid truck given me at Capetown, through the kind co-operation of Sir Alfred Milner – a large double-covered one, capable of holding 12 tons. I took £200 worth of groceries, besides all the bales of clothing I could muster. The truck left Capetown the day before myself, was hitched on to my train at De Aar, and so arrived when I did. The first thing next day was to go down to the goods station, claim the truck, and arrange for its unloading. This morning I have spent arranging all my stores – unpacking and sorting them. It is very hot. I think the essence of delightful work is when you quite forget you have a body, but here the heat keeps you in constant recollection that you are still in the flesh, and it's a great hindrance. I did not have a bad journey from Capetown, though it was rather a lonely one. Going through the Karoo it was very hot, and the second day there were horrible dust-storms, varied by thunder-storms. The sand penetrated through closed windows and doors, filled eyes and ears, turned my hair red and covered everything like a table-cloth. As far as extent and sweep of land and sky go the Karoo is delightful, but it's a vast solitude, and in many parts the very plants grow two or three yards apart, as if they shunned society. From Colesberg on it was a desolate outlook. The land seemed dead and silent as far as eye could reach, absolutely without life, only carcases of horses, mules, and cattle, with a sort of acute anguish in their look, and bleached bones and refuse of many kinds. I saw a few burnt farms, but those unburnt seemed still and lifeless also, and no work is going on in the fields. Really, the line the whole way up is a string of Tommies, yawning at their posts, and these always crowded to the carriage windows to beg for newspapers, or anything, they said, to pass the time. I gave them all I had, and all my novels. . . . But I must pass on to tell you about the Women's Camp, which, after all, is the central point of interest."

The Bloemfontein Camp

January 26th

The exile camp here is a good two miles from the town, dumped down on the southern slope of a kopje, right out on to the bare brown veldt, not a vestige of a tree in any direction, nor shade of any description. It was about four o'clock of a scorching afternoon when I set foot in the camp, and I can't tell you what I felt like, so I won't try.

I began by finding a woman whose sister I had met in Capetown. It is such a puzzle to find your way in a village of bell tents, no streets or names or numbers. There are nearly 2,000 people in this one camp, of which some few are men – they call them "hands up" men – and over 900[1] children.

Imagine the heat outside the tents, and the suffocation inside! We sat on their khaki blankets, rolled up, inside Mrs B.'s tent; and the sun blazed through the single canvas, and the flies lay thick and black on everything; no chair, no table, nor any room for such; only a deal box, standing on its end, served as a wee pantry. In this tiny tent live Mrs B.'s five children (three quite grown up) and a little Kaffir servant girl. Many tents have more occupants. Mrs P. came in, and Mrs R. and others, and they told me their stories, and we cried together, and even laughed together, and chatted bad Dutch

and bad English all the afternoon. On wet nights the water streams down through the canvas and comes flowing in, as it knows how to do in this country, under the flap of the tent, and wets their blanket as they lie on the ground. While we sat there a snake came in. They said it was a puff adder, very poisonous, so they all ran out, and I attacked the creature with my parasol. I could not bear to think the thing should be at large in a community mostly sleeping on the ground. After a struggle I wounded it, and then a man came with a mallet and finished it off.

Mrs P. is very brave and calm. She has six children, ranging from fifteen down to two years, and she does not know where any one of them is.[2] She was taken right away from them; her husband is in detention of some kind at Bloemfontein, but not allowed to see her. She expects her confinement in about three weeks, and yet has to lie on the bare ground till she is stiff and sore, and she has had nothing to sit on for over two months, but must squat on a rolled-up blanket. I felt quite sure you would like her to have a mattress, and I asked her if she would accept one. She did so very gratefully, and I did not rest yesterday till I got one out to her. All her baby linen was in readiness at home, but all is lost. This is but one case, quite ordinary, among hundreds and hundreds. The women are wonderful. They cry very little and never complain. The very magnitude of their sufferings, indignities, loss and anxiety seems to lift them beyond tears. These people, who have had comfortable, even luxurious homes, just set themselves to quiet endurance and to make the best of their bare and terrible lot; only when it cuts afresh at them through their children do their feelings flash out. Mrs M., for instance. She has six children in camp, all ill, two in the tin hospital with typhoid, and four sick in the tent. She also expects her confinement soon. Her husband is in Ceylon. She has means, and would gladly provide for herself either in town or in the Colony, where she has relations, or by going back to her farm. It was not burnt, only the furniture was destroyed; yet here she has to stay, watching her children droop and sicken. For their sakes she did plead with tears that she might go and fend for herself.

I call this camp system a wholesale cruelty. It can never be wiped out of the memories of the people. It presses hardest on the children. They droop in the terrible heat, and with the insufficient, unsuitable food; whatever you do, whatever the

1 These numbers are now nearly doubled.

2 Three months later – Mrs P. has been rejoined to all her children, except two.

authorities do, and they are, I believe, doing their best with very limited means, it is all only a miserable patch upon a great ill. Thousands, physically unfit, are placed in conditions of life which they have not strength to endure. In front of them is blank ruin. There are cases, too, in which whole families are severed and scattered, they don't know where.

Will you try, somehow, to make the British public understand the position, and force it to ask itself what is going to be done with these people? There must be full 15,000[3] of them; I should not wonder if there are not more. Some few have means, but more are ruined, and have not a present penny. In one of two ways must the British public support them, either by taxation through the authorities, or else by voluntary charity.

If the people at home want to save their purses (you see, I appeal to low motives), why not allow those who can maintain themselves to go to friends and relatives in the Colony? Many wish ardently to do so. That would be some relief. If only the English people would try to exercise a little imagination – picture the whole miserable scene. Entire villages and districts rooted up and dumped in a strange, bare place.

To keep these Camps going is murder to the children. Still, of course, by more judicious management they could be improved; but, do what you will, you can't undo the thing itself.

To-day is Sunday, and all the day I have been toiling and moiling over the bales of clothes – unpacking, sorting, and putting up in bundles. We were so glad of such odd things, such as stays and little boys' braces! I found some baby linen for Mrs P. I do not think that there is a single superfluous article. But what a family to clothe!

Now I must tell you their rations: –

Daily:
Meat, $\frac{1}{2}$lb (with bone and fat).
Coffee, 2 oz.
Wholemeal, $\frac{3}{4}$lb.
Condensed milk, one-twelfth of tin.
Sugar, 2 oz.
Salt, $\frac{1}{2}$oz.

That is all, nothing else to fill in. Once they sometimes had potatoes, seven potatoes for seven people, but that has long been impossible. Soap also has been unattainable, and none given in the rations.[4] Some people have money, and may add to the above by purchasing certain things at some little retail shops allowed in the Camp, which charge exorbitant prices,[5] for instance, 6d. for a reel of cotton. But they are, naturally, terribly afraid of parting with their money, feeling it is all they will have to begin life on again, for every one's income is stopped, nothing is coming in. It is, indeed, a dreary prospect. Some few of those who had cash in hand buried it out on their farms for safety, and now, of course, cannot reach it. All say, if released, they would make a living somehow, and shelter beneath the ruined home would be as good as these often rotten tents. It is hard enough that, but countless children's lives would be saved thereby.

We have much typhoid, and are dreading an outbreak, so I am directing my energies to getting the water of the Modder River boiled. As well swallow typhoid germs whole as drink that water – so say doctors. Yet they cannot boil it all, for – first, fuel is very scarce; that which is supplied weekly would not cook a meal a day, and they have to search the already bare kopjes for a supply. There is hardly a bit to be had. Second, they have no extra utensil to hold the water when boiled. I propose, therefore, to give each tent another pail or crock, and get a proclamation issued that all drinking water must be boiled. It will cost nearly £50 to do this, even if utensils are procurable.

In spite of small water supply, and it is very spare, all the tents I have been in are exquisitely neat and clean, except two, and they were ordinary, and such limitations!

January 31st
I suggested a big railway boiler[6] to boil every drop of water before it is served out. This would economise fuel, and be cheaper in the long run, besides ensuring the end desired, for many could not be trusted to boil their own. Next we want forage for the cows. Fifty have been secured, but they only get four buckets of milk out of the poor starved things.[7] What is needed is a wash-house with water laid on from the town, but I see no chance of it. Some people in town still assert that the Camp is a

3 Of course the numbers are now largely increased, over 20,000 in Orange River Colony alone; 25,000 in Transvaal camps, besides the Colony and Natal.

4 With much persuasion and weeks after requisitioning, soap is now given in occasionally in very minute quantities – certainly not enough for clothes and personal washing.
5 In some camps steps are now taken to prevent exorbitant charges in these shops in certain articles.
6 None could be had, so the Government built furnaces and tanks. When the camp doubled this would not supply sufficient, so I left money to put up another.
7 Forage was refused being too precious. After the rains the milk supply was better.

haven of bliss. Well, there are eyes and no eyes. I was at the camp to-day, and just in one little corner this is the sort of thing I found. The nurse, under-fed and overworked, just sinking on to her bed, hardly able to hold herself up, after coping with some thirty typhoid and other patients, with only the untrained help of two Boer girls – cooking as well as nursing to do herself.

Next, I was called to see a woman panting in the heat, just sickening for her confinement. Fortunately, I had a night-dress in my bundle to give her, and two tiny baby gowns.

Next tent, a six months' baby gasping its life out on its mother's knee. The doctor had given it powders in the morning, but it had taken nothing since. Two or three others drooping and sick in that tent.

Next, child recovering from measles, sent back from hospital before it could walk, stretched on the ground, white and wan; three or four others lying about.

Next, a girl of twenty-one lay dying on a stretcher. The father, a big, gentle Boer, kneeling beside her; while, next tent, his wife was watching a child of six, also dying, and one of about five drooping. Already this couple had lost three children in the hospital, and so would not let these go, though I begged hard to take them out of the hot tent. "We must watch these ourselves," he said. I sent _____ to find brandy, and got some down the girl's throat, but for the most part you must stand and look on, helpless to do anything, because there is nothing to do anything with.

Then a man came up and said: "Sister" (they call me "Sister," or "Di Meisie van England"), "come and see my child, sick for nearly three months." It was a dear little chap of four, and nothing left of him but his great brown eyes and white teeth, from which the lips were drawn back, too thin to close. His body was emaciated. The little fellow had craved for fresh milk; but, of course, there had been none till these last two days, and now the fifty cows only give four buckets, so you can imagine what feed there is for them. I sent — for some of this, and made him lay the child outside on a pillow to get the breeze that comes up at sunset. I can't describe what it is to see these children lying about in a state of collapse. It's just exactly like faded flowers thrown away. And one has to stand and look on at such misery, and be able to do almost nothing.

Source: Emily Hobhouse. *Report of a Visit to the Camps of Women and Children in the Cape and Orange River Colonies.* London: Committee of the South African Distress Fund, 1901, pp. 3–5.

Note

Emily Hobhouse (1860–1926) was secretary to the South African Conciliation Committee (formed in November 1899). She visited South Africa in 1900 and reported to the Committee of the Distress Fund for South African Women and Children on the atrocities against the Boers held in British concentration camps. Having outraged political opinion in England by her writing and speaking, she was forcibly prevented from entering South Africa when she attempted to visit again in 1901.

94   Arthur Conan Doyle: "Further Charges Against British Troops" (1902)

Expansive and Explosive Bullets

When Mr Stead indulges in vague rhetoric it is difficult to corner him, but when he commits himself to a definite statement he is more open to attack. Thus, in his "Methods of Barbarism" he roundly asserts that "England sent several million rounds of expanding bullets to South Africa, and in the North of the Transvaal and at Mafeking for the first three months of the war no other bullets were used." Mr Methuen, on the authority of a letter of Lieutenant de Montmorency, R.A., states also that from October 12, 1899, up to January 15, 1900, the British forces north of Mafeking used nothing but Mark IV ammunition, which is not a dum-dum but is an expansive bullet.

Mr Methuen's statement differs, as will be seen, very widely from Mr Stead's; for Mr Stead says Mafeking, and Mr Methuen says north of Mafeking. There was a very great deal of fighting at Mafeking, and comparatively little north of Mafeking during that time, so that the difference is an essential one. To test Mr Stead's assertion about Mafeking, I communicated with General Baden-Powell, the gentleman who is most qualified to speak as to what occurred there, and his answer lies before me: "We had no expanding bullets in our supply at Mafeking, unless you call the ordinary Martini-Henry an expanding bullet. I would not have used them on humane principles, and more-over, an Army order had been issued against the use of dum-dum bullets in this campaign. On the other hand, explosive bullets are expressly forbidden in the Convention, and these the Boers used freely against us in Mafeking, especially on May 12."

I have endeavoured also to test the statement as it concerns the troops to the north of Mafeking. The same high authority says: "With regard to the northern force, it is just possible that a few sportsmen in the Rhodesian column may have had some sporting bullets, but I certainly never heard of them." A friend of mine who was in Lobatsi during the first week of the war assures me that he never saw anything but the solid bullet. It must be remembered that the state of things was very exceptional with the Rhodesian force. Their communications to the south were cut on the second day of the war, and for seven months they were dependent upon the long and circuitous Beira route for any supplies which reached them. One could imagine that under such circumstances uniformity of armament would be more difficult to maintain than in the case of an army with an assured base.

The expansive bullet is not, as a matter of fact, contrary to the Conventions of The Hague. It was expressly held from being so by the representatives of the United States and of Great Britain. In taking this view I cannot but think that these two enlightened and humanitarian powers were ill-advised. Those Conventions were of course only binding on those who signed them, and therefore in fighting desperate savages the man-stopping bullet could still have been used. Whatever our motives in taking the view that we did, a swift retribution has come upon us, for it has prevented us from exacting any retribution, or even complaining, when the Boers have used these weapons against us. Explosive bullets are, however, as my distinguished correspondent points out, upon a different footing, and if the Boers claim the advantages of the Conventions of The Hague, then every burgher found with these weapons in his bandolier is liable to punishment.

Our soldiers have been more merciful than our Hague diplomatists, for in spite of the reservation of the right to use this ammunition, every effort has been made to exclude it from the firing line. An unfortunate incident early in the campaign gave our enemies some reason to suspect us. The facts are these.

At the end of the spring of 1899 some hundreds of thousands of hollow-headed bullets, made in England, were condemned as unsatisfactory, not being true to gauge, etc., and were sent to South Africa for target practice only. A quantity of this ammunition, known as "Metford Mark IV," was sent up to Dundee by order of General Symons for practice in field firing. As Mark IV was not for use in a war with white races all these cartridges were called in as soon as Kruger declared war, and the officers responsible thought they were every one returned. By some blundering in the packing at home, however, some of this Mark IV must have got mixed up with the ordinary, or Mark II, ammunition, and was found on our men by the Boers on October 30. Accordingly a very careful inspection

was ordered, and a few Mark IV bullets were found in our men's pouches, and at once removed. Their presence was purely accidental, and undoubtedly caused by a blunder in the Ordnance Department long before the war, and it was in consequence of this that some hollow-headed bullets were fired by the English early in the war without their knowledge.

What is usually known as the dum-dum bullet is a "soft nosed" one: but the regulation Mark II is also made at the dum-dum factory, and the Boers, seeing the dum-dum label on boxes containing the latter, naturally thought the contents were the soft-nosed, which they were not.

It must be admitted that there was some carelessness in permitting sporting ammunition ever to get to the front at all. When the Derbyshire Militia were taken by De Wet at Roodeval, a number of cases of sporting cartridges were captured by the Boers (the officers had used them for shooting springbok). My friend, Mr Langman, who was present, saw the Boers, in some instances, filling their bandoliers from these cases on the plausible excuse that they were only using our own ammunition. Such cartridges should never have been permitted to go up. But in spite of instances of bungling, the evidence shows that every effort has been made to keep the war as humane as possible. I am inclined to hope that a fuller knowledge will show that the same holds good for our enemies, and that in spite of individual exceptions, they have never systematically used anything except what one of their number described as a "gentlemanly" bullet.

Conduct to Prisoners on the Field

On this count, also, the British soldiers have been exposed to attacks, both at home and abroad, which are as unfounded and as shameful as most of those which have been already treated.

The first occasion upon which Boer prisoners fell into our hands was at the Battle of Elandslaagte, on October 21, 1899. That night was spent by the victorious troops in a pouring rain, round such fires as they were able to light. It has been recorded by several witnesses that the warmest corner by the fire was reserved for the Boer prisoners. It has been asserted, and is again asserted, that when the Lancers charged a small body of the enemy after the action, they gave no quarter – "too well substantiated and too familiar," says one critic of this assertion. I believe, as a matter of fact, that the myth arose from a sensational picture in an illustrated paper. The charge was delivered late in the evening, in uncertain light. Under such circumstances it is always possible, amid so wild and confused a scene, that a man who would have surrendered has been cut down or ridden over. But the cavalry brought back twenty prisoners, and the number whom they killed or wounded has not been placed higher than that, so that it is certain there was no indiscriminate slaying. I have read a letter from the officer who commanded the cavalry and who directed the charge, in which he tells the whole story confidentially to a brother officer. He speaks of his prisoners, but there is no reference to any brutality upon the part of the troopers.

Mr Stead makes a great deal of some extracts from the letters of private soldiers at the front who talk of bayoneting their enemies. Such expressions should be accepted with considerable caution, for it may amuse the soldier to depict himself as rather a terrible fellow to his home-staying friends. Even if isolated instances could be corroborated, it would merely show that men of fiery temperament in the flush of battle are occasionally not to be restrained, either by the power of discipline or by the example and exhortations of their officers. Such instances, I do not doubt, could be found among all troops in all wars. But to found upon it a general charge of brutality or cruelty is unjust in the case of a foreigner, and unnatural in the case of our own people.

There is one final and complete answer to all such charges. It is that we have now in our hands 42,000 males of the Boer nations. They assert, and we cannot deny, that their losses in killed have been extraordinarily light during two years of warfare. How are these admitted and certain facts compatible with any general refusal of quarter? To anyone who, like myself, has seen the British soldiers jesting and smoking cigarettes with their captives within five minutes of their being taken, such a charge is ludicrous, but surely even to the most biassed mind the fact stated above must be conclusive.

In some ways I fear that the Conventions of The Hague will prove, when tested on a large scale, to be a counsel of perfection. It will certainly be the extreme test of self-restraint and discipline – a test successfully endured by the British troops at Elandslaagte, Bergendal, and many other places – to carry a position by assault and then to give quarter to those defenders who only surrender at the last instant. It seems almost too much to ask. The assailants have been terribly punished; they have lost their friends and their officers, in the frenzy of battle they storm the position, and then at the last instant the men who have done all the mischief stand up unscathed from behind their rocks and claim their own personal safety. Only at that moment has the soldier seen his antagonist or been on equal terms with him. He must give quarter, but it must be confessed that this is trying human nature rather high.

But if this holds good of an organised force defending a position, how about the solitary sniper? The position of such a man has never been defined by the Conventions of The Hague, and no rules are laid down for his treatment. It is not wonderful if the troops who have been annoyed by him should on occasion take the law into their own hands and treat him in a summary fashion.

The very first article of the Conventions of The Hague states that a belligerent must (1) Be commanded by some responsible person; (2) Have a distinctive emblem visible at a distance; (3) Carry arms openly. Now it is evident that the Boer sniper who draws his Mauser from its hiding-place in order to have a shot at the Rooineks from a safe kopje does not comply with any one of these conditions. In the letter of the law, then, he is undoubtedly outside the rules of warfare.

In the spirit he is even more so. Prowling among the rocks and shooting those who cannot tell whence the bullet comes, there is no wide gap between him and the assassin. His victims never see him, and in the ordinary course he incurs no personal danger. I believe such cases to have been very rare, but if the soldiers have occasionally shot such a man without reference to the officers, can it be said that it was an inexcusable action, or even that it was outside the strict rules of warfare?

I find in the "Gazette de Lausanne" a returned Swiss soldier named Pache, who had fought for the Boers, expresses his amazement at the way in which the British troops after their losses in the storming of a position gave quarter to those who had inflicted those losses upon them.

"Only once," he says, "at the fight at Tabaksberg, have I seen the Boers hold on to their position to the very end. At the last rush of the enemy they opened a fruitless magazine fire, and then threw down their rifles and lifted their hands, imploring quarter from those whom they had been firing at short range. I was astounded at the clemency of the soldiers, who allowed them to live. For my part I should have put them to death."

Of prisoners after capture there is hardly need to speak. There is a universal consensus of opinion from all, British or foreign, who have had an opportunity of forming an opinion, that the prisoners have been treated with humanity and generosity. The same report has come from Green Point, St Helena, Bermuda, Ceylon, Ahmednager, and all other camps. An outcry was raised when Ahmednager in India was chosen for a prison station, and it was asserted, with that recklessness with which so many other charges have been hurled against the authorities, that it was a hot-bed of disease. Experience has shown that there was no grain of truth in these statements, and the camp has been a very healthy one. As it remains the only one which has ever been subjected to harsh criticism, it may be of use to append the conclusions of Mr Jesse Collings during a visit to it last month:

"The Boer officers said, speaking for ourselves and men, we have nothing at all to complain of. As prisoners of war we could not be better treated, and Major Dickenson (this they wished specially to be inserted), is as kind and considerate as it is possible to be."

Some sensational statements were also made in America as to the condition of the Bermuda Camps, but a newspaper investigation has shown that there is no charge to be brought against them.

Mr John J. O'Rorke writes to the "New York Times," saying, "That in view of the many misrepresentations regarding the treatment of the Boer prisoners in Bermuda, he recently obtained a trustworthy opinion from one of his correspondents there." . . . The correspondent's name is Musson Wainwright, and Mr O'Rorke describes him "as one of the influential residents in the island." He says, "That the Boers in Bermuda are better off than many residents in New York. They have plenty of beef, plenty of bread, plenty of everything except liberty. There are good hospitals and good doctors. It is true that some of the Boers are short of clothing, but these are very few, and the Government is issuing clothing to them. On the whole," says Mr Wainwright, "Great Britain is treating the Boers far better than most people would."

Compare this record with the undoubted privations, many of them unnecessary, which our soldiers endured at Waterval near Pretoria, the callous neglect of the enteric patients there, and the really barbarous treatment of British Colonial prisoners who were confined in cells on the absurd plea that in fighting for their flag they were traitors to the Africander cause.

Executions

The number of executions of Boers as distinguished from the execution of Cape rebels, has been remarkably few in a war which has already lasted twenty-six months. So far as I have been able to follow them, they have been limited to the ex-

ecution of Cordua for broken parole and conspiracy upon August 24, 1900, at Pretoria, the shooting of one or two horse-poisoners in Natal, and the shooting of three men after the action of October 27, 1900, near Fredericstad. These men, after throwing down their arms and receiving quarter, picked them up again and fired at the soldiers from behind. No doubt there have been other cases, scattered up and down the vast scene of warfare, but I can find no record of them, and if they exist at all they must be few in number. Since the beginning of 1901 four men have been shot in the Transvaal, three in Pretoria as spies and breakers of parole, one in Johannesburg as an aggravated case of breaking neutrality by inciting Boers to resist.

At the beginning of the war 90 per cent of the farmers in the northern district of Cape Colony joined the invaders. Upon the expulsion of the Boers these men for the most part surrendered. The British Government, recognising that pressure had been put upon them and that their position had been a difficult one, inflicted no penalty upon the rank-and-file beyond depriving them of the franchise for a few years. A few who, like the Douglas rebels, were taken red-handed upon the field of battle, were condemned to periods of imprisonment which varied from one to five years.

This was in the year 1900. In 1901 there was an invasion of the Colony by Boers which differed very much from the former one. In the first case the country had actually been occupied by the Boer forces, who were able to exert real pressure upon the inhabitants. In the second the invaders were merely raiding bands who traversed many places but occupied none. A British subject who joined on the first occasion might plead compulsion, on the second it was undoubtedly of his own free will.

These Boer bands being very mobile, and never fighting save when they were at an overwhelming advantage, penetrated all parts of the Colony and seduced a number of British subjects from their allegiance. The attacking of small posts and the derailing of trains, military or civilian, were their chief employment. To cover their tracks they continually murdered natives whose information might betray them. Their presence kept the Colony in confusion and threatened the communications of the Army.

The situation may be brought home to a continental reader by a fairly exact parallel. Suppose that an Austrian army had invaded Germany, and that while it was deep in German territory bands of Austrian subjects who were of German extraction began to tear up the railway lines and harass the communications. That was our situation in South Africa. Would the Austrians under these circumstances show much mercy to those rebel bands, especially if they added cold-blooded murder to their treason? Is it likely that they would?

The British, however, were very long-suffering. Many hundreds of these rebels passed into their hands, and most of them escaped with fine and imprisonment. The ringleaders, and those who were convicted of capital penal offences, were put to death. I have been at some pains to make a list

Number	Place	Date		Reason
		1901		
2	De Aar	March	19	Train wrecking.
2	Pretoria	June	11	Boers breaking oath of neutrality.
1	Middelburg	July	10	Fighting.
1	Cape Town	"	13	"
1	Cradock	"	13	"
2	Middelburg	"	24	"
2	Kenhardt	"	25	"
1	Pretoria	Aug.	22	Boer spy.
3	Colesburg	Sept.	4	Fighting.
1	Middelburg	Oct.	10	"
1	Middelburg	"	11	"
1	Vryburg (hanged)	"	12	"
Several	Tarkastad	"	12	"
1	Tarkastad	"	14	"
1	Middelburg	"	15	"
2	Cradock (1 hanged, 1 shot)	"	17	Train-wrecking and murdering native.
2	Vryburg	"	29	Fighting.
1	Mafeking	Nov.	11	Shooting a native.
1	Colesburg	"	12	Fighting, marauding, and assaulting, etc.
1	Johannesburg	"	23	Persuading surrendered burghers to break oath.
1	Aliwal North	"	26	Cape Police deserter.
1	Krugersdorp	Dec.	26	Shooting wounded.
2	Mafeking	"	27	Kaffir murder.

of the executions in 1901, including those already mentioned. It is at least approximately correct:

Allowing 3 for the "several" at Tarkastad on October 12, that makes a total of 34. Many will undoubtedly be added in the future, for the continual murder of inoffensive natives, some of them children, calls for stern justice. In this list 4 were train-wreckers (aggravated cases by rebels), 1 was a spy, 4 were murderers of natives, 1 a deserter who took twenty horses from the Cape Police, and the remaining 23 were British subjects taken fighting and bearing arms against their own country.

Hostages Upon Railway Trains

Here the military authorities are open, as it seems to me, to a serious charge, not of inhumanity to the enemy but of neglecting those steps which it was their duty to take in order to safeguard their own troops. If all the victims of derailings and railway cuttings were added together it is not an exaggeration to say that it would furnish as many killed and wounded as a considerable battle. On at least five occasions between twenty and thirty men were incapacitated, and there are very numerous cases where smaller numbers were badly hurt.

Let it be said at once that we have no grievance in this. To derail a train is legitimate warfare, with many precedents to support it. But to checkmate it by putting hostages upon the trains is likewise legitimate warfare, with many precedents to support it also. The Germans habitually did it in France, and the result justified them as the result has justified us. From the time (October 1901) that it was adopted in South Africa we have not heard of a single case of derailing, and there can be no doubt that the lives of many soldiers, and possibly of some civilians, have been saved by the measure.

I will conclude this chapter by two extracts chosen out of many from the diary of the Austrian, Count Sternberg. In the first he describes his capture:

"Three hours passed thus without our succeeding in finding our object. The sergeant then ordered that we should take a rest. We sat down on the ground, and chatted good-humouredly with the soldiers. They were fine fellows, without the least sign of brutality – in fact, full of sympathy. They had every right to be angry with us, for we had spoiled their sleep after they had gone through a trying day; yet they did not visit it on us in any way, and were most kind. They even shared their drinking-water with us. I cannot describe what my feelings were that night. A prisoner!"

He adds: "I can only repeat that the English officers and the English soldiers have shown in this war that the profession of arms does not debase, but rather ennobles man."

Source: Authur Conan Doyle. *The War in South Africa: Its Cause and Conduct.* New York: McClure, Phillips and Co., 1902. Ch. IX, pp. 108–16.

Note

Best known for his Sherlock Holmes stories, Arthur Conan Doyle (1855–1930) was also an ardent apologist for British involvement in South Africa, which he visited in 1900 as an unofficial supervisor in support of British forces. For all his support for the British efforts in South Africa, he was also a vociferous critic of Belgian oppression in the Congo.

95 Hague Convention (II) with Respect to the Laws and Customs of War on Land (July 29, 1899)

On Means of Injuring the Enemy, Sieges, and Bombardments

Article 22

The right of belligerents to adopt means of injuring the enemy is not unlimited.

Article 23

Besides the prohibitions provided by special Conventions, it is especially prohibited: –

(a) To employ poison or poisoned arms;
(b) To kill or wound treacherously individuals belonging to the hostile nation or army;
(c) To kill or wound an enemy who, having laid down arms, or having no longer means of defence, has surrendered at discretion;
(d) To declare that no quarter will be given;
(e) To employ arms, projectiles, or material of a nature to cause superfluous injury;
(f) To make improper use of a flag of truce, the national flag, or military ensigns and the enemy's uniform, as well as the distinctive badges of the Geneva Convention;
(g) To destroy or seize the enemy's property,

unless such destruction or seizure be imperatively demanded by the necessities of war.

Article 24

Ruses of war and the employment of methods necessary to obtain information about the enemy and the country, are considered allowable.

Article 25

The attack or bombardment of towns, villages, habitations or buildings which are not defended, is prohibited.

Article 26

The Commander of an attacking force, before commencing a bombardment, except in the case of an assault, should do all he can to warn the authorities.

Article 27

In sieges and bombardments all necessary steps should be taken to spare as far as possible edifices devoted to religion, art, science, and charity, hospitals, and places where the sick and wounded are collected, provided they are not used at the same time for military purposes.

The besieged should indicate these buildings or places by some particular and visible signs, which should previously be notified to the assailants.

Article 28

The pillage of a town or place, even when taken by assault, is prohibited.

Source: Convention (II) With Respect to the Laws and Customs of War on Land. The Hague, 1899. Sect. II, ch. 1.

Note

Great Britain was a signatory to the Hague Conventions on international rules of war in 1899.

96 Anonymous: "The Congo State" (1903)

The Congo State
Is a thriving speculation
For the happy Belgian nation

The receipts are great
And getting yearly bigger
– But I'm glad I'm not a nigger
In the Congo State

Source: Punch. May 6, 1903, p. 313.

97   Roger Casement: *The Congo Report* (1903)

Mr Casement to the Marquess of Lansdowne

London, December 11, 1903
[. . .] Perhaps the most striking change observed during my journey into the interior was the great reduction observable everywhere in native life. Communities I have formerly known as large and flourishing centres of population are today entirely gone, or now exist in such diminished numbers as to be no longer recognisable.

[. . .] Bolobo used to be one of the most important native settlements along the South bank of the Upper Congo, and the population in the early days of civilised rule numbered fully 40,000 people, chiefly of the Bobangi tribe. Today the population is believed to be not more than 7,000 to 8,000 souls.

When I visited the Government station at P***, the chief of that post showed me ten sacks of gum which he said had been just brought in by a very small village in the neighbourhood. For this quarter of a ton of gum-copal he said he had paid the village one piece of blue drill – a rough cotton cloth which is valued locally after adding the cost of transport, at $11\frac{1}{2}$ fr. apiece. By the Congo Government "Bulletin Official" of this year (No. 4, April 1903) I found that $339\frac{1}{2}$ tons of gum-copal were exported in 1902, all from the Upper Congo, and that this was valued at 473,490 fr. The value per ton would, therefore, work out at about 561. The fortnightly yield of each village would therefore seem to be worth a maximum of 141 (probably less), for which a maximum payment of $11\frac{1}{2}$ fr. is made. At one village I visited I found the majority of the inhabitants getting ready the gum-copal and the supply of fish which they had to take to P* on the morrow. They were putting it into canoes to paddle across the lake – some 20 miles – and they left with their loads in the night from along side my steamer. These people told me that they frequently received, instead of cloth, 150 brass rods ($7\frac{1}{2}$ fr.) for the quarter of a ton of gum-copal they took fortnightly.

M. P. called on us to get out of the rain, and in conversation with M. Q. in presence of myself and R., said: "The only way to get rubber is to fight for it. The natives are paid 35 centimes per kilog., it is claimed, but that includes a large profit on the cloth; the amount of rubber is controlled by the number of guns, and not the number of bales of cloth. The S. A. B. on the Bussira, with 150 guns, get only 10 tons (rubber) a month: we, the State, at Mombovo, with 130 guns, get 13 tons per month." "So you count by guns?" I asked him. "Partout," M. P. said. "Each time the corporal goes out to get rubber cartridges are given to him. He must bring back all not used; and for every one used, he must bring back a right hand." M. P. told me that sometimes they shot a cartridge at an animal in hunting; they then cut off a hand from a living man. As to the extent to which this is carried on, he informed me that in six months they, the State, on the Momboyo River, had used 6,000 cartridges, which means that 6,000 people are killed or mutilated. It means more than 6,000 for the people have told me repeatedly that the soldiers kill children with the butt of their guns.

The region drained by the Lulongo being of great fertility has, in the past, maintained a large population. In the days prior to the establishment of civilized rule in the interior of Africa, this river offered a constant source of supply to the slave markets of the Upper Congo. The towns around the lower Lulongo River raided the interior tribes, whose prolific humanity provided not only servitors, but human meat for those stronger than themselves. Cannibalism had gone hand in hand with slave raiding, and it was no uncommon spectacle to see gangs of human beings being conveyed for exposure and sale in the local markets. I had in the past, when travelling on the Lulongo River, more than once viewed such a scene. On one occasion a woman was killed in the village I was passing through, and her head and other portions of her were brought and offered for sale to some of the crew of the steamer I was on. Sights of this description are to-day impossible in any part of the country I traversed, and the full credit for their suppression must be given to the authorities of the Congo Government. It is, perhaps, to be regretted that in its efforts to suppress such barbarous practices the Congo Government should have had to rely upon, often, very savage agencies wherewith to combat savagery. The troops employed in punitive measures were – and often are – themselves savages only removed by outward garb from those they are sent to punish.

[. . .] that the Congo Government itself did not hesitate some years ago to purchase slaves (required as soldiers or workmen), who could be obtained for sale by the most deplorable means:

Le chef Ngulu de Wangata est envoyé dans la Maringa, pour m'y acheter des esclaves. Prière à M.M. les agents de l'A.B.I.R. de bien vouloir me signaler les méfaits que celui-ci pourrait commettre en route.

Le Capitaine-Commandant
(Signé) *Sarrazzyn*

Colquilhatville, le 1ᵉʳ ᴹᵃⁱ, 1896

This document was shown to me during the course of my journey. The officer who issued this direction was, I was informed, for a considerable period chief executive authority of the district: and I heard him frequently spoken of by the natives who referred to him by the sobriquet he had earned in the district, "Widjima," or "Darkness." [. . .]

The Concession Companies, I believe, account for the armed men in their service on the ground that their factories and agents must be protected against the possible violence of the rude forest dwellers with whom they deal; but this legitimate need for safeguarding European establishments does not suffice to account for the presence, far from those establishments, of large numbers of armed men quartered throughout the native villages, and who exercise upon their surroundings an influence far from protective. The explanation offered me of this state of things was that, as the "impositions" laid upon the natives were regulated by law, and were calculated on the scale of public labour the Government had a right to require of the people, the collection of these "impositions" had to be strictly enforced. When I pointed out that the profit of this system was not reaped by the Government but by a Commercial Company, and figured in the public returns of that Company's affairs as well as in the official Government statistics as the outcome of commercial dealings with the natives, I was informed that the "impositions" were in reality trade, "for, as you observe, we pay the natives for the produce they bring in." "But," I observed, "you told me just now that these products did not belong to the natives, but to you, the Concessionnaire, who owned the soil; how, then, do you buy from them what is already yours?" "We do not buy the india-rubber. What we pay to the native is a remu-

neration for his labour in collecting our produce on our land, and bringing it to us."

Since it was thus to the labour of the native alone that the profits of the Company were attributed, I inquired whether he was not protected by contract with his employer; but I was here referred back to the statement that the natives performed these services as a public duty required of him by his Government. He was acquitting himself of an "imposition" laid upon him by the Government, "of which we are but the collectors by right of our Concession." "Your Concession, then, implies," I said, "that you have been conceded not only a certain area of land, but also the people dwelling on the land?" This, however, was not accepted either, and I was assured that the people were absolutely free, and owed no service to any one but to the Government of the country. But there was no explanation offered to me that was not at once contradicted by the next. One said it was a tax, an obligatory burden laid upon the people, such as all Governments have the undoubted right of imposing; but this failed to explain how, if a tax, it came to be collected by the agents of a trading firm, and figured as the outcome of the trade dealings with the people, still less how, if it were a tax, it could be justly imposed every week or fortnight in the year, instead of once, or at most, twice a year.

Another asserted that it was clearly legitimate commerce with the natives because these were well paid and very happy. He could not then explain the presence of so many armed men in their midst, or the reason for tying the men, women and children, and of maintaining in each trading establishment a local prison termed a "maison des otages," wherein recalcitrant native traders endured long periods of confinement.

A third admitted that there was no law on the Congo Statute Book constituting his trading establishment a Government taxing station, and that since the product of his dealings with the natives figured in his Company's balance-sheets as trade, and he paid customs duty to the Government on export, and a dividend to the shareholders, and as he himself drew a commission of 2 per cent on his turnover, it must be trade; but this exponent could not explain how if these operations were purely commercial, they rested on a privilege denied to others, for since, as he asserted, the products of his district could neither be worked nor bought by any one but himself, it was clear they were not merchandise, which, to be merchandise, must be marketable. The summing up of the situation by the majority of those with whom I sought to discuss it was that, in fact, it was forced labour conceived in the true interest of the native who, if not controlled in this way, would spend his days in idleness, unprofitable to himself and the general community.

As Z* lies upon the main stream of the Lulongo River, and is often touched at by passing steamers, I chose for the next inspection a town lying somewhat off this beaten track, where my coming would be quite unexpected. Steaming up a small tributary of the Lulongo, I arrived, unpreceded by any rumour of my coming, at the village of A*. In an open shed I found two sentries of the La Lulanga Company guarding fifteen native women, five of whom had infants at the breast, and three of whom were about to become mothers. The chief of these sentries, a man called S – who was bearing a double-barreled shot-gun, for which he had a belt of cartridges – at once volunteered an explanation of the reason for these women's detention. Four of them, he said, were hostages who were being held to insure the peaceful settlement of a dispute between two neighboring towns, which had already cost the life of a man. His employer, the agent of the La Lulanga Company at B – near by, he said, had ordered these women to be seized and kept until the Chief of the offending town to which they belonged should come in to talk over the palaver. The sentry pointed out that this was evidently a much better way to settle such troubles between native towns than to leave them to be fought out among the people themselves.

The remaining eleven women, whom he indicated, he said he had caught and was detaining as prisoners to compel their husbands to bring in the right amount of india-rubber required of them on next market day. When I asked if it was a woman's work to collect india-rubber, he said, "No; that, of course, it was man's work." "Then why do you catch the women and not the men?" I asked. "Don't you see," was the answer, "if I caught and kept the men, who would work the rubber? But if I catch their wives, the husbands are anxious to have them home again, and so the rubber is brought in quickly and quite up to the mark." When I asked what would become of these women if their husbands failed to being in the right quantity of rubber on the next market day, he said at once that then they would be kept there until their husbands had redeemed them. Their food, he explained, he made the Chief of A** provide, and he himself saw it given to them daily. They came from more than one village of the neighborhood, he said, mostly from the Ngombi or inland country, where he often had to catch women to insure the rubber being brought in in sufficient quantity. It was an institution, he explained, that served well and saved much trouble. When his master came each fortnight to A** to take away the rubber so collected, if it was found to be sufficient, the women were released and allowed to return with their husbands, but if not sufficient they would undergo continued detention. The sentry's statements were clear and explicit, as were equally those of several of the villagers with whom I spoke. The sentry further explained, in answer to my inquiry, that he caught women in this way by direction of his employers. That it was a custom generally adopted and found to work well; that the people were very lazy, and that this was much the simplest way of making them do what was required of them. When asked if he had any use for his shot-gun, he answered that it had been given by the white man "to frighten people and make them bring in rubber," but that he had never otherwise used it. I found that the two sentries at A* were complete masters of the town.

The praiseworthy official would be he whose district yielded the best and biggest supply of that commodity; and, succeeding in this, the means whereby he brought about the enhanced value of that yield would not, it may be believed, be too closely scrutinized.

A State without resources is inconceivable. On what legitimate grounds could the exemption of natives from all taxes be based, seeing that they are the first to benefit by the material and moral advantages introduced into Africa? As they have no money, a contribution in the shape of labour is required from them. It has been said that, if Africa is ever to be redeemed from barbarism, it must be by getting the negro to understand the meaning of work by the obligation of paying taxes:

It is a question (of native labour) which has engaged my most careful attention in connection with West Africa and other Colonies. To listen to the right honourable gentleman, you would almost think that it would be a good thing for the native to be idle. I think it is a good thing for him to be industrious; and by every means in our power we must teach him to work. . . . No people ever have lived in the world's history who would not work. In the interests of the natives all over Africa, we have to teach them to work.

Such was the language used by Mr. Chamberlain in the House of Commons on the 6th August, 1901.

Source: Peter Singleton-Gates, (ed.). *The Black Diaries: An Account of Roger Casement's Life and Times, with a Collection of his Diaries and Public Writings.* London: Sidgwick and Jackson, 1959, 96–191.

Note

Roger Casement (1864–1916) lived a third of his life in West Africa, both as representative for a trading company and in the service of the British government. In 1903 he presented his controversial report on the state of affairs in Leopold's Congo to parliament. Later, in "The Putumayo Report" (1910) he would similarly investigate abuses on the rubber plantations in South America. He was executed for treason in 1916 for his role in running guns from Germany to the Irish rebels at the time of the Easter Rising. His writings, collected as *The Black Diaries*, were long suppressed, and only first published in a limited edition in 1959. The Amazon Diaries which served as the basis for Casement's Putumayo Report were published in 1997.

98   E. D. Morel: *History of the Congo Reform Movement* (1910–14)

Origins of the Congo Controversy

Over the Congo itself there hung a dense fog of mystery. Now and again a corner of it would lift. When that happened, scenes of apparently purposeless carnage and delirious chaos were sometimes, and for an instant, visible. On other occasions one had the fleeting impression of a prosperous population and a benign rule. At other times military revolts and military expeditions commanded by Belgian officers and operating far beyond the international confines of the State were momentarily observable. Then the fog would settle down again as impenetrable as ever. The conflict of evidence may be estimated from the fact that one year – 1898 – had seen the appearance of a British Consular Report containing some moderate criticisms of certain features of Congo Free State rule: a book by Captain Guy Burrows, a British officer in the State's employ, dedicated by permission to King Leopold and containing a letter from the King in which he declared that "our only programme is the work of material and moral regeneration": a book by another English writer, Mr. Demetrius C. Boulger, effusively praising the magnificent work accomplished by King Leopold

and his officials; and a book by a Belgian Professor containing both criticism and praise. The next year had witnessed a further protest and denunciation from Morrison, the chief representative of the American missions in the Kasai, and one or two brief condemnatory remarks by a British lay missionary in Uganda who had returned to Europe via the Congo. On the other hand, three volumes had appeared from the pens of a Belgian Senator[1] and two French gentlemen[2] respectively, who had visited the Lower Congo (on the occasion of the opening of the railway connecting the lower and the upper reaches of the river) which, while they contained some criticisms were, in the main, highly complimentary to the Congo administration. In 1900 Mr. E. S. Grogan published contemptuous and outspoken allusions concerning the conditions of the eastern border-region of the Congo Free State, condemning the State as a "vampire growth."

Towards the end of the same year the curtain had been dramatically lifted from the territory exploited by the *Anversoise* Company, the first *Belgian* disclosure of Belgian deeds on the Congo. In these days King Leopold's Press Bureau had not been invented, the corruption of Belgian Editors with Congo gold, and Congo decorations, had not been systematised, and the atrocious self-confessed crimes perpetrated by certain subordinate Belgian agents of the Company, as they averred, under orders, had shocked Belgian Public Opinion. But alas the effect had been fleeting. The outcry was quickly stifled. A powerful and subtle machinery was set immediately to work to discount the emotion produced. Only two men in the Belgian Chamber – Emile Vandervelde and Georges Lorand – had had the courage to protest in the name of Belgian honour. As already noted the President of the *Anversoise* was himself a Member of the Senate, the Guardian of the King's privy purse sat on its board and the Congo Government held half the shares. Even Lorand's reading from the Parliamentary tribune of a letter from a Belgian in another part of the Congo casually mentioning that his soldiers had brought him 1,300 severed hands as testimony to their prowess in punishing recalcitrant rubber collectors, was insufficient to move Belgian Ministers and their solid majority. To Lorand's and Vandervelde's passionate denunciation of a policy

---

1 M. Edmond Picard, afterwards a bitter assailant of the British reformers.
2 Baron de Mandat Grancey and M. Pierre Mille, the latter destined to become my friend and co-worker.

of "pillage, devastation and assassination," all that Belgium's Premier had seen fit to reply was that the Congo Free State as a sovereign independent State was its own master in its own house and for the rest, that the "disinterestedness of its creators will find its reward in the gratitude of the country." The entire Ministerial Press and most of the Liberal papers – notably the *Indépendance Belge* and the *Étoile Belge* – had denounced the two courageous Deputies as personal enemies of the King and "unpatriotic." And so the incident was dismissed.

Looking back now it may appear strange at first sight that Public Opinion in Britain was not more deeply stirred by these successive, if sporadic, revelations spread over nearly five years. But the reasons were many. From the close of 1899 to the period I am writing of (i.e. early in 1901) the Boer War had absorbed the national mind. The Congo was far away. Official circles were averse from stirring up the Congo mud from motives of traditional policy with regard to Belgium. The Foreign Office had a lively dread of King Leopold's power of intrigue. Moreover, the late Queen was opposed to a strong line of action being taken against the son of the man for whom she had entertained such strong affection. I have been assured on good authority that Lord Salisbury was only deterred from acting as vigorously towards Belgium's King over the Stokes affair as he did towards Portugal over Major Serpa Pinto's African promenades, by the Queen's opposition. To similar influence was probably due the fact that Mr. Chamberlain had been unable in 1895–6 to get his colleagues to agree to the setting up of British Consular jurisdiction in the Congo in connection with the ill-treatment of British coloured subjects who had taken service in various capacities under King Leopold's Government. The Liberals had for their part committed themselves deeply and disastrously with King Leopold over the ill-starred Bahr-el-Ghazal agreement of 1894, although it is fair to add that at the time the Cabinet had no knowledge of the outrages of which the Congo was the scene. Indeed, Lord Morley – the Right Honourable John Morley as he was then – frankly admitted three years later at Fox Bourne's meeting called to hear Sjöblom, that in the light of what he then knew, the 1894 agreement was a "great mistake." All the reports received by the Foreign Office from its Consuls in the Congo, from the Governors of the West African possessions, and from British officers or officials in neighbouring British territory between 1896 to the end of 1900, had been suppressed, with the sole exception of the very much abridged and innocuous Pickersgill re-

port of 1898, to which allusion has already been made. Naturally all this only became known to me later, but a reference at this stage of the narrative seemed necessary in order to explain what the British official attitude was when the year 1901 opened. That social influences were quietly exerted in favour of King Leopold is not, I think, doubtful. Stanley, who was still in some measure connected with the Congo Free State, had the *entrée* everywhere in any question affecting that part of the world, and he could never, apparently, bring himself to believe in any of the charges against an enterprise he had so largely contributed in creating. As for any real Public Opinion on the subject, it is no disloyalty to Fox Bourne's memory to say that it did not exist. Fox Bourne was an honest, sincere and genuine philanthropist. His efforts were persistent, protracted and beyond praise. He was perfectly disinterested. He worked for pure zeal on behalf of oppressed peoples all over the world, and, although hampered by failing health, his efforts never relaxed. But the very catholicity of his sympathies was a source of popular weakness in a case of superlative wrongdoing of this kind, and the Aborigines Protection Society of which he was the life and soul, was notorious for criticising every European Government (often quite justly) in its dealings with subject races. Fox Bourne himself was no faddist, although he was prone to think European interference with coloured peoples had no redeeming features, and that the Congo horror was merely the inevitable result, in specially aggravated form, of contact between the White and Black races on African soil. With the assistance of Sir Charles Dilke – that most loyal and generous of public men – he did splendid work, and exposed many an abuse in widely distant lands. But, although he had succeeded in arousing a certain amount of interest in the Congo, it was very restricted and it had no driving force. He and I had our occasional differences of opinion as to tactics. But our co-operation was close and our interchange of letters continuous for nearly nine years, during which our relationship was uniformly friendly. Either had complete confidence in the other and placed his knowledge and information unreservedly at the other's disposal.

I have indicated in a previous chapter some of the doubts which assailed my own mind when I first began to look into the question. Similar doubts, even after the Belgian revelations of the latter part of 1900, must have been uppermost in the minds of men capable of influencing public opinion, who were more or less familiar with the subject and who might have been expected to take an intelligent interest in it, such as Newspaper Editors, politicians and leaders of religious thought. Indeed how those doubts persisted I was soon to learn by my own experience. Nor is it possible to feel real surprise that such should have been the case. Collectively the actual evidence of misgovernment from the Congo was very grave. But it was scattered over a number of years: not accessible in any summarised form. There seemed no connecting link between the various accounts and there was no apparent motive for the crimes reported. There was rebutting evidence – not much, then, at least from the Congo itself, but still some. The periodical denials of King Leopold's Secretaries of State in Brussels had been absolute and conceived in a tone of virtuous indignation. Their protestations of philanthropic intent were so earnest, their profession of a desire to investigate and remedy any abuses which might be found to exist, apparently so sincere, their appeal for fair play towards a poor little struggling "State" hampered by lack of funds and endeavouring to carry out a great civilising work, so eloquently worded that any tendency to harshness of criticism was mitigated. The cloak of philanthropy in which the Congo Free State had been nurtured was not yet worn wholly threadbare: the shreds still clung about it and predisposed people in its favour. Then, had not the King given a most signal proof of the purity of his motives by creating four years previously a permanent Commission "charged with the protection of natives throughout the territory of the State"? Was this Commission not composed of the Godliest men in the Congo, the Superior of the Jesuit Mission, the Revs. George Grenfell and Holman Bentley, of the Baptist Missionary Society; Father de Cleene of the Congregation de Scheut, Dr. Sims of the American Baptist Union, with the Vicar-Apostolic of the Congo, as President? Was it conceivable that if these accusations contained a particle of truth, these holy men would reserve silence? What Editor could resist such arguments, presented in the mellifluent tones of the Consul-General for the Congo Free State in London; promulgated from Brussels in periods of outraged righteousness?

These representations notwithstanding, the embarrassing Belgian revelations of the latter end of 1900, reviving memories of and confirming Glave's and Sjöblom's disclosures of an earlier date, might conceivably have made things awkward for King Leopold, had the Belgian Government adopted for its part a less pronounced attitude. But in identifying itself so wholly with the defence of the Congo Free State Government, in supporting that defence so uncompromisingly, the Belgian Government had adopted a course of action which English public men could with difficulty bring themselves to believe was not due to knowledge of the true state of the case. Vandervelde's indictment was in large measure set down to his socialist views and the personal antagonism he was alleged to bear to the King.

Such, in brief, then, was the position which, I hope and think to have faithfully portrayed, when my own turn came to enter the lists.

Planning the Campaign

From this survey, one central fact of capital importance stood out – in bold relief. Public Opinion had not grasped that the occurrences reported from the Congo were the inevitable results of a fixed policy, carefully thought out, deliberately planned, immovable as the Pyramids. The Public was not aware that any such policy existed. It was not realised that reports from the spot were immaterial to the formation of a reasoned judgement of the true situation in which the Congo was plunged. It was not understood that rebutting or merely negative evidence was worthless, indicating at most that the circumstances either ethnologic or physiological of particular parts of the Congo made the application of the policy impracticable or undesirable. This capital feature in the case was not, and could not be apprehended because the material was lacking. That material, it seemed, I alone possessed. The problem for me then was simply this. Had I the necessary qualifications to so present the case in writing and in speech as to bring conviction to men's minds: and what was the best way to set about it?

I felt intimately assured that it was impossible to rouse anything in the nature of an agitation which would be more than ephemeral, by concentrating solely upon the scattered reports of atrocities perpetrated upon the native population. Moreover these were merely incidental. The central wrong was the reduction of millions of men to a condition of absolute slavery, by a system of legalised robbery enforced by violence. The appeal must be to the mind as well as to the heart. Assume an overwhelming case made out as to the atrocities even on a scale of unparalleled magnitude. However strong, it would be met by promises and protestations of reforms: by the punishment of a few scapegoats; by the promulgation of new laws breathing the quintessence of philanthropy. The Official Bulletins were full of such laws already. The Congo native having been reduced to eternal servitude, it was decided that he should be treated with humanity. His land having been converted into the private property of the King, it was decreed that no one should interfere with his liberty. The only articles in which he could trade with the European having been appropriated by the King and his financial friends, it was decreed that he could trade in anything which was legitimate. Moreover, an element of doubt would always linger as to the thorough reliability of a case built upon statements unverifiable by ordinary processes and made by individuals suspect to many. It should be remembered that there was a complete absence of reports from the consular representatives of the Powers. These resided at Boma, south in the Lower Congo where the policy did not apply. They did not travel in the interior. Or, at any rate if they did, or if reports reached them from the north, nothing transpired outside the Chancelleries. Apart from the observations of chance travellers what were the human elements through whom evidence was procurable? There were only four classes of White men permanently resident in the Congo Free State: the officials (officials were rewarded proportionately to the amount of rubber they succeeded in squeezing out of their districts: but it was decreed that any official guilty of cruel treatment should be severely punished. And the "Magistrates" were the high officials!), the agents of the Thys group of Companies, the agents of the concessionnaire, or privileged companies, and the Missionaries. Of independent European traders or residents there were none. The summary execution of Stokes, and the impossibility of trading in a country where the raw material of trade had been seized by its Government *by law*, had scared away all international-commercial enterprise properly so called. Two or three trading firms lingered on in the Lower Congo doing a retail business. That was all.

Now it was obvious that any disclosures from officials or exofficials, as from agents or ex-agents of the Concessionnaire Companies would be largely discounted on the ground that they emanated from men who were participating in, or had been participators of, the very conditions which they condemned. Moreover the Congo Free State authorities could be trusted to trump up any kind of charge against such people, true or false, and it was at least probable that tactics of that sort would nine times out of ten be successful. The prejudice in the public mind would persist. It would be extremely difficult to make the average man believe the statements of an official with a grievance, and in most cases the average man's judgement would be sound. But not in all. The conditions of the Congo

were peculiar. The newcomer, honest or dishonest, with a clean heart or an evil one, was swept into a maelstrom from which there was no escape, save by a miracle. A raw European, with decent instincts might find himself caught in the meshes of a system which compelled him at least to connive at acts of habitual violence and oppression. But in terms of his contract he would be unable to free himself before his three years' contract was over, however desirous he might be of relinquishing his employment, or of indicating the character of his employers. And by that time, save under exceptionally favourable circumstances, he would either have sunk to the level of the system, or have committed suicide, or died. We shall never know a tithe of the individual White tragedies on the Congo, although a chapter might be written on specific cases familiar to some of us.

Once in the Congo, the new arrival was bound in fetters of steel to a system as pitiless in its way to the Whites as it was to the Blacks. If his past life in Europe contained some blemish he sank into the grip of a system like a stone sinks in water. The Government was itself the hourly violator of the elaborately humane laws published in Brussels for European consumption. The Concessionnaire Companies were the Government's partners in crime and in the profits wrung from "Red Rubber." But the Government took care to maintain a judicial machinery which could be invoked against recalcitrant subordinates.[3] It could be swiftly galvanised into aggressive activity towards subordinates in the event of unlooked-for contumacy. It could be set into operation against subordinates if and when disclosures filtered through to Europe by some means or another. And rare, indeed, under such circumstances would be the occasion when connivance in an act, illegal according to the law, could not be brought home to the wretched scapegoat. His defence would never be published. No one would plead his cause. Thus the Congo "tenderfoot" was absolutely at the mercy of his employers from the moment he stepped out on to the banks of the River. But they surrounded themselves with additional safeguards against his indiscretion. Half of his salary – which was scandalously low – was retained in Brussels to be paid over to him on his return: or withheld. He was bound down strictly in his articles not to communicate any knowledge he might have acquired during his employment. If he made himself a nuisance, his medical and other stores would be unaccountably delayed, and he

3 No high official was ever prosecuted by Congo Courts from the birth to the demise of the Congo Free State.

would be lucky if he suffered no worse inconvenience. He might seek to leave the country. This was peculiarly difficult. The Ocean passage to Europe was £24, and the chances of a subordinate in the Congo service having this amount of money in his possession was remote. Unless he was given a passage on a Missionary steamer out of compassion, the only craft he could travel in on the rivers belonged to the Government. And the Captain of the Government steamer could, of course, refuse to take him. Consulting his own interest he would probably do so; or if he did not he could compel his unwelcome passenger to forage for himself, and what this incurs in Central Africa even under normal conditions some African travellers know to their cost. But if, triumphing over all these and other obstacles too numerous to mention, he had succeeded in actually boarding a boat going down river, he was liable upon arrival at Leopoldville or (had he secured a passage on the railway) at Boma, to be arrested for "desertion," or to see himself detained and under surveillance pending "judicial enquiry" into some alleged breach of "legality." This experience was almost inevitable, for his superior officer would be morally certain to have telegraphed his "dossier" to headquarters. In my experience I never came across but one case of a Belgian subordinate official or agent getting out of the river before the expiration of his period of service, except through illness. As already remarked, after three years' service, the man became identified with the system he worked for, and even if he had kept himself clean – a well-nigh physical and moral impossibility in the rubber districts – such evidence as he then might give was immediately stigmatised by the Congo Authorities in Brussels as that of a dissatisfied ex-servant against whose character much would be hinted if not positively asserted. Nor would the trouble of the unfortunate individual end with his arrival home. Wherever he turned for employment he would find a mysterious influence blocking his chances. If he had spoken out, he was literally hunted down and driven to destitution or emigration. I have known of several such cases. The King's reach was a long one, his attention to detail was marvellous and he never forgave. But no one would have believed all this at the time of which I am writing. And I had only a very faint perception of it myself.

Missionary evidence, on the other hand, is always suspect of a certain class of opinion in Britain. It is not, or used not to be, evidence which commanded public acceptance, although the magnificent manner in which the statements of such of the Protestant missionaries as testified to the truth was eventually vindicated has probably modified that attitude. The Catholic missionaries were mainly Belgians, and it is antagonistic to the Roman system for individual Priests engaged in missionary enterprise to make public declarations on matters affecting the Government under which they live.

Considerations such as these, though not so fully apparent to me then as they have afterwards become, were, nevertheless sufficiently obvious to convince me of the impracticability of leading a crusade against the Congo Free State by invoking humanitarian sentiment alone. After all, the atrocities were merely the effect of a root cause. While that root cause continued to exist, they would continue fatally, inexorably. It was the root cause which needed to be laid bare. It was the policy itself, the whole infernal system, its legal bases, its monstrous claims, its fraudulent accounts and fraudulent statistics, its gross and enormous profits, which required to be dragged into the daylight and pilloried. If one could only make men who counted and the public generally realise that the "Congo Free State" was neither State nor Protectorate, but a personal enterprise thriving upon pillage, whose aims necessitated the servitude and destruction of innumerable human beings, which began and ended with rubber wrung from the bowels of a helpless people then, surely, the fight would be half won, and the American and the European Governments, guarantors of the Congo Free State, trustees for the natives, above all the Government of Great Britain, with its peculiar and special historical liabilities, would be speedily galvanised into action. Thus I thought in my inexperience. And I still think, looking backwards over a long vista of years that King Leopold would have been summoned to the bar of an international conference with the Congo peoples freed from the human vultures fattening on their agony, in a comparatively short time, if a public man of influence possessing a strong moral character had made the question his own and devoted his whole leisure to it. How often in the days that were to come, did I curse my inability to find such a man and lament my own miserable insufficiency.

Such then was the main task: to convince the world that this Congo horror was not only and unquestionably a fact; but that it was not accidental or temporary, or capable of internal cure. To show conclusively that it was deliberate, and that the consequences would be identical in any part of the tropics where similar conceptions might be introduced. To demonstrate that it was at once a survival and a revival of the slave-mind at work, of the slave-trade in being.

Now it was quite evident that this evil, if it were not struck down, would contaminate the whole tropical region of Africa as it had already contaminated a neighbouring region. And if it were to be struck down the appeal must be varied and widened in character, and forces other than humanitarian must be brought into play. There must be the appeal to national honour, which meant that the Public, and especially the philanthropic and religious Public, whose aid Stanley had enlisted with such effect in the early eighties in securing British adhesion to King Leopold's enterprise, must be vividly reminded of the very special national responsibility which rested upon England and Englishmen in the matter. There must be appeal to the Imperial side, the side which would resent King Leopold's filibustering expeditions beyond the Congo Free State's international confines; which would appreciate the danger of perpetual uprisings and unrest on the Congo to the peace and good government of contiguous British territory; which would be affected by the knowledge that arms and ammunition were being poured into the Congo both for the use of hordes of undisciplined soldiery, for the arming of friendly tribes to raid other tribes, for ivory-loot, and for sale or presentation to powerful Chiefs.

There must be appeal to the commercial side. At bottom, the problem in one sense, was economic. The basis of the Congo Free State's policy constituted a complete revolution of accepted economics. The material factor governing the relationship of peoples is the exchange of commodities – in other words, trade. In so far as the scramble for tropical Africa had been inspired by economic considerations (and these played a large part) the latter involved two inter-connected factors. These factors were the creation [of markets] in tropical Africa for the sale to the natives of European merchandise on the one part and the collection and cultivation by the native, in exchange for that merchandise, of the tropical produce increasingly required by European industrialism. Indeed, one of the main arguments advanced in favour of conferring a definite status upon King Leopold's so-called "International Association" had been that it would promote trade, and trade unrestricted by differential tariffs. The support given by the British Chambers of Commerce to Stanley when he conducted his famous pilgrimage through England on the King's behalf, was acquired by the explicitness of the pledges that under the new dispensation trade would be encouraged and untrammelled. The Opposition of the Chambers to the Anglo-Portuguese Treaty for the settlement of the Congo drawn up

by Lord Fitzmaurice and Sir Charles Dilke in 1883–4 was due to legitimate dislike of the fiscal policy adopted by Portugal in her dependencies. This opposition was fanned to a flame by Stanley's campaign. "We made a great mistake. But we relied upon the word of a King." Thus wrote to me in 1901 a member of one of the British Chambers of Commerce which took a prominent part in opposing the Anglo-Portuguese Treaty. When Continental jealousy, provoked by Leopold II, and philanthropic, religious and commercial agitation in England promoted by Stanley, Sir John Kennaway, Lady Burdett-Coutts, the Baptist Union and the Chambers of Commerce had between them succeeded in – as Sir Charles Dilke once put it – "kicking the Treaty out of the House of Commons," the British Government was driven to support King Leopold's enterprise as the only hope "of preventing a practical monopoly of the interior of Africa being obtained by France." But as neither Lord Granville, the Foreign Minister, nor his assistants at the Foreign Office, apparently entertained any belief in King Leopold's philanthropy, "it was decided to bind down the new State by conditions as stringent as those in the defunct Anglo-Portuguese Treaty, to secure freedom of trade and the protection of the natives." These conditions were subsequently embodied in the Congo Free State's international Charter drawn up at Berlin in 1884 and in the Protocols attached to it.

But not only had freedom of trade been destroyed. Trade itself had been declared illegal over three-fifths of the Congo. An embargo had been laid upon the products of the soil which was the raw material of trade. It had been declared the property of the "State" demesne. The land which yielded it had by law been converted into a "Private demesne" (Domaine Privé) of Europe's trustee. Portions of it had been hired out to Concessionnaire Companies. The whole of the land and everything within it had become not a monopoly merely, involving a monopoly of trade: but a gigantic preserve the like of which the world had never seen, exploitable by the sovereign and his financial associates.

The appeal to international commerce to assert its rights was justified in itself because the policy of the Congo Free State was a cynical and outrageous violation of the world's trading rights, as solemnly inscribed in the Congo Free State's international charter of existence, with an enormous region rich in natural products and inhabited by races in which the trading instinct was second nature. But if the appeal was justified from the point of view of international commerce, it was absolutely vital to the purpose of succouring the native peoples of the Congo from their intolerable position. To denounce the cruelties inflicted upon the native population was a mere beating of the air, while the basic cause of the cruelties remained unchallenged. So long as King Leopold's claim to dispossess his African subjects of the natural wealth of the country on the ground that it was his, was not contested, the foundations of his system could weather every assault. So long as King Leopold's claim to call upon his African subjects to gather that natural wealth for himself, his government and his financial associates was undisputed, public discussion of the affairs of the Congo could never advance beyond the stage of charge and counter-charge affecting specific acts of cruelty. So long as Public Opinion acquiesced through lack of appreciation of the facts, in King Leopold converting by simple decree the raw material of Afro-European trade on the Congo into the raw material of taxation, the situation could undergo no real change. This was the key-note of the whole matter. From that wholesale appropriation everything sprang: while that claim persisted as the working basis of the Congo Free State's administrative machinery, the Congo natives were doomed to perpetual slavery and perennial outrage. What in its external aspect appeared at first sight to be a trade question, a question of the way in which the rights of international trade were treated by King Leopold, a question – reduced to its simplest form – of whether John Bull, brother Jonathan, Jacques Bonhomme and Hans Schneider were to be excluded from selling goods to and buying produce from the Bayanzis, Bangalas and Bakubas of the Congo, was something immeasurably greater. In its solution the lives and liberties not of the present generation of Congo natives only, but of millions of Congo natives yet unborn; not of Congo natives alone but of the inhabitants of the African tropics as a whole were inseparably bound up.

It will be instructive to note as the story proceeds, how this simple and irrefutable economic argument, upon which I insisted, in season and out of season for years, and the truth of which is now universally recognised, was represented by the Congo Free State as proof that the Congo reform movement, and myself in particular, were inspired by base, "commercial" motives. It was an inevitable and obvious move, of course. Not less instructive will it be to observe how Belgian Ministers, prominent Belgian Senators, Deputies, and writers, cosmopolitan jurists and continental Editors; the leaders of the French Colonial Party, and the Belgian, French and part of the German Colonial Press, derided and denounced my conclusion as the emendation of an arm-chair theorist. Even here at home, the presentation of the economic case which I had fondly imagined would command immediate acceptance and carry instant conviction, was long misunderstood, and even raised prejudice against me in many quarters, prejudices which lasted a considerable time, and were overcome in some instances only with the greatest difficulty. Again and again I found when referring to the natives' right to trade, in conversation with men I sought to interest in the Congo cause, that they became at once suspicious and aloof. Even Sir Charles Dilke and Mr Fox Bourne queried the wisdom of my insistence upon this fundamental issue. The former, while he never doubted my bona fides, took occasion more than once to dissociate himself publicly and pointedly from what he called the "commercial" side of the case. But he ultimately came round to my way of thinking (as did Fox Bourne) and with his usual loyalty he publicly testified to the fact in a letter published in 1908. I may, perhaps, be pardoned for giving the passage:

Your own chief contribution to the movement, of which you are now properly the head, was that you brought to those of us who originally raised the matter, a firm grasp of a great principle really constituting the spirit of the Berlin Act. You showed us that all depended upon the right of the original black inhabitants of the soil to own their property and carry on trade.

Such, then, was the plan of campaign which commended itself to my judgement if Public Opinion as a whole was to be captured and the emancipation of the Congo natives secured. As the main object of assault and exposure, the "Congo Free State" *itself*: not its officials in Africa and their actions, but its constitution, its claims, its laws and its Sovereign. That attack to be driven home by an appeal addressed to four principles: human pity the world over: British honour: British Imperial responsibilities in Africa: international commercial rights *coincident with and inseparable from native economic and personal liberties.*

To these ends I laboured to the best of my ability with pen and voice for two years, making a few precious and enduring friendships, and a host of bitter enemies. I worked in close association with Sir Charles Dilke and Mr Fox Bourne, gaining much help and guidance from their ripe experience of men and things; and from the encouragement and good counsel of my old friend Mr John Holt and Mrs John Richard Green, who about that time began to honour me with a regard which I have been fortunate in retaining and from which I have derived immeasurable advantage. [During this period, the cause advanced with, as it seemed to me, desperate slowness, but so steadily and surely that in 1903 Mr. Herbert Samuel's resolution was accepted by the Unionist Government, after a debate, in which the strong feeling which animated all Parties was remarkably exemplified, and voted by the House of Commons without a dissentient voice.

By this first and most signal victory, to which I shall refer in detail later on, Great Britain, through its Government, and on the strength of a mandate *proceeding from the manifestation of the will of the entire House of Commons*, became pledged to the cause of Congo emancipation. And it was with poignant if pardonable emotion that my Wife and I in our modest little home at Hawarden, together with kind messages from Sir Charles Dilke, Mr. Herbert Samuel, Mr. Alfred Emmott, and one or two others, read the following lines from a friend who was present on the occasion:

I do not think you were at the debate on the Congo. The reports do not do you justice and you may like to know that your name was referred to in the highest terms by Samuel, Dilke and Emmott, and the reference was warmly cheered. You were referred to as the man who knew more of the subject than anyone else and to whom we should all be grateful.

The story of the progress and development of the movement up to the moment of the debate in the Commons contains many features of interest which may now be dealt with.][4]

Source: E. D. Morel. *History of the Congo Reform Movement* (1910–14), ed. Wm. Roger Louis and Jean Stengers. Oxford: Oxford University Press, 1968. Chs 7 and 8, pp. 52–69.

Note

A work which Morel did not complete, the *History of Congo Reform Movement* is his quasi-autobiographical account of the establishment – and the difficulties and challenges that accompanied that movement – of the Congo Reform Association.

4 [This passage apparently was omitted by accident in the revised version and follows the fair copy of the original].

Part V

Victoria

Chapter Seventeen

The Crystal Palace and the Great Exhibition of 1851

Introduction

The Great Exhibition of 1851 opened on May 1, 1851 at the Crystal Palace, at Sydenham Hill, a massive structure of iron and glass that had been designed and built specifically to house the display of industry and art that was brought from all corners of the globe for the occasion. When the exhibit closed 140 days later, with the closing ceremony on October 15, 1851, more than 6 million people had visited its premises, bringing in a total of £356,000 in admission fees collected at the door.

The Great Exhibition itself followed on a half century of industrial exhibitions, particularly in Paris, but it was no less significant as the premiere of nearly a century of international expositions to come, across Europe, but in particular in Britain, France, and the United States. Whereas the earlier industrial exhibitions in Paris had been intended to foster growth in national manufactures, the international expositions developed in an age that contemplated the increasing importance of free trade and global economic competition, and eventually came to celebrate the imperial and colonial enterprise. The end of the nineteenth century witnessed such a display nearly every year, in London, Glasgow, Paris, Brussels, Amsterdam, and other European capitals, no less than in the colonies themselves, in India, Australia, Africa, and Canada. By the time of the colossal Wembley Exhibition of 1924–5, the exhibitions were decidedly committed to lauding the projects of empire building. Accord-

ing to its Official Guide, the Great Empire Exhibition at Wembley would "reproduce in miniature the entire resources of the British Empire." Wembley, that is, was to be nothing less than a "stock-taking of the whole resources of Empire" (MacKenzie, 1984: 108).

It was the Crystal Palace and the Great Exhibition of 1851, however, that established the determined premises, principles, and parameters for the century of a self-congratulatory and propagandistic display of combined effects of industry and empire that was to follow: the enhancement of trade, the promotion of new technology, the education of the middle classes, and the elaboration of a political stance (Greenhalgh, 1988: 3). But the Crystal Palace was as renowned – if also denounced – as much for its building as for its exhibits. Designed by Joseph Paxton, in response to an idea conceived by Albert, the Prince Consort, it was constructed of the prefabricated elements iron, glass and timber, and paid for by subscriptions provided from throughout Great Britain. Paxton (1801–65) had been previously been known as a landscape gardener and designer of hothouses and at the time was in the employ of the Duke of Devonshire. The distinguishing features of his conservatories found their way into the Crystal Palace as well – much to the dismay of such critics as John Ruskin, who did not appreciate the replacement of such natural materials as stone that had long graced the traditional monuments and cathedrals of Europe. In 1889, Gustave Eiffel, who had made his career as a builder of bridges, would encounter similar disapprobation with his plans for the Eiffel Tower at the 1889 Exposition in Paris. But Paxton's designs for the Crystal Palace eventually won the day – and the enthusiastic admiration of its visitors – from Victoria herself and the Duke of Wellington who were regular attendees to the day-trippers who took advantage of excursions offered by Thomas Cook for the duration of the Great Exhibition.

The Crystal Palace was made up of a single building that covered nearly 19 acres, and enclosed 33 million cubic feet. It housed 14,000 exhibitors and more than eight miles of display tables. A central avenue, with plants and a splendid fountain divided the western nave, which provided space for the British exhibits – half of the total of the displays – from the eastern nave where the exhibits of the non-British and colonial participants were located. The exhibiting categories – which became determinative for subsequent exhibitions – were: Manufactures, Machinery, Raw Materials, and Fine Arts. For all that it had been designed as a temporary structure, the Crystal Palace remained standing until it was destroyed by fire in 1936. But for 140 days during 1851 – making a memorable London Season – fascinated spectators delighted in the sight of "agricultural machinery, Buckingham lace, cinnamon plantations, diamonds, envelope-making machines, felspar porphyritic rocks, the Great Western Railway engine, hydraulic presses, Indian corn, jewels, the Koh-i-Noor diamond, lace, microscopes, a Niagara Falls model, opals, porcelain, quarries, revolvers, Swiss watches, tea plants and tobacco, uranium, vanilla, weapons of chivalry, Young's crossing gates for railroads, and the Zollverein Department" (according to the index to *The Crystal Palace and Its Contents*).

The empire would continue on exhibit in various other venues throughout its life-history. There were, of course, the official exhibitions, and these developed to include not just the raw materials of industrial development, but the peoples as well who populated the imperial territories. While the Hottentot Venus had been taken around England in 1810, by the end of the century, the "noble savages" themselves and their quaint customs had become a regular feature of the expositions that included such favorites as replicas of African villages and reproductions of Cairo streets. Empire fostered not just industry but ethnography. And more permanent institutions – like the Imperial Institute, whose cornerstone was laid in 1887 as a memorial to Victoria's Jubilee that year – were necessary to maintain these areas of development and avenues of progress. The "Empire under one

Roof," as it was called. Profits were to be made as well, as the goods of empire were traded and its bric-à-brac and comestibles became part of late nineteenth century households, and "old curiosity shops."

May Day 1851, and the opening of the Great Exhibition at the Crystal Palace, then, laid the grounds for a popular, political, and profitable display of imperial prowess and power, grounds that would continue to expand in pomp and display through the coming century.

BH

Additional Reading

Coombes, Annie. *Reinventing Africa*. New Haven: Yale University Press, 1994.
Giedion, Siegfried. "The Great Exhibition," in *Space, Time and Architecture: The Growth of a Tradition* (1941). Cambridge, Mass. 1974.
Greenhalgh, Paul. *Ephemeral Vistas: The Expositions Universelles, Great Exhibitions and World's Fairs*. Manchester, 1988.
Hobhouse, Christopher. *1851 and the Crystal Palace* (1937). London, 1950.
MacKenzie, John M. "The Imperial Exhibitions" and "The Imperial Institute," in *Propaganda and Empire: The Manipulation of British Public Opinion, 1880–1960*. Manchester: Manchester University Press, 1984.
Mitchell, Timothy. *Colonizing Egypt*. Cambridge, 1988.

99   Timeline of Significant Events

1832	First Reform Bill
1836–65	Charles Dickens publishes his major novels
1837	Queen Victoria succeeds William IV
1838	Chartist's "People's Charter"
1840	Severe economic depression in England
1845	Famine in Ireland
1846	Repeal of Corn Laws, Free Trade
1848	Chartist movement
	Cholera epidemic; first Public Health Acts
1850	Alfred Tennyson, Poet Laureate
1851	The Great Exhibition at the Crystal Palace
1851–62	Henry Mayhew's *London Labour and the London Poor* published
1854–6	Crimean War
1857	Irish Republican Brotherhood (Fenians) founded
1857–58	Indian Rebellion

1859	Darwin's *The Origins of Species* published
	J. S. Mill's *On Liberty* published
1859–60	Mrs Beeton's *Book of Household Management* published
1861–5	American Civil War
1865	William Booth founds The Christian Mission in the East End of London; in 1878 it becomes the Salvation Army
1867	Second Reform Bill
1869	Opening of Suez Canal
	J. S. Mill's *The Subjection of Women* published
1870	Education Act (Compulsory)
1871	Paris Commune
1876	Alexander Graham Bell invents the telephone
	Queen Victoria becomes Empress of India
1879	Zulu War
1879	Irish Land League formed
1880–1	First Boer War
1884	Scramble for Africa begins
	Gold discovered on the Rand
	Foundation of Fabian Society
	Social Democratic Federation formed
1885	Death of General Gordon
1886	Gladstone's Home Rule Bill
	First Indian National Congress
	Indian and Colonial Exhibition at Royal Albert Hall
1891	Education Act (Free)
1895	Jameson Raid
1887	Queen Victoria's Golden Jubilee
1888	George Eastman develops the "Kodak" box camera
1893	Independent Labour Party formed
1897	Queen Victoria's Diamond Jubilee
1899–1902	Second Boer War
1901	Foundation of Boy Scouts Organization

100   Queen Victoria: "The Opening of the Great Exhibition"

April 29, 1851   We drove to the Exhibition with only the 2 Maids of Honour and 2 Equerries and remained about 2 hours and $\frac{1}{2}$. I came back quite dead beat and my head really bewildered by the myriads of beautiful and wonderful things, which now quite dazzle one's eyes. Such efforts have been made and our people have shown such taste in their manufactures, all owing to the impetus given by the Exhibition and by my beloved one's guidance. We went up into the Gallery, and the sight of it from there into all the Courts, full of all sorts of objects of art, manufacture etc. had quite the effect of fairyland. [. . .]

May 1   This day is one of the greatest and most glorious days of our lives, with which to my pride and joy, the name of my dearly beloved Albert is for ever associated! It is a day which makes my heart swell with thankfulness. [. . .]

The Park presented a wonderful spectacle, crowds streaming through it, – carriages and troops passing, quite like the Coronation, and for *me*, the same anxiety. The day was bright and all bustle and excitement. At $\frac{1}{2}$ p. 11 the whole procession in 9 State carriages was set in motion [. . .] The Green Park and Hyde Park were one mass of densely crowded human beings, in the highest good humour and most enthusiastic. I never saw Hyde Park look as it did, being filled with crowds as far as the eye could reach. A little rain fell, just as we started, but before we neared the Crystal Palace, the sun shone and gleamed upon the gigantic edifice, upon which the flags of every nation were flying. We drove up Rotten Row and got out of our carriages at the entrance on that side. The glimpse, through the iron gates of the Transept, the waving palms and flowers, the myriads of people filling the galleries and seats around, together with the flourish of trumpets as we entered the building, gave a sensation I shall never forget, and I felt much moved [. . .] In a few seconds we proceeded, Albert leading me, having Vicky at his hand and Bertie holding mine. The sight as we came to the centre where the steps and chair (on which I did *not* sit) was placed facing the beautiful crystal fountain was magic and impressive. The tremendous cheering, the joy expressed in every face, the vastness of the building, with all its decorations and exhibits, the sound of the organ (with 200 instruments and 600 voices, which seemed nothing) and my beloved husband, the creator of this peace festival "uniting the industry and art of all nations of the earth," all this was indeed moving, and a day to live for ever. God bless my dearest Albert, and my dear Country, which has shown itself so great today.

Source: David Duff. *Victoria Travels: Journeys of Queen Victoria between 1830 and 1900, with extracts from her journals.* New York: Taplinger 1971, p. 137.

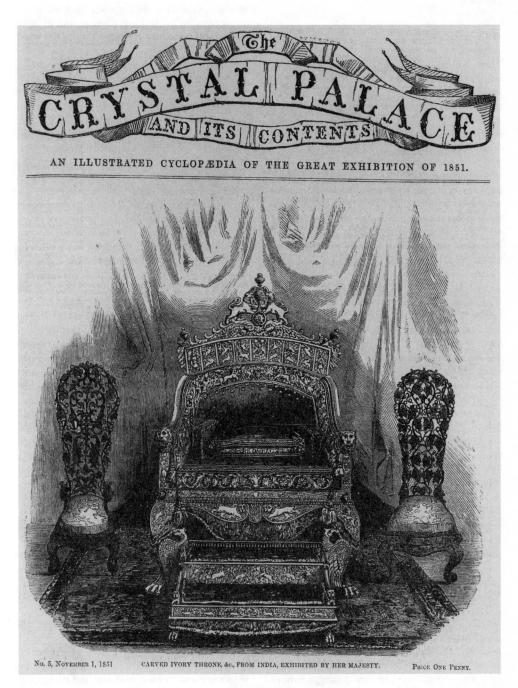

Figure 1   Queen Victoria's carved ivory throne; from *The Crystal Palace and its Contents: An Illustrated Cyclopaedia of the Great Exhibition of 1851.*

101 Lytton Strachey: "Prince Albert and the Great Exhibition" (1921)

Without consulting anyone, he thought out the details of his conception with the minutest care. There had been exhibitions before in the World, but this should surpass them all. It should contain specimens of what every country could produce in raw materials, in machinery and mechanical inventions, in manufactures, and in the applied and plastic arts. It should not be merely useful and ornamental; it should teach a high moral lesson. It should be an international monument to those supreme blessings of civilisation – peace, progress, and prosperity. For some time past the Prince had been devoting much of his attention to the problems of commerce and industry. He had a taste for machinery of every kind, and his sharp eye had more than once detected, with the precision of an expert, a missing cogwheel in some vast and complicated engine. A visit to Liverpool, where he opened the Albert Dock, impressed upon his mind the immensity of modern industrial forces, though in a letter to Victoria describing his experiences, he was careful to retain his customary lightness of touch. "As I write," he playfully remarked, "you will be making your evening toilette, and not be ready in time for dinner. I must set about the same task, and not, let me hope, with the same result. [. . .] The loyalty and enthusiasm of the inhabitants are great; but the heat is greater still. I am satisfied that if the population of Liverpool had been weighed this morning, and were to be weighed again now, they would be found many degrees lighter. The docks are wonderful, and the mass of shipping incredible." In art and science he had been deeply interested since boyhood; his reform of the household had put his talent for organisation beyond a doubt; and thus from every point of view the Prince was well qualified for his task. Having matured his plans, he summoned a small committee and laid an outline of his scheme before it. The committee approved, and the great undertaking was set on foot without delay.

Two years, however, passed before it was completed. For two years the Prince laboured with extraordinary and incessant energy. At first all went smoothly. The leading manufacturers warmly took up the idea; the colonies and the East India Company were sympathetic; the great foreign nations were eager to send in their contributions; the powerful support of Sir Robert Peel was obtained, and

the use of a site in Hyde Park, selected by the Prince, was sanctioned by the Government. Out of 234 plans for the exhibition building, the Prince chose that of Joseph Paxton, famous as a designer of gigantic conservatories; and the work was on the point of being put in hand when a series of unexpected difficulties arose. Opposition to the whole scheme, which had long been smouldering in various quarters, suddenly burst forth. There was an outcry, headed by *The Times*, against the use of the Park for the exhibition; for a moment it seemed as if the building would be relegated to a suburb; but, after a fierce debate in the House, the supporters of the site in the Park won the day. Then it appeared that the project lacked a sufficient financial backing; but this obstacle, too, was surmounted, and eventually £200,000 was subscribed as a guarantee fund. The enormous glass edifice rose higher and higher, covering acres and enclosing towering elm trees beneath its roof: and then the fury of its enemies reached a climax. The fashionable, the cautious, the Protectionists, the pious, all joined in the hue and cry. It was pointed out that the Exhibition would serve as a rallying point for all the ruffians in England, for all the malcontents in Europe; and that on the day of its opening there would certainly be a riot and probably a revolution. It was asserted that the glass roof was porous, and that the droppings of fifty million sparrows would utterly destroy every object beneath it. Agitated nonconformists declared that the Exhibition was an arrogant and wicked enterprise which would infallibly bring down God's punishment upon the nation. Colonel Sibthorpe, in the debate on the Address, prayed that hail and lightning might descend from heaven on the accursed thing. The Prince, with unyielding perseverance and infinite patience, pressed on to his goal. His health was seriously affected; he suffered from constant sleeplessness; his strength was almost worn out. But he remembered the injunctions of Stockmar and never relaxed. The volume of his labours grew more prodigious every day; he toiled at committees, presided over public meetings, made speeches, and carried on communications with every corner of the civilised world – and his efforts were rewarded. On May 1, 1851, the Great Exhibition was opened by the Queen before an enormous concourse of persons, amid scenes of dazzling brilliancy and triumphant enthusiasm.

Victoria herself was in a state of excitement which bordered on delirium. She performed her duties in a trance of joy, gratitude, and amazement, and, when it was all over, her feelings poured themselves out into her journal in a torrential flood. The day had been nothing but an endless succession of glories – or rather one vast glory – one vast radiation of Albert. Everything she had seen, everything she had felt or heard, had been so beautiful, so wonderful that even the royal underlinings broke down under the burden of emphasis, while her remembering pen rushed on, regardless, from splendour to splendour – the huge crowds, so well-behaved and loyal – flags of all the nations floating – the inside of the building, so immense, with myriads of people and the sun shining through the roof – a little side room, where we left our shawls – palm-trees and machinery – dear Albert – the place so big that we could hardly hear the organ – thankfulness to God – a curious assemblage of political and distinguished men – the March from Athalie – God bless my dearest Albert, God bless my dearest country! – a glass fountain – the Duke and Lord Anglesey walking arm in arm – a beautiful Amazon, in bronze, by Kiss – Mr Paxton, who might be justly proud, and rose from being a common gardener's boy – Sir George Grey in tears, and everybody astonished and delighted.

A striking incident occurred when, after a short prayer by the Archbishop of Canterbury, the choir of 600 voices burst into the "Hallelujah Chorus." At that moment a Chinaman, dressed in full national costume, stepped out into the middle of the central nave, and, advancing slowly towards the royal group, did obeisance to Her Majesty. The Queen, much impressed, had no doubt that he was an eminent mandarin; and, when the final procession was formed, orders were given that, as no representative of the Celestial Empire was present, he should be included in the diplomatic cortege. He accordingly, with the utmost gravity, followed immediately behind the Ambassadors. He subsequently disappeared, and it was rumoured, among ill-natured people, that, far from being a mandarin, the fellow was a mere impostor. But nobody ever really discovered the nature of the comments that had been lurking behind the matchless impassivity of that yellow face.

A few days later Victoria poured out her heart to her uncle. The first of May, she said, was "the *greatest* day in our history, the most *beautiful* and *imposing* and *touching* spectacle ever seen, and the triumph of my beloved Albert. . . . It was the *happiest, proudest* day in my life, and I can think of nothing else. Albert's dearest name is immortalised with this *great* conception, *his* own, and my *own* dear country *showed* she was *worthy* of it. The triumph is *immense*."

It was. The enthusiasm was universal; even the bitterest scoffers were converted, and joined in the chorus of praise. Congratulations from public bodies poured in; the City of Paris gave a great *fête* to the Exhibition committee; and the Queen and the Prince made a triumphal progress through the North of England. The financial results were equally remarkable. The total profit made by the Exhibition amounted to a sum of £165,000, which was employed in the purchase of land for the erection of a permanent National Museum in South Kensington. During the six months of its existence in Hyde Park over six million persons visited it, and not a single accident occurred. But there is an end to all things; and the time had come for the Crystal Palace to be removed to the salubrious seclusion of Sydenham. Victoria, sad but resigned, paid her final visit. "It looked so beautiful," she said. "I could not believe it was the last time I was to see it. An organ, accompanied by a fine and powerful wind instrument called the sommerophone, was being played, and it nearly upset me. The canvas is very dirty, the red curtains are faded and many things are very much soiled, still the effect is fresh and new as ever and most beautiful. The glass fountain was already removed [. . .] and the sappers and miners were rolling about the little boxes just as they did at the beginning. It made us all very melancholy." But more cheerful thoughts followed. When all was over, she expressed her boundless satisfaction in a dithyrambic letter to the Prime Minister. Her beloved husband's name, she said, was for ever immortalised, and that this was universally recognised by the country was a source to her of immense happiness and gratitude. "She feels grateful to Providence," Her Majesty conclude, "to have permitted her to be united to so great, so noble, so excellent a Prince, and this year will ever remain the proudest and happiest of her life. The day of the closing of the Exhibition (which the Queen regretted much she could not witness), was the twelfth anniversary of her betrothal to the Prince, which is a curious coincidence."

Source: Lytton Strachey. *Queen Victoria.* New York: Harcourt, Brace, & World, 1949. Ch. 4, pp. 138–43, (Orig. Pub. 1921.)

102   "J. G. Edgar: The Colonial Museum" (1863)

While the Great Exhibition of 1851 was open, and it was yet uncertain that the building would be pulled down, the idea occurred to me that it would be advantageous to the colonies, as well as to people at home, if a Colonial Museum could be established on a large scale in that magnificent edifice. The great mass of people knew very little at that time about the Colonies, nor were they in general interested in them. They were certainly not likely to go much out of their way to visit such a Museum, nor to be willing to pay for seeing it. I wished, however, first to interest them, and then to show them the great value and resources of our Colonial possessions. To accomplish this, I knew that it would be necessary to bring them into the neighbourhood by some greater attractions than the Museum would prove, and then to have an exhibition prepared of a character sufficiently interesting to arrest their attention.

I then edited the Colonial Magazine, and in it I published a paper calling attention to my proposal. I give an extract from it, which will afford an idea of the plan I wished to see carried out:

"In a central compartment we would erect or hang a large globe, with the colonies distinctly marked on it. On the walls we would hang a map of the world, and we would adorn the room with models of trees, stuffed animals, or any other prominent objects, to exhibit the characteristics of the larger colonies. A raised globe would be the most useful.

"Each colony should have a separate compartment, and the compartments should be so arranged, that they should show the relative position of the colonies. The walls of each compartment should be hung with maps, one embracing the quarter of the globe in which the colony exists, so that its exact position should be seen at a glance; while, besides, there should be large maps of each colony and each district, and, in addition, plans of the principal cities and other spots of interest. These would show the geographical position of the colonies. There would also be geological maps, and others showing the different heights of the country, the course of rivers, and the vegetation existing in the different districts. We next come to the means of illustrating the scenery of the country. For this object we would cover the walls with large coloured drawings of the most prominent and interesting scenes characteristic of each district, introducing the vegetation, the style of building, the neighbouring mountains, lakes, or rivers, &c. The views should be placed in order, beginning at one end of the colony, and the exact position of each marked on the maps under which they are placed.

"Besides these large views, we would have others of details, such as sketches of cottages and machinery, or single trees and plants. We would also have drawings of all the birds, the beasts, and reptiles to be found in each colony. There might be even another series to show the various plants, with their leaves and seeds at different periods.

"The country being illustrated as completely as paper and pencil will enable us to do it, we next come to the actual specimens of its natural productions. The minerals would be arranged under the geological maps, with references to show the exact part of the country from which each is taken.

"The seeds, the gums, the roots, would, in like manner, be arranged under the drawings of the trees or plants to which they belong.

"Next to them, under their respective heads, would come the various articles prepared for exportation, or as they are manufactured in the colony. Some means should also be taken to show obviously the principal uses to which they are applied at home. Where it is possible the manufactured articles themselves should be exhibited.

"The flowers and fruit of trees and shrubs should be represented by models of wax or wood, or some other appropriate material, as should all substances which cannot be preserved in their original form. Models of all descriptions of buildings, as well as of trees and plants, should be extensively introduced.

"The beasts, as well as the birds and fish of each district, should appear well stuffed and set up in their proper positions. We would also wish to see models of the face of the country, showing the elevation of certain districts, the height of mountains, and the course of rivers.

"In a word, our aim would be thoroughly to illustrate each colony, so that a person entering the compartment devoted to it would be able at a glance to see its position, its climate and resources. To do this effectually a considerable space will be required, and much art must be employed in the arrangement. Means might be taken to show those colonies which are joined by land and separated by sea, as also to indicate their respective distances. They should be placed also in groups; the North American together; the African, the Asiatic, and the Australasian. A book should also be composed descriptive of the colonies, their various productions, and the uses to which they are put. It might, also, of course, serve as a guide to the museum.

"The museum would be an admirable school for the instruction of youth, and useful lectures might be periodically given on the subject. For the use of public institutions and schools in the country, we would advise the formation of small museums after the model of this large one. Small copies might be made of the colonial drawings and models of prints, and by having a quantity of all the specimens of gums, seeds, etc., sent over, some might be laid aside for that object. These portable museums might be sold in the museum, when the buyers would have an opportunity of testing their correctness."

This paper was widely circulated throughout the colonies, and was sent to all the newspapers. I was much gratified, on visiting the present International Exhibition, to find that the Commissioners of many of the colonies had carried out, in a great degree, the suggestions I had offered, I felt, also, more than ever the great importance such a museum as I proposed would prove at the present day, and the grievous pity it would be to allow so valuable a collection of objects as are there collected to be again separated and lost.

I earnestly hope, therefore, that all who take an interest in the welfare of the colonies, will do their utmost to get such a museum established, and certainly no building could be more fit for it than a portion of that of the International Exhibition. Of course far more system in the arrangement of the objects would be necessary than now exists; more maps, plans, and illustrative drawings are required. An elevated plan of each colony would be valuable; climates might be shown by giving the temperature at different seasons of the year. Here, also, every new product discovered in the colonies should at once be sent, animal, vegetable, or mineral, with a full description of the uses to which it may be put, and the price at which it can be sold in the colony. Notice of the arrival of such articles should be published periodically, either in a paper issued from the museum, or in some other publication. This plan alone would make the museum of great importance, as it would at once bring all colonial products before the notice, not only of the commercial world, but of the public in general. However, the subject is so interesting, and so capable of expansion, that I must not continue it, lest I occupy more space than some of my readers may approve of.

Source: Kingston Annual for Boys, London 1863, pp. 249–52.

Chapter Eighteen

In the Streets: Reforming the Rabble

Introduction

In the Victorian era, one of the central concerns of
the day was the condition of life in Great Britain.
Recent British, European, and colonial uprisings
made politicians and statesmen of every ideological
persuasion distinctly aware of the ways in which
unaddressed social, governmental, and economic
situations could suddenly explode. The enormously rapid growth of Great Britain's industrial-
ized cities created a variety of social and biological
problems. Devastating cholera, typhus, and yellow
fever epidemics had affected a number of cities;
many displaced and under-paid workers turned to
lives of crime; and prostitution and venereal diseases were believed to be rampant social evils that
could potentially affect "respectable" families and
threaten the security and stability of the British
Empire. Some of these social problems were exaggerated; many Victorians were obsessed with
notions of purity and the drive to eradicate sin.
Sensational criminal fictions, tales of fallen women,
and true life crime and punishment narratives fed
the Victorian audience a regular diet of salacious
tales that would shock and comfort the good – who
would be protected by their goodness, identify the
sinful, and attempt to recruit the general audience
to serve in the public and private campaigns for
moral and social reform. The urban poor became
the metropolitan centers' local savages; like many
of the colonial subjects, they were objects of fear
and fascination, and targets of social and administrative experimentation – some of which was necessary and productive, some of which was punitive,

judgmental, and oppressively paternalistic. To be
certain, the empire's poor lived in squalor that
compared to that of the so-called "undeveloped"
nations; and some of the sources of the dire urban
situation were similarly caused by the displacement
of communities and the destruction of traditional
manufacturing and economic systems. Inadequate
housing, clean water, refuse and sanitation facilities
made the urban slums concentration camps. Between the years 1801 and 1841, London's population had more than doubled. And between the
years 1831 and 1844 the mortality rate for Birming-
ham went from 14.6 deaths per thousand to 27.2
deaths per thousand; in the same years the mortality rate for Bristol went from 16.9 to 31 deaths
per thousand, and Liverpool's rates went from 21
to 34.8 deaths per thousand (Britannica Online).
These grim statistics would lead to the organization
of Public Health institutions and the implementation of housing, vaccination, and disease-
prevention programs. The Victorian medical and
social science professionals' productive administrative responses to these modern problems served as
models for health and human services institutions
around the world.

Victorian journalists and photographers, like
Henry Mayhew and John Thompson, invited the
general public to view the wealthy nation's stark
social conditions. Urban reportage and photography were utilized in at least two ways: some producers and receivers of the representations used the
slum images and narratives to lobby on behalf of
the poor; others used the same narratives and images as evidence of impoverished subjects' indolence and sloth. The pressing question of the day

was should or should not the state help those who may or may not be able to help themselves? Parliamentarians and statesmen hotly debated this question and novelists like Charles Dickens, who was influenced by Mayhew's works, pondered it and created realistic and sometimes utopian narratives of salvation and uplift. Dickens's juvenile criminal Oliver Twist, for example, is a secret aristocrat who is rescued by his family heritage by the novel's end. The novel's prostitute with a heart of gold, Nancy, does not fare as well.

The body also provided fertile material for the Victorian imagination. The Romantic era's explorations of sensuality, pleasure, and expanded modes of consciousness were responded to with strict disciplinary regimes to purify, order and control women, racial and ethnic others, and hooligans – the empire's working-class youth. In 1829, Home Secretary Robert Peel ushered through the legislation that would establish the London Metropolitan Police force at 4 Whitehall Place and Scotland Yard. Peel believed a larger, more centralized force would be able to maintain law and order more efficiently and more vigilantly observe the city's "criminal element." His common-name and surname would provide the officers of the law with their nicknames for years to come – bobbies and peelers. Years later in 1878, the plainclothes Criminal Investigation Department (CID) would be formed.

The law and order and sexually moralistic discourses of the Victorian era have maintained their rhetorical power to this day; twentieth-century Prime Minister Margaret Thatcher would regularly hearken back to the allegedly secure and orderly period. A closer examination of the era reveals Victorian people to be as interested in crime, scandal, and sexuality as contemporary audiences are; the deeper and more significant matter of whether or not the ethnically, racially, and sexually different or impoverished "sinners" could become "respectable" or equal citizens in the eyes of the law also continues to be a current question.

MC

Additional Reading

Acton, William. *Prostitution, Considered in Its Moral, Social, and Sanitary Aspects*. London, 1870.

Betjeman, John. *Victorian and Edwardian London from Old Photographs*. New York, 1969.

Bristow, E. J. *Vice and Vigilance: Purity Movements in Britain Since 1700*. Dublin, 1977.

Fisher, Trevor. *Prostitution and the Victorians*. New York, 1997.

Foster, J. *Class Struggle and the Industrial Revolution*. London, 1974.

Foucault, Michel. *Discipline and Punish: The Birth of the Prison*. New York, 1977.

Greenwood, James. *The Wilds of London*. London, 1874.

Jones, David. *Crime, Protest, Community and Police in Nineteenth-Century Britain*. London, 1982.

McHugh, Paul. *Prostitution and Victorian Social Reform*. London, 1980.

Newman, George. *Health of the State*. London, 1907.

Ritchie, James Ewing. *The Night Side of London*. London, 1857.

Simon, Sir John. *English Sanitary Institutions, Reviewed in Their Course of Development and in Some of Their Political and Social Relation*. London, 1890.

Smith, Anna Marie. *New Right Discourse on Race and Sexuality: Britain 1968–1990*. Cambridge, 1994.

Thomis, M. I. and P. Holt. *Threats of Revolution in Britain, 1789–1848*. London, 1977.

Tobias, John Jacob. *Urban Crime in Victorian England* (1967). New York, 1972.

Walkowitz, Judith A. *City of Dreadful Delight: Narratives of Sexual Danger in Late-Victorian London*. London, 1992.

Weeks, Jeffrey. *Sex, Politics, and Society: The Regulation of Sexuality Since 1800*. London, 1981.

Films

William Cowen. *Oliver Twist* (1933).

David Lean. *Oliver Twist* (1948).

Carol Reed. *Oliver!* (1968).

103 Henry Mayhew: Characters from *London Labour and the London Poor* (1851–62)

An Irish Street-Seller

OF THE causes which induced a good-looking Irish woman to become a street-seller I had the following account, which I give in its curious details:

"'Deed thin, sir, it's more than 20 long years since I came from Dublin to Liverpool wid my father and mother, and brother William that's dead and gone, rest his soul. He died when he was fourteen. They was masons in Ireland. Was both father and mother masons, sir? Well, then, in any quiet job mother helped father, for she was a strong woman. They came away sudden. They was in some thrubble, but I never knew what, for they wouldn't talk to me about it. We thravelled from Liverpool to London, for there was no worruk at Liverpool; and he got worruk on buildings in London, and had 18s. a week; and mother cleaned and worruked for a greengrocer, as they called him – he sold coals more than anything – where we lodged, and it wasn't much, she got, but she airned what is such a thrubble to poor people, the rint. We was well off, and I was sent to school; and we should have been better off, but father took too much to the dhrop, God save him. He fell onste and broke his leg; and though the hospital gintlemen, God bless them for good Christians, got him through it, he got little worruk when he came out again, and died in less than a year. Mother wasn't long afther him; and on her death-bed she said, so low I could hardly hear her, 'Mary, my darlint, if you starruve, be vartuous. Remimber poor Illen's funeral.'

"When I was quite a child, sir, I went wid mother to a funeral – she was a relation – and it was of a young woman that died after her child had been borrun a fortnight, and she wasn't married; that was Illen. Her body was brought out of the lying-in hospital – I've often heard spake of it since – and was in the churchyard to be buried; and her brother, that hadn't seen her for a long time, came and wanted to see her in her coffin, and they took the lid off, and then he currused her in her coffin afore him; she'd been so wicked. But he wasn't a good man hisself, and was in dhrink too; still no-body said anything, and he walked away. It made me ill to see Illen in her coffin, and hear him curruse, and I've remembered it ever since.

"I was thin fifteen, I believe, and hadn't any friends that had any tie to me. I was lone, sir. But the neebours said, 'Poor thing, she's left on the shuckrawn' [homeless]; and they helped me, and I got a place. Mistress was very kind at first, that's my first mistress was, and I had the care of a child of three years old; they had only one, because mis-tress was busy making waistcoats. Master was a hatter, and away all day, and they was well off. But some women called on mistress once, and they had a deal of talkin', and bladherin', and laughin', and I don't know how often I was sent out for quarterns of gin. Then they all went out together; and mis-tress came home quite tipsy just afore master, and went upstairs, and had just time to get into bed; she told me to tell master she had one of her sick head-aches and was forced to go to bed; she went on that way for three or four days, and master and she used to quarrel of a night, for I could hear them. One night he came home sooner than common, and he'd been drinking, or perhaps it might be thrubble, and he sent me to bed with the child; and sometime in the night, I don't know what time, but I could only see from a gas-lamp that shined into the room, he came in, for there was no fastenin' inside the door, it was only like a closet, and he began to ask me about mistress.

"When he larned she'd been drinking wid other women, he used dreadful language, and pulled me out of bed, and struck me with a stick that he snatched up, he could see it in the gas-light, it was

little Frank's horse, and swore at me for not telling him afore. He only struck me onste, but I screamed ever so often, I was so frightened. I dressed myself, and lay down in my clothes, and got up as soon as it was light – it was summer time – and thought I would go away and complain to some one. I would ask the neebours who to complain to. When I was going out there was master walking up and down the kitchen. He'd never been to bed, and he says, says he, "Mary, where are you going?' So I told him, and he begged my pardon, and said he was ashamed of what he'd done, but he was half mad; then he began to cry, and so I cried, and mistress came home just then, and when she saw us both crying together, *she* cried, and said she wasn't wanted, as we was man and wife already. Master just gave her a push and down she fell, and he ran out. She seemed so bad, and the child began to cry, that I couldn't lave thin; and master came home drunk that night, but he wasn't cross, for he'd made out that mistress had been drinking with some neebours, and had got to her mother's, and that she was so tipsy she fell asleep, they let her stay till morning, and then some woman set her home, but she'd been there all night. They made it up at last, but I wouldn't stay. They was very kind to me when I left, and paid me all that was owing, and gave me a good pair of shoes, too; for they was well off.

"I had many places for seven years; after that, and when I was out of a place, I stayed wid a widder, and a very dacint woman she was, wid a daughter working for a bookbinder, and the old woman had a good pitch with fruit. Some of my places was very harrud, but shure, again, I met some as was very kind. I left one because they was always wanting me to go to a Methodist chapel, and was always running down my religion, and did all they could to hinder my ever going to mass. They would hardly pay me when I left, because I wouldn't listen to them, they said – the haythens! – when they would have saved my soul. *They* save my soul, indeed! The likes o' thim! Yes, indeed, thin, I had wicked offers sometimes, and from masters that should have known better. I kept no company wid young men. One mistress refused me a karackter, because I was so unhandy, she said; but she thought better of it. At last, I had a faver [fe-ver], and wasn't expected for long [not expected to live]; when I was getting well, everything went to keep me. What wasn't good enough for the pawn went to the dolly [dolly-shop, generally a rag and bottle shop, or a marine store].

"When I could get about, I was so shabby, and my clothes hung about me so, that the shops I went to said, 'Very sorry, but can't recommend you any-where;' and mistresses looked strange at me, and I didn't know what to do and was miserable. I'd been miserable sometimes in place, and had many a cry, and thought how 'lone' I was, but I never was so miserable as this. At last, the old woman I stayed along wid – O, yes, she was an Irishwoman – ad-vised me to sill fruit in the streets, and I began on strawberries, and borrowed 2s. 6d. to do it wid. I had my hilth better than ever thin; and after I'd sold fruit of all kinds for two years, I got married. My husband had a potato can thin. I knew him because he lived near, and I saw him go in and out, and go to mass. After that he got a porter's place and dropped his can, and he porters when he has a chance still, and has a little work in sewing sacks for the corn-merchants. Whin he's at home at his sacks, as he is now, he can mind the children – we have two – and I sells a few oranges to make a thrifle. Whin there's nothing ilse for him to do, he sills fruit in the sthreets, and thin I'm at home. We do middlin, God be praised."

There is no doubt my informant was a modest, and, in her way, a worthy woman. But it may be doubted if any English girl, after seven years of domestic service, would have so readily adapted herself to a street calling. Had an English girl been living among, and used to the society of women who supported themselves by street labour, her repugnance to such a life might have been lessened; but even then, I doubt if she, who had the virtue to resist the offers told of by my Irish informant, could have made the attempt to live by selling fruit. I do not mean that she would rather have fallen into immoral courses than honestly live upon the sale of strawberries, but that she would have struggled on and striven to obtain any domestic labour in preference to a street occupation.

Hindo Beggars

ARE those spare, snake-eyed Asiatics who walk the streets, coolly dressed in Manchester cottons, or chintz of a pattern commonly used for bed-furniture, to which the resemblance is carried out by the dark, polished colour of the thin limbs which it envelopes. They very often affect to be converts to the Christian religion, and give away tracts; with the intention of entrapping the sympathy of elderly ladies. They assert that they have been high-caste Brahmins, but as untruth, even when not acting professionally, is habitual to them, there is not the slightest dependence to be placed on what they say. Sometimes, in the winter, they "do shallow," that is, stand on the kerb-stone of the pavement, in their

thin, ragged clothes, and shiver as with cold and hunger, or crouch against a wall and whine like a whipped animal; at others they turn out with a small, barrel-shaped drum, on which they make a monotonous noise with their fingers, to which mu-sic they sing and dance. Or they will "stand pad with a fakement," i.e. wear a placard upon their breasts, that describes them as natives of Madagas-car, in distress, converts to Christianity, anxious to get to a seaport where they can work their passage back. This is a favourite artifice with Lascars – or they will sell lucifers, or sweep a crossing, or do anything where their picturesque appearance, of which they are proud and conscious, can be effec-tively displayed. They are as cunning as they look, and can detect a sympathetic face among a crowd. They never beg of soldiers, or sailors, to whom they always give a wide berth as they pass them in the streets.

From the extraordinary mendacity of this race of beggars – a mendacity that never falters, hesitates, or stumbles, but flows on in an unbroken stream of falsehood – it is difficult to obtain any reliable in-formation respecting them. I have, however, many reasons for believing that the following statement, which was made to me by a dirty and distressed Indian, is moderately true. The man spoke English like a cockney of the lowest order. I shall not at-tempt to describe the peculiar accent or construc-tion which he occasionally gave to it.

"My name is Joaleeka. I do not know where I was born. I never knew my father. I remember my mother very well. From the first of my remem-brance I was at Dumdum, where I was servant to a European officer – a great man – a prince – who had more than a hundred servants beside me. When he went away to fight, I followed among others – I was with the baggage. I never fought myself, but I have heard the men (Sepoys), say that the prince, or general, or colonel, liked nothing so well as fighting, except tiger-hunting. He was a wonderful man, and his soldiers liked him very much. I travelled over a great part of India with Europeans. I went up coun-try as far as Secunderabad, and learned to speak English very well – so well that, when I was quite a young man, I was often employed as interpreter, for I caught up different Indian languages quickly. At last I got to interpret so well that I was recom-mended to ——, a great native prince who was coming over to England. I was not his interpreter, but interpreter to his servants. We came to London. We stopped in an hotel in Vere Street, Oxford Street. We stayed here some time. Then my chief went over to Paris, but he did not take all his serv-ants with him. I stopped at the hotel to interpret for those who remained. It was during this time that I formed a connexion with a white woman. She was a servant in the hotel. I broke my caste, and from that moment I knew that it would not do for me to go back to India. The girl fell in the family-way, and was sent out of the house. My fellow-servants knew of it, and as many of them hated me, I knew that they would tell my master on his return. I also knew that by the English laws in England I was a free man, and that my master could not take me back against my will. If I had gone back, I should have been put to death for breaking my caste. When my master returned from France, he sent for me. He told me that he had heard of my breaking my caste, and of the girl, but that he should take no notice of it; that I was to return to Calcutta with him, where he would get me employment with some European officer; that I need not fear, as he would order his servants to keep silent on the subject. I salaamed and thanked him, and said I was his servant for ever; but at the same time I knew that he would break his word, and that when he had me in his power, he would put me to death. He was a very severe man about caste. I attended to all my duties as before, and all believed that I was going back to India – but the very morning that my master started for the coast, I ran away. I changed my clothes at the house of a girl I knew – not the same one as I had known at the hotel, but another. This one lived at Seven Dials. I stopped indoors for many days, till this girl, who could read newspapers, told me that my master had sailed away. I felt very glad, for though I knew my master could not force me to go back with him, yet I was afraid for all that, for he knew the King and Queen and had been invited by the Lord Mayor to the City. I liked England better than India, and English women have been very kind to me. I think English women are the handsomest in the world. The girl in whose house I hid, showed me how to beg. She persuaded me to turn Christian, because she thought that it would do me good – so I turned Christian. I do not know what it means, but I am a Christian, and have been for many years. I married that girl for some time. I have been married several times. I do not mean to say that I have ever been to church as rich folks do; but I have been married without that. Sometimes I do well, and sometimes badly. I often get a pound or two by interpreting. I am not at all afraid of meeting any Indian who knew me, for if they said anything I did not like, I should call out 'Police!' I know the law better than I did. Everything is free in England. You can do what you like, if you can pay, or are not found out. I do not like policemen. After the mutiny in 1857 I did very

badly. No one would look at a poor Indian then – much less give to him. I knew that the English would put it down soon, because I know what those rascals over there are like. I am living now in Charles Street, Drury Lane. I have been married to my present wife six years. We have three children and one dead. My eldest is now in the hospital with a bad arm. I swept a crossing for two years; that was just before the mutiny. All that knew me used to chaff me about it, and call me Johnny Sepoy. My present wife is Irish, and fought two women about it. They were taken to Bow Street by a policeman, but the judge would not hear them. My wife is a very good wife to me, but she gets drunk too often. If it were not for that, I should like her better. I ran away from her once, but she came after me with all the children. Sometimes I make twelve shillings a week. I could make much more by interpreting, but I do not like to go among the nasty natives of my country. I believe I am more than fifty years of age."

Negro Beggars

THE negro beggar so nearly resembles the Hindoo that what I have said of one, I could almost say of the other. There are, however, these points of difference. The negro mendicant, who is usually an American negro, never studies the picturesque in his attire. He relies on the abject misery and down-trodden despair of his appearance, and generally represents himself as a fugitive slave – with this exception, his methods of levying contributions are precisely the same as his lighter-skinned brother's.

Some years ago it was a common thing to see a negro with tracts in his hand, and a placard upon his breast, upon which was a wood-cut of a black man, kneeling, his wrists heavily chained, his arms held high in supplication, and round the picture, forming a sort of proscenium or frame, the words: "Am I not a man and a brother?" At the time that the suppression of the slave trade created so much excitement, this was so excellent a "dodge" that many white beggars, fortunate enough to possess a flattish or turned-up nose, dyed themselves black and "stood pad" as real Africans. The imposture, however, was soon detected and punished.

There are but few negro beggars to be seen now. It is only common fairness to say that negroes seldom, if ever, shirk work. Their only trouble is to obtain it. Those who have seen the many negroes employed in Liverpool, will know that they are hard-working, patient, and, too often, underpaid. A negro will sweep a crossing, run errands, black boots, clean knives and forks, or dig, for a crust and a few pence. The few impostors among them are to be found among those who go about giving lectures on the horrors of slavery, and singing variations on the "escapes" in that famous book "Uncle Tom's Cabin." Negro servants are seldom read of in police reports, and are generally found to give satisfaction to their employers. In the east end of London negro beggars are to be met with, but they are seldom beggars by profession. Whenever they are out of work they have no scruples, but go into the streets, take off their hats, and beg directly.

I was accosted by one in Whitechapel, for whom I obtained the following statement:

"My father was a slave, so was my mother. I have heard my father say so. I have heard them tell how they got away, but I forget all about it. It was before I was born. I am the eldest son. I had only one brother. Three years after his birth my mother died. My father was a shoe-black in New York. He very often had not enough to eat. My brother got a place as a servant, but I went out in the streets to do what I could. About the same time that my father, who was an old man, died, my brother lost his place. We agreed to come to England together. My brother had been living with some Britishers, and he had heard them say that over here niggers were as good as whites; and that the whites did not look down on them and ill-treat them, as they do in New York. We went about and got odd jobs on the quay, and at last we hid ourselves in the hold of a vessel, bound for Liverpool. I do not know how long we were hid, but I remember we were terribly frightened lest we should be found out before the ship got under weigh. At last hunger forced us out, and we rapped at the hatches; at first we were not heard, but when we shouted out, they opened the hatches, and took us on deck. They flogged us very severely, and treated us shamefully all the voyage. When we got to Liverpool, we begged and got odd jobs. At last we got engaged in a travelling circus, where we were servants, and used to ride about with the band in beautiful dresses, but the grooms treated us so cruelly that we were forced to run away from that. I forget the name of the place that we were performing at, but it was not a day's walk from London. We begged about for some time. At last, my brother – his name is Aaron – got to clean the knives and forks at a slap-bang [an eating-house] in the city. He was very fortunate, and used to save some bits for me. He never takes any notice of me now. He is doing very well. He lives with a great gentleman in Harewood Square, and has a coat with silver buttons, and a gold-laced hat. He is very proud, and I do not think would speak to me

if he saw me. I don't know how I live, or how much I get a week. I do porter's work mostly, but I do anything I can get. I beg more than half the year. I have no regular lodging. I sleep where I can. When I am in luck, I have a bed. It costs me threepence. At some places they don't care to take a man of colour in. I sometimes get work in Newgate Market, carrying meat, but not often. Ladies give me halfpence oftener than men. The butchers call me 'Othello,' and ask me why I killed my wife. I have tried to get aboard a ship, but they won't have me. I don't know how old I am, but I know that when we got to London, it was the time the Great Exhibition was about. I can lift almost any weight when I have had a bit of something to eat. I don't care for beer. I like rum best. I have often got drunk, but never when I paid for it myself."

Source: Peter Quennell (ed.). *Mayhew's Characters.* London: Kimber 1951, pp. 139–42. P. Quennell (ed.) *London's Underworld*, London: Kimber, 1950, pp. 395–9.

Note

Mayhew's Characters is an excerpt from Henry Mayhew's *London Labour and the London Poor: A Cyclopedia of the Conditions and Earnings of Those That Will Work and Those That Cannot* (London, 1851–62). Mayhew (1812–87) was a journalist and sociologist; he also wrote a number of plays, fairy tales, and novels. He is best known for being the founder and co-editor of *Punch* (1841–1992). Some of Mayhew's significant and related works include, *Deeds Not Words* (London, 1850), and *Criminal Prisons of London and Scenes of Prison Life* (London, 1862).

104   Anonymous: "The Voice of the Hooligan" (1899)

THE *Contemporary* for December contains a remarkable article by Mr Robert Buchanan, in which he launches his bolts against the ferocious and contemptible Jingoism of the time which inspires Mr Rudyard Kipling and supplies material for the vapouring of the Yellow Press. Ever since "the criminal crusade of the Crimean War," says Mr Buchanan, the enthusiasm of humanity has been gradually dying away to be replaced by a spirit of blind and animal brutality, tempered by panic and cowardice, and debased by bragging.

Hooligan Imperialism

Here is the picture which Mr Buchanan contrasts with the "Gospel of humanity as expressed in the language of poets like Wordsworth and Shelley, and in the deeds of men like Wilberforce and Mazzini":

The Aristocracy, impoverished by its own idleness and luxury, rushes wildly to join the Middle-class in speculations which necessitate new conquests of territory and constant acts of aggression. The Mob, promised a merry time by the governing classes, just as the old Roman mob was deluded by bread and pageants – *panem et circenses* – dances merrily to patriotic War-tunes, while that modern monstrosity and anachronism, the Conservative Working Man, exchanges his birthright of freedom and free thought for a pat on the head from any little rump-fed lord that steps his way and spouts the platitudes of Cockney patriotism. The Established Church, deprived of the conscience which accompanied honest belief, supports nearly every infamy of the moment in the name of the Christianity which it has long ago shifted quietly overboard. There is an universal scramble for plunder, for excitement, for amusement, for speculation, and above it all the flag of a Hooligan Imperialism is raised, with the proclamation that it is the sole mission of Anglo-Saxon England, forgetful of the task of keeping its own drains in order, to expand and extend its boundaries indefinitely, and, again in the name of the Christianity it has practically abandoned, to conquer and inherit the Earth.

The political life based on this is equally rotten. Since Mr Gladstone's death we possess no politician, with the single exception of Mr Morley, who demands for the discussion of public affairs any conscientious and unselfish sanction whatever:

We possess instead a thousand pertinacious counsellors, cynics like Lord Salisbury or trimmers like Lord Rosebery, for whom no one in his heart of hearts feels the slightest respect. Our fashionable Society is admittedly so rotten, root and branch, that not even the Queen's commanding influence can impart to it the faintest suggestion of purity or even decency. As for our popular Literature, it has been in many of its manifestations long past praying for; it has run to seed in fiction of the baser sort, seldom or never with all its cleverness touching the quick of human conscience; but its most extraordinary feature at this moment is the exaltation to a position of almost unexampled popularity of a writer who in his single person adumbrates, I think, all that is most deplorable, all that is most retrograde and savage, in the restless and uninstructed Hooliganism of the time.

The Hero of Hooliganism

It is needless to say that this Hooligan bard is Mr Rudyard Kipling. Encouraged by the journalistic praise lavished on the fragments of verse with which he had ornamented his prose effusions, Mr Kipling decided to challenge criticism as "the approved and authoritative Poet of the British Empire." He set himself to sing Tommy Atkins, and the hero – in no way, Mr Buchanan thinks, resembling the real soldier – is a drunken, swearing, coarse-minded Hooligan for whom, nevertheless, our sympathy is earnestly entreated. Against Mr Kipling's ideal of the swaggering and filthy-minded butcher scarcely a word of protest has been raised:

Are we to assume, then, that there are no refined gentlemen among our officers, and no honest, self-respecting human beings among their men? Is the life of a soldier, abroad as at home, a succession of savage escapades, bestial amusements, fuddlings, tipplings, and intrigues with other men's wives, redeemed from time to time by acts of brute courage and of *sang froid* in the presence of dangers? Is the spirit of Gordon quite forgotten, in the service over which he shed the glory of his illustrious name? If this is really the case, there is surely very little in the Anglo-Saxon military prestige which offers us any security for the stormy times to come. That Englishmen are brave and capable of brave deeds is a truism of which we need no longer to be assured; but bravery and brave deeds are not national possessions – they are the prerogative of the militant classes all over the earth. Englishmen in times past were not merely brave, they could be noble and magnanimous; their courage was not only that of the bulldog, but of the patriot, the hero, and even the philanthropist: they had not yet begun to mingle the idea of a national Imperialism with the political game of Brag. I am not contending for one moment that the spirit which inspired them then has altogether departed; I am sure, on the contrary, that it is living yet, and living most strongly and influentially in the heart of the Army itself; but if this is admitted and believed, it is certain that the Tommy Atkins of Mr Rudyard Kipling deserves drumming out of all decent barracks as a monstrosity and a rogue.

The truth is, however, that these lamentable productions were concocted, not for sane men or self-respecting soldiers, not even for those who are merely ignorant and uninstructed, but for the "mean whites" of our eastern civilisation, the idle and loafing Men in the Street, and for such women, the well-drest Doll Tearsheets of our cities, as shriek at their heels. Mr Kipling's very vocabulary is a purely Cockney vocabulary, even his Irishmen speaking a dialect which would cause amazement in the Emerald Isle, but is familiar enough in Seven Dials.

Here is Mr Buchanan's view of the new Imperialism – the Hooligan Imperialism of which Lord Rosebery is the self-appointed prophet:

I write neither as a Banjo-Imperialist nor as a Little Englander, but simply as a citizen of a great Nation, who loves his country and would gladly see it honoured and respected wherever the English tongue is spoken. It will scarcely be denied, indeed it is frankly admitted by all parties, that the Hooligan spirit of Patriotism, the fierce and quasi-savage militant spirit as expressed in many London newspapers and in such literature as the writings of Mr Kipling, has measurably lowered the affection and respect once felt for us among European nations.

The True Imperialism

The ideal of true Imperialism, which would neither bully and grab with Lord Rosebery in Africa, and cringe with him before Russia, still exists, and Mr Buchanan thinks it has still a chance:

True Imperialism should be strong, but the strength should be that of Justice, of Wisdom, of brotherly love and sympathy; for the power which is bred of a mere multitude equipped with the engines of slaughter will, in the long run, avail nothing against the eternal Law which determines that the righteous only shall inherit the earth. We are a People still, though we seem for the time being to be forgetting the conditions on which we received our charter, and deep in the heart of England survives the sentiment of a world-wide nationality, as expressed in the passionate lines of a modern poet.

"Hands across the Sea!
Feet on British ground!
The Motherhood means Brotherhood the whole
    world round!
From the parent root,
Sap, and stem, and fruit

Grow the same, or soil or name. –
Hands across the Sea!"

There sounds the true Imperial feeling, which will survive, I think, long after the repulsive school of Patriotism which I have called (for want of a better name) the Hooligan school, is silent and forgotten. Let me at least hope that it may be so – that Englishmen, after their present wild orgy of militant savagery, may become clothed and in their right minds. There is time to pause yet, although they are already paying the penalty, in blood, in tears, in shame.

Source: The Review of Reviews. vol. 20 July–Dec. 1899, p. 581.

105   General William Booth: "Why 'Darkest England'?" (1890)

This summer the attention of the civilized world has been arrested by the story which Mr Stanley has told of "Darkest Africa" and his journeyings across the heart of the Lost Continent. In all that spirited narrative of heroic endeavour, nothing has so much impressed the imagination, as his description of the immense forest, which offered an almost impenetrable barrier to his advance. The intrepid explorer, in his own phrase, "marched, tore, ploughed, and cut his way for one hundred and sixty days through this inner womb of the true tropical forest." The mind of man with difficulty endeavors to realize this immensity of wooded wilderness, covering a territory half as large again as the whole of France, where the rays of the sun never penetrate, where in the dark, dank air, filled with the steam of the heated morass, human beings dwarfed into pygmies and brutalized into cannibals lurk and live and die. Mr Stanley vainly endeavors to bring home to us the full horror of that awful gloom. He says:

Take a thick Scottish copse dripping with rain; imagine this to be a mere undergrowth nourished under the impenetrable shade of ancient trees ranging from 100 to 180 feet high; briars and thorns abundant; lazy creeks meandering through the depths of the jungle, and sometimes a deep affluent of a great river. Imagine this forest and jungle in all stages of decay and growth, rain pattering on you every other day of the year; an impure atmosphere with its dread consequences, fever and dysentery;

gloom throughout the day and darkness almost palpable throughout the night; and then if you can imagine such a forest extending the entire distance from Plymouth to Peterhead, you will have a fair idea of some of the inconveniences endured by us in the Congo forest.

The denizens of this region are filled with a conviction that the forest is endless – interminable. In vain did Mr Stanley and his companions endeavor to convince them that outside the dreary wood were to be found sunlight, pasturage and peaceful meadows.

They replied in a manner that seemed to imply that we must be strange creatures to suppose that it would be possible for any world to exist save their illimitable forest. "No," they replied, shaking their heads compassionately, and pitying our absurd questions, "all like this," and they moved their hands sweepingly to illustrate that the world was all alike, nothing but trees, trees and trees – great trees rising as high as an arrow shot to the sky, lifting their crowns intertwining their branches, pressing and crowding one against the other, until neither the sunbeam nor shaft of light can penetrate it.

"We entered the forest," says Mr Stanley, "with confidence; forty pioneers in front with axes and bill hooks to clear a path through the obstructions, praying that God and good fortune would lead us." But before the conviction of the forest dwellers that the forest was without end, hope faded out of the hearts of the natives of Stanley's company. The men became sodden with despair, preaching was useless to move their brooding sullenness, their morbid gloom.

The little religion they knew was nothing more than legendary lore, and in their memories there dimly floated a story of a land which grew darker and darker as one travelled towards the end of the earth and drew nearer to the place where a great serpent lay supine and coiled round the whole world. Ah! then the ancients must have referred to this, where the light is so ghastly, and the woods are endless, and are so still and solemn and grey; to this oppressive loneliness, amid so much life, which is so chilling to the poor distressed heart; and the horror grew darker with their fancies; the cold of early morning, the comfortless grey of dawn, the dead white mist, the ever-dripping tears of the dew, the deluging rains, the appalling thunder bursts and the echoes, and the wonderful play of the dazzling lightning. And when the night comes with its thick palpable darkness, and they lie huddled in their damp little huts, and they hear the tempest overhead, and the howling of the wild winds, the grinding and groaning of the storm-tost trees, and the dread sounds of the falling giants, and the shock of the trembling earth which sends their hearts with fitful leaps to their throats, and the roaring and a rushing as of a mad overwhelming sea – oh, then the horror is intensified! When the march has begun once again, and the files are slowly moving through the woods, they renew their morbid broodings, and ask themselves: How long is this to last? Is the joy of life to end thus? Must we jog on day after day in this cheerless gloom and this joyless duskiness, until we stagger and fall and rot among the toads? Then they disappear into the woods by twos, and threes, and sixes; and after the caravan has passed they return by the trail, some to reach Yambuya and upset the young officers with their tales of woe and war; some to fall sobbing under a spear-thrust; some to wander and stray in the dark mazes of the woods, hopelessly lost; and some to be carved for the cannibal feast. And those who remain compelled to it by fears of greater danger, mechanically march on, a prey to dread and weakness.

That is the forest. But what of its denizens? They are comparatively few; only some hundreds of thousands living in small tribes from ten to thirty miles apart, scattered over an area on which ten thousand million trees put out the sun from a region four times as wide as Great Britain. Of these pygmies there are two kinds; one a very degraded specimen with ferretlike eyes, close-set nose, more nearly approaching the baboon than was supposed to be possible, but very human; the other very handsome, with frank open innocent features, very prepossessing. They are quick and intelligent, capable of deep affection and gratitude, showing remarkable industry and patience. A pygmy boy of eighteen worked with consuming zeal; time with him was too precious to waste in talk. His mind seemed ever concentrated on work. Mr Stanley said:

"When I once stopped him to ask him his name, his face seemed to say, 'Please don't stop me. I must finish my task.'

"All alike, the baboon variety and the handsome innocents, are cannibals. They are possessed with a perfect mania for meat. We were obliged to bury our dead in the river, lest the bodies should be exhumed and eaten, even when they had died from smallpox."

Upon the pygmies and all the dwellers of the forest has descended a devastating visitation in the shape of the ivory raiders of civilization. The race that wrote the Arabian Nights, built Bagdad and Granada, and invented Algebra, sends forth men with the hunger for gold in their hearts, and Enfield muskets in their hands, to plunder and to slay. They exploit the domestic affections of the forest dwellers in order to strip them of all they possess in the world. That has been going on for years. It is going on to-day. It has come to be regarded as the natural and normal law of existence. Of the religion of these hunted pygmies, Mr Stanley tells us nothing, perhaps because there is nothing to tell. But an earlier traveler, Dr Kraff, says that one of these tribes, by name Doko, had some notion of a Supreme Being, to whom, under the name of Yer, they sometimes addressed prayers in moments of sadness or terror. In these prayers they say: "Oh Yer, if Thou dost really exist why dost Thou let us be slaves? We ask not for food or clothing, for we live on snakes, ants, and mice. Thou hast made us, wherefore dost Thou let us be trodden down?"

It is a terrible picture, and one that has engraved itself deep on the heart of civilization. But while brooding over the awful presentation of life as it exists in the vast African forest, it seemed to me only too vivid a picture of many parts of our own land. As there is a darkest Africa is there not also a darkest England? Civilization, which can breed its own barbarians, does it not also breed its own pygmies? May we not find a parallel at our own doors, and discover within a stone's throw of our cathedrals and palaces similar horrors to those which Stanley has found existing in the great-Equatorial forest?

The more the mind dwells upon the subject, the closer the analogy appears. The ivory raiders who brutally traffic in the unfortunate denizens of the forest glades, what are they but the publicans who flourish on the weakness of our poor? The two tribes of savages, the human baboon and the handsome dwarf, who will not speak lest it impede him in his task, may be accepted as the two varieties who are continually present with us – the vicious, lazy lout, and the toiling slave. They, too, have lost all faith of life being other than it is and has been. As in Africa, it is all trees, trees, trees with no other world conceivable; so is it here – it is all vice and poverty and crime. To many the world is all slum, with the Workhouse as an intermediate purgatory before the grave. And just as Mr Stanley's Zanzibaris lost faith, and could only be induced to plod on in brooding sullenness of dull despair, so the most of our social reformers, no matter how cheerily they may have started off, with forty pioneers swinging blithely their axes as they force their way into the wood, soon become depressed and despairing. Who can battle against the ten thousand million trees? Who can hope to make headway against the innumerable adverse conditions which doom the dweller in Darkest England to eternal and immutable misery? What wonder is it that many of the warmest hearts and enthusiastic workers feel disposed to repeat the lament of the old English chronicler, who, speaking of the evil days which fell upon our forefathers in the reign of Stephen, said "It seemed to them as if God and his Saints were dead."

An analogy is as good as a suggestion; it becomes wearisome when it is pressed too far. But before leaving it, think for a moment how close the parallel is, and how strange it is that so much interest should be excited by a narrative of human squalor and human heroism in a distant continent, while greater squalor and heroism not less magnificent may be observed at our very doors.

The Equatorial Forest traversed by Stanley resembles that Darkest England of which I have to speak, alike in its vast extent – both stretch, in Stanley's phrase, "as far as from Plymouth to Peterhead"; its monotonous darkness, its malaria and its gloom, its dwarfish de-humanized inhabitants, the slavery to which they are subjected, their privations and their misery. That which sickens the stoutest heart, and causes many of our bravest and best to fold their hands in despair, is the apparent impossibility of doing more than merely to peck at the outside of the endless tangle of monotonous undergrowth; to let light into it, to make a road clear through it, that shall not be immediately choked up by the ooze of the morass and the luxuriant parasitical growth of the forest – who dare hope for that? At present, alas, it would seem as though no one dares even to hope! It is the great Slough of Despond of our time.

And what a slough it is no man can gauge who has not waded therein, as some of us have done, up to the very neck for long years. Talk about Dante's Hell, and all the horrors and cruelties of the torture-chamber of the lost! The man who walks with open eyes and with bleeding heart through the shambles of our civilization needs no such fantastic images of the poet to teach him horror. Often and often, when I have seen the young and the poor and the helpless go down before my eyes into the morass, trampled underfoot by beasts of prey in human shape that haunt these regions, it seemed as if God were no longer in His world, but that in His stead reigned a fiend, merciless as Hell, ruthless as the grave. Hard it is, no doubt, to read in Stanley's pages of the slave-traders coldly arranging for the surprise of a village, the capture of the inhabitants, the massacre of those who resist, and the violation of all the women; but the stony streets of London, if they could but speak, would tell of tragedies as awful, of ruin as complete, of ravishments as horrible, as if we were in Central Africa; only the ghastly devastation is covered, corpse-like, with the artificialities and hypocrisies of modern civilization.

The lot of a negress in the Equatorial Forest is not, perhaps, a very happy one, but is it so very much worse than that of many a pretty orphan girl in our Christian capital? We talk about the brutalities of the dark ages, and we profess to shudder as we read in books of the shameful exaction of the rights of feudal superior. And yet here, beneath our very eyes, in our theaters, in our restaurants, and in many other places, unspeakable though it be but to name it, the same hideous abuse flourishes unchecked. A young penniless girl, if she be pretty, is often hunted from pillar to post by her employers, confronted always by the alternative – Starve or Sin. And when once the poor girl has consented to buy the right to earn her living by the sacrifice of her virtue, then she is treated as a slave and an outcast by the very men who have ruined her. Her word becomes unbelievable, her life an ignominy, and she is swept downward ever downward, into the bottomless perdition of prostitution. But there, even in the lowest depths, excommunicated by Humanity and outcast from God, she is far nearer the pitying heart of the One true Saviour than all the men who forced her down, aye, and than all the Pharisees and Scribes who stand silently by while these fiendish wrongs are perpetrated before their very eyes.

The blood boils with impotent rage at the sight of these enormities, callously inflicted, and silently borne by these miserable victims. Nor is it only women who are the victims, although their fate is the most tragic. Those firms which reduce sweating to a fine art, who systematically and deliberately defraud the workman of his pay, who grind the faces of the poor, and who rob the widow and the orphan, and who for a pretense make great professions of public-spirit and philanthropy, these men nowadays are sent to Parliament to make laws for the people. The old prophets sent them to Hell – but we have changed all that. They send their victims to Hell, and are rewarded by all that wealth can do to make their lives comfortable. Read the House of Lords' Report on the Sweating System, and ask if any African slave system, making due

allowance for the superior civilization, and therefore sensitiveness, of the victims, reveals more misery.

Darkest England, like Darkest Africa, reeks with malaria. The foul and fetid breath of our slums is almost as poisonous as that of the African swamp. Fever is almost as chronic there as on the Equator. Every year thousands of children are killed off by what is called defects of our sanitary system. They are in reality starved and poisoned, and all that can be said is that, in many cases, it is better for them that they were taken away from the trouble to come.

Just as in Darkest Africa it is only a part of the evil and misery that comes from the superior race who invade the forest to enslave and massacre its miserable inhabitants, so with us, much of the misery of those whose lot we are considering arises from their own habits. Drunkenness and all manner of uncleanness, moral and physical, abound. Have you ever watched by the bedside of a man in delirium tremens? Multiply the sufferings of that one drunkard by the hundred thousand, and you have some idea of what scenes are being witnessed in all our great cities at this moment. As in Africa streams intersect the forest in every direction, so the ginshop stands at every corner with its River of the Water of Death flowing seventeen hours out of the twenty-four for the destruction of the people. A population sodden with drink, steeped in vice, eaten up by every social and physical malady, these are the denizens of Darkest England amidst whom my life has been spent, and to whose rescue I would now summon all that is best in the manhood and womanhood of our land.

But this book is no mere lamentation of despair. For Darkest England, as for Darkest Africa, there is a light beyond. I think I see my way out, a way by which these wretched ones may escape from the gloom of their miserable existence into a higher and happier life. Long wandering in the Forest of the Shadow of Death at our doors, has familiarized me with its horrors; but while the realization is a vigorous spur to action it has never been so oppressive as to extinguish hope. Mr Stanley never succumbed to the terrors which oppressed his followers. He had lived in a larger life, and knew that the forest, though long, was not interminable. Every step forward brought him nearer his destined goal, nearer to the light of the sun, the clear sky, and the rolling uplands of the grazing land. Therefore he did not despair. The Equatorial Forest was, after all, a mere corner of one quarter of the world. In the knowledge of the light outside, in the confidence begotten by past experience of successful endeavor, he pressed forward; and when the 160 days' struggle was over, he and his men came out into a pleasant place where the land smiled with peace and plenty, and their hardships and hunger were forgotten in the joy of a great deliverance.

So I venture to believe it will be with us. But the end is not yet. We are still in the depths of the depressing gloom. It is in no spirit of light-heartedness that this book is sent forth into the world. The magnitude of the evils and the difficulty of dealing with them are immense.

If this were the first time that this wail of hopeless misery had sounded on our ears the matter would have been less serious. It is because we have heard it so often that the case is so desperate. The exceeding bitter cry of the disinherited has become to be as familiar in the ears of men as the dull roar of the streets or as the moaning of the wind through the trees. And so it rises unceasing, year in and year out, and we are too busy or too idle, too indifferent or too selfish, to spare it a thought. Only now and then, on rare occasions, when some clear voice is heard giving more articulate utterance to the miseries of the miserable men, do we pause in the regular routine of our daily duties, and shudder as we realize for one brief moment what life means to the inmates of the Slums. But one of the grimmest social problems of our time should be sternly faced, not with a view to the generation of profitless emotion, but with a view to its solution.

Is it not time? There is, it is true, an audacity in the mere suggestion that the problem is not insoluble that is enough to take away the breath. But can nothing be done? If, after full and exhaustive consideration, we come to the deliberate conclusion that nothing can be done, and that it is the inevitable and inexorable destiny of thousands of Englishmen to be brutalized into worse than beasts by the condition of their environment, so be it. But if, on the contrary, we are unable to believe that this "awful slough," which engulfs the manhood and womanhood of generation after generation, is incapable of removal; and if the heart and intellect of mankind alike revolt against the fatalism of despair,

then, indeed, it is time, and high time, that the question were faced in no mere dilettante spirit, but with a resolute determination to make an end of the crying scandal of our age.

What a satire it is upon our Christianity and our civilization, that the existence of these colonies of heathens and savages in the heart of our capital should attract so little attention! It is no better than a ghastly mockery – theologians might use a stronger word – to call by the name of One who came to seek and to save that which was lost those Churches which in the midst of lost multitudes either sleep in apathy or display a fitful interest in a chasuble. Why all this apparatus of temples and meeting-houses to save men from perdition in a world which is to come, while never a helping hand is stretched out to save them from the inferno of their present life? Is it not time that, forgetting for a moment their wranglings about the infinitely little or infinitely obscure, they should concentrate all their energies on a united effort to break this terrible perpetuity of perdition, and to rescue some at least of those for whom they profess to believe their Founder came to die?

Before venturing to define the remedy, I begin by describing the malady. But even when presenting the dreary picture of our social ills, and describing the difficulties which confront us, I speak not in despondency but in hope. "I know in whom I have believed." I know, therefore do I speak. Darker England is but a fractional part of "Greater England." There is wealth enough abundantly to minister to its social regeneration so far as wealth can, if there be but heart enough to set about the work in earnest. And I hope and believe that the heart will not be lacking when once the problem is manfully faced, and the method of its solution plainly pointed out.

Source: General William Booth *In Darkest England and The Way Out*. London: The Salvation Army, 1890. Part I, ch. 1, pp. 15–23.

Chapter Nineteen

"Moral Musculature": Schoolboys and Boy Scouts

Introduction

Schoolboys

First published in 1857, Thomas Hughes's *Tom Brown's Schooldays* had run into nearly 50 editions by 1890, at which time the popular public school program had well become "to create universal Tom Browns" who would, as Henry Newbolt would lyricize it in "Vitaï Lampada," "play on, play on, and play the game!." Hughes himself had been a student at Rugby from 1834 to 1842 under the headmastership of the renowned educational reformer Thomas Arnold (1795–1842). Arnold, educated at Oxford in the early part of the century was appointed to the position at Rugby in 1828, and held it until his death 14 years later. At Rugby Arnold introduced the system of prefects that had the older boys monitoring the new students and emphasized not just the teaching of Greek and Latin classics, but athleticism and team sports as well, as being necessary to the making of "gentlemen." Bullying especially was discouraged. Newbolt, who studied nearly half a century later at Clifton School in Bristol, made that school spirit the subject of many of his poems, verses which celebrated the continuation of the public school tradition in the fields of empire, what J. A. Mangan has referred to as the "games ethic," a code that involved the combined development of mind and body, a "moral musculature," as it came to be called. Playing games, that is, on the English playing-field would prepare the young men of England to "play the game" on the battlefields of empire. If "Tommy Atkins" personified the ordinary soldier of the imperial army, Tom Brown's schooling created the officer class. That ethos of manliness, courage, and compassion permeated the popular representations of the direct connection between education and empire, from Rudyard Kipling's *Kim* (1901) in which Kimball O'Hara must be properly trained to the "game," to A. E. W. Mason's *The Four Feathers* (1901) that traces Harry Faversham's quest to redeem in the Sudan the four white feathers of cowardice with which his comperes and fiancee have scorned him. A century later, the "bully" of Tom Brown's Rugby would re-enter the novelistic annals in George MacDonald Fraser's fictional Flashman series. Harry Flashman, Tom Brown's school foe, goes on in these tales to participate in the Afghan Wars, the Charge of the Light Brigade, in the Indian Rebellion, the West African slave trade, and against the "redskins" in the United States. What had become of Tom Brown's schoolmates?

Boy Scouts

It was on those same playing-fields of colonial battle that Robert Baden-Powell (1857–1941) elaborated his project for the "boy scouts," continuing the traditions and ethos of "moral musculature." Baden-Powell had toured India, fought in the Sudan in 1884–5, and during the Boer War defended Mafeking against the extended Boer siege of that town. The first trial camp for scouts was held in 1907, and by 1913, when Baden-Powell made his "tour of the world," he visited troops across the reaches of the British Empire. His last stop, in South Africa, locates the Boy Scout movement as an important outcome of the social, political, and military history of British empire-making on that tip of the continent. With his sister, Agnes, he also founded the Girl Guides in 1910. If, as Kipling versified, the motto of the Boy Scouts must be, "All patrols look out," it is the analogous slogan of "Be Prepared" that animates the young women who look to the Guides for a way of their own to join the work of empire and exercise their "moral muscles."

BH

Additional Reading

Bratton, J. S. "Of England, Home and Duty: The Image of England in Victorian and Edwardian Juvenile Fiction," in John M. MacKenzie (ed.). *Imperialism and Popular Culture*. Manchester, 1986.

Castle, Kathryn. *Britannia's Children: Reading Colonialism through Children's Books and Magazines*. Manchester, 1996.

Mangan, J. A. *The Games Ethic and Imperialism*. New York, 1986.

Richards, Jeffrey. "Boy's Own Empire: Feature Films and Imperialism in the 1930s," in *Imperialism and Popular Culture*.

Films

Robert Stevenson. *Tom Brown's Schooldays* (1940).
Gordon Parry. *Tom Brown's Schooldays* (1951).
Richard Lester. *Royal Flash* (1975).

106   Donald Hughes: "The Short Cut" (n.d.)

In Queen Victoria's golden day,
Beneath the mild and settled rule,
The grand old game I used to play,
With decent chaps in a public school.
And I soon found out, as I played the game,
That you need not score a large amount,
But the shortest cut to the heights of fame
Is to get to know the chaps who count.

In Oxford's fields, I found it true,
For the Captain was my closest friend,

And so I acquired my Cricket Blue,
Though I always batted near the end.
It is good to bowl with an action high
Or to smite the leather hard and far,
But it's better to wear the proper tie
And to keep your end up at the bar.
Leave lesser men to their golf-clubs then
Or to play with racquets and a net.
For this is the game for gentlemen
Till on our race the sun shall set.
The greatest glory of our land
Whose crimson covers half the maps
Is in the field where the wickets stand
And the game is played by DECENT CHAPS.

> *Source:* Leslie Ronald Frewin. *The Poetry of Cricket: An Anthology*. London: MacDonald, 1964; cited in J. A. Mangan. *The Games Ethic and Imperialism: Aspects of the Diffusion of an Ideal.* London: Viking, 1986.

107   Sir Henry Newbolt: *Poems: New and Old* (1912)

"Vitaï Lampada"

There's a breathless hush in the Close to-night –
    Ten to make and the match to win –
A bumping pitch and a blinding light,
    An hour to play and the last man in.
And it's not for the sake of a ribboned coat,
    Or the selfish hope of a season's fame,
But his Captain's hand on his shoulder smote –
    "Play up! Play up! and play the game!"

The sand of the desert is sodden red, –
    Red with the wreck of a square that broke; –
The Gatling's jammed and the Colonel dead,
    And the regiment blind with dust and smoke.
The river of death has brimmed his banks,
    And England's far, and Honour a name,
But the voice of a schoolboy rallies the ranks:
    "Play up! Play up! and play the game!"

This the word that year by year,
    While in her place the School is set,
Every one of her sons must hear
    And none that hears it dare forget.
This they all with a joyful mind
    Bear through life like a torch in flame,
And falling fling to the host behind –
    "Play up! Play up! and play the game!"

"The Schoolfellow"

Our game was his but yesteryear;
  We wished him back; we could not know
The selfsame hour we missed him here
  He led the line that broke the foe.

Blood-red behind our guarded posts
  Sank as of old the dying day;
The battle ceased; the mingled hosts
  Weary and cheery went their way:

"To-morrow well may bring," we said,
  "As fair a fight, as clear a sun."
Dear lad, before the word was sped,
  For evermore thy goal was won.

"The School at War"

All night before the brink of death
  In fitful sleep the army lay,
For through the dream that stilled their breath
  Too gauntly glared the coming day.

But we, within whose blood there leaps
  The fulness of a life as wide
As Avon's water where he sweeps
  Seaward at last with Severn's tide,

We heard beyond the desert night
  The murmur of the fields we knew,
And our swift souls with one delight
  Like homing swallows Northward flew.

We played again the immortal games,
  And grappled with the fierce old friends,
And cheered the dead undying names,
  And sang the song that never ends;

Till, when the hard, familiar bell
  Told that the summer night was late,
Where long ago we said farewell
  We said farewell by the old gate.

"O Captains unforgot," they cried,
  "Come you again or come no more,
Across the world you keep the pride,
  Across the world we mark the score."

Source: Sir Henry Newbolt. *Poems: New and Old.* London: J. Murray 1912, pp. 95–6, 107, 109–10.

---

108   Rudyard Kipling: "A Boy Scout's Patrol Song" (1913)

These are *our* regulations –
  There's just one law for the Scout
And the first and the last, and the present and the
    past,
And the future and the perfect is "Look out!"
  I, thou and he, look out!
  We, ye and they, look out!
  Though you didn't or you wouldn't
  Or you hadn't or you couldn't;
  You jolly well *must* look out!

Look out, when you start for the day,
  That your kit is packed to your mind;
There is no use going away
  With half of it left behind.
Look out that your laces are tight,
  And your boots are easy and stout,
Or you'll end with a blister at night.
  (*Chorus*) *All* Patrols look out!

Look out for the birds of the air,
  Look out for the beasts of the field –
They'll tell you how and where
  The other side's concealed.
When the backbird bolts from the copse,
  Or the cattle are staring about,
The wise commander stops
  And (*chorus*) All Patrols look out!

Look out when your front is clear,
  And when you feel you are bound to win.
Look out for your flank and rear –
  That's where surprises begin.
For the rustle that isn't a rat,
  For the splash that isn't a trout,
For the boulder that may be a hat
  (*Chorus*) All Patrols look out!

For the innocent knee-high grass,
  For the ditch that never tells,
Look out! Look out ere you pass –
  And look out for everything else!
A sign mis-read as you run
  May turn retreat to a rout –
For all things under the sun
  (*Chorus*) All Patrols look out!

Look out when your temper goes
  At the end of a losing game;
When your boots are too tight for your toes;
  And you answer and argue and blame.

It's the hardest part of the Law,
  But it has to be learned by the Scout –
For whining and shirking and "jaw"
  (*Chorus*) All Patrols look out!

Source: Rudyard Kipling. *Collected Verse*. Herts:
Wordsworth Editions, 1994, pp. 273–4.

---

109 Sir Robert Baden-Powell: *Boy Scouts Beyond the Seas*: "*My World Tour*" (1913)

Native Outbreaks

But with these warlike natives you can never tell
when they may not break out. The only thing is
to Be Prepared beforehand, and then you will be
perfectly safe.

If every farm had its little fort or fortified building *always ready*, and its men and women and boys
all trained to shoot, there would be very few of the
murders and raids which have been so common
in the country when the defenceless state of the
farmers invited attack.

And this is one of the reasons why we encourage
Scouts to learn marksmanship – just on the same
principle that they learn boxing – not in order that
they should go and attack everyone they see, but
that they should be able to defend themselves and
those who are dear to them should it ever be necessary to do so.

Some day you may want to go out to an Oversea
Dominion, and it may very easily cost you your life
if you don't know how to use a rifle:

Majuba Hill

In the early morning our train stops at the little
town of Newcastle, the last town in Natal towards
the Transvaal border.

Like Newcastle in England and Newcastle in
New South Wales, this place has its coal mines, and
like them also it has its Boy Scouts. The Scouts
only paraded in small numbers, as most of them
were away on their holidays in camp or at the sea-
side, but those that were present were a nice, prom-
ising-looking lot, very clean and cheery.

Alongside them were also the Newcastle Girl
Guides, equally smart, and evidently doing their
work well.

To one of these I had the pleasure of presenting
the medal for gallantry in life saving. Three children had got into difficulties when bathing, and
were drowning when a lady dashed to their rescue,
but she in her turn got swept out of her depth, and
she, too, was in great danger of being drowned
when the Girl Guide, Carrie Cross, sprang in to
her assistance.

Although but a poor swimmer, this girl did not
lose her head in the midst of the excitement where
four people were drowning, but she gallantly went
to their rescue without any thought of the danger
to herself. She succeeded in getting hold of the
lady, and in bringing her safely to shore after a
plucky struggle. The children were unfortunately
drowned.

For her gallant conduct the Guide received the
Silver Cross for life saving.

After leaving Newcastle, the line winds and
climbs up the hills to the ridge which divides Natal
from the Transvaal. The pass over this ridge is
called Laings Nek, and formed a strong position for
defence by the Boers in both the Boer campaigns of
1881 and of 1900, and there many a gallant soldier
lost his life.

In the 1881 campaign, after trying in vain to
drive the Boers out of their trenches on Laings
Nek, Sir George Colley, the British General, took
a portion of his force by night up to the top of the
Majuba mountain, which overlooks the Laings Nek
position.

As you will have read in "Scouting for Boys," it
was a Boer woman who first noticed the British on
the top of the mountain, and pointed it out to the
Boer Commandant.

Boers and British

You would think a fellow a pretty average rotter if,
after a hard match at football, he showed a nasty
feeling about it, that is, if, as a winner, he swag-
gered over the other side as being a lot of ninnies, or
if, as a loser, he bore a grudge against the fellows
who had won.

The manly way is for both sides to shake hands
and be the best of friends after a game – the harder
the game has been the better they can admire each
other, and the better friends they can be.

It is just the same after a war.

And that's what I was so glad to find in South
Africa; the Boers and British have learnt to admire
each other, and have settled down together as
friends, and all the better friends for the better
knowledge of each other gained in a long-fought
campaign. "The past is past," they say, "let us look

to the future." And that is the manly way to look at it.

The troubles which have arisen from time to time between the British and Boer inhabitants of South Africa have not been due so much to ill-feeling on the part of the two peoples against each other, as to their two Governments getting at loggerheads and not understanding the question – that is, *not seeing things from the other's point of view.*

The fault lies sometimes with one Government, sometimes with the other.

The people, in both cases loyal to their own Government, had to follow suit, and so had to fight each other – thus ill-feeling naturally resulted from, though it did not begin, the fighting.

Both peoples were originally from the same stock in northern Europe before they came to South Africa.

Both have earned their rights equally in South Africa, as can be seen from the following score-sheet:

Score-sheet

THE BOERS
First colonised the Cape and Western Provinces.
Colonised the Orange Free State, Transvaal.
Defeated Dingaan, Mosilikatze.
Cultivated the veldt, raised cattle and horses and mules, ostriches, farm produce.
Produced men like Van Riebeck, Van der Stel, Pretorius, Kruger.

THE BRITISH
First annexed the Cape and colonised Eastern Province.
Colonised Natal, Rhodesia.
Defeated Cetewayo, Lobengula, Sekukuni.
Made railways, harbours, gold and diamond mines.
Produced men like Livingstone, Harry Smith, Cecil Rhodes, Bartle Frere.

Even in their quarrels the results have come out pretty equal – the British were defeated in 1881, the Boers in 1900.

So the honours are equally due to both.

Where each had such history and such rights, what was wanted was one single, broad-minded Government for both, in place of two Governments continually misunderstanding each other.

This has now come about; the two Governments are formed into one.

There is therefore no longer any need for quarrelling; the two people can now settle down together again, but as one instead of two nations, and can work together in friendship for the good of the whole land.

There may be a few old-timers on both sides who will grumble about the past till they die. Let us hope that this may be soon.

In the meantime there is a younger and more sensible lot growing up, who can see the other fellow's point of view. They will look to the good of the country as their first duty, putting their own personal feelings on one side. In this way they will raise South Africa to be really a great State among the other nations of the world.

In this grand work the Boy Scouts – Boer and British – are already taking a step by being brothers in that great brotherhood, and in Being Prepared to do their best for their country.

Old Table Mountain

The last I saw of our Overseas lands on my tour round the world was the top point of Table Mountain.

A cloud had come over it out of a clear blue sky just before our ship steamed out of Capetown Docks, and as we slid out to sea with our bow pointed homewards nothing was visible of the mountain; he had completely hidden himself under a curtain of cloud.

But as we drove farther and farther away and could no longer see the shore, up above the cloud his strong, grey head appeared just as if to give us a smiling farewell before we sailed away for good.

I have seen the old mountain many, many times, but (as I wrote of him fifteen years ago) he always seems to me to have something human about him, something divine.

I have been eight times in South Africa. Each time I started out from under the shadow of the great mountain, and went far across the veldt to very distant scenes, doing the work that had to be done, sometimes in sunshine, sometimes in rain; often well, sometimes ill.

Sometimes the work was difficult or unpleasant, sometimes easy and delightful – it all had to be done – and then at the end of it I returned back to the old mountain. I always looked out for his rugged old head as I came south, and felt the trip was over only when I was back upon his shoulder again.

But it always seemed to me very much like our life. We start out from the hand of the Great Maker, and go for our trip in the world, sometimes in trouble, at other times in prosperity; sometimes praised, sometimes found fault with; sometimes having to tackle the greatest difficulties, and at others finding things running as smoothly as oil.

But in the end we come back to our Maker, whether we have done evil or good.

Some who have done evil are afraid as they come back – they fear death – but the fellow who *has done his best* comes back with no fear upon him; he can truthfully say to God: "I have tried to do my duty – I have done my best," and no man can do more than that; and he can go to his rest tired and satisfied.

For a Boy Scout' this is easy.

You know that your duty is *to do your best* to carry out

1st – Your Scout's promise,
2nd – The Scout Law.

Remember what both these are; try to carry them out, then you will have done your Duty.

Europe

From South Africa we hail back, up the West Coast past Nigeria and Sierra Leone with their Boy Scouts, to Europe. We coast along past Gibraltar, Spain, Portugal and France, in all of which Boy Scouts are to be found.

After a few hours only in England, I went on for a little holiday in Norway and here, as everywhere else, I found our brother Scouts "going strong."

Source: Sir Robert Baden-Powell. *Boy Scouts Beyond the Seas: "My World Tour."* London: C. Arthur Pearson, 1913, pp. 236–41.

---

110 Agnes Baden-Powell: "Camp Fire Yarn no. 33" (1912)

Our Empire: How it Grew – How it must be Held

Hints to Instructors

The use of a large map of the Empire is very desirable for illustrating this. The Arnold Forster, the Navy League, or the League of the Empire Maps are very good.

Look up the local history of your neighbourhood, and give your Guides the more interesting and dramatic bits of it, on the actual scene of the events if possible.

Any of you who have travelled much about this country by train, going for your holidays and so on, know how two or three hours will take you a good

long distance, and six or eight hours will take you to the other end of England.

Well, if instead of hours you travelled for as many days, even six or eight days would take you a very little way over our Empire. It would take you into Canada, but you would want several more days – not hours – to get across that country. Eighteen days' hard travelling day and night would take you to India or South Africa, but both of these are little more than half-way to Australia. And all that distance off, across the seas, on the other side of the world, we have a British country into which you could put nine Great Britains and Irelands.

9	United Kingdoms = 1 Australia
10	United Kingdoms = 1 Canada
6	United Kingdoms = 1 India and Burma
5	United Kingdoms = East Africa, Uganda, and Sudan
5	United Kingdoms = South Africa
1	United Kingdoms = New Zealand
$1\frac{1}{2}$	United Kingdoms = Nigeria

Then there are numbers of smaller colonies or dependencies, such as Guiana (nearly as big as the United Kingdom), North Borneo, New Guinea, Somaliland, Straits Settlements, Gold Coast, West Indies, Tasmania, etc., and numbers of islands in every sea. Our Colonies together are something like forty times the size of the United Kingdom.

Our fellow-subjects amount to four hundred million, and make up *one quarter of the whole human beings in the world,* and comprise almost every known race. Almost every known species of wild animal occurs in British territory. It is a magnificent Empire over which the Union Jack flies, but it is still only at the beginning of its development. The territories are there, but the people are only coming. The white population of all these Dominions only amounts to a little over a quarter of the population of these crowded little islands. We have nearly forty-four million here; and of these people over four and a half million live in London. In Glasgow or Liverpool there are nearly eight hundred thousand people.

Many of you, as you grow up, will probably find your way to some of these splendid and fruitful Colonies, and help to make them into big prosperous countries. Your Guide's training will come in very useful to you there. But when you go there you must be prepared to work, and to work hard, and to turn your hand to any kind of job.

How our Empire Grew

The British Empire is composed of the British Isles and those overseas Dominions in the table above.

Nothing in history is comparable to this enormous prosperous realm known as the British Empire, with the sea for its streets, and with a sacred duty to carry light into all the dark places over the whole world. The British Empire is three times as big as the whole of Europe, and four times as big as the United States of America.

When we first went to America it took Sir Walter Raleigh, Captain John Smith, and other great pioneers four or five months to get there in their little cockle-shells of ships, some of them only 30 tons burden – no bigger than a Thames barge. Nowadays you can go there in five or six days, instead of months, in steamers of 30,000 tons.

Think of the pluck of those men in tackling a voyage like that with a very limited supply of water and salt food. And when they got to land with a handful of men, they had to overcome the savages, and in some cases other Europeans, like the Dutch, the Spaniards, and the French; and then they had hard work to till the ground, to build settlements, and to start commerce. Hard sailoring, hard soldiering, hard colonizing by those old British sea-dogs – that is what made British character with grit in it.

All these immense Colonies did not come to the English of themselves; they were got for us by the hard work and the endurance and bravery of our forefathers.

In CANADA the Army has had famous men who served in the campaigns which placed the Dominion under the Union Jack. They can point to their glorious deeds when they took Fort Ogdensburg, and in the hard fighting at Lundy's Lane. They were in the Red River Expedition, and helped in the suppression of Riel's Rebellion.

In SOUTH AFRICA more than a hundred years ago we established our rule of freedom and fairplay in struggles with the Hottentots and the Dutch, in which the Cape Mounted Rifles fought valiantly. The Natal Carabineers were the finest regiment of that colony, and the regiment of Rhodesian Horse behaved gallantly in helping us against the Matabele and many savage tribes.

AUSTRALIA happily had no wars in her conquest, but was got for us by our sailor men (like Captain Cook), who outstripped all other nations in their plucky navigation of immense, unknown oceans. The Australian soldiers came to the help of Britain in the Sudan and also in the South African War.

The NEW ZEALANDERS had a long ten years' contest with the native Maoris. Their Riflemen and City Guards are the sons of the Englishmen who fought for us at Ranagiri and Gate Pahs.

The vast extent of INDIA has all been conquered bit by bit to form one enormous country loyal to our King, and the natives furnish us with a splendid army, composed of the brave Sikhs and Gurkas, the troops of Gwalior and the Frontier Force, and the "Guides," a crack corps of picked men, always ready for instant service.

EAST AFRICA, Uganda, and the Sudan beyond Egypt, and Somaliland have also been fought for and won in quite recent times.

And now in all these countries we are spreading the blessings of peace and justice, doing away with slavery and oppression, and developing commerce and manufactures.

Other nations could formerly only look on and wonder, but now they, too, are pressing forward in the race for empire and commerce, so that we cannot afford to sit still or let things slide.

We have had this enormous Empire handed down to us by our forefathers, and we are responsible that it develops and goes ahead, and, above all, that we make ourselves fit and proper subjects to help it to go ahead. It won't do so of itself, any more than it would have become ours of itself. If we don't do this, some other nation will take it from us.

Patriotism

We all want to help our country, and wish to be of use for the advancement of the Empire.

The Rev. J. Purvis, in addressing some Guides, said: "As you are moulding your minds and your bodies at the present time, so will they act in the future, either as a drag or for the advancement of this glorious nation."

Let every Guide think of her country and help its advancement.

A girl patriot who helped her country at the time of the American War was the Duchess of Sutherland, who, when she was only twelve years old, raised a Sutherland regiment. This brave girl then reviewed her men, 1,000 strong, from the windows of her aunt's house in Edinburgh, only regretting that she could not be in command.

Patriots

In our country we do not lack heroines, and can boast of many who have endured terrible sufferings and have gone through all kinds of dangers for duty and their country.

READ – So long as tongues can speak, the stories of the valiant deeds of these patriots will be told to eager listeners and proud hearts.

We have a long-ago heroine in our Queen Boadicea, who governed in Norfolk. When she found that the Romans had taken possession of London, she gathered together a very large army of Britons to try and turn out the enemy. She cleverly took the opportunity when the Roman chief had gone away to fight up in the north. She bravely rallied a large force, and urged them to march on London. The queen led her army on, and, inspirited by her, they attacked the Romans suddenly, and massacred the whole garrison.

However brave or great the deed seems, a woman is no heroine if it cost her nothing to do it.

You should read Whittier's account of the brave old American lady, Barbara Fritchie, who, even when over ninety years of age, risked her life in defending the flag of her country. You would all admire the noble self-sacrifice of Lady Catherine Douglas for her king. It was when King James the First of Scotland and his queen had arrived to stay in the abbey at Perth for some great festivities, and were just preparing to retire for the hight, that they were alarmed by the tramp of soldiers in the abbey garden. The rebel Graham had come with three hundred armed men to kill the king. The terrified ladies of the Court attempted to close the door, but the lock was found to have been broken, and the great bar which bolted the door had been removed. One of the maids of honour, Lady Catherine Douglas, bravely, and without hesitation, thrust her arm into the staple-rings in the door and the wall so as to bar the door, and for a short time held the door shut. With rough soldiers trying to force the door, what could a girl's tender arm do against them? It was soon broken. The soldiers got in, and finally found the king, who had hidden himself. The queen tried to save him by throwing herself between him and the ruffians; but they were roughly separated and the king murdered before her eyes.

In this way patriots cheerfully face immense peril without thought of applause or reward.

We have a great many heroines among the stout-hearted Scots. Read about the "White Rose of Scotland," who was associated with Perkin Warbeck; also Helen of Kirkconnell, who is immortalized by Wordsworth. Then there was Christian Grainger, who was in the castle where the Scottish regalia were kept when it was besieged by the insurgents. She was so loyal that she determined that the rebels should not get the crown even if they took the castle, so she managed to conceal the golden sceptre and the jewelled crown and the sword of state beneath her skirts and cloak, and in the confusion of the fighting she contrived to escape and deliver up her precious goods to their rightful keepers.

She managed to get them to Dunnottar Castle. But later the insurgents attacked that place too, and took the marischal prisoner. Still, the lieutenant, Ogilvy, protected the jewels, and when the troops besieged the castle, he smuggled the regalia away to a church, where they remained hidden for eight years.

Guarding your country by a deed of valour is not out of the power of quite a small child. Do you remember how the little Dutch boy saved his country from a dreadful flood? Parts of Holland lie below the sea-level, and so people build walls and banks to keep out the water. This little boy was, just as you might be, simply walking home from school, but he saw that the water was coming through the bank, and that the sea waves were washing the hole larger every moment. What could a little child do to save the whole country? There was no one near to help him; but he quickly stuffed his coat into the hole, and thrust his arm in to fill the gap, and there he held it all the long, dark hours of the night. Was it not brave and good of him never to leave off trying? His friends came to find him next morning, cold and weak, but also a conquering hero, for, had he not acted so quickly, and stayed there so courageously, all the crops would have been ruined, the houses flooded, and no one would have been able to live.

And then there is the story of how Agoustina of Saragossa bravely took her husband's place when he was killed by the enemy's shot during the famous siege. She fired his gun, and turned the tide of the battle at a critical moment, so helping to save her town. You can read about it in Charlotte Yonge's "Book of Golden Deeds."

The girls of the nation have the moulding of the men of the future. This great Empire is entrusted to their care, and what it will be in the future is just what the girls try to make it. Girls have great power and influence, and can serve their country even better than men can, by forming the minds and characters of the children.

Helping Police

Girl Guides can be of special use in assisting the police in towns. In the first place, every Guide ought to know where the fixed police points are – that is, where a constable is always stationed, apart from the policemen on their beats. She ought to know where to find the fire alarm; where the nearest fire brigade station is, and the nearest hospital or ambulance station, and chemist.

On seeing an accident, if you cannot help at it you should run and inform the nearest policeman, and ask him how you can help him – whether you can call a doctor, a cab, and so on. If you hear a policeman's whistle sounding, run and offer to help him; it is your duty, as he is a king's servant.

If you find a lost child or lost dog, or any lost property, you should take them at once to the police station.

Sir H. Poland, KC, had his watch snatched by a pickpocket the other day. The thief darted away down the street; but a small boy jumped on to a bike and followed him, crying, "Stop thief!" till he was caught – with the watch on him.

Not only can boys help the police, but girls also. Within the last few months I have noticed many cases of girls going to the assistance of constables who were in difficulties with violent men. In each case the girl got the policeman's whistle and blew it for him until assistance arrived. These heroines were Miss Edith Harris at Southampton, Miss Bessie Matthews in Clerkenwell, Mrs. Langley at Brentford, Frances Wright, and Dorothy Chambers.

Hints to Instructors

Read up thrilling incidents in the history of our Colonies, and let the Guides each choose a part, and act scenes or tableaux of the decisive events.

Source: Agnes Baden-Powell. *The Handbook for Girl Guides, or How Girls Can Help Build the Empire.* London: Thomas Nelson and Sons, 1912, pp. 405–13.

Chapter Twenty

"Jingoes" vs "Little Englanders": The Debate over Empire

Introduction

Within months of its publication in February 1899 in *McClure's Magazine*, Rudyard Kipling's poem, "The White Man's Burden," had provoked dozens of complementary and contestatory poems and essays: "The Brown Man's Burden," "The Poor Man's Burden," "The Black Man's Burden," "Two Burdens," "The Wrong Man's 'Burden',", and "The Burden of Profit," to cite some few examples. The "burden" of empire weighed heavily not just on imperial shoulders but in its rhetorical, lyrical, and political debates as well. What was that burden? According to W. E. Gladstone, in a speech presented at the Mechanics Institute in 1855, it was not "love of gold," the "propagation of the gospel," "increasing . . . the revenus of the mother country," nor the "addition of territory to the country," not a matter of "reputation" or "patronage," nor the "establishment of an exclusive trade," but rather, in the words of the MP John Roebuck, cited by Gladstone, "'the object of colonisation is the creation of so many happy Englands.'" Nearly 50 years later, the radical political economist J. A. Hobson attacked imperialism and the "essentially illicit nature of this use of public resources of the nation to safeguard and improve private investments."

By the end of the century, however, and despite the series of "Reform Bills," it was not at all clear just how "happy" England herself really was. And there were those who considered that too much investment in the colonies and empire had been made at the dire expense of the island's inhabitants. Gladstone's prime ministerial rival, Benjamin Disraeli, in turn, insisted in his 1872 Crystal Palace speech that one of the great objects of the Tory party was precisely to "uphold the Empire of England." But the political debate over the maintenance and extension of British imperial dominion was not just a matter of personal rivalry, between the two statesmen, but between the "jingoes" and the "little Englanders." The latter opposed what MP Robert Wallace referred to as the "seamy side of 'imperialism.'" The former extolled the expansion of capital and the rewards to be reaped from it for the home country. The debate translated as well into that between advocates of free trade and campaigners for protectionism – an issue that had been dividing England since at least the passage of the Corn Laws in the late eighteenth century, and had significantly inspired Adam Smith's *Wealth of Nations*. It could also be rendered as the difference between "empire" and "kingdom," as evidenced in the controversy raised by Disraeli's Royal Titles Bill in 1876. Should England allow missionaries to proselytize in India, intervene in "native" customs by banning sati, thuggee, or, later, polygamy and child marriage in that land? Should she buy shares in the Suez Canal, extend her Egyptian protectorate to include the Sudan, contest Leopold in the

Congo, or "pay – pay – pay" to support the families of the recruits fighting in the Anglo-Boer War?

What were the costs of empire? And who really carried the burden?

BH

Additional Reading

Adelson, Roger. *London and the Invention of the Middle East: Money, Power, and War, 1902–1922.* New Haven, 1995.
Hall, Catherine. "Rethinking Imperial Histories: The Reform Act of 1867," *New Left Review* 208, 1994, pp. 3–29.
Lenin, V. I. *Imperialism: The Highest Stage of Capitalism.*
Marx, Karl. "On the Question of Free Trade," speech delivered in Brussels. 1848. With preface by Frederick Engels to the 1888 English edition pamphlet.
Strachey, Lytton. "Mr. Gladstone and Lord Beaconsfield," *Queen Victoria*. London, 1921.
Zwick, Jim. "'The White Man's Burden' and its Critics." http://www.rochester.ican.net/~fjzwick/kipling/. In Jim Zwick, (ed), Anti-Imperialism in the United States 1898–1935. http://www.rochester.ican.net/~fjzwick/ail98-35.html. July 1996.

Film

Alfred E. Green. *Disraeli* (1929).

111   Queen Victoria's Prime Ministers

1837–41	William Lamb, Lord Melbourne	Whig
1841–6	Sir Robert Peel	Tory
1846–52	Lord John Russell	Whig
1852	Lord Derby	Tory
1852–5	Lord Aberdeen	Coalition Whig/ Peelite
1855–8	William Temple, Lord Palmerston	Whig
1858–9	Lord Derby	Tory
1859–65	Lord Palmerston	Whig
1865–6	Lord John Russell	Liberal
1866–8	Lord Derby/ Benjamin Disraeli	Conservative
1868–74	William Ewart Gladstone	Liberal
1874–80	Benjamin Disraeli	Conservative
1880–5	Gladstone	Liberal
1885–6	Lord Salisbury	Conservative
1886	Gladstone	Liberal
1886–92	Lord Salisbury	Conservative
1892–4	Gladstone	Liberal
1894–5	Lord Rosebury	Liberal
1895–1901	Lord Salisbury	Conservative

112   Rudyard Kipling: "The White Man's Burden" (1899)

Take up the White Man's burden –
  Send forth the best ye breed –
Go, bind your sons to exile
  To serve your captives need;
To wait, in heavy harness,
  On fluttered folk and wild –
Your new-caught sullen peoples,
  Half devil and half child.

Take up the White Man's burden –
  In patience to abide,
To veil the threat of terror
  And check the show of pride;
By open speech and simple,
  An hundred times made plain,
To seek another's profit
  And work another's gain.

Take up the White Man's burden –
  The savage wars of peace –
Fill full the mouth of Famine,
  And bid the sickness cease;
And when your goal is nearest
  (The end for others sought)
Watch sloth and heathen folly
  Bring all your hope to nought.

Take up the White Man's burden –
  No iron rule of kings,
But toil of serf and sweeper –
  The tale of common things.
The ports ye shall not enter,
  The roads ye shall not tread,
Go, make them with your living
  And mark them with your dead.

Take up the White Man's burden,
  And reap his old reward –
The blame of those ye better
  The hate of those ye guard –
The cry of hosts ye humour
  (Ah, slowly?) toward the light: –
"Why brought ye us from bondage,
  Our loved Egyptian night?"

Take up the White Man's burden –
  Ye dare not stoop to less –

Nor call too loud on Freedom
    To cloak your weariness.
By all ye will or whisper,
    By all ye leave or do,
The silent sullen peoples
    Shall weigh your God and you.

Take up the White Man's burden!
    Have done with childish days –
The lightly-proffered laurel,
    The easy ungrudged praise:
Comes now, to search your manhood
    Through all the thankless years,
Cold, edged with dear-bought wisdom,
    The judgment of your peers.

Source: McClure's Magazine, February 12, 1899.

113   W. E. Gladstone: "Our Colonies" (1855)

THE greatest difficulty which besets me in comply-
ing with the request you have done me the honour
to make to me, is, that I scarcely know how to select
such an amount of material as time would permit
me to lay before you, from the vast redundance
which the subject offers. I believe you are aware
that the request which was presented to me was,
that I should address you upon the same subject,
and to the same effect as I have already addressed
your friends and neighbours at Hawarden, namely,
the subject of our Colonies. Now, that little word
includes in itself ample matter of the most interesting discussion; so vast, that even the minor
branches of it have given occasion for the most
important and most interesting treatises in their
distinct and separate forms. If, for example, I name
such a question as the discovery of gold in Australia
– such a question as the laws which govern and
regulate emigration – such a question as the history
of Negro slavery, and the means through which it
has been brought to an end – such a question,
again, as the treatment of the aboriginal tribes
inhabiting and bordering upon the various settlements of this great empire – or, to name only one
more, such a question as the great subject of the
transportation of British criminals to distant
British possessions – each one of these, apart from
every other, is not only sufficient to occupy the
utmost period which I could possibly ask this night
from your indulgence, but has been found suffi-

cient to occupy nights upon nights, weeks upon
weeks, and months upon months, of the thoughts
of the ablest writers, and the discussions of both
your legislative houses. You will, therefore, I am
sure, excuse me, if I at once announce that I can lay
before you nothing but the rudest and the very
slightest sketch of a subject so vast in its range, and
you will also, I am certain, grant to me the indulgence which I have occasion to ask, when I observe
that such a sketch, necessarily passing by and omitting much that is important, is liable to doubtful
and unfavourable interpretation through its scanti-
ness of exposition. I am sure that you will allow me
to request your favour and indulgence if I seem to
you to give rise to inferences which perhaps a fuller
explanation might tend very much to obviate, while
upon my part it will be most agreeable to offer to
any gentleman may ask for it any explanation which
it may be in my power to give, without proceeding
to such a length as to inflict upon the meeting a
second dissertation.

But when I speak of the magnitude and importance of the question, it is true that after all it is not
every extended or every important question which
is of legitimate interest to a British audience. Nothing, however, can be easier than to show in detail
that the great subject of the Colonies of the British
empire has now come to constitute a question of the
most just and legitimate interest to every Englishman, and does amply justify the zeal and favour
which you testify to the discussion by your
crowded attendance here to-night. Let me only, for
one moment, advert to what is sufficient, although
it be slight in its bulk, to establish what I say.

In the middle of last century, the American colonial empire of England was, to use a hackneyed
phrase, but yet one which in this instance is the
simple and literal truth, the envy and the admiration of the world. It was then thought that nothing
had been seen for centuries upon centuries at all to
compare with that empire. And yet the American
population at the time of the outbreak of the war of
independence (it was not known with precision,
but as it was believed) amounted to nearly or about
two millions of souls. And what is the state of
things now? Why the single colony of Canada, not
to say the whole colonial empire of Great Britain,
not to say even the whole of British America, but
the single colony of Canada contains a population
nearly equal to the whole of the thirteen American
colonies of that time. Such is the magnitude and
importance to which that Empire has swelled.

Look again at the question from this point of
view: There is scarcely any European language of
note or importance which is not spoken in our

colonies. I do not mean merely spoken by families, or by the inhabitants of a particular village or district here or there, but by the great masses of the population. The subjects of the Queen in Malta, and those whom she protects in the Ionian Islands, speak the beautiful languages of Italy and Greece. A considerable portion of the Canadians, the people of the populous Island of the Mauritius, the people of St Lucia, and other of the West Indian Islands, speak the language of the great French nation. In British Guiana and at the Cape of Good Hope Dutch is spoken. In the important colony of Trinidad Spanish is the vernacular tongue. And thus the Queen of England, of an Island which once was looked upon as a separated and remote extremity of the habitable globe, possesses an empire under which are arrayed not only the barbarous tribes who speak tongues almost innumerable, but those who speak all the most cultivated, and all the most distinguished and famous languages of highly civilised Europe.

Look at the question for a moment from another point of view: Consider the great subject of emigration. That which was formerly a matter of remote knowledge and concern – that which even twenty or thirty years ago was regarded only as a means of getting rid of the offscourings of our population – has now become, on the contrary, a matter of close and domestic interest to many of the most intelligent, and many of the best conditioned and most respected, families in this country. In the year 1815, the whole number of emigrants who left the shores of England was 2,000. The average emigration of England in the fifteen years, from 1815 to 1830, was 20,000. The average for the years between 1830 and 1844 rose from 20,000 to 80,000. Between 1844 and 1854, the average rose to 267,000, and in the year 1852 the sum total reached no less a number than 368,000 people, over 1,000 persons thus quitting the shores of this country every day to find a home in the British colonial empire. You thus see that the increase in the quantity of the emigration was of a most remarkable character. The change in the quality is still more worthy of your notice. Because, for a long time, emigration was nothing but the resort of the most necessitous; but now, on the contrary, in a great many cases – I dare say there may be those here who would be able to bear testimony to it in instances within their own domestic sphere, or their own private knowledge – in a great many cases, indeed, it is not the needy and the necessitous, but it is the most adventurous, the most enterprising, the most intelligent man, the most valuable member of society in the sphere in which he moves, who goes to seek his fortune in those distant lands. This great change in the character of our emigration is capable of being brought in some degree to the test of figures, because we all know that the greater part, or nearly the whole emigration, while it was only made up of our pauperism, was not only a pauper but likewise an Irish emigration. Consequently, in former years, out of the gross total which I have read to you an immense proportion consisted of the natives of Ireland. Necessity has now ceased to press upon the natives of that country as it formerly pressed upon them. The Irish emigration also has changed its quality; but while the Irish emigration has changed, the English and Scotch emigration, which formerly was quite inconsiderable, and which is by no means and has never been merely or mainly an emigration of paupers and necessitous persons, has gained enormously upon the Irish emigration; and in the first nine months of the present year, closing with the 30th of last September, while the Irish who left this country were 67,000, of English and Scotch about 70,000 appear to have proceeded to the colonies. Thus I have given, I will not say even an outline, but at least a faint indication of the title which this great question may perhaps have to your attention.

Now, this is the shape in which it presents itself to my mind. I ask myself these two questions, both of them of the deepest interest to our country, – In the first place, why is it desirable that England, or that any other country, should possess colonies at all? and, in the second place, if it is desirable that they should be possessed, in what manner ought these colonies to be founded, and to be governed? When we entered upon this question at Hawarden, I confined myself almost wholly to the former of these subjects, the comparatively abstract argument, whether it be desirable that a country should possess colonies, and for what reason it is to be desired? With your permission, I will now endeavour to vary a little the form of our discussion, or rather, I should say, of my statement. I will endeavour to touch but lightly and summarily upon that more abstract part of the question, and will enter more at large upon the branch of the subject which will naturally assume an historical form – that which relates to the answer to be given to the second of the questions that I have described, namely, how should colonies be founded and governed? because that is a question which stands in more immediate relation with our own country, with our past, with our present, and with our future colonial policy. And I do not scruple to introduce it here, because I am happy to think that though it may justly be called a political question, and a question of the highest politics, yet it is in no sense a question of party. The time has been when these matters were so treated. I am bound to say I trust and believe that that time has passed away; that the truths relating to this great subject are beginning to be generally acknowledged, and the English people to be thoroughly united as to the mode of fulfilling one of the highest functions which Providence appears to have committed to its hands, namely, that of conducting the work of colonisation, that is to say, the peopling of a great portion of the habitable globe. I will then, in the first place, run very lightly over various notions that have at different times prevailed – notions which I think we ought now to note only for the purpose of letting it be observed that we do not embrace them, but which have an historical importance, on account of their having prevailed and having influenced in various degrees the actions of men and of states in former times. It is asked, why should we possess colonies at all? and the great bulk of the people, perhaps even to this day, have a strong impression that it is a very good thing that we do possess colonies, but it has not been their vocation or their special duty, though entertaining that opinion, to consider the special reasons for which it is desirable that we should possess them. Now, I will state in a summary manner here what I dwelt upon at more length upon a former occasion, because I think it is a fact that deserves to be recorded in the history not only of colonies, but of mankind, and one which teaches us an admirable moral and political lesson. The vast colonisation of modern times, which took its course from the eastward to the westward, across the Atlantic, must have been prompted by some powerful motive. What was that motive? It was the love of gold; it was the love and desire of gold that drew forth from Italy, from Spain, from France, from England, and from Portugal, those men whose bold and adventurous spirit tracked the stormy Atlantic, and founded successively, amidst dangers and difficulties indescribable, those colonies which have now grown into the great states of Northern and Southern America. They went to America in search of gold. They found no gold; but observe how, in this instance, by the wise dispensation of Providence, the very delusions of mankind were made to serve their great interests. They found no gold, or little gold – gold was found in South America; but, after all, the colonisation of South America is not to be named for its importance in the same day or in the same year with that of North America. In North America there was no discovery of precious metals at all

worth naming, but there was discovery of a great and powerful country, teeming with all the resources of nature, offering a home to mankind, and offering to them also the opportunity of the most extended field for the development of human energy and industry in every branch. They went in search of gold – they found no gold when they got there; but observe, there is about the idea of obtaining gold a certain fascination, so that even in these days, when the principles of political economy come to be better understood, and when we begin at last to know that a pound's worth of gold is of no greater value than a pound's worth of anything else – there is even in these days a fascination in the prospect of obtaining gold that excites and so to speak tickles the imagination, and practically acts upon man with a violence that nothing can equal. Much more so was it in those times when, according to the crude economical ideas which prevailed, it was believed, in many cases, that gold constituted the only true wealth of mankind. Therefore, this false idea, that gold was to be found in immense quantities in North America, did a work which the true idea never could have done, for depend upon it, those who went to North America never would have gone there if they had known that when they got there they would have nothing to do except to use the hatchet, the plough, and the spade, and pursue the works of industry in the same way as they had been used to do in Europe. So that their very delusion was made an instrument in the hands of Providence for forwarding the peopling of those vast countries of the earth. Gold then was the great mainspring of that immense movement; still, along with the idea that gold was to be obtained in immense quantities on the other side of the Atlantic was certainly mingled, in some minds at least, the desire for the propagation of the gospel. Yet it does not appear that these notions were very happily associated, for certainly, as far as we can see, the temporal and secular motive obtained an immense preponderance over the higher and spiritual motive, and the history of European civilisation in the West is a history of anything rather than the history of the propagation of the gospel. I do not intend now to enter upon that great question. I only mention it as one that would amply reward inquiry, especially in the relation it bears to another extended and painful subject, that of an institution which has left a deep stain upon, I will not say the name of Christianity but upon the history of its professors, the institution, if so it is to be called, of negro slavery. That, of course, would open a very wide field, distinct from that upon which we are now engaged; but I pass on to lay before you the other motives which have either led in a great degree to the promotion of colonisation across the Atlantic, or which have been alleged as reasons why colonisation is a task fit to be pursued.

Some have said, and more have thought, that colonies were to be founded for the sake of increasing and improving, by their direct contributions, the revenue of the mother country; and of this idea you have instances even to this day in the colonies of Spain and perhaps also in some of the colonial possessions of Holland. But that has never been the view with which the work of British colonisation has been carried on, and the unfortunate attempt which was made to derive a revenue from the colonies in the case of America, in the middle of last century, will demand our notice at a later period of my statement. Others again have thought that it must be desirable to possess colonies, because colonies constitute a large addition to the territory of the country. Undoubtedly the possession of territory is valuable, provided you know how to make use of it, but it is not desirable for this nation, or for any nation to possess an extent of territory without bounds and without reference to your power of turning it to account. On the contrary, according to the territory you possess is necessarily the expense that you must undertake for the purpose of defending that territory. The lust and love of territory have been among the greatest curses of mankind. The territory of colonies, rightly used, undoubtedly is of the utmost value, but it is a vain and mischievous idea to suppose that because you can acquire a certain portion of the space which the surface of the globe offers to man, you are, therefore, without reference to your power of using it, acquiring something that is valuable to possess. Then, again, people have a notion that for the reputation of this country it is desirable to possess colonies. I do not at all deny that the possession of colonies does contribute to the just reputation of this country, and does add to its moral influence, power, and grandeur; but if it is meant by this doctrine that it is desirable to have colonies in order that we may make a show in the world with which we have no substance to correspond, that I think you will agree with me is not a good reason for desiring an extension of a colonial empire. It never can be in the interest of this country, or any country in the world, to be taken for more than it is worth. What we should desire is to be valued at what we are worth – not at less and not at more. There has, again, been a notion more vulgar, I must say, than any of these, that it was desirable to possess colonies in order that the executive government of this country might have that patronage at

its command which was thought necessary to its being carried on, and which the public appointments and places in these colonies placed at its disposal. Many of us may be old enough to recollect occasions when persons whom it was not convenient or not decorous to provide for at home, have received appointments in the colonies. But of such cases there will I trust be no recurrence. Patronage in some form and degree may be inseparable from the institutions of civilised life: but I do not envy that man who hopes that in times like these – perhaps in any times, but certainly who hopes that in times like these – government can be carried on through the influence of patronage. It is a wretched instrument; it is a feeble instrument on which to rely; and it is also an instrument very apt to lower the moral tone of those who rely upon it. But, be that as it may, it is not the question before you, inasmuch as it would be impossible to induce any free colony of England in the present day to submit to that exercise of patronage for the purposes of the mother country. Therefore we must entirely dismiss from our consideration the idea that the colonial empire of this country is to be maintained for the sake of increasing the quantity of patronage at the command of the Government at home.

But an idea far more important and effective to a far greater extent has been the idea that the colonies ought to be maintained for the purpose of establishing an exclusive trade, the whole profit of which should be confined to the mother country, and should be enjoyed by the mother country. This was in fact the basis of the modern colonial system of Europe. I do not speak now of the political system, but it was the basis of the commercial laws of the countries which had colonies: that the industry of the colonists, instead of having a fair field and equal favour given to it, was attempted to be made entirely subservient to the interests and the profit of the mother country. It was placed in an unfair position. People were told in fact that they might go to the colonies, but that whatever they produced in the colonies must be sent to the British market – nay, that it must be sent in British vessels to the British market – nay, that whatever was produced must be sent to the British market in British vessels and in the state of raw produce, because if sent in other vessels, although it were sent better and cheaper, it would not be for the interest of the British shipowner, and if sent in a manufactured state it would not be for the interest of the British manufacturer. It is not now the question to be discussed whether it might have been desirable to establish a trading monopoly with your colonies at the time you founded them, for some short period, in order to apply a strong temporary stimulus, and to induce the people to enter upon enterprises which, at their commencement, are most difficult, and might be said, therefore, with some plausibility, to have required a special inducement. That is not the question. A trading monopoly to a country for a strictly limited time is rather in the nature of a patent, with respect to which, whether the principle be on the whole expedient for the community, or be not, we cannot say that the patent involves any very offensive or unjust principle of restriction. But the idea of the commercial relation with colonies was founded on this – and after the expectation of great treasures of gold were dissipated the colonial system was mainly maintained for this by the powers which were interested in it – that it might be the basis of exclusive trade between the mother country and the colonies, by which the colonies were to derive just so much profit as would enable them to carry on their affairs, and the mother country was to appropriate all the rest. Now, look at the effect of an idea of such a nature. When colonies were founded upon a principle of this sort, the government at home proceeded as if the colony could only benefit one other country by its trade. It proceeded upon the false notion which was at the bottom of our own commercial laws some time ago, and which still is at the bottom of the commercial laws of many other nations of the globe, the notion that there can be any other basis whatever for trade except the benefit of both parties concerned; the idea that any trade is possible where all the gains are at one side; the idea above all that whatever was gained by one was taken from the other. That is the great fallacy of the protective system, the system which prevails still in many countries in Europe. The truth, on the contrary, with respect to trade being, that not only what one man gains another does not lose, but that when one man gains, the other man must gain also. There is no possible mainspring of trade, except the benefit of both the parties who are engaged in carrying it on. But the vain and false notion that the greatest benefit was to be obtained from the trade of a colony by keeping it all to yourself, and that if you allowed a foreign country to come in and get a share of that trade it would be something taken away from you without a compensation, completely perverted the colonial, and in no small degree the political, system of Europe. Because the immediate consequence of it was this – the patriotism of Europe took a most mischievous direction. It never had been supposed that there could be a general commerce between Europe and America, or between Europe and the tropics. The statesmen and the people of each

country, immediately set about to consider how each of them could get hold of the greatest portion of its neighbour's colonial possessions. England, I am sorry to say, was not the most backward in the race. England had the character, during the last century, of being, perhaps, the most rapacious, certainly the most successful in rapacity, of all the European powers. The colours now drawn on the map, if only they are compared with the history of the different colonies, will show you that she possesses a vast number of colonies which she did not found, but that nobody else possesses any colony which she did found. Undoubtedly, we were not able to keep the North American colonies which we founded ourselves, but that was owing to our faults of policy, and was not a question of possession between us and any foreign power. But as regards the question between England and the other powers of Europe, the other great colonising states, I have already referred to the very inspiring consideration, that almost all the languages of Europe are spoken in the different colonies of the Queen of England, and the origin and explanation of that fact is to be found in this, that at different times we appropriated by force of arms what had belonged to other people. Not alone in our own case, however, but generally, the doctrine of a permanent trading monopoly with the colonies was not merely false as a system of political economy, but it was, likewise, most mischievous in a political point of view, partly because these restraints were offensive to colonists, but yet more because it became the foundation of intrigue and of war among the different European countries, it led to many of the wars, and some of the most important wars, which desolated Europe and America during the last century, and although it ended in a very considerable acquisition of territory by us, yet it brought an acquisition of another kind, namely, an acquisition of debt, which, I think, it is very doubtful whether we should not have done well to dispense with, at the cost of foregoing the advantage of the territories we obtained. These, then, roughly stated, are all reasons which have prevailed at different times, and have been the basis, in a great degree, of the colonial policy of different statesmen, in different ages, and in different countries.

Now, as I repudiate any and all of these reasons for desiring the possession of colonies, it is but fair that I should endeavour to state why I think colonies are desirable for a country circumstanced as England is. I have stated, that I do not think them desirable simply to puff up our reputation, apart from the basis and substance on which it rests. It is plain that they are not to be desired for revenue, because they do not yield it. It is plain that they are not to be desired for trading monopoly, because that we have entirely abandoned. It is plain they are not to be desired for patronage, properly so called, within their limits, because they will not allow us to exercise patronage, and I am bound to say, I do not think the public men of this country have any desire so to exercise it. With respect to territory, it is perfectly plain that mere extension of territory is not a legitimate object of ambition, unless you can show that you are qualified to make use of that territory for the purposes for which God gave the earth to man. Why then are colonies desirable? In my opinion, and I submit it to you with great respect, they are desirable both for the material and for the moral and social results which a wise system of colonisation is calculated to produce. As to the first, the effect of colonisation undoubtedly is to increase the trade and employment of the mother country. Take the case of the emigrant going across the Atlantic. Why does he go across the Atlantic? Because he expects – and in general he is the best judge of his own interests – to get better wages across the Atlantic than he can get at home. If he goes across the Atlantic to get better wages, he leaves in the labour market at home fewer persons than before, and consequently raises the rate of wages at home by carrying himself away from the competition with his fellows. By going to the colony and supplying it with labour he likewise creates a demand for capital there, and by this means he creates a trade between the colony and the mother country. The capital and labour thus employed in the colony raise and export productions, for which commodities are wanted in return. Of these commodities a very large proportion is usually sought from the parent country; you will almost always find that a colony is founded under circumstances where the country to which the settlers go, produces the very commodities which are wanted in the country which they left. Therefore, so far as trade, and the gain connected with trade, are concerned, it is perfectly obvious that the foundation of a colony, where it is the natural result of the circumstances of the country – for I am no advocate for the arbitrary foundation by an artificial effort of government, irrespective of all circumstances – but where it is the natural and spontaneous result of the circumstances in which the country is placed – is simply a great enlargement of the material resources of that country. Trade and employment may be increased by any one of three ways. They may be increased by the opening of new fields in foreign countries; they may be increased by the opening of such fields in your own country; or they may be increased by the opening of them in your colonies. If employment and trade with foreign countries are increased, you get the profit of the trade. But then you are undoubtedly liable to the disadvantage that the passing of unwise and bad laws in these foreign countries may greatly restrict and hamper the extension of your trade. Thus you are exposed to the utmost disadvantage, not because a proceeding of this kind makes the trade with foreign countries less lucrative than the trade with the colonies; there never can exist permanently or for any length of time two trades lucrative in different degrees, for if the trade with the colony is more lucrative than the trade with a foreign country, it is quite plain that the balance will soon be restored, because those who carry on the worst trade with the foreign country will go into the better trade with the colony until the gains of the two are equalised. But the difference is this, in the case of a foreign country your trade often may be injuriously crippled and kept down so as to suffer by the bad laws of the country with which you are trading, while with respect to the colony you have no such danger, both because the sentiment of rivalry usually does not prevail, and because the commercial laws are under the control of the mother country; so that when you found colonies, and trade with them, you are practically sure that that trade will have fair play, and that the natural field which is open for its extension will not be narrowed by the unwise proceedings of men. That is a great advantage of colonial trade. An immense advantage it is. The consequence of it has been that your colonies, although they contain but a very small proportion of the inhabitants of the countries with which you trade, yet, notwithstanding, furnish you with a very considerable proportion of that trade. If, upon the other hand, you open new fields of employment at home, such as the creating of a new trade – suppose, for example, we take such a case as happened in Scotland not so many years ago, when the ironstone of the great district which surrounds Glasgow was discovered, an event which has happened within the memory of many, it was the opening of an immense field of new employment and the creation of an immense new trade. When, therefore, you open a new field of employment at home you get the profit to trade, you give a security to the trade that it will not be interrupted or hemmed in by bad laws; and likewise, when you have got that increase of population to which increase of trade cannot fail to lead, you also get the additional advantage that those who carry it on become part and parcel of the same community with yourselves, and directly contribute towards bearing the burthens necessary for the support of the country. Thus, the material advantages of colonial enterprise and trade, though inferior to those of extended trade at home, present some recommendations that foreign trade does not possess. But these are incidental differences. Every legitimate, that is unforced, extension of trade is beneficial; and there is no doubt that as regards the trade and employment of the people, the possession of colonies like those of England, which are peopled by the spontaneous operation of natural causes – that is to say, by the free judgment of the people, each man carrying his labour or his capital to the market where he thinks he may get the best price for either – there is no doubt that, in a material point of view, the possession of such colonies is eminently beneficial, not because it creates a more profitable trade than other trades, but because it creates a perfectly new trade, and a trade which would not otherwise exist.

But I do not concede that the material benefit of colonies is the only consideration which we are able to plead. Their moral and social advantage is a very great one. If we are asked why, on these grounds, it is desirable that colonies should be founded and possessed, I answer by asking another question – Why is it desirable that your population at home should increase? Why is it that you rejoice, always presuming that the increase of population goes hand in hand with equally favourable or more favourable conditions of existence for the mass of the people – why is it that you rejoice in an increase of population at home? Because an increase of population is an increase of power, an increase of strength and stability to the state, and because it multiplies the number of people who, as we hope, are living under good laws, and belong to a country to which it is an honour and an advantage to belong. That is the great moral benefit that attends the foundation of British colonies. We think that our country is a country blessed with laws and a constitution that are eminently beneficial to mankind, and if so, what can be more to be desired than that we should have the means of reproducing in different portions of the globe something as like as may be to that country which we honour and revere? I think it is in a work by Mr Roebuck that the expression is used, "that the object of colonisation is the creation of so many happy Englands." It is the reproduction of the image and likeness of England – the reproduction of a country in which liberty is reconciled with order, in which ancient institutions stand in harmony with popular freedom, and a full recognition of popular rights, and in which religion and law have found one of their most favoured homes. Well,

as it is the destiny of man to live in society, under laws and institutions, it is desirable that he should live under good laws and institutions; but if we suppose the case of a country with very bad institutions, colonisation by such a country would be a curse to mankind instead of a blessing, and the reproduction of its tyranny on other shores would not be a cause, in a social or moral point of view, for satisfaction. It is because we feel convinced that our constitution is a blessing to us, and will be a blessing to our posterity, as it has been to our forefathers, that we are desirous of extending its influence, and that it should not be confined within the narrow borders of this little island; but that if it please Providence to create openings for us upon the broad fields of distant continents, we should avail ourselves in reason and moderation of those openings to reproduce the copy of those laws and institutions, those habits and national characteristics, which have made England so famous as she is. But it is quite time that I should pass on to the second of the two questions I proposed.

If it be desirable, upon the grounds I have stated, that a country circumstanced as England is should be possessed of colonies, or should enter upon the work of colonisation and pursue it with all the vigour at her command – in what manner ought those colonies to be founded, and in what manner ought they to be governed? Now, I think that this question will be examined in the form most interesting and instructive if I try it by reference to the standards which history affords; and there is one people famous in ancient times, a people, too, that may possibly have future fame in store for it – I mean that Greek race, to which we all of us owe infinitely more than we are really aware of. That Greek race so celebrated and renowned in history was nowhere more remarkable than it was in the work of colonisation. This deserves your attention especially, because the Greek idea of colonisation appears to have been lost with the Greeks themselves. At any rate, no country known to us appears so fully to have realised or to have given such remarkable effect to that idea. But while I think that we have much to learn from it, I do not pretend to say that it is a perfect idea for the times in which we live; but I think it was as perfect an idea as the nature of things admitted in the times of the glory and prosperity of Greece. Now, the Greeks were originally a people that lay in a nutshell; their proper and prevailing name – the word "Greek" being comparatively a modern one – in the earliest times, is the Hellenic race. The Hellenic race originally were a tribe utterly insignificant in numbers, and inhabiting a part of the mountainous regions or of the plains of Thessaly; but by their indomitable energy they spread themselves over the whole country lying to the South between themselves and the Southern point of the Peloponnesus, from thence into the Greek islands, again into Asia Minor, where they founded states not inferior to those of Greece herself, and then again, in immense numbers, to the westward, where (in Sicily) they became masters of the country, and founded states, having a population which now is hardly possible for us to credit, for it is actually stated that Sicily, at the time of the Greek colonisation, contained eight millions of inhabitants. But, at any rate, they peopled Sicily, and brought it to a point of prosperity that it is very far from having maintained for many generations; and they likewise peopled the South of Italy in such strength that the South of Italy acquired the name of Great Greece. And what was the principle of Greek colonisation? It may be summed up in one word – it was perfect freedom and perfect self-government. Colonies were founded from Greece, not by the action of government, not by the meeting of cabinets or by the acts of ministers, but by the spontaneous energy of the members of the community themselves, who went forth to those spots in the globe where they thought they could do better for themselves than they found they could do at home; and rude and simple as that course of proceeding was, yet, when you compare it with the laboured and artificial appliances of modern times, undoubtedly its results were wonderful. For these men who went forth across the sea over to Asia, Thrace, Sicily, and Italy carried with them the recollection and the love of the country from which they came; they carried with them its laws, its religion, its manners, its language, its institutions. They reflected its manners and its image. It was the creation of so many mirrors in which the parent Greece was thrown back upon herself, and the whole of that result, and the immense prosperity of those states was due to this – that those colonies were founded in perfect freedom. The notion of interference by the mother country, the notion of the mother country undertaking to show to those colonies how they should regulate their own affairs – those notions which have been so pernicious to us, and of which we are only now and by slow degrees getting rid – were totally unknown to that remarkable people. The consequence was this – that although there was no direct political connexion, no direct administrative connexion, yet there was always to be found union in heart and character. The country founded in freedom, by virtue of that freedom developed itself with the utmost rapidity to strength, and a har-

mony of feeling and of affection always remained between it and the city from which its founders came. That was the principle of the Greek colonisation, and, as I have stated, its results were astonishing. Take the case of Sicily. It is difficult, undoubtedly, to give entire and implicit credence to the reports as they were told, but it is stated, as I have mentioned, that Sicily was inhabited by 8,000,000 of inhabitants after the Greek colonisation, and that the city of Syracuse was inhabited by no less than 1,200,000 persons, a greater number of persons than at present compose the population of the magnificent capital of France. That town of Syracuse at the present day has dwindled down comparatively to a village. It is far less than half the size of Chester, but at that time it was a city of the first order; and I only quote it, first of all, to show the immense material results that followed upon the principle of free colonisation; and secondly, to show that it was not only material results but moral results which were also secured, and that the unity of action and affection, and the great increase of influence and of power which followed upon the extension of their race, was best obtained by abstaining from any attempt at interference with them, and by allowing the colony to grow and thrive under the light and warmth of the sun of heaven.

Such was the Greek colonisation. It was impossible that at that time a political connexion between the mother country and the colony could be maintained, for two reasons. In the first place, a line of communication was very difficult to carry on. The art of navigation was in its infancy; and so rude were the notions and the practice of it, that for ages the habit of those who were at sea was to creep along the coasts from point to point, to haul up their vessels on the shore at night, and launch them again in the morning, that they might continue their voyage. Of course we may judge that, under these circumstances, periodical or even regular communication was a thing almost impossible. Such were the hazards of it – such was the fear of the horrors of the sea – that the condition of the ancients in that respect was not for a moment to be compared with that of the age in which we live, or with that of those who preceded us by 200 or 300 years. There is one remarkable passage in Homer, which will give an idea of the way in which these things presented themselves; speaking of the distance of Egypt from Greece, he says, "It is so far off that not even the birds could in their flight get there within a year." And you may well judge that when such notions prevailed, or a state of society which rendered such notions possible – because undoubtedly this is figurative or exaggerated language, inasmuch as Egypt was known to and sometimes visited by the Greeks in the days of Homer – you may well conceive what would be the difficulty of such communications between the mother country and its colonies, as are needed in order to carry on the functions of government. It is, therefore, not surprising that they did not attempt to maintain a regular communication. Another reason why it could not be done was this, that the development of political institutions at home was not sufficiently advanced for the purpose. Government was so much of a makeshift; it was so difficult for it to fulfil its purposes, even with regard to the community at its own doors; it was usually so narrow in its basis, and so perplexed and weakened by the miserable institution of slavery which prevailed throughout those heathen times; so that the government being unable to discharge its own domestic functions with any great degree of stability and regularity, it was, of course, much more difficult for it to exercise power over a people of cities and states at a distance, and with whom regular communication was almost impossible. It was, therefore, impossible for the Greeks to maintain a system of colonisation and colonial connexion, such as undoubtedly it is in our power to maintain. The physical difficulties that beset infant colonies from the want of material support were, in consequence, very great; many perished in the cradle; multitudes also survived, and through freedom became great and glorious.

But let us now consider modern colonisation. I will here – for it is absolutely necessary to reject much material which presents itself upon very side – confine myself to the case of England; again I will confine myself mainly to what may be called the free colonies of England, and will call upon you simply to notice some of the broadest and most palpable distinctions between the policy of this country at different times, and the many and fundamental features which mark the difference of that policy at one time from what it was at another. And here it is very singular that until within the last five-and-twenty years, I should have to say, things have been regularly going down. You remember the fable of the poets which described the early ages of the world as being four in number – of which the first was the golden; the second, the silver; the third, the brazen; and the fourth, the iron age. Well, I should say that our colonisation – not speaking of our commercial system, but of the political system – our colonisation and the right relation between the mother country and the colony began with the golden age; it then came to its silver age; and from its silver age it came to its brazen age. We have now entered into its fourth age, and I am happy to say I am very confident that that will not be an iron age, but that if it is not a golden one, it will, at all events, exhibit a considerable reaction, and return towards the better system which distinguished our early colonial history. I take for the golden age the seventeenth and part of the eighteenth centuries. Our colonisation may be said, practically to have begun with the former – in the end of the reign of Elizabeth and the beginning of the reign of James the First; and the reason why I venture to dignify this period with the epithet of the golden age is this, that the colonial connexion at that time was conceived in the true spirit of British freedom. The idea of a colony, as it was entertained, was the idea of a subaltern corporation, comprehended within the great incorporation of the nation or state. As you are all aware, the municipal body – take the municipality of Chester, or any other, as an instance – is not interfered with by Parliament so long as its action is confined to concerns properly local, but is permitted to exercise a discretion, and to manage those things according to the sense of the local community. Even so the idea of the statesmen of the seventeenth century appears to have been that a colony was essentially a municipal corporation, and as a municipal corporation ought to be allowed the management of its own affairs. So it was in a great degree with the colonies that were founded under the elder Stuarts. This idea and this disposition to be most liberal in the grant of constitutions to our colonies rose to their very highest point at the period, or shortly after the period, of the restoration of Charles the Second, when the constitution of Rhode Island was given by the Crown. The reign of Charles the Second is a period upon which, for some reasons, we must look back with great pain and shame. It is hardly possible to find a more discreditable sovereign in the long list of British monarchs than Charles the Second. The position of subserviency to Louis the Fourteenth, in which, through his foreign policy, he placed this country, must make his name ever raise a blush upon the face of an Englishman. But it was a great epoch in legislation, and it certainly was remarkable for this, that there appears never to have been a time when the principle of colonial government was better understood in this country than in the early part, at least, of the reign of Charles the Second. Now, I will describe the spirit of the British policy of that period in words which require to be introduced with no apology, for they are the words of Edmund Burke. He described the colonial policy which presided over the foundation and government of the American States in these few words. He said, "Through a wise and salutary neglect, a generous nature has been suffered to take her own way to perfection." Of course, you will readily understand the meaning of that refined expression of Mr Burke. By a wise and salutary neglect he meant an omission to meddle, connected, no doubt more or less, with the conviction that meddling was mischievous, and that the colonists themselves were the best judges of their own affairs. It is very remarkable that at the time when the liberties of the English people at home were in a critical and hazardous condition – during the very century in which they received their development, through the midst of a disastrous and blood-stained struggle – at that very time the principles of colonial government should have been better understood than at a later day. At the same time the secret of that fact is not very difficult to penetrate. If we are asked why the governments of James the First, Charles the First, and Charles the Second, did not meddle so much as has been done in later times with the affairs of the colonies, I believe the answer may be readily given. No doubt there was at that time, as at all times, a strong vigorous spirit of English good sense, which kept the country out of scrapes, as it has done upon many occasions; but I believe a main reason was that those governments had quite enough to do at home. They found it difficult enough to govern the country, and to solve the problems which presented themselves for solution at home; and perhaps their conduct towards the colonies was the consequence quite as much of their necessities as of their superior wisdom. But, whatever the cause may have been, the result undoubtedly was that the colonies at that period were left practically in the enjoyment of a freedom almost as complete, for every practical purpose, as that which the Greek colonies formerly enjoyed. The political connexion continued. The colony had the honour and the advantage of belonging to the British Empire – it had the advantage of British laws, wherever the colonists did not themselves seek to modify them in conformity with local circumstances – it had the right of calling upon England to defend it in case of need, and to recognise it as her offspring entitled to her protection. These were advantages attaching to our colonial system which, as I said before, it was impossible for the Greek system to attain. The great point, however, was, that under both systems the colonies had freedom, and that freedom produced its effects – first, a wonderfully rapid growth of greatness and prosperity; and second, the utmost warmth of attachment and affection to the mother country.

I now come to consider the silver age, which undoubtedly presents a very great decline as compared with the golden age. I call that period the silver age which immediately precedes the American war. At that period the notion of commercial monopoly, as constituting the whole value of colonies, had caused much squabbling, so to speak, amongst the various nations for the possession of each other's colonies; and the expenses of the transatlantic war having become heavy, the people of England thought it only fair that their fellow-countrymen in America should contribute something towards the expenses of the struggle. The period of that war is one of the most remarkable in our history, and one, in my opinion, of the most useful for us to contemplate, for it is full of salutary lessons. In general, people conceive of the American war as a thing gone by. They know we inherit from it a considerable debt – I think it left us saddled with something like 160 or 180 millions of permanent debt at the end of the war more than when it began – but the debt is not all it has left us, it has left us also great lessons. We use that war now chiefly as a means of glorifying ourselves at the expense of our fathers. We think to ourselves that we never would have committed such folly had we lived in those times. I am doubtful about that. However, though it was not so easy to discern then, as many suppose, we can now plainly enough see that the American war was a gross folly – a grievous folly: we have paid for it most severely – we have paid for it in an enormous amount of debt – we have paid for it in an amount of military and political disgrace greater than England had for many centuries been called upon to undergo, in the abandonment of America under the pressure of American and French arms – we paid for it most of all in the loss of the hearts of the Americans. Before we began the system of meddling and peddling in her affairs, the attachment of the colony was strong to this country; but when they saw a disposition to deprive them of their time-honoured hereditary privileges – when they saw that Englishmen, so jealous of their own liberties at home, were disposed to stint and narrow the enjoyment of such liberties by their brethren who had crossed the Atlantic, indeed, but yet were still thoroughly Englishmen in their hearts and feelings, no doubt a bitterness of sentiment sprang up, and that bitterness was not the fault of the Americans, it was the unhappy result of our errors and of the circumstances of the time. The unhappy consequences of this feeling, aggravated in the course of that long, bloody, and obstinate struggle, were that at the time when American independence was acknowledged the affections of the country towards us had received a desperate blow. For a long time the name of Englishman was odious, and naturally odious in America. The name of England was associated with oppression, and those among the Americans who were known to entertain a strong feeling of affection towards her were odious in the eyes of their fellow-countrymen. That temporary estrangement of feeling, which was almost total, and which even now, notwithstanding the healing influence of time, has necessarily left some traces behind, was a part of the mighty price we have paid for the error involved in a misconception of the right manner of governing our colonies.

I want here to press yet further that which I have already said, that the true value of colonies, for all moral and social purposes, arises in their unity of character and affection with the mother country. There are 30,000,000 of people, or near that number, now constituting the great American republic; and it is really very doubtful whether the influence of England in Europe and the world at large is greater because there are 30,000,000 men in America, the great bulk of whom sprang from the loins of England. It is hard to say whether the existence of America takes from or adds to the weight of England as a member of the great family of nations. In some respects it takes from it, in others it adds to it. But suppose that, instead of mutual curses and disagreements – suppose that, instead of that bloody struggle – suppose that, instead of a violent laceration of the ties that bound the colony to the mother country, America had continued to grow and prosper as a colony, under the beneficent influence of England, or even that America had separated from England as friend from friend, breaking only the link of administrative connexion, but retaining the same feeling as of old in her heart, and carrying with her into a state of freedom, nothing but a recollection of benefits received in the laws and institutions she had inherited, do you not think that the existence of America, even in this state of independence, yet allied to us by language and by laws, would have immensely increased the influence of England in the world? It was a sad loss, I think, we underwent in consequence of that error. If this be so, it is important to us to know, if it is to be a lesson to us, how the error arose, and whose the error was. The error was the attempt by England to levy taxes upon the people of America – not certainly for purposes exclusively English, but for the purpose of defraying part of the expense of wars into which England had entered for the benefit, so she believed, of America, as well as of herself. But some

people think that that was not the error of the English people. Let there be no mistake on this: if there is one thing in history more clear than another, it is that the English nation, at the beginning of the American war, were united almost to a man in favour of the prosecution of the war. All wars, almost without an exception, have been popular in this country during the first year – or even during the second and third; but the American war was especially popular in its earlier stages; and of that I will give you a most conclusive proof from the history of Mr Burke. Mr Burke was elected for Bristol in 1774; he was rejected in 1780, when next he presented himself to the constituency; and in his speech in 1780, explaining his conduct, he stated, among other reasons for not visiting them more frequently, or as often as they thought he ought to have done, that his main reason was the state of feeling in Bristol with respect to the American war. Before people knew how the fortune of arms would turn, there was a difference of opinion in Bristol; naturally enough, Bristol carried on a great trade with America, and there were parties there opposed to hostilities; but when, shortly after war had broken out, the English became successful in the field, that party was entirely put down. And you should know that the English were usually successful over the Americans in the field. It is not necessary to go into the causes – the fact implies no reproach to American bravery, because America had none of the advantages of that time of a military system. The military organisation was all on the side of England. But it was not the want of success in the field that defeated us in the American war; it was this – that though we most commonly beat America in the field, we were no nearer than before to the subjugation of the country. We possessed the ground where the camps were pitched, but we possessed nothing else. The enemy was in the heart of every man, woman and child; and driving their soldiery out of the field, did not establish our power in the hearts of a people who were fighting for their freedom. Thus, the struggle was wound up, naturally enough, by foreign intervention on behalf of America. But let us see, was the error the error of the Government, or was it the error of the people? Listen to Mr Burke, speaking in 1780:

To open my whole heart to you on this subject, I do confess, however, that there were other times besides the two years in which I did visit you when I was not wholly without leisure for repeating that mark of my respect. But I could not bring my mind to see you. You remember, that in the beginning of this American war (that era of calamity, disgrace, and downfall – an era which no feeling mind will ever mention without a tear for England) you were greatly divided, and a very strong body, if not the strongest, opposed itself to the madness which every art and every power were employed to render popular, in order that the errors of the rulers might be lost in the general blindness of the nation. This opposition continued until after our great but most unfortunate victory at Long Island. Then all the mounds and banks of our constancy were borne down at once, and the frenzy of the American war broke in upon us like a deluge. This victory, which seemed to put an immediate end to all difficulties, perfected us in that spirit of domination which our unparalleled prosperity had but too long nurtured. We had been so very powerful and so very prosperous that even the humblest of us were degraded into the vices and follies of kings. We lost all measure between means and ends, and our headlong desires became our politics and our morals. All men who wished for peace, or retained any sentiments of moderation, were overborne or silenced.

And again, a little further on:

A representative worthy of you ought to be a person of stability. I am to look, indeed, to your opinions; but to such opinions as you and I must have five years hence. I was not to look to the flash of the day. I knew that you chose me, in my place, along with others, to be a pillar of the state, not a weathercock on the top of the edifice, exalted for my levity and versatility, and of no use but to indicate the shiftings of every fashionable gale. Would to God, the value of my sentiments on Ireland and on America had been at this day a subject of doubt and discussion! No matter what my sufferings had been, so that this kingdom had kept the authority I wished it to maintain, by a grave foresight, and by an equitable temperance in the use of its power.

Here you have the unquestionable testimony of that remarkable man to the state of feeling that prevailed even in Bristol – in a city so dependent upon its trade with America – in reference to the error of that unhappy, that miserable war. So long as success continued to gild it, the war was popular; but when difficulties came to present themselves – when misfortunes thickened on the country – when France took up arms – when Spain followed the example – when Russia and the other powers of Europe, though they did not take up arms, yet sufficiently indicated by their measures their adverse disposition, then the popular mind recovered its balance, and in 1780 Mr Burke found the people

of Bristol not so disinclined to hear the accents of his wisdom on the subject of the American war as they had been but a short time before. Nor is this a mere tale of the past. The case of this American war – considering how universally it is now admitted that a great error was committed in beginning and in continuing it – is one upon which we can all look back with great advantage, for all generations and all times, as a most emphatic lesson of caution, of circumspection, and of moderation.

But we must pass on from that age in which the American war took place, and which I call the "Silver Age," because at that time the error of interfering with colonial affairs appears only to have been partial, occasional, and for special reasons; and I come to the "Brazen Age," commencing (to take it roughly) about the year 1783, and ending about the year 1840, when we began to have a dawn of better things. And as in the first period of English colonisation the principle was that "through a wise and salutary neglect a generous nature should be suffered to find her own way to perfection," so now the principle was rather conceived to be that through incessant interference a generous nature should be prevented from taking her own way to perfection. The idea now came to be entertained that it was absolutely necessary that from a certain spot in the city of London the local affairs of the colonies should be directed. It is difficult to believe to what an extent we carried this interference with the affairs of our colonial fellow-subjects. But some of the principal particulars may be cursorily enumerated. In the first place, it was thought that we in England, should retain in our hands, and on no account give the colonists, a disposal of the unoccupied lands of the colonies. Then it was thought, that besides the taxes raised by the colonists themselves to support the colonial government, we must have another set of revenues, called crown revenues, that is to say, to provide for the contingency that the people of the colony might be so ignorant and barbarous as to make no provision for the very first necessities of their own government. The next step was to keep standing armies to discharge the functions of police, the consequence of which was enormous expense to this country, in the first place, and the greatest mischief to the discipline of the army, in the next. They were parcelled out here, there, and everywhere, in such small bodies that they lost the unity of action which an army acquires by being trained and disciplined in masses, and the consequence has been that the army of England, which on the peace establishment is, as compared with other armies, but small in number, has never been able to make an appearance in the field, proportionate even to that reduced number. That was one of the consequences of our mistaken notions on colonial policy. Another mistake in practice was that of requiring the people of the colonies to establish a civil list – to establish a certain range of salaries for their governors, and judges, and secretaries, and other officers for public purposes. Why was it necessary that these things should be required of them? Did the government at home suppose that the colonists themselves did not recognise the necessity of law and order? If they recognised these, they were sure of themselves to provide judges and other officers necessary for their enforcement; and if they did not, the way taken was not the way to make them understand their interest in having them. Another faulty rule was the establishment for each colony of a certain tariff of differential duties, dictating by means of our commercial laws what price should be paid for commodities coming to our colonies from any quarter of the globe. We compelled the North American to pay an extra price for West India sugar; and then we compensated him by making the West Indian pay an additional price for North American wood; so that instead of the commercial interchange being made a blessing or a benefit, we made it an interchange of evils and reciprocal inflictions. Lastly, we used to exercise patronage for our own purposes in the colonies as far as we could venture; and whenever there were a set of people who were not quite presentable at home, whom the English would not quietly endure to see appointed to office in this country, it was commonly thought they were quite good enough to hold office, often with a handsome salary, in some remote colony.

That was the colonial policy of modern times. But it is well worth while to inquire how it came into operation. Consider how the colonies were composed during the time after we conceded American independence. We had three classes of colonies in which the application of free institutions was not very easy. One class was that of the slave-holding colonies, and there it was impossible that institutions of a free character could apply. Another class consisted of conquered colonies; and of course in the case of a conquered colony, where, according to the very meaning of the words, you had just subdued the population, who could not be for a moment supposed to be over well affected to your government, it was not likely that free institutions could easily be planted there, or take root kindly under British authority. The third class consisted of penal colonies. There, again, the mass of the population being composed of convicts transported for offences against the laws, were not very

hopeful subjects for the exercise of political privileges. The free colonies at this time had almost all disappeared. Therefore, I am very far from calling upon you to censure the statesmen of the period when this bad system came gradually into vogue. I think it was mainly the misfortune of the American war, and our having lost our free colonies, and there remaining to us little or nothing except colonies undoubtedly little fit for freedom, which brought us, almost unawares, into that bad system. I am sure there was no man more likely than Mr Pitt to extend a wise, enlightened, and liberal system of government to our colonies, if the circumstances had been favourable to such a system. But they were unfavourable – first, for the reasons I have already mentioned; and secondly, because the effect of the great war in which England and all Europe became engaged, necessarily was to absorb the whole of the public mind and of the time and thoughts of public men, and to compel them in a great degree to neglect almost everything connected with the objects and the arts of peace. But at last the day of reckoning, which is usually also the day of awakening, came. The rebellion of Canada in the year 1837–8 was a cause in which the colonists took up arms to enforce a number of demands, few or none of which we should ever have thought of refusing two or three hundred years before. If all the demands of the Canadian colonists had been conceded, they would not have possessed so much liberty as we ourselves voluntarily gave the people of the American settlements in what we now think the unenlightened time of Charles the Second. It would be very easy to illustrate this subject at greater length, but the lapse of time has been so rapid and I have already detained you at such length, that I shall only enter into it generally and slightly. I shall just mention this, because it is short and intelligible, that the Canadian rebellion cost us, to say nothing of the strife, nothing of the bitterness, nothing of the shedding of human blood, four or five millions of money – and that almost immediately after the rebellion was put down we began to concede all the demands which had been made by the colony, one after another, as fast as we could. We conceded them not from terror, but because, on seriously looking at the case, it really was found that, after all, we had no possible interest in withholding them. You have no cross interest with your colonies. It is hardly possible, in any instance, for their interests to come across yours. What is best for them is best for you. Your great interest is in their prosperity, and the best way to win their affections is to do that which promotes their prosperity. There is, however, one very curious case, and only one, which I shall mention, as illustrating the consequences of the system which prevailed, and the embarrassments which originated in our intermeddling with colonial affairs. The Assembly of Lower Canada, composed chiefly of Frenchmen, resisted us. A large portion of the population took up arms, and were put down by the exercise of British power. After it was put down, we made all the concessions which we might have made without bloodshed, or strife, or heartburning. Some time after that date, namely in 1848, a bill was introduced in Canada, called the Canada Rebellion Losses Bill. The purpose of that bill was understood to be to give compensation at the expense of the public to some of those who had suffered losses in the rebellion in resisting the Queen's troops. You will admit that this was a very bad and dangerous precedent. What effect must it have upon the authority of the law – what effect must it have upon the discipline of the army, if, after rebels against the authority of law have been put down, you introduce an Act of Parliament to compensate the rebels for their losses in and by rebelling? And yet let us look at the case for a moment from the rebels' point of view. The rebels were entitled to say, "why did we rebel? We rebelled because you refused to concede what you have since admitted to be a just demand." Now observe the painful dilemma in which we were placed. Either, upon the one hand, after having virtually admitted that we were wrong in resisting the demands of the rebels, we were to insist upon their suffering for our stupidity and folly – or upon the other hand we were to set an abominable precedent by admitting and recognising the fact that men who with arms in their hands had resisted the law and the ministers of the law, and the troops called out in support of the law, were to be authorised by that same law to receive compensation for the losses which their conduct had brought upon them. It was a difficult question. I for one felt the pressure of the difficulty. I thought the Rebellion Losses Bill ought not to pass, but the case was hardly one which, either way, admitted of any satisfactory solution. Many wiser men than I thought that, grievous as the evil was, the bill should pass; and it did pass, and we were obliged to put our dignity in our pockets upon that occasion. I hope no such occasion will recur, because I hope the conduct which brought it about will never be repeated.

I have only now to call your attention to the general effect of the system. Our scheme of governing the colonies from Downing-street completely alienated – no, I will not say completely alienated, but it decidedly tended to alienate – the hearts of

the people from this country. It led to a system in each colony by which a knot of people combined together and called themselves the British party. A knot of people set themselves about the men who held leading offices in the colony, they professed great zeal in supporting the executive, and called themselves the British party. They were always extremely loud in their professions of zeal, and generally had one or more newspapers to support them. In the meantime where were all the rest of the community? Unfortunately all the rest of the community were deemed anti-British; and the name that ought to be dearest of all names to every colonist became the arbitrary distinction of a few, as opposed to the mass of the community. Now, it is a positive fact that this was invariably, or with very rare exceptions indeed, the way in which the affairs of the colonies were administered. On the one side was the governor, with a little body of official persons, and another little body of individuals picked out of the community, a good many of them having relations in these offices. These were tugging one way, supported by the power of the British government – and on the other side was tugging the whole mass of the colonial population. That is the system upon which we managed our colonial affairs. This now is all changed. The principle is recognised, and fully recognised, that the local affairs of free colonies – for I do not enter into the question of colonies disabled by any peculiar or temporary cause for full freedom – shall be fully managed by the colonies themselves. And now I wish to discharge a debt of justice. There were some men in this country who had undoubtedly proceeded far in advance of their fellow-legislators with regard to colonial affairs. I mention them, because, for the most part, they were men with whose political opinions it was my fate commonly or very frequently to differ. Moreover, I think that as the time of the greatest colonial freedom I have mentioned – namely, the reign of Charles the Second – was eminently a Tory time, it is but fair, and in the spirit of equal justice, that we should now render their due to men of quite a different political connexion – namely, some of the Radical members of the British Parliament. Mr Hume, Mr Roebuck, who is still amongst us, and a gentleman whose name has only within the last few weeks been added to the list of the departed – Sir William Molesworth; these were all of them, in my opinion, great benefactors to their country, by telling the truth upon the right method of colonial government, and that at a time when the truth was exceedingly unpopular. They showed great resolution in saying things for which they were looked upon at the time as little better than either traitors or madmen; but either they were not traitors and madmen then, or we are all traitors and madmen now, because what they then scarcely ventured to utter amid universal disapprobation, no man in his senses would, in the British Parliament, now dare – I speak not without exceptions, but generally – or if he dared would desire to contradict. Of Sir William Molesworth, let me say, on account of the circumstances which will justify a special reference to him, that I have the greatest satisfaction in owning the benefit and instruction which, during many years, I derived from communication with him on colonial questions, and in acknowledging how much I have learned from the speeches which he delivered on the subject of colonial policy, from time to time, in the House of Commons. He was a man of clear and comprehensive mind, of singular diligence and industry, well grounded in the principles of colonial policy and in the history of our colonies, and full of resolution and determination in making his opinions known, while at the same time he promulgated those opinions in a manner entirely free from the taint of party spirit, and not arousing against him a hostile sentiment, greatly increased the benefits which his large research enabled him to confer upon the country. And I feel perfectly satisfied that the speeches which he delivered will – though he is dead and gone – long continue to be consulted, and his name to be had in honour on account of the valuable matter they contain – not only with reference to facts on almost all colonial questions, of which he was a perfect master, but likewise with reference to the principles upon which the colonial empire of this great country ought to be governed. To him I wish to pay that debt of justice, and also to others, some departed and some still alive, who have also led us on in this work.

It is now, then, coming to be understood that the affairs of the colonies are best transacted and provided for by the colonists themselves, as the affairs of England are best transacted by Englishmen. And upon this understanding we act more and more, and with still increasing advantage. We do not attempt to force English institutions on the colonies. But then it will be asked, "do you not intend to have English institutions in the colonies?" Certainly, by all means let us have English institutions in the colonies to the utmost extent to which their circumstances render possible. The main question is, who is to be judge of that extension? Now, I say we are not good judges whether laws useful and convenient to this country ought to prevail in the colonies or not; we are not such good judges of this as the colonies themselves. But more, I say this –

experience has proved that if you want to strengthen the connexion between the colonies and this country – if you want to increase the resemblance between the colonies and this country – if you want to see British law held in respect and British institutions adopted and beloved in the colonies, never associate with them the hated name of force and coercion exercised by us, at a distance, over their rising fortunes. Govern them upon a principle of freedom – let them not feel any yoke upon their necks – let them understand that the relations between you and them are relations of affection; even in the matter of continuing the connexion, let the colonists be the judges, for they are the best judges as to whether they ought to continue to be with you or not, and rely upon it you will reap a rich reward in the possession of that affection unbroken and unbounded in all the influence which the possession of such colonies will give you, and in all the grandeur which it will add to your renown. Defend them against aggression from without – regulate their foreign relations (these things belong to the colonial connexion, but of the duration of that connexion let them be the judges) – and I predict that if you leave them that freedom of judgment it is hard to say when the day will come when they will wish to separate from the great name of England. Depend upon it they covet a share in that name. You will find in that feeling of theirs the greatest security for the connexion. You may learn from the London book-sellers that the greatest purchasers of books relating to old English history now are the Americans. The Americans who come over to this country seek out and visit the scenes where the most remarkable events in British history have occurred; they cannot forget that they are the descendants of the men who have made that history just as much as you are. Make the name of England yet more and more an object of desire to the colonies. Their natural disposition is to love and revere it, and that reverence is by far the best security you can have for their continuing not only to be subjects of the crown – not only to render it allegiance, but to render it that allegiance which is the most precious of all – the allegiance which proceeds from the depths of the heart of man. You have experienced some proof of that in the occurrences of the present and past year. You have seen various colonies, some of them lying at the Antipodes, offering to you their contributions to assist in supporting the wives and families of your soldiers, the heroes that have fallen in the war. This I venture to say may be said, without exaggeration, to be among the first fruits of that system upon which within the last twelve or fifteen years you have founded a rational mode of administering the affairs of your colonies without gratuitous interference. You have every encouragement for the extension of that system. There is so much union of feeling among the public, in Parliament, and throughout the country upon it, that now, I trust, we may look forward with the utmost confidence to its prevalence and its progress; and, for my part, I shall ever thankfully rejoice to have lived in a period when so blessed a change in our colonial policy was brought about; a change which, I think, is full of promise, and profit to a country having such claims on mankind as England, but also a change of system, let me add, in which we have done no more than make a transition from misfortune and from evil, almost in some cases one would say from madness and from crime, back to the rules of justice, of reason, of nature, and of common sense.

> Source: W. E. Gladstone. Address delivered to the Members of the Mechanics Institute, at Chester, November 12, 1855. In Paul Knaplund. *Gladstone and Britain's Imperial Policy*. Hamden, CT: Archon Books, 1996, pp. 185–227.

Note

William Ewart Gladstone (1809–98) was a British statesman and served four times as Prime Minister, from 1868 to 1874, from 1880 to 1885, in 1886, and finally from 1892 to 1894. His early allegiance to the Tory Party eventually evolved into a more liberal position, and his rivalries with Disraeli represented an important feature of the Victorian political landscape. Among other vexed imperial concerns with which Gladstone took issue were the occupation of Egypt in 1882 and the struggle over Irish Home Rule.

114   Benjamin Disraeli: "Conservative and Liberal Principles" (1872)

My Lord Duke and Gentlemen – I am very sensible of the honour which you have done me in requesting that I should be your guest to-day, and still more for your having associated my name with the important toast which has been proposed by the Lord Mayor. In the few observations that I shall presume to make on this occasion I will confine myself to some suggestions as to the present state of the Constitutional cause and the prospects which you, as a great Constitutional party, have before you. Gentlemen, some years ago – now, indeed, not an inconsiderable period, but within the memory of many who are present – the Tory party experi-

enced a great overthrow. I am here to admit that in my opinion it was deserved. A long course of power and prosperity had induced it to sink into a state of apathy and indifference, and it had deviated from the great principles of that political association which had so long regulated the affairs and been identified with the glory of England. Instead of the principles professed by Mr Pitt and Lord Grenville, and which those great men inherited from Tory statesmen who had preceded them not less illustrious, the Tory system had degenerated into a policy which found an adequate basis on the principles of exclusiveness and restriction. Gentlemen, the Tory party, unless it is a national party, is nothing. It is not a confederacy of nobles, it is not a democratic multitude; it is a party formed from all the numerous classes in the realm – classes alike and equal before the law, but whose different conditions and different aims give vigour and variety to our national life.

Gentlemen, a body of public men distinguished by their capacity took advantage of these circumstances. They seized the helm of affairs in a manner the honour of which I do not for a moment question, but they introduced a new system into our political life. Influenced in a great degree by the philosophy and the politics of the Continent, they endeavoured to substitute cosmopolitan for national principles; and they baptized the new scheme of politics with the plausible name of "Liberalism." Far be it from me for a moment to intimate that a country like England should not profit by the political experience of Continental nations of not inferior civilisation; far be it from me for a moment to maintain that the party which then obtained power and which has since generally possessed it did not make many suggestions for our public life that were of great value, and bring forward many measures which, though changes, were nevertheless improvements. But the tone and tendency of Liberalism cannot be long concealed. It is to attack the institutions of the country under the name of Reform, and to make war on the manners and customs of the people of this country under the pretext of Progress. During the forty years that have elapsed since the commencement of this new system – although the superficial have seen upon its surface only the contentions of political parties – the real state of affairs has been this: the attempt of one party to establish in this country cosmopolitan ideas, and the efforts of another – unconscious efforts, sometimes, but always continued – to recur to and resume those national principles to which they attribute the greatness and glory of the country.

The Liberal party cannot complain that they have not had fair play. Never had a political party such advantages, never such opportunities. They are still in power; they have been for a long period in power. And yet what is the result? I speak not I am sure the language of exaggeration when I say that they are viewed by the community with distrust and, I might even say, with repugnance. And, now, what is the present prospect of the national party? I have ventured to say that in my opinion Liberalism, from its essential elements, notwithstanding all the energy and ability with which its tenets have been advocated by its friends – notwithstanding the advantage which has accrued to them, as I will confess, from all the mistakes of their opponents, is viewed by the country with distrust. Now in what light is the party of which we are members viewed by the country, and what relation does public opinion bear to our opinions and our policy? That appears to me to be an instructive query; and on an occasion like the present it is as well that we should enter into its investigation as pay mutual compliments to each other, which may in the end, perhaps, prove fallacious.

Now, I have always been of opinion that the Tory party has three great objects. The first is to maintain the institutions of the country – not from any sentiment of political superstition, but because we believe that they embody the principles upon which a community like England can alone safely rest. The principles of liberty, of order, of law, and of religion ought not to be entrusted to individual opinion or to the caprice and passion of multitudes, but should be embodied in a form of permanence and power. We associate with the Monarchy the ideas which it represents – the majesty of law, the administration of justice, the fountain of mercy and of honour. We know that in the Estates of the Realm and the privileges they enjoy, is the best security for public liberty and good government. We believe that a national profession of faith can only be maintained by an Established Church, and that no society is safe unless there is a public recognition of the Providential government of the world, and of the future responsibility of man. Well, it is a curious circumstance that during all these same forty years of triumphant Liberalism, every one of these institutions has been attacked and assailed – I say, continuously attacked and assailed. And what, gentlemen, has been the result? For the last forty years the most depreciating comparisons have been instituted between the Sovereignty of England and the Sovereignty of a great Republic. We have been called upon in every way, in Parliament, in the Press, by articles in newspapers, by pamphlets, by every means which can influence opinion, to contrast the simplicity and economy of the Sovereignty of the United States with the cumbrous cost of the Sovereignty of England.

Gentlemen, I need not in this company enter into any vindication of the Sovereignty of England on that head. I have recently enjoyed the opportunity, before a great assemblage of my countrymen, of speaking upon that subject. I have made statements with respect to it which have not been answered either on this side of the Atlantic or the other. Only six months ago the advanced guard of Liberalism, acting in entire unison with that spirit of assault upon the Monarchy which the literature and the political confederacies of Liberalism have for forty years encouraged, flatly announced itself as Republican, and appealed to the people of England on that distinct issue. Gentlemen, what was the answer? I need not dwell upon it. It is fresh in your memories and hearts. The people of England have expressed, in a manner which cannot be mistaken, that they will uphold the ancient Monarchy of England, the Constitutional Monarchy of England, limited by the co-ordinate authority of the Estates of the Realm, but limited by nothing else. Now, if you consider the state of public opinion with regard to those Estates of the Realm, what do you find? Take the case of the House of Lords. The House of Lords has been assailed during this reign of Liberalism in every manner and unceasingly. Its constitution has been denounced as anomalous, its influence declared pernicious; but what has been the result of this assault and criticism of forty years? Why, the people of England, in my opinion, have discovered that the existence of a second Chamber is necessary to Constitutional Government; and, while necessary to Constitutional Government, is, at the same time, of all political inventions the most difficult. Therefore, the people of this country have congratulated themselves that, by the aid of an ancient and famous history, there has been developed in this country an Assembly which possesses all the virtues which a Senate should possess – independence, great local influence, eloquence, all the accomplishments of political life, and a public training which no theory could supply.

The assault of Liberalism upon the House of Lords has been mainly occasioned by the prejudice of Liberalism against the land laws of this country. But in my opinion, and in the opinion of wiser men than myself, and of men in other countries beside this, the liberty of England depends much upon the landed tenure of England – upon the fact that there is a class which can alike defy despots and mobs, around which the people may always rally, and which must be patriotic from its intimate connection with the soil. Well, gentlemen, so far as these institutions of the country – the Monarchy and the Lords Spiritual and Temporal – are concerned, I think we may fairly say, without exaggeration, that public opinion is in favour of those institutions, the maintenance of which is one of the principal tenets of the Tory party, and the existence of which has been unceasingly criticised for forty years by the Liberal party. Now, let me say a word about the other Estate of the Realm, which was first attacked by Liberalism.

One of the most distinguishing features of the great change effected in 1832 was that those who brought it about at once abolished all the franchises of the working classes. They were franchises as ancient as those of the Baronage of England; and, while they abolished them, they proposed no substitute. The discontent upon the subject of the representation which has from that time more or less pervaded our society dates from that period, and that discontent, all will admit, has now ceased. It was terminated by the Act of Parliamentary Reform of 1867–8. That Act was founded on a confidence that the great body of the people of this country were "Conservative." When I say "Conservative," I use the word in its purest and loftiest sense. I mean that the people of England, and especially the working classes of England, are proud of belonging to a great country, and wish to maintain its greatness – that they are proud of belonging to an Imperial country, and are resolved to maintain, if they can, their empire – that they believe, on the whole, that the greatness and the empire of England are to be attributed to the ancient institutions of the land.

Gentlemen, I venture to express my opinion, long entertained, and which has never for a moment faltered, that this is the disposition of the great mass of the people; and I am not misled for a moment by wild expressions and eccentric conduct which may occur in the metropolis of this country. There are people who may be, or who at least affect to be, working men, and who, no doubt, have a certain influence with a certain portion of the metropolitan working classes, who talk Jacobinism. But, gentlemen, that is no novelty. That is not the consequence of recent legislation or of any political legislation that has occurred in this century. There always has been a Jacobinical section in the City of London. I don't particularly refer to that most distinguished and affluent portion of the metropolis which is ruled by my right honourable friend the Lord Mayor. Mr Pitt complained of and suffered

by it. There has always been a certain portion of the working class in London who have sympathised – perverse as we may deem the taste – with the Jacobin feelings of Paris. Well, gentlemen, we all know now, after eighty years' experience, in what the Jacobinism of Paris has ended, and I hope I am not too sanguine when I express my conviction that the Jacobinism of London will find a very different result.

I say with confidence that the great body of the working class of England utterly repudiate such sentiments. They have no sympathy with them. They are English to the core. They repudiate cosmopolitan principles. They adhere to national principles. They are for maintaining the greatness of the kingdom and the empire, and they are proud of being subjects of our Sovereign and members of such an Empire. Well, then, as regards the political institutions of this country, the maintenance of which is one of the chief tenets of the Tory party, so far as I can read public opinion, the feeling of the nation is in accordance with the Tory party. It was not always so. There was a time when the institutions of this country were decried. They have passed through a scathing criticism of forty years; they have passed through that criticism when their political upholders have, generally speaking, been always in opposition. They have been upheld by us when we were unable to exercise any of the lures of power to attract force to us, and the people of this country have arrived at these conclusions from their own thought and their own experience.

Let me say one word upon another institution, the position of which is most interesting at this time. No institution of England, since the advent of Liberalism, has been so systematically, so continuously assailed as the Established Church. Gentlemen, we were first told that the Church was asleep, and it is very possible, as everybody, civil and spiritual, was asleep forty years ago, that that might have been the case. Now we are told that the Church is too active, and that it will be destroyed by its internal restlessness and energy. I see in all these efforts of the Church to represent every mood of the spiritual mind of man, no evidence that it will fall, no proof that any fatal disruption is at hand. I see in the Church, as I believe I see in England, an immense effort to rise to national feelings and recur to national principles. The Church of England, like all our institutions, feels it must be national, and it knows that, to be national, it must be comprehensive. Gentlemen, I have referred to what I look upon as the first object of the Tory party – namely, to maintain the institutions of the country, and reviewing what has occurred, and referring to the present temper of the times upon these subjects, I think that the Tory party, or, as I will venture to call it, the National party, has everything to encourage it. I think that the nation, tested by many and severe trials, has arrived at the conclusion which we have always maintained, that it is the first duty of England to maintain its institutions, because to them we principally ascribe the power and prosperity of the country.

Gentlemen, there is another and second great object of the Tory party. If the first is to maintain the institutions of the country, the second is, in my opinion, to uphold the Empire of England. If you look to the history of this country since the advent of Liberalism – forty years ago – you will find that there has been no effort so continuous, so subtle, supported by so much energy, and carried on with so much ability and acumen, as the attempts of Liberalism to effect the disintegration of the Empire of England.

And, gentlemen, of all its efforts, this is the one which has been the nearest to success. Statesmen of the highest character, writers of the most distinguished ability, the most organised and efficient means, have been employed in this endeavour. It has been proved to all of us that we have lost money by our colonies. It has been shown with precise, with mathematical demonstration, that there never was a jewel in the Crown of England that was so truly costly as the possession of India. How often has it been suggested that we should at once emancipate ourselves from this incubus. Well, that result was nearly accomplished. When those subtle views were adopted by the country under the plausible plea of granting self-government to the Colonies, I confess that I myself thought that the tie was broken. Not that I for one object to self-government. I cannot conceive how our distant colonies can have their affairs administered except by self-government. But self-government, in my opinion, when it was conceded, ought to have been conceded as part of a great policy of Imperial consolidation. It ought to have been accompanied by an Imperial tariff, by securities for the people of England for the enjoyment of the unappropriated lands which belonged to the Sovereign as their trustee, and by a military code which should have precisely defined the means and the responsibilities by which the colonies should be defended, and by which, if necessary, this country should call for aid from the colonies themselves. It ought, further, to have been accompanied by the institution of some representative council in the metropolis, which would have brought the Colonies into constant and continuous relations with the Home Government. All this,

however, was omitted because those who advised that policy – and I believe their convictions were sincere – looked upon the Colonies of England, looked even upon our connection with India, as a burden upon this country, viewing everything in a financial aspect, and totally passing by those moral and political considerations which make nations great, and by the influence of which alone men are distinguished from animals.

Well, what has been the result of this attempt during the reign of Liberalism for the disintegration of the Empire? It has entirely failed. But how has it failed? Through the sympathy of the Colonies with the Mother Country. They have decided that the Empire shall not be destroyed, and in my opinion no minister in this country will do his duty who neglects any opportunity of reconstructing as much as possible our Colonial Empire, and of responding to those distant sympathies which may become the source of incalculable strength and happiness to this land. Therefore, gentlemen, with respect to the second great object of the Tory party also – the maintenance of the Empire – public opinion appears to be in favour of our principles – that public opinion which, I am bound to say, thirty years ago, was not favourable to our principles, and which, during a long interval of controversy, in the interval had been doubtful.

Gentlemen, another great object of the Tory party, and one not inferior to the maintenance of the Empire, or the upholding of our institutions, is the elevation of the condition of the people. Let us see in this great struggle between Toryism and Liberalism that has prevailed in this country during the last forty years what are the salient features. It must be obvious to all who consider the condition of the multitude with a desire to improve and elevate it, that no important step can be gained unless you can effect some reduction of their hours of labour and humanise their toil. The great problem is to be able to achieve such results without violating those principles of economic truth upon which the prosperity of all States depends. You recollect well that many years ago the Tory party believed that these two results might be obtained – that you might elevate the condition of the people by the reduction of their toil and the mitigation of their labour, and at the same time inflict no injury on the wealth of the nation. You know how that effort was encountered – how these views and principles were met by the triumphant statesmen of Liberalism. They told you that the inevitable consequence of your policy was to diminish capital, that this, again, would lead to the lowering of wages, to a great diminution of the employment of the people, and ultimately to the impoverishment of the kingdom.

These were not merely the opinions of Ministers of State, but those of the most blatant and loud-mouthed leaders of the Liberal party. And what has been the result? Those measures were carried, but carried, as I can bear witness, with great difficulty and after much labour and a long struggle. Yet they were carried; and what do we now find? That capital was never accumulated so quickly, that wages were never higher, that the employment of the people was never greater, and the country never wealthier. I ventured to say a short time ago, speaking in one of the great cities of this country, that the health of the people was the most important question for a statesman. It is, gentlemen, a large subject. It has many branches. It involves the state of the dwellings of the people, the moral consequences of which are not less considerable than the physical. It involves their enjoyment of some of the chief elements of nature – air, light, and water. It involves the regulation of their industry, the inspection of their toil. It involves the purity of their provisions, and it touches upon all the means by which you may wean them from habits of excess and of brutality. Now, what is the feeling upon these subjects of the Liberal party – that Liberal party who opposed the Tory party when, even in their weakness, they advocated a diminution of the toil of the people, and introduced and supported those Factory Laws, the principles of which they extended, in the brief period when they possessed power, to every other trade in the country? What is the opinion of the great Liberal party – the party that seeks to substitute cosmopolitan for national principles in the government of this country – on this subject? Why, the views which I expressed in the great capital of the county of Lancaster have been held up to derision by the Liberal Press. A leading member – a very rising member, at least, among the new Liberal members – denounced them the other day as the "policy of sewage."

Well, it may be the "policy of sewage" to a Liberal member of Parliament. But to one of the labouring multitude of England, who has found fever always to be one of the inmates of his household – who has, year after year, seen stricken down the children of his loins, on whose sympathy and material support he has looked with hope and confidence, it is not a "policy of sewage," but a question of life and death. And I can tell you this, gentlemen, from personal conversation with some of the most intelligent of the labouring class – and I think there are many of them in this room who can bear witness to what I say – that the policy of the Tory party – the hereditary, the traditional policy of the Tory party, that would improve the condition of the people – is more appreciated by the people than the ineffable mysteries and all the pains and penalties of the Ballot Bill. Gentlemen, is that wonderful? Consider the condition of the great body of the working classes of this country. They are in possession of personal privileges – of personal rights and liberties – which are not enjoyed by the aristocracies of other countries. Recently they have obtained – and wisely obtained – a great extension of political rights; and when the people of England see that under the constitution of this country, by means of the constitutional cause which my right honourable friend the Lord Mayor has proposed, they possess every personal right of freedom, and, according to the conviction of the whole country, also an adequate concession of political rights, is it at all wonderful that they should wish to elevate and improve their condition, and is it unreasonable that they should ask the Legislature to assist them in that behest as far as it is consistent with the general welfare of the realm?

Why, the people of England would be greater idiots than the Jacobinical leaders of London even suppose, if, with their experience and acuteness, they should not long have seen that the time had arrived when social, and not political improvement is the object which they ought to pursue. I have touched, gentlemen, on the three great objects of the Tory party. I told you I would try to ascertain what was the position of the Tory party with reference to the country now. I have told you also with frankness what I believe the position of the Liberal party to be. Notwithstanding their proud position, I believe they are viewed by the country with mistrust and repugnance. But on all the three great objects which are sought by Toryism – the maintenance of our institutions, the preservation of our Empire, and the improvement of the condition of the people – I find a rising opinion in the country sympathising with our tenets, and prepared, I believe, if the opportunity offers, to uphold them until they prevail.

Before sitting down, I would make one remark particularly applicable to those whom I am now addressing. This is a numerous assembly; this is an assembly individually influential; but it is not on account of its numbers, it is not on account of its individual influence, that I find it to me deeply interesting. It is because I know that I am addressing a representative assembly. It is because I know that there are men here who come from all districts and all quarters of England, who represent classes and powerful societies, and who meet here not merely for the pleasure of a festival, but because they believe that our assembling together may lead to national advantage. Yes, I tell all who are here present that there is a responsibility which you have incurred to-day, and which you must meet like men. When you return to your homes, when you return to your counties and to your cities, you must tell to all those whom you can influence that the time is at hand, that, at least, it cannot be far distant, when England will have to decide between national and cosmopolitan principles. The issue is not a mean one. It is whether you will be content to be a comfortable England, modelled and moulded upon Continental principles and meeting in due course an inevitable fate, or whether you will be a great country, – an Imperial country – a country where your sons, when they rise, rise to paramount positions, and obtain not merely the esteem of their countrymen, but command the respect of the world.

Upon you depends the issue. Whatever may be the general feeling, you must remember that in fighting against Liberalism or the Continental system you are fighting against those who have the advantage of power – against those who have been in high places for nearly half a century. You have nothing to trust to but your own energy and the sublime instinct of an ancient people. You must act as if everything depended on your individual efforts. The secrect of success is constancy of purpose. Go to your homes, and teach there these truths, which will soon be imprinted on the conscience of the land. Make each man feel how much rests on his own exertions. The highest, like my noble friend the chairman, may lend us his great aid. But rest assured that the assistance of the humblest is not less efficient. Act in this spirit, and you will succeed. You will maintain your country in its present position. But you will do more than that – you will deliver to your posterity a land of liberty, of prosperity, of power, and of glory.

Source: Speech delivered at the Crystal Palace, June 24, 1872. Earl of Beaconsfield. *Selected Speeches*, Ed. T. E. Kebbel, vol. II. London: 1882, Longmans, pp. 523–35.

115 Benjamin Disraeli: "Royal Titles Bill, March 9, 1876"

In moving the second reading of this Bill I take the opportunity of noticing a question which was ad-

dressed to me a few days ago by the honourable member for Banbury. I thought at the time that the question was unfair and improper. The question was whether I was then prepared to inform the House of the title which Her Majesty would be advised to adopt with respect to the matter contained in the Bill before us, and my answer was, that I was not then prepared to give the information to the House. It appeared to me that that appeal, as I ventured to remark, was unfair and improper, because, in the first place, on a controversial matter, it required me to make a statement respecting which I could offer no argument, as the wise rules of this House, as regards questions and answers, are established. I should, therefore, have had to place before the House, on a matter respecting which there is controversy, the decision of the Government, at the same time being incapacitated from offering any argument in favour of it. I thought the question was improper, also, in the second place, because it was a dealing with the royal prerogative that, to say the least, was wanting, as I thought, in respect. Both sides of the House agree that we are ruled by a strictly constitutional Sovereign. But the constitution has invested Her Majesty with prerogatives of which she is wisely jealous, which she exercises always with firmness, but ever, when the feelings and claims of Parliament are concerned, with the utmost consideration. It is the more requisite, therefore, that we should treat these prerogatives with the greatest respect, not to say reverence. In the present case if Her Majesty had desired to impart to the House of Commons information which the House required, the proper time would certainly be when the Bill in question was under the consideration of the House. It would be more respectful to the House, as well as to the Queen, that such a communication should be made when the House was assembled to discuss the question before them; and such information ought not to be imparted, I think, in answer to the casual inquiry of an individual member.

From the beginning there has been no mystery at any time upon this matter. So far as the Government are concerned they have acted strictly according to precedent, and it has not been in my power until the present evening to impart any information to the House upon the subject on which they intimated a wish to be informed. But, upon the first night, when I introduced this Bill, I did say, alluding to the prerogative of the Queen, and Her Majesty's manner of exercising that prerogative, that I did not anticipate difficulties upon the subject. To this point, in the course of the few observations I have to make, I shall recur; but, before doing so, I shall make some remarks upon the objections which have been made to a title which it has been gratuitously assumed that Her Majesty, with respect to her dominions in India, wishes to adopt. It is a remarkable circumstance that all those who have made objections on this subject, have raised their objections to one particular title alone. One alone has occurred to them – which *prima facie* is rather an argument in favour of its being an apposite title. No doubt other objections have been urged in the debate, and I will refer to them before proceeding to the other part of my remarks. It has been objected that the title of Emperor and Empress denotes military dominion; that it has never or rarely been adopted but by those who have obtained dominion by the sword, retained it by the sword, and governed by the sword; and, to use the words of a right honourable gentleman who took part in the recent debate – "Sentiment clothes the title of Emperor with bad associations."

Now, the House must at once feel what vague and shadowy arguments – if they can be called arguments – are these: "Sentiment clothes the title of Emperor with bad associations." I very much doubt whether sentiment does clothe the title of Emperor with bad associations. I can remember, and many gentlemen can remember, the immortal passage of the greatest of modern historians, where he gives his opinion that the happiness of mankind was never so completely assured or so long a time maintained as in the age of the Antonines, and the Antonines were emperors. The honourable gentleman may be of opinion that an imperial title is a modern invention, and its associations to him may be derived from a limited experience, of which he may be proud. But when so large a principle is laid down by one distinguished for his historical knowledge, that "Sentiment clothes the title of Emperor with bad associations," I may be allowed to vindicate what I believe to be the truth upon this matter. Then a second objection was urged – it was said, "This is a clumsy periphrasis in which you are involving the country if you have not only royal but imperial majesties." Now, the right honourable gentleman who made the remark, ought to have recollected that there would be no clumsy periphrasis of the kind. The majesty of England requires for its support no epithet. The Queen is not Her Royal Majesty. The Queen is described properly as Her Majesty. Therefore the clumsy periphrasis of "Royal and Imperial" Majesty could never occur.

There is, however, a stronger and more important objection which has been brought to this title

of Empress. Put briefly and concisely it is this – that we diminish the supremacy of the queenly title by investing Her Majesty, though only locally, with an imperial dignity. I deny that any imperial dignity is superior to the queenly title, and I defy anyone to prove the reverse. (Hear.) I am happy to have that cheer; but I hear and read every day of an intention to invest Her Majesty with a title superior to that which she has inherited from an illustrious line of ancestors. It is necessary, therefore, to notice this statement. In times which will guide us in any way upon such a subject, I doubt whether there is any precedent of an emperor ranking superior to a crowned head, unless that crowned head was his avowed feudatory. I will take the most remarkable instance of imperial sway in modern history. When the Holy Roman Empire existed, and the German Emperor was crowned at Rome and called Cæsar, no doubt the princes of Germany, who were his feudatories, acknowledged his supremacy, whatever might be his title.

But in those days there were great kings – there were kings of France, and kings of Spain, and kings of England – they never acknowledged the supremacy of the Head of the Holy Roman Empire, and the origin, I have no doubt, of the expression of the Act of Henry VIII, where the crown of England is described as an imperial crown, was the determination of that eminent monarch that at least there should be no mistake upon the subject between himself and the Emperor Charles V. These may be considered antiquarian illustrations, and I will not dwell upon them, but will take more recent cases at a time when the intercourse of nations and of Courts was regulated by the same system of diplomacy which now prevails. Upon this question, then, I say there can be no mistake, for it has been settled by the assent, and the solemn assent, of Europe. In the middle of the last century a remarkable instance occurred which brought to a crisis this controversy, if it were a point of controversy. When Peter the Great emerged from his anomalous condition as a powerful sovereign – hardly recognised by his brother sovereigns – he changed the style and title of his office from that of Czar to Emperor. That addition was acknowledged by England and by England alone. The rulers of Russia as Emperors remained unrecognised by the great comity of nations; and after Peter the Great they still continued to bear the titles of Czar and Czarina; for more than one female sovereign flourished in Russia about the middle of the century. In 1745, Elizabeth, Czarina of Russia, having by her armies and her councils interfered considerably in the affairs of Europe – probably (though I am not sure of this) influenced by the circumstances that the first Congress of Aix la Chapelle, in the middle of the last century, was about to meet – announced to her allies and to her brother sovereigns that she intended in future to take the title of Empress, instead of Czarina. Considerable excitement and commotion were caused at all the Courts and in all the Governments of Europe in consequence of this announcement; but the new title was recognised on condition that Her Majesty should at the same time write a letter, called, in diplomatic language, a reversal, acknowledging that she thereby made no difference in the etiquette and precedence of the European Courts, and would only rank upon terms of equality with the other crowned heads of Europe. Upon these terms France, Spain, Austria, and Hungary admitted the Empress of Russia into their equal society.

For the next twenty years, under Peter III, there were discussions on the subject; but he also gave a reversal, disclaiming superiority to other crowned heads in taking the title of Emperor. When Catherine II came to the throne, she objected to write this reversal, as being inconsistent with the dignity of a crowned sovereign; and she herself issued an edict to her own subjects, announcing, on her accession, her rank, style, and title; and distinctly informing her subjects that, though she took that style and title, she only wished to rank with the other sovereigns of Europe. I should say that the whole of the diplomatic proceedings of the world from that time have acknowledged that result, and there can be no question on the subject. There was an attempt at the Congress of Vienna to introduce the subject of the classification of sovereigns; but the difficulties of the subject were acknowledged by Prince Metternich, by Lord Castlereagh, and by all the eminent statesmen of the time; the subject was dropped; the equality of crowned heads was again acknowledged, and the mode of precedence of their representatives at the different Courts was settled by an alphabetical arrangement, or by the date of their arrival and letters of credit to that Court at once and for ever. The question of equality between those sovereigns who styled themselves Emperors and those who were crowned heads of ancient kingdoms, without reference to population, revenue, or extent of territory, was established and permanently adopted.

Now, Sir, the honourable gentleman the member for Glasgow (Mr Anderson) said the other day, "If Empress means nothing more than Queen, why should you have Empress? If it means something else, then I am against adopting it." Well, I have proved to you that it does not mean anything else. Then, why should you adopt it? Well, that is one of those questions which, if pursued in the same spirit, and applied to all the elements of society, might resolve it into its original elements. The amplification of titles is no new system, no new idea; it has marked all ages, and has been in accordance with the manners and customs of all countries. The amplification of titles is founded upon a great respect for local influences, for the memory of distinguished deeds, and passages of interest in the history of countries. It is only by the amplification of titles that you can often touch and satisfy the imagination of nations; and that is an element which Governments must not despise. Well, then, it is said that if this title of Empress is adopted, it would be un-English. But why un-English? I have sometimes heard the ballot called un-English, and indignant orators on the other side have protested against the use of an epithet of that character which nobody could define, and which nobody ought to employ. I should like to know why the title is un-English. A gentleman the other day, referring to this question now exciting Parliament and the country, recalled to the recollection of the public the dedication of one of the most beautiful productions of the English muse to the Sovereign of this country; and speaking of the age distinguished by an Elizabeth, by a Shakespeare, and by a Bacon, he asked whether the use of the word *Empress*, applied by one who was second in his power of expression and in his poetic resources only to Shakespeare himself, in the dedication of an immortal work to Queen Elizabeth was not, at least, an act which proved that the word and the feeling were not un-English? Then, of course, it was immediately answered by those who criticised the illustration that this was merely the fancy of a poet. But I do not think it was the fancy of a poet. The fancy of the most fanciful of poets was exhausted in the exuberant imagination which idealised his illustrious Sovereign as the "Faëry Queen." He did not call her Empress then – he called her the "Faëry Queen." But when his theme excited the admiration of royalty – when he had the privilege of reciting some of his cantos to Queen Elizabeth, and she expressed a wish that the work should be dedicated to her – then Spenser had, no doubt, to consult the friends in whom he could confide as to the style in which he should approach so solemn an occasion, and win to himself still more the interest of his illustrious Sovereign. He was a man who lived among courtiers and statesmen. He had as friends Sidney and Raleigh; and I have little doubt that it was by the advice of Sidney and Raleigh that he addressed his Sovereign as Empress, "The Queen of England, of Ireland, and of Virginia," the hand of Sir Walter Raleigh being probably shown in the title of the Queen of Virginia; and it is not at all improbable that Elizabeth herself, who possessed so much literary taste, and who prided herself upon improving the phrases of the greatest poet, revised the dedication. That example clearly shows that the objection of this assumed adoption by Her Majesty of the title of Empress as un-English could hardly exist in an age when the word was used with so much honour – in an age of "words which wise Bacon and brave Raleigh spake."

I think it is obvious from these remarks, made upon the assumption that the title which Her Majesty would be pleased to adopt by her Proclamation would be "Empress," that the title would be one to which there could be no objection. I am empowered, therefore, to say that the title would be "Empress," and that Her Majesty would be "Victoria, by the Grace of God, of the United Kingdom of Great Britain and Ireland, Queen, Defender of the Faith, and Empress of India." Now, I know it may be said – it was said at a recent debate and urged strongly by the right honourable gentleman the member for Bradford (Mr W. E. Forster) – that this addition to Her Majesty's style, and in this addition alone, we are treating without consideration the colonies. I cannot in any way concur in that opinion. No one honours more than myself the Colonial Empire of England; no one is more anxious to maintain it. No one regrets more than I do that favourable opportunities have been lost of identifying the colonies with the royal race of England. But we have to deal now with another subject, and one essentially different from the colonial condition. The condition of India and the condition of the colonies have no similarity. In the colonies you have, first of all, a fluctuating population; a man is member of Parliament, it may be, for Melbourne this year, and next year he is member of Parliament for Westminster. A colonist finds a nugget, or he fleeces a thousand flocks. He makes a fortune. He returns to England, he buys an estate; he becomes a magistrate; he represents Majesty; he becomes high sheriff; he has a magnificent house near Hyde Park; he goes to Court, to *levées*, to drawing-rooms: he has an opportunity of plighting his troth personally to his Sovereign; he is in frequent and direct communication with her. But that is not the case with the inhabitant of India.

The condition of colonial society is of a fluctuating character. Its political and social elements change. I remember, twenty years ago, a distinguished statesman(?) who willingly would have seen a Dukedom of Canada. But Canada has now no separate existence. It is called the "Dominion," and includes several other provinces. There is no similarity between the circumstances of our colonial fellow-subjects in India. Our colonists are English; they come, they go, they are careful to make fortunes, to invest their money in England; their interests in this country are immense, ramified, complicated, and they have constant opportunities of improving and employing the relations which exist between themselves and their countrymen in the metropolis. Their relations to the Sovereign are ample; they satisfy them. The colonists are proud of those relations; they are interested in the titles of the Queen; they look forward to return when they leave England; they do return; in short, they are Englishmen.

Now let me say one word before I move the second reading of this Bill, upon the effect it may have upon India. It is not without consideration, it is not without the utmost care, it is not until after the deepest thought, that we have felt it our duty to introduce this Bill into Parliament. It is desired in India; it is anxiously expected. The princes and nations of India, unless we are deceived – and we have omitted no means by which we could obtain information and form opinions – look to it with the utmost interest. They know exactly what it means, though there may be some honourable members in this House who do not. They know in India what this Bill means, and they know that what it means is what they wish. I do myself most earnestly impress upon the House to remove prejudice from their minds and to pass the second reading of this Bill without a division. Let not our divisions be misconstrued. Let the people of India feel that there is a sympathetic chord between us and them, and do not let Europe suppose for a moment that there are any in this House who are not deeply conscious of the importance of our Indian Empire. Unfortunate words have been heard in the debate upon this subject: but I will not believe that any member of this House seriously contemplates the loss of our Indian Empire. I trust, therefore, that the House will give to this Bill a second reading without a division. By permission of the Queen, I have communicated, on the part of my colleagues, the intention of Her Majesty, which she will express in her Proclamation. If you sanction the passing of this Bill, it will be an act, to my mind, that will add splendour even to her throne, and security even to her empire.

Source: Earl of Beaconsfield. *Selected Speeches*, Ed. T. E. Kebbel, vol. II. London: Longmans, 1882, pp. 231–9.

Note

Benjamin Disraeli (1804–81), or the Earl of Beaconsfield, who was also popularly known as "Dizzy," was both statesman and novelist. His novels include *Sybil, or the Two Nations* (1845) and *Tancred, or the New Crusade* (1847). He served twice as England's Prime Minister (1868 and 1874–80), and is remembered as Victoria's "favorite" PM. He was largely responsible for Victoria's acquisition of the title "Empress" in 1876, and his purchase of controlling shares in the Suez Canal guaranteed England's continued involvement in Egypt.

Chapter Twenty-one

From Ingénue to Empress: The Reign
of Queen Victoria

Great Britain's Queen Victoria was a young girl of 19 when she ascended the throne in 1837, the date which officially inaugurates the Victorian era. Victoria's imperial reign was spectacular in a number of ways; for one, it was the longest in the history of the British monarchy. In a sense, the Queen who would become Empress was as important a royal ruler as the formidable Elizabeth I; Victoria, however, was primarily associated with the domestic arena, whereas Elizabeth I – the Queen who declared the nation her spouse – was skilled in the political arena. Queen Victoria was largely disinterested in the political questions of the day, particularly those taking place on the home front. Land and Labour Reform movements disinterested her, the suffrage question offended her; and the Socialists' and Chartists' demands for a more democratic government were contrary to her personal and political investments. The Queen supported Prime Minster Benjamin Disraeli's reform platform in 1867, partly because she was so pleased with the Conservative leader's imperial efforts and accomplishments (and in part, to snub William Ewart Gladstone, whom she disfavored). Disraeli was a dynamic champion of expansionism; during his first and second reigns as Prime Minister, a number of territories had been seized, put under "protection," or annexed. These newly acquired possessions substantially contributed to Great Britain's size and the Queen's international stature; they would also be the cause of various little wars, and in the future, more devastating ones.

In 1875, Disraeli purchased 44 per cent of the Suez Canal Company's shares, a maneuver that assured Great Britain's dominance in the region and dismissed the nation's primary competitors, the French. Disraeli shared the news of the successful purchase with the Queen in his characteristic theatrical fashion: the Suez, India, and the passage to the East were personal gifts for his Queen. In the following years, the Transvaal was annexed (1877) and the Western Pacific High Commission was established in the same year; Cyprus was occupied by the British in 1878; and in 1879, the British attempted to expand territories in Zululand and Afghanistan. Substantial territories were also gained in West Africa, Fiji, and the Malay States. The Queen and the flamboyant Prime Minister shared a fascination with India and a general love of empire, as well; in 1876 Disraeli sponsored the bill that would symbolize the jewel in the crown that the Eastern possession was for Victoria, by declaring the Queen Empress of India.

Both of Victoria's Royal Jubilees were designed to celebrate Great Britain's empire in a grand manner. However, the Golden Jubilee of 1887 occurred in the not too distant shadow of colonial crises, including the Zulu (1879), Second Afghan (1878–80), and First Boer (1881) Wars, the Arabi Rebellion (1882), and the death of Gordon at Khartoum (1885). The even more sensational Diamond Jubilee of 1897 occurred when Great Britain was the predominant European imperial power. Victoria's

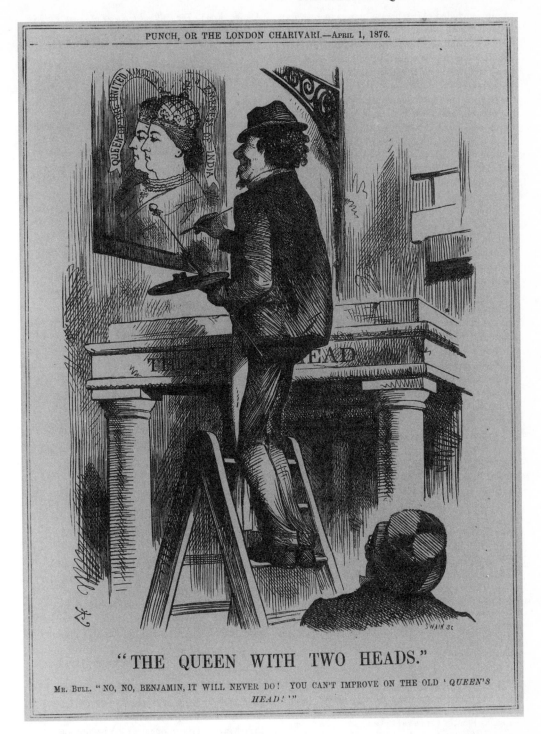

"THE QUEEN WITH TWO HEADS."

MR. BULL. "NO, NO, BENJAMIN, IT WILL NEVER DO! YOU CAN'T IMPROVE ON THE OLD 'QUEEN'S HEAD!'"

Plate 6   Cartoon from *Punch*, April 1, 1876.

empire included 47 separate governments and Britain's naval, military, and economic superiority were unparalleled. These combined strengths contributed to many statesmen's, politicians', and citizens' enjoyment of Great Britain's status as the world power and police-force. Jingoistic songs like "Soldiers of the Queen" and "Rule Britannia" were popularized and both high and popular cultural forms celebrated the era's expansionist zeal. For boys, travel and adventure narratives and magazines represented tantalizing tales of imperial duty and glory; while for girls, "scientific" domestic advice in household management books and distinctly gendered magazines encouraged the young women of empire to perform their imperial and national duties on the home front. In addition to the booms in print culture and literary genres, the Jubilee celebrations also made evident the growing power and visibility of commodity culture. The *Punch* advertisement for "Jubilicon" on page 394, and the other miraculous Jubilee products satirizes the omnipresent marketing and avid consumption of material goods. The Royal administration helped to create the frenzy for goods; for example, at Queen Victoria's Hyde Park celebration for children, 30,000 young subjects were presented their own Jubilee mug. Official flags, dishes, and other mementos were also distributed; and commercial merchants followed suit, marketing products ranging from Jubilee candies to condiments.

Despite the festivities, celebrations and boisterous declarations of national greatness, progress, and perfection, troubles were on the horizon for the Queen and the British Empire. The Second Boer War would damage Great Britain's sense of moral and military superiority. And poverty and the unresolved problems related to massive urban growth; intermittently violent suffrage and land, labor, and government reform campaigns; and fermenting nationalist movements in India, Ireland, and elsewhere would reverberate the somber tones that were already audible in Rudyard Kipling's Jubilee "Recessional."

MC

Additional Reading

Brown, Ray B. and Michael T. Marsden. *The Cultures of Celebration*. Bowling Green, 1994.
Chapman, Caroline and Paul Raban. *Debrett's Queen Victoria's Jubilees*. London, 1977.
Diamond, Frances. *Crown and Camera: The Royal Family and Photography, 1842–1910*. Harmondsworth, 1987.
Handelman, Don. *Models and Mirrors: Towards an Anthropology of Public Events*. New York, 1990.
Hardie, Frank. *The Political Influence of Queen Victoria*. London, 1935.
Hibbert, Christopher. *Daily Life in Victorian England*. New York, 1975.
Lant, Jeffrey I. *Insubstantial Pageant: Ceremony and Confusion at Queen Victoria's Court*. New York, 1980.
Mackenzie, J. M. *Propaganda and Empire: The Manipulation of British Public Opinion, 1880–1961*. Manchester, 1984.
Mangan, J. A. *Making Imperial Mentalities*. Manchester, 1990.
Thompson, Dorothy. *Queen Victoria: Gender and Power*. London, 1990.
Weintraub, Stanley, *Victoria, Biography of a Queen*. London, 1987.

Films

Herbert Wilcox. *Sixty Glorious Years* (1937).
Herbert Wilcox. *Victoria the Great* (1938).
Jean Negulesco. *The Mudlark* (1950).
John Madden. *Mrs Brown* (1997).

116 Timeline of Significant Events in the Life of Queen Victoria

1819 May	Birth of Alexandrina Victoria, only child of Edward, Duke of Kent
1837 May	Accession of Queen Victoria
1838 June	Queen's Coronation in Westminster Abbey
1840 Feb.	Marriage of Queen Victoria and Prince Albert of Saxe-Coburg-Gotha
1840 June	Assassination attempt on Queen
1840 Nov.	Birth of Princess Victoria Adelaide Mary Louise
1841 Nov.	Birth of Albert Edward, Prince of Wales
1842 July	Second attempt on Queen's life
1843 April	Birth of Princess Alice Maud Mary
1844 Aug.	Birth of Prince Ernest Albert
1846 May	Birth of Princess Helena Augusta Victoria
1847 Jan.	Queen established Irish Famine fund
1848 Mar.	Birth of Princess Louise Caroline Alberta
1849 May	Third attempt on Queen's life
1850 May	Birth of Prince Arthur William Patrick Albert
1851 May	Queen opens Great Exhibition
1853 April	Birth of Prince Leopold George Duncan Albert
1854 June	Queen opens Crystal Palace

1857 April	Birth of Princess Beatrice Mary Victoria Feodora
1857 May	Queen decorates soldiers wounded in Crimean War
1857 June	Queen makes first presentation of the Victoria Cross
1858 Nov.	Queen proclaimed direct ruler of India
1861 June	Queen institutes Order of the Star of India
1861 Dec.	Death of Albert, the Prince Consort; Queen Victoria retires from public life for 10 years
1872 Aug.	Queen presents gift to Stanley for finding Livingstone
1876 May	Queen Proclaimed Empress of India
1877 Jan.	Formal ceremony proclaiming Queen Empress of India in Delhi
1882 Mar.	Fourth attempt on the Queen's life
1887 Feb.	Queen's Jubilee celebrated in India
1887 June	Celebration of the Queen's Golden Jubilee
1893 May	Queen opens the Imperial Institute
1897 June	Celebration of the Queen's Diamond Jubilee
1901 Jan.	Death of the Queen at Osborne House, Isle of Wight

117   Alfred, Lord Tennyson: "To the Queen" (1889)

O LOYAL to the royal in thyself,
And loyal to thy land, as this to thee –
Bear witness, that rememberable day,
When, pale as yet, and fever-worn, the Prince
Who scarce had pluck'd his flickering life again
From halfway down the shadow of the grave,
Past with thee thro' thy people and their love,
And London roll'd one tide of joy thro' all
Her trebled millions, and loud leagues of man
And welcome! witness, too, the silent cry,
The prayer of many a race and creed, and clime –
Thunderless lightnings striking under sea
From sunset and sunrise of all thy realm,
And that true North, whereof we lately heard
A strain to shame us "keep you to yourselves;
So loyal is too costly! friends – your love
Is but a burthen: loose the bond, and go."
Is this the tone of empire? here the faith
That made us rulers? this, indeed, her voice
And meaning, whom the roar of Hougoumont
Left mightiest of all peoples under heaven?

What shock has fool'd her since, that she should speak
So feebly? wealthier – wealthier – hour by hour!
The voice of Britain, or a sinking land,
Some third-rate isle half-lost among her seas?
There rang her voice, when the full city peal'd
Thee and thy Prince! The loyal to their crown
Are loyal to their own far sons, who love
Our ocean-empire with her boundless homes
For ever-broadening England, and her throne
In our vast Orient, and one isle, one isle,
That knows not her own greatness: if she knows
And dreads it we are fall'n. – But thou, my Queen,
Not for itself, but thro' thy living love
For one to whom I made it o'er his grave
Sacred, accept this old imperfect tale,
New-old, and shadowing Sense at war with Soul,
Ideal manhood closed in real man
Rather than that gray king, whose name, a ghost,
Streams like a cloud, man-shaped, from mountain peak,
And cleaves to cairn and cromlech still; or him
Of Geoffrey's book, or him of Malleor's, one
Touch'd by the adulterous finger of a time
That hover'd between war and wantonness,
And crownings and dethronements: take withal
Thy poet's blessing, and his trust that Heaven
Will blow the tempest in the distance back
From thine and ours: for some are scared, who mark,
Or wisely or unwisely, signs of storm,
Waverings of every vane with every wind,
And wordy trucklings to the transient hour,
And fierce or careless looseners of the faith,
And Softness breeding scorn of simple life,
Or Cowardice, the child of lust for gold,
Or Labour, with a groan and not a voice,
Or Art with poisonous honey stol'n from France,
And that which knows, but careful for itself,
And that which knows not, ruling that which knows
To its own harm: the goal of this great world
Lies beyond sight: yet – if our slowly-grown
And crown'd Republic's crowning common-sense,
That saved her many times, not fail – their fears
Are morning shadows huger than the shapes
That cast them, not those gloomier which forego
The darkness of that battle in the West,
Where all of high and holy dies away.

Source: Selections from Tennyson. London and New York: Macmillan, 1889, p. 346.

Note

Alfred, Lord Tennyson (1809–92) was appointed Poet Laureate of Great Britain in 1850; he wrote a number of poems and odes to the Queen, including a previous "To the Queen" (1851), and "Carmen Sæculare. An Ode in Honour of the Jubilee of Queen Victoria" (1887).

118   Queen Victoria: Journal and Letter Selections, 1896–8

Journal   20 June 1896
Fifty-nine years since I came to the throne! What a long time to bear so heavy a burden! God has guided me in the midst of terrible trials, sorrows, and anxieties, and has wonderfully protected me. I have lived to see my dear country and vast Empire prosper and expand, and be wonderfully loyal!

                                        11 September 1896
After luncheon saw Mr. Balfour [First Lord of the Treasury]. We talked over many important topics.

I am much struck, as is everyone, by Mr. Balfour's extreme fairness, impartiality, and large-mindedness. He sees all sides of a question, is wonderfully generous in his feelings towards others, and very gentle and sweet-tempered.

                                        23 September 1896
To-day is the day on which I have reigned longer, by a day, than any English sovereign, and the people wished to make all sorts of demonstrations, which I asked them not to do until I had completed the sixty years next June. But notwithstanding that this was made public in the papers, people of all kinds and ranks, from every part of the kingdom, sent congratulatory telegrams, and they kept coming in all day.

                                        28 September 1896
Dear little David [the Duke of York's son, Prince Edward, later Duke of Windsor] with the baby came in at the end of luncheon to say good-bye. David is a most attractive little boy, and so forward and clever. He always tries at luncheon time to pull me up out of my chair, saying "Get up, Gangan," and then to one of the Indian servants, "Man pull it," which makes us laugh very much.

                                        3 October 1896
At twelve went down to below the terrace, near the ballroom, and we were all photographed by Downey by the new cinematograph process, which makes moving pictures by winding off a reel of films. We were walking up and down.

                                        23 November 1896
After tea went to the Red drawing-room, where so-called "animated pictures" were shown off, includ-ing the groups taken in September at Balmoral. It is a very wonderful process, representing people, their movements and actions, as if they were alive.

To Bigge   30 January 1897
Sir A. Bigge may tell the Prince of Wales that there is not the slightest fear of the Queen's giving way about the Emperor William's coming here in June. It would never do for many reasons, and the Queen is surprised that the Empress should urge it.

Journal   22 April 1897
At half-past six the celebrated and famous actress Sarah Bernhardt, who has been acting at Nice and is staying in this hotel [at Cimiez], performed a little piece for me in the drawing-room at her request. The play was called *Jean Marie*, by Adrien Fleuriet, quite short, only lasting half an hour. It is extremely touching, and Sarah Bernhardt's acting was quite marvellous, so pathetic and full of feeling. She appeared much affected herself, tears rolling down her cheeks. She has a most beautiful voice, and is very graceful in all her movements . . . When the play was over, Edith Lytton presented Sarah Bernhardt to me, and I spoke to her for a few moments. Her manner was most pleasing and gentle. She said it had been such a pleasure and honour to act for me. When I expressed the hope that she was not tired, she answered, "Cela m'a reposée."

                                          24 May 1897
My poor old birthday again came round, and it seems sadder each year, though I have such cause for thankfulness, and to be as well as I am, but fresh sorrow and trials still come upon me. My great lameness, etc., makes me feel how age is creeping on. Seventy-eight is a good age, but I pray yet to be spared a little longer for the sake of my country and dear ones.

Before breakfast the little children, Lenchen and Beatrice, gave me flowers and took me to my birth-day table, which was covered with presents.

                                          20 June 1897
This eventful day, 1897 [the Diamond Jubilee], has opened, and I pray God to help and protect me as He has hitherto done during these sixty long event-ful years!

At eleven I, with all my family, went to St George's Chapel, where a short touching service took place . . . The service began with the hymn, "Now thank we all our God," followed by some of the usual morning prayers. Dear Albert's beautiful *Te Deum* was sung, and the special prayer for Accession Day followed, with a few others. Felt rather nervous about the coming days, and that all should go off well.

21 June 1897

The 10th anniversary of the celebration of my fifty years Jubilee . . . Passed through dense crowds [between Paddington Station and Buckingham Palace], who gave me a most enthusiastic reception. It was like a triumphal entry . . . The windows, the roofs of the houses, were one mass of beaming faces, and the cheers never ceased. On entering the park, through the Marble Arch, the crowd was even greater, carriages were drawn up amongst the people on foot, even on the pretty little lodges well-dressed people were perched. Hyde Park Corner and Constitution Hill were densely crowded. All vied with one another to give me a heartfelt, loyal, and affectionate welcome. I was deeply touched and gratified [. . .]

Dressed for dinner. I wore a dress of which the whole front was embroidered in gold, which had been specially worked in India, diamonds in my cap, and a diamond necklace, etc. The dinner was in the Supper-room at little tables of twelve each. All the family, foreign royalties, special Ambassadors and Envoys were invited.

22 June 1897

A never-to-be-forgotten day. No one ever, I believe, has met with such an ovation as was given to me, passing through those six miles of streets . . . The crowds were quite indescribable, and their enthusiasm truly marvellous and deeply touching. The cheering was quite deafening, and every face seemed to be filled with real joy.

At a quarter-past eleven, the others being seated in their carriages long before, and having preceded me a short distance, I started from the State entrance in an open State landau, drawn by eight creams, dear Alix, looking very pretty in lilac and Lenchen sitting opposite me. I felt a good deal agitated, and had been so all these days, for fear anything might be forgotten or go wrong . . .

Before leaving I touched an electric button, by which I started a message which was telegraphed throughout the whole Empire. It was the following: "From my heart I thank my beloved people, May God bless them!" At this time the sun burst out. Vicky was in the carriage nearest me, not being able to go in mine, as her rank as Empress prevented her sitting with her back to the horses, for I had to sit alone. Her carriage was drawn by four blacks, richly caparisoned in red . . . The denseness of the crowds was immense, but the order maintained wonderful. The streets in the Strand are now quite wide, but one misses Temple Bar. Here the Lord Mayor received me and presented the sword, which I touched. He then immediately mounted his horse in his robes, and galloped past bare-headed, carrying the sword, preceding my carriage, accompanied by his Sheriffs. As we neared St Paul's the procession was often stopped, and the crowds broke out into singing *God Save the Queen*. In one house were assembled the survivors of the Charge of Balaclava.

In front of the Cathedral the scene was most impressive. All the Colonial troops, on foot, were drawn up round the Square. My carriage, surrounded by all the Royal Princes, was drawn up close to the steps, where the Clergy were assembled, the Bishops in rich copes, with their croziers, the Archbishop of Canterbury and the Bishop of London each holding a very fine one. A *Te Deum* was sung . . .

[On returning to Buckingham Palace] I stopped in front of the Mansion House, where the Lady Mayoress presented me with a beautiful silver basket full of orchids. Here I took leave of the Lord Mayor. Both he and the Lady Mayoress were quite *émus*.

6 July 1897

Mr Whitelaw Reid [Special United States Envoy for the Diamond Jubilee, afterwards American Ambassador in London] was full of the kindest expressions to me personally, and said that the people in America were so much attached to me, and spoke of me as "the good Queen," and that there was in fact a very friendly feeling towards this country, the various disputes and disagreements being really entirely superficial.

30 September 1897

Took leave with much regret of Georgie and May, who are leaving the first thing tomorrow morning. Every time I see them I love and like them more and respect them greatly. Thank God! Georgie has got such an excellent, useful, and good wife!

30 January 1898

Spoke to [Cosmo Gordon Lang, then Vicar of Portsea, afterwards Archbishop of Canterbury] for some time after dinner. He is a very interesting and clever man, a Scotchman, and was at Oxford. He has a very hard time at Portsea, having 40,000 parishioners, and the population is not very pleasant, particularly the artizans, who are very difficult, sceptical, and full of prejudices. The sailors are true and warm-hearted, but, as well as the soldiers, somewhat difficult to manage. Mr Lang has thirteen curates to assist him, and they all live together.

To Chamberlain   **6 February 1898**

The Queen thanks Mr Chamberlain for his letter enclosing the despatch from New Zealand inviting the Duke and Duchess of York to visit that Colony.

The Queen duly appreciates the loyal and kind

ROYAL ANNIVERSARY SOAP is a detergent and astringent cleanser.

ROYAL ANNIVERSARY SOAP creates a terrific lather.

ROYAL ANNIVERSARY SOAP will remove the rust from chain armour.

ROYAL ANNIVERSARY SOAP is a veritable toilet gem.

ROYAL ANNIVERSARY SOAP is more efficient than scouring-paper.

ROYAL ANNIVERSARY SOAP takes the skin off the face wholesale.

ROYAL ANNIVERSARY SOAP completely annihilates the complexion.

ROYAL ANNIVERSARY SOAP has the stimulating effect of a curry-comb.

ROYAL ANNIVERSARY SOAP will clean a cart-wheel.

ROYAL ANNIVERSARY SOAP will flay an infant.

ROYAL ANNIVERSARY SOAP has been supplied by the LORD CHAMBERLAIN to all Her Majesty's illustrious foreign guests.

ROYAL ANNIVERSARY SOAP.—An Indian Maharajah writes:—" I have used it only once, but the effect has been truly marvellous. My face which was a dusky brown is now a creamy white. Nobody knows me."

ROYAL ANNIVERSARY SOAP.—A German Potentate writes:—" It is a composition most truly astonishing. Yesterday I was pale. To-day I have all the appearance of a Red Indian. No clothes-brush could have produced such a result. I am hooted at wherever I show myself."

THE IMPERIAL INSTITUTE PILL is not a popular medicine.

THE IMPERIAL INSTITUTE PILL should be approached cautiously by the invalid.

THE IMPERIAL INSTITUTE PILL is better out of every household.

THE IMPERIAL INSTITUTE PILL is composed entirely of dangerous and deleterious drugs.

THE IMPERIAL INSTITUTE PILL effectively instals influenza.

THE IMPERIAL INSTITUTE PILL instantly sets up lumbago.

THE IMPERIAL INSTITUTE PILL rapidly increases neuralgia.

THE IMPERIAL INSTITUTE PILL quickly renovates toothache.

THE IMPERIAL INSTITUTE PILL developes constant rheumatism.

THE IMPERIAL INSTITUTE PILL induces aggravated sciatica.

THE IMPERIAL INSTITUTE PILL will be found a most excellent substitute for Jungle fever.

THE IMPERIAL INSTITUTE PILL will give a passing ailment a chronic character.

THE IMPERIAL INSTITUTE PILL utterly destroys all sleep.

THE IMPERIAL INSTITUTE PILL.— A Country Curate writes:—" I purchased a box, and persuaded an aged Uncle and Aunt, both in a feeble state of health, to try them, with the result that one had a paralytic stroke, and the other became afflicted with permanent convulsions. They are both now inmates of the County Lunatic Asylum. Don't send me any more."

JUBILICON is an entirely New and Startling Digestive Preparation.

JUBILICON may be regarded as a Universal food.

JUBILICON contains all the Nutritive Properties of Soup, Fish, Joint, two Entrées, Sweets, Vegetables, and Cheese.

JUBILICON creates a perfect furore in a menagerie.

JUBILICON is immensely relished by the Rhinoceros.

JUBILICON infallibly delights the Baby.

JUBILICON forms an excellent Dog Biscuit.

JUBILICON can, with confidence, be set before Epicures.

JUBILICON may be taken before daybreak.

JUBILICON can be swallowed after midnight.

JUBILICON should be served at all hours.

JUBILICON, mixed with Dublin Stout, affords an admirable Porridge.

JUBILICON mingled with Ink, produces an efficient Boot-Blacking.

JUBILICON, gives a wonderfully fresh appearance to brass candlesticks.

JUBILICON will Restore the Appetite of the jaded Invalid.

JUBILICON can be regarded as a Serviceable Furniture Polish.

JUBILICON can be utilised as a fuel in a quick-drawing Kitchener.

JUBILICON may be taken as a cough lozenge.

JUBILICON, if scattered freely on the pavement, will prevent accidents in slippery weather.

JUBILICON.—A Country Squire writes: " At a hunting breakfast last season, acting on the advice of a friend, I set nothing before each of my guests but a bowl of JUBILICON, made, according to the directions, with hot water. I have never seen any of their faces again, and I am now cut by the whole county."

PROCESSION. — OPPORTUNITY TO VIEW. A few excellent seats to witness HER MAJESTY'S progress to the Abbey on the 21st, are still to be had on the chimney-pots of a Nobleman's Mansion commanding a fine view of one of the leading thoroughfares. Price, Five guineas a seat, except for that on the kitchen chimney, for which, as there will be necessarily a fire lighted below, only Three guineas will be charged. Early application desirable to Earl of ——, 417, Piccadilly.

ILLUMINATION.—SUGGESTION WANTED. A Royal Enthusiast, who is desirous of contributing to the general gala rejoicing at the proposed universal illumination, on the occasion of Her Most Gracious MAJESTY'S Jubilee, and has purchased a box containing ten of Price's Night Lights, one of which he intends to utilise for the purpose, would be thankful to anyone who would advise him how to display it to the best advantage. Whether it should be over the hall-door, or in the drawing-room balcony, or placed conspicuously in the attic-window. Advertiser will be thankful for any hints to guide him in the settlement of his problem. Address, BLAZER, Flare St., Hackney Wick.

Figure 2 Advertising panel from *Punch*, June 25, 1887.

wish of the New Zealanders to see her grandchildren. But there are very strong reasons against it, which she feels cannot be disregarded. The Duke of York is the only surviving son of the Prince of Wales, and the only available Prince in this country, besides the Prince of Wales himself and the Duke of Connaught (both very much overworked) able to perform all that is expected of them, and to help the Queen, now in her seventy-ninth year, who has lost the able and affectionate help of her dear son-in-law Prince Henry of Battenberg. But this is not all. Life is so uncertain, that the risk of sending the Duke of York so far away and exposing him to the innumerable dangers of fatigue, climate, etc., are too great; and it would indeed be tempting providence were we to send him so far away.

Source: Christopher Hibbert *Queen Victoria in Her Letters and Journals.* London: Murray, 1984, pp. 333–6.

---

119   Mark Twain: "Queen Victoria's Jubilee" (1897)

So far as I can see, a procession has value in but two ways – as a show and as a symbol; its minor function being to delight the eye, its major one to compel thought, exalt the spirit, stir the heart, and inflame the imagination. As a mere show, and meaningless – like a Mardi-Gras march – a magnificent procession is a sight worth a long journey to see; as a symbol, the most colorless and unpicturesque procession, if it have a moving history back of it, is worth a thousand of it.

After the Civil War ten regiments of bronzed New York veterans marched up Broadway in faded uniforms and bearing faded battle flags that were mere shot-riddled rags – and in each battalion as it swung by, one noted a great gap, an eloquent vacancy where had marched the comrades who had fallen and would march no more! Always, as this procession advanced between the massed multitudes, its approach was welcomed by each block of people with a burst of proud and grateful enthusiasm – then the head of it passed, and suddenly revealed those pathetic gaps, and silence fell upon that block; for every man in it had choked up, and could not get command of his voice and add it to the storm again for many minutes. That was the most moving and tremendous effect that I have ever witnessed – those affecting silences falling between those hurricanes of worshiping enthusiasm.

There was no costumery in that procession, no color, no tinsel, no brilliancy, yet it was the greatest spectacle and the most gracious and exalting and beautiful that has come within my experience. It was because it had history back of it, and because it was a symbol, and stood for something, and because one viewed it with the spiritual vision, not the physical. There was not much for the physical eye to see, but it revealed continental areas, limitless horizons, to the eye of the imagination and the spirit.

A procession, to be valuable, must do one thing or the other – clothe itself in splendors and charm the eye, or symbolize something sublime and uplifting, and so appeal to the imagination. As a mere spectacle to look at, I suppose that the Queen's procession will not be as showy as the Tsar's late pageant; it will probably fall much short of the one in Tannhäuser in the matter of rich and adorable costumery; in the number of renowned personages on view in it, it will probably fall short of some that have been seen in England before this. And yet in its major function, its symbolic function, I think that if all the people in it wore their everyday clothes and marched without flags or music, it would still be incomparably the most memorable and most important procession that ever moved through the streets of London.

For it will stand for English history, English growth, English achievement, the accumulated power and renown and dignity of twenty centuries of strenuous effort. Many things about it will set one to reflecting upon what a large feature of this world England is to-day, and this will in turn move one, even the least imaginative, to cast a glance down her long perspective and note the steps of her progress and the insignificance of her first estate. In this matter London is itself a suggestive object lesson.

I suppose that London has always existed. One cannot easily imagine an England that had no London. No doubt there was a village here 5,000 years ago. It was on the river somewhere west of where the Tower is now; it was built of thatched mud huts close to a couple of limpid brooks, and on every hand for miles and miles stretched rolling plains of fresh green grass, and here and there were groups and groves of trees. The tribes wore skins – sometimes merely their own, sometimes those of other animals. The chief was monarch, and helped out his complexion with blue paint. His industry was the chase; his relaxation was war. Some of the Englishmen who will view the procession to-day are carrying his ancient blood in their veins.

It may be that that village remained about as it began, away down to the Roman occupation, a couple of thousand years ago. It was still not much of a town when Alfred burned the cakes. Even when the Conqueror first saw it, it did not amount to much. I think it must have been short of distinguished architecture or he would not have traveled down into the country to the village of Westminster to get crowned. If you skip down 350 years further you will find a London of some little consequence, but I believe that that is as much as you can say for it. Still, I am interested in that London, for it saw the first two processions which will live longer than any other in English history, I think; the date of the one is 1415, that of the other is 1897.

The compactly built part of the London of 1415 was a narrow strip not a mile long, which stretched east and west through the middle of what is now called "the City." The houses were densest in the region of Cheapside. South of the strip were scattering residences which stood in turfy lawns which sloped to the river. North of the strip, fields and country homes extended to the walls. Let us represent that London by three checker-board squares placed in a row; then open out a New York newspaper like a book, and the space which it covers will properly represent the London of to-day by comparison. It is the difference between your hand and a blanket. It is possible that that ancient London had 100,000 inhabitants, and that 100,000 outsiders came to town to see the procession. The present London contains five or six million inhabitants, and it has been calculated that the population has jumped to 10,000,000 to-day.

The pageant of 1415 was to celebrate the gigantic victory of Agincourt, then and still the most colossal in England's history.

From that day to this there has been nothing that even approached it but Plassey. It was the third and greatest in the series of monster victories won by the English over the French in the Hundred Years' War – Crecy, Poitiers, Agincourt. At Agincourt, according to history, 15,000 English, under Henry V, defeated and routed an army of 100,000 French. Sometimes history makes it 8,000 English and 60,000 French; but no matter, in both cases the proportions are preserved. Eight thousand of the French nobility were slain and the rest of the order taken prisoners – 1,500 in number – among them the Dukes of Orléans and Bourbon and Marshal Boucicaut; and the victory left the whole northern half of France an English possession. This wholesale depletion of the aristocracy made such a stringent scarcity in its ranks that when the young peasant girl, Joan of Arc, came to undo Henry's mighty work fourteen years later she could hardly gather together nobles enough to man her staff.

The battle of Agincourt was fought on the 25th of October, and a few days later the tremendous news was percolating through England. Presently it was sweeping the country like a tidal wave, like a cyclone, like a conflagration. Choose your own figure, there is no metaphor known to the language that can exaggerate the tempest of joy and pride and exultation that burst everywhere along the progress of that great news.

The king came home and brought his soldiers with him – he and they the idols of the nation, now. He brought his 1,500 captive knights and nobles, too – we shall not see any such output of blue blood as that to-day, bond or free. The king rested three weeks in his palace, the Tower of London, while the people made preparations and prepared the welcome due him. On the 22d of December all was ready.

There were no cables, no correspondents, no newspapers then – a regrettable defect, but not irremediable. A young man who would have been a correspondent if he had been born 500 years later was in London at the time, and he remembers the details. He has communicated them to me through a competent spirit medium, phrased in a troublesome mixture of obsolete English and moldy French, and I have thoroughly modernized his story and put it into straight English, and will here record it. I will explain that his Sir John Oldcastle is a person whom we do not know very well by that name, nor much care for; but we know him well and adore him, too, under his other name – Sir John Falstaff. Also, I will remark that two miles of the Queen's progress to-day will be over ground traversed by the procession of Henry V; all solid bricks and mortar, now, but open country in Henry's day, and clothed in that unapproachable beauty which has been the monopoly of sylvan England since the creation. Ah, where now are those long-vanished forms, those unreturning feet! Let us not inquire too closely. Translated, this is the narrative of the spirit-correspondent, who is looking down upon me at this moment from his high home, and admiring to see how the art and mystery of spelling has improved since his time!

Narrative of the Spirit Correspondent

I was commanded by my lord the Lord Mayor to make a report for the archives, and was furnished with a fleet horse, and with a paper permitting me to go anywhere at my will, without let or hindrance, even up and down the processional route, though no other person not of the procession itself was allowed this unique privilege during the whole of the 21st and the 22d.

On the morning of the 22d, toward noon, I rode from the Tower into the city, and through it as far as St Paul's. All the way, on both sides, all the windows, balconies, and roofs were crowded with people, and wherever there was a vacancy it had been built up in high tiers of seats covered with red cloth, and these seats were also filled with people – in all cases in bright holiday attire – the woman of fashion barring the view from all in the rear with those tiresome extinguisher hats, which of late have grown to be a cloth-yard high. From every balcony depended silken stuffs of splendid and various colors, and figured and pictured rich tapestries. It was brisk, sharp weather, but a rare one for sun, and when one looked down this swinging double wall of beautiful fabrics, glowing and flashing and changing color like prisms in the flooding light, it was a most fair sight to see. And there were frequent May poles, garlanded to their tops, and from the tops swung sheaves of silken long ribbons of all bright colors, which in the light breeze writhed and twisted and prettily mingled themselves together.

I rode solitary – in state, as it might be – and was envied, as I could see, and did not escape comment, but had a plenty of it; for the conduits were running gratis wine, and the results were accumulating. I got many ribald compliments on my riding, on my clothes, on my office. Everybody was happy, so it was best to seem so myself, which I did – for those people's aim was better than their eggs.

A place had been reserved for me on a fine and fanciful erection in St Paul's Churchyard, and there I waited for the procession. It seemed a long time, but at last a dull booming sound arose in the distance, and after a while we saw the banners and the head of the procession come into view, and heard the muffled roar of voices that welcomed it. The roar moved continuously toward us, growing steadily louder and louder, and stronger and stronger, and with it the bray and crash of music; and presently it was right with us, and seemed to roll over us and submerge us, and stun us, and deafen us – and behold, there was the hero of Agincourt passing by!

All the multitude was standing up, red-faced, frantic, bellowing, shouting, the tears running down their faces; and through the storm of waving hats and handkerchiefs one glimpsed the battle banners and the drifting host of marching men as through a dimming flurry of snow.

The king, tall, slender, handsome, rode with his visor up, that all might see his face. He was clad in his silver armor from head to heel, and had his great two-handed sword at his side, his battle-ax at his pommel, his shield upon his arm, and about his helmet waved and tossed a white mass of fluffy plumes. On either side of him rode the captive dukes, plumed like himself, but wearing long crimson satin gowns over their armor; after these came the French marshal similarly habited; after him followed the fifteen hundred French knights, with robes of various colors over their armor, and with each two rode two English knights, sometimes robed in various colors, sometimes in white with a red cross on the shoulder, these white-clad ones being Knights Templars. Every man of the three thousand bore his shield upon his left arm, newly polished and burnished, and on it was his device.

As the king passed the church he bowed his head and lifted his shield, and by one impulse all the knights did the same; and so as far down the line as the eye could reach one saw the lifted shields simultaneously catch the sun, and it was like a sudden mile-long shaft of flashing light; and, Lord! it lit up that dappled sea of color with a glory like "the golden vortex in the west over the foundered sun"! (The introduction of this quotation is very interesting, for it shows that our literature of to-day has a circulation in heaven – pirated editions, no doubt. – M.T.)

The knights were a long time in passing; then came 5,000 Agincourt men-at-arms, and they were a long time; and at the very end, last of all, came that intolerable old tun of sack and godless ruffler, Sir John Oldcastle (now risen from the dead for the third time), fat-faced, purple with the spirit of bygone and lamented drink, smiling his hospitable, wide smile upon all the world, leering at the women, wallowing about in his saddle, proclaiming his valorous deeds as fast as he could lie, taking the whole glory of Agincourt to his single self, measuring off the miles of his slain and then multiplying them by 5, 7, 10, 15, as inspiration after inspiration came to his help – the most inhuman spectacle in England, a living, breathing outrage, a slander upon the human race; and after him came, mumming and blethering, his infamous lieutenants; and after them his "paladins," as he calls them, the mangiest lot of starvelings and cowards that was ever littered, the disgrace of the noblest pageant that England has ever seen. God rest their souls in the place appointed for all such!

There was a moment of prayer at the Temple, the procession moved down the country road, its way walled on both sides by welcoming multitudes, and so, by Charing Cross, and at last to the Abbey for the great ceremonies. It was a grand day, and will remain in men's memories.

That was as much of it as the spirit correspondent could let me have; he was obliged to stop there because he had an engagement to sing in the choir, and was already late.

The contrast between that old England and the present England is one of the things which will make the pageant of the present day impressive and thought-breeding. The contrast between the England of the Queen's reign and the England of any previous British reign is also an impressive thing. British history is two thousand years old, and yet in a good many ways the world has moved further ahead since the Queen was born than it moved in all the rest of the two thousand put together. A large part of this progress has been moral, but naturally the material part of it is the most striking and the easiest to measure. Since the Queen first saw the light she has seen invented and brought into use (with the exception of the cotton gin, the spinning frames, and the steamboat) every one of the myriad of strictly modern inventions which, by their united powers, have created the bulk of the modern civilization and made life under it easy and difficult, convenient and awkward, happy and horrible, soothing and irritating, grand and trivial, an indispensable blessing and an unimaginable curse – she has seen all these miracles, these wonders, these marvels piled up in her time, and yet she is but seventy-eight years old. That is to say, she has seen more things invented than any other monarch that ever lived; and more than the oldest old-time English commoner that ever lived, including Old Parr; and more than Methuselah himself – five times over.

Some of the details of the moral advancement which she has seen are also very striking and easily graspable.

She has seen the English criminal laws prodigiously modified, and 200 capital crimes swept from the statute book.

She has seen English liberty greatly broadened – the governing and lawmaking powers, formerly the possession of the few, extended to the body of the people, and purchase in the army abolished.

She has seen the public educator – the newspaper – created, and its teachings placed within the reach of the leanest purse. There was nothing properly describable as a newspaper until long after she was born.

She has seen the world's literature set free, through the institution of international copyright.

She has seen America invent arbitration, the eventual substitute for that enslaver of nations, the

standing army; and she has seen England pay the first bill under it, and America shirk the second – but only temporarily; of this we may be sure.

She has seen a Hartford American (Doctor Wells) apply anæsthetics in surgery for the first time in history, and for all time banish the terrors of the surgeon's knife; and she has seen the rest of the world ignore the discoverer and a Boston doctor steal the credit of his work.

She has seen medical science and scientific sanitation cut down the death rate of civilized cities by more than half, and she has seen these agencies set bounds to the European march of the cholera and imprison the Black Death in its own home.

She has seen woman freed from the oppression of many burdensome and unjust laws; colleges established for her; privileged to earn degrees in men's colleges – but not get them; in some regions rights accorded to her which lifted her near to political equality with man, and a hundred breadwinning occupations found for her where hardly one existed before – among them medicine, the law, and professional nursing. The Queen has herself recognized merit in her sex; of the 501 lordships which she has conferred in sixty years, one was upon a woman.

The Queen has seen the right to organize trade unions extended to the workman, after that right had been the monopoly of guilds of masters for six hundred years.

She has seen the workman rise into political notice, then into political force, then (in some parts of the world) into the chief and commanding political force; she has seen the day's labor of twelve, fourteen, and eighteen hours reduced to eight, a reform which has made labor a means of extending life instead of a means of committing salaried suicide.

But it is useless to continue the list – it has no end.

There will be complexions in the procession today which will suggest the vast distances to which the British dominion has extended itself around the fat rotundity of the globe since Britain was a remote unknown back settlement of savages with tin for sale, two or three thousand years ago; and also how great a part of this extension is comparatively recent; also, how surprisingly speakers of the English tongue have increased within the Queen's time.

When the Queen was born there were not more than 25,000,000 English-speaking people in the world; there are about 120,000,000 now. The other long-reign queen, Elizabeth, ruled over a short 100,000 square miles of territory and perhaps 5,000,000 subjects; Victoria reigns over more territory than any other sovereign in the world's history ever reigned over; her estate covers a fourth part of the habitable area of the globe, and her subjects number about 400,000,000.

It is indeed a mighty estate, and I perceive now that the English are mentioned in the Bible:

"Blessed are the meek, for they shall inherit the earth."

The Long-Reign Pageant will be a memorable thing to see, for it stands for the grandeur of England, and is full of suggestion as to how it had its beginning and what have been the forces that have built it up.

I got to my seat in the Strand just in time – five minutes past ten – for a glance around before the show began. The houses opposite, as far as the eye could reach in both directions, suggested boxes in a theater snugly packed. The gentleman next to me likened the groups to beds of flowers, and said he had never seen such a massed and multitudinous array of bright colors and fine clothes.

These displays rose up and up, story by story, all balconies and windows being packed, and also the battlements stretching along the roofs. The sidewalks were filled with standing people, but were not uncomfortably crowded. They were fenced from the roadway by red-coated soldiers, a double stripe of vivid color which extended throughout the six miles which the procession would traverse.

Five minutes later the head of the column came into view and was presently filing by, led by Captain Ames, the tallest man in the British army. And then the cheering began. It took me but a little while to determine that this procession could not be described. There was going to be too much of it, and too much variety in it, so I gave up the idea. It was to be a spectacle for the kodak, not the pen.

Presently the procession was without visible beginning or end, but stretched to the limit of sight in both directions – bodies of soldiery in blue, followed by a block of soldiers in buff, then a block of red, a block of buff, a block of yellow, and so on, an interminable drift of swaying and swinging splotches of strong color sparkling and flashing with shifty light reflected from bayonets, lance heads, brazen helmets, and burnished breastplates. For varied and beautiful uniforms and unceasing surprises in the way of new and unexpected splendors, it much surpassed any pageant that I have ever seen.

I was not dreaming of so stunning a show. All the nations seemed to be filing by. They all seemed to be represented. It was a sort of allegorical suggestion of the Last Day, and some who live to see that day will probably recall this one if they are not too much disturbed in mind at the time.

There were five bodies of Oriental soldiers of five different nationalities, with complexions dif-

ferentiated by five distinct shades of yellow. There were about a dozen bodies of black soldiers from various parts of Africa, whose complexions covered as many shades of black, and some of these were the very blackest people I have ever seen yet.

Then there was an exhaustive exhibition of the hundred separate brown races of India, the most beautiful and satisfying of all the complexions that have been vouchsafed to man, and the one which best sets off colored clothes and best harmonizes with all tints.

The Chinese, the Japanese, the Koreans, the Africans, the Indians, the Pacific Islanders – they were all there, and with them samples of all the whites that inhabit the wide reach of the Queen's dominions.

The procession was the human race on exhibition, a spectacle curious and interesting and worth traveling far to see. The most splendid of the costumes were those worn by the Indian princes, and they were also the most beautiful and richest. They were men of stately build and princely carriage, and wherever they passed the applause burst forth.

Soldiers, soldiers, soldiers, and still more and more soldiers and cannon and muskets and lances – there seemed to be no end to this feature. There are 50,000 soldiers in London, and they all seemed to be on hand. I have not seen so many except in the theater, when thirty-five privates and a general march across the stage and behind the scenes and across the front again and keep it up till they have represented 300,000.

In the early part of the procession the colonial premiers drove by, and by and by after a long time there was a grand output of foreign princes, thirty-one in the invoice.

The feature of high romance was not wanting, for among them rode Prince Rupert of Bavaria, who would be Prince of Wales now and future king of England and emperor of India if his Stuart ancestors had conducted their royal affairs more wisely than they did. He came as a peaceful guest to represent his mother, Princess Ludwig, heiress of the house of Stuart, to whom English Jacobites still pay unavailing homage as the rightful queen of England.

The house of Stuart was formally and officially shelved nearly two centuries ago, but the microbe of Jacobite loyalty is a thing which is not exterminable by time, force, or argument.

At last, when the procession had been on view an hour and a half, carriages began to appear. In the first came a detachment of two-horse ones containing ambassadors extraordinary, in one of them Whitelaw Reid, representing the United States; then six containing minor foreign and domestic princes and princesses; then five four-horse carriages freighted with offshoots of the family.

The excitement was growing now; interest was rising toward the boiling point. Finally a landau driven by eight cream-colored horses, most lavishly unholstered in gold stuffs, with postilions and no drivers, and preceded by Lord Wolseley, came bowling along, followed by the Prince of Wales, and all the world rose to its feet and uncovered.

The Queen Empress was come. She was received with great enthusiasm. It was realizable that she was the procession herself; that all the rest of it was mere embroidery; that in her the public saw the British Empire itself. She was a symbol, an allegory of England's grandeur and the might of the British name.

It is over now; the British Empire has marched past under review and inspection. The procession stood for sixty years of progress and accumulation, moral, material, and political. It was made up rather of the beneficiaries of these prosperities than of the creators of them.

As far as mere glory goes, the foreign trade of Great Britain has grown in a wonderful way since the Queen ascended the throne. Last year it reached the enormous figure of £620,000,000, but the capitalist, the manufacturer, the merchant, and the workingmen were not officially in the procession to get their large share of the resulting glory.

Great Britain has added to her real estate an average of 165 miles of territory per day for the past sixty years, which is to say she has added more than the bulk of an England proper per year, or an aggregate of seventy Englands in the sixty years.

But Cecil Rhodes was not in the procession; the Chartered Company was absent from it. Nobody was there to collect his share of the glory due for his formidable contributions to the imperial estate. Even Doctor Jameson was out, and yet he had tried so hard to accumulate territory.

Eleven colonial premiers were in the procession, but the dean of the order, the imperial Premier, was not, nor the Lord Chief Justice of England, nor the Speaker of the House. The bulk of the religious strength of England dissent was not officially represented in the religious ceremonials. At the Cathedral that immense new industry, speculative expansion, was not represented unless the pathetic shade of Barnato rode invisible in the pageant.

It was a memorable display and must live in history. It suggested the material glories of the reign finely and adequately. The absence of the chief creators of them was perhaps not a serious disadvantage. One could supply the vacancies by imagination, and thus fill out the procession very

effectively. One can enjoy a rainbow without necessarily forgetting the forces that made it.

Source: Mark Twain (1835–1910). *Europe and Elsewhere.* New York, and London: Harper Bros, 1923, pp. 193–210.

120 Rudyard Kipling: "Recessional" (1897)

GOD of our fathers, known of old,
Lord of our far-flung battle-line,
Beneath whose awful Hand we hold
    Dominion over palm and pine –
Lord God of Hosts, be with us yet,
Lest we forget – lest we forget!

The tumult and the shouting dies;
    The Captains and the Kings depart:
Still stands Thine ancient sacrifice,
    An humble and a contrite heart.
Lord God of Hosts, be with us yet,
Lest we forget – lest we forget!

Far-called, our navies melt away;
    On dune and headland sinks the fire:
Lo, all our pomp of yesterday
    Is one with Nineveh and Tyre!
Judge of the Nations, spare us yet,
Lest we forget – lest we forget!

If, drunk with sight of power, we loose
    Wild tongues that have not Thee in awe,
Such boastings as the Gentiles use,
    Or lesser breeds without the Law –
Lord God of Hosts, be with us yet,
Lest we forget – lest we forget!

For heathen heart that puts her trust
    In reeking tube and iron shard,
All valiant dust that builds on dust,
    And guarding, calls not Thee to guard,
For frantic boast and foolish word –
Thy mercy on Thy People, Lord!

Source: Rudyard Kipling (1865–1936). *Collected Verse.* Herts: Wordsworth Editions, 1994, pp. 193–210.

Note

Of related interest is Kipling's story, "The Jubilee in Lahore," in *Kipling in India.* London, 1966.

Glossary

Words and phrases are listed in the form in which they appear in the text.

ad valorem Latin: "in proportion to value."

Alcoran an archaic form of Koran/Qu'ran, the sacred book of Islam.

ali sadar probably an office relating to the Indian civil court; see **sudder**.

amil an official in colonial Egypt and India; usually a revenue collector.

amuldar cf. "amildar": an Indian revenue collector; answerable to a **buggshi** as an overseer and manager of local expenditure.

aperire terram gentibus Latin: "to open up the land to the peoples."

atta a type of wheaten flour used to make cakes in India.

baboo see document 16.

banjarah in British India, a native supplier of goods, particularly grain and salt.

banyan-tree also spelt "banian," the Indian fig tree.

beetle-nut cf. "betel-nut" the nut of the Areca Palm tree; both the nut and the leaf of this tree are chewed throughout South-East Asia, and produce a strong red colour which stains the mouth and gums of the user.

Beloochees cf. "Balochi" (also spelt Baluchi/Beluchi) a group of tribes inhabiting the province of Balochistan, conquered by Persia in the nineteenth century, and now in western Pakistan.

bercundauz/burkundaz cf. "burkundauze," in British India an armed retainer, policeman or other kind of native employee.

Bey in colonial Egypt, a Turkish word for a governor of a province or district.

brandy-pawny/brandy-pawnee an Anglo-Indian expression for a brandy and water.

budgerow an Anglo-Indian word for a type of keelless barge, often seen along the Ganges.

bungalow see document 71.

buggshi/buxey cf. "buggess," the name used in the British colonies of the Indian Archipelago for a native soldier in the service of a European army; more specifically, an officer who worked under a provincial administrator in India as paymaster of the native troops and general administrator of local, public expenditure.

Burra Beebee in British India, a title of respect accorded a local "grande dame" or great lady; also, generally, female head of a household (the equivalent of "memsahib").

cabay a long sleeveless tunic of muslin or linen worn in India.

cromlech in Scotland, a group of prehistoric standing stones.

cassava a starchy, tuberous root; an important food source in tropical countries from which a type of tapioca is made.

catwall cf. "cotwal," in British India the name for a police officer or local magistrate; also used as a collective name for native administrators of justice, as well as the name of the residence or building in which these persons resided.

cazee a corruption of "cadi" or "kadi" – the Arabic name for a Muslim judge in religious matters, a revered member of the community who based his judgements on the Qu'ran.

chapattie/chupattie a type of flat, unleavened Indian bread, cooked like a pancake on a griddle.

chawbuck an Indian horse-whip.

chowkeydar in colonial India a local village official; often a watchman or guardian of property, such as burial grounds.

chuckledar probably a corruption of the word "chuckler," a member of a very lowly southern Indian caste. Alternatively, a corruption of the word for district "chucklah," meaning a native official who worked for that district.

coup de Jarnac French: meaning a treacherous or unexpected attack which changes the outcome of events; (from the name of a French nobleman, Guy Chabot, Sieur de Jarnac, who during a duel disabled his opponent and then killed him when he was down and defenceless).

coup de main French: literally "a stroke of the hand" – a sudden, and decisive, military attack.

crore a unit of ten million rupees, equivalent to 100 **lakhs**.

cusa-grass cf. cuscus-grass: the sweet-smelling root of an Indian grass which was used in India to make screens and fans against the hot sun.

dak (bungalow) see document 71.

darogha/daroga in British India a local, native official of various kinds – particularly a police official, manager or excise inspector.

dhingee cf. dinghy, in India a native rowing boat.

duan in colonial India, a native provincial judge, who dealt with civil matters.

durbar in colonial India and British West Africa, a public audience held either by a British viceroy or governor; also a court reception or audience for the hearing of petitions, held by an Indian prince or native ruler.

fakeer cf. fakir, a Hindu religious ascetic or mendicant.

feddan in Egypt, a measure of land equivalent to just over an acre.

fellah an Egyptian peasant.

feringhee an Indian word, often contemptuous, for a European.

fuzee/fusee here, a variant spelling of "fusil," a type of light musket or firearm.

Garbhadhan a Hindu ceremony performed for a married woman, after menstruation, in order to favour conception; the ceremony was also performed at the first indication of pregnancy.

Gentoo Anglo-Indian slang for a Hindu – i.e. a non–Muslim.

ghat/ghaut Anglo-Indian for a pathway leading to a landing-stage on a river; also a mountain pass.

ghee a butter made from boiled buffalo milk used in cooking in India.

goor a type of coarse, unrefined sugar, often made as an offering to Hindu gods.

Goorka/Gurkha a Hindu person from Nepal; also the name for such a person serving in the British army.

Grand Signior cf. *Grand Seigneur*, the French title for the Sultan of Turkey, meaning "a great lord."

gum-kopal a hard resin tapped from tropical trees, which is often used as a varnish.

harcarra/harkara cf. "hircarra," in British East India, a spy, messenger or courier, often on camelback.

havildar a Sepoy non-commissioned officer, equivalent to the British rank of sergeant; often charged with the supervision of a small village.

hedeya a corruption of "hadiyah," a present or offering made to a prince or ruler.

howder/howdah a seat used on elephants in India, often with a railing surrounding it and a canopy above.

jageerdar/jaghirdar the holder of a jaghire or assignment of the government's share of the produce of a particular Indian district; often awarded for the upkeep of a military base in that area.

jamadar/jemadar a post held by a native officer in India, equivalent to an English lieutenant. The name was also used for the head of a detachment of police or a household of servants.

Jingo the popular name for a bombastic patriot, derived from the nickname for the supporters of aggressive British foreign policy, which led to the sending of British ships into Turkish waters against Russia in 1878.

juggernat cf. "juggernaut," a name, originating in Hindu mythology, for the god Krishna; in annual religious festivals held in India an image of the god was drawn through the streets and devotees were said to throw themselves under the wheels of the vehicle.

kaffir originally an Arabic word for "unbeliever" or "infidel," this word was adopted in colonial southern Africa as a derogatory term for any Black African.

kaloon cf. "caleoon"/"calyoon" a type of hubble-bubble pipe, similar to an Arab hookah.

kamdar possibly a corruption of "kardar," a native agent of the British government in India.

karoo bush originally from the Hottentot, this was the term used to describe the dry, barren tracts of South African bushland.

kellidar in British India, a native governor or commander of a fort.

khareeta cf. "kareeta," the special silk bag used for carrying a letter to and from an Indian noble; also the letter itself.

Khedive taken from the Persian for "sovereign," this was the title given to viceroys of Egypt during the period of Ottoman rule from 1867 to 1914.

kopje in South Africa, an Afrikaans word for a small hill.

kraal in South Africa, an Afrikaans word for a pen or enclosure for livestock.

kurbash cf. "kourbash," a whip made of hippopotamus hide and used as an instrument of punishment in Egypt, Turkey, and the Sudan.

lac/lakh Anglo-Indian for a unit of one hundred thousand; one hundred lakhs of rupees were equivalent to one **crore**.

lakhiraj cf. "lakerage," permission given by the colonial adminstration to natives in India to farm land rent-free.

Lee-Metford a standard rifle adopted by the British War Office in 1888; it was a precursor to the Lee-Enfield rifle introduced in the 1890s. Metford refers to the type of ammunition (Metford Mark IV) used – a kind of exploding bullet – which was the subject of considerable debate. See document 94.

Little Englander   an adherent of the movement against British colonial expansion, who sought to limit the growth of the British Empire.

mahratta/maratha   a member of a warlike Hindu people from Maharashtra in central and south-western India.

maxim   a type of single-barrelled machine gun, invented in the nineteenth century by Sir Hiram Maxim and used by British troops during the Boer War.

meer-kat/meerkat   a small South-African mongoose, often kept as a housepet.

Mens aequa in arduis   Latin: literally "equanimity in arduous enterprises" – i.e. "keep your head."

mohur/mohurrir   a major gold coin of British colonial India, worth 15 rupees.

moonsiff/munsif   an Indian native judge of the lowest rank who dealt with civilian matters.

moratto   a corruption of the word **mahratha**.

mulct   a fine or penalty.

mundul   in British India, a native headman of a village.

munsubbar   an honorific title in India, originally given to a commissioned native officer, according to the number of horsemen under his command.

Mussulman   an obsolete word for a Muslim.

nabob/nawwab/naib   see document 16.

nautch   an East-Indian form of highly stylized, traditional dance; also the name for a professional girl-dancer who performs it.

nazim   possibly a corruption of "nizam," the hereditary title of a reigning prince of Hyderabad.

Osmanli   an Ottoman or Turk.

otter/otto of roses   cf. attar of roses – a highly concentrated extract of oil made especially from the damask rose and used as the base for many other perfumes.

pagoda   a coin of gold or silver formerly used in southern India.

palankeen/palanquin   an Indian word for a covered litter, carried by four to six men on their shoulders, and between poles, with one passenger inside.

pariah dog   in India a stray, mongrel dog that scavenges around the towns and villages; from the Tamil word for a member of a lowly Indian caste.

peg   in British India, a slang word for a brandy-and-soda.

peon   in eighteenth-century British India, a foot-soldier or native constable.

per fas, per nefas   Latin: "justly," and "unjustly."

phousdar   also spelt "foujdar," in British India, the native commander of an army detachment; a title of office in the military government of an Indian province.

pice   a Hindi word for a copper coin of low denomination.

pollygar   cf. "poligar," in British India the name for the feudal chiefs of rural districts, later applied to the native governor of that district. Elsewhere the title used was **zemindar**.

pundit   see document 16.

punkah/punka   a large fan – either made from palm leaves and held in the hand or made of cloth and attached to a frame and worked by use of a pulley cord.

purdah   in its original meaning – a screen or curtain used to separate women off from men and prying eyes; also used to describe the veil worn by Indian women of high caste.

riaz   possibly a corruption of "rayah," in Ottoman Egypt, the name for a Christian subject, who paid a poll tax in lieu of being conscripted into the army.

ryot/riot   a Hindi word for an Indian peasant or tenant farmer.

sahib   see document 71.

sandjak/sanjak   under the Ottoman Empire, a Turkish word for an administrative district – a subdivision of a vilayet; also the title given to the person who administered that district.

sati/suttee   from the Hindi/Urdu meaning "faithful" or "good," the act of self-immolation on her husband's funeral pyre by a Hindu widow.

Sepoy   a native Indian soldier in the service of the British army.

serai   from **caravanserai**, a Turkish word for an overnight stopping place or inn for travellers.

Shasters/Shastras   the sacred writings of the Hindus, which became the basis for Hindu law and everyday religious practise.

sherif/shereef   a Muslim title for a prince or sovereign; also used as an honorific for a chief magistrate or local governor.

sowar   an Anglo-Indian word for a native mounted soldier or policeman.

sub lodice teguntur   Latin: meaning literally "under the blanket," i.e. kept out of sight/not discussed in public.

subah   an Anglo-Indian word for a province in the Mogul empire.

Sublime Porte   the government of the Ottoman empire; taken from the French equivalent for the Turkish *baba ali* "Imperial Gate."

sudder/suddur/sadar Anglo-Indian usage, particularly in Bengal, for a senior official or chief government department; also used as an abbreviation for the chief Sudder Court of a district and the building wherein its officials resided.

sadar ameen cf. "sudder ameen," the second rank of native Indian judge who served at the Sudder Court.

suwarry cf. "sowarry," in colonial British India, the mounted retinue or cortege of attendants of a high government official.

taluqdar/talukdar in British India, the owner of a hereditary estate; also the name given to the official who administered this area.

terai a wide-brimmed felt hat with ventilation holes, worn by Europeans in tropical climates.

terra incog Latin: cf. "terra incognita" – literally "unknown land," i.e. "unfamiliar."

thuggee a form of attack and/or murder, often involving strangulation, performed as part of robbery or assassination by members of an Indian organization; from the Hindi word for "thief." See also document 22.

tila cf. Hindi *til*, the sesame plant, which produces an oil used in cooking in India.

titunji in Egypt, the official pipe-bearer of the Khedive.

Tommy a nickname for a British soldier; its popular use evolved during the nineteenth century from "Thomas Atkins," a specimen name used in army manuals to identify an average, conscripted soldier.

tufa a type of porous, volcanic rock.

vakeel/vakil in colonial India, a native lawyer or barrister; also a government minister or representative.

vis naturae Latin: "a power of nature."

wideawake the nickname for a broad-brimmed, soft felt hat with a low crown.

woo the balmy cf. the phrase "to go to the balmy," a slang expression found in Dickens, meaning to have a sleep or nap.

zemindar/zamindar in India, the owner or holder of a large agricultural estate; under British colonial rule during the eighteenth century, such landowners were recognized as the landed aristocracy of India. See also **pollygar**.

compiled by Helen Rappaport

Index

Illustrations and maps are indicated by page references in *italics*, Glossary entries in **bold**.